THE ODYSSEY

A NEW VERSE TRANSLATION

BACKGROUNDS

THE ODYSSEY IN ANTIQUITY

CRITICISM

W.W. NORTON & COMPANY, INC.
also publishes

THE NORTON ANTHOLOGY OF AMERICAN LITERATURE
edited by Nina Baym et al.

THE NORTON ANTHOLOGY OF ENGLISH LITERATURE
edited by M. H. Abrams et al.

THE NORTON ANTHOLOGY OF LITERATURE BY WOMEN
edited by Sandra M. Gilbert and Susan Gubar

THE NORTON ANTHOLOGY OF MODERN POETRY
edited by Richard Ellmann and Robert O'Clair

THE NORTON ANTHOLOGY OF POETRY
edited by Alexander W. Allison et al.

THE NORTON ANTHOLOGY OF SHORT FICTION
edited by R. V. Cassill

THE NORTON ANTHOLOGY OF WORLD MASTERPIECES
edited by Maynard Mack et al.

THE NORTON FACSIMILE OF
THE FIRST FOLIO OF SHAKESPEARE
prepared by Charlton Hinman

THE NORTON INTRODUCTION TO LITERATURE
edited by Carl E. Bain, Jerome Beaty, and J. Paul Hunter

THE NORTON INTRODUCTION TO THE SHORT NOVEL
edited by Jerome Beaty

THE NORTON READER
edited by Arthur M. Eastman et al.

THE NORTON SAMPLER
edited by Thomas Cooley

HOMER

THE ODYSSEY

A NEW VERSE TRANSLATION
BACKGROUNDS
THE *ODYSSEY* IN ANTIQUITY
CRITICISM

≫ ≪

Translated and Edited by

ALBERT COOK

BROWN UNIVERSITY

W · W · NORTON & COMPANY · INC · *New York*

W. W. Norton & Company, Inc., 500 Fifth Avenue, New York, N.Y. 10110

Copyright © 1974, 1967 by Albert Cook

Library of Congress Catalog No. 76-141587

ISBN 0-393-04161-1
ISBN 0-393-09971-7 pbk.

PRINTED IN THE UNITED STATES OF AMERICA

3 4 5 6 7 8 9 0

Contents

79384

Foreword

I hope this collection will help the student to see many sides of the *Odyssey*; that is its purpose.

In the light of that purpose, two features of the translation itself should be emphasized: first, that it tries to render the poem not only literally, but line by line, so that almost always the expressions in a given line of Greek are those in the corresponding English line. Second, it is, I believe, wholly faithful to the formulaic character of the poem that so many commentators today have stressed. The poem is built of hundreds of repeated lines, groups of lines, and half lines. In this translation those many repetitions are faithfully and exactly retained in all cases.

Under "Backgrounds," various kinds of information are provided—on the language of the poem, the lands and peoples it discusses, its poetic conventions, and the kind of society it depicts. "The Homeric Question" summarizes much of the data involved in the nagging and complex problem of the exact circumstances of the poem's composition. This question has taken up thousands of pages of scholarly discussion over the past two centuries, and the interested student, once he has learned Greek, may wish to go farther into the special jungle of this problem.

Under "The *Odyssey* in Antiquity" and "Criticism," the rest of this collection is taken up with commentary from Aristotle to the present. The brief selections under "Scholia" and "Eustathius" offer very small samples of the kind of comment a Byzantine bishop and various anonymous scholars in ancient and medieval times thought that the poem called for. Their quirky concerns stand in striking contrast to the passing homage of Racine, Goethe, and Ezra Pound, and also to the deliberate and sensitive meditations on the poem by the modern commentators with which this collection concludes.

Grateful acknowledgment is made to my research assistant Phillip Bodrock for careful aid; to Bernard Knox and James Hutton for editorial advice; to John Benedict for continuously imaginative editorial supervision; to Clint Goodson for resourceful bibliographical help, for translating the pieces by Germain and Adorno, and for access to his own recent studies, included here; and to Edwin Dolin and Charles Doria for material offered in advance of publication elsewhere.

Preface on the Translation

To hear and re-create the sound and sense of his original is always the task of the translator, whether of the impressionist or the literalist camp. Except when the sense of the original is tied up in lost or unsurfaceable data (the jokes of Aristophanes), or when the sound is so elaborately structured as to be wholly inimitable (*The Divine Comedy*, or possibly any case of regular rhyme), there is no reason why the literalist cannot aspire to as full a re-creation as the impressionist—and therefore to a fuller one, since he has the advantage of confining himself to bringing over as much of the designative sense as possible. Of course he too misses by a considerable margin; and of course he faces any translator's problem of catching the flow of overtones and sequences of sense—and of sound.

For both sound and sense, the Homeric line is a unit, and this literal translation seeks as its major goal to preserve that crucial unit in its integrity while trying to catch something of Homer's flow. A line with a syllabic base (almost always in the range of twelve to seventeen syllables) is one possible option for an equivalent to the Homeric hexameter.

For sense, the heavily formulaic character of Homer recommends that one render words, lines, and phrases as nearly identically as possible. This conviction suggests that one should not opt for a variety in translating *kalos* ("fine," "beautiful," "lovely," "pretty," "fair," and so on) but choose one and stick to it most of the time. I chose "lovely." The English words "ocean" and "sea" must do duty for more than two Homeric words; and the translator is forced, if he would utilize both, to overlook the fact that the proper name "Ocean" in Homer designates something special. Distinguishing *Okeanos* by a slightly Anglicized proper name "Oceanos" [1] and rendering *pontos* as "ocean"

---

1. My middle-of-the-road position on spelling Greek names results in a mixture between Latin norm for English and true Greek transliteration. In this way I have tried to combine the familiarity of the Latin usage

seems preferable to calling it "sea" along with *hals* and *thalassa*, or to picking a metaphoric archaism like "the deep."

For *demos*, there are implications of a geographical "region," one sufficiently more restricted than a French *pays* for us to render the word "district." Sometimes the area is primarily meant, and "land" is the closest term; and sometimes the inhabitants, the "people," are primarily indicated. In this case I have settled for "district" as a normative use, and the other three when their emphases seemed the primary ones. English convention could be ignored in some cases. If *glaukopis* probably means "bright-eyed," [2] we can ignore the English tradition of rendering it "gray-eyed." And the same with the more hallowed "wine-dark," a rendering based on a specious phenomenological inference. There is no color word in the Greek.

The choices are not always easy of course. An obscure attribution of Hermes, *Argeiphontes*, presents three choices: "slayer of Argos," "the one who appears swiftly," or the opaque expression itself, *Argeiphontes*. On the hunch that the expression would not have sounded opaque to the normal reader of Homer in antiquity, I have followed the inclination of much contemporary opinion toward the first rendering.

Or again, in simple grammar, we get *theos*, masculine, "god," and *thea*, feminine, "goddess." What do we do with *theos*, with or (more usually) without feminine adjective when it is applied to a goddess? The distinction between *thea* and *theos*, confined almost exclusively to Homer, is an elusive one not to be accounted for wholly by metrical convenience. Unless the translator is prepared to identify *thea* and *theos* as "goddess," he is forced to strengthen the common-gender tinge of "god" and use that one word for the one word *theos*, masculine or feminine. "God" does sound a little odd when applied to a female immortal; *theos* is rare enough in the feminine to have struck an ancient reader as comparably odd.

The literalist provides the reader, or at least the student, with

with the Hellenic flavor of a Greekish new-spelling. Hitting between *Oceanus*, or merely *Ocean*, on the Latin side, and *Okeanos* on the Greek, I have produced *Oceanos*, a case I am less happy with than I am with *Telemachos* for the young man who has been known for centuries in English as *Telemachus*. But I believe the principle of combination (producing usually a Latin-like base and a Greek-like termination) is fairly consistent.

2. Manu Leumann, *Homerische Wörter* (Basel, 1950), pp. 148-152.

the comfortable assurance that for the vast designative tapestry of the original a pink thread may sometimes do duty for a red one, or a blurred one for a blurred one—but never a blue one for a red one, and never a polychrome burst for a single color of the original. The impressionist, on the other hand, for all the rationales he can muster, can never free himself of the charge leveled by T. S. Eliot at Gilbert Murray (who translates rather more literally than most of the impressionists now active): "So here are two striking phrases which we owe to Mr. Murray; It is he who has sapped our soul and shattered the cup of all life for Euripides. . . . Professor Murray has simply interposed between Euripides and ourselves a barrier more impenetrable than the Greek language."

Any rendering builds a wall. One can only hope to build a translucent one. We always need masonry, but also bricks that are translucent to begin with.

ALBERT COOK

The Text of
The Odyssey

I

Tell me, Muse, about the man of many turns, who many
Ways wandered when he had sacked Troy's holy citadel;
He saw the cities of many men, and he knew their thought;
On the ocean he suffered many pains within his heart,
Striving for his life and his companions' return.   5
But he did not save his companions, though he wanted to:
They lost their own lives because of their recklessness.
The fools, they devoured the cattle of Hyperion,
The Sun, and he took away the day of their return.
Begin the tale somewhere for us also, goddess, daughter of Zeus.[1]   10
Then all the others, as many as escaped sheer destruction,
Were at home, having fled both the war and the sea.
Yet he alone, longing for his wife and for a return,
Was held back in a hollowed cave by the queenly nymph
    Calypso,[2]
The divine goddess, who was eager for him to be her husband.   15
But when in the circling seasons the year came around,
The gods spun the thread for him to return to his home,
To Ithaca; and he did not escape struggle there either,
Even among his dear ones. All the gods pitied him,
Except Poseidon,[3] who contended unremittingly   20
With godlike Odysseus, till the man reached his own land.
But the god had gone to the far-off Ethiopians—
The Ethiopians, remotest of men, divided asunder,
Some where Hyperion sets, and some where he rises.
He was taking part in the sacrifice of bulls and rams,   25
And enjoyed being present at a feast there. The others
Were gathered together in the halls of Olympian Zeus.

1. I.e., the muse of epic poetry. Zeus, the son of Cronos, was king of the
gods and specifically the god of the sky and of weather.
2. Daughter of Atlas.
3. Son of Cronos and brother of Zeus; god of the sea, especially hostile
toward Odysseus.

The father of men and gods began to speak among them.
In his heart he was remembering excellent Aigisthos [4]
30 Whom Agamemnon's son, far-famed Orestes,[5] had slain.
Thinking of that man, he made his speech to the immortals:
"Well now, how indeed mortal men do blame the gods!
They say it is from us evils come, yet they themselves
By their own recklessness have pains beyond their lot.
35 So this Aigisthos married beyond his lot the lawful
Wife of the son of Atreus, and killed him on his return;
Knowing he would be destroyed, since we told him beforehand:
We had sent sharp-eyed Hermes, the slayer of Argos,[6]
To tell him not to kill the man and not to woo his wife,
Or payment would come through Orestes, descendant of
40   Atreus,
As soon as he came of age and longed for his own land.
So Hermes told him; but, though of good mind himself, he
    did not
Change Aigisthos' mind. And now he has paid for it all."
Then the bright-eyed goddess Athene [7] answered him:
45 "Our father, son of Cronos,[8] highest of all rulers,
As for that man, he surely lies in a fitting death.
May anyone else also perish who would do such deeds.
But the heart within me is torn over skillful Odysseus,
The hard-fated man, who long suffers griefs far from his dear
    ones
50 On a flood-circled island where the navel of the sea is.
The island is wooded, a goddess there has her dwelling,
The daughter of destruction-minded Atlas,[9] who knows
The depths of the whole sea, and holds up by himself
The enormous pillars that hold apart earth and heaven.
55 His daughter has kept back the wretched and grieving man,
And perpetually, with tender and wheedling speeches,

4. Cousin of Agamemnon and lover of Clytemnestra; after Agamemnon's
murder he became king of Mycenae.
5. Agamemnon was leader of the Greeks at Troy; killed by Clytemnestra
on his return home; Orestes killed Clytemnestra and Aigisthos to avenge
his father's murder.
6. Hermes was son of Zeus; messenger of the gods and guide of the dead.
The obscure compound *Argeiphontes* could also mean "appear rapidly" or
"appear brightly."
7. Goddess of reason and the arts and special patron of Odysseus.
8. One of the older gods; the father of Zeus, Poseidon, Hera, Hades.
9. The supporter of the pillars of heaven.

She charms him to forget Ithaca. Odysseus, however,
Wanting to catch sight even of smoke leaping up
From his land, is longing to die. But your own heart
Does not turn toward it, Olympian one. Did Odysseus   60
Not please you in broad Troy by the ships of the Argives
When he made sacrifice? Why, then, are you so angry at him,
      Zeus?"
In answer to her, cloud-gathering Zeus spoke out:
"My child, what sort of word has got past the bar of your teeth?
How could I at any time forget godlike Odysseus,   65
Who stands out among mortals for thought, and for the
      sacrifices
He has given the immortal gods who possess broad heaven?
But Poseidon, who holds up the earth, remains obstinately
Enraged about the Cyclops whom he blinded in the eye,
Godlike Polyphemos, who possesses the greatest strength   70
Of all the Cyclopes.[1] The nymph Thoosa gave him birth,
The daughter of Phorcys,[2] ruler over the barren sea,
In hollow caves, after she had lain with Poseidon.
For that, to be sure, earth-shaking Poseidon has not
Killed Odysseus but does make him wander far from his
      homeland.   75
Well, come now, let all of us here carefully devise
His return, so he may arrive; and Poseidon will slacken
His rage, for counter to all the immortals he cannot
Carry on strife alone against the will of the gods."
Then the bright-eyed goddess Athene answered him: 80
"Our father, son of Cronos, highest of all rulers,
If this course is now really dear to the blessed gods,
That many-minded Odysseus return to his own home,
Then let us urge on the runner Hermes, slayer of Argos,
To the island of Ogygia,[3] in order that with all speed   85
He may tell the fair-braided nymph an unerring plan
For the return of stout-hearted Odysseus, so he may go back.
And I myself will go to Ithaca, so that I the better
May urge his son on and place a strength in his mind

1. A lawless race of giants met by Odysseus.
2. A lesser sea divinity.
3. The legendary island home of Calypso.

90 To call the long-haired Achaians [4] into an assembly
And to speak out to all the suitors, who are always slaying
His throngs of sheep, and his shamble-footed, crumple-horned
    cattle.
I shall send him on to Sparta, and also to sandy Pylos,
To learn of his dear father's return, if he may hear somehow,
95 And so a noble renown among men may belong to him."
When she had said this, she bound under her feet the lovely
    sandals,
The ambrosial golden ones that bear her either over water
Or over the limitless land swift as blasts of the wind.
She grasped the valiant spear, pointed with sharp bronze,
Ponderous, big, and stout, with which she daunts the ranks
100   of men,
Of heroes at whom she is angry, the daughter of a mighty father,
She went down in a rush from the summits of Olympos
    and stood
In the district of Ithaca before Odysseus' gates
At the courtyard threshold. In her fist she held the bronze spear,
105 Likening herself to a stranger, the Taphian leader Mentes.
She came upon the bold suitors. They at the moment
Were delighting their hearts with a diceboard before the doors,
Seated on the skins of oxen they had killed themselves.
Heralds attended on them, and capable servants also;
110 Some of these were mixing wine and water in bowls.
Others were cleaning off the tables with porous sponges,
And setting them, and dividing up the meat in many pieces.
Godlike Telemachos was by far the first to see her,
For he sat among the suitors, crushed in his own heart,
115 Seeing his noble father in his mind, if from somewhere
He would come and make those suitors scatter through the
    halls,
So that he himself might have honor and command his own
    goods.
Thinking this over while seated with the suitors, he sighted
    Athene.
He went straight to the gate, and he resented in his heart
120 That the stranger stood so long at the door. Standing near her
He took her right hand and received the bronze spear;

4. A collective appellation of the Greeks besieging Troy.

Speaking out to her, he uttered wingèd words:
"Greetings, stranger, you shall be welcomed among us. And
    when
You have eaten dinner, you will tell what it is you need."
When he had said that, he led on, and Pallas [5] Athene followed.   125
And when they had got inside of the lofty house,
He stood the spear he was carrying against the long pillar
Inside the well-polished spearcase, where many other
Spears of stout-hearted Odysseus were also standing.
He led her on and seated her in an armchair, spreading
    linen beneath,   130
Lovely and skillfully wrought. A stool was under her feet.
He placed a broidered seat alongside, apart from the others,
The suitors, lest the stranger might be disturbed at the uproar
When mingling with the insolent, and lose appetite for dinner,
And so he might ask her of the father who had gone away.   135
A handmaid poured water from a pitcher she was carrying,
A lovely golden one, over into a silver basin,
For washing the hands; she set up a polished table alongside.
A respected housekeeper served bread she was carrying,
Laying out many dishes, gracious with the provisions.   140
A carver lifted up and set out trenchers of meats
Of all sorts, and set out gold goblets alongside for them.
A herald served them attentively, pouring out the wine.
The bold suitors came in. And then they themselves
Sat down one after another in seats and in armchairs.   145
Heralds were pouring water for them over their hands.
And serving maids were heaping bread up on trays.
Young men were filling bowls up to the brim for drinking,
They stretched forth their hands to the food that was spread
    out ready.
But when the suitors had taken their fill of food and drink,   150
Other matters came to their minds for attention:
Singing and dancing, which are the graces of a banquet.
Into Phemios' [6] hands a herald placed a lyre
Of supreme beauty; he sang for the suitors under compulsion.
Playing his instrument, he struck up a lovely song.   155
Telemachos, however, addressed bright-eyed Athene,
Holding his head close so that the others might not hear:

5. An epithet of Athene.
6. Son of Terpis ("Pleasure") and bard at Odysseus' palace.

"Dear stranger, will you resent it if I say something?
These men are concerned with this, the lyre and singing,
160 At their ease, since they devour scot-free another man's living,
A man whose white bones somewhere are rotting in the rain,
Lying on a shore, or a wave tumbles them in the sea.
If they ever see that man returning to Ithaca,
They will all pray to be nimbler on their feet
165 Rather than to be richer in clothing and in gold.
As it is, an evil fate has killed him, surely; there is
No comfort for us even if some one of the men on earth
Says he will come. The day of his return is lost.
But come now, tell me this, and explain truthfully:
170 What men are you from? Where are your city and parents?
On what sort of ship did you come? How did the sailors
Bring you to Ithaca? What men did they claim to be?
For I do not think you could have got here at all on foot.
Tell me this exactly, so that I may well know
175 Whether you come on a first visit or are a friend
Of my father's, since many other men come to our home,
And since he was himself well acquainted among men."
Then the bright-eyed goddess Athene addressed him:
"All right, then, I will tell you this quite truthfully.
180 I declare I am Mentes, son of skillful Anchialos,
And I rule over the Taphians, who are fond of rowing.
Just now I have come this way by ship, with companions,
Sailing on the wine-faced sea to men of alien tongue,
To Temese for bronze, and I carry glittering iron.
185 My vessel stands here by the fields far off from the city,
In the harbor of Reithron, below wooded Neion.
We declare we are guest friends of one another through our
     fathers
Originally; if you will, go and ask Laertes,[7]
The old warrior, who they say no longer comes
190 To the city, but suffers griefs off by himself on his field,
With an old servant woman, who serves him food and drink
Whenever a weariness overcomes his limbs
As he creeps along the knoll of the vine-bearing garden.
But I have come now because they said the man really was in
     the district,

7. Father of Odysseus and former king of Ithaca.

Your father. But him have the gods hindered on his journey.   195
The godly Odysseus has not yet died on the earth,
But he is still alive somewhere, held back on the broad ocean
On a flood-circled island, and troublesome men hold him,
Savages, who somehow keep him back against his will.
Well, I will now tell you a prophecy, how the immortals   200
Cast it in my heart, and how I think it will end,
Though I am not a prophet, and have no clear skill with
    birds.[8]
Not much longer now, surely, will he be away
From his dear fatherland; not even if iron bands hold him.
He will devise how to return, since he has many resources.   205
But come now, tell me this, and explain it truthfully,
If, big as you are, you are really the son of Odysseus himself.
You resemble him strangely in your head and your fine eyes,
Since we had contact quite often with one another
Before he embarked for Troy, where the other noblest   210
Men of the Argives were headed in their hollow ships.
Since then I have not seen Odysseus, nor has he seen me."
Then the sound-minded Telemachos answered her:
"All right, stranger, I shall speak quite truthfully.
My mother calls me the son of the man. But I myself   215
Do not know. No one has ever been certain of his father.
Ah, would that I were the fortunate son of some man
Whom old age came upon with all his possessions!
As it is, he has been the most ill-fated of mortal men,
The man they say I was born of, since you ask me this."   220
And then the bright-eyed goddess Athene addressed him:
"The gods have not set it down that your race hereafter
Be nameless, since Penelope bore such a man as you.
But come, tell me this, and explain it truthfully,
What feast, what gathering is this? What is your need here?   225
A banquet or a marriage? The guests have brought no share to it.
How overweening they seem to be, how presumptuous
To be feasting in the hall! A man with any sense
Who came on these shameful things would be angry to see
    them."
Then the sound-minded Telemachos answered her: 230

8. An augur would make divinations based on the behavior of birds, as
in Book 2, lines 146-60, and elsewhere.

"Stranger, since you ask me this and inquire about it,
This house was once supposed to be wealthy and blameless,
So long as that very man was still here in the district.
Now the gods have wished otherwise and decreed misfortune;
235 They have made that person vanish more completely than all
Men. No, I would not grieve this way if he had died,
If with his companions he had gone under in the land of the
      Trojans,
Or in the arms of his friends, after he had wound up the war.
Then all the Achaians would have made him a funeral mound,
240 And he would have won great glory for his son, too, hereafter;
As it is, the storm winds have snatched him off without glory.
He is gone, vanished and unperceived, and has left me
Pains and laments. Yet I no longer moan and grieve for that man
Only, since the gods have fashioned other evil cares for me.
245 All of the noblemen who rule over the islands,
Dulichion and Samê and also wooded Zakynthos,
And all those who are masters in craggy Ithaca,
Are paying court to my mother and wearing down my home.
She neither refuses the hateful marriage nor can she
250 Make an end of it. But they are wasting my home away
As they devour it. Soon they will tear me to pieces myself."
Pallas Athene was greatly disturbed and spoke out to him:
"Ah well, you do need Odysseus who is gone away
Very much indeed, to lay hand to these shameless suitors.
255 Would that he came now to the outer doors of the house
And stood there with a helmet and a shield and two spears,
And were the sort of man he was when I first saw him
In our very own home drinking and taking his pleasure,
As he went from Ephyre, leaving Ilos the son of Mermeros.
260 Odysseus had traveled there upon a rapid ship
Seeking after a man-killing drug, so that he might
Smear bronze-tipped arrows with it, but the man did not
Give it, since he dreaded the ever-living gods.
But my father gave it to him; he loved him terribly.
265 As that sort of man might Odysseus contend with the suitors!
They would all be swift in their doom and bitter in marriage.
Well, all these matters lie in the laps of the gods,
Whether he will return and pay them off or not,
In his own halls. So I bid you to consider
270 In what way you may drive the suitors out of the hall.

Come now, pay attention and take note of my words:
Tomorrow call the Achaian warriors to assembly;
Make a declaration to all. Let the gods witness it.
Order the suitors to disperse to their own affairs.
And your mother, if her spirit urges her to marry,   275
Let her go back to the hall of her father who is great in power.
They will prepare a wedding and set in array
The many gifts that ought to go with a dear daughter.
For yourself, I strongly advise you, if you will listen,
To fit out the ship that is best with twenty oarsmen   280
And go in search of your father who has been gone so long,
On the chance some mortal may tell you of him, or you hear
   from Zeus
The voice that best of all brings report to men.
First go to Pylos and question the godly Nestor.[9]
From there go on to Sparta and blond Menelaos,[1]   285
Who has come back the last of the bronze-clad Achaians.
If you do hear your father is alive and will return,
Though worn down, you might bear out yet another year.
But if you hear that he is dead and exists no more,
Return home then to your own dear fatherland,   290
Heap up a monument for him, and perform the many
Rites that are fitting, and give your mother to a husband.
When you have accomplished all this and brought it to pass,
Then you may consider in your heart and in your mind
How you may slaughter the suitors in your halls,   295
Either by cunning or openly. There is really no need
To indulge in childishness. You are not that age.
Or have you not heard how much glory godly Orestes seized
Among all men when he killed his father's murderer,
The cunning Aigisthos, who killed his renowned father?   300
You too, my dear friend, since I see you are handsome and
   great;
Be brave, so that a man born in the future would praise you.
Well, by now I should be going down to my swift ship
And the companions who are impatiently awaiting me.
Be concerned yourself. Pay attention to my words."   305
Then the sound-minded Telemachos answered her:

9. The aged king of Pylos and chief adviser for the Greeks at Troy.
1. Brother of Agamemnon and husband of Helen; co-commander of the
Greeks at Troy.

"Stranger, you have spoken these friendly words wisely
Like a father to his son, and I shall never forget them.
Come now, wait a while, though you are eager for the journey,
310 So that once you are bathed, delighted in your own heart,
You may board your ship rejoicing in spirit, with a gift,
An honorable and lovely one that will be a keepsake
From me, of the kind that fond guest friends give each other."
Then the bright-eyed goddess Athene answered him:
315 "Do not hold me back now, longing as I am for the journey.
Whatever gift your own heart bids to you give me,
Give it to me to carry home when I return again.
And pick a lovely one. It will be worth the exchange to you."
Having spoken so, bright-eyed Athene went off.
320 She flew upward like a bird. Into his spirit
She had put strength and courage. She put him in mind
Of his father more than before. When he thought it over,
He was amazed in his spirit; he thought she was a god.
And at once the godlike mortal went toward the suitors.
325 A renowned singer was singing to them. They were sitting
In silence listening. He sang of the baleful return
Of the Achaians from Troy that Pallas Athene laid on them.
The daughter of Icarios, prudent Penelope,
From her upper chamber hearkened to the divine song.
330 She descended the lofty stairway from her dwelling,
Not alone, but two servants followed along with her.
And when the godly woman had come to the suitors,
She stood by the pillar of the stoutly fashioned roof,
Holding the glistening headbands before her cheeks.
335 A devoted servant maid stood near her on either side.
Then, weeping, she addressed the godlike singer:
"Phemios, you know many other ravishments for mortals,
The deeds of men and of gods that singers glorify.
Sing one of these as you sit among them. And let the men
340 Drink wine in silence. But stop singing this baleful song
Which forever wears away my own heart in my breast,
Since an unforgettable grief affects me heavily.
I long for a person so dear, remembering always
That man whose glory is wide through Greece and middle
    Argos."
345 Then the sound-minded Telemachos answered her:
"Mother, for what reason do you begrudge the trusty singer's

Giving pleasure with whatever his thought rouses in him? Singers
Are not guilty; I suppose Zeus is guilty, who gives
To bread-earning men, to each one as he wishes.
It is no wrong for this man to sing about the evil fate   350
Of the Danaans.[2] Men acclaim that song the most
Which has come round newest of all to those who hear it,
Let your mind and spirit resign you to listening.
Odysseus is not alone to have lost his day of return
In Troy. Many other mortals perished there also.   355
Well, come into the house, and apply yourself to work,
To the loom and the distaff, and give orders to your servants
To set at the work. This talk will concern all the men,
But me especially. For the power in the house is mine."
She was amazed at him, and back into the house she went.   360
The sound-minded speech of her son she took to heart.
She entered the upper chamber with her serving women,
And then wept for Odysseus, her dear husband, until
Bright-eyed Athene cast sweet sleep upon her eyelids.
The suitors were making a din through the shadowy halls.   365
They all gave voice to the prayer of lying in her bed.
Sound-minded Telemachos began speaking to them:
"Suitors of my mother, with your excessive insolence,
Let us now take our pleasure and dine. And let there be
No noise, since it is lovely to listen to a singer   370
Of the kind this one is, who resembles the gods in his voice.
And at dawn tomorrow let us all go and take our seats
In council, so that I may tell you something outright;
Get out of the halls and partake of other dinners,
Eating your own goods, visiting each other's homes.   375
And if it seems better and preferable to you
To consume one man's livelihood scot-free,
Waste on. But I shall call on the eternal gods for help,
So that Zeus may grant there to be acts of retribution,
And then scot-free within this house you may die."   380
So he said, and they all set their teeth on their lips
And wondered at Telemachos that he spoke so courageously.
Antinoos,[3] the son of Eupeithes, addressed him first:

2. The Greeks (Achaians) collectively; seen as descendants of a mythical
king, Danaos.
3. The ringleader and most insolent of Penelope's suitors.

"Well, Telemachos, the gods themselves must be teaching you
385 To be presumptuous and speak courageously.
May the son of Cronos over sea-circled Ithaca
Not make you king, your paternal right by birth."
Sound-minded Telemachos addressed him in answer:
"Antinoos, even if you are offended at what I say,
390 Still I would wish this very thing done if Zeus were to give it.
Would you call this the worst thing to happen among men?
It would not be bad at all to be king. There comes at once
An opulent home for the man, and he is himself more honored.
Yes, there are also other kings of the Achaians,
395 Many in sea-circled Ithaca, young ones and old ones.
And one of them shall have this, since godly Odysseus is dead.
But as for me, I shall be lord over our household,
And over the servants whom godly Odysseus won for me."
Eurymachos, son of Polybos, addressed him in answer:
400 "Telemachos, all this lies in the laps of the gods,
Who of the Achaians shall rule in sea-circled Ithaca.
May you have your own possessions and be lord in your own
    home.
May a man never come, while Ithaca is inhabited,
Who would tear your possessions away from you by force.
405 But I want to ask you, my brave man, about this stranger.
Where did the man come from, and what country did he claim
To be from? Where are his birthplace and his father's land?
Does he bring some message that your father is coming home?
Or did he come here seeking some personal need of his own?
410 He started up so, and went at once, nor did he wait
For us to find him out. Yet his face did not look like a
    coward's."
Then sound-minded Telemachos addressed him in answer:
"Eurymachos, surely my father's return has been lost.
I put no trust in a message, wherever it comes from,
415 And I give no heed to any divination my mother
Might ask of a diviner, calling him to the hall.
The stranger is a guest friend of my father's from Taphos.
He declares he is Mentes, son of skillful Anchialos,
And he rules over the Taphians, who are fond of rowing."
420 So Telemachos said, but in his mind knew the immortal god.
The men turned then to dancing and delightful song
And took their pleasure, and waited for evening to come.

As they took their pleasure black evening came upon them.
Then they went away, each to his own home to sleep.
But Telemachos, where his bedroom was, built aloft   425
In the very lovely courtyard in a place with a view all around,
Went to bed pondering many things in his mind.
Eurycleia went in with him and carried the flaming torches,
The devoted daughter of Ops, Peisenor's son.
Laertes bought her once as one of his possessions   430
When she was still in her first youth; he gave twenty cattle for
    her,
And honored her the same as the devoted wife in the halls.
But he had never lain with her, for he feared his wife's wrath.
Going with him, she carried the flaming torches. She loved him
Most of all the servants, and had tended him as a child.   435
She opened up the doors of the stoutly fashioned bedroom.
He sat down on the bed and took off his soft tunic
And put it in the hands of the shrewd-minded old woman.
She folded up the tunic, put it in smooth order
And hung it on a peg beside the jointed bed.   440
Then she went out of the bedroom, drew the door shut with a
    ring
Of silver, and drew the bolt full length by its thong.
There all night long, wrapped up in the sheepskin,
He pondered in his mind the course that Athene had shown.

II

And when the early-born, rosy-fingered dawn appeared,
The dear son of Odysseus rose up out of his bed,
Put on his clothes, and set the sharp sword round his shoulder,
Bound the lovely sandals beneath his shining feet
5 And went on out of the bedroom, like a god to look at.
At once he ordered the heralds with their piercing voices
To summon the long-haired Achaians to an assembly.
The heralds made summons, and they gathered together
    quickly.
And when they were gathered and had come together
10 He went to the assembly and held his bronze spear in his fist—
Not alone, but the swift-footed dogs went along with him.
Moreover, Athene shed a divine grace around him.
The people all marveled at him as he was coming up.
He sat down in his father's seat, and the old men gave way.
15 Then the hero Aigyptios began to speak among them,
A man bent with age who knew numberless things.
He too had a dear son, who went with godlike Odysseus
In the hollow ships to Ilion [1] that abounds in horses,
The spearman Antiphos. But the savage Cyclops killed him
20 In his hollowed cave, and prepared him as his final meal.
Three other sons he had; one fell in with the suitors,
Eurynomos; and two stayed always on their father's lands.
But still he remembered the other one, in grief and sorrow.
For him he wept as he spoke and addressed the assembly:
25 "Listen to me now, Ithacans, in what I say.
Our assembly has not once met or sat in session
From the time godly Odysseus went off in the hollow ships.
And now who has called it together? And to which of the
    young men
Or of those who are older, has there come so great a need?
30 Has he heard some message about an army coming on

1. Another name for Troy.

That he might plainly tell us, since he was the first to hear it?
Does he declare and announce some other public matter?
Noble he seems to me, well favored. For him may Zeus
Bring about whatever good thing he desires in his mind."
So he said, and Odysseus' dear son was glad for his statement. 35
Nor did he stay seated longer but he felt a desire to speak.
He stood up in the midst of the assembly. The herald Peisenor,
Who was full of sound advice, put the scepter in his hand.
Then he began to speak, first addressing the old man:
"Old sir, this man is not far, you yourself shall soon know it, 40
He who gathered the people: it is I. The pain comes most to me.
I heard no message about an army coming on
That I might plainly tell you, since I was the first to hear it;
I declare and announce no other public matter
But my own need, that an evil has befallen my home,   45
And a double one: I lost my noble father, who ruled as king
Over all of you here once, and was mild as a father.
And now there is a much greater evil too, that will soon
Fully tear my whole house apart and destroy all my living.
Suitors are assailing my mother against her will,   50
The dear sons of the men who are the noblest in this place.
They shudder to make a trip to the house of her father
Icarios, so he might set his daughter's dowry himself,
And give her to the man she wants, him who pleases her most.
But they cluster to our house day after day.   55
Slaughtering oxen and sheep and fat goats,
They carry on their revels and drink the sparkling wine
Wantonly. Many things are wasted. And there is no man
Of the kind Odysseus was, to ward off harm from the house.
Nor are we at all the kind to ward it off. Even hereafter 60
We shall be pitiable and not have acquired strength.
I would ward it off myself, if I had the power.
Unendurable deeds have been done; in no pretty way
Has my house been destroyed. Be indignant yourselves!
Be ashamed toward the other men of our neighborhood   65
Who live around us. Fear, too, the wrath of the gods,
Lest, aghast at all the evil deeds, they work some change.
I beseech you, both by Olympian Zeus, and by Themis,[2]
Who disbands and also convokes the assemblies of men,

2. Goddess of Just Order.

70 Leave off, my friends; and let me wear away alone
    In my woeful grief, unless my noble father Odysseus
    Was ever hostile to the well-greaved [3] Achaians and did them
        harm;
    For this you pay me back, are hostile and do me harm
    By urging these men on. It would be better for me
75 If you were to devour my property and my herd yourselves;
    If you were to eat them, there might be some recompense.
    In that case we should carry the story around the town,
    Demanding back our goods, till they were all given back.
    As it is, you are heaping incurable pains on my heart."
    So he spoke, in anger. He threw the scepter down on the
80   ground,
    Bursting out in tears. And pity gripped all the people.
    Then all the others there were silent. No one could bear
    To reply to Telemachos with severe words;
    Antinoos alone addressed him in reply:
    "High-talking Telemachos, unchecked in your anger, what is
85   this
    You say to shame us? You would like to fix blame on us!
    The Achaian suitors are not guilty toward you.
    No, it is your dear mother, who knows advantages well.
    It is the third year already, and will soon be a fourth,
90 Since she has slighted the spirit in the Achaians' hearts.
    She gives hope to all, and she promises every man,
    Sending out messages. But her thought wishes otherwise.
    And she has devised in her mind this other deceit.
    She set a great loom in the halls and on it she wove
95 A large and delicate fabric. She told us at once:
    'Young men, my suitors, since godly Odysseus is dead,
    Wait, though you are eager for this marriage of mine, till I
        finish
    This robe, so that the yarn will not waste in vain,
    The burial sheet of warrior Laertes for the time
100 The ruinous fate of long-sorrowful death seizes him,
    Lest one of the Achaian women in the district blame me
    If he who had won so much lie without covering!'
    So she said, and the bold heart was persuaded within us,
    Then every day she kept weaving on the great loom.
105 And in the nights she undid it when she had the torches set up.

    3. A greave is a stiff protector worn on the lower leg.

So three years she has fooled the Achaians and persuaded them.
But when the fourth year came and the seasons came on,
Right then one of the women, who perceived it clearly, told it,
And we happened upon her undoing the shining fabric.
So she has finished it, though unwilling and under duress.   110
The suitors answer you this way in order that for yourself
You may know it in your heart; that all the Achaians may know
    it.
Send your mother away; command her to marry
Whatever man her father bids and who pleases her.
But if she incites the sons of the Achaians much longer,   115
Attending in her heart to the gifts Athene gave her
Beyond others, skill at beautiful tasks, a noble mind,
And wiles, such as we have heard of none of the women
Of old, the fair-braided Achaians who existed before,
Tyro and Alcmene and Mycene of the lovely crown [4]—   120
No one of them had ideas the like of Penelope's.
Yet in this she has not had a propitious idea,
Because truly they will devour your living and your possessions
As long as she keeps this purpose that the gods
Have now placed in her heart. For herself she makes great
    renown,   125
But for you, the longing for a plentiful livelihood.
We are not going first to our lands or anywhere else
Till she marries whichever of the Achaians she wishes."
Then sound-minded Telemachos addressed him in answer:
"Antinoos, in no way can I force her who bore and raised me   130
Out of the house against her will, while elsewhere on earth
My father is alive or dead. It would be a bad thing to pay
Icarios a large fine if I sent my mother off on my own.
From her father I should then suffer ills, and a god would give
Others, when my mother had invoked the dread Erinyes,[5]   135
As she went away from the house. The resentment of men
Would be upon me. So I shall never utter such a word.
And if your own spirit can feel the resentment,
Get out of the halls, partake of other dinners,
Eating your own goods, visiting each others' homes.   140

4. Tyro, bride of Poseidon, grandmother of Nestor and Jason; Alcmene,
mother of Heracles; Mycene, daughter of the river Inachos and patroness
of Mycenae.
5. Goddesses who fulfill curses and avenge crimes.

But if this seems better and preferable to you,
To use up one man's livelihood scot-free,
Waste on. But I shall call on the eternal gods for help,
So that Zeus may grant there to be acts of retribution,
145 And then scot-free within this house you may die."
So Telemachos spoke, and broad-seeing Zeus sent him
Two eagles from above from the crest of the mountain flying.
They for a time flew down along with the blasts of the wind,
Stretching their wings out close to one another.
150 But when they came to the midst of the many-voiced assembly,
Then they whirled about and beat their wings rapidly.
They went to the heads of all and destruction was in their look,
As they tore each other's cheeks and throats on both sides
    with their claws.
Then they sped off on the right, past the men's homes and city.
They were amazed at the birds when they saw them with their
155   own eyes.
They turned over in their hearts what was going to happen.
Then the old warrior Halitherses addressed them,
The son of Nestor. He alone excelled those of his age
For knowing about birds and explaining the auspices.
160 Well disposed toward them, he spoke out and addressed them:
"Listen to me now, Ithacans, in what I say.
I declare this especially to make it known to the suitors.
A great trouble for them is gathering force. Odysseus
Will not long be far from his dear ones. In fact already, perhaps,
165 He is nearby, breeding murder and fate for these men,
All of them. And it will also be ill for many of the rest
Of us who inhabit sunny Ithaca. Yet far beforehand
Let us consider how we may stop them. Let the men
Stop themselves. And surely this is better for them.
170 Not as a novice do I prophesy, but as one who knows,
And I say everything has come to pass for that man,
As I explained to him when the Argives went off
To Ilion, and with them went many-minded Odysseus.
I said he would suffer many ills, lose all his friends,
175 And then unknown to all in the twentieth year
He would get home. Now all these things are indeed coming
    to pass."
Eurymachos, son of Polybos, addressed him in answer:
"Old man, go on now and prophesy to your children,

Go on home, lest they suffer some ill afterward.
I am much better at prophesying about this than you.   180
And there are many birds that wander beneath the beams
Of the sun, and not all are in accord with fate. Odysseus
Has perished far off, and would that you too had perished
Along with him. You would not say so much in augury,
Nor would you so incite the angered Telemachos,   185
Expecting a gift for your house, if he provide one.
I will tell you this right out. And it will come to pass:
If, when you know so many ancient matters, you prevail
Over a younger man, and with your speeches urge him to rage;
First, this will be very tormenting to the man himself,   190
And he will be able to do absolutely nothing about it.
But on you, old man, we shall set a charge you will grieve
In your heart to pay off. It will be a hard pain for you.
I shall advise Telemachos myself in the presence of all:
Let him bid his mother go back to her father's house.   195
They will work out a marriage and array many bridal gifts,
As many as should go along with a dear daughter.
Before then I do not think the sons of the Achaians will cease
From the wearisome suit, since we fear no one anyway—
No, not Telemachos, however full of speeches he is,   200
And we do not give heed, old man, to the augury you tell,
Which is unfulfilled; and you are still the more hated.
Moreover, the goods shall be vilely eaten, and their equal
Shall never exist,[6] so long as she herself puts the Achaians off
About her marriage. But we are waiting day after day   205
And compete over her excellence, and we do not go
Among the other women it is fit for each of us to marry."
Then sound-minded Telemachos addressed him in answer,
"Eurymachos, and all the rest of you noble suitors,
I will not implore you about this or speak out any more.   210
Already the gods know this, and all the Achaians.
But come, give me a fast ship and twenty companions
Who can complete a journey with me, thither and back.
I am going to Sparta and also to sandy Pylos
To learn of the return of my father, who is gone so long,   215
On the chance some mortal may tell of him, or I hear from
   Zeus

6. Obscure in Greek. It means, probably, that there will be no equal
recompense for them.

The voice that most of all brings report to men.
If I do hear my father is living and will return,
Then, though worn down, I could bear out yet another year.
220 But if I hear that he is dead and exists no more,
I will then return to my own dear fatherland,
Heap up a monument for him and perform the many
Rites that are fitting, and give my mother to a husband."
When he had said just this, he sat down. There stood up
among them
225 Mentor, who was a companion of excellent Odysseus;
When he went on the ships he turned over his whole home to
him,
To obey the old man [7] and steadfastly to protect all.
Well disposed to them, he spoke out and addressed them:
"Listen to me now, Ithacans, in what I say.
230 Let no scepter-bearing king be deliberately
Kind and mild any longer, or keep his mind on the right,
But may he be perpetually harsh and act unjustly,
Since there is no one who remembers the godly Odysseus
Of the people he ruled; and he was mild as a father.
235 No, I do not make objection about the bold suitors
That they do violent deeds, with evil weaving of thought,
For they stake their own heads when they devour violently
The home of Odysseus, who, they say, will return no more.
But now I blame the rest of the people, for the way you all
240 Sit in silence, that you do not address these few suitors
With speeches, and restrain them, being yourselves so many."
Leocritos, son of Euenor, addressed him in answer:
"Stubborn Mentor, crazed in your mind, what is this you say
Urging them to put us down? But it is disastrous
245 To fight over a banquet, and with men greater in number.
Yes, even if Ithacan Odysseus himself were to come
Upon the noble suitors banqueting in his house
And plan in his heart to drive them out of the hall,
His wife, though she longed for it much, would not rejoice
250 At his coming, but he would meet his wretched fate right there,
If he fought against many. You have not spoken properly.
But come, let the people disperse, each one to his tasks;
Mentor and Halitherses will hasten the man on his way.

7. Probably Laertes, though some take it as meaning that the household
shall obey Mentor.

They have been his father's companions from the beginning.
And yet I believe he will stay a long time in Ithaca   255
And listen for the news, but will never complete this journey."
So he spoke, and he dismissed the assembly quickly.
And they did disperse, each one to his own dwelling.
But the suitors went into the dwelling of godly Odysseus.
Telemachos went off apart to the sands of the sea,   260
Washed his hands in gray salt water, and prayed to Athene:
"Hear me, you who yesterday came as a god to our house
And bade me to go in a ship onto the murky sea
To learn of the return of my father who is gone so long,
But the Achaians delay over all these things,   265
And the wickedly presumptuous suitors most of all."
So he spoke in prayer. Athene came close to him,
Likening herself to Mentor in form and in voice.
And speaking out to him, she uttered wingèd words:
"Telemachos, hereafter you will not be a coward or senseless.   270
If there is really instilled in you the good might of your father
And you are as he was to achieve both word and deed,
Then the journey will not be fruitless or unachieved.
But if you are not the offspring of him and Penelope,
Then I have no hope that you will achieve what you wish.   275
Few indeed are the sons who are equal to their fathers;
Most are worse, but few are better than their fathers.
But since you will not be a coward hereafter or senseless,
And the shrewdness of Odysseus has not quite forsaken you,
There is hope in that case you will bring these deeds to pass.   280
Therefore let the plan and the thought of the suitors go,
Mad as they are, since they are neither thoughtful nor just.
They do not know at all about the death and black fate
That is really near them, to destroy them all on a single day.
The journey you desire will not be distant for long.   285
Since I am for you the companion I was for your father,
I will get a fast ship ready for you and come with you myself.
But go on back to your house and talk with the suitors,
Lay up provisions and fit everything in containers;
Wine in jugs, and barley, the marrow of men,   290
In close-sewn skins. And I myself will soon gather
Willing companions around the district. There are
Many ships in sea-circled Ithaca, new and old.
I myself will look them over and see which is best for you.

295 We will soon get it ready and send it on the broad ocean."
So spoke Athene, the daughter of Zeus. Telemachos
Did not tarry long when he heard the voice of the god.
He went on to his home, troubled in his own heart,
And he did indeed find the bold suitors in the halls,
300 Flaying goats and singeing fat hogs in the courtyard.
Antinoos with a laugh went straight to Telemachos,
Took his hand, and spoke right out directly to him:
"High-talking Telemachos, unchecked in your anger,
Give heed in your breast to no other evil word or deed,
305 But do eat for my sake, and drink, just as before.
The Achaians will accomplish for you all these things,
A ship and chosen rowers, so you may get swiftly
To hallowed Pylos for word about your illustrious father."
Then sound-minded Telemachos addressed him in answer:
310 "Antinoos, there is no way I could dine in silence
With you, insolent men, and enjoy myself securely.
Or is it not enough, you suitors, that beforehand you wasted
Many noble possessions of mine while I was still a child?
And now that I am big and learn about the story,
315 Hearing it from others, and the spirit does wax within me,
I shall try some way to fling evil fates upon you,
Either by going to Pylos or here in this very district.
I am going, and the journey I speak of will not be fruitless—
As a passenger, for I have the disposal of neither
Ship nor rowers; that, I suppose, is the way it seemed better
320   to you."
He spoke and drew his hand from Antinoos' hand
Lightly. The suitors busied themselves through the house with
     dinner.
They spoke in mockery and made abusive speeches,
And this is what one of the overbearing young men would say:
325 "Well, Telemachos is devising slaughter for us.
He will bring some defenders either from sandy Pylos
Or even from Sparta, since he wants to so terribly,
Or else he wishes to go to Ephyre, the fertile land,
In order that he may get a life-killing drug there,
330 Put it in a bowl, and do away with us all."
And then another of the overbearing young men would say
"Who knows but that he too, going in the hollow ship

Far from his dear ones, will die wandering like Odysseus?
That way he would increase our labor even more!
For we would divide up all the possessions; the house, moreover, 335
We would give to his mother to have, and to whoever weds
    her."
So they spoke. He entered his father's high-roofed chamber,
A broad one, where gold and bronze lay piled up,
Clothing in coffers and abundance of fragrant oil,
And in it were large jars of aged, sweet-tasting wine   340
Standing, which contained an unmixed godly drink,
Set in a row beside the wall, if ever Odysseus
Should homeward return, though he had suffered many pains.
Bolt-fitted planks were upon it, stoutly fashioned,
Double doors, and a housekeeper by night and by day   345
Held it, who guarded all in her resourcefulness of mind,
Eurycleia, daughter of Ops, Peisenor's son.
Then Telemachos spoke to her and called her to the chamber:
"Good mother, come draw wine off for me into jars with handles,
Sweet wine, except for the most savory that you keep,   350
Thinking of that ill-fated man, in case he comes from some-
    where,
Zeus-born Odysseus, and wards off destiny and death.
Fill up twelve of them, and fit them all with lids,
And pour barley for me into well-stitched leather bags.
Let there be twenty measures of mill-crushed barley flakes.   355
Keep this to yourself. Let it all be readied together.
I shall take it away in the evening myself at the time
When my mother enters the upper room and thinks of rest.
I am going to Sparta and also to sandy Pylos
To learn of my dear father's return, if I may hear somehow." 360
So he spoke, and his dear nurse Eurycleia cried out,
And while she was sobbing she uttered wingèd words:
"How, dear child, does this thought come to be in your mind?
And where do you wish to go upon the broad earth,
Being a belovèd only child? Zeus-born Odysseus has died   365
Far from his fatherland in a country of strangers.
From the moment you are gone they will devise evils against
    you,
How by deceit you may die. Then they will divide all this
    themselves.
No, remain here among your own. There is no need

370 For you to wander and suffer ills on the barren ocean."
Then sound-minded Telemachos addressed her in answer:
"Take cheer, nurse; this plan is not without a god.
But swear you will tell nothing of this to my dear mother
Before the eleventh or the twelfth day has come,
375 Unless she misses me and hears that I am gone off,
So that she might not weep and injure her lovely skin."
So he spoke; and the old woman swore by the gods she would
    not,
A great oath; and then when she swore and completed the oath,
Right away she drew off wine for him in the jars with handles
380 And poured barley for him into well-stitched leather bags.
Telemachos went to the house and joined the suitors.
Then the bright-eyed goddess Athene had another thought.
Likening herself to Telemachos, she went all through the city.
She stood beside each mortal man and she uttered a speech
385 And bade them to gather at evening by the swift ship.
And then she asked Noemon, glorious son of Phronios,
For his swift ship. And he granted it graciously.
The sun went down and all the ways were shadowed.
Then she had the swift ship dragged to the sea. And in it
390 She put all the tackle that well-timbered ships carry.
She moored it at the verge of the bay. His noble companions
Were gathered together. The goddess urged each one on.
Then the bright-eyed goddess Athene had another thought.
And she went on to the halls of godlike Odysseus.
395 There she diffused sweet slumber down on the suitors,
And confused them as they drank. The goblets fell from their
    hands.
They rose up to go sleep through the city. And not long
Did they sit, when once slumber fell on their eyelids.
Then the bright-eyed goddess Athene spoke to Telemachos,
400 Calling him out of the well-situated halls,
Likening herself to Mentor in form and in voice:
"Telemachos, already your well-greaved companions
Are seated at the oars awaiting your urging.
Let us go, so that we may not long delay from the journey."
405 So did Pallas Athene speak, and she led on
Speedily. He went along in the god's footsteps.
But when they had got down to the ship and the sea,
They found the long-haired companions there on the sand.

And Telemachos addressed them in his holy might:
"Over here, friends. Let us load on provisions. Already   410
All are gathered in the chamber. My mother has not found out,
Nor the other serving maids. One alone has heard the tale."
So he spoke, and led them, and they went along with him.
When they had brought everything to the well-timbered ship,
They stowed it away as Odysseus' dear son ordered them.   415
Telemachos then boarded the ship, but Athene went first
And sat down in the stern of the ship. Close beside her
Telemachos sat. They let the stern cables loose,
And themselves boarded and sat down at the oarlocks.
Bright-eyed Athene sent them a driving breeze,   420
A driving West Wind roaring on the wine-faced sea.
Telemachos, as he urged his companions on, told them
To grasp the tackle. And they hearkened to his urging.
They stood a fir-wood mast in the hollow mast-block;
They raised it up, and with forestays they made it fast.   425
Then they hauled up the white sails with well-plaited oxhide
    ropes.
A wind swelled the midsail, and the purple wave
About the stem sounded loud as the ship went on.
She ran into the wave, accomplishing her course.
When they had tied down the tackle on the swift black ship,   430
They set up mixing bowls filled to the brim with wine,
And poured libations to the deathless, ever-living gods,
And of all especially to the bright-eyed daughter of Zeus.
All night the ship pierced her course, and at morning too.

III

The sun rose up, leaving the beautiful water,
Into the bronze-covered heaven, to shine for immortals
And also for mortal men upon the grain-giving earth.
They came to Pylos, the well-established city
5 Of Neleus.[1] On the sands of the sea those men were sacrificing
Bulls all of black to the earth-shaker with blue locks.
There were nine groups, and in each one five hundred men
Were sitting. And for each group they put forward nine bulls.
While these were eating the entrails and burning the thighs to
the god,
10 The others sailed straight in, furling into place the sails
Of the balanced ship; they pulled her up, and got out them-
selves.
Telemachos got out of the ship, and Athene went ahead.
The bright-eyed goddess Athene addressed him first:
"Telemachos, there is no longer the least need for you to be
modest,
15 For just this did you sail on the ocean to learn about your father,
Where the earth has hidden him and what fate he has met.
But come now, go straight to Nestor, breaker of horses.
We will see what advice he has hidden in his breast.
Entreat him yourself to speak unerringly.
20 He will not speak falsely. For he is very sound of mind."
Then sound-minded Telemachos addressed her in answer:
"Mentor, how then shall I go? How shall I approach him?
For in quick responses I have no experience.
Modesty becomes a young man addressing an elder."
25 Then the bright-eyed goddess Athene spoke to him:
"Telemachos, some thoughts you will have in your mind,
And a god will suggest others. For I do not think
You were born and raised without the favor of the gods."

1. Founder of Pylos; son of Poseidon and father of Nestor.

So did Pallas Athene speak, and she led the way
Speedily. He went along in the god's footsteps.   30
They came to the conclave and sessions of the men of Pylos,
Where Nestor sat with his sons, and about him companions
Prepared a feast, roasting some meat and skewering the rest.
When these men saw the strangers, they all came over in a body
And hailed them with gestures and asked them to sit down.   35
First Peisistratos, Nestor's son, came near,
Took the hands of both men and sat them down at the feast
In soft fleeces upon the sands of the salt sea,
Beside his brother Thrasymedes and his father.
He gave them shares of the entrails and poured out wine   40
In a golden goblet. Pledging her, he addressed
Pallas Athene, daughter of aegis-bearing [2] Zeus.
"Say a prayer now, stranger, to Lord Poseidon,
Whose feast you have come upon in arriving hither.
But when you have poured a libation and prayed, which is
    fitting,   45
Then give this man also a cup of honey-sweet wine
To pour a libation, since I believe he too says prayers
To the immortals. All men have need of the gods.
But he is younger, and equal in age to myself.
Therefore I will first give you the gold cup of libation."   50
When he had said this, he put the cup of sweet wine in her
    hand.
Athene was pleased at the sound-minded, judicious man
Because he had given her first the gold cup of libation.
At once she said many things in prayer to Lord Poseidon:
"Listen, Poseidon, you who hold up the earth. Bear no grudge   55
Against us as we are praying to bring these deeds to pass.
First of all, grant renown to Nestor and his sons.
And then give the others, all the men of Pylos together,
A pleasing recompense for their illustrious hecatomb. [3]
Grant that Telemachos and I may go back, when we have done 60
That which we came here in the swift black ship to do."
So she prayed then. But she herself brought it all to pass.
She gave Telemachos the lovely two-handled cup.
The dear son of Odysseus prayed in the same way.

2. The aegis was a weapon, or later a breastplate, carried only by Zeus and
Athene.
3. Sacrifice of a hundred oxen.

When the others had roasted the outer pieces of meat and
65   unskewered them,
They divided the portions and dined on the hearty feast.
But when they had taken their fill of food and drink,
Nestor, the Gerenian horseman, began speaking to them:
"Now is the best time to inquire, and to ask
70   Strangers who they are, after they have enjoyed food.
Strangers, who are you? Whence have you sailed the watery
     ways?
For some sort of gain, or do you wander at hazard
The way pirates do who wander over the sea,
Risking their lives, bearing evil to foreigners?"
75   Then sound-minded Telemachos addressed him in answer,
Taking courage, for Athene herself had put in his mind
Courage to ask him about the father who had gone away,
And so that a noble renown among men might belong to him:
"Nestor, son of Neleus, great pride of the Achaians,
80   You ask where we are from. And I will inform you.
We have come from Ithaca, which is under Mount Neion.
It is a private affair, not a public one, that I speak of.
I seek widespread report of my father, if somehow I may hear,
Of the stout-hearted, godly Odysseus, who once, they say,
85   Sacked the city of the Trojans, fighting at your side.
Of all the other men who waged war on the Trojans,
We have heard where each one perished by a woeful death.
But the son of Cronos made that man's death not to be heard
     of.
No one is able to say clearly just where he perished,
90   Whether on the mainland he went under to hostile men
Or on the open sea in Amphitrite's [4] waves.
So I now embrace your knees to ask if you are willing
To tell about that man's woeful death, if you saw it
With your own eyes, perhaps, or heard the tale from another
95   Wanderer. For excessive sorrow did his mother bear him!
Sweeten nothing out of pity or respect for me,
But tell me straight out how you encountered the sight.
I beseech you, if ever my father noble Odysseus
Promised you any word or deed and carried it out
100   In the Trojans' land, where you Achaians suffered troubles;

4. A sea goddess, here identified with the sea itself.

Recall that for me now and tell me unerringly."
Then Nestor, the Gerenian horseman, answered him:
"Ah friend, since you have reminded me of the woe we suffered
In that land, we sons of the Achaians, unchecked in our anger;
How much, both in the ships upon the murky sea,   105
Wandering for booty wherever Achilles led,
And how much, too, we fought around the great city
Of Lord Priam! ⁵ There at that time all the best were slain!
There lies warlike Ajax, there lies Achilles,⁶
There Patroclos,⁷ a counselor equal in weight to the gods: 110
There lies my dear son, at once mighty and excellent,
Antilochos, outstanding as a runner and as a fighter.
Many other ills we endured besides these. Who
Of mortal men could ever recount all of them?
Not if you stayed five years, no, not six, could you ask   115
To the end of the ills the godly Achaians endured there.
Before that you would tire and return to your fatherland.
Nine years we busied ourselves weaving ills for them
By all sorts of wiles. The son of Cronos barely brought it to pass.
And no one there ever wanted to be compared to him openly   120
For craftiness, since godly Odysseus far surpassed
In all sorts of wiles—your father, if it is true
You are that man's offspring. Awe holds me to look upon you.
Yes, indeed, your speech is like his. You would not think
A man so young could speak in such a likely way.   125
There the whole time I myself and godly Odysseus
Never once spoke diversely in assembly or in council,
But holding one spirit in mind and in prudent counsel,
We advised the Argives how it should come out by far the best.
And when we had sacked the lofty city of Priam   130
And gone off in the ships, and a god had scattered the Achaians,
Then Zeus plotted out in his mind a woeful return
For the Argives, since they were not all prudent or just.
Therefore many of them encountered an evil fate
Because of the destructive wrath of the bright-eyed daughter   135
Of a strong father, who set strife on the two sons of Atreus.
The two of them called all the Achaians to a council,

5. The aged king of Troy killed by the Greeks.
6. Ajax was son of Telamon, second to Achilles in prowess; Achilles, captain
of the Myrmidons and the greatest hero of the Greeks at Troy.
7. The closest friend of Achilles; his death inspired Achilles to return to
battle.

Rashly, in no orderly way, at the sun's setting,
And the sons of the Achaians came, weighed down with wine.
140 They told the story of why they had gathered the people.
Then Menelaos commanded all the Achaians
To take thought of a return on the broad back of the sea.
But that did not please Agamemnon at all, for he wanted
To hold back the people and to offer sacred hecatombs
145 So as to appease the dreadful rage of Athene.
The fool, he did not know she was not to be persuaded.
The mind of the ever-living gods is not quickly turned.
And so they stood there and replied to each other
With harsh speeches. And the well-greaved Achaians rose up
150 With a wondrous noise. The plan pleased them diversely.
We spent the night turning over harsh thoughts in our minds
Against one another. For Zeus was shaping an evil woe.
At dawn some of us dragged the ships to the bright salt water;
We put our possessions and the deep-girdled women in.
155 But half of the people held back, staying on behind
With Atreus' son Agamemnon, shepherd of the people.
The other half embarked and went on. Swiftly indeed
They sailed, and a god smoothed out the great-gulfed ocean.
When we came to Tenedos we sacrificed to the gods,
160 Wanting to go home. But Zeus intended no return yet,
Cruel, as he stirred up evil strife for the second time.
Some turned their bobbing ships around and went their way,
Those about skillful devious-minded Lord Odysseus;
And they again favored Agamemnon, son of Atreus.
165 But I, with the massed ships that were following me,
Kept fleeing, since I knew the god was intending evil.
The warlike son of Tydeus fled and aroused his companions.
Blond Menelaos came along with us later on.
He found us in Lesbos thinking over the long voyage,
170 Whether we should take our way above rugged Chios
By the island of Psyra, keeping that on our left,
Or should go below Chios along by windy Mimas.
We besought the god to make a portent appear, and he did
Show us one and ordered us to cleave the middle sea
175 To Euboia, so we might soonest flee from under misfortune.
A sharp breeze rose up and blew. Our ships swiftly
Ran over the fish-laden courses. During the night
They put in at Geraistos. We dedicated the thighs

Of many bulls to Poseidon, when we had measured the great sea.
It was the fourth day when the companions of Diomede,[8]   180
Tydeus' horse-taming son, moored their balanced ships in
    Argos.
As for me, I held toward Pylos. Never did the breeze
Lull, from the very first time the god set it on to blow.
So I arrived, dear child, with no news. I know nothing
About them, which Achaians were saved, and which perished. 185
As much as I could learn sitting in my own halls,
You shall find out, as is right. I will not conceal it from you.
They say the spear-wielding Myrmidons [9] came safely,
Whose leader was the famous son of great-hearted Achilles,
And safely came Philoctetes, Poeas' glorious son.   190
Idomeneus [1] led all his companions to Crete,
Who escaped from the war. The ocean deprived him of none.
You have heard about the son of Atreus, though you live far
    away—
How he arrived, how Aigisthos plotted his woeful death.
Ah, but that man did pay for it terribly.   195
And how good it is for a man to leave behind when he dies
A son, since that son avenged his father's murderer,
The cunning Aigisthos, who killed his renowned father!
You too, my dear friend, since I see you are handsome and
    great;
Be brave, so that a man born in the future would praise you."   200
Then sound-minded Telemachos addressed him in answer:
"Nestor, son of Neleus, great glory of the Achaians,
Yes, that man avenged himself well. And the Achaians
Will bring him wide renown and a song for men to come.
Would that the gods might invest me with so great a power,   205
To take vengeance on the suitors for their painful transgression,
Men who in their pride devise reckless deeds against me.
But the gods have not spun the thread of so great a bliss
For my father and me. Now it must be endured, all the same."
Nestor, the Gerenian horseman, then answered him: 210
"Dear friend, since you have mentioned this and spoken of it
    to me,
They do say that there are many suitors for your mother

8. Ruler of Argos; a major Greek hero at Troy.
9. Followers of Achilles.
1. The grandson of Minos and king in Crete.

Who are devising evils in your halls against your will.
Tell me, are you willingly subjected? Or do the people
215 Despise you in the district, yielding to the voice of a god?
Who knows if he may come some day and punish their violence,
Either himself alone or all the Achaians together?
For if only the bright-eyed Athene did wish to favor you
The way she cared once for glorious Odysseus,
220 In the Trojans' land where we Achaians suffered troubles—
I never saw the gods so openly showing favor
The way Pallas Athene stood openly by that man—
If she did wish to favor you and care in her heart that way,
Then some of those men would surely forget the marriage."
225 Then sound-minded Telemachos addressed him in answer:
"Old man, I think this word will never be fulfilled.
You have said a great deal. Wonder holds me. Not for my hope
Would this happen, not even if the gods wished it to."
Then the bright-eyed goddess Athene spoke to him:
"Telemachos, what sort of word has got past the bar of your
230   teeth?
A god may easily if he wish save a man, even from afar.
I should rather myself be distressed with many pains
And travel homeward to see the day of my return
Than to arrive and perish at my hearth, as Agamemnon
235 Was killed by the guile of Aigisthos and his own wife.
Yet not even the gods can ward off from a man they love
The death that is common to all at whatever time
The ruinous fate of long-sorrowful death seizes him."
Then sound-minded Telemachos addressed her in answer:
240 "Mentor, let us speak of this no more, though we care for him.
There is no longer a real return for that man. Already
The immortal gods have devised for him death and black fate.
But now I want to ask and inquire about another story
From Nestor, since he knows justice and prudence beyond
      others.
245 For they say he has three times ruled the generations of men.
Like an immortal he strikes me to look upon.
O Nestor, son of Neleus, do utter the truth:
How did Atreus' son, broad-ruling Agamemnon, die?
Where was Menelaos? What sort of destruction did cunning
250 Aigisthos plot for him, when he killed a far better man?
Or was it not in Achaian Argos, but did he wander

Somewhere else among men, and the other took courage and
   murdered?"
Then Nestor, the Gerenian horseman, answered him,
"All right, my child, I shall tell you all of the truth.
Surely you may think for yourself how this would have happened ₂₅₅
If Atreus' son, blond Menelaos, arriving from Troy,
Had come upon Aigisthos still alive in the halls.
They would not have spread a heap of earth over him when he
   died.
But the dogs and also the birds would have devoured him
As he lay on a plain far from the city. And none   ₂₆₀
Of the Achaian women would have wept, for he devised a huge
   deed.
While we stayed there bringing many combats to an end,
He, secure in a nook of horse-nourishing Argos,
Enchanted Agamemnon's wife with many words.
Actually, she at first rejected the sorry act,   ₂₆₅
Godly Clytemnestra, since she practiced good sense.
And there was a singer with her, too, whom the son of Atreus
When he went off to Troy had strongly ordered to guard his
   wife.
But when the fate of the gods bound her to be overcome,
Then Aigisthos brought the singer to a desert island   ₂₇₀
And left the man to become a prey and a spoil for birds.
And a willing man led to his house a willing woman.
He burned many thighs on the holy altars of the gods
And set up many ornaments of woven work and gold,
Having achieved a huge deed he had never hoped in his heart. ₂₇₅
Now we sailed on together as he went from Troy,
The son of Atreus and I, knowing each what pleased the other.
When we reached holy Sunion, headland of Athens,
There Phoebos Apollo ² slew the pilot of Menelaos,
Visiting him with his soothing shafts while the man   ₂₈₀
Was holding in his hands the rudder of the coursing ship,
Phrontis, Onetor's son, who surpassed the tribes of men
In piloting a ship wherever the storm winds rushed.
So he was held back there, though pressing on for the journey,
Till he should bury his companion and perform due rites. ₂₈₅
But when he had gone again upon the wine-faced sea
In the hollow ships and, as he sped along, had reached

2. Son of Zeus and brother of Artemis; the god of sun and light.

Maleia, the sheer mountain, broad-seeing Zeus devised
A hateful journey and poured on a blast of shrill winds
290 And monstrous swollen waves as big as mountains.
He separated the ships there and brought some of them near
    Crete
Where the Cydonians dwelt by the streams of the Iardanos.
A certain smooth rock stands there sheer to the sea
At the extreme point of Gortyn in the murky ocean,
Where the south wind pushes a great wave up against the left
295   peak
To Phaistos and a small stone holds back a great wave.
Some ships did get there, and the men barely escaped
    destruction,
But the waves shattered the ships upon the reefs.
Yet the wind and the water carried and brought five
300 Of the dark blue-prowed ships right on up to Egypt.
So he gathered there a great deal of provisions and gold
And wandered with his ships among men of alien tongue.
Meanwhile Aigisthos plotted these woeful things at home.
For seven years he ruled Mycenae,[3] the rich in gold
When he had killed Atreus' son, and the people were subdued
305   under him.
In the eighth year, an evil for him, godly Orestes
Came back from Athens and killed his father's murderer,
The cunning Aigisthos, who had killed his renowned father.
When he had killed him, he gave the Argives a funeral feast
310 Both for his hateful mother and for cowardly Aigisthos.
That day Menelaos, good at the war cry, came to him bringing
Many possessions, as great a burden as his ships could bear.
As for you, too, my friend, do not wander long from your home
And leave behind in your home the possessions and the men
315 Presumptuous as they are, lest they divide and devour
All your possessions, and you have gone on a fruitless journey.
But I exhort you and urge you to proceed on
To Menelaos. For he has come recently from elsewhere,
From men from whom no one would expect in his heart
320 To return, whom storm winds had once led astray
Into a sea so great that not even the birds
Could get through in a year, it is so great and dire.
But go on now with your ship and your companions.

3. The chief city of bronze-age Greece and residence of Agamemnon.

If you wish to go by land, a chariot and horses are here;
My own sons are here also, who will be your guides   325
To godly Lacedemon, where blond Menelaos lives.
Beseech him yourself that he may speak unerringly.
He will not speak falsely. For he is very sound of mind."
So he said. The sun went down and darkness came on.
Then the bright-eyed goddess Athene spoke to them.   330
"Old sir, indeed you have told all this properly.
Come now, cut up tongues for offering and mix wine,
So when we have poured a libation to Poseidon and the other
Immortals, we may think of sleep. It is the hour for it.
Light is already gone under the dusk. Nor does it seem right   335
To sit a long time at the gods' feast, but to go on."
So spoke Zeus's daughter, and they hearkened to her voice.
Heralds poured out water for them over their hands.
Young men were filling bowls up to the brim with drink;
And served round to all, putting the first drops in the cups.   340
They cast the tongues on the fire and did libation standing.
But when they had poured libation and drunk as much
As the spirit moved, Athene and godlike Telemachos
Both then wanted to go on to the hollow ship.
Nestor restrained them and addressed them with a speech: 345
"May Zeus and the other immortal gods prevent
Your going away from my house to the swift ship
As from someone wholly without raiment, or destitute,
Who does not have coverlets and many rugs in his house
Either for himself or for his guests to sleep in softly.   350
But there are coverlets and lovely rugs at my disposal.
Not indeed will the dear son of this man Odysseus
Lie down on his ship's deck so long as I am alive
And so long as children are left to me in the halls
To entertain guests, whoever comes to my house."   355
Then the bright-eyed goddess Athene answered him:
"Dear old sir, you have said this well: It does seem right
That Telemachos obey you, as it is much better thus.
But now he will go along with you here, so he may sleep
In your halls. I myself will go to the black ship   360
So I may cheer our companions and tell them the details.
I declare I am the only older man among them,
The others follow along in friendship, younger men,
All the same age as great-hearted Telemachos.

365 There may I lay myself down in the hollow black ship
    Right now. But at dawn to the great-hearted Kaucones
    I am going, where a debt is owed me, not a recent one,
    Or a small one. And since this man has come to your house,
    Send him off with a chariot and your son. Give him the horses
370 That are nimblest at running and the best in strength."
    When she had said this, bright-eyed Athene went off,
    Likening herself to a sea eagle. Wonder seized all the Achaians.
    The old man was amazed when he saw it with his eyes,
    He took Telemachos' hand and spoke right out directly:
375 "My friend, I do not suppose you would be craven and cowardly
    If the gods so accompany a young man like you as guides.
    This is no other of those who holds the halls of Olympos
    Than the daughter of Zeus, the glorious Tritogeneia.[4]
    Among the Argives she honored your noble father too.
380 Come, mistress, be gracious and grant me a noble renown
    For myself and my children and my respected wife.
    I shall sacrifice to you a yearling heifer of broad brow,
    Untamed, that a man has never led under the yoke.
    I will sacrifice her, and deck her horns with gold."
385 So he spoke in prayer, and Pallas Athene heard him.
    Nestor, the Gerenian horseman, led them on,
    His sons and his sons-in-law, to his beautiful home;
    But when they arrived at the famous home of the ruler,
    They sat down one after another in seats and in armchairs.
390 As they came, the old man mixed up for them a bowl
    Of wine, sweet to drink, that in the eleventh year
    The serving maid had opened and untied the seal string from.
    The old man mixed it in a bowl. As he poured libation
    He prayed much to Athene, daughter of aegis-bearing Zeus.
395 But when they had poured libation and drunk their fill,
    They went to lie down to sleep, each in his own house.
    But there Nestor, the Gerenian horseman, bedded down
    Telemachos, the dear son of godly Odysseus,
    In the jointed bed under the resounding portico.
400 Beside him was Peisistratos of the good ash spear, chief of men,
    Who of the children in his halls was still unmarried.
    But he himself slept in a nook of the lofty house,
    And his lady wife prepared him a bed and a resting place.
    And when the early-born, rosy-fingered dawn appeared,

4. A name of Athene referring obscurely to her birth.

Nestor, the Gerenian horseman, rose up out of his bed.   405
He went out and sat himself down on the polished stones
That belonged to him out in front of his lofty portals,
White ones, glistening with oil. Upon them of old
Neleus used to sit, an adviser equal in weight to the gods,
But already he had succumbed to his fate and gone to Hades.[5]   410
Then Gerenian Nestor, bulwark of the Achaians, sat there,
Bearing the scepter. His sons were gathered round in a group
As they came from their bedrooms, Echephron and Stratios,
Perseus and Aretos and the godlike Thrasymedes.
And then sixth among them came the hero Peisistratos.   415
They led godly Telemachos in and sat him at their side.
The Gerenian horseman Nestor began to speak among them:
"Dear children, fulfill my wish very speedily,
So that first of the gods I may propitiate Athene,
Who came in clear form to the lavish feast of the god.   420
Come now, let one man go to the plain for an heifer,
So it come with all speed, and the herd of the oxen drive her.
Let one of you, going to great-hearted Telemachos'
Black ship, lead all his companions, and leave just two.
Let one of them summon the goldsmith Laerkes to come   425
Hither, so he may gild the heifer's horns round with gold,
And all you others stay here in a group. Tell the maids
Within to prepare a feast through the famous halls.
Bring seats and logs for the place, and shining water."
So he said, and they all got busy. The heifer came   430
From the plain, and there came from the swift, balanced ship
The companions of great-hearted Telemachos. The smith came
Carrying bronze implements in his hands, the tools of the trade,
An anvil and a hammer and well-made fire tongs
With which he worked gold. And Athene came to take part   435
In the sacrifice. The old charioteer Nestor gave gold,
And then the other gilded it round and decked the heifer's
     horns,
So that the goddess would be pleased to see the decoration.
Stratios and godly Echephron led the heifer by the horns.
Aretos came from the chamber carrying water for washing   440
In a flower-chased vessel. He held barley grains in a basket
In his other hand. And Thrasymedes, the steady in battle,

---

5. That is, to the ruler of the underworld. In Homer, Hades is a person,
not a place.

Stood by, holding in his hand a sharp ax to strike the heifer.
Perseus held the blood-bowl. The old charioteer Nestor led off
445 By washing his hands and sprinkling barley. As he started,
He prayed much to Athene, throwing hairs of its head in the
     fire.
And when they had prayed and tossed the barley offering on,
At once Nestor's son, high-spirited Thrasymedes,
Stood close and struck it. The ax slit the tendons
Of the neck. The heifer's strength was loosed; the women
450   shrieked,
His daughters and daughter-in-law and the respected wife
Of Nestor, Eurydice, eldest of Clymenos' daughters.
At that point they lifted it up from the wide-traveled earth
And held it. Peisistratos, chief of the men, cut its throat.
455 When black blood flowed from it and the spirit left the bones,
They quickly dismembered it and at once cut up
The whole thighs duly and covered them over with fat,
Making a double fold, and put the raw meat thereon.
The old man burned it on split wood. He poured sparkling wine
Over that. The young men beside him held the five-pronged
460   forks
In their hands. When the thighs were burned and they had
     eaten of the entrails,
They cut up the rest in small pieces and pierced it on spits,
And they roasted it, holding the sharp-pointed spits in their
     hands.
Meanwhile, the lovely Polykaste, youngest daughter
465 Of Nestor, the son of Neleus, washed Telemachos.
And when she had washed him and anointed him richly with oil,
She put a lovely mantle on him and a tunic.
And he left the bathtub in body like the immortals;
He went and sat down by Nestor, shepherd of the people.
470 When they had roasted the outer flesh and pulled it off,
They sat feasting. Noble men did watchful service
Pouring out the wine into the golden goblets.
But when they had taken their fill of food and drink,
Nestor, the Gerenian horseman, began speaking to them:
"Come my sons, bring the lovely-haired horses, and yoke them
470   up
To the chariot for Telemachos, so he may speed on his way."
So he said, and they listened to him right away and obeyed.

Nimbly they yoked swift horses to the chariot,
And the woman who kept them put in food and wine
And cooked meat, such as kings eat who are nourished by Zeus. 480
Telemachos got into the beautiful chariot.
Nestor's son, Peisistratos, chief of the men, along with him
Got into the chariot and took the reins in his hands.
He whipped to start up. Not against their will the pair flew
To the plain, and they left the sheer citadel of Pylos.   485
All day they shook the yoke, holding it up on either side.
The sun went down and all the ways were shadowed.
They arrived at Pherai and to the home of Diocles,
Son of Ortilochos, whom Alpheus [6] sired as his son.
There they slept the night, and he gave them the fare of a guest. 490
But when the early-born, rosy-fingered dawn appeared,
They yoked up the horses and mounted the inlaid chariot.
And they drove out of the forecourt and the resounding portico.
He whipped to start up. Not against their will the pair flew.
They reached the wheat-bearing plain. From then on they strove 495
To finish their journey. So the swift horses bore onward.
The sun went down and all the ways were shadowed.

6. A river god.

IV

They came to hollow Lacedemon, full of ravines,
And drove on to the halls of glorious Menelaos.
They found him holding a wedding feast with his many clans-
men
For a son and an excellent daughter in his own house.
5 He was sending the girl to the son of rank-breaking Achilles.
He had betrothed her first in Troy and had nodded
For her to be given; the gods were fulfilling the marriage.
He was then sending her off with horses and chariots
To the famous city of the Myrmidons, whom the man ruled,
And he was bringing the daughter of Alektor from Sparta for
10 his son,
The dearly beloved, valiant Megapenthes, born to him
From a slave girl; the gods no longer granted childbirth to Helen
When she had once given birth to her charming daughter
Hermione, who had the form of golden Aphrodite.
15 So they banqueted under the great high-roofed hall,
The neighbors and clansmen of glorious Menelaos,
Enjoying themselves. Among them a divine singer sang
And played on the lyre. And a pair of tumblers about them
Started off at the song and whirled about in their midst.
20 Then the two of them stood in the gateway of the house,
The hero Telemachos and the illustrious son of Nestor,
They and their horses. The lord Eteoneus came forth
And saw them, the capable servant of glorious Menelaos.
He went through the halls to tell the shepherd of the people,
25 And he stood close to him and uttered wingèd words;
"Menelaos, nourished by Zeus, some strangers are here,
Two men, and they resemble the race of mighty Zeus.
Tell me, shall we unharness their swift horses for them
Or send them to reach another who will befriend them?"
30 Greatly disturbed, blond Menelaos spoke to him:
"Eteoneus, son of Boethoüs, you were never a fool

Before. But now you mouth foolishness like a child.
We ourselves, indeed, ate many guest offerings
Of other men as we came here, if only in the future
Zeus were ever to make woe cease. But unhitch the horses   35
Of the strangers. Go bring them forward to be entertained."
So he said, and the man passed quickly through the hall and
    called
Other capable servants to follow along with him.
They unhitched the sweating horses from under the yoke
And they haltered them in the mangers for horses.   40
They threw in emmer grains, and they mixed white barley in,
And leaned the chariot against the resplendent walls.
Then they led the men to the godly house. When they saw
The hall of the Zeus-nourished king, they wondered at it.
There was a gleam like that of the sun or of the moon   45
Beneath the high-roofed hall of glorious Menelaos.
But when they had taken their joy of looking with their eyes,
They went out and got washed in the well-polished bathtubs.
And when the maidservants had washed them and rubbed them
    with oil,
They put woolen cloaks around them and also tunics,   50
And they sat on armchairs beside Menelaos, son of Atreus.
A handmaid poured water from a pitcher she was carrying,
A lovely golden one, over into a silver basin,
For washing the hands. She set up a polished table alongside.
A respected housekeeper served bread she was carrying,   55
Laying out many dishes, gracious with the provisions.
A carver lifted up and set out trenchers of meats
Of all sorts, and set out gold goblets alongside for them.
Making a sign to the two men, blond Menelaos addressed them:
"Take some of the food and enjoy yourselves; and when   60
You have partaken of dinner, we shall ask what men
You may be. The race of your parents is not lost in you;
But you are of the race of men who are scepter-bearing kings,
Nourished by Zeus, since mean men would not produce sons
    like these."
So he spoke, and he took in his hands and set before them   65
The fat roast ox-back he had been given as an honor himself.
They stretched forth their hands to the food that was spread out
    ready.
But when they had taken their fill of food and drink,

Then Telemachos spoke out to the son of Nestor,
70 Holding his head close so that the others might not hear:
"Son of Nestor, you who have delighted my heart,
Notice the flash of bronze through the echoing halls,
Of gold and of amber, of silver and of ivory;
The court of Olympian Zeus must be like this inside,
75 So many wonders are here. Awe holds me when I look at them."
Blond Menelaos was aware of him as he spoke.
He addressed his voice to them and uttered wingèd words:
"Dear children, surely no mortal may contend with Zeus.
Immortal are his dwelling and his possessions.
80 But of men few if any could contend with me
In possessions. Yes, I suffered much and wandered much
When I brought them in the ships and arrived in the eighth
   year.
I wandered to Cyprus, to Phoenicia, and to the Egyptians;
I reached the Ethiopians, the Sidonians, and the Erembi,
85 And Libya, where the lambs are born sprouting horns at once.
The sheep give birth three times within a complete year.
No lord there, and also no shepherd, is at all lacking
In cheese and in meats, and not in sweet milk either;
But the flocks always furnish abundant milk for suckling.
90 I wandered thereabouts getting a great livelihood
While another man killed my brother unawares,
Secretly, through the cunning of his accursèd wife.
So it is not in delight that I rule over these possessions.
You will have heard about this from your fathers, whoever
95 They may be, since I suffered much, and ruined a home,
A good habitation, containing many noble things.
Would I might dwell in my halls with just a third share
Of those things, and the men were safe who perished then
In broad Troy, far away from horse-nourishing Argos!
100 But nevertheless I frequently sit in our halls
Mourning and grieving over all of them; sometimes
I please my mind with lamentation and sometimes
I cease from it. For quick is the glut of cold lamentation.
I do not, though I am grieved, mourn for them all so much
105 As I do for one man, who makes food and sleep hateful to me
When I think of him, since none of the Achaians suffered as
   much
As Odysseus suffered and bore. For him there were destined

To be troubles, and for me a perpetually ceaseless grief
Over him, since he has long been gone, and we do not know
If he lives or is dead. I suppose they are mourning him now,   110
The old Laertes and constant Penelope,
And Telemachos, whom he left as a newborn child in his
      house."
So he spoke, and roused in him a longing to mourn his father.
A tear fell on the ground from his eyelids as he heard of his
      father,
And he held the purple mantle up before his eyes   115
With both of his hands. Menelaos perceived him
And turned it over in his mind and in his heart
Whether he should allow him to mention his father himself
Or should first inquire and test him in the details.
While he pondered these matters in his mind and in his heart, 120
Helen[1] came out of the high-roofed fragrant bedroom,
She who resembled Artemis[2] of the golden shafts.
Adreste went with her and set up a well-made couch for her,
And Alcippé carried in a rug of soft wool.
Phylo carried a silver basket that Alcandré   125
Had given her, the wife of Polybos, who dwelt
In Egyptian Thebes, where the most goods are stored in the
      houses.
He gave two bathtubs of silver to Menelaos
And a pair of cauldrons and ten talents of gold.
His wife on her own presented the loveliest gifts to Helen;   130
She gave her a gold distaff, a basket with wheels underneath
Made of silver, and the rims of it were finished with gold.
The servant Phylo brought it in and set it out before her,
Stuffed with artfully arranged thread, and on it
There lay a distaff holding dark violet wool.   135
She sat in the chair; a footstool was beneath for her feet.
Right away she asked her husband in words for the details:
"Menelaos, nourished by Zeus, do we know who these people
Who have come to our home claim to be among men?
Shall I dissemble or speak the truth? My heart bids me to.   140
I think I have never yet seen anyone so like him,
A man or a woman; wonder holds me as I see this man,
For the way he looks like great-hearted Odysseus' son

1. Wife of Menelaos; carried off by Paris to Troy.
2. Daughter of Zeus and sister of Apollo.

Telemachos, whom he left as a newborn child in his house.
145 He did so when you Achaians, because of my bitch-faced self,
Went up under Troy intending a strenuous war."
And blond Menelaos addressed her in answer:
"My wife, I also now think it is just as you suppose.
His feet are the same as that man's, his hands are the same,
150 And the glances of his eyes, and his head, and the hair upon it.
Yes, just now I was remembering about Odysseus
And telling how much that man suffered in his grief
For my sake, and he shed quick tears from under his eyebrows,
Holding up the purple mantle in front of his eyes."
155 Peisistratos, son of Nestor, addressed him in answer:
"Son of Atreus, Zeus-nourished Menelaos , chief of the people,
This is really the son of the man, as you say.
But he is prudent; and in his heart he is ashamed
To come so the first time and make a show of bold talk
160 Before you, in whose voice we both delight as in a god's.
Now, the Gerenian horseman Nestor sent me out
To go along with him as a guide. He longed to see you,
So that you might provide him with something, a word or a
    deed.
The son of a father who is gone away has many pains
165 Within his halls, if there be no other helpers for him,
As now for Telemachos he is gone away, and there are
No others in the district who might ward off misery."
And blond Menelaos addressed him in answer:
"Well now, he comes to my house as the son of a man indeed
170 Very dear to me, one who suffered many trials for my sake,
And I thought when he came I would befriend him above all
Of the Argives, if broad-seeing Olympian Zeus had granted
A return for us both in our swift ships over the sea.
I would have settled him in a city in Argos and made a house,
175 Bringing him from Ithaca with his goods and his son
And all of his people, when I had sacked one city
Of those settled nearby that are ruled over by me.
When they were here we would often have mingled. Nothing
    else
Could have parted us two in our friendship and delight,
180 At least till the black cloud of death had veiled us about.
But the god himself must somehow have been jealous
To have made that wretched man alone fail to return."

So he said, and roused desire for lamentation in them all.
The Argive Helen wept, she who was born of Zeus,
And Telemachos wept, and Menelaos too, son of Atreus;   185
Nor did the son of Nestor keep his eyes without tears,
For in his heart he remembered excellent Antilochos,
Whom the glorious son of the brilliant Dawn had slain.
As he called that man to mind, he uttered wingèd words:
"Son of Atreus, old Nestor used to declare you to be   190
Sound-minded above mortals when we in his halls
Called you to mind and asked one another about you,
And now, if it may be, listen to me; I for my part
Do not enjoy mourning at dinner. And besides,
The early-born dawn will be here. I do not at all blame   195
Weeping for any mortal who dies and meets his fate.
This indeed is the sole honor for sorrowful mortals,
To cut the hair for them and let a tear fall from our cheeks.
Yes, my brother is dead, too, by no means the worst
Of the Argives. You probably knew him; I for my part   200
Never met him or saw him. They say Antilochos
Was better than others in fighting and in speed of running."
Then blond Menelaos addressed him in answer:
"My friend, you have said as much as a sound-minded man
Would say and perform, even one who was born before you.   205
You are the son of a great father, to speak so sound-mindedly.
Easily known is the seed of a man for whom the son of Cronos
Weaves the thread of wealth when he marries and when he is
    born,
Such as he has now steadily given Nestor all his days;
So the man himself may grow sleekly old in his halls,   210
And his sons may be wise and may excel with spears;
But let us cease the lamentation that was made before,
And let us once more think about dinner; let them pour
Water on our hands. There will be stories after dawn
For Telemachos and me to talk out with one another."   215
So he said, and Asphalion poured water over their hands,
The capable servant of glorious Menelaos.
And they stretched forth their hands to the food that was spread
    out ready.
Then Helen, who was born of Zeus, had another thought.
Right away she dropped a drug in the wine they were drinking,   220
A soothing pain-killer, that made one forget all his ills,

And whoever swallowed it down when it was mixed in the bowl
Would not shed a tear down his cheeks the whole day long,
Not if his mother and his father were both to die,
225 Not if right in front of him his brother or his dear son
Were slaughtered with a sword, and he see it with his own eyes.
Drugs of such devices did the daughter of Zeus have,
Good ones, which Polydamna gave her, wife of Thon,
From Egypt, where the grain-giving earth bears the most drugs,
230 Many of them good in mixture, and many harmful;
And each man is a physician, knowledgeable beyond
All men. For they are truly of the race of Paieon.[3]
But when she had put it in and called for wine to be poured,
She answered with a speech and spoke out once again:
235 "Zeus-nourished Menelaos, son of Atreus, and you men too,
Who are children of noble men—well, Zeus as a god gives
Good and evil now to one man and now to another;
For he can do all things. But come, sit and dine now in the hall,
And enjoy the tales. I shall tell an appropriate one.
240 Now I shall not be able to tell or enumerate all
Of the many trials there were for stout-hearted Odysseus;
But what a deed this one was the mighty man did and dared
In the land of the Trojans where you Achaians suffered troubles·
When he had submitted himself to disfiguring blows,
245 He threw a poor covering over his shoulders, and in the likeness
Of a servant he entered the enemy's broad-streeted city.
He likened himself in his concealment to another mortal,
To a beggar, he who by the Achaians' ships was nothing like
    that.
In that guise he entered the city of the Trojans. They all
250 Overlooked him. I alone recognized him as he was.
And I questioned him. He eluded me cunningly.
But when I was washing him and rubbing him with oil,
And had put garments on him and sworn a mighty oath
That I would not reveal Odysseus to the Trojans before
255 He should make his way back to the huts and the swift ships,
Then he told me the entire purpose of the Achaians.
Many of the Trojans he killed with the long-edged sword,
And went back to the Argives, and brought much information;
Then the other Trojan women lamented loudly. My heart,
    though,

3. A legendary physician of the gods; later, Apollo.

Rejoiced, since already the heart within me was turned   260
To go back home, and I bemoaned the madness Aphrodite
Gave me when she led me there far from my own fatherland,
Abandoning my daughter, my bedchamber, and my husband,
Who was lacking in nothing, either of mind or of form."
The blond Menelaos addressed her in answer: 265
"Yes, indeed, my wife, you have said all this properly.
Already I have learned the purpose and the thought of many
Men, of heroes, and I have traveled to many lands,
But never yet did I see with my own eyes such a man
As stout-minded Odysseus was, in his own heart,   270
Nor such a deed as that mighty man did and dared
In the polished horse, where all the noblest of us Argives
Sat inside bearing murder and destiny for the Trojans;
And then you came there. Some god must have beckoned you,
One of those who wished to bring glory to the Trojans;   275
Yes, and Deiphobos,[4] like a god, followed you as you went.
Three times you walked round the hollow decoy, handling it,
And called out the best of the Danaans, naming them by name,
Making your voice like that of the wives of all the Argives.
I and the son of Tydeus and godlike Odysseus,   280
As we sat in their midst, heard you as you shouted.
And the two of us were eager to make a start,
Either to get outside or to reply at once from within.
But Odysseus held us back and restrained us, though we wanted
    to.
Then all the other sons of the Achaians were silent   285
And Antilochos alone wished to give you answer
With a speech. But Odysseus steadily pressed the man's mouth
With his powerful hands, and he saved all the Achaians.
He held him until Pallas Athene led you away."
Then sound-minded Telemachos addressed him in answer: 290
"Menelaos, Zeus-nourished son of Atreus, chief of the people,
The more painful it is! This did not ward off his sad death
Nor would have, if the heart had been of iron within him.
But come, send us off to bed, so that right away
We may take the pleasure of lying down under sweet sleep."   295
So he said, and Argive Helen called to the serving maids
To put bedsteads down in the colonnade and to throw on
Lovely purple rugs, and to spread blankets above them,

4. Son of Priam and Hecuba; a prominent Trojan warrior.

And to put down woolen mantles on top of all that.
300 They went out of the hall bearing each a torch in her hand
And covered the bedsteads. And a herald led the strangers out.
So they went to sleep right there in the forecourt of the house,
The hero Telemachos and the illustrious son of Nestor.
The son of Atreus slept in a nook of the lofty house,
And by him lay Helen of the long gown, a goddess among
305   women.
And when the early-born, rosy-fingered dawn appeared,
Menelaos, good at the war cry, rose up out of his bed,
Put on his clothes, set the sharp sword round his shoulder,
Bound the lovely sandals beneath his shining feet,
310 And went on out of the bedroom like a god to look at.
He sat by Telemachos, and spoke out to him directly:
"Hero Telemachos, what need brought you hither
To godly Lacedemon, upon the broad back of the sea,
A public one or your own? Tell me this unerringly."
315 Sound-minded Telemachos addressed him in answer:
"Menelaos, Zeus-nourished son of Atreus, chief of the people,
I came to see if you might tell me some news of my father.
My house is being eaten up, my fertile lands are ruined,
My home is full of enemy men who perpetually slay
My throngs of sheep and my shamble-footed, crumple-horned
320   cattle,
Suitors of my mother, who possess presumptuous pride.
So now I embrace your knees to ask if you are willing
To tell me about that man's woeful death, if you saw it
With your own eyes, perhaps, or heard the tale from another
325 Wanderer. For excessive sorrow did his mother bear him!
Sweeten nothing out of pity or respect for me,
But tell me straight out how you encountered the sight,
I beseech you, if ever my father, noble Odysseus,
Promised you any word or deed and carried it out
330 In the Trojan's land where you Achaians suffered troubles,
Remember that for me now, and tell me unerringly."
Greatly disturbed, blond Menelaos spoke to him:
"Well now, they who are themselves without courage
Have wished to lie down in the bed of a stouthearted man!
335 As when a deer in the thicket of a mighty lion
Has put her newborn milk-sucking fawn to sleep,
And goes questing over the spurs and the grassy gorges

For grazing, and just then he comes into his own lair
And upon the two of them brings a wretched fate;
So upon these men will Odysseus bring a wretched fate.   340
Father Zeus and Athene and Apollo, I wish
He might be as he once was in well-established Lesbos,
When he stood up and wrestled in a fight with Philomelides,
Threw him down mightily, and all the Achaians rejoiced—
As that sort of man might Odysseus contend with the suitors.   345
They would all be swift in their doom and bitter in marriage.
As for what you ask and beseech me about, I myself
Will say nothing at all off the point, nor will I deceive.
But what the unerring old man of the sea told me,
Not a word of that shall I hide from you or conceal.   350
The gods were still holding me in Egypt, though I was striving
To return here, as I had not sacrificed full hecatombs for them.
The gods have always wished their injunctions to be kept in
     mind.
Well, there is a certain island in the much-surging ocean,
Over before the Nile, and they call it Pharos,   355
Just so far away as a hollow ship in a day
Could reach it, with a shrill breeze blowing on behind.
There is a well-sheltered harbor in it, from which men launch
Balanced ships on the ocean, when they have drawn black water
     on board.
There the gods held me twenty days. No breezes ever   360
Came blowing upon the sea, the ones that become
Escorts for ships over the broad back of the sea.
And all the food would have been spent, and the men's
     strength,
If one of the gods had not felt sorry for me and pitied me,
The daughter of mighty Proteus, old man of the sea,   365
Eidothëe; her heart I aroused especially,
When she met me walking alone apart from my companions,
For they were always roaming around the island fishing
With bent fishhooks, and hunger wore on their stomachs.
She stood close to me, spoke, and uttered a speech: 370
'Are you a fool, stranger? Are you too slack of mind?
Do you willingly let go and enjoy suffering pain?
So long a time are you held back on the island and cannot
Find a way out, and the heart dwindles in your companions.'
So she said, and I addressed her in answer: 375

'I shall tell you right out, whatever goddess you are,
That I do not hold back at all willingly, but I must have
Trespassed against the immortals who possess broad heaven.
But you tell me now yourself—the gods know all—
380 Which of the immortals constrains and binds me from my way;
And tell about my return, how I may go on the fish-laden
   ocean?'
So I said; she, the divine goddess, answered at once:
'All right, stranger, I shall speak out truthfully.
A certain unerring old man of the sea comes here,
385 The immortal Egyptian, Proteus, who knows
The depths of the whole sea, a subject to Poseidon.
They say he is my own father and sired me.
If somehow you could hide in an ambush and catch him,
He will tell you your course and the measures of your way,
390 About a return, how you may go on the fish-laden ocean,
And he may tell you, too, if you wish, you who are nourished by
   Zeus,
Whatever good and evil has been done in your halls
While you have been gone on the long and burdensome jour-
   ney.'
So did she speak, and I addressed her in answer:
395 'Show me now yourself the ambush for the divine old man,
Lest somehow he see me or learn of me first and escape,
As it is hard for a god to be subdued by a mortal man.'
So I said, and she, the divine goddess, answered at once:
'All right, I shall speak straight out to you truthfully.
400 At the time when the sun strides the middle of heaven,
Then the unerring old man of the sea comes from the sea
Under the blowing West Wind, hidden in a black ripple;
And when he gets out he sleeps down inside the hollow caves.
Around him the foot-swimming seals of the lovely sea's daughter
405 Sleep in a flock, when they have risen out of the hoary sea,
Exhaling a bitter smell of the sea that has many depths;
There I will lead you myself when the dawn appears
And will lay you down in due order. Make a good choice
Of three companions who are your best in the well-timbered
   ships,
410 And I shall tell you all the cunning of this old man.
At first he will number the seals and go over them,
But when he has counted them by fives and looked at them all,

He will lie in their midst like a shepherd amid flocks of sheep.
And when you first see him lying down to rest,
At that very moment give heed to your strength and might.   415
Hold him struggling there, though he be violent to escape.
He will try it by becoming all the many creatures
That move on the earth; and then water, and divinely kindled
    fire.
But hold him firmly yourselves and constrain him the more.
When at last he questions you with a speech as himself   420
And is the way he was when you saw him resting,
Then, hero, hold back your strength and release the old man,
And ask him which one of the gods oppresses you,
And about a return, how you may go on the fish-laden ocean.'
When she had said this, she vanished into the ocean's surging
    waves.   425
But I went to the ships where they were standing on the sands.
The heart within me brooded about much as I went.
But when I arrived at the ship and at the sea,
And had prepared dinner, and ambrosial night came on,
Then did we lie down to sleep by the surf of the sea.   430
And when the early-born, rosy-fingered dawn appeared,
I went on along the strand of the wide-pathed sea,
Supplicating the gods very much. And I brought along
Three companions whom I most trusted for every course.
Meanwhile she had gone down under the broad bosom of the
    sea   435
And she took four skins of the seals out of the ocean;
All of them were new-flayed. And she planned a trick on her
    father.
When she had scooped out beds in the sands of the sea,
She sat waiting. We came up very close to her.
She bedded us down in a row and threw a skin over each;   440
There the ambush would have been most dreadful. The dire
    smell
Of the sea-nourished seals oppressed us dreadfully,
For who would lie down to sleep with a monster of the sea?
But she saved us herself and thought up a great remedy;
She brought and put under each one's nostrils, ambrosia   445
That has a sweet aroma, and it destroyed the smell of seal,
And we waited with enduring heart the whole morning.
The seals came up in a flock from the sea. Then in a row

They lay down to sleep along the surf of the sea.
450 At full light the old man came from the sea and found his seals
Well nourished; he went over them all and counted their
number,
And us he numbered first among the seals, nor did it occur
To his heart that there was a trick. Then he lay down himself.
But we rushed on him with a shout and threw our hands
455 Around him. The old man did not forget his wily skill.
First of all he became a lion with a mighty beard,
And then a serpent, and a panther, and a great boar.
Then he became watery water, and a lofty-leaved tree.
But we held on firmly with an enduring heart,
460 And when the old man of cunning skill was exhausted,
He spoke out to me and questioned me with a speech:
'Which of the gods, son of Atreus, has devised plots for you
That you catch me in ambush against my will? What do you
need?'
So he spoke, and I for my part addressed him in answer:
465 'You know, old man—why do you say this and put me off?—
How long I am held back on this island and can find
No way out, and the heart is dwindling within me.
But you yourself tell me now—the gods know all—
Which of the immortals constrains me and binds me from my
way,
470 And my return, how I may go on the fish-laden ocean?'
So I said, and right away he addressed me in answer:
'Surely before embarking you ought to have made fair sacrifices
To Zeus and the other gods, so that you may very soon
Reach your fatherland, sailing on the wine-faced sea.
475 For it will not be your lot to see your friends and to reach
Your well-established home and your own fatherland
Until you come once again to the waters of the Nile,
The Zeus-fallen [5] river, and there perform sacred hecatombs
To the immortal gods who possess broad heaven.
480 Then the gods will give you the journey you desire.'
So he said, but my own heart was shattered within me,
Because he ordered me back onto the murky ocean,
To go to the Nile, a long and burdensome journey.
Yet this is what I answered, addressing him with a speech:

5. This probably means "rain-fed," since it is "Zeus" who "rains" in
ancient Greece.

'So shall I perform it, old man, just as you direct me.   485
But come now, tell me this, and speak out truthfully:
Did all the Achaians arrive safe and sound with their ships,
Those whom Nestor and I left when we went from Troy,
Or did any of them perish on his ship by a harsh death?
Or in the arms of his friends, after he had wound up the war?'   490
So I said, and he straightway addressed me in answer:
'Son of Atreus, why do you ask me all this? There is no need
For you to know it or learn my thoughts. And I say that you
Will not long be tearless when you have found it all out.
Many of them were overcome, and many are left.   495
But two leaders alone of the bronze-clad Achaians
Died on the return. As for the battle, you were there yourself.
A single man, perhaps still alive, is held back on the broad
   ocean.
Ajax [6] was overcome in the midst of his long-oared ships.
Poseidon at first brought him up close to Gyrai,   500
The great headlands, and rescued him out of the sea.
And he would have escaped his fate, though hated by Athene,
If he had not thrown out a bold word and lost his senses.
He said he had escaped the sea's great gulf against the god's will,
And Poseidon heard him as he uttered his great boast;   505
Straightway then he took his trident in his muscular hands,
Struck the headland of Gyrai, and split some of it off;
One part stayed on the spot; the fragment fell in the ocean,
The one Ajax was perched on when he lost his senses,
And it carried him down to the boundless wave-breaking ocean. 510
So he perished there, when he had drunk the salty water.
Your brother, though, escaped the fates and eluded them
In his hollow ships. And the queenly Hera [7] saved him.
But just at the time when he was set to arrive at the sheer
Mountain of Malea, a tempest snatched him up   515
And carried him heavily groaning on the fish-laden ocean,
To the verge of the land where the halls of Thyestes were
Beforehand, but now Thyestes' son Aigisthos lived there.
And when from that place, too, a safe return appeared,
The gods turned the breeze back again and sent him homeward. 520
Rejoicing, he set foot on the soil of his fatherland,

6. This is the "second" Ajax, son of Oileus, not the better-known son
of Telamon.
7. Queen of the gods; wife and sister of Zeus.

And he kept kissing the fatherland as he touched it. Many warm
   tears
Poured from his eyes when in gladness he saw his land.
But a watchman saw him from a watch point, whom cunning
525 Aigisthos had led and stationed there, and promised a reward,
Two talents of gold, and he watched there for a year
Lest the man should slip by him and recall his impetuous might.
He went through the halls to tell the shepherd of the people.
Right away Aigisthos thought up a crafty design.
530 He picked out the twenty best men in the district and set
An ambush, and bid them make dinner on the other side.
And he went to call Agamemnon, shepherd of the people,
With horses and chariot, planning his horrid plans.
He led him in unaware of his destruction,
535 And after feasting him, slew him, as one kills an ox at the crib.
None of the comrades was left who followed the son of Atreus,
And none of Aigisthos' but they were killed in the halls.'
So he said, but my own heart was shattered within me.
And I wept as I sat on the sand, and wished in my heart
540 Not to live any longer and see the light of the sun.
But when I had enough of weeping and groveling,
Then the unerring old man of the sea addressed me:
'Son of Atreus, do not weep any more so persistently
And so long, since we shall find no result from that,
545 But try to arrive as soon as you can at your fatherland.
You may find the man alive, or Orestes will have gone ahead
And killed him, and you may come upon his funeral.'
So he said, and the heart within me and the bold spirit
Were warmed again in my breast, even though I was grieved.
550 And speaking out to him, I uttered wingèd words:
'These men I know of. But tell me about the third man,
The one who was held back upon the broad sea, still alive,
Or he is dead. Though I am grieved, I want to hear of him.'
So I said, and right away he addressed me in answer:
555 'That is the son of Laertes, whose home is in Ithaca,
I saw him on an island shedding a swelling tear
In the halls of the nymph Calypso, who by compulsion
Is holding him back, and he cannot reach his fatherland,
For he has no ships there with oars, and no companions
560 Who might convey him over the broad back of the sea.
And for you it is not decreed, Zeus-nourished Menelaos,

In horse-pasturing Argos to die and to meet your fate.
But the immortals will send you to the Elysian plain
And the end of the earth, where blond Rhadamanthys [8] is,
And where the easiest living exists for men.   565
No snow is there, not much winter, and never rain,
But instead clearly blowing breezes of the West Wind
Does Oceanos [9] always send on to put a fresh breath in men,
Because you have Helen and are for them a son-in-law of Zeus.'
When he had said this, he went down under the wave-breaking
    ocean.   570
But I went to the ships with my godlike companions,
And the heart within me was troubled as I went.
But when we arrived at the ships and at the sea
And had prepared a dinner and ambrosial night came on,
Then did we lie down to sleep by the surf of the sea.   575
And when the early-born, rosy-fingered dawn appeared,
First of all we dragged our ships to the godly sea
And set up masts and sails upon the balanced ships,
Then we ourselves boarded and sat down at the oarlocks.
Seated in a row, we beat the hoary sea with our oars.   580
Back at the Egyptian Nile, the Zeus-fallen river,
I beached the ships and sacrificed complete hecatombs.
When I had calmed down the wrath of the ever-living gods
I set up a mound for Agamemnon so his fame would be
    unquenched.
When I completed this, I left. The immortals gave me   585
A breeze, and they sent me quickly to my dear fatherland—
But come, stay on for the time being here in my halls,
Until the eleventh day comes, and also the twelfth.
Then I will send you off well; I will give you glorious gifts,
Three horses and a well-polished chariot. And then   590
I will give you a lovely libation cup, so you may pour
To the immortal gods, remembering me all your days."
Then sound-minded Telemachos addressed him in answer:
"Son of Atreus, do not hold me back here a long time.
I myself would surely stay sitting here with you   595
For a year, and no longing for home or parents would take me;
So terribly pleased am I to be listening to your words
And stories. Already my companions in hollowed Pylos

8. A judge over the dead.
9. The mythical ocean encircling the earth.

Are worrying, and you have held me back here for some time.
600 As for the gift you would give me, let it be a keepsake.
I will not bring horses to Ithaca, but I shall leave them here
As an adornment for yourself. You rule a broad plain
And in it there is much clover and galingale,
Wheat in it, and emmer grain, and broad-growing white barley.
605 In Ithaca there are no broad courses or any meadow;
It has pasture for goats and is pleasanter than a horse pasture.
But none of the islands that lie by the sea has good meadows
Or a place for driving horses, and Ithaca surpasses them all."
So he said, and Menalaos, good at the war cry, smiled.
610 He caressed him with one hand, and spoke out to him directly:
"You are of good blood, dear child, to judge by what you say,
And so I will exchange these for you, since I çan.
Of the gifts that lie stored as keepsakes in my house,
I shall give you the one that is loveliest and of highest worth.
615 I shall give you a well-fashioned mixing bowl. It is all
Of silver, and its rim is finished round with gold,
The work of Hephaistos. The hero Phaidimos gave it,
King of the Sidonians, when his house took me in
As I had returned that far. I would like to give it to you."
620 And so they said such things to one another,
While the dinner guests went to the halls of the godly king.
They drove in sheep and brought in wine that is good for men,
And their wives with beautiful shawls sent them bread.
So they were busying themselves about dinner in the halls.
625 Meanwhile the suitors out in front of the hall of Odysseus
Were amusing themselves by throwing weights and javelins
On the leveled terrace, as before, in their insolence.
Antinoos sat by, and the godlike Eurymachos,
Leaders of the suitors, who for excellence were far the best.
630 Noemon, the son of Phronios, came close to them
And addressed Antinoos, questioning him with a speech:
"Antinoos, do we or do we not know in our minds
When Telemachos is coming back from sandy Pylos?
He has gone off in my ship. A need for it has arisen
635 To cross over to Elis of the broad dancing-place
Where I have twelve brood mares, and suckling mules, tough
    workers,
That are untrained; one of these I would drive and tame."

So he said. They were amazed at heart. They did not think
He had gone to Nelean Pylos, but was somewhere there
Around in the fields with the sheep or with the swineherd.   640
Then Antinoos, son of Eupeithes, addressed him:
"Tell me unerringly when he went away and what
Young men went with him. Were they the chosen of Ithaca
Or his own slaves and hirelings? He could have done this too.
Tell me this exactly, so that I may know it well,   645
Did he take the black ship by force from you against your will,
Or did you give it willingly when he begged you with a speech?"
Noemon, son of Phronios, addressed him in answer:
"I gave it to him willingly. What would another man do
When a man of such a kind had cares in his heart   650
And requested it? It would be hard to refuse the gift.
The young men who are best in the district, next to us,
Went with him. And I noticed Mentor boarding as leader,
Or a god who in every way resembled him.
And I wonder at this; I saw godlike Mentor here   655
Yesterday morning. Yet he was gone then in the ship to Pylos."
When he had said this, he went off to the halls of his father.
And in both of them the bold spirit was amazed.
They sat the suitors down together and stopped their contests.
Antinoos, son of Eupeithes, spoke out to them,   660
Troubled. For his heart, black all round, was greatly filled
With rage. And his eyes resembled a shining fire:
"Well now, this voyage is a great deed carried out very boldly
By Telemachos. We thought he would not carry it out.
In spite of us all, he went off, the young child, just like that,   665
When he had dragged down the ship and chosen the best in the
     district.
He will begin to be a trouble even more. Yet may Zeus
Destroy his power before he gains the measure of manhood.
But come now, give me a swift ship and twenty companions,
So that I may lie in ambush and watch for him as he comes   670
In the channel between Ithaca and rugged Samos,
That this voyage for his father may be a grievous one."
So he said, and they all spoke out and assented.
They stood up at once then and went to the house of Odysseus,
Nor was Penelope for a long time unaware   675
Of the plots that the suitors were pondering in their hearts:

Medon, the herald, told her, who had listened to their plans
When he was outside the courtyard; they were weaving their de-
    ceit within.
He went through the halls to announce it to Penelope,
And Penelope addressed him as he stepped down on the thresh-
680   old:
"Herald, why did the noble suitors send you out?
To bid the maidservants of the godly Odysseus
To cease from their labors and fix a dinner for them?
May they never go wooing or come together elsewhere;
685 May they dine here now for the last and final time.
You who often gather and consume a large living,
The wealth of skilled Telemachos, did you not hear
From your fathers long ago, when you were children,
The sort of man Odysseus was among your parents?
690 He never performed or said anything unjust
In the district—this is the way of godly kings,
Who might despise one mortal and love another—
But he never acted recklessly against any man.
Now your own hearts and your disgraceful deeds
695 Are clear. There are no thanks afterward for deeds well done."
Then Medon, sound-minded in knowledge, addressed her:
"Well, my queen, may this be your greatest misfortune.
But the suitors are devising another one greater by far
And more disastrous. May the son of Cronos not bring it to
    pass!
700 They are eager to murder Telemachos with the sharp sword
As he comes homeward. He went off to hear of his father
To divine Pylos, and also to godly Lacedemon."
So he said; right there her knees and her own heart went slack.
Speechlessness seized her for a long time. Her two eyes
705 Were filled with tears, and her resonant voice was held back.
She answered him at last with a speech and addressed him:
"Herald, why did my son go away? There was no need
At all to embark in the swift-faring ships, that are
Horses of the sea for men and cross over much water.
710 Was it so that not even his name might be left among men?"
Then Medon, sound-minded in knowledge, answered her:
"I do not know whether some god incited him
Or his own spirit roused him to go to Pylos to learn
If his father will return or has met his fate."

When he had said this, he went into the house of Odysseus.   715
But heartbreaking anguish poured over her. No longer
Could she bear sitting on a chair, and many were in the house.
But she sat down on the threshold of the richly adorned bed-
     room,
Lamenting piteously, and the serving maids moaned about her,
All the many that were in the halls, young and old.   720
When she had moaned heavily, Penelope spoke out to them:
"Hear me, my friends. For Olympian Zeus has given me pain
Beyond all the women who were born and raised in my time;
Beforehand I lost a noble lion-hearted husband,
Who excelled in all the virtues among the Danaans,   725
A noble man whose glory is wide through Greece and middle
     Argos.
And now storms have snatched away my beloved son
Unnoticed from the halls; nor did I hear of his rushing off.
Cruel ones—why did each of you at least not put it in her mind
To wake me out of bed, when you clearly knew in your heart   730
The time he was going down to the hollow black ship?
If I had found out he was considering the voyage,
Then, though eager for voyage, he would surely have stayed
     here,
Or else he would have left me in the halls a dead woman.
But let someone speedily call the old man Dolios,   735
My servant, whom my father gave me before I came here,
Who tends my garden with its many trees; so he shall right
     away
Sit down beside Laertes and explain all this to him;
If somehow that man may weave some plan in his mind
And may go out and complain to the people about these men   740
Who wish to destroy his stock and that of godly Odysseus."
Then the beloved nurse Eurycleia addressed her:
"Dear bride, you may slay me with the pitiless sword,
Or leave me in the house. I will not hide the story from you.
I knew all this. I provided all that he ordered,   745
Bread and sweet wine. He put me under a great oath
Not to tell you until either the twelfth day should come,
Or you should miss him yourself and hear of his rushing off,
So you might not weep and injure your lovely skin.
But do take a bath and put clean clothes on your skin.   750
Then ascend to the upper chamber with the serving women

And pray to Athene, daughter of aegis-bearing Zeus,
For she can save him in that case, even from death.
Do not trouble the troubled old man. I do not think
755 The offspring of Arkesios' son is entirely hated
By the blessed gods; there may yet be someone to own
The high-roofed dwelling and the rich fields far away."
So she said, and soothed the other's weeping: she held her eyes
    from weeping.
She did take a bath and put clean clothes on her skin,
760 Ascended to the upper chamber with the serving women,
Put barley for sprinkling in a basket, and prayed to Athene.
"Hear me, unwearying child of aegis-bearing Zeus,
If ever in his halls Odysseus of many devices
Burned the fat thighs of an ox or a sheep for you,
765 Remember them now for me and save my dear son.
Ward the suitors off in their evil presumption."
She wailed as she said this. And the goddess heard her prayer.
The suitors were making a din through the shadowy halls,
And this is what one of the overbearing young men would say:
770 "Yes, indeed, the much-wooed queen is planning a wedding
For us, and does not know that murder is prepared for her son."
So one would say, and they did not know how it was prepared.
And Antinoos spoke out to them and addressed them:
"You fools, keep away from all insolent speeches
775 Entirely, lest someone announce them inside as well.
But come, let us stand up, and accomplish in silence
The very plan that suited the minds of all of us."
When he had said this, he selected the twenty men that were
    best
And they went on down to the swift ship and the strand of the
    sea.
780 First of all they dragged the ship into a depth of salt water,
Then set up a mast and sails upon the black ship.
They fitted the oars into the straps made of leather
All in order—and then stretched out the white sails.
Proud-spirited servants carried equipment on for them.
785 High in flowing water they moored her, and got out themselves.
There they took dinner and waited for evening to come.
The prudent Penelope there in her upper chamber
Lay without eating, not partaking of food or drink,
Pondering whether her excellent son might escape death,

Or would go under to the presumptuous suitors.   790
As much as a lion deliberates in a crowd of men,
Fearing when they draw the stealthy circle about him;
So much did she ponder, and balmy sleep came upon her.
She sank back, and slept, and her limbs were all slackened.
Then the bright-eyed goddess Athene had another thought.   795
She made an image and likened it in form to a woman,
To Iphthime, daughter of great-hearted Icarios
That Eumelos, whose house of dwelling was in Pherai, married.
She sent her to the halls of the godly Odysseus,
So that she could make the grieving and wailing Penelope   800
Cease from her tearful wailing and lamentation.
She went into the bedroom by the thong of the bolt,
Stood over her head, and addressed a speech to her:
"Are you asleep, Penelope, sorrowing in your own heart?
No, the gods who live without care do not allow you   805
To mourn or to grieve, since your son is still set
To return. For he is in no way sinful before the gods."
And then the prudent Penelope answered her,
Slumbering very sweetly within the gates of dreams:
"My kinswoman, why have you come here? Never before   810
Did you visit, since the halls you dwell in are far, far away.
Do you bid me to desist from sorrow and from pains,
The many that beset me in my mind and in my heart?
Beforehand I lost a noble, lion-hearted husband,
A noble man whose glory is wide through Greece and middle
      Argos.   815
Who excelled in all the virtues among the Danaans,
And now my dear son has gone off in a hollow ship,
A foolish child who has no good knowledge of toils or of
      councils,
And I am more grieved about him than about the other.
I tremble for him and fear lest he suffer something   820
In the land of those he has gone to, or on the ocean,
For there are many hostile men who contrive against him,
Wanting to kill him before he reaches his fatherland."
The shadowy image answered and addressed her:
"Take courage; do not fear excessively in your mind.   825
Such is she who goes as his guide, she whom other men
Have prayed to stand by them, and she has the power,
Pallas Athene. She takes pity on your lamenting

And has sent me forth now to say these things to you."
830 Then the prudent Penelope spoke forth to her:
"If indeed you are a god, and have heard the voice of a god,
Come tell me also about that sorrowful man,
Whether he still lives somehow and sees the light of the sun,
Or has already died and is in the halls of Hades."
835 The shadowy image answered her and addressed her:
"About that man I shall not tell you in full detail
Whether he is dead or alive. It is bad to utter windy things."
When it had said this, it slipped through the bolt of the
        doorpost
Into the blasts of the wind. The daughter of Icarios
840 Rose up out of sleep. And her own heart was gladdened,
So clear had the dream rushed upon her in the gloom of the
        night.
The suitors had boarded and were sailing on the watery ways,
Devising in their minds sheer murder for Telemachos.
There is a rocky island in the middle of the sea,
845 Halfway between Ithaca and rugged Samos,
Asteris, not large. Its harbors have coves for ships,
On both sides. There the Achaians lay waiting in ambush.

V

Dawn, out of her bed, from beside the noble Tithonos,[1]
Rose up to bring light to immortals and to mortals.
The gods took their seats in assembly. And in their midst
Was high-thundering Zeus, who has the greatest might.
Athene spoke to them, reminding them of the many cares   5
Of Odysseus. His being in the nymph's home concerned her.
"Father Zeus, and you other blessed, ever-living gods,
Let no scepter-bearing king be deliberately
Kind and mild any longer, or keep his mind on the right,
But may he be perpetually harsh and act unjustly;   10
Since there is no one who remembers the godly Odysseus
Of the people he ruled; and he was mild as a father.
He is staying on an island suffering strong pains
In the halls of the nymph Calypso, who by compulsion
Is holding him back, and he cannot reach his fatherland,   15
For he has no ships there with oars and no companions
Who might convey him over the broad back of the sea.
And now they are striving to kill his beloved son
As he comes homeward. He went off to hear of his father,
To divine Pylos, and also to godly Lacedemon."   20
And cloud-gathering Zeus addressed her in answer:
"My child, what sort of word has got past the bar of your teeth?
Why did you not think out this idea by yourself,
That Odysseus might indeed take vengeance on them when he
    came?
Guide Telemachos yourself, skillfully; you can do it,   25
So that he may arrive unscathed at his fatherland,
And so the suitors may go in their ship back where they came
    from."
He said that, and addressed in turn his dear son Hermes:
"Hermes—for in other matters you are my messenger—

1. The mortal husband of Dawn, granted immortality but not perpetual youth.

30 Tell the nymph of the fair braids my unerring plan,
   A return for stout-hearted Odysseus, how he may go back
   Without an escort of gods or one of mortal men.
   Yes, and he, on a strongly-bound raft, suffering troubles,
   Will arrive at rich-loamed Scheria on the twentieth day,
35 To the land of the Phaeacians, who are close kin to the gods,
   And they will honor him most heartily as a god.
   They will send him in a ship to his dear fatherland
   When they have given him bronze and gold and sufficient
      clothing,
   Much more than Odysseus would ever have taken from Troy
40 If he had come safe and sound and got his share of the booty.
   And so it is his lot to see his dear ones and arrive
   At his high-roofed home and his own fatherland."
   So he said, and the runner, slayer of Argos, did not disobey.
   At once, then, he bound beneath his feet the lovely sandals,
45 The ambrosial golden ones that carry him over water
   Or the limitless land, swift as the blasts of the wind.
   And he took the wand with which he entrances the eyes
   Of those men he wishes, and wakes up others who are sleeping.
   The strong god, slayer of Argos, flew on with that in his hands.
50 He passed Pieria, and fell from the air on the ocean,
   Then he hastened upon the wave as a sea gull does
   That over the terrible gulfs of the barren sea
   Dips its rapid wings, while catching fish, in the brine.
   Like one of these, Hermes bore himself over many waves.
55 But when he arrived at the island that was far away,
   He stepped from the violetlike ocean onto the dry land,
   And went on till he came to the great cave wherein the nymph
   Of the fair braids was dwelling. He came upon her within.
   On the hearth a big fire was burning, and the smell from afar
60 Of cedar and easy-split citron was exhaled through the island
   As it blazed. She within, singing in a lovely voice,
   Moved to and fro at the loom and wove with a gold shuttle.
   Wood was growing in abundance around the cave,
   Alder and black poplar and fine-scented cypress,
65 Where the birds with their long wings went to sleep,
   Horned owls and hawks and, with their long tongues,
   Salt water crows, who are busy with things of the sea.
   And right on the spot round the hollow cave had been drawn
   A trained vine in bloom that was blossoming with clusters.

Four springs one after another flowed with white water   70
All close together; one turned one way, one another.
All around soft meadows of violet and wild parsley
Were blooming. And even an immortal who might come there
Would wonder to look and be delighted in his mind.
As he stood there, the Runner, the slayer of Argos, wondered,   75
But when he had wondered in his heart at it all,
He went right away into the broad cave. As she faced him,
Calypso, the divine goddess, did not fail to know him by sight,
For the gods never fail to know one another,
The immortals, not even one who lives in a far-off home.   80
And he did not come upon the great-hearted Odysseus within;
The man was weeping, seated on the beach where he had been
    before,
Shattering his heart with tears and laments and groans.
He was looking out on the barren sea, shedding tears.
But Calypso, the divine goddess, questioned Hermes,   85
When she had seated him upon a bright, glistening chair.
"Hermes of the golden wand, my respected friend,
Why have you come to me? You have not come often before.
Say what you have in mind. My spirit bids me to do it
If I am able to do it and if it can be done;   90
But follow me, so I may entertain you as a guest."
When she had said this, the goddess set a table alongside
Full of ambrosia, and she mixed up ruddy nectar.
Then the Runner, the slayer of Argos, ate and drank.
When he had dined and satisfied his heart with food,   95
He spoke out and addressed her in answer with a speech:
"You, a goddess, ask me, a god, why I come. And I
Will tell you the story unerringly, since you ask me.
Zeus ordered me to come here against my own will.
Who would willingly cross so much indescribable   100
Salt water? There is no city of mortals nearby
Who offer sacrifices and choice hecatombs to the gods.
But in no way is it possible for another god
To slip by or frustrate the purpose of aegis-bearing Zeus.
He says you have with you the wretchedest man of all   105
Those men who were fighting around the city of Priam
For nine years; and in the tenth year sacked the city
And went home. But on the return they sinned against Athene,
Who roused up against them an ill wind and great waves.

110 Then all the others, his noble companions, perished.
But the wind and the water carried and brought him here.
Zeus now orders you to send him off as fast as you can.
For it is not right he should waste here far from his dear ones.
No, his fate is still to see his dear ones and come
115 To his high-roofed home and his own fatherland."
So he said, and Calypso, the divine goddess, went cold;
And she spoke out to him and uttered wingèd words:
"You are cruel, you gods, jealous above all others,
Who begrudge it to goddesses when they sleep with men
120 Openly, if one wants to make a man her dear husband.
So when the rosy-fingered Dawn chose Orion,
You gods, who live at ease, begrudged him to her
Till the chaste golden-throned Artemis in Ortygia
Came upon him and slew him with her soothing shafts.
125 And so when fair-braided Demeter yielded in her heart
To Iasion,[2] and lay with him in love and in bed
In a thrice-plowed fallow, it did not take Zeus long
To find out; he slew him, hurling a dazzling thunderbolt.
So now you gods begrudge a mortal man's being with me.
130 I myself saved him as he was bestriding his keel
All alone, when Zeus with a dazzling thunderbolt
Crushed his swift ship, and sank it in the middle of the
      wine-faced sea.
Then all the others, his noble companions, perished.
But the wind and the water carried and brought him here.
135 I have loved him and nourished him and I have declared to him
I would make him immortal and ageless all his days.
But in no way is it possible for another god
To slip by or frustrate the purpose of aegis-bearing Zeus.
Let him go, if that god commands him and drives him
140 Out on the barren ocean. I myself will send him nowhere,
For I have no ships here with oars, and no companions
Who might convey him over the broad back of the sea.
But I shall advise him graciously, and shall conceal nothing,
So that he may arrive unscathed at his fatherland."
145 And then the Runner, the slayer of Argos, spoke to her:
"Send him off this way now, and respect the wrath of Zeus,

2. Probably an early cult figure, an agricultural god who may have been
united with Demeter, the grain goddess, in a primitive rite on a plowed
field (as suggested in these lines).

So that afterward he will not be enraged and hold it against
   you."
When he had said this, the strong slayer of Argos departed,
And the queenly nymph went to great-hearted Odysseus,
Since she had indeed given ear to the message of Zeus.   150
She found him seated on the shore. His eyes never
Were dry of tears, but his sweet life was flowing away
As he mourned for a return, since the nymph no longer pleased
   him.
But he slept the nights with her by necessity
In the hollow cave, an unwilling man with a willing woman.   155
During the days, sitting up on the rocks and on the beaches,
Shattering his heart with tears and laments and groans,
He kept looking over the barren ocean, shedding tears.
The divine goddess stood close to him and addressed him:
"Ill-fated man, do not mourn here longer beside me, do not let 160
Your life waste away, for I shall now graciously send you off.
But come, cut long pieces of wood and fit them with a bronze
   ax
For a wide raft. And fashion half-decks upon it
High up, so that it may bear you over the murky sea.
And in it I shall put food and water and ruddy wine   165
That are satisfying and will check your hunger.
I shall dress you in clothes and send a breeze behind you,
So that you may arrive unscathed at your fatherland,
If the gods are willing, who possess broad heaven,
Who are more powerful than I at planning and achieving."   170
So she said, and godly Odysseus, who had borne much, went
   cold,
And he spoke out to her and uttered wingèd words:
"You devise this, goddess, for some other reason, not to get me
   there,
And you bid me to traverse in a raft the great gulf of the sea,
Terrible and disastrous, which not even balanced ships,   175
In their swift course, may cross, exulting in the breeze of Zeus.
I would not for my part board the raft against your will
Unless you will put up with swearing me a great oath, goddess,
That you will not plot some other bad trouble against me."
So he said, and the divine goddess Calypso smiled,   180
She caressed him with one hand, and spoke out to him directly:
"Ah, you are a real rogue, skilled in tricks that are not futile,

To have conceived and uttered a speech of this sort.
May the earth and broad heaven above witness this oath,
185 And the flowing water of Styx,[3] which is the greatest
And most dreadful oath there is for the blessed gods:
I will not plot any other bad trouble against you,
But I am thinking and considering the very things
I would plan for myself should an equal need come upon me.
190 Yes, and this is my fitting intention. The heart
In my breast is not of iron, but a pitying one."
When she had said this, the divine goddess led the way
Nimbly. And he went along in the footsteps of the god.
The god and the man arrived at the hollow cave
195 And he sat down there on the chair out of which Hermes
Had risen up. The nymph set out every sort of dish
To eat and drink, of the kind that mortal men eat.
She herself sat down facing the godly Odysseus,
And handmaids placed ambrosia before her and nectar.
They stretched forth their hands to the food that was spread out
200   ready,
And when they had taken their pleasure of eating and drinking
Calypso, the divine goddess, began a speech to him:
"Zeus-born son of Laertes, much-contriving Odysseus,
Do you really want to go home to your dear fatherland
205 Right at once, now? Well, even so, luck be with you!
If you knew in your mind how many sorrows it is
Your fate to fulfill before reaching your fatherland,
Then you would stay right here with me and keep this home
And you would be immortal, even though you would desire
210 To see your wife, whom you long for always every day.
I declare I am not a bit inferior to that woman
In form or in shape, since it is not at all seemly
For mortals to contend with immortals in looks and in form."
Odysseus of many devices addressed her in answer:
215 "Lady goddess, be not angry at me this way. I myself know
All this, that beside you the prudent Penelope
Seen face to face is less striking in form and size.
For she is a mortal and you are immortal and ageless.
Yet even so I am wishing and longing all my days
220 To go home and to see the day of my return.
And if one of the gods wrecks me on the wine-faced sea,

3. River of the Underworld by which the gods swore oaths.

I shall bear it in my breast, with a long-grieving heart.
For I have suffered much already and endured much,
On the waves and in war; and let this be added to those."
So he said, and the sun went down, and darkness came on.   225
The two of them went into a nook of the hollow cave
And took pleasure of love, abiding with one another.
And when the early-born, rosy-fingered dawn appeared,
Then Odysseus at once put on his cloak and his tunic,
And the nymph herself put on a great shining mantle   230
Finely made and pleasing, and a lovely gold sash
Around her waist, and a veil upon her head above.
Then she took thought about sending great-hearted Odysseus
    away;
She gave him a great ax fitted to the palms,
A bronze one, sharpened at both ends; upon it there was   235
A beautiful olive wood handle, well fitted in place.
Then she gave him a well-polished adz and led the way
To the verge of the island where tall trees were growing,
Alder and poplar, and fir that was tall to the heavens,
Dry for a long time, well seasoned, that would float lightly for
    him.   240
And when she had shown him where the tall trees were growing,
Calypso, the divine goddess, went back to her home.
But he cut beams, and the work went quickly for him.
He felled twenty in all and hewed them with the bronze ax,
Planed them skillfully, and set a straight line upon them.   245
Meanwhile, the divine goddess Calypso brought along augers,
And he then bored them all and fitted them to one another.
Then he made it fast with pegs and with fastenings;
And just the way a man who is a well-skilled craftsman
Rounds off the hull of a broad ship for carrying freight,   250
The same measure did Odysseus make for his own broad raft.
He made it by setting deck planks on and fitting them
To the close-set ribs. And he finished it off with long gunwales.
Then he made a mast and a yardarm fitted to it.
He made a rudder, too, so that he might steer straight.   255
And he plaited it all through with wicker osiers
To be a bulwark against the wave. And he set much wood upon
    it.
Meanwhile the divine goddess brought along a piece of cloth
For making sails, and he fashioned those well too.

260 Upon it he tied braces and halyards and tackle and sheets,
And with levers he dragged it down to the godly sea.
It was the fourth day, and he had finished everything.
On the fifth day the divine Calypso sent him from the island
After she had clothed him in fragrant garments and bathed him.
265 The goddess put on board for him a skin of dark wine,
And another, a big one of water, and food, too,
In a bag. And she put many satisfying morsels in for him.
And then she sent on a soothing and gentle breeze.
Delighted at the breeze, godly Odysseus stretched his sails
270 And he steered on with the rudder skillfully
As he sat. Nor did sleep fall upon his eyelids
While he watched the Pleiades and late-setting Boötes,
And the Bear, which they call, too, by the name of the Wagon,
Which turns in one place and also points at Orion,
275 And alone has no share in the washings of Oceanos.
The divine goddess Calypso bade him to keep that star
Upon his left hand, as he fared over the sea.
He sailed seventeen days, faring on the sea,
And on the eighteenth there appeared the shadowy mountains
280 Of the land of the Phaeacians where it was nearest him.
It seemed to be just like a shield on the murky sea.
But the earth-shaking ruler, coming back from the Ethiopians,
Saw him from afar, from the mountains of the Solumoi;
He was seen sailing the ocean. The god in his heart
285 Got very angry. He shook his head and addressed his spirit:
"Well, the gods have now made quite a different plan
About Odysseus, while I was with the Ethiopians;
He is near the Phaeacians' land, where it is his lot
To escape the great bound of woe which has come upon him.
290 And I think I will still drive him into quite enough evil."
When he had said this, he gathered clouds and troubled the
      ocean,
Grasping the trident in his hands. He stirred up whole storms
Of all the winds and covered earth and ocean alike
With clouds. And night rose up from the heavens.
The East Wind fell down, and the South Wind and the hard-
295   blowing West Wind,
And the North Wind that makes clear skies, rolling a great
      wave.
Then Odysseus' knees and his own heart went slack;

He was distressed, and he spoke to his own great-hearted spirit:
"Ah, wretched as I am, what will happen at last to me now?
I fear that the goddess spoke all unerringly   300
When she said I would have a fill of pains on the ocean
Before reaching my fatherland. It has all come to pass,
With such large clouds has Zeus crowned heaven about
And has disturbed the ocean; and storms are rushing on
Of all the winds. Now my sheer destruction is sure.   305
Thrice and four times blessed are the Danaans who perished
In broad Troy then, doing the pleasure of the sons of Atreus.
Would that I myself had died and had met my fate
On that day when numbers of the Trojans did hurl
Bronze-tipped spears at me over the dead son of Peleus: 310
I would have gotten my rites; the Achaians would have spread
    my glory.
But now I am fated to get caught in a miserable death."
A great wave dashed on him as he said that, pushing
Fearfully from its peak, and it spun the raft about.
He himself fell far from the raft. The rudder   315
Shot out of his hands. A fearful storm of intermingled
Winds came up and broke the mast in the middle.
The sail and the yardarm fell into the ocean.
It put him under the water a long time, and he could not
Quickly rise up from the rush of the great wave,   320
For the clothes weighed him down that divine Calypso gave
    him.
At last he did come up, and spat out of his mouth
The bitter brine that flowed plenteously off his head.
Nor did he forget the raft, though he was wearied.
But as he rushed into the waves he caught hold of it   325
And sat in the middle, shunning the end of death.
A great wave carried it here and there along the current.
As when the North Wind at harvest time carries thistles
Over the plain, but they hold close to one another,
So the winds carried it here and there over the sea.   330
Sometimes the South Wind threw it to the North Wind to carry
And sometimes the East Wind yielded it to the South Wind for
    pursuit.
But Cadmos' daughter saw him, Ino [4] of the lovely ankles,

4. She leaped into the sea to save her son, and was made a goddess; her
father, Cadmos, was founder of Thebes.

Leucothea, who earlier had a mortal voice
335 And now in the sea swells gets honor from the gods.
She took pity on Odysseus as he was driven about in his pains.
Like a shearwater she rose in flight from the sea,
Perched on the raft, and addressed a speech to him:
"Ill-fated man, why is the earth-shaker Poseidon
340 So strikingly angry that he spawns you these many ills?
He will not wear you down, however he may desire it.
But do as follows: you do not seem foolish to me:
Take off these clothes and leave the raft for the winds
To carry; and swim with your hands, and strive for reaching
345 The Phaeacians' land, where it is your fate to escape.
And here now, stretch this veil out across your chest.
It is immortal. Have no fear of suffering or dying,
But when you have touched the mainland with your hands,
Untie it again and throw it into the wine-faced sea,
350 Far from the mainland, and turn yourself the other way."
When she had said this, the goddess gave him the veil.
She plunged back herself into the surging waves of the ocean
Like a shearwater. And a black wave covered her.
Godly Odysseus, who had borne much, meditated;
355 And he spoke, grieving, to his own great-hearted spirit:
"Alas for me, I fear one of the immortals is weaving
A snare for me, to have bade me get off the raft;
I shall not yet obey her, since I saw with my own eyes
The land far off where she said was a refuge for me.
360 But this I shall do, and it seems to be best to me.
So long as the beams are fitted to their fastenings,
I will stay here and hold out while I suffer pain.
But when a wave does shake my raft into pieces,
I shall swim, since there is nothing better to think of."
365 While he pondered these things in his mind and in his heart,
Earth-shaker Poseidon stirred up a great wave,
A terrible disastrous one, overarching; it dashed him.
As when a blustering wind shakes up a heap
Of dry husks, and scatters them in all directions,
370 So it scattered the raft's long beams. And Odysseus
Bestrode one spar as if he were riding a horse.
He took off the clothes that divine Calypso gave him,
And he stretched the veil right away beneath his chest.
He fell headlong down in the sea, spreading out his hands

And striving to swim. The lord who disturbs the earth saw him; 375
He shook his head and spoke out to his own spirit;
"So wander now on the ocean, after suffering many ills,
Until you may mingle with men who are nourished by Zeus.
Yet I do not expect you will find fault with your misfortune."
When he had said this, he whipped up his lovely-maned horses [5] 380
And arrived at Aigai, where his renowned dwelling is.
But Athene, daughter of Zeus, had another thought.
She bound up the courses of all the other winds
And bade them die down and all go to sleep.
She stirred up a rapid North Wind and broke waves before it   385
Till Zeus-born Odysseus could mingle with the Phaeacians,
Who love rowing, when he had warded off destinies and death.
Then for two nights and two days upon the thick wave
He wandered, and his heart many times saw destruction ahead.
But when fair-braided Dawn finished the third day,   390
Then at that point the wind died down and there was
A windless calm, and he sighted land nearby,
Scanning sharply, as he raised himself from the great wave.
As when it appears delightful to sons if their father
Lives, who lies in sickness and undergoes strong pains,   395
Long wasting away, and some dread god has assailed him,
Whom now the gods have delightfully freed from misfortune;
So delightful did land and forest appear to Odysseus.
Vigorously he swam to set foot on the mainland.
But when he was as far off as a shout may carry,   400
And had heard against the reefs the noise of the sea—
For the great wave was dashing upon the dry mainland.
Fearfully spraying, it covered all with saltwater foam;
For there were indeed no secure harbors for ships, or channels,
But headlands there were, jutting out, and reefs and cliffs;   405
Then Odysseus' knees and his own heart went slack,
And, grieving, he addressed his own great-hearted spirit:
"Alas, that Zeus has granted me to see unhoped-for land
And I have come to the end of cleaving this gulf,
And no way of escape appears from the hoary sea.   410
But offshore there are sharp reefs, and the wave about them
Moans as it surges, and the rock runs on up smooth.
The sea is deep close in, and there is no way
To stand with both feet and to escape misfortune,

5. Poseidon is fabled to ride a horse chariot through the waves.

415 For a great wave perhaps may snatch me as I am getting out
    And hurl me on rough rock, and my trying would be in vain.
    But if I can swim along still further and can find
    Spits of land jutting out and harbors of the sea,
    Then I fear that a storm will seize me back again
420 And bear me heavily groaning onto the fish-laden ocean,
    Or some god may drive a great monster on me from the sea,
    Of the kind that in numbers the renowned Amphitrite [6] feeds;
    For I know how angry the renowned earth-shaker is at me."
    He pondered these matters in his mind and in his heart
425 Till a great wave bore him up on the rugged shore.
    There his skin would all have been stripped off and his bones
        broken
    If the bright-eyed goddess Athene had not put a thought in his
        mind;
    He caught at the rock with both hands as he dashed upon it,
    And held onto it moaning, till a great wave came along.
430 And he avoided it so, but it struck him again with its backwash,
    And dashed on him and threw him far into the ocean.
    As when an octopus is pulled out of its den,
    Numerous pebbles are caught in its suckers,
    So against the rocks the skin from his stout hands
435 Was stripped off. And the great wave covered him over.
    Then surely wretched Odysseus would have died in excess of
        fate
    If bright-eyed Athene had not given him presence of mind.
    Getting up out of the wave that spewed on the mainland,
    He swam along it outside, looking for land, if he might happen
440 On spits of land jutting out and harbors of the sea.
    But when as he swam on he came up to the mouth
    Of a fair-flowing river, there the best place seemed to him to be.
    It was bare of rocks, and it had a shelter from the wind.
    He perceived it flowing and prayed to it in his heart.
445 "Hear me Lord,[7] whoever you are; I approach you with many
    Prayers, fleeing the rebukes of Poseidon out of the ocean.
    A man should be respected even by the immortal gods
    When anyone approaches, wandering, as now I,
    Who have suffered much, approach your knees and your flowing.
450 Have pity, Lord. I declare I am a suppliant to you."

    6. A goddess of the sea.
    7. The rivers are gods in Homer.

So he said. At once the river stopped flowing and held the wave.
It made a calm in front of him and rescued him
At the issue of the river. Then he bent both his knees
And his stout hands. For his own heart was downed by salt
　　water.
All his skin was swollen, and much seawater oozed   455
From his mouth and his nostrils. Breathless and voiceless
He lay with slight strength, and dread fatigue came upon him.
But when he caught his breath and the spirit in his mind
Awakened, he unbound the god's veil from himself
And he let it go into the sea-mingling river.   460
A great wave bore it back down the stream. Ino quickly
Took it in her own hands. He slipped out of the river,
Lay down on a rush bed, and kissed the grain-giving earth.
Then, grieving, he spoke to his own great-hearted spirit:
"Ah, what do I suffer; what will happen to me at last?   465
If I watch through the troublesome night beside the river,
I fear that the evil frost and gentle dew together
May subdue my winded spirit in its slight strength,
For a cold breeze blows from the river just before dawn.
But if I ascend the slope to the shadowy wood   470
And go to sleep in the thick bushes; even if fatigue
And cold let go of me and sweet sleep does come upon me,
I fear I may become a spoil and a prey to wild beasts."
So, as he thought, this seemed to him to be better.
He went on into the wood; he found it near the water   475
In the clearing around, and came upon two bushes growing
From the same place, one of wild olive, one of tame.
Nor did the moist force of the blowing winds breathe through
　　them,
And the shining sun never struck them with its beams,
Nor did rain ever reach through to them, so thick   480
Did they grow over and under each other. Odysseus
Went in beneath them. He quickly gathered a broad bed
With his own hands. Leaf-shedding had been quite plentiful,
Enough to give shelter for two or three men
In the winter season, even if it were especially hard.   485
Godly Odysseus, who had borne much, rejoiced to see it.
He lay down in the middle, heaping the fallen leaves over him,
As a man may cover a torch with black embers
At the edge of a field, where no neighbors may be by,

490 And save the fire's seed, so he need not light it from elsewhere.
So Odysseus covered himself with leaves. Athene
Shed sleep on his eyes, so it might release him quite soon
From toilsome fatigue, and she covered his eyelids over.

VI

And so godly Odysseus, who had suffered much, slept there,
Worn out with fatigue and sleepiness. Yet Athene
Went on to the district and city of the Phaeacians,
Who at one time dwelt in Hyperia of the broad dancing-place,
Close to the Cyclopes, presumptuous men   5
Who used to injure them, and were more powerful in strength.
Then godlike Nausithoos [1] rose up and led them off
And settled them in Scheria, far from bread-earning men.
He set a wall around the city, built houses,
Made temples to the gods, and divided up the fields.   10
But already he had succumbed to his fate and gone to Hades.
Alcinoos ruled at the time, who had his thoughts from the gods.
The bright-eyed goddess Athene went to his home,
Devising a return for great-hearted Odysseus.
She entered the highly wrought bedroom where there was
    sleeping   15
A girl like the immortals in shape and in form,
Nausicaa,[2] daughter of great-hearted Alcinoos,
And beside her two servants, who had beauty from the Graces,
On either side of the door posts. The bright doors were shut.
She rushed to the girl's bed like a blast of the wind,   20
Stood over her head and spoke a word to her,
Likening herself to the daughter of Dymas, famous for ships,
Who was the girl's own age and delighted her heart.
In the likeness of her, bright-eyed Athene spoke out:
"Nausicaa, how did your mother have such a careless child?   25
Your shining garments are lying uncared for,
And your wedding is near, when you yourself will need
Lovely clothes to put on, and to give to the men who will lead
    you;
Through them does a noble reputation arise

1. The colonizer of Scheria; son of Poseidon.
2. Daughter of Alcinoos and Arete.

30 Among men, and a father and queenly mother rejoice.
But let us go washing as soon as dawn appears.
I will follow as a helper so you may array yourself
Very soon, since you will not be a maiden much longer.
Already in the land the best men of all the Phaeacians,
35 Where your own family is too, are wooing you.
But come, and urge your illustrious father at dawn
To harness up mules and a wagon to carry you
And the girdles and the gowns and the shining mantles.
It is much better for you to go that way yourself
40 Than by foot. For the place of washing is far from the city."
When she had said this, the bright-eyed Athene went off
To Olympos, where they say the gods' seat is forever
Secure. It is not shaken with winds and is never wet
With rain, nor does snow fall there, but a cloudless clarity
45 Spreads far upon it, and a white gleam runs over it.
In that place the blessed gods enjoy themselves day after day.
The bright-eyed one went off there when she had prompted the girl.
And right away the fair-throned Dawn came and awakened
The fair-gowned Nausicaa. At once she wondered at her dream,
50 And went through the halls to announce it to her parents,
Her dear father and mother. She found them within.
Her mother sat at the hearth with her serving women
Turning sea purple yarn on the distaff. She came on her father
At the door as he was going with his illustrious kings
55 To council, where the noble Phaeacians were summoning him.
She stood very close to her dear father and addressed him:
"Papa dear, won't you have a chariot harnessed for me,
A high one with good wheels, so I may take the splendid clothes
And wash them at the river, the ones I have lying dirty?
60 Yes, and it is fitting for you to be with the chief men
And hold council, wearing clothes on your skin that are clean.
And five dear sons have been born to you in the halls,
Two of them are married; three are blooming youths
Who are always wanting to wear freshly washed garments
65 To go dancing; all these cares are on my mind."
So she said. But she was ashamed to speak of lusty marriage
To her dear father. He saw all, and replied with a word:
"I do not begrudge you mules or anything else, child—
Come, the servants will harness you a chariot,

A high one, with good wheels, fitted with a hood."   70
When he had said this, he ordered the servants, and they
   obeyed.
Outside they set up a well-running wagon for mules.
They brought up mules and yoked them to the chariot.
The girl brought the shining garments from the bedroom
And she put them upon the well-polished chariot.   75
Her mother put all sorts of satisfying food
In a chest, and put in dainties, and poured wine
In a goatskin bag. Her daughter got up on the chariot.
And she gave her moist olive oil in a golden flask
So she and her serving women might anoint themselves.   80
And she took hold of the whip and the glistening reins
And whipped them to go; there was clatter of the two mules.
They drew it strenuously and bore the clothes and the girl,
Not alone: along with her other serving women went also.
And when they came to the beautiful stream of the river   85
Where there were plentiful places to wash and much
Lovely water flowed forth to clean what had got very dirty,
There they unharnessed the mules from the chariot
And shooed them out along the eddying river
To graze on honey-sweet field-grass. From the chariot   90
They took the clothes in their hands, carried them to the black
   water,
And trod them in pits, swiftly vying with one another.
But when they had washed and cleaned all the dirty clothes,
They spread them in a row on the strand where especially
The ocean washed pebbles up along the shore.   95
They bathed and anointed themselves richly with olive oil.
Then they had their dinner along the banks of the river
And waited for the clothes to dry in the gleam of the sun.
When she herself and the serving maids had enjoyed the food,
They played with a ball, having taken off their shawls.   100
White-armed Nausicaa began the sport with them.
Just as arrow-shooting Artemis goes along mountains,
Along the lofty Taygetos or Erimanthos,
Delighting in the boars and in the swift deer;
And field-haunting nymphs, daughters of aegis-bearing Zeus,   105
Play with her, and Leto [3] rejoices in her mind;
She holds her head and her forehead higher than all

3. Mother of Apollo and Artemis.

And is easily outstanding, but all are lovely:
So the unwed girl stood out among her serving maids.
110 But when she was ready to go back home again
And had hitched up the mules and folded the lovely clothes,
Then the bright-eyed goddess Athene had another thought:
Odysseus would wake up, he would see the fair-faced girl,
And she would conduct him to the city of the Phaeacians.
115 Then the princess threw the ball to a serving maid;
She missed the maid and shot it into a deep eddy.
They gave a long shout. And godly Odysseus woke up.
He sat there and deliberated in his mind and heart:
"Ah me, to what land of mortals have I come this time?
120 Are these men proud and savage and without justice,
Or are they friendly to strangers and have a god-fearing mind?
How the sound of girls' voices has surrounded me,
Of nymphs, who hold the lofty peaks of mountains,
And the sources of rivers and the grassy meadows!
125 Or am I somewhere near men who are of clear speech?
Well, come, I shall make a trial myself and see."
When he had said this, godly Odysseus came from under the
   bushes.
From the thick wood he broke off in his stout hand a branch
With leaves, that it might cover the skin round a man's loins,
130 And he went like a mountain-bred lion, who, relying
On his strength, goes rained on and blown on, but his eyes
   within
Are burning, and he chases after oxen or sheep
Or after the wild deer, and his belly bids him
To try for sheep and to go into their thick fold—
135 So was Odysseus about to mingle with the fair-braided girls,
Although he was naked. For need had come upon him.
Frightfully begrimed with brine did he appear to them.
One ran one way, one another, on the jutting shores.
The daughter of Alcinoos alone stayed; Athene
140 Had put courage in her mind and taken fear from her limbs.
She stood in one place, facing him. Odysseus wondered
Whether he should grasp the fair-faced girl's knees in prayer
Or supplicate her where he was at a distance, with soothing
   words,
To show him the city and also to give him clothes.
145 As he thought it over, it seemed better to him

To supplicate her at a distance with soothing words,
Lest if he grasped her knees the girl's mind be angered.
Right at once he made a soothing and wily speech:
"I am at your knees, mistress. Are you some god or a mortal?
If you are one of the gods who possess broad heaven,   150
I myself would liken you in look and size and form
Most closely to Artemis, the daughter of great Zeus.
And if you are one of the mortals who dwells on the land,
Three times blessed are your father and your queenly mother,
And three times blessed your kinsmen. Surely their hearts   155
Must be warmed forever with happiness on your account,
Beholding so fine a flower stepping into the dance.
Blessed above all others within his heart is the man
Who, laden down with bride-gifts, may lead you home.
Never before have I seen with my eyes such a person,   160
Either man or woman. Awe holds me as I look.
On Delos [4] once by the altar of Apollo I caught sight
Of such a one, the sapling of a date palm coming up.
For I went there also, and a large company followed me
On that journey whereon evil cares lay in store for me.   165
When I saw that, I was stunned in spirit a long time, lady,
Since such a shaft never rose from the ground; the same way
That I wonder at you, and am stunned, and dreadfully fear
To touch your knees. And a difficult sorrow comes on me.
Yesterday, on the twentieth day, I fled the wine-faced ocean.   170
All during that time did the waves and rapid storms carry me
From the island of Ogygia. Now a god has cast me here
To suffer some evil in this place. I do not think
It will stop, but the gods will perform many things yet first.
Do have pity, mistress. As one who has endured many evils   175
I come to you first. I know not one of the others,
Of the men who possess this city and this land.
Point the town out to me. Give me a rag to throw on,
If perhaps when you come here you had some wrapper for the
    clothing.
May the gods grant you as much as you wish in your mind.   180
May they provide you a husband and also a home,
And noble sympathy. Nothing is better or higher than that,
When a man and wife have a home who are sympathetic
In their thoughts. It gives many pains to their enemies

4. A small island sacred to Apollo.

185 And joys to their friends. And they know it best themselves."
Then white-armed Nausicaa spoke to him in answer:
"Stranger, since you seem like a man neither evil nor senseless,
And Olympian Zeus himself controls prosperity for men,
For the noble and the evil, as he wishes for each,
190 So perhaps he gave you this, and still you have to bear it.
And now, since you have come to our city and our land,
You will not want for clothing, or for anything else
That befits a long-suffering suppliant who encounters us.
I will show you the town and tell you the name of the people.
195 The Phaeacians possess this city and this land.
I am the daughter of great-hearted Alcinoos,
On whom the strength and might of the Phaeacians depend."
So she said, and she called out to her fair-braided servants,
"Come here to me, servants. Where do you flee when you see a
   man?
200 Surely you don't think him to be one of our enemies?
There is no man so vigorous and no mortal born
Who would come to the land of the Phaeacian men
Bringing hostility. For they are very dear to the gods.
And we dwell far away in the much-surging ocean,
205 The remotest of men. And no other mortal has congress with us.
Now this man, a wretched wanderer, has come here,
Whom we must look after, for all strangers and beggars
Are in the care of Zeus, and a gift, even small, is friendly.
Come, maidens, give food and drink to the stranger.
210 Wash him in the river where there is shelter against the wind."
So she said, and they stood and urged one another,
And they took Odysseus down to a shelter, as Nausicaa,
Daughter of great-hearted Alcinoos, had ordered.
They put down a mantle and a tunic and clothes for him,
215 And gave him liquid olive oil in a golden flask,
And bade him to wash himself in the streams of the river.
Then godly Odysseus addressed the servant maids:
"Maidens, stand off where you are, so that I myself
May wash the brine from my shoulders and with olive oil
220 May anoint me all over. Oil has been long from my skin;
I do not want to wash in front of you. I am ashamed
To come out naked in the midst of fair-braided girls."
So he said, and they went apart and spoke to the girl.
But Odysseus in the river washed off of his skin

The brine that he had on his back and his broad shoulders,   225
And he wiped from his head the scurf of barren salt water.
When he had fully washed and had rubbed himself richly,
He put on the clothes that the unwed girl had provided,
And Athene, she who was born from Zeus, made him
Bigger to look at and stouter, and on his head   230
Made his hair flow in curls, like the hyacinth flower.
As when some man overlays gold upon silver,
A skilled man whom Hephaistos [5] and Pallas Athene have taught
Art of all kinds, and he turns out graceful handiwork;
So she poured grace upon his head and his shoulders.   235
Then he sat off apart, when he had gone along the beach of the
     sea,
Gleaming with beauty and graces. And the girl marveled.
And then she spoke out to her fair-braided serving maids:
"Listen to me, white-armed servants, in what I say.
Not against the will of all the gods who hold Olympos   240
Does this man mix with the Phaeacians, who are equal to gods.
Beforehand he appeared to me to be unseemly,
And now he seems like the gods who possess broad heaven.
Would that a man of this sort might be called my husband
And be dwelling here, and it might please him to stay   245
In this place. But, maidens, give the stranger food and drink."
So she said, and they listened closely and obeyed her.
They set out before Odysseus food and drink.
Godly Odysseus, who had suffered much, ate and drank
Greedily, for he had been a long time without eating.   250
But white-armed Nausicaa had another thought.
She folded up the clothes, put them on the lovely chariot,
Harnessed the stout-hooved mules, got in herself,
And urged Odysseus on, speaking out to him directly:
"Rise up now, stranger, to go to the city, so I may   255
Convey you to my skillful father's home, where I think
You may get to know all the noblest of the Phaeacians.
Well, this is what you should do—you do not seem to me to be
     foolish.
As long as we are passing the fields and the farms of men,
Come speedily along with the serving maids behind the mules   260
And the chariot. And I myself shall lead the way.
But when we walk into the city—about it there is a high

5. Son of Zeus and husband of Aphrodite; god of fire and the forge.

Tower wall, and there is a lovely harbor on either side of the city
And a narrow entrance, and bobbing ships from the voyage
265 Are pulled in there—it is a slip for one and all.
There is the assembly place, round a fine temple to Poseidon,
Fashioned from deep-bedded stones that have been quarried.
And there they take care of the tackle of the black ships,
Cables and sails, and they sharpen oars off to a point.
270 For the Phaeacians the bow and the quiver are of no concern,
But sails and the oars of ships and the balanced ships;
Delighting in these, they traverse the hoary sea.
I shun an unseemly repute among them, lest one
Rebuke me hereafter. For there are presumptuous men in the
     district,
275 And this is what some meaner one, if he met us, might say:
'Who is this great and handsome stranger that follows
Nausicaa? Where did she find him? He will be her husband.
She must have brought him off his own ship wandering
From distant men, since there are not any near at hand;
280 Or else some much-invoked god has come at her prayer,
Descending from the sky and will have her all her days.
Better so, if she went herself and found a husband
From elsewhere. For she despises these men in the district,
The Phaeacians, though many men who are noble woo her.'
285 So they will say. And these reproaches will come against me.
I myself would blame anyone else who should do such things,
Who against the will of her dear ones, a father and mother still
     alive,
Should mingle with men before coming to open marriage.
Stranger, understand quickly what I say, so you may
290 Very soon get an escort and a return from my father.
Near the road you will find a shining grove of Athene,
One of poplars; a spring flows in it, a meadow is about it.
There is my father's preserve and his fruitful vineyard,
The same distance from the city that a shout would carry.
295 Sit there a while and wait till the time that we
Come to the town and arrive at the house of my father.
But when you consider that we have arrived at the house,
Then go to the city of the Phaeacians and ask
For the house of my father, great-hearted Alcinoos.
300 It is easy to recognize; even a foolish child
Could lead you. There is none of the Phaeacians' houses

Made to resemble the home of Alcinoos,
Who is a hero. But when the house and courtyard enclose you,
Go very swiftly through the hall until you reach
My mother. She sits at the hearth in the fire's gleam,   305
And turns sea purple yarn on the distaff, a wonder to see,
Propped against a pillar. And serving maids sit behind her.
And there the chair of my father is propped up against hers,
Where, seated like an immortal, he drinks his wine.
Pass him by and throw your hands around the knees   310
Of my mother, so you may speedily rejoice and see
The day of your return, even if you are from very far away.
And if that woman thinks kindly of you in her heart,
Then there is hope for you of seeing your dear ones and reaching
Your well-established home and your own fatherland."   315
When she had said this, she lashed with her shiny whip
At the mules, and they quickly left the streams of the river.
They ran along well and nimbly bent their legs.
She managed the reins so that the servants and Odysseus
Might follow on foot. And she skillfully applied the lash.   320
The sun went down and they came to the famous grove
Sacred to Athene, and there godly Odysseus sat down.
Then at once he prayed to the daughter of great Zeus:
"Hear me, unwearied one, child of aegis-bearing Zeus,
Hear me now, since you did not hear me before   325
When I was smitten and the famous earth-shaker smote me.
Grant that I come to the Phaeacians as a pitied man and a
    friend."
So he said in prayer; and Pallas Athene heard him,
But she did not yet appear to him face to face. For she feared
Her father's brother. He was contending vehemently   330
With godlike Odysseus till the man reached his own land.

And so godly Odysseus, who had suffered much, prayed there
While the strength of the two mules bore the girl toward the
   town.
And when she had arrived at her father's famous house
She halted them in the gateway, and her brothers were standing
5 About her like immortals; they unhitched the mules
From the chariot and carried the clothing on inside.
She herself went to her bedroom. An old woman of Apeire
Was kindling a fire for her, the chambermaid Eurymedousa,
Whom once the bobbing ships took away from Apeire,
10 And they chose her as a prize for Alcinoos because he ruled
All the Phaeacians. The people obeyed him like a god.
She waited on white-armed Nausicaa in the halls,
And kindled the fire for her, and set out her dinner within.
And then Odysseus got up to go to the city. Athene,
15 With kind thoughts for Odysseus, shed a thick mist about him,
Lest some great-hearted Phaeacian should confront him,
Taunt him with a speech, and ask him who he might be.
But when he was ready to enter the charming city,
Then the bright-eyed goddess Athene confronted him.
20 Likenening herself to a virginal young girl with a pitcher,
She stood in front of him, and godly Odysseus asked:
"My child, would you lead me to the home of Alcinoos,
The man who is the ruler over these people?
For I have come here as a long-suffering stranger
25 From afar, from a distant land; so I know no one
Of the men who possess this city and its fields."
Then the bright-eyed goddess Athene addressed him:
"Yes, father stranger, I will show you the home
You ask of, since it lies close to my blameless father's.
30 But come very silently and I shall lead the way.
Do not catch any man's eye or question anyone.
Those here do not easily endure strange men,

And they do not befriend or welcome one coming from
    elsewhere.
Putting their confidence in the swift and speedy ships,
They traverse the great gulf, since the earth-shaker gave it to
    them,   35
And their ships are as swift as any wing or thought."
When she had said this, Pallas Athene conducted him
Speedily; he went along in the footsteps of the goddess.
But the Phaeacians, famous for ships, did not perceive him
As he went through the town among them, for fair-braided
    Athene,   40
The dreadful goddess, did not allow it; she shed
A divine fog about him, with kind thoughts in her heart.
Odysseus wondered at the harbors and the balanced ships,
The meeting places of the heroes themselves, and the walls,
Long and lofty, fitted with stakes, a wonder to behold.   45
When they came to the illustrious house of the king,
The bright-eyed goddess Athene began to speak among them:
"Father stranger, this is the house that you requested me
To point out to you. You will find kings nourished by Zeus
Eating dinner there. Go in and do not be frightened   50
In your heart. A man who is bold in all his deeds
Thrives better, even when he comes from somewhere else.
You will first come upon the mistress in the halls.
Arete¹ is the name she is called, and her ancestors
Are the same ones who begot King Alcinoos.   55
First Nausithoos was born of earth-shaker Poseidon
And of Periboea, the best for her form, among women,
The youngest daughter of great-hearted Eurymedon,
Who ruled as king over the high-spirited Giants.
But he destroyed his reckless people, and was himself destroyed. 60
Then Poseidon lay with the girl and fathered a son,
Great-spirited Nausithoos, who ruled the Phaeacians.
Nausithoos begat Rhexenor and Alcinoos.
Apollo of the silver bow slew the first while still sonless
And a bridegroom in the hall: he left one sole daughter,   65
Arete. And her did Alcinoos make his wife.
He honored her as no other woman on earth is honored,
Of all women who now have a household under men.
So she was highly honored in heart, and she still is,

1. Queen of the Phaeacians; wife of Alcinoos and mother of Nausicaa.

70 By her beloved children and by Alcinoos himself
And by the people who look on her as on a god
And welcome her with speeches as she goes through the town.
Nor is she herself at all lacking in any noble thought.
She dissolves disputes for those of whom she thinks well, even
   for men.
75 And if that woman has kind thoughts for you in her heart,
There is hope for you of seeing your dear ones and reaching
Your lofty-roofed house and your own fatherland."
When she had said this, bright-eyed Athene went away
Over the barren ocean, and left charming Scheria;
80 She arrived at Marathon, and at Athens with its broad streets,
And entered the stout house of Erechtheus. Meanwhile
   Odysseus
Went to the famous house of Alcinoos. His heart
Pondered much as he stood there before reaching the bronze
   threshold.
There was a gleam like that of the sun or of the moon
85 Beneath the high-roofed hall of great-hearted Alcinoos.
Bronze walls were run round it on every side to the corner
From the threshold, and there was a frieze of dark blue about it.
Golden portals shut up the stout home within,
And silver door posts were set upon the bronze threshold,
90 And a silver lintel above, and a golden handle.
And on either side there were gold and silver dogs
That Hephaistos with his skillful faculties had formed
To watch over the house of great-hearted Alcinoos;
They were immortal, and ageless for all their days.
Inside, armchairs had been propped round the wall here and
95   there
To the corner from the threshold in unbroken line. And cloths
Were strewn there, fine and well-woven, the work of women.
And there the leaders of the Phaeacians were seated
When they ate and drank. They possessed unfailing abundance.
100 And there were golden youths on well-built pedestals
That stood there holding in their hands flaming torches
Illuminating the nights for the diners through the halls.
And there were fifty serving maids through the hall, women
Who grind up in a mill grain of an apple hue,
105 And who do weaving on looms and turn the distaff
Seated, the way the leaves of the tall poplar turn;

And from the close-woven linen the moist oil drops off.
As the Phaeacians are knowing beyond all other men
To drive a swift ship in the ocean, so their women
Are skilled in weaving. Athene has endowed them highly   110
With skill in beautiful tasks and with noble minds.
Outside the courtyard is a great garden before the portals,
One of four measures. A fence runs round it on both sides.
And in that place tall blossoming trees are growing.
Pears, and pomegranates, apple trees with shining fruit,   115
And sweet fig trees and blossoming olive trees.
Of these the fruit never perishes and never leaves off
In winter or summertime, all the year round. But always
A blowing West Wind makes some grow and ripens others.
Pear matures upon pear, apple upon apple,   120
Grape cluster on grape cluster, and fig on fig,
And there is rooted a vineyard that bears much fruit,
One part of which, light-parched in a level place,
Dries in the sun, and others they harvest at vintage.
Still others they tread. First there are the unripe grapes   125
Shedding flowers, and others are darkening underneath.
Well-ordered vegetable beds in the last row there
Grow things of all kinds and shine green in unceasing
    abundance.
And in it are two springs: one through the whole garden
Is dispersed, and the other rises by the courtyard threshold   130
Before the lofty house, whence the townspeople draw water.
Such were the gods' glorious gifts to Alcinoos' house.
As he stood there, godly Odysseus, who had endured much,
    marveled.
And when he had marveled in his heart at everything,
He went speedily over the threshold into the hall.   135
He found the leaders and counselors of the Phaeacians pouring
Libations to the far-sighted god, the slayer of Argos.
They poured him the last cup whenever they remembered sleep.
But godly Odysseus, who had endured much, went through the
    hall,
Clad in the large mist that Athene had shed about him,   140
Until he reached Arete and King Alcinoos.
Odysseus threw his hands about the knees of Arete,
And then the divine mist poured away from him.
They grew silent through the hall when they saw the man

145 And wondered to behold him. Odysseus pleaded with her:
      "Arete, daughter of Phrexenor, who was equal to a god,
      I, who have suffered much, fall at your knees and your husband's
      And all those dining here: may the gods grant them to live
      With blessings; and may each one turn his possessions over
150 To his children in his halls, and any prize the people have given.
      But call up an escort for me to reach my fatherland
      Soon, as I have long suffered woes apart from my dear ones."
      When he had said this, he sat down on the hearth in the ashes
      By the fire. And they all became silent in stillness.
155 After a pause the old hero Echeneus spoke out,
      A man who was oldest by birth of the Phaeacian men,
      Who excelled in speaking and knew many ancient things.
      In good will he spoke out to them and addressed them:
      "Alcinoos, this does not seem to be very good,
160 To let a stranger sit on the ground by the hearth in the ashes.
      Those here are holding back and waiting for your word.
      Come now, have the stranger stand up, and sit him down
      In a chair studded with silver; give your herald bidding
      To mix up more wine so we may pour a libation
165 To bolt-hurling Zeus, who protects pious suppliants.
      Let a housekeeper give the stranger dinner from what is within."
      When Alcinoos in his sacred strength had heard this,
      He took the hand of skillful, various-minded Odysseus,
      Raised him from the hearth, and seated him on a shining chair.
170 He had his son stand up, the manly Laodamas,
      Who sat nearest to him and whom he loved especially.
      And a handmaid poured water from a pitcher she was carrying,
      A lovely golden one, over into a silver basin,
      For washing the hands; she set up a polished table alongside.
175 A respected servant served bread she was carrying,
      Laying out many dishes, gracious with the provisions.
      Godly Odysseus, who had suffered much, ate and drank,
      Then Alcinoos in his might spoke out to the herald:
      "Pontonoos, mix up a bowl and serve out the wine
180 To all through the hall so we may pour a libation
      To bolt-hurling Zeus, who protects pious suppliants."
      So he said, and Pontonoos mixed the mind-honeying wine
      And distributed the first drops into the cups of all.
      When they had poured and drunk as much as the spirit wished,
185 Alcinoos spoke out to them and addressed them:

"Hear me, leaders and counselors of the Phaeacians,
So I may say what the spirit in my breast bids me to.
Now that you have dined, go home and go to bed,
And at dawn when we have beckoned more of the elders,
Let us welcome the stranger in the halls and offer   190
Fine sacrifices to the gods; then let us take thought
For a convoy, so this stranger without pain or distress
Under our convoy may arrive at his fatherland,
And speedily rejoice, even if he is from very far away.
May he undergo no evil or suffering in mid-passage   195
Before coming upon his land; but then he will suffer
Whatever his fate and the grave Spinners [2] have spun for him
With his birth thread at the time when his mother bore him.
And if he has come down as one of the immortals from heaven,
Then it is something else that the gods are contriving in this.   200
Always before have the gods appeared to us plainly
Whenever we have offered the famous hecatombs,
And they dined along with us seated where we are;
Even if some wayfarer meets them when he is alone
They conceal it not at all, since we are close to them,   205
As are the Cyclopes and the wild tribes of the Giants."
Odysseus of many devices spoke to him in answer:
"Alcinoos, concern yourself with something else. As for me,
I am not like the immortals who possess broad heaven,
Either in body or form, but am like mortal men.   210
Whomever you may know among men who have borne
The most woe, I would equal myself to them in griefs,
And indeed I myself might tell of still further ills
Of the great number I have endured at the will of the gods.
But permit me to eat dinner, burdened as I am with cares,   215
For there is nothing at all more shameless than the hateful belly
Which bids a man to remember it by compulsion,
Even one who is much worn down and has sorrow in his mind,
As I now have sorrow in my mind. It perpetually
Bids me to eat and drink and makes me forget   220
All I have undergone, and commands me to fill up.
But arouse yourselves at the appearance of dawn
And bring me, wretched as I am, to my fatherland.
Indeed I have suffered much. May my life abandon me

2. Often identified with the three Fates—Clotho, Lachesis, and Atropos
—who have in charge the "thread" of a man's life.

Once I have seen my goods, my servants, and my great high
225   house."
So he said, and they all assented and gave orders
To guide the stranger off, since he had spoken properly.
When they had poured and drunk as much as the spirit wished,
They went on off to sleep, each one to his own house.
230 But godly Odysseus was left behind in the hall.
And with him Arete and Alcinoos, godly in form,
Were sitting. Servants put the dishes of the meal in order.
Arete of the white arms began to speak among them.
She recognized the mantle, tunic, and clothes when she saw
        them,
235 Lovely ones, that she made herself with her serving women.
And she spoke out to him and uttered wingèd words:
"Stranger, I should first like to ask you a question myself:
Who are you? What men are you from? Who gave you these
        clothes?
Did you not say you got here wandering on the ocean?"
240 Odysseus of many wiles addressed her in answer:
"It is difficult, queen, to speak out in full detail
About troubles, when the celestial gods have given me so many.
But this I will tell you that you ask and question me of.
A certain island, Ogygia, lies far off in the sea,
245 Where the daughter of Atlas dwells, wily Calypso
Of the fair braids, a dread goddess. With her no one
Has intercourse, either of gods or of mortal men.
But some god led me to her hearth, wretched as I am,
All alone, when Zeus with a dazzling thunderbolt
Crushed my swift ship, and sank it in the middle of the wine-
250   faced sea.
Then all the others, my noble companions, perished,
But I alone took in my hands the keel of the bobbing ship
And was carried nine days. And on the tenth black night
The gods brought me near the island Ogygia, where Calypso
255 Of the fair braids dwells, dread goddess. She took me in
And kindly befriended me, nourished me, and said
She would make me immortal and ageless all my days,
But she did not persuade the heart within my breast.
I waited there steadily seven years. And always I moistened
260 With my tears the ambrosial clothes that Calypso gave me.
But when the eighth year in its cycle came around,

Then she urged me and bid me to go away,
Because of a message from Zeus, or else her mind had changed.
She sent me on a strongly-bound raft, gave me much
Bread and sweet wine, clothed me in ambrosial garments,   265
And then she sent on a soothing and gentle breeze.
Seventeen days, faring upon the ocean, I sailed,
And on the eighteenth there appeared the shadowy mountains
Of your land. And my own heart was delighted in me,
Ill-fated as I was. And yet I was to have still more to do   270
With the great distress earth-shaker Poseidon raised against me.
He stirred up winds and hindered me from the voyage
And he raised an indescribable sea so the wave did not
Allow me, heavily groaning, to be borne on the raft.
Then a tempest scattered it, and I myself   275
Cleft this gulf as I swam on through, until the wind
And water carried me and brought me near your land.
Then the wave as I tried to get out would have driven me on
     land,
Throwing me against great rocks and a joyless place,
But I withdrew and swam the other way until I came   280
To the river, where the best place seemed to me to be,
Smooth of rocks, and where there was shelter from the wind.
I fell out struggling for life, and ambrosial night
Came on. Back away from the Zeus-fallen river
I stepped out and went to sleep in the bushes and heaped   285
Leaves about me. A god poured down boundless sleep.
There in the leaves, wearied in my own heart I slept
All the night long, and till dawn and the middle day,
And the sun declined, and then sweet sleep let me free.
Then I noticed your daughter's serving maids playing   290
On the strand. She herself was among them, like the goddesses.
I begged her, and she did not fail of such noble intent,
As one would not expect a young person he encountered
To demonstrate. For the very young are always thoughtless.
She gave me sufficient food and sparkling wine   295
And had me washed in the river and gave me these clothes.
This is the truth I have told you, though I am distressed."
Then Alcinoos spoke out and answered him:
"Stranger, of this at least my daughter did not properly
Take thought, in that she did not lead you to our house,   300
With her serving women. For you besought her first."

Odysseus of many wiles addressed him in answer:
"Do not, hero, reproach your blameless daughter for my sake.
She bade me to follow along with the serving women,
305 But I did not want to, as I was afraid and ashamed
Lest somehow your heart be offended at seeing me.
Very suspicious are we tribes of men on the earth."
Then Alcinoos spoke out and answered him:
"Stranger, my own heart in my breast is not such
310 As to rage easily. Everything proper is best.
Would that by father Zeus, Athene, and Apollo,
Being such as you are, and of a mind like my own,
You might have my daughter and be called my son-in-law,
And stay here. I would give you a home and property
315 If you willingly stayed. No Phaeacian would hold you back
Against your will. May that not be pleasing to father Zeus.
I appoint your convoy for a day, so you may know it well,
That is, tomorrow. Then you may lie overcome in sleep.
And they will row on a calm sea until you arrive
320 At fatherland, home, and whatever is dear to you,
Even if it is very much farther off than Euboea,
Which those of our people say to be farthest off
Who saw it when they brought blond Rhadamanthys
To go and see Tityos, the son of Gaia.
325 They went there and accomplished it without difficulty
On the same day, and completed the voyage back home.
You too shall know in your own mind how much the best
Our ships and our youths are who toss up the sea with their
        oars."
So he said, and godly Odysseus, who had borne much, rejoiced.
330 He said a prayer then, and spoke right out directly:
"Father Zeus, may Alcinoos bring to pass all
That he has said; may his fame be unquenchable
On the grain-giving earth; may I reach my fatherland."
So they addressed such speeches to one another.
335 And white-armed Arete bade her serving women
To put bedsteads down in the colonnade, and to throw on
Lovely purple rugs, and to spread blankets above them
And to put down woolen mantles on top of all that.
They went from the hall with torches in their hands.
340 And when they had spread down the thick bed busily,
They stood beside Odysseus and urged him with speeches:

"Come rise up, stranger, the bed is made for you."
So they said. It seemed welcome to him to lie down.
So godly Odysseus, who had endured much, slept there
In the jointed bed under the resounding portico.   345
Alcinoos slept in a nook of the lofty house;
His lady wife beside him prepared a bed and a resting place.

VIII

And when the early-born, rosy-fingered dawn appeared,
Alcinoos rose up out of bed in his sacred strength.
And Odysseus, the Zeus-born sacker of cities, rose up.
Alcinoos in his sacred strength led them to the assembly place
5 Of the Phaeacians, which was made for them beside the ships.
When they got there they sat down on the polished stones
Close together. Pallas Athene went on through the town,
Likening herself to a herald of skillful Alcinoos,
Devising a return for the great-hearted Odysseus.
10 And she said something to each man, standing beside him:
"Come hither, leaders and counselors of the Phaeacians;
Go to the assembly, so you may learn about the stranger
Who has recently come to skillful Alcinoos' house,
Having wandered the ocean, like the immortals in form."
When she had said this, she aroused the strength and the heart
15   of each.
Speedily the assembly and its seats filled up with men
As they gathered. And many marveled to behold
The skillful son of Laertes. On his behalf Athene
Shed a divine grace over his head and his shoulders,
20 And she made him loftier and stouter to behold,
So that he might become cherished by all the Phaeacians,
And fearful, and respected, and might carry out many
Of the contests in which the Phaeacians tested Odysseus.
But when they were gathered and had come together,
25 Alcinoos spoke out to them and addressed them:
"Hear me, leaders and counselors of the Phaeacians,
That I may say what the spirit in my breast bids me to.
This stranger—I know not who he is—reached my house,
From the men of the dawn or of the evening,[1] wandering.
30 He urges a convoy and beseeches that it be assured,
And let us ourselves, as before, speed on a convoy,

1. That is, of East and West.

For never did anyone else who came to my halls
Wait here and long lament for the sake of a convoy.
Come then, let us drag a black ship on its first voyage
To the godly sea, and let two and fifty young men   35
Be picked through the land of those who are far the best up to
    now.
And when you have fastened the oars well in the oarlocks,
All of you get out of it. Then come to my house and partake
Of a hasty meal. I shall make good provision for all.
This I command the young men. And as for you others,   40
You scepter-bearing kings, come to my lovely home,
So that we may entertain the stranger in the halls.
Let no one refuse. Summon the godlike singer
Demodocos.[2] The gods have granted him to please beyond
    others
With whatever kind of song his spirit urges him to sing."   45
When he had said this, he led on, and the scepter-bearing kings
Followed along. A herald brought in the godly singer.
The two and fifty young men were selected
And went, as he bade them, to the strand of the barren sea.
But when they got down to the ship and to the sea   50
They dragged the black ship into a depth of salt water
And set up a mast and sails upon the black ship.
Then they fitted the oars into the straps made of leather
All in order and then stretched out the white sails.
Then they anchored her high in flowing water, and then   55
They entered the great house of skillful Alcinoos.
The porticoes and courts and rooms were filled with the men
As they gathered. There were many, both old and young.
And among them Alcinoos sacrificed twelve sheep,
Eight shining-tusked sows and two shamble-footed heifers.   60
They flayed them and prepared them and made a delightful
    banquet.
Then a herald came near, leading the trusty singer
Whom the Muse loved dearly and gave both good and ill.
She blinded him in the eyes but gave him a sweet song.
Pontonoos set out a silver-studded armchair for him   65
In the midst of the banqueters, propping it on a tall pillar.
The herald hung his clear-toned lyre from a peg
There above his head and showed him how to take it

2. The blind bard of the Phaeacians.

In his hands. He put a basket and lovely table alongside
70 And a cup of wine for when the spirit should bid him to drink.
They stretched forth their hands to the food that was spread out
    ready,
And when they had taken their fill of food and drink
The Muse bade the singer to sing famous deeds of men
From the lay whose fame had by then reached broad heaven,
75 The quarrel of Odysseus and Achilles, son of Peleus,
How once they wrangled at an abundant feast of the gods
With terrible words, but the lord of men, Agamemnon,
Was pleased in his mind that the best Achaians were wrangling.
For so Phoebos Apollo had told him by an oracle
80 In divine Pytho [3] where he had gone over the stone threshold
Seeking an oracle. For then the beginning of trouble was rolling
On the Trojans and Danaans through the plans of great Zeus.
This did the far-famed singer sing. But Odysseus
Took his great purple mantle in his stout hands,
85 Pulled it over his head, and concealed his handsome face;
He was ashamed before the Phaeacians for shedding tears
    under his eyebrows.
And whenever the godlike singer paused in his singing,
He lifted the mantle over his head and wiped the tears,
Took a two-handled cup, and poured libation to the gods.
90 But whenever he started again and the Phaeacian nobles
Urged him on to sing, since they were pleased with his stories,
Odysseus again covered his head over and moaned.
Now, as he shed tears, he escaped the notice of all the others.
But Alcinoos alone took note of him and perceived him,
95 While seated near him, and heard him as he deeply groaned.
At once he addressed the Phaeacians, who are fond of rowing:
"Listen, leaders and counselors of the Phaeacians,
Now we have sated our spirits with a well-shared feast
And the lyre, the consort of an abundant banquet;
100 Now let us go out and make trial in all sorts
Of contests, so that the stranger may tell his friends
When he returns home how much we surpass others
In boxing and wrestling, in jumping and also in running."
When he had said this, he led, and they followed along.
105 The herald hung the clear-toned lyre up on its peg,
Took Demodocos' hand, and led him from the hall.

3. The oracle of Apollo at Delphi.

He led him along the same path that the other
Phaeacian nobles took to gaze upon the contests.
They went to the assembly, and a large crowd followed along,
Myriads. And many young noblemen stood up.   110
Acroneus rose up, Ocyalos and Elatreus,[4]
Nauteus and Prymneus and Anchialos and Eretmeus,
Ponteus and Proireus, Thoon and Anabesineus,
And Amphialos, son of Polyneus, son of Tecton,
And Euryalos too, the equal of man-slaying Ares,[5]   115
Naubolos' son, who was best in form and in body
Of all the Phaeacians, after excellent Laodamas.
And the three sons of excellent Alcinoos stood up,
Laodamas and Halios and godlike Clytoneus.
And first they made a trial at a running race.   120
And their running was strained from the turning post on, and
   all
Flew speedily together, raising dust on the plain.
The best of them at running was excellent Clytoneus.
By as much as the range of two mules in a fallow field
He ran ahead and reached the crowd, and they were left behind. 125
Then they made a trial of painful wrestling.
And in that Euryalos surpassed all the best.
In jumping, Amphialos was most outstanding of all.
And Elatreus was by far the best of all with the weight.
In boxing it was Laodamas, Alcinoos' good son.   130
And when they had all delighted their minds with the contests,
Laodamas, the son of Alcinoos, addressed them:
"Come, friends, let us ask the stranger if there is any contest
That he knows and is skilled in. He is not bad in form,
In his thighs and in his calves and both hands above them, 135
And his neck is stout, and his strength great, nor does he lack
His prime; but he is broken down by many evils.
I think for my part there is nothing worse than the sea
To shatter a man, even though he be very strong."
Then Euryalos answered him and addressed him: 140
"Laodamas, indeed you have said this properly.
Go challenge him now yourself and say what you said."
And when the good son of Alcinoos heard that,

4. These are all names formed on marine terms: Ship-top, Swift-sea,
Rower, etc.
5. Son of Zeus; the god of war.

He went and stood in the middle and addressed Odysseus:
145 "Father stranger, come here too, and try the contests,
If you have ever learned any—you seem to know about contests.
Yes, there is no greater glory for a man as long as he lives
Than what he achieves by his feet or by his hands.
Come now, have a try; scatter the cares from your heart.
150 Your journey is not far off, and already the ship
Is drawn down for you, and the companions are ready."
Odysseus of many wiles addressed him in answer:
"Laodamas, why do you taunt me in calling me to this?
Troubles are more in my mind than contests are.
155 As a man who has endured much before and suffered much,
I am now sitting in your assembly, seeking
A return, beseeching your king and all the people."
Euryalos answered and rebuked him to his face:
"No, stranger, I would not say you were like a man skilled
160 In contests of the many sorts that exist among men,
But are like one who is used to a ship with many oarlocks,
A leader of sailors who are also merchantmen
With his mind on a load, an overseer of cargoes
And of gain got by greed. You do not resemble an athlete."
165 Odysseus of many wiles answered, glowering at him:
"You have spoken not well, stranger; you are like a fool,
And so the gods do not grant delightful gifts
To all men, in shape or in mind or in speaking.
One man is rather insignificant in look;
170 But a god crowns his speech with grace, and men behold him
And are pleased. And he speaks without faltering,
With soothing deference, and he stands out in the gathering.
And they look upon him like a god as he goes through the city.
And another man will be like the immortals in look,
175 But there is no gracefulness to crown his speech;
And so you are striking in look, and not even a god
Could make you otherwise. But you are of futile mind.
You have aroused the spirit inside my own breast,
As you spoke unbecomingly. I am not unskilled in contests,
180 As you have said, but I think I was among the first
So long as I relied on my vigor and my hands.
But now I am held in pains and misfortune. I have suffered
  much,

Passing through the wars of men and the troublesome waves.
But even though I have felt many ills, I will try the contests,
For your speech gnaws my heart. What you say urges me on." 185
So he said. Springing up with cloak and all, he took a weight,
A broad one, not by a trifle larger and stouter
Than the ones the Phaeacians threw among themselves.
He whirled it around and shot it from his stout hand.
The stone whirred, and the Phaeacians, who have long oars,   190
Men famous for ships, crouched down upon the ground
At the stone's rush. It flew past the marks of all,
Speeding quickly from his hand. Athene set the distance,
Likened in body to a man; she spoke out directly:
"Even a blind man, stranger, could make out this mark   195
By feeling it, since it is not mingled at all with the throng,
But is first by far. Take heart, at least for this contest.
None of the Phaeacians will reach or exceed this mark."
So she said, and godly Odysseus, who had borne much, rejoiced,
Pleased to behold a helpful companion in the game.   200
Then he addressed the Phaeacians in a lighter spirit:
"Reach this mark now, young men. I believe someone else
May soon hereafter hurl an equal distance, or greater.
Of all the rest, come and try what your heart and spirit
Bid you to try—since you have got me highly angered—   205
In boxing or wrestling or running—I say nothing against it—
Any of the Phaeacians except Laodamas himself,
For he is my host. And who could contend with a friend?
That man would be indeed a senseless and worthless person
Who should bring competition in contests upon his host 210
In a foreign land. He would cut all short for himself.
But of the others I do not refuse or slight a one.
I should like to know them and try them out face to face.
I am not bad in any of the many kinds of games among men.
I know well how to handle a well-polished bow;   215
I would be first, shooting in a crowd, to hit my man
Among the enemy, even if many companions
Were standing close to me and shooting at people.
Philoctetes alone surpassed me with the bow
In the land of the Trojans when we Achaians were shooting.   220
But I say I am far more outstanding than any
Of the mortals who now eat bread upon the earth.

I should not want to contend with men of earlier times,
Either with Heracles or Oichalian Eurytos,[6]
225 Who contended even with immortals in archery.
For that, great Eurytos died quickly; old age did not
Come on him in his halls, for Apollo got angry
And killed him because he challenged him to shoot.
I shoot farther with a spear than anyone else with an arrow.
230 In running alone do I fear that some Phaeacians
Might surpass me. I was very disgracefully overcome
In the numerous waves, since there was no lasting
Provision on my ship. Therefore my knees are slackened."
So he said, and the others were silent in stillness.
235 Alcinoos alone addressed him in answer:
"Stranger, you have said this to us not ungracefully,
But you would like to show the excellence that belongs to you,
Angry that this man has stood up to you in the games
And blamed you, as no man would reproach your excellence
240 Who knew in his mind how to speak sensibly.
But come now, give heed to my word, so you may tell it
To another hero when you are in your halls
Dining beside your wife and your own children,
And remember our excellence in such deeds as Zeus
245 Bestows on us steadily since the time of our fathers.
We are not blameless in boxing or in wrestling,
But we do run nimbly in races and are best in ships.
Feasting is dear to us always, the lyre, and dances,
Changes of clothes and hot baths, and the bed.
250 But you who are the best dancers of the Phaeacians, come
And frolic, so the stranger may report to his friends,
When he returns home, how much we surpass others
In seamanship and running and dancing and in song.
Let someone go at once and bring for Demodocos
255 The clear-toned lyre which is lying somewhere in our halls."
So said the godlike Alcinoos, and a herald rose
To bring the hollow lyre from the home of the king.
The umpires appointed for the district stood up,
Nine in all, who attended well to details of the games.
260 They smoothed a dancing place and broadened a lovely ring;

6. A legendary archer, slain by Apollo in a contest; Heracles was the most
famous of Greek legendary heroes, noted especially for his performance
of twelve nigh-impossible labors.

The herald came near, carrying the clear-toned lyre
For Demodocos. He went to the middle then. Young men
In their first youth stood round him, skillful in the dancing,
And beat the godly floor with their feet. Odysseus
Gazed at their flashing feet and wondered in his heart.   265
Then playing the lyre, the man struck up a beautiful song
Of the love of Ares and fine-crowned Aphrodite,[7]
How they first had lain together in the home of Hephaistos,
Secretly. He gave her many gifts and shamed the marriage bed
Of her lord Hephaistos. A messenger came at once to him,   270
Helios,[8] who perceived them lying together in love.
Hephaistos, when he heard the spirit-hurting story,
Went into his bronze works plotting evil in his mind
And put a great anvil on the anvil block, and hammered bonds
Unbreakable and indissoluble, that would hold them there fast.   275
And when in his anger he had fashioned a snare for Ares,
He went into his bedroom where his own precious bedstead
   stood
He spread bonds all around the bedposts in a circle
And he spread many out from the rafters up above,
Subtle as spider web, that no one would ever see,   280
Even of the blessed gods, so well for deceit did he make them.
And when he had put the whole snare around in the bedding,
He made as if to go to Lemnos, the well-built citadel
That is the dearest by far to him of all the lands.
Nor did Ares of the golden rein keep a blind watch   285
When he saw the famed craftsman Hephaistos going off.
He went to the home of the highly renowned Hephaistos,
Craving for the love of Cytherea [9] with the fine crown.
She had recently come from her father, the mighty son
Of Cronos, and had sat down. And he went into the house,   290
Took her hand, and spoke right out directly to her:
"Come, darling, let us enjoy the couch and the bed ourselves.
Hephaistos is no longer in the district. Already
He is gone off to Lemnos among the wild-speaking Sintians."
So he said. It struck her as delightful to go to bed.   295
The two of them went to sleep in the bed clothes. And the
   bonds

7. Daughter of Zeus; the goddess of love.
8. The sun god.
9. Another name for Aphrodite; from Cythera, an island where a shrine
to her was located.

Fashioned by various-minded Hephaistos were spread about
   them,
So they could not move or raise their limbs at all.
And then they knew it when they could no longer escape.
300 The far-famed double cripple came up close to them;
He had turned back again before reaching the land of Lemnos,
As the Sun had kept watch for him and told him the story.
He went into his home, troubled in his own heart.
He stood in the doorway, and a wild anger seized him.
305 Terribly he shouted and cried out to the gods:
"Father Zeus and you other blessed ever-living gods,
Come see deeds to laugh at that are not to be endured,
How Aphrodite, the daughter of Zeus, dishonors me always,
Lame as I am, and loves the destructive Ares
310 Because he is handsome and nimble of foot, while I
Was born feeble. I know no other cause of that
Than my two parents; would that they had never had me!
But you shall see how the two of them have gone into my bed
And are making love there. It grieves me to see it.
But I suppose they would not like to be that way a moment
315   more,
Though they love one another much. Nor will they soon
Want to sleep, but the snare and the bond will constrain them
To the point where our father gives me back all the bride gifts
I paid to him for the sake of the bitch-faced maiden,
320 Since his daughter is lovely, but does not restrain her heart."
So he said, and the gods gathered in the bronze-floored hall.
Poseidon came, who holds up the earth, and Hermes,
The helper; the far-darting Lord Apollo came.
Of the feminine goddesses each stayed home out of shame.
325 The gods, givers of good things, stood in the doorways.
Unquenchable laughter rose up among the blessed gods
To see the devices of many-minded Hephaistos.
This is what one of them would say as he looked to his neigh-
   bor:
"Evil deeds do not win. The slow man finds out the swift,
330 As even now Hephaistos, who is slow and a cripple,
With his devices caught Ares, swiftest of the gods
Who possess Olympos. He owes the adulterer's fine."
This was the sort of thing they said to one another.
The son of Zeus, Lord Apollo, addressed Hermes:

"Hermes, son of Zeus, runner and giver of good things,   335
How would you like to be constrained in strong bonds
And sleep in a bed alongside golden Aphrodite?"
Then the Runner, the slayer of Argos, answered him:
"Far-darting Lord Apollo, I wish that might come about!
Three times as many endless bonds might hold me fast   340
And all you gods and all the goddesses might look at me,
But I should be sleeping alongside golden Aphrodite."
So he said, and laughter arose among the immortal gods.
Laughter did not touch Poseidon; he kept imploring
Hephaistos, renowned for his works, to release Ares;   345
And he spoke out to him and uttered wingèd words:
"Release him, and I will promise for him what you ask:
He will pay all that is proper among the immortal gods."
Then the widely renowned double cripple addressed him:
"Poseidon, holder of earth, do not ask me to do this.   350
The pledges of the worthless are worthless to be kept as
    pledged.
How should I constrain you before the immortal gods
If Ares should go off, avoiding the debt with the bond?"
Then the earth-shaker Poseidon spoke to him:
"Hephaistos, even if Ares gets out from under the debt   355
And goes off in flight, I shall pay it to you myself."
Then the widely renowned double cripple answered him:
"It is not seemly or right to deny your request."
When he had said this, Hephaistos in his force undid the bond.
When the two were released from the bond, strong as it was, 360
They rushed off right at once. He went away to Thrace,
And Aphrodite of the lovely smile got to Cyprus,
To Paphos, where she had a sacred grove and fragrant altar.
There the Graces washed her and anointed her with immortal
Olive oil, such as is poured on the ever-living gods;   365
And they put her in charming clothes, a wonder to see.
This was what the widely renowned singer sang. Odysseus
Was delighted in mind as he listened, and so were the others,
The Phaeacians, who have long oars, men famous for ships.
Alcinoos bade Halios and Laodamas   370
To dance alone, since no one would contend with them.
And so when they had taken a lovely ball in their hands,
A purple one that skillful Polybos had made them,
One of them threw it up to the shadowy clouds,

375 Doubling himself backward. The other rose high off the earth
And easily caught it before touching ground with his feet.
And when they had tried their skill at throwing the ball straight
     up,
The two of them danced upon the much-nourishing earth,
Rapidly changing position. The other youths beat time,
380 Standing in a ring; and a great sound of stamping arose.
Then godly Odysseus spoke to Alcinoos:
"Lordly Alcinoos, illustrious among all peoples,
You did claim that these dancers were most excellent,
And it has been shown true. Awe holds me as I look."
385 So he said, and Alcinoos in his sacred strength rejoiced.
Right away he spoke to the Phaeacians, who are fond of rowing:
"Listen, leaders and counselors of the Phaeacians,
The stranger seems to me to be very prudent.
Come now, let us give him a guest's gift, as is seemly.
390 There are in the district twelve distinguished kings,
Rulers who hold sway, and I am myself the thirteenth.
Each of you give him a well-washed mantle and tunic
And bring him a talent of precious gold. Let us at once
Bring all these together so the stranger may hold them
395 In his hands and go to dinner rejoicing in his heart.
But let Euryalos propitiate him in person
With words and a gift, since he spoke an improper speech."
So he said, and they all assented and gave the order,
And each one sent off a herald to bring the gifts.
400 Then Euryalos answered him and addressed him:
"Lordly Alcinoos, illustrious among all peoples,
I will propitiate the stranger just as you bid me,
And I shall give him this sword all of bronze, whose hilt
Is silver, and a sheath of newly sawn ivory
405 Circles it about. It is worth a great deal for him."
When he had said this, he placed a silver-studded sword in his
     hands;
And he spoke out to him and uttered wingèd words.
"Greetings, father stranger: if any terrible word
Has come out, let storms at once snatch it and carry it off.
May the gods grant that you see your wife and reach your fa-
410   therland,
Since you have long suffered troubles far from your dear ones."
Odysseus of many devices addressed him in answer:

"Kind greetings to you, friend. May the gods grant blessings to
    you,
And may there come to you henceforth no longing for this
    sword
Which you have given me, appeasing me with words."   415
So he said, and put the silver-studded sword over his shoulders.
The sun went down, and the glorious gifts for him were brought.
Noble heralds carried them to the home of Alcinoos.
The sons of excellent Alcinoos, when they had taken them,
Lay the beautiful gifts before their respected mother.   420
Alcinoos led the way for them in his sacred strength.
When they had entered, they sat down on the high armchairs,
And Alcinoos in his might spoke to Arete:
"My wife, bring a fine coffer here, the best there is,
And put a well-washed mantle and tunic in it yourself,   425
Warm the bronze cauldron round the fire for him and heat up
    water
So that when he has bathed, he may look at all the gifts,
Well arrayed, that the excellent Phaeacians have brought,
And enjoy dinner and listen to the strain of a song.
I shall present him myself with this beautiful cup   430
Of gold, so that he may remember me all his days
When he pours in his halls to Zeus and the other gods."
So he said, and Arete gave the word to her handmaids
To set a big cauldron over the fire as quickly as they could.
They stood a cauldron for bath water on a blazing fire,   435
Poured in water, took wood, and kindled it beneath.
The fire circled the cauldron's belly, and the water heated.
Meanwhile Arete brought the lovely coffer for the stranger
From the chamber, and put in it the splendid gifts,
The clothing and the gold that the Phaeacians had given.   440
She herself put in a mantle and a lovely tunic.
And she spoke out to him and uttered wingèd words:
"Look to the lid yourself, and quickly fasten the knot,
Lest someone rob you of it on your trip, at a time when
You are resting in sweet sleep as you go in the black ship."   445
When godly Odysseus, who had endured much, heard that,
He at once fitted the lid on and quickly fastened the knot,
The subtle one that queenly Circe [1] had once taught his mind.
At the same moment a housekeeper called him to go

1. An enchantress living in Aiaia; daughter of the sun.

450 To the bathtub to be washed. He saw the hot water
With gladdened heart, as he had received no such treatment
Since he had left the home of Calypso with the lovely locks.
The care he got all that while was as it would be for a god.
When the handmaids had washed him and anointed him with
    oil,
455 They threw a lovely mantle around him and a tunic,
And out of the bathtub he stepped, and he went amid the men
As they were drinking wine. Nausicaa, who had her beauty
From the gods, stood by the column of the stoutly made roof
And wondered at Odysseus as she took him in with her eyes.
460 She spoke out to him, and she uttered wingèd words:
"Farewell, stranger; and even when you are in your fatherland
May you remember me as the one you first owe the ransom of
    life."
Odysseus of many devices addressed her in answer:
"Nausicaa, daughter of great-hearted Alcinoos,
465 May Zeus, the thunderer, husband of Hera, now grant
That I go homeward and see the day of my return,
And that there, too, I may pray to you as to a god
Forever all my days. For you saved my life, maiden."
He spoke, and sat on an armchair beside King Alcinoos.
470 They were already passing out portions and mixing wine,
And a herald came near, leading the trusty singer
Demodocos, honored by the people. And he set him
In the midst of the diners, propped against a tall pillar.
Then Odysseus of many devices addressed the herald
475 When he had cut some off the back—but more was left on it—
Of a shining-tusked boar; and swelling fat was about it.
"Herald, take this portion over to Demodocos
So he may eat, and I will embrace him, grieved as I am,
For among all the men on the earth singers are sharers
480 In honor and respect, because the Muse has taught them
Poems, and she cherishes the tribe of singers."
So he said; the herald brought the meat and put it in the hands
Of the hero Demodocos. He took it and rejoiced in his heart.
They stretched forth their hands to the food that was spread out
    ready,
485 And when they had taken their fill of food and drink,
Odysseus of many devices addressed Demodocos:
"Demodocos, I give you praise above all mortal men,

Either a Muse, a child of Zeus, has taught you, or Apollo.
Very becomingly did you sing the fate of the Achaians,
All they acted and endured, all the Achaians suffered,   490
As though you had somehow been there yourself or heard one
    who was.
Come, change your subject and sing of the stratagem
Of the wooden horse Epeios made with Athene's help,
The trap that godly Odysseus once led to the citadel,
When he had filled it up with the men who sacked Ilion.   495
If you do tell me these matters in proper form,
Then at once I will proclaim among all men
How a propitious god endowed a divine singer."
So he said. Inspired by the god, he began and showed forth his
    song,
Starting from where some of the Argives on the well-timbered
    ships   500
Boarded and sailed off, when they had set fire to the huts,
And the others who were round the famous Odysseus already
Were seated in the assembly of the Trojans concealed within
    the horse,
For the Trojans themselves dragged it to their citadel.
So it stood, and they made many ill-considered speeches   505
Seated about it. Three plans there were that pleased them:
To strike through the hollow wood with the pitiless sword,
To drag it to the peak and throw it off the rocks,
Or to let the great ornament be a charm for the gods.
Even then it was destined to end in just this way.   510
Fate was, they should be destroyed, since the city enfolded
The great wooden horse, where all the best men of the Argives
Were seated, bringing death and destiny on the Trojans.
He sang how the sons of the Achaians sacked the city,
When they had poured from the horse and abandoned the
    hollow ambush;   515
He sang how one man ravaged one place and one another,
In the lofty city, and Odysseus like Ares went
To the halls of Deiphobos, with godlike Menelaos.
There he said the man dared fight his most dreadful battle
And won, that time too, through great-hearted Athene.   520
This did the renowned singer sing. And Odysseus
Melted, and a tear from under his eyelids wet his cheeks,
As a woman weeps embracing her beloved husband

Who has fallen before his own city and his own people,
525 Warding off from city and children the pitiless day,
And she sees the man dying and breathing heavily,
And falls down upon him and piercingly shrieks. The enemy
From behind strike her back and her shoulders with spears
And lead her off in bonds to have trouble and woe,
530 And her cheeks are wasted for her most wretched grief;
Just so did Odysseus shed a piteous tear under his eyebrows.
Then, as he shed tears, he escaped the notice of all the others
But Alcinoos alone took note of him and perceived him
While seated near him, and heard him as he deeply groaned.
535 At once he addressed the Phaeacians, who are fond of rowing.
"Hear me, leaders and counselors of the Phaeacians,
And let Demodocos hold off now from the sharp-toned lyre.
For he does not give everyone pleasure when he sings this.
Since we have been dining and the divine singer rose,
540 The stranger has not at all ceased his woeful lament,
For grief has very much compassed his mind about.
But come, let him hold off, so we may all alike take pleasure,
Hosts and the guest, since it is much more pleasant so.
All this has been done for the sake of our respected guest,
545 The convoy and the precious gifts we give him in friendship.
A guest and a suppliant is held equal to a brother
By a man who has even a little grasp with his wits.
And so in your cunning notions do not yourself now conceal
What I ask you about. It is better for you to speak.
550 Tell the name which your mother and father called you there,
And the others who dwell in that city and about it,
For no one among men is wholly without a name,
Neither a worthless man nor a noble, from the time he was
    born;
Parents when they have children bestow them on everyone.
555 Tell me your land and your district and your city,
So that the ships that are steered by thought may convey you
    there,
For there exist no pilots among the Phaeacians,
And there are no rudders at all such as other ships have,
But the ships themselves know the intentions and minds of
    men.
560 They know the cities and fertile fields of all men
And very swiftly, shrouded in mist and a cloud,

They traverse the gulf of the sea. There is no fear
At all for them that they suffer harm or be lost.
But once I heard my father Nausithoos
Say this: he asserted that Poseidon bore a grudge   565
Against us, because our convoys are safe for all men.
He said a well-made ship of the Phaeacian men
Coming back sometime from an escort on the murky ocean
Would be dashed, and a great mountain would hide our city
    round.
So the old man said. And the god will either fulfill it   570
Or it will be unfulfilled, as his spirit desires.
Come tell me this, and speak out truthfully.
Where have you wandered, and what places have you reached
Among men: tell of them and their well-inhabited cities,
Those that were difficult and savage and without justice,   575
And those who were friendly to strangers and have a godfearing
    mind.
Tell also why you lament and grieve in your heart
When you hear the fate of Ilion and the Danaan Argives.
That did the gods fashion, and they spun the thread of death
For men, so that it would be a song for those to come.   580
Did some kinsman of yours perish before Ilion,
A nobleman, son-in-law, or father-in-law,
Those who are dearest, next to one's blood and family,
Or perhaps some companion of sympathetic mind,
A noble one? Since not inferior to a brother   585
Is a companion who possesses a prudent mind."

Odysseus of many devices addressed him in answer:
"Lordly Alcinoos, exalted among all your people,
Indeed it is pleasant to listen to such a singer
As this one is, who resembles the gods in his voice.
5 I would say myself there is no more delightful result
Than when happiness so prevails through a whole district
And when diners seated in order through the halls
Listen to a singer, and the tables nearby are full
Of bread and meat, and the wine pourer draws wine off
10 From the bowl, carries it around, and pours it in the cups.
To my mind this seems to be the loveliest thing.
But your heart turns toward me to ask of my woeful cares,
So that I may grieve still further as I lament.
What then shall I tell you first, what tell last,
15 Since the heavenly gods bestowed many cares upon me?
Well now, I shall tell you my name first, so that you too
May know it, and then, when I have escaped the pitiless day
I may be your guest friend, though I dwell far off in my halls.
I am Odysseus, son of Laertes, who for my wiles
20 Am of note among all men, and my fame reaches heaven.
I dwell in sunny Ithaca. A mountain is on it,
Neritos, with trembling leaves, conspicuous.
Many islands lie about it quite close to one another,
Dulichion and Samê and wooded Zakynthos;
25 She herself sits low-lying, farthest out to sea
Toward dusk, and they are apart toward dawn and the sun,
Rugged but good for bringing up young men. And I
Can look upon nothing sweeter than a man's own land.
Well, Calypso, the divine goddess, kept me in one place,
30 In a hollow cave, desiring that I be her husband.
The same way in her halls would the wily Aiaian
Circe have held me back, desiring that I be her husband.
But they never persuaded the heart within my breast.

So nothing grows sweeter than a man's own fatherland
And his parents, even if he dwell in a fertile home   35
Far off in a foreign land apart from his parents.
But come, let me tell you of the much-troubled return
That Zeus put upon me when I went away from Troy.
The wind bearing me from Ilion brought me near the Cicones,[1]
To Ismaros. There I sacked the city and killed its men.   40
From the city we took the wives and many possessions
And divided them so none for my sake would lack an equal
    share.
Then I gave the order for us to take rapid flight,
But the men, great fools as they were, did not obey;
They had drunk much wine there and slain many sheep   45
Along the strand, many shamble-footed, crumple-horned cattle.
Meanwhile the Cicones went and called other Cicones
Who were their neighbors, at once more numerous and brave,
Who dwelt on the mainland, skilled in fighting with men,
From horses, and, when necessary, on foot.   50
As thick as leaves and flowers grow in their season,
They came, in early morning. Then an evil fate of Zeus was with
    us
In our dread destinies, so we might suffer many pains.
They took their stand and fought a battle by the swift ships,
And they threw bronze-tipped spears at one another.   55
So long as it was morning and the sacred day increased,
We stayed and warded them off, many as there were.
But when the sun declined to the time of ox-loosing,
Then the Cicones turned back the Achaians and routed them.
Six from each ship of my well-greaved companions   60
Perished. The rest of us escaped death and destiny.
Then we sailed on further, grieving in our hearts,
Glad to escape death, having lost our dear companions.
My bobbing ships, however, did not proceed further
Till someone had thrice called for each of our wretched com-
    panions   65
Who had died on the plain, slaughtered by the Cicones.
Cloud-gathering Zeus raised a North Wind against the ships
In an immense storm, and covered land and ocean alike
Over with clouds. And night rose up out of heaven.
The ships were borne headlong, and the force of the wind   70

1. Thracian allies of the Trojans raided by Odysseus.

Ripped the sails up into three fragments and four.
We lowered them onto the ships, fearing destruction,
And rowed the ships forward to the mainland hastily.
There for two whole nights and two days continually
75 We lay, eating our hearts with pain and fatigue alike.
But when fair-braided Dawn had brought the third day to the full,
We set up our masts and hoisted the white sails
And took our seats. The wind and the pilots steered them,
And I would have arrived unscathed at my fatherland,
80 But as I rounded Malea a rushing wave
And a North Wind pushed me off and drove me past Cythera.
Thence for nine days I was borne by destructive winds
On the fish-laden ocean. But the tenth day I set foot
On the land of the Lotus-eaters, who eat a flowery food.
85 Then we went onto the dry land and drew off water,
And at once my companions took dinner beside the swift ships.
But when we had partaken of food and of drink,
I sent my companions forth to go and find out
Who these were of the men who eat bread on the earth.
90 I picked out two men and sent on a third as a herald.
They went off at once and mingled with the Lotus-eaters.
And the Lotus-eaters did not plot destruction
For our companions, but gave them the lotus to taste of.
Whoever among them ate the honey-sweet fruit of the lotus
95 Wished no longer to bring word back again or return,
But wanted to remain there with the Lotus-eaters
To devour the lotus and forget about a return.
Back weeping to the ships I led them, by compulsion,
Dragged them and bound them in the hollow ships under the benches,
100 And I called all my other trusty companions
To hasten and to get on board the rapid ships,
Lest someone perchance eat the lotus and forget a return.
They got in at once and took their seats at the oarlocks.
Seated in order, they beat the hoary sea with their oars.
105 Then we sailed further on, grieving in our hearts,
To the land of the Cyclopes, an overweening
And lawless people, who, trusting in the immortal gods,
Do not sow plants with their hands and do not plow
But everything grows for them unplowed and unsown,

Wheat and barley and vines that produce a wine grape   110
Of large clusters, and a rain from Zeus makes them grow.
They have neither assemblies for holding council nor laws,
But they inhabit the crests of the lofty mountains,
In hollow caves, and each one dispenses the laws
For his children and his wives and is not concerned for the
     others.   115
A fertile island stretches there from the harbor
Of the land of the Cyclopes, not near and not far away,
A wooded one. And on it numberless wild goats flourish,
For there is no beaten path of men to keep them away.
Nor do hunters land upon it, who in the woods   120
Undergo pains and chase them over the mountain peaks.
And it is not held, either, with flocks or with plowed lands,
But it lies unsown and unplowed day after day
Bereft of men, and it nourishes bleating goats.
There are no vermilion-prowed ships for the Cyclopes,   125
As there are no shipwrights among them who might work
At good-timbered ships to accomplish it all for them
So they may visit cities among men, as frequently
Men do cross the sea in ships toward one another;
And these would have worked to make the island well settled
     for them,   130
As it is not really bad, and would bear all things in season.
There are meadows in it along the banks of the hoary sea,
Soft, moist ones. And there would be fine, unwithering vines
And smooth plowing, and they would mow the deep-standing
Grain in season, as it is very rich beneath the surface.   135
There a sheltered harbor is, where there is no need of a rope
Or of throwing out anchor stones or fastening cables,
But they could put in and stay a time till the hearts
Of the sailors urged them on and breezes should be blowing.
And shining water flows down from the head of the harbor,   140
A spring under a cave. Poplars grow about it.
There we sailed on in. And some god guided us
Through the murky night. There was not light enough to see.
Dark air was deep about the ships, nor did the moon
Show forth from heaven, but it was contained in clouds.   145
There no one looked upon the island with his eyes,
And we did not behold the great waves rolling up
On the mainland, before we beached our well-timbered ships.

When the ships had been beached, we took down all the sails,
150 And got out ourselves beside the surf of the sea.
We fell asleep there and awaited the godly dawn.
And when the early-born, rosy-fingered dawn appeared,
We wondered at the island and traveled all around it.
The nymphs, daughters of aegis-bearing Zeus, roused up
155 Mountain goats, so that my companions might have dinner.
At once we took curved bows and long-socketed goat spears
Out of the ships. We divided into three groups
And went shooting. At once the god gave us satisfying game.
The men of twelve ships followed along with me. Nine goats
160 Fell the lot of each ship. They picked ten out just for me.
So then for the whole day till the setting of the sun
We sat dining on the endless meat and sweet wine,
For the red wine from the ships had not yet been exhausted,
But was still there. Each group had drawn off much in jars
165 When we sacked the holy citadel of the Cicones.
We were looking over to the land of the Cyclopes nearby,
To their smoke, to their sound and that of their sheep and goats.
But when the sun went down and the darkness came on,
We lay down to sleep beside the surf of the sea.
170 And when the early-born, rosy-fingered dawn appeared,
I called an assembly and spoke out to them all:
'Stay here now, the rest of you, my trusty companions;
But I will go myself with my ship and companions
To inquire about these men, whoever they may be,
175 Whether they are proud and savage and without justice
Or are friendly to strangers, and have a god-fearing mind.'
When I had said this, I went on the ship and called my companions
To go on board themselves and to undo the stern cables.
At once they got on and took their seats at the oarlocks;
180 Seated in order, they beat the hoary sea with their oars.
And when we had arrived at the place that was nearby,
There we saw a cave on the verge, close to the sea
High up, overhung with laurel. Many animals
Usually slept there, sheep and goats; a courtyard
185 Was built high around it out of deep-bedded stones
And tall pines and oak trees with lofty foliage.
There a monstrous man usually slept, who alone
And aloof tended the animals. He did not consort

With the others, but stayed apart and had a lawless mind.
And indeed he was formed as a monstrous wonder. He looked 190
Not like a grain-eating man but like a wooded crest
On lofty mountains that appears singled out from the others.
And then I ordered the rest of my trusty companions
To remain there beside the ship and to guard the ship.
But I myself picked out twelve of my best companions   195
To go on. Now I had a goatskin flask of black wine,
A sweet wine that Maron gave me, Euanthes' son—
The priest of Apollo, who watches over Ismaros—
Because we protected him along with his wife and son,
And reverenced him. He dwelt in the tree-filled grove   200
Of Phoebos Apollo. And he gave me glorious gifts:
He gave me seven talents of well-fashioned gold,
And he gave me a mixing bowl all of silver, and then
Into two-handled jars, twelve in all, he drew off wine
Sweet and unmixed, a godly drink, nor was any   205
Maidservant or serving man in the house aware of it,
But himself and his wife and one single housekeeper.
And whenever they drank that honey-sweet red wine,
He would fill one cup and pour it into twenty measures
Of water, and a sweet aroma came from the bowl   210
Of marvelous fragrance: to abstain then would not have been
    easy.
I filled a great skin with it and brought it, and also I put
Provisions in a bag. At once my bold spirit
Sensed that the man would approach, clad in his great strength,
The wild man who had clear in his mind neither justice nor
    laws.   215
Speedily we came to the cave and did not find him
Within. But he was tending rich flocks in a pasture.
We entered the cave and gazed at each separate thing.
Baskets were weighed down with cheeses, and the folds were
    thronged
With lambs and kids. All were divided in groups,   220
And confined; here the first born, there the middlers,
The dew-fleeced apart too. All the pails flowed with whey,
The vessels and the pans, well wrought, in which he milked
    them.
Then at first my companions besought me with speeches
To go back again, when we had picked some cheeses and then   225

When we had hastily driven the kids and lambs out of the pens
On board the swift ship, to set sail upon the salt water.
But I did not listen—that would have been far better—
So I might see the man and he give me the gifts of a guest.
But when he appeared, he was not to be joyful to my com-
230   panions.
We kindled a fire there, sacrificed, and ourselves
Also picked out some cheeses and ate, and awaited him
Seated inside, till he did come driving sheep. He carried
A stout burden of dry wood to use for his supper.
235 Throwing it down inside the cave, he made a din;
And we drew back in fear into a nook of the cave.
But into the broad cavern he drove his fat flocks,
All those that he usually milked, and he left the males
By the entrance, rams and he-goats, in the deep yard outside.
240 Then he put a great doorstone on, raising it aloft,
A mighty one. And twenty-two excellent wagons
With four wheels could not pry it up from the ground,
So great was the towering rock he set on the entrance.
He sat down and milked the sheep and the bleating goats,
245 All in due order, and set each young one to his mother;
And at once when he had curdled half the white milk,
He skimmed it off and put it up in wicker baskets,
And half of it he stood in pails so he would have it
To drink when he reached for it, to have it for supper.
250 And when he had hurried at attending to all his tasks,
He kindled a fire, and looked at us, and spoke to us:
'Strangers, who are you? Whence have you sailed the watery
     ways?
For some sort of gain, or do you wander at hazard
The way pirates do who wander over the sea
255 Risking their lives, bearing evil to foreigners?'
So he said, and our own hearts were shattered within us,
In terror at his deep voice and the monster himself.
Yet even so I answered him with a speech and addressed him
     thus:
'We are Achaians coming from Troy, driven off course
260 By all kinds of winds over the great gulf of the sea;
Wanting to go homeward, we came by other passages,
By another way. So Zeus I suppose wished to devise it.
We declare we are the men of Agamemnon, son of Atreus,

The glory of whom is now the most under heaven,
So great a city did he sack, and he destroyed many   265
People. And so we have arrived here and come up to your
    knees
To see if you may provide some guest gift or otherwise
Give a present, such as is the custom among guest friends,
Mighty one, revere the gods. We are your suppliants.
Zeus is the protector of suppliants and guest friends,   270
The god of guests, who accompanies respectful guests.'
So I said, and he answered me at once in his pitiless spirit:
'You are a fool, stranger, or have come from afar,
To bid me to be afraid or to shrink from the gods.
Cyclopes have no regard for aegis-bearing Zeus,   275
Or the blessed gods since we are mightier by far.
Nor to shrink from the hatred of Zeus would I spare
You or your companions, unless the spirit moved me.
But tell me where you have come and put your well-made
    ships,
Whether on the mainland or nearby, so I may know.'   280
So he said, testing us; I who knew much was not deceived.
I addressed him in return with guileful words:
'The earth-shaker Poseidon has shattered my ship,
Throwing it on the rocks at the borders of your land,
Driving it on the cape, but a wind bore it from the ocean.   285
And I escaped with these men from sheer destruction.'
So I said; in his pitiless spirit he answered nothing,
But he leaped up, stretched his hands to my companions,
Snatched up two together, and dashed them like whelps to the
    earth.
Their brains flowed out onto the ground and wet the earth.   290
Then he tore them limb from limb and made them his meal.
He ate like a mountain-reared lion, and did not leave off
Their entrails and their flesh and their marrowed bones.
We wailed and held our hands out to Zeus when we
Had seen the cruel deeds. Helplessness held our hearts.   295
And when the Cyclops had filled up his great belly
By eating human flesh and then drinking unmixed milk,
He lay down in the cave, stretched full length through the sheep.
And in my great-hearted spirit I made a plan myself
To go closer to him, draw the sharp sword from my thigh   300
And wound him in the chest where the midriff holds the liver,

Striking with my hand. But another spirit restrained me;
For there we too would have perished in sheer destruction,
Since from the lofty entrance we could not push away
305 The mighty rock with our hands that he had set upon it.
And so we lamented then and awaited the godly dawn.
And when the early-born, rosy-fingered dawn appeared,
He kindled a fire and milked his glorious flocks,
All in due order, and set each young one to his mother.
310 And when he had hurried at tending to all his tasks,
He again snatched two men together and made them his meal.
When he had finished, he drove the rich flock from the cave,
Taking the great doorstone off easily. And then
He put it back, as one would put the lid on a quiver.
315 With a great whistling, the Cyclops turned his fat flock
To the mountain. I was left deeply devising evil,
If I might somehow avenge me and Athene give me glory.
And this seemed to me in my heart to be the best plan.
In the fold a great club of the Cyclops was lying,
320 A green one of olive wood. He had cut it to carry
When it was dry. As we beheld it, we thought it
To be as large as the mast of a black, twenty-oared ship,
A wide freighter that traverses the great gulf:
So great was its length, so great its breadth to behold.
325 I stood by and cut off a piece the size of a cubit,
Gave it to my companions and told them to plane it;
They made it smooth, and I stood by and sharpened it to a
    point.
I took it at once and brought it to a glow in the blazing fire;
Then I hid it well, placing it under the dung
330 Which was strewn through the cave in great abundant heaps.
Then I ordered the others to cast lots for a choice
Of the one who would dare to raise the pole along with me
And bore it in his eye when sweet sleep had come upon him.
The lots fell to those I would have wished to choose myself,
335 Four men, and I picked myself as the fifth among them.
He came at evening driving the flocks with their lovely fleece.
At once he drove the fat flocks into the broad cave,
All, and did not leave any outside in the deep yard;
Either he suspected something or a god bade him so.
340 Then he put the great doorstone on, raising it aloft,

And he sat down and milked the sheep and the bleating goats,
All in due order, and set each young one to his mother.
And when he had hurried at attending to all his tasks,
He again snatched two men together and made them his meal.
Then I addressed the Cyclops, standing close to him,   345
Holding in my hands an ivy bowl of black wine:
'Here, Cyclops, drink wine, now you have eaten human flesh,
So you may see what sort of wine this is that our ship contained.
I brought it for libation to you that you might pity me
And send me home. Your rage may be borne no longer;   350
Cruel wretch, how could anyone else come to you later on
Of the number of mankind, since you have not acted properly.'
So I said. He took and drank it. He was fearfully pleased
As he drank the sweet wine, and he asked me for a second.
'Kindly grant me something more and tell me your name   355
At once now, so I may give you a guest gift to delight you.
Yes, indeed, for the Cyclopes the grain-giving land bears
Large-clustered wine grapes, and a rain of Zeus makes them
    grow,
But this is a runnel of nectar and ambrosia.'
So he said. And I gave him more of the sparkling wine.   360
Thrice I brought it and gave it, thrice he thoughtlessly drank.
And when the wine had overcome the mind of the Cyclops,
At that point I addressed him with soothing words:
'Cyclops, do you ask me my famous name? Well, I
Will tell you. Then give me the guest gift you promised.   365
Noman is my own name. Noman do they call me,
My mother and my father and all my companions.'
So I said, and he answered at once in his pitiless spirit:
'Noman I shall eat last among his companions
And the others first. This will be my guest gift to you.'   370
With that he leaned over and fell down on his back. And then
He lay with his massive neck twisted. All-subduing
Sleep seized him. Wine poured out of his gullet,
And chunks of human flesh. He belched out drunkenly.
And then I drove the pole up under a mass of ashes   375
Until it should heat. And I encouraged all my companions
With speeches, lest one of them should draw back from me in
    fear.
But just when the olive pole was ready to catch fire,

Green as it was, and was glowing dreadfully,
At that moment I came closer and took it out of the fire. My
380   companions
Stood about. And some god breathed great courage into them.
They lifted the olive pole that was sharp at its tip
And thrust it in his eye; I myself, leaning on it from above,
Twirled it around as a man would drill the wood of a ship
With an auger, and others would keep spinning with a strap
385   beneath,
Holding it at either end, and the auger keeps on going.
So we held the fire-sharpened pole in his eye
And twirled it. The blood flowed around it, hot as it was.
The fire singed his eyebrows and eyelids all around
390 From the burning eye. Its roots swelled in the fire to bursting,
As when a smith plunges a great ax or an adz
Into cold water and the tempering makes it hiss
Loudly, and just that gives the strength to the iron;
So did his eye sizzle around the olive pole.
395 He wailed a great terrible wail; the rock resounded,
And we were afraid and rushed back, while he drew
The pole out of his eye spattered with much blood;
Then he threw it from him with his hands, maddened by pain,
And let out a great roar for the Cyclopes, who dwelt
400 All around him in caves throughout the windy peaks.
When they heard the shout they trailed in from every side;
They stood around the cave and asked what bothered him:
'Polyphemos, how is it you are hurt so much as to shout so
Through the ambrosial night and to make us sleepless?
405 No mortal drives your flocks against your will, does he?
And no one is murdering you by craft or by force?'
Mighty Polyphemos addressed them from the cavern:
'Friends, Noman is murdering me by craft, not by force.'
And they answered him and addressed him with wingèd words:
410 'If no one is compelling you when you are alone,
There is no way to escape a sickness from great Zeus.
Come now and pray to our father Lord Poseidon.'
So they said and went away; and my own heart laughed
At how my name had deceived him, and my faultless device.
415 The Cyclops, though, was in pain as he groaned, and felt pangs.
Groping with his hands, he took the stone from the entrance
And sat in the entrance himself, stretching out his hands

To see if he could catch someone going outdoors with the sheep;
So foolish did he in his mind think me to be.
And I myself kept planning what way might be far the best   420
If I could find some release from death for my companions
And for myself. I wove all sorts of wiles and deceit
As for very life, since a great ill was near at hand.
This seemed to me in my heart to be the best plan:
The males of the sheep were well nourished and shaggy coated,   425
Handsome and large, with a fleece of dark violet.
These I joined fast in silence with easily twisted twigs
On which the monster Cyclops slept, lawless in his mind.
I bound them in threes, and the middle one would carry a man.
The other two went on either side, protecting my companions.   430
So three sheep bore each mortal man. As for myself,
There was a lead ram, by far the finest of all the sheep,
Whose back I grasped and lay under his shaggy belly
Curled up. And with my hand twisted in his marvelous
    wool
I held on relentlessly with an enduring heart.   435
So then, lamenting, we awaited the godly dawn.
And when the early-born, rosy-fingered dawn appeared,
At that moment he drove the male flocks to pasture,
And the females were bleating unmilked around the pens.
Their udders were swollen. And then the master, afflicted   440
By bad pains, felt over the backs of all the sheep
As they stood erect. And the fool did not perceive
How the men were bound under the breasts of the thick-fleeced
    sheep.
Last of all the lead ram of the flock went outdoors
Encumbered by his wool and by me with my rapid thoughts.   445
The mighty Polyphemos felt him over and addressed him:
'Friend ram, why of all the sheep do you move this way as
    the last
Out of the cave? You were not left behind by the sheep be-
    fore;
You were much the first to pasture on the tender flowers of
    grass
With your long strides, and you came first to the rivers' streams, 450
And you were the first to desire to return to the fold
At evening. But now you are last of all. Ah, you long
For the eye of your master that an evil man put out

With woeful companions, overcoming his mind by wine,
455 Noman, who I say has not yet escaped destruction.
And if you could sympathize and become able to speak,
To say in what place that man is evading my rage,
Then once he were struck, his brains should be dashed through
      the cave
In all directons on the threshold. And then my heart
460 Should be relieved of the ills worthless Noman brought me.'
When he had said this, he sent the ram from him out the en-
      trance.
When I had gone a short way away from the cave and the yard,
I first got loose from the ram and then freed my companions.
Speedily we drove the long-legged sheep, rich in fat,
465 Rounding the many of them up, until we came
To the ship. We were welcome to our dear companions,
We who escaped death. The others they would have lamented,
      wailing,
But I did not allow it and nodded with my eyebrows to each
Not to weep. I ordered them to put the many sheep
470 With lovely fleece quickly on the ship and sail the salt water.
They got on board at once and took their seats at the oarlocks;
Seated in order, they beat the hoary sea with their oars.
And when I was as far off as a man's shout would carry,
I addressed the Cyclops myself with taunting speeches:
475 'Cyclops, you were not destined to eat in your hollow cave,
For your powerful might, the companions of a strengthless man.
And truly it was destined for your evil deeds to find you out,
Cruel wretch, since you did not shrink from eating the guests
In your house. Zeus and the other gods have paid you for that.'
480 So I said. Then he got the more angry in his heart.
He broke off the crest of a great mountain and threw it,
And it fell down in front of the dark blue-prowed ship,
Just short, and it missed hitting the end of the rudder.
The sea was heaved up by the rock as it descended,
485 And a great back-washing wave bore the ship at once to land,
As it swelled from the ocean, and drove it to hit the mainland.
And I took hold of a very long pole in my hands
And pushed on out. I called to urge on my companions,
Nodding with my head, to throw themselves on the oars,
490 So we could flee misfortune. Falling to it, they rowed.
When we had crossed twice as much water and were far away,

Then I would have shouted to the Cyclops, but my companions
    around me
From all sides tried to restrain me with soothing speeches:
'You wretch, why did you want to provoke the wild man,
Who, even now, when he threw his missile into the ocean,   495
Has brought the ship back to land? And we really thought we
    would die there.
And if he had heard anyone speaking or shouting out
He would have broken our brains and our ship timbers
Casting a jagged piece of sparkling rock. So powerfully does he
    throw!'
So they said, but they did not sway my great-hearted spirit.   500
But in my angry spirit I answered him back:
'Cyclops, if someone among mortal men should inquire
Of you about the unseemly blindness in your eye,
Say that Odysseus, sacker of cities, blinded it,
The son of Laertes, whose home is in Ithaca.'   505
So I said. He moaned and answered me with a tale:
'Well then, the decrees uttered of old have come upon me.
Once there was a prophet here, a man fine and great,
Telemos, Eurymos' son, who excelled in prophecy,
And grew old prophesying among the Cyclopes,   510
Who said all these things in the future would come to pass,
That I would be deprived of my sight at Odysseus' hands.
But I always expected some mortal great and handsome
To arrive in this place decked out in great strength.
And now, a man small and worthless and feeble   515
Has blinded my eye when he overcame me with wine.
Come here now, Odysseus, so I may present you with gifts,
And urge the famed earth-shaker to give you an escort,
For I am his son, and he declares he is my father.
He himself, if he wishes, will heal me. No one else   520
Can do it, of the blessed gods or of mortal men.'
So he said, and I myself addressed him in answer:
'Would I might as surely be able to make you devoid
Of breath and life and send you to the hall of Hades,
As I am sure not even the earth-shaker will heal your eye.'   525
So I said, and then he prayed to Lord Poseidon,
Stretching his hand up to the heaven filled with stars:
'Hear me, earth-holding Poseidon of the dark-blue locks,
If truly I am yours, and you declare you are my father,

530 Grant that the city-sacker Odysseus not go homeward,
The son of Laertes whose home is in Ithaca.
But if it is his fate to see his dear ones and arrive
At his well-established home and his fatherland,
May he come late and ill, having lost all his companions,
535 On someone else's ship, and find troubles at home.'
So he said in prayer. The god with the dark-blue locks heard
    him.
And then once more he lifted up a far bigger stone.
Whirling it, he shot it and thrust it with boundless strength
And threw it down behind the dark blue-prowed ship,
540 Just short, and it missed hitting the end of the rudder.
The sea was heaved up by the rock as it descended.
A wave bore the ship forward and drove it to hit land.
And when we arrived at the island, where the other
Well-timbered ships were waiting, gathered, and our
    companions
545 Sat lamenting all around, forever awaiting us;
As we came there, we beached our ship upon the sand
And got out ourselves beside the surf of the sea.
Taking the flocks of Cyclops out of the hollow ship,
We divided them so none would lack an equal share for my
    sake.
550 But my well-greaved companions chose the ram especially
For me alone, when the flocks were divided. On the strand
We slew it and burned the thighs to black-clouded Zeus,
The son of Cronos, who rules all. But he received not the rites;
Instead he kept on plotting how all the well-timbered ships
555 And the companions faithful to me might be destroyed.
So then the whole day till the setting of the sun
We sat dining on endless meat and sweet wine.
But when the sun went down and darkness came on,
We lay down to sleep beside the surf of the sea.
560 And when the early-born, rosy-fingered dawn appeared,
I myself called to my companions and bade them
To go on board themselves and to undo the stern cables;
At once they got on and took their seats at the oarlocks.
Seated in order, they beat the hoary sea with their oars.
565 Then we sailed further on, grieving in our hearts,
Glad to escape death, having lost our dear companions.

X

"Then we came to the island of Aeolia, where dwelt
Aeolos,[1] Hippotas' son, who is dear to the immortal gods,
On a floating island. All about it there was
An unbreakable bronze wall, and up it the stone ran smooth.
And there are twelve children of his living in his halls;   5
Six of them are daughters and six are blooming sons.
So he gave the daughters to the sons to be their wives.
They always take their meals with their dear father
And devoted mother. Numberless dishes lie ready for them;
The redolent house resounds all round with the flute   10
In the day, and at night beside their respected wives
They sleep in blankets and upon their jointed bedsteads.
And so we came to their city and their lovely halls.
A whole month he befriended me and asked in detail
About Ilion, the Argives' ships, and the Achaians' return,   15
And I told him everything in its due order.
But when I inquired about the way and asked him
To send us, he did not refuse, and he made a conveyance.
He gave me the skin of a nine-year-old ox he had flayed,
And in it he had bound the courses of the blustering winds.   20
For the son of Cronos had made him steward of the winds,
So he could make the one he wished rise up or subside.
He bound it in the hollow ship with a shining cord
Of silver, so it would not blow at all, not a little.
Then he set a breeze of the West Wind blowing for me   25
That would carry the ship and the men onward. He was not
Destined to complete it. We were lost by our own foolishness.
Nine days we sailed alike by night and by day;
On the tenth the soil of our fatherland already appeared,
And we were close enough to see men tending the fire.   30
Then sweet sleep came upon me in my weariness,
For I always saw to the ship's sheet, and did not give it

1. Lord of the winds.

To another companion, so we might reach the fatherland
  quicker.
But my companions addressed one another with speeches
35 And said that I was bringing gold and silver home
As gifts from Aeolos, the great-hearted son of Hippotas.
This is what one, looking at his closest neighbor, would say:
'Well now, how beloved and honored this man is
Among all those men at whose city and land he arrives.
40 He is bringing much fine treasure out of Troy
As booty. And we, who have accomplished the same journey,
Are going homeward, all of us, with empty hands.
Now Aeolos has given him these things as a favor
In friendship. Come, let us see quickly what they are,
45 How much there is of gold and silver in the skin.'
So they said, and evil advice won my companions over.
They undid the skin, and the winds all rushed out.
At once a storm seized them and bore them onto the ocean,
Far away from our fatherland, weeping. And I,
50 As I awoke, wondered in my own blameless heart
Whether I should drop from the ship and perish in the ocean
Or endure silently and stay among the living still.
But I endured and waited, and lay with head covered
In my ship. The ships were borne in a bad storm of wind
55 Back to the island Aeolia, and my companions groaned.
Then we went onto the dry land and drew off water,
And at once my companions took dinner beside the swift ships.
But when we had partaken of food and of drink,
I took a herald and a companion along with me
60 To the famous halls of Aeolos. And I found him
Having a meal along with his wife and his children.
When we came to the hall we sat beside the columns
On the threshold. They wondered in their hearts, and asked
  right out:
'How have you come, Odysseus? What evil god has attacked
  you?
65 We did send you off kindly, so that you might reach
Fatherland and home and whatever is dear to you.'
So they said, and I spoke out, grieved in my heart:
'My evil companions ruined me; and besides them, a wretched
Sleep. But give relief, friends. You have the power.'
70 So I said, addressing them with gentle words.
But they grew silent. The father answered with a speech:

'Go quickly from the island, most shameful of living men.
It is not lawful for me to help or to send on his course
Any man who is despised by the blessed gods.
Go, since you came to this place despised by the gods.'   75
When he had said this, he sent me deeply groaning from his
    halls.
Then we sailed further on, grieving in our hearts.
The spirit of the men was worn down by the rowing, painful
Through our folly, since conveyance appeared no more.
Six days did we sail alike by night and by day.   80
And on the seventh we came to Lamos' sheer citadel,
Lestrygonian [2] Telepylos, where a shepherd driving in the flock
May call to a shepherd, and the one driving out answers.
And there a sleepless man could have earned double pay
For tending cattle and for pasturing bright sheep,   85
For the courses of the day and night are close together.
There, when we came to the famous harbor, about which a rock
Is set towering on both sides without a break,
And crags jutting out against one another
Are projecting at its mouth, and the entrance is slight,   90
There all the others brought their bobbing ships on inside.
The ships were tied up inside the hollow harbor
Close to one another, for no wave rose in it,
Either great or small, but there was a white calm all around.
But I myself alone brought my black ship outside   95
There on the verge and tied the cables to a rock.
I got up and stood on a rugged point of outlook.
There nothing that was done by oxen or man appeared,
But we saw a lone smoke column rising from the land.
Then I sent my companions to go and find out   100
Who these were of the men who eat bread on the earth.
I picked out two men and sent a third as a herald.
They went off, going by a smooth path where wagons
Brought wood down to the town from the high mountain.
And they happened on a girl getting water before the city,   105
The goodly daughter of Lestrygonian Antiphates.[3]
She was going down to Artacia, a spring with a lovely stream.
From there they carried water on to the city.
Standing beside her, they spoke out to her and asked

2. The Lestrygonians were a tribe of savage giants whose king was Lamos.
3. A king of the Lestrygonians.

110 Who the king of these men was and over whom he ruled.
She at once pointed out the high-roofed house of her father.
When they entered the glorious hall, they found his wife
As big as the crest of a mountain, and they loathed her.
Right away she called renowned Antiphates from assembly,
115 Her husband, who planned a woeful destruction for the men.
Snatching one companion at once, he made a meal of him.
The other two rushed in flight and came to the ships.
But he sent a shout through the town. They heard it, the
      mighty
Lestrygonians, and ran out from all directions,
120 Thousands of them, like giants and not like men.
From the cliffs they threw boulders the size of a man's load.
And at once an evil din rose up among the ships
Of men being destroyed and ships being crushed together.
Spearing the men like fish, they bore off their gruesome meal.
125 While they were destroying the men in the very deep harbor,
I myself drew my sharp sword from along my thigh
And with it cut the cable of the dark blue-prowed ship.
At once I called and urged my companions on
To throw themselves on the oars so we could flee misfortune.
130 They all strained together, in fear of destruction.
To my joy my own ship escaped from the overhanging rocks
Onto the ocean. But the others were lost there all together.
From there we sailed further on, grieving in our hearts,
Glad to escape death, having lost our dear companions.
135 We came to the island of Aiaia. There did dwell
Fair-braided Circe, dread god with a singing voice,
The blood sister of destructive-minded Aietes.[4]
They were both descended from the sun who gives light to
      mortals,
And from their mother Perse, whom Oceanos had for a child.
140 There we put in silently to land on the shore with the ship
Into a sheltered harbor, and some god guided us.
When we had got out there, for two days and two nights
We lay still, eating our hearts with pain and fatigue alike.
But when fair-braided Dawn had brought the third day to the
      full,
145 I myself took hold of my spear and my sharp sword
And went up speedily from the ship to a place of lookout,

4. King of Colchis; father of Medea.

To look for the works of mortals or to hear their sound.
I went up onto the rugged lookout and stood there,
And smoke appeared to me from the wide-traveled earth
In the halls of Circe through dense thickets and a wood.   150
Then I deliberated in my mind and my heart
About going and finding out, since I had seen the lurid smoke.
As I thought about it, it seemed to be better so:
First to go to the swift ship and the strand of the sea
To give my companions a meal, then send to inquire.   155
But when on my way I got close to the bobbing ship,
Some one of the gods pitied me, as I was alone,
And he sent me in my very path a great stag
With high horns who was going down from the wood grove
To the river to drink. For the strength of the sun gripped him.   160
As he was coming out, I hit him along the spine
In the middle of his back. The bronze spear went right through
    him.
He fell with a cry in the dust and his spirit flew off.
I put my foot on him and drew out the bronze spear
From his wound. Then I laid it there along the ground   165
And left it. Thereupon I pulled up brushwood and twigs;
I twined a rope of a fathom in length, well twisted
From both ends, and tied the feet of the vast creature,
Carried it across my back, and went to the black ship
Leaning on my spear, since I could not carry it on one shoulder 170
With my other hand, for the animal was very large.
I threw it down before the ship, roused my companions,
Stood by each man, and spoke to him with soothing words:
'My friends, though we are grieving, we shall not yet go down
To the halls of Hades before the fated day arrives.   175
Come now, while there is food and drink in the swift ship,
Let us take thought of food and not waste away in hunger.'
So I said, and they swiftly hearkened to my words.
Uncovering their heads by the strand of the barren sea,
They gazed at the stag, for the animal was very large.   180
And when they had taken their joy of looking with their eyes,
They washed their hands and prepared a glorious feast,
And so the whole day till the setting of the sun
We sat dining on endless meat and on sweet wine.
And when the sun went down and the darkness came on,   185
We lay down to sleep beside the surf of the sea.

And when the early-born, rosy-fingered dawn appeared,
I called an assembly and spoke out to them all:
'Hear my speech, my companions, though you have suffered ills;
190 My friends, we do not know where dusk is, or dawn,
Nor where the sun that gives light to mortals sets under earth
Nor where it rises. Let us consider quickly
If there is any plan left. I do not think there is.
When I went up to the rugged lookout I saw
195 An island that an endless sea girds all around.
The island itself is low lying. I saw with my own eyes
A smoke in the middle through dense thickets and woods.'
So I said, and the heart of each man was shattered
To remember the deeds of Lestrygonian Antiphates
200 And of Cyclops, great-hearted in strength, the eater of men.
So they wailed piercingly, and they shed swelling tears,
And yet no result came from their lamentation.
But I numbered all my well-greaved companions
Into two groups and appointed a leader for each.
205 I led one of them, godlike Eurylochos [5] the other.
Quickly we shook the lots in a bronze-fitted helmet.
The lot of great-hearted Eurylochos leaped out.
He went off, and along with him went twenty-two companions,
Lamenting. And they left us grieving behind them.
210 In the glen they found the hall of Circe, constructed
Out of polished stone in a place with a view all around.
About her were wolves of the mountains and also lions
That she had charmed herself when she gave them evil drugs.
Nor did these creatures rush upon the men, but instead
They reared up on them and fawned over them with their long
215   tails.
As when dogs fawn about their master when he comes
From dinner, and he always brings blandishments for their
       temper,
So did the wolves with powerful claws and the lions
Fawn about them. They were afraid when they saw the dread
       creatures.
220 So they stood in the forecourt of the fair-braided goddess
And they heard Circe singing in a lovely voice within
As she went to and fro at a great immortal web, such as are

5. The chief companion of Odysseus.

The works of goddesses, fine woven, pleasing, and bright.
Then Polites, chief of the men, began speaking to them:
He was dearest to me of my companions, and the most devoted. 225
'My friends, some woman within, as she tends a great web,
Sings beautifully, and the whole ground echoes about;
A god or a woman; well, let us quickly call out.'
So he said to them, and they did call out, shouting.
At once she opened the shining doors and came out   230
And called. They all went with her in their ignorance.
Eurylochos hung back, thinking it to be a trick.
She led them in and sat them in seats and in armchairs.
She mixed for them cheese and barley and green honey
With Pramnian wine. And she stirred into the food   235
Woeful drugs that make one forget his fatherland wholly.
But when she had given it and they had drunk, she at once
Struck them with her wand and shut them up into sties.
They had the heads of swine and the voice and the hair
And the body, but the mind was steady as before.   240
So they were penned in, weeping, and to them Circe
Threw two kinds of acorns and the fruit of the cornel tree
To eat, such as swine who sleep on the ground always eat.
Eurylochos came back at once to the swift black ship
To tell the news of his companions and their harsh fate.   245
He was not able to speak a word, though he wanted to,
Struck in his heart with a great grief; and his eyes
Were filled with tears, and his heart brooded on weeping.
And when all had questioned him and were amazed,
He recounted the ruin of our other companions: 250
'We went, as you bid, through the thicket, noble Odysseus,
And in the glen we found lovely halls constructed
Of polished stones in a place with a view all around.
There a woman tending a great web sang clearly,
A god or a woman. They called out to her, shouting.   255
At once she opened the shining doors and came out
And called. They all went with her in their ignorance.
But I hung back myself, thinking it to be a trick.
They all vanished together. Nor did one of them
Appear. And I sat for a long time and kept watching.'   260
So he said. And I threw my silver-studded sword
On my shoulders, a big bronze one, and a bow about me,

I ordered him to lead me back by the same path.
But he clutched my knees with both of his hands and begged
　me;
265 And lamenting to me, he uttered wingèd words:
'You whom Zeus nourished, do not lead me there against my
　will;
Leave me here. I think you will not come back or lead back
Any of your companions. No, let us quickly flee
With these men, for we may still avoid the fatal day.'
270 So he said, and, answering him, I addressed him:
'All right, Eurylochos, you stay here in this place,
Eating and drinking by the hollow black ship.
But I will go myself; strong necessity is on me.'
When I had said this, I went up from the ship and the sea.
275 And when I was about to go through the sacred glen
To come to the great house of Circe of the many drugs,
Hermes of the golden wand came across my path
As I was going to the house, resembling a young man
With his first beard, at the most pleasing time of youth.
280 He took my hand and spoke right out directly to me:
'Where are you going, alone through the hills, hapless man,
Ignorant of the place? These companions of yours are confined
In Circe's house as swine, and keep to their dense lairs.
Are you going there to free them? I do not think
285 You will return yourself, but will stay where the others are.
Well, I will release you from evil and rescue you.
Here, take this excellent drug to the halls of Circe
And enter; so it may ward off from your head the evil day.
I shall tell you all of Circe's pernicious wiles.
290 She will make you a mixture and drop drugs into the food.
But she will not be able to charm you so. The excellent drug
I shall give you will not permit it. I will tell you the details.
At the moment when Circe hits you with her very long wand,
Draw your sharp sword at once from along your thigh
295 And rush upon Circe as if intending to kill her.
She will be afraid of you and ask you to go to bed.
And from that point on do not refuse the bed of the god,
So she may free your companions and guide you yourself.
But order her to swear a great oath by the blessed gods
300 That she plot no other bad trouble against your person,

Lest when you are naked she make you unmanly and a
    coward.'
When he had said this, the god, the slayer of Argos, gave me
    the drug
He had plucked out of the earth, and showed me its nature.
It was black at the root, but its flower was like milk.
The gods call it moly. It is difficult to dig   305
For mortal men. But gods are able to do all things.
Then Hermes went away toward tall Olympos
Along the wooded island. And to the halls of Circe
I proceeded. My heart was greatly disturbed as I went.
I stood in the courtyard of the goddess with the lovely hair.   310
As I stood there I shouted, and the goddess heard my voice.
She came out right away and opened the shining doors
And called. I followed her, grieving in my heart.
She led me in and seated me on a silver-studded chair,
Lovely and cleverly wrought. A footstool was beneath my feet. 315
She made me a mixture in a golden cup to drink
And put in a drug, devising evil in her heart.
When she gave it and I drank and it did not charm me,
She struck me with a wand and spoke right out directly:
'Come to the sty now. Lie down with the others, your
    companions.'   320
So she said, but I drew the sharp sword from along my thigh
And rushed on Circe as if intending to kill her,
She gave a great shout, ran up under and took my knees;
And lamenting to me, she uttered wingèd words:
'What men are you from? Where are your city and parents?   325
Wonder holds me that you drank this drug and were not
    charmed.
No other man at all has been able to bear this drug
Once he had drunk it and let it pass the bar of his teeth.
You have in your breast some mind that is not to be charmed.
Surely you are the Odysseus of many turns, who,   330
The gold-wanded slayer of Argos always told me
Would come on his way out of Troy in a swift black ship.
Well, come, put your sword in the sheath and let us now
Go up to our bed so that when we have lain together
In love and in bed we may rely on one another.'   335
So she said; and answering her, I addressed her:

'Circe, how can you request that I be mild to you,
Who in your halls have turned my companions to swine
And now with wiles on your mind you request me
340 To go into your bedroom and to enter your bed,
That when I am naked you may make me unmanly and a
      coward.
I myself do not want to enter your bed, goddess,
Unless you will put up with swearing me a great oath,
That you will not plot some other bad trouble against me.'
345 So I said, and she swore at once as I had asked her.
And when she had sworn the oath and completed it,
I went up to the bed of the beautiful Circe.
Serving maids busied themselves around her halls,
Four of them, who are servants for her in the house.
350 These women are born from the springs and from the groves,
And from the sacred rivers that flow down to the sea.
One of them threw lovely blankets upon the armchairs,
Purple ones about them, and underneath she put linen.
Another one out in front of the armchairs arranged tables
355 Of silver and set out golden baskets before them.
The third one mixed sweet mind-honeying wine
In a bowl of silver and set out golden goblets.
The fourth one carried water and lit up a large fire
Underneath a great cauldron. And the water was warmed.
360 And when the water was boiling in the gleaming bronze,
She set me in a bathtub and washed me, from the great
      cauldron pouring
Water mixed to a pleasing warmth on my head and shoulders
Till it took the spirit-destroying fatigue from my limbs.
And when she had washed and anointed me richly with oil
365 And had thrown a lovely mantle about me and a tunic,
She led me in and seated me on a silver-studded armchair,
Lovely and cleverly wrought. A footstool was beneath my feet.
A handmaid poured water from a pitcher she was carrying,
A lovely golden one over into a silver basin,
370 For washing the hands; she set up a polished table alongside.
A respected housekeeper served bread she was carrying,
Laying out many dishes, gracious with the provisions,
And bade me eat. But no pleasure was in my heart.
I sat thinking other thoughts. My heart foreboded ills.

Circe, when she perceived that I sat there and did not   375
Reach my hands to the food, and that powerful grief held me,
Came and stood nearby and uttered wingèd words:
'Why do you sit this way, Odysseus, as one with no voice,
Eating your heart out, and do not touch food or drink?
Perhaps you expect another trick. There is no need   380
To fear; I have already sworn you a powerful oath.'
So she said, and in answer to her, I addressed her:
'Circe, what man is there, if he be righteous,
Who could endure to be partaking of food and drink
Before he got his companions free and saw them with his eyes? 385
If really in good faith you bid me to eat and drink,
Free them, so my eyes may behold my trusty companions.'
So I said, and Circe walked on out through the halls
Holding a wand in her hand; she opened the gates of the sty
And drove out the men, who looked like swine nine years old. 390
They stood opposite us. She went in their midst
And with another drug she rubbed each one of them.
The hair fell off their limbs that the baleful drug
The queenly Circe gave them before had made grow there.
They became men again, younger than they were before   395
And far more handsome and larger to behold.
They recognized me, and each one grasped my hands.
The longed-for weeping came on them all. The house about
Terribly resounded, and the goddess herself felt pity.
The divine goddess stood close to me and addressed me: 400
'Zeus-born son of Laertes, much-contriving Odysseus,
Go on now to your swift ship and the strand of the sea,
And first of all, draw your ship up on the mainland,
Put your property and all your gear into caves.
Then come back yourself and bring your trusty companions.'   405
So she said. Then the bold heart was persuaded within me
And I went down to the swift ship and the beach of the sea.
There I found my trusty companions on the swift ship,
Lamenting piteously, shedding large tears.
As when calves of the fields all skip around together   410
In front of the drove of cows that are coming into the dung
    yard
When they are filled up on grass, and the pens no longer
Hold them, but they run in throngs around their mothers,

Lowing on and on, so did those men act when their eyes saw
    me:
415 They shed tears, weeping. And it seemed to their hearts
As though they had come to the fatherland and the very city
Of rugged Ithaca, where they were born and brought up.
And lamenting to me, they uttered wingèd words:
'At your return, Zeus-nourished one, we have rejoiced
420 As if we had come to Ithaca, our fatherland.
Come and tell about the ruin of our other companions.'
So they said. And I addressed them with soothing words:
'First of all, let us draw the ship up onto the mainland
And bring our possessions and all our gear into caves.
425 Then press on yourselves and follow me all together
So you may see our companions in Circe's sacred halls,
Eating and drinking; they have unfailing abundance.'
So I said, and they quickly hearkened to my words.
Eurylochos alone tried to hold back all my companions,
430 And addressing them, he uttered wingèd words:
'Ah, wretched men, where are we going? Why long for these ills,
And go down to the halls of Circe, who will make us all
Into swine or wolves or lions, so that we may guard
The great house for her, and by necessity,
The way the Cyclops acted when our companions came
To his middle yard, and bold Odysseus went with them,
And they were all destroyed because of his recklessness.'
So he said, and I pondered myself in my mind
About drawing my sharp-pointed sword from my stout thigh,
440 To cut his head off and to bring it to the ground,
Though he was very close kin to me. But my companions
Restrained me on every side with soothing words:
'You who were born of Zeus, let us leave this man here
Beside the ship, if you bid it, and guard the ship,
445 And you lead the way for us to Circe's sacred halls.'
When they said this they went up from the ship and the sea.
Nor was Eurylochos left beside the hollow ship,
But he followed, for he feared my striking rebuke.
Meanwhile Circe in her halls had kindly washed the rest
450 Of our companions and anointed them richly with oil.
She threw woolen mantles and tunics about them.
And we came upon them all dining well in the halls.
When they had seen and looked at each other face to face,

They wept, lamenting, and the halls rang around.
The divine goddess stood near me and addressed me: 455
'Zeus-born son of Laertes, Odysseus of many wiles,
Raise this swelling lament no longer. I myself know
How many pains you have suffered on the fish-laden ocean
And how many wrongs hostile men did to you on land.
So come now and eat victuals and drink wine   460
Until you have taken the spirit into your breast again
As it was when you first left your fatherland
Of rugged Ithaca. Now, wasted and without spirit,
You remember hard wandering always, and your spirit has never
Been in gladness, since you have suffered very much!'   465
So she said, and the bold spirit was persuaded in us.
There day by day till the year was brought to a close
We stayed, dining on endless meat and on sweet wine.
But when the year was up and the seasons turned round
As the moons were declining, and the long days came round to
     an end,   470
Then my trusty companions called me out and said to me:
'You fool, at this time now remember your fatherland,
If it is decreed that you be saved and arrive
At your well-established home and your fatherland.'
So they said, and the bold spirit was persuaded within me.   475
So then the entire day till the setting of the sun
We stayed, dining on endless meat and on sweet wine.
But when the sun went down and the darkness came on
They lay down to sleep through the shadowy halls,
And I went up to the beautiful bed of Circe   480
And took her knees in prayer. The goddess heard my voice.
Then I spoke out to her and uttered wingèd words:
'Circe, fulfill for me the promise you made,
To send me home; the spirit is eager in me already
And in my other companions, who consume my precious heart   485
In complaining around me whenever you are absent.'
So I said, and the divine goddess at once answered:
'Zeus-born son of Laertes, Odysseus of many devices,
Do not stay any longer in my home unwillingly.
Yet you must first achieve another journey and come   490
To the halls of Hades and dread Persephone,[6]
So you may consult the soul of Theban Tiresias,

6. Daughter of Zeus and Demeter; queen of the underworld.

The blind prophet in whom there is a steadfast mind.
To him alone, even when dead, did Persephone grant
495 A mind that could understand. The others flit, shadows.'
So she said, and my own heart was shattered within me.
Seated on the bed, I lamented, nor did my heart
Wish still to live and to see the light of the sun.
500 But when I was sated with lamenting and wallowing,
I answered her and addressed her with a speech:
'O Circe, who will be my guide on this journey?
No one ever got to the place of Hades in a black ship.
So I said, and at once the divine goddess answered:
505 'Zeus-born son of Laertes, Odysseus of many devices,
Give heed to no longing for a guide upon your ship,
But set up a mast and stretch out the white sails,
And then sit down. The blast of the North Wind will carry it for you.
And when in your ship you have traversed Oceanos,
Where the scrubby strand and groves of Persephone are,
510 Both tall poplars and willows that lose their fruit,
Beach your ship there by deep-whirling Oceanos;
But go on yourself to the moldy hall of Hades.
There into Acheron flow Puriphlegethon
And Cocytus, which is a branch of the Styx's [7] water,
515 And a rock and a concourse of the two resounding rivers.
Then go up near there, hero, as I bid you to;
Dig a pit the size of a cubit on all sides.
Pour a libation about it for all the dead,
First of honey mixture, and then of sweet wine,
520 And the third one of water; sprinkle white barley on it.
Beseech the feeble heads of the dead with many prayers,
Saying that when you go to Ithaca you will sacrifice
Your best barren cow in your halls, heap a pyre with goods,
And consecrate apart for Tiresias alone
525 A sheep all of black that stands out among your flocks.
And when you have besought the famed tribes of the dead with prayers,
Sacrifice a ram and also a black female,
Bending their heads to Erebos; [8] turn the other way yourself,

7. Rivers of the Underworld. Their names mean Distress, Fire-flaming, Lament, and Hate.
8. Outer darkness for the dead.

Setting on for the streams of the river. And there many
Souls will come of the corpses of those who have died.   530
And then urge your companions on and command them
To take sheep which lie slain with the pitiless sword,
To flay them and burn them and pray to the gods,
To mighty Hades and dread Persephone.
You yourself draw your sharp sword from beside your thigh.   535
Stay put, and do not let the feeble heads of the dead
Go near the blood till you learn from Tiresias.
At once, then, leader of the people, the prophet will come,
Who will tell you the course and measures of the way
And about a return, how you may go on the fish-laden ocean.'   540
So she said, and at once the golden-throned Dawn came.
She clothed me in garments, a mantle and a tunic,
And the nymph herself put on a great shining mantle
Finely made and pleasing, and a lovely gold sash
Around her waist, and she put a veil on her head.   545
I went through the halls and urged my companions on,
Standing by each man and speaking with soothing words:
'Slumber now no longer as you lie in sound, sweet sleep,
But let us go. Queenly Circe has already informed me.'
So I said, and the bold spirit in them was persuaded.   550
But I did not lead my companions from there unscathed.
There was one very young man, Elpenor, not overly
Courageous in battle and not steadfast in his mind,
Who apart from my companions in Circe's sacred halls,
Longing for coolness, lay down drunk with wine.   555
Hearing the noise and din of his companions moving,
He rose up suddenly and wholly forgot in his mind
To go back down again by way of the long ladder.
But he fell right down off the roof. And his neck
Was broken from the joint. His soul went down to Hades.   560
Then I addressed a speech to the men as they were going:
'You think, perhaps, you are going home to your dear
Fatherland. Circe has decreed another way for us,
To the halls of Hades and dread Persephone,
So that we may consult the soul of Theban Tiresias.'   565
So I said, and their own hearts were shattered within them;
They sat on the spot lamenting and tearing their hair.
And yet no result came from their lamentation.
And when we had gone grieving to the swift ship

570 And to the strand of the sea, shedding large tears,
    Circe had meantime gone alongside the black ship
    And bound down a ram and also a black female.
    She passed by nimbly; for who could see with his eyes
    A god who did not wish it, whether going this way or that?

XI

"And when we came down to the ship and to the sea,
First of all we dragged the ship to the godly water
And set up the mast and the sails upon the black ship.
We took sheep and brought them on board, and we ourselves
Went on, grieving and pouring down swelling tears.   5
Then a driving wind full in the sails, a fine companion,
Did the fair-braided Circe, dread god with a singing voice,
Send on for us from behind the dark blue-prowed ship.
And when we had tended to the gear through the ship, piece by
    piece,
We took our seats. The wind and a pilot steered her.   10
The sails were stretched all day long as she fared on the ocean.
The sun went down and all the ways were shadowed.
She arrived at the bounds of deep-flowing Oceanos.
There is the land and city of Cimmerian men,
Who are shrouded in mist and cloud. Never does the sun   15
Look down upon them, glittering with his rays—
Never when he climbs up into the starry heaven
Or when he turns back from the heaven to the earth,
But deadly night is stretched out for hapless mortals.
Arriving there, we beached the ship and took out the flocks. 20
Then we ourselves went along the stream of Oceanos
Until we arrived at the place that Circe had said.
There Perimedes and Eurylochos held the victims.
I myself drew my sharp sword from along my thigh,
Dug a pit the size of a cubit on all sides,   25
And poured a libation about it for all the dead,
First of honey mixture, and then of sweet wine,
And the third one of water; I sprinkled white barley on it.
I besought the feeble heads of the dead for many things,
Saying that when I went to Ithaca I would sacrifice   30
My best barren cow in my halls, heap a pyre with goods,
And consecrate apart for Tiresias alone

A sheep all of black that stands out among my flocks.
And when I had besought the tribes of the dead with prayers
   and vows,
35 Then I took the sheep and cut their throats into the pit.
And the black-clouded blood poured out. And out of Erebos
The souls gathered of the corpses of those who had died,
Brides and bachelors and old men who had suffered much,
And tender maidens whose hearts were fresh in sorrow,
40 And many who had been wounded by bronze-tipped spears,
Men slain in battle wearing gore-spattered armor,
Many of whom hovered round the pit on every side
With a tremendous shout. And sallow fear seized me.
Then I urged my companions on and commanded them
45 To take the sheep which lay slain with the pitiless sword,
To flay them and burn them and then pray to the gods,
To mighty Hades and to dread Persephone.
I myself drew my sharp sword from beside my thigh
And stayed put, and did not let the feeble heads of the dead
50 Go near the blood till I could learn from Tiresias.
First came the soul of our companion Elpenor,
For he had not yet been buried beneath the wide-traveled earth;
We ourselves had left his body in the hall of Circe,
Unwept and unburied, since another labor drove us on.
55 I wept when I saw him and pitied him in my heart.
So I spoke out to him, and uttered wingèd words:
'Elpenor, how did you get here under the murky dusk?
You went faster by foot than I did with the black ship.'
So I said, and he wailed and answered me with a speech:
60 'Zeus-born son of Laertes, Odysseus of many devices,
The ill fate of some god destroyed me, and abundant wine.
When I lay down in the hall of Circe I did not think
To go back down again upon the long ladder,
But I fell straight down off the roof. And my neck
65 Was broken from the joint and my soul came down to Hades.
Now I beseech you by those left behind who are not here,
By your wife and the father who reared you when you were small,
And by Telemachos, whom you left alone in your halls,
For I know on your way from here out of the hall of Hades
70 You will stop the well-made ship at the island of Aiaia.
There at that time, lord, I ask you to remember me.
Do not go and leave me henceforth unwept and unburied

And turn not from me, lest I bring on you the wrath of the gods,
But burn me with all the armor that belongs to me
And heap a tomb for me by the strand of the hoary sea,   75
Hapless man that I am, so that those to come may learn of me.
Do this for me, and set my oar fast on the mound
With which when alive I rowed among my companions.'
So he said, and then I addressed him in answer:
'Wretched man, I shall do this for you and carry it out.'   80
Exchanging grim words this way with one another,
We sat, and on one side I held my sword over the blood.
On the other side the phantom of my companion told me much.
Then there came the soul of my mother who had died,
Anticleia,[1] daughter of great-hearted Autolycos,   85
Whom I had left alive when I went to sacred Ilion.
I wept when I saw her and pitied her in my spirit,
But though I grieved heavily, I did not let her
Get near the blood first till I could learn from Tiresias.
Then the soul of Theban Tiresias came up,   90
Holding a gold scepter; he knew me and spoke to me:
'Zeus-born son of Laertes, Odysseus of many devices,
Why, hapless man, have you left the light of the sun
And come here to see the dead and a joyless place?
But draw back from the pit and hold back your sharp sword   95
So I may drink the blood and speak to you unerringly.'
So he said. I drew back and thrust the silver-studded sword
Into the sheath. And when he had drunk the black blood,
The excellent prophet addressed me with a speech:
'You seek a honey-sweet return, noble Odysseus;   100
A god will make it disastrous for you. I do not think
You will elude the earth-shaker; against you he has laid up a
    grudge,
In his heart, enraged that you blinded his beloved son.
You may get there yet, even so, though you suffer ills;
If you are willing to check your spirit and your companions',   105
At the time when you first bring the well-made ship up close
To the isle of Thrinacria, fleeing the violet ocean,
And you find grazing there the cattle and goodly sheep
Of the Sun, who sees everything and hears everything.
If you let them go unmolested and think of your return   110
You may yet get to Ithaca, though you do suffer ills.

1. Wife of Laertes and mother of Odysseus.

If you molest them, then I prophesy destruction
For your ship and companions. And even if you escape yourself
You will return late and ill, having lost all your companions,
115 On another's ship. You will find troubles in your house,
Presumptuous men who consume your livelihood
While wooing your godlike wife and giving her bridal gifts.
But when you get there, then you will avenge the violence of
  those men,
But when you have killed the suitors in your own halls,
120 Whether by guile or openly with the sharp sword,
Thereupon take a well-fitted oar and go on
Till you arrive at the place of men who do not know
The sea and eat a food that has not been mixed with salt,
And where they do not know about ships with purple cheeks,
125 Or about well-fitted oars that are the wings for ships.
I will tell you a very plain token; do not forget it:
When another wayfarer has confronted you
And says you have a winnowing fan [2] on your gleaming
  shoulder,
Then set your well-fitted oar fast in the earth
130 And carry out fine sacrifices to Lord Poseidon,
A ram, a bull, and a boar, the mounter of sows.
Then go back home and sacrifice sacred hecatombs
To the immortal gods who possess broad heaven,
To all of them in order. Far from the sea will death come,
135 Ever so gently to your person and slay you
When you are worn out with sleek old age. And the people
  about you
Will be happy. I tell you this unerringly.'
So he said, and then I addressed him in answer:
'Tiresias, the gods themselves have perhaps spun this thread,
140 But come tell me one thing, and speak out truthfully:
I see here the soul of my mother who has died.
She sits in silence close to the blood and does not dare
To look her son in the face or speak out to him.
Tell me, lord, how may she know me as who I am?'
145 So I said, and at once he addressed me in answer:
'Easily shall I say the word and put it in your mind.
Whomever you permit of the souls of the dead
To approach the blood closer will speak without error to you.

2. A tool for sifting grain.

The one you begrudge it to will go back away.'
When he had said this, the soul of Lord Tiresias went   150
Within the halls of Hades, after it spoke what was decreed.
I waited there steadily until my mother
Came up and drank the black-clouded blood. She knew me
At once, and, lamenting, she uttered wingèd words:
'My child, how have you come down under the murky dusk   155
While yet alive? This is dangerous for the living to see.
In between us there are great rivers and dread streams,
Oceanos first, that it is not possible to cross
On foot; one must possess a well-made ship.
Have you just got this far in wandering from Troy   160
A long time with ship and companions? Have you not yet come
To Ithaca and seen the wife within your halls?'
So she said, and then I addressed her in answer:
'Mother, need led me down to the place of Hades
To consult the soul of Theban Tiresias.   165
I have not yet come close to Achaia. I have not yet
Set foot on our land, but wander always, possessing woe,
From the very first time I followed godly Agamemnon
To Ilion with its fine horses to fight the Trojans.
But tell me one thing, and speak out truthfully: 170
What fate overcame you of long-sorrowful death?
A lengthy sickness, or did Artemis who shoots arrows
Visit you and slay you with her gentle shafts?
Tell me of the father and the son I left behind.
Is my honor still with them, or does some other man   175
Already have it, and they say I will return no more?
Tell me about the purpose and thought of my wedded wife;
Does she stay with my son and steadily guard all,
Or has the best man of the Achaians wed her already?'
So I said, and at once my queenly mother answered me: 180
'Too long that woman in her enduring spirit waits
Within your halls. And the miserable nights
And the days always waste away for her as she sheds tears.
No one else yet holds your fine honor, but Telemachos
Possesses the acres securely, and he dines   185
On well-shared feasts, whereof it befits a judge to partake.
All invite him. But your father remains in one place
In the country and does not visit the city. No bed
He has, no bedclothes and mantles and glistening blankets,

190 But he sleeps all winter where servants do in the house,
In the ashes by the fire, and he puts bad clothes on his flesh.
But when the summer comes and the blossoming autumn,
Everywhere along the knoll of the wine-bearing vineyard
His beds of fallen leaves have been strewn on the ground.
195 He lies there grieving; great sorrow grows in his mind
As he longs for your return. Hard old age has come upon him.
And so I myself have perished and have met my fate.
And the far-sighted one who shoots arrows did not
Visit me in the hall and slay me with her gentle shafts,
200 Nor did sickness come on me, such as especially
With grim wasting away takes the spirit from the limbs.
But longing for you and your counsels, noble Odysseus,
And your kindliness, reft my honey-sweet spirit away.'
So she spoke. And pondering in my mind, I wished
205 To take hold of the soul of my mother who had died.
Three times I tried and my spirit bade me to grasp her.
And three times like a shadow or a dream she flew
Out of my hands. Sharp grief grew ever greater in my heart.
So I spoke out to her and uttered wingèd words:
210 'Mother, why do you not wait as I strive to grasp you,
So that even in the place of Hades we might throw our dear
    hands
Round each other and take pleasure in cold lamentation?
Or is this some phantom that noble Persephone
Sends me, so that I may grieve and lament still more?'
215 So I said, and my queenly mother answered at once:
'Alas, my child, ill-fated beyond all mortals,
Persephone, daughter of Zeus, does not beguile you;
But this is the rule for mortals, whenever one dies.
No longer do the sinews hold the bones and the flesh,
220 But the mighty power of burning fire subdues them
When first the spirit has abandoned the white bones,
And the soul, flying off like a dream, flutters.
But be eager to go to the light as fast as you can,
And note all this to tell it to your wife hereafter.'
225 So we exchanged words with one another. Women
Came up, and noble Persephone sent them forth,
All of whom were the wives and daughters of excellent men.
They gathered in clusters around the black blood.
And I thought about how I might question each one.

This seemed to me in my heart to be the best plan: 230
To draw the long-pointed sword from beside my stout thigh
And not allow all to drink the black blood together.
They came on in succession, and each one
Announced her descent. I inquired of them all.
First I saw Tyro [3] there, who had a fine father,   235
Who claimed to be descended from blameless Salmoneus.
She said she was the wife of Cretheus, son of Aeolos;
She had fallen in love with a river, the godly Enipeus,
Which flows loveliest by far of the rivers on earth,
And she frequented the lovely streams of the Enipeus.   240
Likened to him, the earth-shaker who holds up the earth
Lay beside her at the mouth of the eddying river.
The purple wave stood up around them like a mountain
Arching, and it hid the god and the mortal woman.
He loosened her virgin sash and shed sleep down upon her.   245
And when the god had completed the deed of love
He took her hand and spoke out to her directly:
'Rejoice in this love, woman, and when the year comes round
You will bear glorious children; not barren are the beds
Of the immortals. Take care of them and bring them up.   250
And now go to your home; stay quiet and do not mention it.
Behold, I am Poseidon, the shaker of the earth.'
When he had said this, he went down under the wave-
    breaking ocean.
She was pregnant and gave birth to Pelias and Neleus,[4]
Who became mighty servants of great Zeus, both of them.   255
Pelias in Iolcos of the broad dancing-place,
Dwelt rich with flocks, and the other in sandy Pylos.
And to Cretheus the queen of women bore other sons,
Aeson [5] and Pheres and Amythaon, whose delight was in horses.
After her I saw Antiope, Asopos' daughter,   260
Who declared she had lain in the embrace of Zeus
And gave birth to two sons, Amphion and Zethos,
Who first founded the seat of Thebes with the seven gates
And built its rampart, since without a rampart they could not,
Though mighty, inhabit Thebes of the broad dancing-place.   265

3. Grandmother of Jason and Nestor.
4. Pelias, Pheres, and Amythaon are uncles of Jason; Neleus, father of
Nestor.
5. Father of Jason.

And after her I saw Alcmene, Amphitryon's wife,
Who bore Heracles of steadfast boldness and a lion's heart
After she had lain in the embrace of great Zeus;
And Megara, the daughter of haughty-spirited Creon,[6]
Whom Amphitryon's son, ever unwearied in his strength, had
270   wed.
I saw the mother of Oedipos,[7] lovely Epicaste,
Who did an enormous deed in the ignorance of her mind
And married her son. He slew his own father
And married her. The gods soon made these things known to
       men.
275 But he suffered pains in his much-beloved Thebes,
And ruled the Cadmeians through the destructive plans of the
       gods;
And she went to the place of the mighty gatekeeper Hades.
She hung up a high noose from the lofty roofbeam,
Possessed by her grief. For him she left many pains
280 Behind her, the kind a mother's Furies bring to pass.
And I saw the Beautiful Chloris,[8] whom Neleus once
Married for her beauty, and gave numberless bridal gifts.
She was the youngest daughter of Amphion, son of Iasos,
Who once ruled by force in Minyan Orchomenos.
285 She was queen over Pylos; she bore him glorious children,
Nestor, Chromios, and honored Periclymenos,
And she bore, besides, goodly Pero, a wonder to mortals,
Whom all her neighbors wooed. Nor would Neleus give her
To one who could not drive away from Phylace
290 The crumple-horned, broad-browed cattle of mighty Iphiclos,
Difficult as they were. An excellent prophet [9] alone
Undertook to drive them. The hard fate of the gods bound him,
And difficult bonds, and the cowherds of the fields.
But when the months and the days were finished out
295 Of the year coming back around, and the seasons came on,
Then mighty Iphiclos released him when he had told all
That was decreed. And a plan of Zeus was accomplished.
I saw Leda also, the wife of Tyndareus,[1]
Who bore to Tyndareus two sons of mighty mind,

6. A king of Thebes.
7. A king of Thebes; son of Laios and Epicaste (in Homer).
8. Mother of Nestor.
9. The seer Melampos, whom Iphiclos first captured and then released.
1. Father of Clytemnestra.

Horse-taming Castor and Polydeuces, who is good at boxing,   300
Both of whom the grain-giving earth holds alive.
Even beneath the earth they have honor from Zeus.
One time they live, on alternate days, and another time
They are dead. Honor equal to the gods is allotted them.
And after her I saw Iphimedeia, the wife   305
Of Aloeus, who said she had lain with Poseidon,
And she had two sons that were born short-lived,
The godlike Otos and the far-famed Ephialtes,
Who were the tallest men nourished by the grain-giving earth,
And by far the handsomest, next to famous Orion,   310
For after nine seasons these men were nine cubits
In breadth, and they were also nine fathoms in height.
They made threats to the immortals upon Olympos
That they would start the combat of an impetuous war.
They strove to put Ossa on Olympos, and to put on Ossa ,   315
Leaf-quivering Pelion, so that heaven might be scaled.
And they would have done it had they reached the measure of
     their prime;
But the son of Zeus,[2] whom fair-haired Leto bore, destroyed
Both of them, before the whiskers beneath their temples
Had flowered and their chins got thick with blossoming down.   320
I saw Phaedra and Procris and lovely Ariadne,[3]
Daughter of destruction-minded Minos, whom Theseus
Once was leading out of Crete to the knoll of sacred Athens
But did not enjoy her, for Artemis slew her beforehand
In flood-circled Dia for what Dionysos testified.   325
Maire and Clymene I saw and hateful Eriphyle,[4]
Who took precious gold in return for her own husband.
I cannot tell or mention all of the women
I saw in numbers there, wives and daughters of heroes.
Ambrosial night would wane first. Now it is time   330

2. Apollo.
3. Phaedra: daughter of the Cretan king Minos and wife of the Athenian
hero Theseus after he killed the Minotaur. Procris: daughter of Erechtheus,
king of Athens, unfaithful to a husband who accidentally killed her.
Ariadne: Phaedra's sister who, after helping Theseus out of the labyrinth
and escaping with him, was abandoned by him on the island where Artemis
killed her.
4. Maire: a nymph of Artemis, killed for breaking her vow of chastity.
Clymene: wife of a king of Minyan Orchemenos. Eriphyle: wife of Am-
phiaraos, whom she persuaded to join the siege of Thebes, where he
knew he would be killed.

For me to sleep, whether I go to my companions on the swift
   ship
Or stay here. The convoy shall be your concern, and the gods'."
So he said. And they all became silent in stillness.
They were held in rapture through the shadowy halls.
335 Then white-armed Arete began to speak among them:
"Phaeacians, how does this man appear to you to be,
In form and in size, and in his mind well-balanced within?
He is my guest, and yet each has a share in the honor.
Let us not hasten to send him off, and do not stint
340 Of gifts to a man so needy, since, by favor of the gods,
Many possessions lie stored for you in your halls."
And the old hero Echeneus spoke out among them,
Who was an elder among the Phaeacian men:
"My friends, our prudent queen has not spoken to us
345 Wide of the mark or of repute. Do as she says.
On Alcinoos here the word and the deed depend."
Then Alcinoos spoke to him and gave him an answer:
"So shall this word come about, if I be indeed
Alive and rule the Phaeacians, who are fond of rowing.
350 Let the stranger, though greatly desiring a return,
Still endure to wait till tomorrow until I complete
The entire gift. The convoy will concern all the men,
And me especially, as I have power in the land."
Odysseus of many wiles addressed him in answer:
355 "Lordly Alcinoos, exalted among all your people,
Even if you should bid me to stay here for a year
And urged on an convoy and gave glorious gifts,
I would want to do it, since it would be better by far
To reach one's dear fatherland with a fuller hand;
360 Then I would be more respected and loved by all
The men who might see me return to Ithaca."
Alcinoos gave him an answer and spoke to him:
"Odysseus, as we look on you we would not think you
To be a deceiver and cheat the way many men are
365 Whom the black earth nourishes, and are widely dispersed,
Fashioning falsehoods out of what no one could see;
There is grace in your words and your thoughts are noble.
As a singer would, you have skillfully told the tale
Of all the Argives' sad troubles and of your own.
370 But come, tell me this and speak out truthfully:

Did you see any of the godlike companions that went
Along to Ilion with you and there met a fate?
This night is prodigiously long. It is not yet time
To sleep in the hall. Do tell me your wondrous deeds.
I would hold out until the godly dawn, so long   375
As you could endure to recount your cares in the hall."
Odysseus of many wiles addressed him in answer:
"Lordly Alcinoos, exalted among all your people,
There is a time for many tales and also a time for sleep.
But if you are still longing to listen, I would not myself   380
Refuse you in this, to tell other more piteous things,
The cares of my companions who perished afterward,
Who escaped from the grievous war cry of the Trojans
But died on returning at the will of an evil woman.
Moreover when holy Persephone had scattered the souls   385
Of the womanfolk off in all directions,
The soul came of Agamemnon, son of Atreus,
Grieving; and others gathered about who had died
And had met their fate with him in the house of Aigisthos.
He recognized me at once when he had drunk the black blood.   390
He wailed piercingly and shed a swelling tear,
Stretching his hands toward me in striving to reach me.
But his strength was not still steadfast and he had no force
Such as there used to be before in his supple limbs.
I wept to see him and pitied him in my heart.   395
And speaking out to him, I uttered wingèd words:
'Glorious son of Atreus, lord of men, Agamemnon,
What fate has overcome you of long-sorrowful death?
Was it that Poseidon overcame you in your ships,
Raising up a dreadful blast of disastrous winds?   400
Or did hostile men ravage you upon the mainland
As you were cutting off cattle and the fine fleece of sheep,
Or as you were fighting over their city and their women?'
So I said, and he at once addressed me in answer:
'Zeus-born son of Laertes, Odysseus of many devices,   405
Poseidon did not overcome me in my ships,
Raising up a dreadful blast of disastrous winds.
Nor did hostile men ravage me on the mainland.
But Aigisthos fashioned for me my death and my fate.
With my cursèd wife he killed me, inviting me to his house,   410
Feasting me, the way a man slaughters an ox in a crib.

So I died a most grievous death, and my other companions
They killed without blenching, as boars with shining tusks
Are killed in the house of a rich and very powerful man
415 At a marriage or a joint feast [5] or a fruitful banquet.
You have encountered already the slaughter of many men
Slain singly, and also in a mighty combat,
But you would most have grieved in your heart to see that,
How we lay in the hall about the mixing bowls
420 And the full tables, and the whole ground swam with blood.
Most pitiful of all, I heard the voice of Priam's daughter,
Cassandra, whom wily Clytemnestra murdered
Next to me. But I reached my hands to the earth,
Then threw them as I died around the blade. The bitch-faced
    woman
425 Turned away; as I went to Hades she could not bear
To shut my eyes with her hands and close up my mouth.
So there is nothing more dreadful and shameless than a
    woman
Who would set out within her mind such deeds at these,
The sort of disgraceful deed which that woman plotted,
430 Devising murder for her wedded husband. I thought
Indeed that I would come home welcome to my children
And my servants. But she, with utter evil on her mind,
Poured shame upon herself and upon womenkind to come
Hereafter, even on one who might do good deeds.'
435 So he said, and then I addressed him in answer:
'Alas, broad-seeing Zeus has terribly hated
The descent of Atreus from the outset because of the plans
Of women. Many men perished because of Helen;
Clytemnestra made a plot against you while you were far away,
440 So I said, and he at once addressed me in answer:
'So never be mild yourself, henceforth, even to your wife.
Reveal to her no entire story that you know well,
But tell a part of it and let the rest be concealed.
But your own death, Odysseus, will not at all be from your wife.
445 Highly trustworthy and of good care in her mind
Is Icarios' daughter, the prudent Penelope.
We left her as a young bride when we went off to war
And she had an infant child at her breast, who now
Is seated, I suppose, amid the number of the men;

5. To the *eranos* each guest brought an equal share.

Blessed, for his dear father will see him when he comes,   450
And the man will embrace his father, as is right.
My wife never allowed me to fill my eyes up
With my son. She killed me beforehand, my very self.
I will tell you another thing and put it in your mind:
Hold your ship on course secretly, not openly,   455
To your fatherland. There is no longer any trust in women.
But come, tell me this and speak out truthfully:
If perhaps you men have heard of my son as still living
In Orchomenos or else in sandy Pylos
Or perhaps with Menelaos in broad Sparta.   460
For godly Orestes is not yet dead on the earth.'
So he said, and I addressed him in answer:
'Son of Atreus, why do you ask me this? I know nothing
Whether he is dead or alive. It is bad to utter windy things.'
The two of us stood there exchanging dreadful speeches   465
In that way, grieving, and shedding our swelling tears.
The soul of Achilles, son of Peleus, came up;
The soul of Patroclos and of excellent Antilochos,
And of Ajax who was the finest in body and form
Of all the Danaans, after the excellent son of Peleus.   470
The soul of the swift-footed offspring of Aeacos [6] knew me,
And in lamentation he uttered wingèd words:
'Zeus-born son of Laertes, Odysseus of many devices,
Rash man, what still greater deed will you plot in your mind?
How have you dared to come down to Hades, where the dead 475
Dwell senseless, the phantoms of mortals who are worn out?'
So he said, and I addressed him in answer:
'Achilles, son of Peleus, bravest of the Achaians,
I came in need of Tiresias, if he might tell me
Some plan whereby I might come to craggy Ithaca;   480
For I have not yet come close to Achaia, I have not yet
Set foot on my land, but have ills always. Achilles,
No man in the past or hereafter is more blessed than you.
When you were alive before, the Argives honored you
Equal to the gods. Now you greatly rule over the dead,   485
Being here as you are. So do not grieve now you are dead,
   Achilles.'
Thus I spoke, and he at once addressed me in answer:
'Noble Odysseus, do not commend death to me.

6. Grandfather of Achilles.

I would rather serve on the land of another man
490 Who had no portion and not a great livelihood
Than to rule over all the shades of those who are dead.
Come now and tell me the story of my noble son,
Did he follow to battle and become a chief or not?
Tell me about blameless Peleus, if you have heard anything;
495 Does he have honor still with the many Myrmidons,
Or do they show him no honor through Hellas and Phthia
Because old age constrains him in his hands and feet?
For I am no protector under the rays of the sun
Of the kind I was at one time when in broad Troy
500 I slew their best men, defending for the Argives.
If I could come that way just a while to my father's house,
Then I would make my might and invincible hands hateful
To any of those who compel him and force him from honor.'
So he said, and I for my part addressed him in answer:
505 'No, I have not heard anything about blameless Peleus.
But about your beloved son Neoptolemos
I shall tell you the whole truth, as you request me.
I brought him myself on my hollow, balanced ship,
Out of Scyros after the well-greaved Achaians.
510 And when we declared our proposals about the city of Troy,
He always spoke first, and he did not err in his speech.
I believe godlike Nestor and I alone did surpass him.
And when on the plain of the Trojans we Achaians fought
He would never remain in the throng or the crowd of men.
515 He ran far out front, yielding in his strength to no one.
In the dreadful combat he slaughtered numerous men.
I shall not myself mention and tell of them all,
The great host he killed, blameless among the Argives.
Yes, how he slaughtered with the sword the son of Telephos,
520 The hero Eurypylos! Many companions about him
Of the Ceteians were killed for the gifts of a woman.
He was the handsomest man I saw next to godly Memnon.
And when we, the best of the Argives, went into the horse
That Epeios had made, the whole rule was laid on me
525 Of opening and closing the door of the stout decoy.
There the other leaders and counselors of the Danaans
Wiped their tears, and the limbs of each trembled beneath him.
But that man I never saw with my eyes at all
Go pallid on his fair flesh or wipe off the tears

From his cheeks. He besought me very frequently   530
To let him go out of the horse. He kept stroking his sword's
   hilt
And his bronze-heavy spear; and he planned ills for the Trojans.
And when we had sacked the lofty city of Priam,
He went on board the ship with a noble portion and prize,
Unscathed; he had not been hit by the sharp bronze spear   535
Or wounded in close combat, such as many times
Happens in war; Ares does rage helter-skelter.'
So I said; the soul of the swift-footed son of Aeacos
Moved on with great strides through the asphodel meadow
In joy that I said his son was illustrious.   540
The other souls of the shades of those who had died
Stood there grieving, and each one asked of his cares.
Alone did the soul of Ajax, son of Telamon,
Stand off apart, angered about the victory
That I had won over him when judgment was made by the
   ships   545
About the armor of Achilles. His queenly mother had set it.
The sons of the Trojans judged it, and Pallas Athene.
Would I had not won in a contest of that kind!
For the sake of those arms the earth closed over the great head
Of Ajax, who by his form and his deeds had surpassed   550
The other Danaans, after Peleus' blameless son.
I myself spoke out to him with soothing words:
'Ajax, son of blameless Telamon, are you destined
Not to forget, even in death, your anger at me
For the cursèd armor? The gods gave it as a trouble to the
   Argives,   555
Since you died, such a bulwark of them. The Achaians
Grieved constantly for you when you perished, just as much
As for Peleus' son Achilles. There was no one else
To blame but Zeus, who terribly hated the host
Of Danaan spearsmen, and set your fate upon you.   560
But come hither, lord, so that you may hear our speech
And our story. Subdue your strength and your bold heart.'
So I said, but he answered me nothing and went with the other
Souls of the shades of the dead to Erebos.
And he would have spoken in anger, just as I to him,   565
But the spirit within my own breast desired
To see the souls of the other men who had died.

There I saw Minos, the illustrious son of Zeus,
With a golden scepter dealing out justice to the dead,
570 Seated. And they kept asking that lord about laws,
While they sat and stood in the wide-gated house of Hades.
After him I caught sight of the enormous Orion,
Driving beasts together through the asphodel meadow
That he had slaughtered himself on the lovely mountains,
575 Holding in his hands an all-bronze club, ever unbroken.
And I saw Tityos, the renowned son of Gaia,
Lying on the ground. He lay more than nine measures long.
And two vultures, perched on both sides, rent at his liver,
Plunging into the caul. He could not ward them off with his
      hands,
580 For he had dragged off Leto, the glorious mistress of Zeus,
As she came to Pytho through fair-lawned Panopeus.
And I saw Tantalos, who had difficult pains,
Standing in a lake. He was plunged up to his chin,
And pressed on in his thirst, but he could not reach to take
      a drink.
585 As often as the old man bent over striving to drink
The water disappeared, swallowed, and at his feet
Black earth appeared; and some god kept drying it up.
Trees with lofty foliage from their tops shed fruit,
Pears, pomegranates, and apples with shining fruit,
590 And sweet figs and blossoming wild olives;
And when the old man straightened to stretch his hands for
      them,
The wind kept tossing them toward the shadowy clouds.
And then I saw Sisyphos, who had difficult pains
Pushing a monstrous stone up with both of his hands.
595 And indeed he made a leaning effort with hands and feet
To push the stone up the crest. But when it was about
To go over the top, then it turned back down with its force;
The shameless stone rolled on down again to the plain.
Then he pushed it back again, exerting himself, and the sweat
600 Flowed off his limbs and dust rose up around his head.
After him I caught sight of powerful Heracles,
A phantom. For he himself with the immortal gods
Enjoys abundance and has Hebe of the fair ankles,
Child of great Zeus and of Hera with the golden sandals.
605 There was a shrieking about him of the dead as of birds

Terrified on all sides. And he like the gloomy night
Held his bare bow with an arrow on the string,
Peering dreadfully like one who is ever about to shoot.
Terrible was the sword strap circling him round the chest,
A golden belt on which wonderful things were fashioned,   610
Bears and savage boars and lions with glaring eyes,
Battles and combats and slaughters and murders of men.
May he never make or never have made any other,
The man who conceived that belt in his own skill.
He knew me at once when he saw me with his eyes,   615
And lamenting to me, he uttered wingèd words:
'Zeus-born son of Laertes, Odysseus of many devices,
Wretched man, what an evil fate you too are carrying on,
Such as I bore myself beneath the rays of the sun!
I was a child of Zeus, son of Cronos, but I had   620
Boundless woe, for I was subdued to a mortal,
Inferior by far, who put difficult tasks on me.
He sent me here once to bring the dog. He did not think
Any task would be more difficult for me than this.
But I did take the dog and lead him out of the place of Hades.   625
Hermes escorted me, and bright-eyed Athene.'
When he had said this, he went back into the hall of Hades.
But I stayed there on the spot in case anyone came
Of the heroes, men who had perished in time before,
And I still would have seen men of old whom I wished to see,   630
Theseus and Perithous,[7] glorious children of the gods,
But first numberless bands of the dead came on
With a tremendous shout, and sallow fear seized me
Lest noble Persephone send the Gorgon [8] head
Of the dread monster from the hall of Hades against me.   635
At once I went on the ship and called my companions
To board it themselves and to untie the stern cables.
They boarded it at once and sat down at the oarlocks,
And a wave of the stream bore it to the river Oceanos;
First there was rowing, and after that a fair breeze.   640

7. Proverbial friend of Theseus.
8. The dead head of a fearful monster (possibly not the same as the
later Gorgon).

"And when the ship had left the stream of the river
Oceanos, and reached the wave of the wide-pathed sea
And the island Aiaia, where the home and the dancing floors
Of the early-born dawn are, and the risings of the sun;
5 When we arrived there, we beached the ship on the sands
And got out ourselves beside the surf of the sea.
We fell asleep there and awaited the godly dawn.
And when the early-born, rosy-fingered dawn appeared,
I sent my companions off to the halls of Circe
10 To bring the body of Elpenor, who had died.
At once we cut logs where the shore jutted highest out,
And we buried him, lamenting and shedding a swelling tear.
When his dead body had been burned, and the gear of his
     body,
We heaped up a mound, dragged a grave marker up on it,
15 And set up his well-shaped oar on top of the mound.
We talked out the details, nor did we escape the notice
Of Circe as we came from Hades, but very swiftly
She adorned herself and came. Servants with her carried
Bread, many pieces of meat, and sparkling red wine.
20 The divine goddess took her stand in our midst and spoke:
'Rash you are, who have gone alive into the hall of Hades,
Dying twice, when other men die a single time:
Well, come, eat of the provisions and drink wine
All day long in this place, and as soon as dawn appears
25 You shall set sail. I shall show you the way and point out
All the details, lest by some troublesome complication
You be hurt and suffer pain on land or on the sea.'
So she said, and the bold heart was persuaded within us.
So then for the entire day till the setting of the sun
30 We sat there dining on the endless meat and sweet wine.
But when the sun went down and the darkness came on
The men lay down by the stern cable of the ship.

She took me by the hand aside from my dear companions,
Sat me down, lay next to me, and asked me the details,
And I told everything to her in its due order.   35
Then the queenly Circe addressed a speech to me:
'So all this has been brought to an end. Now listen
To what I tell you; a god himself shall remind you.
First you will come to the Sirens, who enchant
All men, whenever anyone comes upon them.   40
Whoever in ignorance nears them and hears the voice
Of the Sirens—for that man, his wife and infant children
Do not stand by or rejoice at his homeward return,
But the Sirens enchant him with their clear-toned song,
Seated in a meadow. About is a large heap of bones,   45
Of men rotting, and the skin is shrinking around them.
But go on past; soften honey-sweet wax and smear it
In the ears of your companions lest any of the rest
Should listen. And if you yourself desire to listen,
Let them bind you upon the swift ship hand and foot   50
Erect at the mast; and let the rope ends be made fast from it,
So that you may hear and enjoy the Sirens' song.
If you implore your companions and call on them to free you,
Then have them bind you in further fastenings.
And when your companions have got on past those women,   55
At that point I shall no longer tell you in full detail
Which one of two ways will be yours, but you yourself
Must decide in your heart. I will tell you the alternatives:
In one place there are overhanging rocks; and against them
The great wave of dark blue-eyed Amphitrite roars.   60
Those, indeed, do the blessed gods call the Wandering Rocks,
Where nothing that flies can get by, not even the timid
Doves that carry ambrosia to father Zeus.
And the sheer rock always takes away one of them,
But the Father sends another to make up the number.   65
No ship of men that arrives there ever escapes,
But sea waves and storms of destructive fire carry off
The timbers of the ships and the bodies of the men alike.
One seafaring ship alone did sail past the place,
The Argo, known to all men, as it sailed from Aietes,[1]   70
And it would swiftly have been dashed there on the great rocks
But Hera sent it past, since Jason was dear to her.

1. King of Colchis, father of Medea. The *Argo* was Jason's ship.

The other way there are two crags; one reaches to broad heaven
With its sharp peak, and a dark blue cloud surrounds it
75 That never recedes, nor ever does a clear sky
Hold the peak of it, either in summer or in autumn.
No mortal man could ever climb it or get on top,
Not even if he had twenty hands and twenty feet,
For the rock is sheer, as though polished all around,
80 And in the middle of the crag is a murky cave
Turned facing to the dusk toward Erebos, and there,
Noble Odysseus, you should steer your hollow ship.
Nor could a vigorous man shooting with a bow
From the hollow ship reach to the open cave.
85 There within dwells Scylla, who barks dreadfully,
And her voice comes as loud as that of an unweaned puppy,
But she herself is an evil monster, nor would anyone
Take pleasure to see her, not if a god should confront her.
There are twelve feet on her, all dangling in air;
90 She has six very long necks, and on each one
A terrible head, and on it three rows of teeth
Thick-set and in a cluster, and full of black death.
She is withdrawn to her middle down in the hollow cave;
She holds her heads outside of the dreadful abyss,
95 And there she fishes and reaches all around the crag
For dolphins and dogfish and whatever larger sea creature
She may catch that roaring Amphitrite feeds by the thousands.
There no sailors may ever claim to have escaped past
Unharmed with their ship. She carries off in each head
100 A mortal she has snatched up from a dark blue-prowed ship.
The second crag you will see lying lower, Odysseus,
Close to the other. And you could shoot an arrow across it.
Upon it is a large wild fig tree blooming with leaves;
There divine Charybdis sucks black water back under.
105 Three times daily she sends it up, three times sucks back
Terribly. Do not happen to be there when she sucks,
For not even the earth-shaker could save you from evil then,
But sail to the crag of Scylla very rapidly
And drive your ship on past, since it is better by far
110 To miss six companions on the ship than all at once.'
So she said, and I spoke out to her in answer:
'Come now, goddess, tell me this unerringly,
May I get away from destructive Charybdis somehow

And ward off the other, once she has despoiled my companions?'
So I said, and the divine goddess answered at once: 115
'You rash man, do the works of war concern you again
And toil? Will you not yield to the immortal gods?
She is not mortal for you, but an immortal evil,
Dreadful, oppressive, wild, and not to be fought.
And there is no defense. It is best to flee from her.   120
But if you linger and helm yourself beside the rock,
I fear that she may search and light on you again
And take away as many mortals as she has heads.
No, drive very strongly on, cry aloud for Cratais,
The mother of Scylla, who bore her as a bane for mortals.   125
Then she will stop her from reaching out a second time.
You will arrive at the isle of Thrinacria. There many
Oxen of the Sun and goodly sheep are pasturing,
Seven herds of cattle and as many lovely flocks of sheep,
Fifty in each. No offspring are born from them,   130
Nor do they ever wane. Goddesses and shepherds over them,
The fair-braided nymphs, Phaethusa and Lampetie,
Whom divine Neaira bore to Hyperion, the Sun.
When their queenly mother had borne them and raised them,
She sent them to the isle of Thrinacria to live far off,   135
To guard the sheep and crumple-horned cattle of their father.
If you let them go unmolested and think of your return,
You may get to Ithaca, though you do suffer ills.
But if you molest them, then I prophesy destruction
For your ship and companions. And even if you escape
    yourself   140
You will return late and ill, having lost all your companions.'
So she said, and at once the golden-throned Dawn came on.
The divine goddess herself returned then up the island,
But I went on to the ship and urged my companions
To go on board themselves and to undo the stern cables.   145
At once they got on and took their seats at the oarlocks.
Seated in order, they beat the hoary sea with their oars.
A driving wind full in the sails, a fine companion,
Did the fair-braided Circe, dread god with a singing voice,
Send on for us from behind the dark blue-prowed ship.   150
At once when we had tended to the gear through the ship piece
    by piece
We took our seats. The wind and a pilot steered her.

Then, grieving in my heart, I spoke to my companions:
'My friends, not one person or two alone need to know
155 The prophecies that the divine goddess Circe told me.
But I will tell them, so you may know whether we
Shall die or might avoid death and escape fate.
She ordered us first to avoid the voice of the marvelous
Sirens, and also their meadow full of flowers.
160 Me alone she ordered to hear their voice; but bind me
In hard bonds so that I may stay firm in my place
Erect at the mast. And let the rope-ends be fastened from it.
And if I implore you and call you to untie me
Then constrain me yourselves in further fastenings.'
165 So I declared, and made known the details to my companions.
Meanwhile the well-made ship arrived speedily
At the isle of the Sirens. A fair breeze drove it on.
Then at that point the wind died down, and there was
A windless calm, and some god put the waves to sleep.
170 My companions stood up and furled the sails on the ship.
They threw them in the hollow ship; then, seated at the oars,
They made the water white with the blades of smooth fir.
But I cut up a great disc of wax with the sharp sword
Into small pieces and kneaded it with my stout hands.
175 At once the wax softened when my great force had compelled it,
And the gleam of the Sun, Hyperion's lordly child.
I smeared it in all my companions' ears one by one,
And they bound me on the ship by my hands and feet
Erect on the mast and fastened rope ends from it.
180 Taking their seats, they beat the hoary sea with their oars.
But when it was as far off as a man's shout would carry,
While we pushed swiftly on, the fast-sailing ship did not get
    past
The Sirens—as it drew near, they struck up their clear-toned
    song:
'Come near, much-praised Odysseus, the Achaians' great glory;
185 Bring your ship in, so you may listen to our voice.
No one ever yet sped past this place in a black ship
Before he listened to the honey-toned voice from our mouths,
And then he went off delighted and knowing more things.
For we know all the many things that in broad Troy
190 The Argives and the Trojans suffered at the will of the gods.
We know all that comes to be on the much-nourishing earth.'

So they said, sending their lovely voice out. My heart
Desired to listen, and I told my companions to free me,
Signaling with my eyebrows. Falling to it, they rowed.
Standing up at once, Perimedes and Eurylochos   195
Bound me in further bonds and constrained me more,
And when we had got on past them and could no longer
Listen to the cry of the Sirens or their voice,
At once my trusty companions took out the wax
I had smeared in their ears and freed me from my bonds.   200
But when we had left the island, then at once
I saw smoke and a great wave and heard a noise.
As the men were afraid, the oars flew from their hands;
They all splashed down on the current. And the ship held
In place, since they could no longer drive the sharp-bladed oars
    with their hands.   205
But I went on through the ship, urging my companions
With soothing speeches, standing close to each man:
'Friends, so far we are not unacquainted with evils,
And this is really no greater evil upon us than when the
    Cyclops
Penned us in his hollow cave by his powerful force.   210
Yet even from there, through my prowess and my plan and
    thought,
We escaped, and I think perhaps we shall remember this too.
Come now, do as I tell you, let us all obey.
Beat the deep breakers of the sea with your oars,
Seated at the oarlocks, so that Zeus somehow   215
May grant that we escape and avoid this destruction.
To you, pilot, I give this command. And put it
In your heart as you tend the rudder of the hollow ship.
Keep the ship on the outside of this smoke and this wave,
And make for the crag lest the ship get away from you   220
As it rushes out there and you plunge us all into evil.'
So I said, and they obeyed my words right away.
I said no more of Scylla, the unavoidable danger,
Lest somehow in their fear over me my companions
Should cease from the rowing and crowd themselves within.   225
And then I forgot the hard injunction of Circe
When she ordered me in no way to arm myself.
I put on my famous armor, took two long spears
In my hands, and went up on the deck of the ship

230 At the prow, for from that place I expected rocky Scylla
    First to be sighted, who bore me woe for my companions.
    I could not discern her anywhere. My eyes were tired
    As I peered everywhere out toward the murky rock.
    And we sailed on through the narrow passage, lamenting.
235 There was Scylla, and on the other side godly Charybdis
    Sucked back terribly the salt water of the sea.
    Whenever she disgorged, like a basin in a large fire,
    She seethed, all stirred up. And from overhead, foam
    Fell down on both sides of the peaks of the crags,
240 And when she swallowed down the salt water of the sea
    She appeared all stirred up within, and the rock roared
    Terribly about, and the earth appeared underneath
    In dark blue sand. Sallow fear seized the men.
    We looked toward her in fear of our destruction.
245 Meanwhile Scylla snatched off of the hollow ship
    Six of my companions, who were mightiest in strength.
    But when I looked into the swift ship toward my companions
    I saw already their hands and their feet from above
    As they were lifted on high. They called to me with a cry,
250 Calling me then by name for the last time, grieving in heart.
    As a fisher on a promontory with a very long rod
    Throws down morsels as a lure for the little fish
    And sends down into the ocean the horn of a field ox;
    Then when he catches one writhing, throws it ashore;
255 So they, writhing, were raised up toward the rocks.
    There at the entrance she ate them as they shrieked,
    Reaching their hands toward me in their dread struggle.
    That was the most piteous thing I saw with my eyes
    Of all that I suffered as I sought out the paths of the sea.
260 But when we had fled the rocks and terrible Charybdis
    And Scylla, we arrived at once at the blameless island
    Of the god, where the beautiful broad-browed cattle were,
    And the many goodly flocks of Hyperion, the Sun.
    Then, while I was still on the ocean in the black ship,
265 I heard a lowing of cattle coming to the fold
    And a bleating of sheep. Then there fell on my heart the speech
    Of the blind prophet Theban Tiresias,
    And of Aiaian Circe, who enjoined me many times
    To avoid the isle of the Sun, who delights mortal men.
270 So then I addressed my companions, grieving in my heart:

'Hear my speech, though you have suffered ills, my companions,
So I may tell you the prophecies of Tiresias
And of Aiaian Circe, who enjoined me many times
To avoid the isle of the Sun, who delights mortal men.
They said a most dreadful evil would come on us there.   275
So let us drive the black ship on past that island.'
So I said, and their own hearts were shattered within them.
Eurylochos answered me at once with a hateful speech:
'You are tough, Odysseus, with your superior strength; your limbs
Do not get tired, but they are made all of iron for you   280
Who will not let your companions, worn out with fatigue
And sleepiness, set foot on land, where, moreover,
On the flood-circled island we might make a pleasant dinner,
But you bid us to wander as we are through the sudden night,
Carried away from the island upon the murky ocean.   285
And hard winds come up out of the night, the destroyers
Of ships. Where might one escape sheer destruction
If suddenly a storm of wind by chance came on,
Of the South Wind or the hard-blowing West Wind, that most
Tear ships to pieces beyond the will of the ruling gods?   290
No, but indeed, let us now give in to the black night.
Let us prepare dinner as we stay by the swift ship.
At dawn we shall get in and proceed on the broad ocean.'
So Eurylochos said, and my other companions agreed.
Then I knew that some god had devised evils,   295
And I spoke out to him, uttering wingèd words:
'Eurylochos, indeed you compel me, single as I am.
Come then, all of you, and swear me a mighty oath.
If we find some herd of cattle or a great flock
Of sheep, that no one in evil recklessness   300
Will slaughter any cow or sheep. But be secure
And eat the provisions that immortal Circe gave.'
So I said, and they at once swore an oath as I bid them.
And when they had sworn the oath and completed it,
They set the well-fashioned ship in a hollow harbor   305
Near sweet water. My companions got out and away
From the ship and then prepared dinner skillfully.
But when they had taken their fill of food and drink,
They then remembered and wept for our dear companions
Whom Scylla had snatched out of the hollow ship and eaten.   310

Balmy sleep came upon them as they were weeping.
When it was the third part of night and the stars had gone by,
Cloud-gathering Zeus raised a wind to blow against them
In a tremendous storm, and he covered land and ocean alike
315 Over with clouds. And night rose up out of heaven.
And when the early-born, rosy-fingered dawn appeared,
We beached the ship, dragging her into a hollow cave
Where the fair dancing-floors and the haunts of the nymphs
    were.
And then I made an assembly and addressed them a speech:
320 'My friends, since there is food and drink in the swift ship,
Let us hold off from the cattle, lest we suffer something.
These are the cattle and goodly sheep of a dreadful god,
The Sun, who sees everything and hears everything.'
So I said, and the bold spirit was persuaded in them.
325 The South Wind blew steadily a whole month; no other
Wind came up then except the East Wind and the South.
So long as they possessed grain and red wine
They held off from the cattle in their desire for life.
But when all the provisions had been used up from the ship,
330 They went out on the hunt, roving from necessity
For fish and birds, with bent hooks, for whatever came
Into their own hands. Hunger wore down their bellies.
Then I went away, up into the island so that I might pray
To the gods, for one to show me the way to return.
When I had gone through the island and got clear of my
335   companions,
I washed my hands where there was shelter from the wind,
And I prayed to all of the gods who possess Olympos.
But they poured sweet sleep on me over my eyelids.
And Eurylochos unfolded a bad plan to my companions:
340 'Hear my speech, companions, though you have suffered ills.
There are all kinds of hateful deaths for wretched mortals,
But most piteous is to die and meet one's fate by hunger.
Come then, let us drive the best of the cattle of the Sun
And sacrifice them to the immortals who hold broad heaven,
345 And if we ever get to Ithaca, our fatherland,
We shall at once build a rich temple to Hyperion,
The Sun, and put in it many noble ornaments.
But if he is at all enraged for his straight-horned cattle
And wishes to destroy the ship, and the other gods follow,

I would rather gasp once into a wave and lose my life   350
Then to be starved a long time on a desert island.'
So Eurylochos said, and the other companions agreed.
At once they drove the best of the cattle of the Sun
From nearby. For not far away from the dark blue-prowed
    ship
Did the fine crumple-horned, broad-browed cattle pasture.   355
They surrounded them and made prayers to the gods,
When they had plucked tender leaves from an oak with high
    foliage,
For they did not have white barley on the well-timbered ship.
But when they had prayed and had slaughtered and flayed
    them,
They cut out the thighs and covered them over with fat.   360
They made two folds and lay the raw flesh upon them,
Nor did they have wine to pour on the burning sacrifices,
But used water for libation and roasted all the entrails.
And when the thighs were burned and they had eaten the
    inward parts,
They cut the rest in pieces and pierced it on spits.   365
And then balmy sleep flew away from my eyelids.
I went down to the swift ship and the strand of the sea.
And when I got up close to the bobbing ship,
The sweet aroma of roasting came over to me.
Then I groaned and cried out to the immortal gods: 370
'Father Zeus, and you other blessed, ever-living gods,
To my ruin, indeed, have you lulled me in relentless sleep;
And my companions, while waiting, have devised an enormous
    deed.'
Then a messenger came swiftly to Hyperion the Sun,
Long-gowned Lampetie, to say we had killed his cattle.   375
At once he addressed the immortals, angered in his heart:
'Father Zeus, and you other blessed, ever-living gods,
Take vengeance on the companions of Laertes' son Odysseus,
Who have presumptuously killed my cattle, in which I
Took delight when I went into the starry heaven   380
And when I turned back again from heaven to earth.
If they do not pay fitting recompense for the cattle,
I will go down to the place of Hades and shine among the
    dead.'
Cloud-gathering Zeus spoke out to him in answer:

385 'O Sun, do indeed shine among the immortals
    And among mortal men on the grain-giving earth.
    I shall smite their swift ship soon with a gleaming bolt
    Into small pieces, and burn it in the middle of the wine-faced
        ocean.'
    I heard these things from Calypso of the fair hair,
390 Who said she had heard them herself from the runner Hermes.
    And when I had got down to the ship and the sea,
    I rebuked them one after another on the spot. Nor could we
    Find any remedy. The cattle were already dead.
    Then at once the gods showed forth portents to the men;
395 The skins were creeping, meat lowed upon the spits,
    Both roast and raw, and there came up the voice as of cattle.
    And so for six days did my trusty companions
    Feast on the fine cattle of the Sun they had driven off.
    But when Zeus, son of Cronos, had added the seventh day,
400 At that point the wind ceased raging in a tempest.
    We boarded at once and set out upon the broad ocean,
    When we had set the mast up and hoisted the white sails.
    And when we had left the island behind, no other land
    Appeared at all, but only heaven and the sea.
405 Then the son of Cronos halted a dark blue cloud
    Over the hollow ship, and the ocean darkened beneath it.
    She ran on not too long a time. For at once there came
    The shrieking West Wind raging in a great tempest,
    And a storm of wind broke the forestays of the mast,
410 Both of them, and the mast fell backward, and all the tackle
    Was thrown into the hold. On the stern of the ship
    It hit the pilot's head. And in an instant it crushed
    All the bones of his head together. Like a diver
    He dropped down from the deck, and the bold spirit left his
        bones.
415 Zeus at that instant thundered and threw a bolt on the ship.
    It whirled all around, struck by Zeus's thunderbolt,
    And was filled with brimstone. My companions fell from the
        ship,
    And they resembled sea crows around the black ship
    As they were borne on the waves; a god took away their return.
420 I wandered through my ship until the surge had loosed
    The planks from the keel, and the wave carried it stripped.
    It broke the mast off the keel, and then the backstay,

Which had been made out of oxhide, was flung up on it.
Then I bound both the keel and the mast together.
Seated on them, I was carried by the destructive winds.   425
And then the West Wind ceased raging in a tempest
And the South Wind came quickly, bearing pains for my heart,
That I should still remeasure my course to destructive
   Charybdis.
All night long I was carried, and with the rising sun
I came to the crag of Scylla and to dreadful Charybdis.   430
And she had sucked back the salty water of the sea,
But I raised myself high up against the tall wild fig tree
And held myself fastened to it like a bat. Nor anywhere
Could I plant my feet firmly or climb up on it,
For its roots held far off and its branches were high swaying,   435
Tall and great, and they shadowed Charybdis over.
I held there steadily, till she should disgorge back
The mast and keel again. I longed for them, but they came late.
At the time when a man gets up from the assembly for dinner,
One who judges many quarrels of youthful adversaries,   440
At that time did the timber appear out of Charybdis.
I let my hands and feet be brought down from above
And plunged right on in the midst of the lengthy timbers.
Seated upon them, I rowed on with my hands.
The father of men and gods no longer let Scylla   445
See me, or I would not have escaped sheer destruction.
Nine days I was borne thence, and on the tenth night
The gods brought me near the island of Ogygia, where lives
Fair-braided Calypso, dread god with a singing voice.
She befriended me and cared for me. Why tell this story?   450
Already I have told it in your house yesterday
To you and your goodly wife. It is hateful to me
To tell over again a story that has been clearly told."

So he said, and they all became hushed in silence.
They were held in rapture through the shadowy halls.
Then Alcinoos gave him an answer and spoke to him:
"Odysseus, since you have come to my bronze-based home
  5 With its high roof, I think you will not be driven off course
In your return back, though you have suffered much.
And I say this in urging every man of you,
All those who in my halls are forever drinking
The sparkling wine of the elders and listening to the singer.
 10 Clothes are laid up for the stranger in a polished chest,
And highly wrought gold and all sorts of other gifts
That the members of the Phaeacian council brought here.
Come now, let us give him a great cauldron and a basin,
Man by man. Then we shall collect among the people and
    get paid back.
 15 It is hard for a single man to give freely for nothing."
So Alcinoos spoke, and his speech was pleasing to them.
They all went off, each to his house, to lie down to sleep.
And when the early-born, rosy-fingered dawn appeared,
They hastened to the ship and brought bronze that is a help for
    men.
 20 Alcinoos in his sacred strength stored it well under the benches,
Going himself through the ship so it might not hamper
Any of the rowing crew as they sped with the oars.
They went to the home of Alcinoos and partook of dinner.
Alcinoos in his sacred strength sacrificed an ox for them
 25 To black-clouded Zeus, son of Cronos, who rules all.
When they had burned the thighs, they dined on the illustrious
    feast
And enjoyed it. Among them the godly singer played,
Demodocos, who was honored by the people. But Odysseus
Turned his head many times to the resplendent sun,
 30 Impatient for it to set. So eager was he to return;

As when a man longs for dinner whose wine-faced oxen
Have drawn the jointed plow on his fallow land all day:
He is glad when the light of the sun goes down on him
As he heads for dinner, and his knees fail as he goes;
So was Odysseus glad when the sun's light went down.   35
At once he addressed the Phaeacians, who are fond of rowing.
And to Alcinoos especially did he make known his speech:
"Lordly Alcinoos, exalted among all your people,
Pour a libation and send me home unharmed. Farewell to you!
What my own heart was wanting has now been brought to pass,   40
An escort and friendly gifts; and may the heavenly gods
Make them blessed for me! On my return may I find
My wife at home blameless, with my friends safe and sound.
You, though, stay here and give pleasure to your wedded wives
And to your children. May the gods grant excellence   45
Of all sorts to you, and no evil be among your people."
So he said, and they all assented and gave the order
To escort the stranger, since he had spoken properly.
Then Alcinoos in his might spoke out to a herald:
"Pontonoos, mix up a bowl and pass out wine   50
To all through the hall, so we may pray to Father Zeus,
And escort the stranger to his own fatherland."
So he said, and Pontonoos mixed the mind-honeying wine.
He passed it to all in turn. From the seats where they were
They poured libation to the blessed gods   55
Who possess broad heaven. Godly Odysseus stood up,
Placed a cup with two handles in Arete's hand,
And speaking out to her he uttered wingèd words:
"May you constantly fare well, my queen, till old age
And death come upon you, which do exist for men.   60
But I am going now. Enjoy yourself in this house,
With your children and your people and King Alcinoos."
When he had said this, godly Odysseus went over the threshold.
Alcinoos in his might sent a herald along with him
To lead him to the swift ship and the strand of the sea.   65
And Arete sent serving women along with him,
One of whom held a well-washed mantle and tunic,
Another she sent with her to bring the stout chest along,
And still another was carrying bread and red wine.
And when they had come down to the ship and the sea,   70
At once his noble escorts took those things and placed them

Inside the hollow ship, all of the food and drink.
They spread out a blanket and linen cloth for Odysseus
On the deck of the hollow ship, so he might sleep without
    waking,
75 Upon the stern. He himself boarded too and lay down
In silence. Each of them sat down at the oarlocks
In order. They loosed the cable from the pierced stone.
As soon as they leaned on the oars and flung up salt water with
    the blade,
For him there fell down upon his eyelids a balmy sleep,
80 Unwaking, most sweet, nearest in semblance to death.
As for the ship, the way four yoked stallions on a plain
All rush on together under the blows of a whip,
Leap up high, and pursue their journey rapidly;
So was her stern raised up, and behind her there surged
85 A great purple wave of the loud-roaring sea.
She ran safely and steadily, nor could the circling
Hawks, the nimblest of winged things, have kept up,
So rapidly did it run as it cut the waves of the sea
Carrying a man who had plans like those of the gods,
90 Who in time past had suffered very many pains in his heart,
Passing through the wars of men and the troublesome waves,
But at this time he slept without a tremor, forgetting what he
    had suffered.
When the brightest star rose up that most of all
Comes on to announce the light of early-born dawn,
95 At that time did the seafaring ship reach the island.
There is a certain harbor of Phorcys, the old man of the sea,
In the land of Ithaca; and there, jutting out on it,
Are two headlands broken off, sloping down to the harbor.
They give shelter against the great wave from hard-blowing
    winds
100 Outside. And inside of it well-timbered ships remain
Without a cable when they reach the measure of mooring.
At the head of the harbor is an olive with long leaves,
And close to that is a pleasant and shadowy cavern
Sacred to the nymphs who are called Naiades.
105 And in it there are mixing bowls and two-handled jars
Of stone. And the bees store up their honey in them.
There are very long stone looms in it, where the nymphs
Weave sea purple mantles, a wonder to behold,

And ever-flowing waters are there. It has two doors,
One toward the North Wind, accessible to men,   110
And the other one divine is toward the South Wind, nor may
    men
Approach by that one, but it is a path for immortals.
The men, who knew it beforehand, drove the ship in there;
And then she was beached on the mainland, half her whole
    length
As she ran in, so fast was she pushed on by the rowers' hands.   115
They got out of the well-benched ship onto dry land.
First they raised Odysseus out of the hollow ship,
The linen sheet and the glistening blanket and all;
They set him down on the sand overcome with sleep.
They lifted out the goods the noble Phaeacians had given   120
As he was going home through great-hearted Athene's help,
And then put them in a heap by the base of the olive tree,
Out of the path lest by chance some wayfaring man
Might find and despoil them before Odysseus woke up.
Then they started back homeward. Nor did the earth-shaker   125
Forget the curses he had made originally
Against godlike Odysseus. And he asked about Zeus's plan:
"Father Zeus, I myself shall no longer be honored
Among the immortal gods when mortals do not respect me,
The Phaeacians, who are of my very own descent.   130
For I just now said Odysseus would suffer many ills
Before he got home; I have never deprived him of a return
Entirely, since you promised this first and nodded agreement.
Yet these men have brought him asleep on the ocean in a swift
    ship,
Have set him down in Ithaca and given him prodigious gifts,   135
Bronze and gold and woven clothing aplenty,
Much more than Odysseus ever would have taken from Troy
If he had arrived unharmed with his share of booty."
Cloud-gathering Zeus addressed him in answer:
"Well now, wide-powered earth-shaker, what a speech you have
    made!   140
The gods do not at all insult you. It would be hard
To attack with insults the oldest and finest god—
And if some man, yielding to his strength and might,
Does not honor you, vengeance is yours forever after.
Do as you wish and as is pleasing to your own heart."   145

And then the earth-shaker Poseidon answered him:
"Black-clouded one, I would do at once as you say.
But always I respect and do deference to your heart.
And now I would like to dash the beautiful ship
150 Of the Phaeacians as it comes from escort on the murky sea,
So that henceforth they may hold back and refrain from escort
For men; and I would hide their city round with a great
      mountain."
Cloud-gathering Zeus addressed him in answer:
"Dear friend, in my heart this seems to me the best course:
155 When all the people are away from the city and catch sight
Of the ship coming on, make it into a stone near the land
Resembling the swift ship, so that all the men may be
Amazed; and hide the city round with a great mountain."
And when earth-shaker Poseidon had heard this speech,
160 He went on to Scheria where the Phaeacians dwell
And stayed there. The seafaring ship came very near,
Running on nimbly. The earth-shaker came near it,
And he turned it to stone and rooted it beneath,
Pressing it with the flat of his hand. Then he departed.
165 The Phaeacians with their long oars, men famous for ships,
For their part addressed wingèd words to one another.
This is what a man who saw it would say to his neighbor:
"Ah me, who has detained the swift ship in the ocean
As it was coming home? It has just appeared all in view."
170 So one man would say. They did not know how this was done.
Then Alcinoos spoke out to them and addressed them:
"Ah well, the prophecies have come upon me, spoken of old
By my father, who used to say Poseidon resented us
Because we are secure escorts for everyone.
175 He said a beautiful ship of the Phaeacian men
Coming back sometime from an escort on the murky ocean
Would be dashed, and a great mountain would hide our city
      round."
So the old man said. Now it has all come to pass.
But come now. Let us all observe what I shall say:
180 Give up escorting mortals when anyone comes
To our city, and let us sacrifice to Poseidon
Twelve chosen bulls so that he may take pity
And not hide our city round with a very tall mountain."
So he said; they were afraid, and prepared the bulls.

And so the leaders and counselors of the land   185
Of the Phaeacians were praying to Lord Poseidon,
Standing round the altar. But godly Odysseus woke up
From sleeping on his fatherland soil and did not recognize it,
For he had been gone a long time. A god shed a mist round
    him,
Pallas Athene, the daughter of Zeus, so she could make him   190
Unrecognizable, and tell him the details,
Lest his wife recognize him, and his townsmen and friends,
Before the suitors had paid for all their transgressions.
And so everything appeared of a changed form to its lord;
Continuous pathways and harbors with mooring all round,   195
Towering rocks and trees that were blossoming.
He sprang up, stood still, and looked on his fatherland soil,
And then he uttered a groan and struck both his thighs
With the flat of his hands. And he made a speech, lamenting:
"Woe is me, to the land of what mortals have I come this time?   200
Are the men proud and savage and without justice
Or are they friendly to strangers and have a god-fearing mind?
Where am I carrying these many goods? Where do I myself
Wander? Would that they had stayed with the Phaeacians
In that place. But I would have come on another of the
    exalted kings   205
Who would have befriended me and sent me on my return.
As it is I do not know where to put these things. Nor can I
Leave them here, lest they become a prey to others.
Well now, the leaders and counselors of the Phaeacians
Were not wholly prudent and just when they led me off   210
To another land. They did say they would lead me
To sunny Ithaca, and they did not bring it to pass.
May the Zeus of suppliants pay them back, who watches
Over all men and punishes whoever errs.
All right, I shall number the goods and look at them   215
Lest they have taken some from me and gone on the hollow
    ship."
When he had said this, he counted the beautiful cauldrons
And the basins and the gold and the lovely woven clothes.
He missed none of them. But he bemoaned his fatherland,
Dragging himself along the strand of the loud-roaring sea   220
And grieving much. And Athene came up close to him,
Likening her body to a young man's, a feeder of sheep,

All tender, the way the children of rulers are.
She wore a well-made double-folded mantle on her shoulders
225 And had sandals under her glistening feet, a javelin in her hands.
Odysseus rejoiced to see her and came up facing her.
And speaking out to her, he uttered wingèd words:
"My friend, since you are the first one I find in this place,
Greetings. And may you not confront me with an evil mind.
230 But save these things and save me; I pray to you
As to a god, and I come up to your precious knees.
Tell me this one thing, truly, so I may know it well;
What land is this, what people? What men are native here?
Is it some sunny island, perhaps, or some shore
235 Of the rich-loamed mainland that lies sloping to the sea?"
Then the bright-eyed goddess Athene spoke to him:
"You are simple, stranger, or have come from far away
If you ask what this land is. To no great degree
Is it nameless. Very many men know which it is,
240 Both all those who are living toward dawn and the sun
And also all those who live back toward the murky dusk.
Indeed it is rough and not for driving horses,
Nor is it excessively poor, though not broad in shape.
In it is produced immense food and also wine.
245 Rain holds it perpetually and the fertile dew.
It is a good goat pasture and cow pasture. Woods
Are all over it, and it affords year-round watering places.
And so, stranger, the name Ithaca has reached even to Troy,
Which they say is far off from the Achaian land."
So she said, and godly Odysseus, who had endured much,
250   rejoiced,
Glad at his fatherland soil, that Pallas Athene,
The daughter of aegis-bearing Zeus, told him of,
And speaking out to her, he uttered wingèd words.
He did not speak the truth, but he held back his story,
255 Forever managing the very shrewd thought in his breast:
"I have heard of Ithaca even in broad Crete,
Far over the ocean. And now I have come myself
With these goods; leaving as much again to my children,
I fled, since I had killed the dear son of Idomeneus,
260 Swift-footed Ortilochos, who in broad Crete
Surpassed all bread-earning men with his swift feet,
Because he wanted to deprive me of all my booty

From Troy, for which I had suffered pains in my heart,
Passing through the wars of men and the troublesome waves,
And because I was not graciously willing to serve his father   265
In the Trojans' land, but led other men as companions.
I hit him with the bronze-tipped spear as he was coming back
From a field, lying in ambush with a companion by the path.
A very dark night held the heavens, nor did any man
Perceive us, and I took away his life unnoticed.   270
But when I had killed the man with the sharp bronze spear
I went on a ship at once and pleaded with the noble
Phoenicians, and I gave them booty to their heart's desire.
I asked them to bring me to Pylos and put me to shore,
Or close to godly Elis, where the Epeians are ruling.   275
But then the force of the wind drove them away from there,
Much against their will, for they did not want to deal falsely.
Wandering from there we arrived at this place by night.
With haste we rowed into the harbor, nor did any of us
Have dinner in mind, though we wanted much to take it;   280
But getting off the ship, we all lay down as we were.
Then sweet sleep came on me, fatigued as I was,
And they took my goods out of the hollow ship
And set them down where I was lying on the sands.
Embarking for well-inhabited Sidonia,   285
They went off, and I was left grieving in my heart."
So he said, and the bright-eyed goddess Athene smiled.
She reached her hand to him and likened her body to a woman's,
Lovely and tall and skilled in glorious tasks;
And speaking to him, she uttered wingèd words: 290
"Cunning would he be and deceitful, who could overreach you
In various wiles, and even if a god should confront you.
Versatile-minded wretch, insatiate in wiles, you would not
Cease from deceits though you are in your own land,
Or from fraudulent stories that from the ground up are dear to
    you.   295
Come, let us say no more of this, as both of us are skilled
In shrewdness, since you are by far the best of mortals
In plans and in stories, and I among all the gods
Am famed for planning and shrewdness, and you did not know
Pallas Athene, daughter of Zeus, who always stands   300
Beside you and guards you in all sorts of troubles
And made you beloved by all of the Phaeacians.

And now I have come here so I may weave a plot with you
And hide all the goods the noble Phaeacians gave you
305 When you came homeward by my plan and my thought.
And I shall tell you how many cares it is your lot to put up with
In the well-made halls. But endure them, for you must,
And do not declare to any one of them all,
Men or women, that you came here wandering. But in silence
310 Suffer many pains, submitting to the violence of men."
Odysseus of many wiles addressed her in answer:
"It is hard, goddess, for a mortal who meets you to recognize
    you,
Even one who is knowing. You liken yourself to anything.
I know this well, that you were mild to me before,
315 While we sons of the Achaians were making war in Troy,
But when we had sacked the lofty city of Priam,
And went off in ships and a god scattered the Achaians,
I did not see you then, daughter of Zeus, or discern you
Boarding my ship to ward any pain off from me.
320 But having always a heart cut asunder in my breast
I wandered until the gods freed me from evil,
Till the time when in the rich land of the Phaeacians
You cheered me with words and led me yourself to the city.
Now I embrace your knees for your father—I do not think
325 I have come to sunny Ithaca, but turn on through
Some other land. And I think you ridicule me
By saying this, so that you may deceive my mind.
Tell me truly if I have reached my dear fatherland."
And then the bright-eyed goddess Athene answered him:
330 "You have an idea like this forever in your breast.
And so I cannot forsake you when you are wretched,
Because you are polite, ready-minded, and of steadfast thought.
Gladly another man who had come in his wandering
Would push on to see his wife and children in his halls.
335 But it is not dear to you to find out or inquire
Before you may yet try your wife out; and she sits
As ever in the halls. Woeful for her always
The days and the nights waste away as she sheds tears.
I never failed to believe it myself, but in my heart
340 Knew you would return, having lost all your companions.
And yet I did not want to quarrel with Poseidon,

My father's brother, who laid up a grudge against you in his
    heart,
Enraged at you for having blinded his dear son.
Come, I will show you Ithaca's site, to convince you.
This is the harbor of Phorcys, the old man of the sea;   345
This at the harbor's head the olive with long leaves,
And close to it the charming and shadowy cavern
Sacred to the nymphs who are called Naiades.
This is the broad, high-roofed cave where you used to offer
Many acceptable hecatombs to the nymphs.   350
And that is Neriton, the mountain clothed over with woods."
When she had said this, the goddess scattered the mist;
    ground showed.
Then godly Odysseus, who had suffered much, rejoiced,
Glad at his own land, and he kissed the grain-giving soil.
At once he prayed to the nymphs, holding up his hands: 355
"Nymphs, Naiades, daughters of Zeus, I never thought
I would see you myself. And now, do take pleasure
In my kindly prayers. I shall give gifts as before,
If Zeus's daughter, driver of the spoil, graciously allows
Me to live myself and makes my dear son grow up."   360
Then the bright-eyed goddess Athene spoke to him:
"Take cheer. Do not give heed to this in your mind,
But right away now we shall place the goods in a nook
Of the marvelous cavern, so they may stay there safe for you,
And let us ourselves discuss how it may be for the best."   365
When she had said this, the goddess entered the shadowy cave,
Searching out the recesses in the cave. And Odysseus
Brought everything nearer, the gold and unyielding bronze
And the well-made clothes that the Phaeacians gave him.
Pallas Athene, the daughter of aegis-bearing Zeus,   370
Put them in well and placed a stone at the entrance.
They both sat down at the base of the holy olive tree
And talked about destruction for the presumptuous suitors.
The bright-eyed goddess Athene was the first to speak:
"Zeus-born son of Laertes, Odysseus of many devices,   375
Take thought about how you may lay hands on the shameless
    suitors
Who for three years have held sway over your hall,
Wooing your godlike wife and giving her bridal gifts.

But she always grieves in her heart for your return.
380 She gives them all hope and makes promises to each man,
Sending out messages, but her mind plans other things."
Odysseus of many devices addressed her in answer:
"Well now, I might surely have perished in my halls
By the evil fate of Agamemnon, son of Atreus,
385 If you, goddess, had not duly told me the details.
Come, devise a plan, that I may do vengeance on them.
Stand beside me yourself, putting in me such courageous might
As we had when we undid Troy's shining diadems.
And if you stood as then pressing on so beside me, bright-eyed
    one,
390 I myself would do battle against three hundred men
With you, honored goddess, when you would earnestly help
    me."
Then the bright-eyed goddess Athene answered him:
"Yes, I shall surely stand strongly beside you, nor shall you
    miss me
When we are busy with these matters, and I think
395 Some of the suitors who devour your livelihood
Shall spatter the immense ground with their blood and brains.
Come, I shall make you unrecognizable to all mortals.
I shall shrivel the lovely flesh on your supple limbs,
Destroy the blond hair from your head, and cloak you about
400 In rags a man seeing you wear would loathe you for.
And I shall mar your eyes that were beautiful beforehand,
So that you may appear ill-favored to all the suitors,
And to your wife and your child that you left in the halls.
But first of all go on up yourself to the swineherd
405 Who is guardian of your swine, kindly disposed to you also,
And a friend to your son and the constant Penelope.
You will find him staying with the swine.They pasture
Beside the rock of the Raven and the spring Arethusa.
They eat the satisfying acorn and drink black water,
410 The things that nourish abundant fat on swine.
Stay there, remain beside him and ask him everything,
So that I may go to Sparta that is lovely in women
And summon Telemachos, your dear son, Odysseus,
Who went to Menelaos in Lacedemon of the broad dancing-
    place
415 To learn tidings about you, if you were still alive."

Odysseus of many wiles addressed her in answer:
"Why did you, who know all in your mind, not tell him?
So that he too might wander and undergo pains
On the barren sea and others eat his livelihood?"
Then the bright-eyed goddess Athene answered him: 420
"As for him, do not really take him too much to heart.
I escorted him myself so he might gain noble renown
When he went there. But he has no trouble; he sits secure
In the halls of Atreus' son, and he has endless bounty.
The young men do wait in ambush for him with a black ship,   425
Wanting to kill him before he reaches his fatherland.
But I do not think that will be; sooner shall the earth contain
Some one of the suitors who devour your livelihood."
When she had said this, Athene touched him with a wand.
She shriveled the lovely flesh on his supple limbs,   430
Destroyed the blond hair on his head, and put the skin
Of an aged old man around all of his limbs.
And she marred his eyes that were beautiful beforehand.
She threw other clothing about him; a foul rag and a tunic,
Dirty and full of holes, begrimed with foul smoke,   435
And she clothed about him the great skin of a swift deer,
Bare of hair, and she gave him a staff and a sorry wallet
Thick with holes; a rope shoulder strap was on it.
When they had this plan the two of them parted. And she
Went to godly Lacedemon after the child of Odysseus.   440

XIV

Then he went over the rugged path from the harbor
Up wooded country through the heights, to where Athene
Had showed him the way to the godly swineherd, who, of all the
    servants
Godly Odysseus owned, best took care of his livelihood.
5 He found him seated in the forecourt where the courtyard
Was built up lofty in a place with a view all around,
Lovely and large, circled round, that the swineherd himself
Had built for the swine when his master had gone away,
Secretly from his mistress and the old man Laertes,
10 Out of quarried stones; and he coped it with a prickly shrub.
Outside when he had hewn off the black part of an oak
He drove in stakes, stout and close set, right through on either
    side,
And inside of the courtyard he made twelve pig sties
Close to one another, beds for the swine. In each
15 Fifty swine that sleep on the ground were shut up,
The females for breeding. And the males slept on the outside,
Fewer by far. The godlike suitors diminished those
By eating them, since the swineherd always sent
The best one out of all the well-nourished hogs.
20 Three hundred and sixty there were of them in all.
And dogs that resembled wild beasts slept always beside them,
Four of them, that the swineherd, chief of the men, had reared.
He himself was fitting sandals about his feet,
And cutting oxhide of good color. The other men
25 Were gone off in different directions with the droves of swine,
Three of them. And he had sent the fourth one off to the city
To bring a pig to the presumptuous suitors, under constraint,
So they might sacrifice it and glut their hearts on meat.
The yelping dogs sighted Odysseus suddenly
30 And ran on after him barking, and Odysseus
Sat down in cunning, and the staff fell from his hand.

And then by his own pen he would have suffered a sorry pain,
But the swineherd came up quickly on nimble feet,
Rushed in the front gate, and the leather fell from his hand.
He shouted at the dogs and scattered them this way and that   35
With showers of stones. And he addressed his master:
"Old man, in a little while the dogs would suddenly
Have torn you to pieces, and you would have heaped reproach
    on me.
To me also have the gods given other pains and griefs.
As I groan and lament over my godlike master,   40
I sit here and keep fattening swine for other men
To eat. But that man, perhaps, longing for food,
Wanders to the city and the land of alien men,
If he is indeed still alive and sees the light of the sun.
But follow me, old man, let us go to the hut, so for yourself   45
When you are satisfied in your heart with food and wine,
You may tell where you come from and how many cares you
    have endured."
When he had said this, the godly swineherd led him into the
    hut.
He brought him in and sat him down; and heaped shaggy
    brushwood
And spread on it the hide of a hairy wild goat   50
Great and shaggy, which was his own bedding. Odysseus
    rejoiced
That he had received him so. He spoke out directly:
"Stranger, may Zeus and the other gods grant you whatever
You wish the most, since you have received me kindly."
And you addressed him in answer, swineherd Eumaeos: 55
"Stranger, it would not be right for me to dishonor
A stranger, not if one worse than you came. In Zeus's care
Are all strangers and beggars. And a gift that comes from us,
Even a small one, is friendly, because the rule for servants is
    always
To be afraid when young masters hold power over them.   60
And indeed, the gods have hindered the return of the man
Who kindly befriended me and gave me possessions,
A home and a portion and a wife wooed by many,
Such things as a good-hearted master gives his servant
Who toils much for him, and a god also fosters the work,   65
As he fosters for me too this work at which I abide.

And so my master would have given me much, had he aged here.
But he is dead. Would that the whole race of Helen had died
On their knees, since she undid the knees of many men.
70 But that man went off for the honor of Agamemnon
Toward Ilion that abounds in horses to fight with the Trojans."
When he had said this he quickly bound his tunic with his belt
And went to the sties where the herds of pigs were shut up.
Then he took two, bore them off, and sacrificed them both.
75 He singed them and cut them up and pierced them on spits.
When he had roasted it all he brought it over to Odysseus,
Hot on the very spits, and sprinkled white barley on it,
And in a bowl made of ivy he mixed up honey-sweet wine;
He sat across from him and spoke out, urging him on:
80 "Eat now, stranger, the food that is furnished to servants,
Plain pork. But the suitors eat the fatling swine
And in their minds do not think of divine surveillance or pity,
For the blessed gods are not fond of cruel deeds;
No, they reward justice and the righteous deeds of men.
85 And even the hostile and unfriendly men that approach
The country of others, and Zeus gives booty to them,
When they fill up the ships and go to return home—
Even on their minds does a strong fear of the surveillance fall.
But these men know—they have heard some voice of a god—
Of that man's woeful death, and so they do not wish to pay
90   court
Justly, or to return to their own goods, but at their ease
They presumptuously devour his goods, and there is
No restraint. As many days and nights as there are from Zeus
I think they have never made one sacrifice, or two.
95 They presumptuously draw off the wine and waste it.
His living was unspeakably great. Not so much was there
For any of the heroes, not upon the black mainland
Or Ithaca itself. Not twenty mortals together
Have so much wealth. I shall tell you all about it myself.
There are twelve herds on the mainland, as many flocks of
100   sheep,
As many of swine and as many extensive droves of goats
That strangers pasture, and also his own herdsmen.
There are eleven extensive droves of goats here in all
That pasture at the verge, and good men watch over them.
105 Each one always brings them an animal every day,

Whichever of the well-nourished goats seems to be best.
I watch over these swine and protect them myself
And I make a good choice and send them the best of the
  swine."
So he said. The other gratefully ate meat and drank wine,
Reaching for it in silence. And he was sowing ill for the suitors. 110
But when he had dined and satisfied his heart with eating
The other filled a cup from which he drank himself and gave
  it to him
Full of wine. He took it and rejoiced in his spirit.
And speaking out to the other, he uttered wingèd words:
"My friend, who was it that bought you with his resources,   115
And he so very rich and so mighty as you say?
You say he was destroyed for the honor of Agamemnon.
Tell me, if I might somehow know him for the man he is.
Zeus knows, perhaps, and the other immortal gods,
If I might give news of having seen him; I have wandered
  much."   120
Then the swineherd, the chief of the men, answered him:
"Old man, no wanderer who came here bringing news of him
Could ever convince his wife and his dear son.
Yet anyway, wanderers who need entertainment
Tell lies, and they are not willing to speak the truth.   125
Whoever in wandering reaches the land of Ithaca
Comes to my mistress and utters deceptive stories.
She receives him, befriends him, and asks for the details,
And as she laments, the tears fall from her eyelids,
As is right for a woman when her husband has perished abroad. 130
And you too, old man, would quickly fashion a story
If someone gave you a mantle and a tunic and clothes.
By now the dogs and swift birds have probably
Torn the skin from his bones and the soul has left him,
Or fish have eaten him in the ocean and his bones   135
Are lying on a mainland wrapped over with much sand.
So he has perished there, and afterward many cares
Have been made for all his friends, most for me; I shall not
  again
Find another master so mild anywhere I go,
Not if I should reach my mother's and father's home again,   140
Where I was first born and they themselves brought me up.
Nor should I yet mourn them so much, though I do want

To see them with my eyes in my own fatherland.
But longing takes hold of me for Odysseus who is gone away.
145 I am in awe to speak his name, stranger, though he is not here.
For he loved me exceedingly and cared for me in his heart.
But I call him 'honored sir' even when he is far away."
Godly Odysseus, who had endured much, spoke to him then:
"My friend, since you wholly deny it, you do not still think
150 That man will come, and your heart is ever unbelieving;
I shall still say it, not just that way, but with an oath:
Odysseus shall return. Let me have reward for good news
Right away when that man arrives at his own halls;
Clothe me in a mantle and a tunic, lovely clothes.
155 Before then, though I need them much, I will take nothing.
Hateful to me as the gates of Hades is that man
Who yields to poverty and tells deceitful stories.
May Zeus now be my witness, first of the gods, and this guest
          table,
And the hearth of the blameless Odysseus, to which I have come.
160 Truly, all these things shall come to pass as I say.
Within the light of this very month will Odysseus be coming
          here:
While one moon is waning and another is on the rise
He will return home and do vengeance on anyone
Who here dishonors his wife and his glorious son."
165 And you addressed him in answer, swineherd Eumaeos:
"Old man, I shall not reward you for this good news,
Nor will Odysseus still come home. But at your ease,
Drink. Let us think of quite other things. Do not
Remind me of these matters. The heart in my breast
170 Is grieved when anyone mentions my beloved master.
Well, we will let the oath go, but may Odysseus
Come, as I wish myself, and Penelope wishes,
And the old man Laertes, and godlike Telemachos.
I mourn ceaselessly now for the son Odysseus fathered,
175 Telemachos. When the gods had reared him like a young tree,
And I thought among men he too would be not inferior
To his own dear father, wondrous in body and form,
Then one of the immortals hurt his mind, balanced within,
Or else some man. He went after hearsay about his father
180 To sacred Pylos. And the noble suitors lie in ambush
For him as he comes home so that out of Ithaca

The race of godlike Arkesios [1] might perish nameless.
Well, let us forget that man, whether he is captured
Or escapes, and the son of Cronos holds his hand over him.
But come now, old man, tell me about your own cares,   185
And tell me this really so I may know it well.
What men are you from? Where are your city and parents?
On what sort of ship did you come? How did sailors
Bring you to Ithaca? What men did they claim to be?
For I do not think you could have got here at all on foot."   190
Odysseus of many wiles addressed him in answer:
"All right, I shall tell you this quite truthfully.
And now a long time for the two of us might there be
Both food and sweet wine while we stayed within the hut
To feast in quiet while others performed the work: 195
Easily in that case even for an entire year
I would not come to an end of telling the cares of my heart,
All the many things I have suffered at the will of the gods.
I declare I am of the race of those who live in broad Crete,
The son of a wealthy man. And many other sons   200
Were both born and nourished in his hall, legitimate,
From his wife. A bought mother bore me, a concubine.
But Castor, son of Hylax, of whose race I declare I am,
Honored me as he did the sons rightfully born.
Then among the Cretans he was honored as a god in the land   205
For his prosperity and his wealth and his glorious sons.
But the fates of death came and carried him off
To the halls of Hades. His haughty-spirited sons
Divided his living up and cast lots for it.
Yet they gave me a very poor part and assigned me a dwelling.   210
I took a wife among men who had a large portion,
Because of my excellence, since I was not a good-for-nothing
Or a coward in battle. And now it has all left me.
Nevertheless I think if you look at the stubble
You can know what the grain was. For a great deal of distress
    holds me.   215
Ares and Athene gave me the courage and power
To break the ranks of men, whenever I picked for ambush
Excellent men, sowing evils for enemies;
Never did my bold spirit look forward to death
But I leapt forward by far the first and took with my sword   220

1. Grandfather of Odysseus.

Any man of the enemy who yielded to me in running.
Such was I in war. Labor was not dear to me
Or household-tending, that raises glorious children.
No, ships with good oars were always dear to me
225 And battles, and well-made javelins and arrows,
Woeful things, that for others are to be shuddered at.
But to me things are precious, I think, that a god put in my
    mind,
For one man delights in one task, one man in another.
Before the sons of the Achaians arrived at Troy
230 Nine times I had been a leader of men on swift-faring ships
Against alien men, and many things fell in my hands.
Of them, some satisfying things I chose, but got many
Afterwards by lot. At once my house increased, and then
I became respected and feared among the Cretans.
235 But when broad-seeing Zeus devised that hateful journey
Which has undone the knees from under many man,
Then they kept urging me and renowned Idomeneus
To lead them in ships to Ilion. There was no means
For us to refuse; the stern talk of the people held.
240 There for nine years we sons of the Achaians waged war.
In the tenth we sacked the city of Priam and went
Home in our ships, and a god scattered the Achaians.
But Zeus, the counselor, planned evil for my poor self.
A single month I remained delighting in my children
245 And my wedded wife and possessions. But then my heart
Ordered me to equip the ships well and embark
On a voyage to Egypt with my godlike companions.
I equipped nine ships, and my crew collected quickly.
For six days then my trusty companions dined with me
250 And I presented as victims many animals
To offer the gods and to prepare as dinner for themselves,
And on the seventh day, as we set off from broad Crete,
We sailed on in a fair, steadily blowing North Wind
Easily, as if down a stream. Nor did anyone
255 Give trouble on my ships, but we sat there unharmed
And without disease, and the wind and pilots steered them.
On the fifth day we came to the fair-flowing river of Egypt.
I beached my bobbing ships by the Egyptian river
And then I called upon my trusty companions
260 To remain there beside the ships and to guard the ships,

And I ordered spies to go up on places of lookout.
But they gave in to excess; relying on their own strength,
They sacked the beautiful fields of the Egyptians
At once and carried their women and infant children off.
They killed the men. And soon the noise reached the city.   265
They perceived the shouting, and at the appearance of dawn
Came on. The whole plain was filled with foot soldiers and
    horses
And the flash of bronze. Zeus, who hurls the thunderbolt,
Threw evil panic among my companions, nor could any
Bear to stay face to face; ills surrounded us on all sides.   270
Then they slaughtered many of us with the sharp bronze
And led some off alive to work for them under constraint.
But Zeus himself put the following idea
In my mind: I wish I had died and met my fate
There in Egypt, for trouble was still to welcome me.   275
I at once took the well-made helmet off my head and the shield
From my shoulders and threw the spear out of my hand.
Then I came up in front of the horses of the king.
I took his knees and kissed them. He pitied me and spared me.
He put me on the chariot and led me weeping to his home.   280
Very many men rushed upon me with ashwood spears,
Wanting to kill me, for they were angered highly.
But he held them off and showed awe for the wrath of Zeus,
Who protects strangers and gets highly incensed at evil deeds.
Then I stayed seven years there, and I gathered many   285
Goods among the Egyptian men, for they all gave me some.
But when the eighth year in its course came round for me,
Then a Phoenician man came, skilled in deceits,
A sharp dealer who had worked many evils among men.
He led me and induced me by his cunning till we came   290
To Phoenicia, where his own home and possessions lay.
There I stayed with him till the completion of the year.
But when the months and the days had been filled out
Of the year coming round again, and the seasons came on,
He put me on a seafaring ship to Libya   295
On the false plan that I should bring cargo with him,
But so that he might sell me there and get an immense price.
Though suspicious, I followed him onto the ship, by constraint.
The ship ran under a fair, steadily blowing North Wind
On the main above Crete. Then Zeus planned their destruction.   300

And when we had left Crete, no other point
Of land appeared, but just the heaven and the sea.
Then the son of Cronos halted a dark blue cloud
Over the hollow ship, and the ocean darkened beneath it;
305 Zeus at that instant thundered and threw a bolt on the ship.
The whole ship quivered, struck by the bolt of Zeus,
And it was filled with brimstone. All fell from the ship.
The men like sea crows all about the black ship
Were borne in the waves. A god took away their return.
310 Though I had many pains in my heart, Zeus himself
Put the enormous mast of the dark blue-prowed ship
Into my hands so I might still escape from distress.
Embracing it, I was carried in the destructive winds.
I was carried nine days, and on the tenth black night
315 A great rolling wave brought me near the Thesprotians' land,
Where the hero Pheidon, king of the Thesprotians,
Saved me without reward. His dear son came on me,
Overcome by cold and fatigue, and led me to his home,
Taking me by the hand till we reached his father's halls.
320 He clothed me about in garments, a mantle and tunic.
There I heard of Odysseus. That man said he had entertained
And befriended him as he was going to his fatherland.
And he showed me all the possessions Odysseus had gathered
Of bronze and of gold and of heavily wrought iron.
325 They would support each man in turn to the tenth generation,
So many were the treasures that lay in the lord's halls.
He said the man had gone to Dodona [2] in order to hear
The plan of Zeus from the lofty-leaved oak of the god
As to how he might return to the rich land of Ithaca,
330 Openly or in secret, as already he had been long away.
He swore to me personally, pouring libation in his house,
That a ship had been drawn down and companions were
    ready
Who would conduct him to his beloved fatherland.
But he sent me off first. For a ship happened to come
335 Of Thesprotians headed for Dulichion, rich in wheat.
And thither he bade them to convey me attentively
To King Akastos. But an evil plan for me pleased their minds.
That I should still come wholly to the woe of grief.
And when the seafaring ship had sailed a great way from land,

2. A shrine of Zeus.

At once they were contriving my day of slavery.   340
They took off my tunic, my mantle, and my clothes
And put another evil rag and tunic around me,
The torn one that you see yourself before your eyes.
At evening they reached the tilled fields of sunny Ithaca,
And there they tied me up on the well-timbered ship,   345
Tightly with a well-twisted cord. They themselves
Went off hastily to the strand of the sea and took dinner.
But the gods themselves bent the bonds back for me
Easily. I covered my head over with the rags,
Went down the smooth loading plank, and slid to my breast   350
Into the sea. Then I stroked through it with both hands,
Swimming. Very quickly I got out and away from them.
Then I came up where there was a copse of much-flowering
   wood
And lay crouched down. They were groaning greatly
As they wandered around. But it did not seem any good to
   them   355
To search further, and so they went back again
On board the hollow ship. And the gods themselves concealed
   me
Easily. They led me and brought me to the homestead
Of a man with knowledge. For it is still my fortune to live."
And you addressed him in answer, swineherd Eumaeos: 360
"Ah, wretched stranger, you have stirred my heart very much
As you tell the details of how you suffered and wandered.
But this I think is not in order, nor will you convince me
When you speak about Odysseus. Why does a man like you
   need
To lie fruitlessly? Well do I myself also know   365
Of my master's return, that he has been very much hated
By all the gods, as they did not subdue him among the Trojans
Or in the arms of his friends, after he had wound up the war.
Then all the Achaians would have made him a funeral mound,
And he would have won great glory for his son, too, hereafter.   370
As it is, the storm winds have snatched him off without glory.
But I myself live apart among the swine. Nor do I
Go to the city unless prudent Penelope happens
To urge me to come when a message comes from somewhere,
But then the men sit there and ask for the details,   375
Both those who grieve for the master who is gone so long

And those who enjoy devouring a livelihood scot free.
But for myself, I do not like to ask or inquire
Since the time an Aetolian cheated me with a story—
380 One who had killed a man and wandered far on the earth.
He came to my home and I embraced him in friendship.
He said he saw him among the Cretans with Idomeneus
Repairing his ships that storms had broken to pieces.
And he said he would come toward summer or harvest time
385 Bringing many possessions, with his godlike companions.
And you, much-grieved old man, since some god led you to me,
Do not blandish me or charm me at all with lies,
As I shall not respect and befriend you for that, but in fear
Of Zeus, the god of strangers, and pity for your person."
390 Odysseus of many wiles addressed him in answer:
"Surely you have an unbelieving spirit in your breast,
When I do not bring a man like you round by oath, or
　　　persuade you.
But come, let us make an agreement. Let the gods
Who hold Olympos be henceforth witnesses for both.
395 If your master does return to this very home,
You will dress me in clothes a mantle and a tunic and send me
On a trip to Dulichion, where I would like in my heart to be.
But if your master does not come as I say he will,
You may urge the servants to throw me from a great rock,
400 So any other beggar may shrink from deceiving."
The godly swineherd spoke out to him in answer:
"Stranger, there would surely be much honor and excellence
For me among men both at present and in after time
If when I led you to the hut and gave you a guest's gifts
405 I then should kill you and take your dear life away!
Then I might zealously pray to Zeus, son of Cronos!
But now is the time for dinner. May my companions soon
Be here inside, so we may make a tasty dinner in the hut."
In this way they addressed such words to one another.
Then did the swine approach, and the men who were
410　　swineherds.
The men shut them up in their sties to go to sleep,
And an immense clamor arose from the pigs that were
　　　penned up.
Then the godly swineherd called to his companions:
"Bring the best swine, so I may slaughter it for the stranger

From far away. And we too may enjoy it, who have long   415
Had sorrow as we labored for the swine with shining tusks,
And other men do devour our hard work scot free."
When he had said this, he split wood with the pitiless bronze,
And they led in a very fat pig five years of age.
Then they stood it by the hearth, nor did the swineherd   420
Forget the immortals, for he had good understanding.
He began by cutting the hairs of the head off the shining-tusked
    boar,
Threw them into the fire, and prayed to all the gods
That many-minded Odysseus return to his own home.
He stood up and hit it with a chunk left from the oak he had
    split,   425
And the life left it. They cut its throat and singed it.
At once they divided it; the swineherd took a first part
From all the limbs and laid the raw pieces on the rich fat.
And he threw some in the fire, sprinkling on barley meal.
The rest of it they cut up small and pierced it on spits,   430
Roasted it carefully, and pulled it all off.
They put it in a mass on platters, and the swineherd
Stood up to carve it. He understood what was right.
Dividing it, he apportioned it all in seven parts.
One he gave with a prayer to the nymphs and to Hermes,   435
The son of Maia, and the others he distributed to each.
To Odysseus he did honor with the whole long back
Of the shining-tusked swine, and pleased his master's heart.
Odysseus of many wiles spoke out and addressed him:
"Eumaeos, would you might be as dear to Father Zeus   440
As you are to me, that you honor a man like me with good
    things!"
And you addressed him in answer, swineherd Eumaeos:
"Eat, marvelous stranger, and enjoy these things
That are here. A god gives one thing and lets another go
As he wishes in his heart. For he can do all things."   445
So he said, and offered the first parts to the ever-living gods.
He poured sparkling wine, put the cup in the hands of
    Odysseus,
The sacker of cities, and sat down with his own share.
Mesaulios passed bread to them, a man that the swineherd
Had got by himself alone while his master was gone,   450
Secretly from his mistress and the old man Laertes;

He bought him from the Taphians with his own resources.
They stretched forth their hands to the food that was spread
   out ready,
But when they had eaten their fill of food and drink
455 Mesaulios took the bread off, and they hurried
Away for sleep, satiated with bread and meat.
A bad night came on, dark of a moon. Zeus rained
All night, and a great watery West Wind steadily blew.
Odysseus spoke to them, testing the swineherd out,
460 If he would take off his mantle and give it to him, or urge
Another of his companions to, since he cared much for him.
"Listen now, Eumaeos, and all you other companions,
I have a boast, and will tell a story, for crazing wine
Bids it, that sets even a man of many thoughts on
465 To sing and to laugh gently, and it drives him to dance,
And he brings out a story that would be better untold.
But since I was the first to speak up, I shall not hide it:
Would that I were in my prime and my strength were steadfast
As when we prepared and led our ambush up under Troy!
470 Odysseus led, and Menelaos, son of Atreus.
I was third leader among them. They ordered it themselves.
But when we arrived before the city and the sheer wall,
We lay around the town in the thick brushwood
Among the reeds and the marsh, crouching under our armor,
475 And as the North Wind fell off, a bad night came,
A freezing one. And snow came from above like hoar frost,
Cold, and ice clustered all around on our shields.
Then the other men all had mantles and tunics.
They slept securely, covering their shoulders with their shields.
480 But I, when I went, left my mantle with my companions,
Foolishly, since I thought I would not freeze in any case.
I went along with only my shield and a shining apron.
When it was the third part of night and the stars had gone past,
I shouted out then to Odysseus, who was near at hand,
485 Nudging him with my elbow. He hearkened quickly:
'Zeus-born son of Laertes, Odysseus of many devices,
I shall not be long among the living, but the cold
Overcomes me. I have no mantle. Some god tricked me
To have just one tunic. And there is no way out any longer.'
490 So I said. And then he had this purpose in his heart,
Such a man was he for deliberation and fighting.

Speaking in a little voice, he addressed a speech to me:
'Silence now, lest someone else of the Achaians hear you.'
And he held his head on his elbow and said his speech:
'Listen, friends, a godly dream came to me in my sleep.   495
We have come too far from the ships. Would there were
    someone
To go tell Agamemnon, son of Atreus, shepherd of the people,
That he might urge on more of the men from beside the
    ships.'
So he said. Then Thoas rose up, son of Andraemon,
Hastily. And he took his purple mantle off   500
And ran off to the ships. In that man's clothing I
Lay gladly. Then Dawn of the golden throne appeared.
So would I were now in my prime and my strength steadfast!
Then might someone in the swineherds' lodge give me a
    mantle,
For two reasons: friendship and respect for a good man.   505
Now men dishonor me for the bad clothes I wear on my skin."
Then you addressed him in answer, swineherd Eumaeos:
"Old man, the story is excellent that you have told.
And no profitless word did you speak improperly.
So you shall not want for clothes or for anything else,   510
Of the things that befit a long suffering suppliant one meets—
For now. But at dawn you shall bundle your own rags on,
As there are not many mantles and changes of tunic
To put on here, just a single one for each mortal man.
But when the beloved son of Odysseus comes,   515
He himself will give you clothes, a mantle and tunic,
And will send you wherever your heart and spirit bid."
When he had said this, he rose up and made a bed for him
Near the fire. And on it he threw skins of sheep and goats.
There Odysseus lay down. He threw on him a mantle   520
Great and thick, which lay beside him as a change
To put on when any terrible storm arose.
So Odysseus slept. And beside him those young men
Were sleeping. But to lie there was not pleasing
To the swineherd, to be sleeping apart from the swine.   525
He went out to go and get ready. Odysseus was pleased
That the man took care of his livelihood when he was away.
First the man threw a sharp sword around his stout shoulders
And put on a very thick mantle that warded off wind.

530 Then he put on the fleece from a great well-nourished goat.
He grasped a sharp javelin, a defense against dogs and men,
And he went on to lie down where the shining-tusked swine
  slept
Beneath a hollow rock under shelter from the North Wind.

XV

Pallas Athene had gone to Lacedemon of the broad dancing-
   place
To remind the illustrious son of great-hearted Odysseus
About his return and to urge him to go back.
She found Telemachos and the noble son of Nestor
Lying in the forecourt of glorious Menelaos.   5
The son of Nestor was overcome with soft sleep,
But sweet sleep did not hold Telemachos. In his heart
Concern for his father kept him awake through the ambrosial
   night.
Bright-eyed Athene stood close to him and addressed him:
"Telemachos, it is no longer good to wander far from home,   10
And leave behind in your home the possessions and the men,
Presumptuous as they are, lest they divide and devour
All your possessions and you have gone on a fruitless journey.
But right away urge Menelaos who is good at the war cry,
To send you on, so you may still find your blameless mother
   at home.   15
For already her father and her kinsmen are calling on her
To marry Eurymachos. He outdoes all the other
Suitors with presents and greatly augments the bridal gifts.
Let her bear no goods from your home against your will.
You know what sort of heart there is in a woman's breast.   20
She wishes to increase the house of the man she weds;
She no longer remembers or inquires of her former
Children or of her dear wedded husband who is dead.
But you should go yourself, and turn each piece of property
Over to whichever of the maids appears best to you,   25
Till the gods reveal to you an illustrious wife.
I will say something else to you; store it in your mind.
The best of the suitors lie ready in ambush against you
In the strait between Ithaca and the rugged Samê,
Wanting to kill you before you reach your fatherland.   30

But I do not think that will be: sooner shall the earth contain
Some one of the suitors who devour your livelihood.
But keep your well-made ship far from the islands
And sail by night as well. Whoever of the immortals
35 Guards and protects you will sent a breeze behind you.
And when you arrive at the first shore of Ithaca
Send your ship on to the city, and all your companions,
But first of all go on up yourself to the swineherd
Who is guardian of your swine, and kindly disposed to you also.
40 Rest the night there. And send him on inside the city
To give the message to the prudent Penelope
That you are safe for her and have arrived from Pylos."
And when she had said this, she went off to tall Olympos.
Then he woke the son of Nestor out of his sweet sleep,
45 Nudging him with his foot, and addressed a speech to him:
"Wake, Peisistratos, son of Nestor! Lead the single-hooved
    horses,
And harness them to the chariot, so we may hurry away."
Then Peisistratos, son of Nestor, replied to him:
"Telemachos, though we press on our way, we cannot
50 Drive through the dusky night. Soon it will be dawn,
But wait till the hero, son of Atreus, spear-famed Menelaos
Has brought the gifts and put them on the chariot
And has addressed us with gentle words and sent us off.
For a guest remembers all of his days the man
55 Who has received him as a guest and shown friendliness."
So he said, and at once Dawn of the golden throne came.
Menelaos, good at the war cry, came up close to them
When he had got out of bed from beside the fair-haired Helen.
And when the beloved son of Odysseus noticed him,
60 The hero hurried and put the glistening tunic on
Over his skin and threw a great mantle on his stout shoulders.
Telemachos, beloved son of godly Odysseus,
Went outside, stood beside him, and addressed him:
"Zeus-nourished Menelaos, son of Atreus, chief of the people,
65 Send me off right away to my dear fatherland,
For already my heart is longing to return home."
Then Menelaos, good at the war cry, answered him:
"Telemachos, I shall not hold you back here a long time,
Wanting to return as you do. I would resent another
70 Who, receiving a guest, acted excessively friendly

Or excessively hostile. All things are better when in measure.
It is equally bad when a man urges a guest to go off
Unwillingly, and when he holds back one who strains to go.
One must welcome a guest who stays, send one off who wishes.
Well, wait till I have brought the lovely gifts and put them   75
On the chariot, till your eyes behold them, and I tell the
    women
To make dinner in the halls out of the abundance inside.
It is glory, splendor, and refreshment all together
For men, after dining, to go far on the unbounded earth.
If you would like to wind through Hellas and middle Argos,   80
So that I should go with you, I will yoke up horses for you;
And lead you to the cities of men. No one will send us off
The way we are, but will give us some one gift at least to carry,
Some sort of cauldron of good bronze or a basin
Or a pair of mules or a golden libation cup."   85
Sound-minded Telemachos addressed him in answer:
"Zeus-nourished Menelaos, son of Atreus, chief of the people,
I would rather go right now to our home. For I did not
Leave a guard behind for my possessions when I went.
I fear I may perish myself in seeking my godlike father   90
Or have some noble treasure perish from my halls."
And when Menelaos, good at the war cry, heard him
He at once called to his wife and his serving women
To make dinner in the halls out of the abundance inside.
Eteoneus, son of Boethoüs, came up close to him   95
When he got out of bed, as the man did not live far from him.
Menelaos, good at the war cry, told him to kindle a fire
And to roast some meat. The other heard and did not disobey.
And he himself went off to his fragrant chamber,
Not alone, but Helen went with him, and Megapenthes.   100
And when they had reached the place where the treasures lay,
The son of Atreus took out a two-handled cup
And ordered his son Megapenthes to carry a mixing bowl
Of silver. And Helen took her stand alongside the coffers,
Where there were all the embroidered robes she had made
    herself.   105
Helen, godlike among women, picked one up and brought it,
The one that was largest and loveliest in embroidery.
It shone like a star; it lay beneath all the rest.
They went on further through the house till they reached

₁₁₀ Telemachos. And blond Menelaos addressed him:
"Telemachos, may Zeus, Hera's loud-thundering husband,
Fulfill for you the return you desire in your mind.
And of the gifts that lie stored as keepsakes in my house
I will give you the one that is loveliest and of highest worth.
₁₁₅ I shall give you a well-fashioned mixing bowl. It is all
Of silver, and its rim is finished round with gold,
The work of Hephaistos; the hero Phaidimos gave it,
King of the Sidonians, when his house took me in
As I had returned that far. I would like to give it to you."
₁₂₀ When he had said this, the hero, son of Atreus, put
The two-handled cup in his hands, and stout Megapenthes
Carried the shining mixing bowl out and set it before him,
The silver one. Helen of the fair cheeks stood alongside
With the robe in her hands; she said her speech right out:
₁₂₅ "'I, too, give you a gift, dear child, this remembrance
From the hands of Helen for your own wife to wear at the
　　　time
Of your lovely marriage. And until then, let it lie
In the hall with your dear mother. And may you come, I pray,
Rejoicing to your well-built home and your fatherland."
When she had said this, she put it in his hands. He took it and
₁₃₀ 　rejoiced.
The hero Peisistratos took the things and put them
In the wagon box, and he marveled in his heart at them all.
Blond-headed Menelaos led them to his house.
And they took their places in seats and in armchairs.
₁₃₅ A handmaid poured water from a pitcher she was carrying,
A lovely golden one, over into a silver basin,
For washing the hands; she set up a polished table alongside.
A respected housekeeper served bread she was carrying,
Laying out many dishes, gracious with the provisions.
Near her, the son of Boethoüs carved meat and served it in
₁₄₀ 　portions,
And the son of glorious Menelaos poured the wine.
They stretched forth their hands to the food that was laid out
　　　ready
But when they had taken their fill of food and drink,
Then Telemachos and the glorious son of Nestor
₁₄₅ Hitched the horses up, mounted the inlaid chariot,
And drove out of the forecourt and resounding portico.

With them went blond Menelaos, the son of Atreus,
Holding in his right hand the mind-honeying wine
In a gold cup, so both might pour libation and go.
He stood before the horses and spoke with a pledging gesture: 150
"Farewell, young men. And to Nestor, shepherd of the people,
Give greetings. To me he was always mild as a father
While we sons of the Achaians waged war in Troy."
Then sound-minded Telemachos answered him:
"All this that you say, you who are nourished by Zeus,   155
We shall certainly tell that man when we arrive.
Would that thus, returning to Ithaca and finding
Odysseus at home, I might tell him how I come from you
As one who got all your friendship and also bear many noble
    treasures."
A bird flew to the right of him, as he was speaking,   160
An eagle bearing a huge, bright goose in his claws,
A tame one from the courtyard. The men and the women
Followed them shrieking. He came up close to them
And rushed off to the right before the horses. When they saw it,
They rejoiced, and the spirit was warmed in all their minds.   165
Peisistratos, son of Nestor, began speaking to them:
"Consider, Zeus-nourished Menelaos, chief of the people,
Whether a god has shown this portent to the two of us or to
    you."
So he said, and Menelaos, dear to Ares, pondered
So that he might give a proper judgment when he had thought.   170
Helen of the long gown began speaking before he could:
"Listen to me, and I shall prophesy the way the immortals
Have put it in my heart, and how I think it will end.
Just as this bird seized the goose reared in our home
When he came from the mountain where his descent and his
    birth are,   175
So Odysseus who has suffered many ills and wandered much
Will return homeward and do vengeance. Or else already
He is at home and breeds evil for all the suitors."
Then sound-minded Telemachos answered her:
"May Zeus, Hera's thundering husband, make it so.   180
And then, even there, I should pray to you as to a god."
He spoke and lashed the whip at the two horses. They swiftly
Rushed to the plain, pressing on through the city.
All day they shook the yoke, holding it up on either side.

185 The sun went down and all the ways were shadowed.
    They arrived at Pherai to the home of Diocles,
    Son of Ortilochos, whom Alpheus sired as his son.
    There they rested at night, and he gave them the gifts of a guest.
    And when the early-born, rosy-fingered dawn appeared,
190 They yoked up the horses and mounted the inlaid chariot
    And drove out of the forecourt and resounding portico.
    He whipped them to go, and both flew on, not unwilling.
    Soon thereupon they reached the sheer citadel of Pylos.
    Then Telemachos addressed the son of Nestor:
195 "Son of Nestor, will you promise me, if you can, to carry out
    What I ask? We declare we are guest friends in unbroken line
    Through our fathers' friendship. And we are the same age.
    This trip will bring us to greater congeniality.
    You who are nourished by Zeus, do not carry me on past the
        ship,
200 But leave me there, lest the old man keep me unwilling
    In his house, wanting to befriend me. I must arrive quicker."
    So he said, and the son of Nestor deliberated in his heart
    How he might promise him this and duly carry it out.
    And thus it seemed to him to be best as he thought about it.
205 He turned the horses to the swift ship and the strand of the sea
    And unloaded the beautiful gifts on the ship's stern,
    The clothing and the gold Menelaos had given him.
    Then urging him on, he uttered wingèd words:
    "Board quickly now and call all your companions,
210 Before I reach home and announce it to the old man.
    For this I know well in my mind and in my heart,
    How overbearing his heart is. He will not let you go,
    But he would come here to invite you himself. I think
    He would not go back empty handed, but still would be very
        angry."
215 When he had said this, he drove the fair-maned horses back
    To the town of Pylos and rapidly reached his home.
    But Telemachos urged his companions on and called them:
    "Put the gear in order, my companions, on the black ship,
    And let us get on board ourselves, so we may press on the
        journey."
220 So he said, and they listened to him and obeyed him.
    At once they got on board and took their seats at the oarlocks.
    So he busied himself, prayed, and sacrificed to Athene

At the stern of the ship. And a man came up close to him,
An alien who had killed a man and was fleeing from Argos,
A seer. He was descended from the race of Melampos   225
Who dwelt once long ago in Pylos, the mother of sheep,
A rich man who dwelt among the Pylians in a very large house.
But then he reached the country of others, fleeing from his
     fatherland
And from great-hearted Neleus, noblest man of the living,
Who held as many goods by force, till the completion   230
Of the year. The first one, meanwhile, in the halls of Phylacos
Was bound in a harsh bond, having suffered strong pains
For the daughter of Neleus and for the deep madness
That Fury, the hard-smiting goddess, had put in his mind.
Still, he fled from fate and he drove the lowing cattle   235
To Pylos from Phylace. He paid the godlike Neleus
With a wretched deed and brought the woman for his brother
To the halls. And then he went to the land of other men,
To horse-nourishing Argos. There it was fated for him
To dwell while ruling over many of the Argives.   240
Then he married a wife and set up a high-roofed house,
And had Antiphates and Mantios, mighty sons.
Antiphates fathered great-spirited Oikles;
Oikles had Amphiaraos, rouser of the people,
Whom aegis-bearing Zeus loved in his heart and Apollo   245
Loved with all affection. Still, he did not reach the threshold of
     age,
But perished in Thebes on account of gifts to a woman.
The sons born to him were Alcmaeon and Amphilochos.
And Mantios fathered Polypheides and Kleitos,
But Dawn of the golden throne seized Kleitos away   250
On account of his beauty, that he might be with the immortals,
And Apollo made high-spirited Polypheides a prophet,
By far the best of mortals, after Amphiaraos died.
He migrated to Hyperesia in anger at his father,
Where he dwelt and prophesied to all mortal men.   255
This man's son came up, whose name was Theoclymenos,
And stood close to Telemachos. He found him
Pouring a libation and praying by the swift black ship,
And speaking out to him, he uttered wingèd words:
"My friend, since I find you sacrificing in this place   260
I pray you by the burnt offerings, by the god, and then

By your own head and by the companions who follow you,
To tell me unerringly what I ask; do not hide it.
What men are you from? Where are your city and parents?"
265 Then sound-minded Telemachos answered him:
"Indeed I shall speak to you, friend, quite truthfully.
My descent is from Ithaca, my father is Odysseus,
If he ever was. He has already died by a woeful death.
So now I have taken companions and a black ship
270 And come to find out about my father who is gone so long."
And then the godly Theoclymenos spoke to him:
"I have gone from my fatherland too, having killed a man
Of my tribe. He has many kinsmen and relatives
In horse-nourishing Argos; they rule the Achaians mightily.
275 Escaping from them, I flee death and black fate,
Since it is now my lot to wander among men.
Do put me on your ship, since as a fugitive I beseech you,
So they may not kill me. I believe I am pursued."
Then sound-minded Telemachos answered him:
"Since you wish to be on the balanced ship, I shall not push you
280 off.
Come, you shall be befriended there, with what we have."
When he had said this, he took his bronze spear from him
And put it along on the deck of the bobbing ship.
And the man himself got on board the seafaring ship.
285 Then he sat him down on the stern and at his side he sat
Theoclymenos. And they loosed the stern cables.
Telemachos called to his companions and urged them
To take hold of the gear. And they hastily obeyed.
They stood a fir-wood mast in the hollow mast block;
290 They raised it up, and with forestays they made it fast.
Then they hauled up the white sails with well-plaited oxhide
ropes.
Bright-eyed Athene sent on a driving breeze for them,
Rushing rapidly through the air so the ship might soon
Arrive as it ran over the salt water of the sea.
295 They went past the Springs and the fair-flowing Chalcis.
The sun went down and all the ways were shadowed.
She came close to Pheai drawn on by the breeze of Zeus,
And passed godly Elis, where the Epeians rule.
And then he drove it on forward to the Sharp Islands,
300 Wondering whether he should flee death or be taken.

Meanwhile, both Odysseus and the godly swineherd
Were dining in the hut. The other men dined with them.
But when they had taken their fill of food and drink
Odysseus addressed them, trying the swineherd out,
Whether he would still kindly befriend him and ask him to stay 305
There in the fold, or would urge him on to the city:
"Listen now, Eumaeos, and all you other companions,
I am longing to go off to the town at dawn
To beg, so I may not wear down you and your companions.
But advise me well and send a good guide along with me   315
Who may lead me there. I myself from necessity
Shall stray to the city to try to get a cup and a loaf.
And when I come to the dwelling of godly Odysseus,
I would like to give a message to prudent Penelope
And mingle with the presumptuous suitors, to see   315
If they who have countless dishes give me a dinner.
Right away in their midst I could do whatever service they
    wished.
I shall speak out to you; put it in your mind and hear me:
Through the favor of the runner Hermes, who provides
Grace and glory for the actions of all men,   320
No other mortal could ever rival my service
At kindling a fire and splitting up dry wood,
At carving and roasting and pouring out wine,
The sort of service humble men do for noble ones."
Greatly disturbed, you spoke to him, swineheard Eumaeos: 325
"Alas, stranger, what is this thought that has come about
In your mind? You must surely long to die on the spot
If you wish to enter the company of the suitors,
Whose presumption and might reaches iron heaven.
Not men of your sort are the servants under them,   330
But young men, clothed well in mantles and in tunics,
Perpetually sleek on their heads and fair of face,
The ones who serve them. And their well-polished tables
Are loaded down with bread and with meats and with wine.
But stay, no one is troubled at your being here,   335
Not I or any other of the companions who are with me.
But when the beloved son of Odysseus comes,
He will clothe you in garments, a mantle and a tunic,
And he will send you wherever your heart and spirit bid."
Then godlike Odysseus, who had suffered much, answered him: 340

"Eumaeos, would that you might be as dear to father Zeus
As to me, that you stop me from straying and from dire woe.
There is nothing worse for mortal man than wandering.
But for the cursed belly's sake men have evil cares,
345 Anyone that straying and trouble and pain come upon—.
Now, since you hold me back and bid me, as I am, to stay,
Come, tell me about the mother of godly Odysseus,
And the father whom he left on the threshold of old age when
    he went.
Are they perchance still living under the rays of the sun,
350 Or are they already dead and in the halls of Hades?"
Then the swineherd addressed him, a chief of the men:
"All right, stranger, I shall tell you that quite truthfully:
Laertes is still alive; he forever prays to Zeus
That the spirit may waste from his limbs in his own halls.
355 He mourns terribly for his son who is gone away
And for his wise wedded wife who, when she perished,
Brought the greatest grief on him and put him in raw old age.
She did perish for grief over her renowned son
By a miserable death, and may no one who dwells here die
360 That way who is kind to me and acts in a kindly way.
And so as long as that woman lived, even though she grieved,
I always liked to ask and inquire about her,
Because she brought me up along with long-gowned Ktimene,
Her goodly daughter, whom she bore youngest of her children.
365 I was reared along with her; she honored me little less.
But when both of us arrived at youth that is full of love,
They married her off in Samê, and they took countless gifts,
But me she clothed in a mantle and a tunic, clothes
That were very lovely, gave me sandals for my feet
And sent me off to the fields. But she loved me much in her
370   heart.
As it is, I am now deprived of these things. Yet for me
The blessed gods foster the work at which I abide.
From them have I eaten and drunk and given to respected men.
And of the mistress there is nothing pleasant to be heard,
375 Neither word nor deed, since an evil has fallen on the house,
These presumptuous men. The servants greatly miss
Speaking in their mistress' presence and hearing tidbits,
And eating and drinking, and then carrying something off
To the fields, the things that always warm servants' hearts."

Odysseus of many wiles addressed him in answer: 380
"Well, swineherd Eumaeos, what a little one you were
When you wandered far from your parents and your fatherland!
But come, tell me this, and speak quite truthfully:
Was the broad-streeted city of that people destroyed
In which your father and your queenly mother were dwelling,   385
Or while you were alone with cattle or with sheep
Did hostile men take you in ships and bring you for sale
To the home of this man, and he gave a worthy price?"
Then the swineherd addressed him, the chief of the men:
"Stranger, since you ask me and inquire of these matters,   390
Listen in silence now, and take pleasure; drink wine
While you are sitting. These nights are immense. One can sleep
And one can listen if he enjoys it. There is no need
To lie down before it is time. And much sleep is a weariness.
As for the others, let any man leave and go to sleep   395
By what the heart and the spirit bid, and when dawn appears
Let him eat and follow the swine that are the master's;
But let us two be in the hut drinking and dining,
And we shall take pleasure in one another's sad sorrows
As we recall them; for a man takes pleasure even in pains,   400
One who has suffered very much and wandered much.
And I will tell you this of which you ask and inquire.
There is a certain island called Syria, as you may have heard,
Above Ortygia where the turnings of the sun are.
It is not very populous, and yet it is good,   405
Rich in cattle and sheep, full of wine, with much grain.
Poverty never comes to the land, nor any other
Disease exists there that is sad for wretched mortals.
But when the tribes of men grow old in the city
Apollo of the silver bow comes with Artemis   410
And slays them by visiting them with his soothing shafts.
In that place are two cities. They are wholly divided asunder.
My father used to rule as the king over both of them,
Ktesios, son of Ormenos, who resembles the immortals.
There the Phoenicians came, men who are famous for ships,   415
Sharp dealers, who brought in a black ship countless trinkets.
There was a Phoenician woman in my father's house,
Lovely and tall and skilled at excellent tasks.
The very wily Phoenicians deceived her.

One lay with her first, as she was washing clothes by the hollow
420　ship,
In the bed and in affection which deceives the minds
Of womankind, even one who is good in what she does.
Then he asked her who she was and where she was from,
And she at once pointed out my father's high-roofed house.
425　'I declare I am from Sidon that is full of bronze,
And I am the daughter of Arybas, a man of overflowing wealth,
But Taphian men, pirates, snatched me away
As I was coming from the fields. They brought me here and
　　sold me
To the home of this man. And he gave a worthy price.'
430　Then the man who had secretly lain with her said to her:
'Well then, would you follow along with us back to your home,
So you may see the high-roofed house of your father and mother,
And themselves? For they still exist, and are called wealthy.'
Then the woman spoke to him and answered with a speech:
435　'This too, might come about, sailors, if you are willing
To pledge me an oath and take me back home safe and sound.'
So she said, and they all swore an oath as she asked.
But when they had sworn and had completed the oath,
The woman addressed them again and answered with a speech:
440　'Keep silence, now, and let none of your company
Speak out to me as he comes upon me in the street
Or at the well, perhaps; lest someone go to the house
And tell the old man, and when he learns he bind me
In a hard binding and devise destruction against you.
But keep my words in your mind; hurry your buying for the
445　journey,
And when the ship gets filled up with the goods of life,
Let one quickly come with a message for me to the house.
For I shall bring gold, too, whatever comes to my hand.
And I would willingly give other things, too, as fare,
450　For I am rearing the son of this nobleman in his halls.
Such a clever one he is, who runs along when I go outdoors.
I might bring him into the ship, and he would gain for you
A boundless price if you brought him to alien men.'
When she had said this, she went off to the lovely home.
455　They remained there with us for an entire year
And traded to get many goods in the hollow ship.
When the hollow ship was loaded for them to go,

They sent a messenger to give the woman word.
He came, a very shrewd man, to the home of my father
Bearing a gold chain strung round with amber beads.   460
The serving maids in the hall and my queenly mother
Felt it with their hands and looked at it with their eyes
And offered his price. He nodded to the woman in silence.
When he had nodded, he went off to the hollow ship.
She took me by the hand and led me from the house outdoors.   465
In the forecourt she found the cups and the tables
Of the men who attended on my father, banqueting.
They were gone to the session and assembly of the district.
At once she concealed three tankards under her bosom
And bore them off. I followed in my thoughtlessness.   470
The sun went down and all the ways were shadowed.
We went swiftly and arrived at the famous harbor
Where there was a swift-sailing ship of the Phoenician men.
They boarded it then and sailed on the watery ways,
When they had boarded us both. And Zeus sent on a breeze.   475
For six days we sailed alike by night and by day.
But when Zeus, the son of Cronos, added the seventh day,
Artemis, who pours forth arrows, struck the woman,
And she crashed as she fell in the hold like a tern of the sea,
And they threw her out to become the prey of seals   480
And fishes. But I was left grieving in my heart.
The wind and the water carried and brought them near Ithaca,
Where Laertes bought me with his resources.
In that way did I see this country with my eyes."
Then Zeus-born Odysseus answered him with a speech: 485
"Eumaeos, you have stirred the heart very much in my
    breast
As you tell the details of the pain you suffered in your heart.
But Zeus has provided good for you along with evil
When, having suffered much, you reached the home of a man
Who was mild, and who furnished you with food and drink   490
Kindly. And you live a good life. But as for me,
I reach here after wandering to many cities of men."
And so they told such stories to one another.
And the two of them did not sleep much time, but a little.
For soon the fair-throned Dawn came on. Telemachos'
    companions   495
At the mainland, slacked their sails, and took the mast down

Speedily, and pulled the ship to the mooring with the oars.
They threw out the anchor stones and tied the stern cables.
They themselves got out at the surf of the sea,
500 And they prepared a dinner and mixed sparkling wine.
But when they had taken their fill of food and drink,
Sound-minded Telemachos began speaking to them:
"You men, bring the black ship over now toward the town,
And I myself shall hurry to the fields and the herdsmen.
I shall go to the town at evening when I have seen my own
505   lands.
And at dawn I shall provide for you as the journey's pay
A good banquet of meat and of wine sweet to drink."
Then godlike Theoclymenos addressed him:
"But where shall I head, dear child? To what man's house
510 Shall I go, of those who rule over rocky Ithaca,
Or shall I go straight to your mother's house and yours?"
Then sound-minded Telemachos answered him:
"In another case I myself should advise you to go
To our house, for there is no lack of hospitality. Still,
515 It would be worse for you, since I am gone, and my mother
Will not see you. She does not appear often in the house
To the suitors, but apart from them weaves a web in her
    room.
But I shall tell you about another man you may go to:
Eurymachos, noble son of skillful Polybos,
520 Whom the Ithacans look upon as equal to a God.
He is far the most excellent man and is the most eager
To marry my mother and have the honor of Odysseus.
But in that, Olympian Zeus who dwells in the upper air, knows
If he will bring an evil day to pass for them before the marriage."
525 A bird flew to the right of him as he was speaking,
A hawk, swift messenger of Apollo. In his claws
He was plucking a dove he held and strewing its feathers on the
    ground
Between the ship and Telemachos himself.
Theoclymenos called him aside from their companions,
530 Took his hand, and spoke right out directly to him:
"Telemachos, not without a god did that bird fly to the right.
I knew when I saw it head on it was a bird of omen.
There is no other descent more royal than yours
In the land of Ithaca. You are the strongest always."

Then sound-minded Telemachos answered him: 535
"Would that this speech, stranger, might be fulfilled.
And then you would soon know friendship and many gifts
From me, so that someone who met you would call you
    blessed."
And then he shouted to Peiraeos, his trusty companion:
"Peiraeos, son of Klytos, in all else you hearken to me   540
Most of all the companions who followed me to Pylos.
And now bring this guest for me into your house.
Befriend him kindly and honor him until I come."
Then Peiraeos, renowned for his spear, answered him:
"Telemachos, even if you stay here for a long time   545
I will conduct this man, and he shall not lack hospitality."
When he had said this, he went on the ship and called his com-
    panions
To get on board themselves and untie the stern cables.
They got on board at once and took seats at the oars.
Telemachos bound the lovely sandals beneath his feet   550
And took a valiant spear pointed with sharp bronze
From the deck of the ship. They untied the stern cables
And pushed it off and sailed to the city, as Telemachos,
The beloved son of godly Odysseus, had commanded.
His feet bore him forward fast, as he strode, till he reached   555
The farmyard where the numberless swine were, beside which
    slept
The noble swineherd whose mind was mild to his masters.

Then both Odysseus and the godly swineherd in the hut
Were preparing breakfast at dawn when they had kindled a fire,
And had sent out shepherds along with the droves of swine.
The dogs, prone to bark, fawned around Telemachos
5 And did not bark as he approached. Godly Odysseus noticed
The fawning dogs, and the sound of footsteps carried to him.
Right away to Eumaeos he uttered wingèd words:
"Eumaeos, surely some companion is coming here
Or some other acquaintance, since the dogs do not bark
10 But fawn around him. And I hear the low noise of his feet."
The speech was not yet fully said when his dear son
Was standing in the doorway. The swineherd started, dumbstruck.
From his hands the bowls fell that he was tending to
As he mixed the sparkling wine. He went over to his master
15 And kissed him on the head and on both lovely eyes
And both of his hands. A swelling tear fell from him,
As a father receives lovingly the dear son he sees
Coming in the tenth year from a faraway land,
His precious only son, for whom he suffered many pains;
20 So then the godly swineherd embraced and kissed all over
The godlike Telemachos, as if he had escaped from death.
And while he was sobbing he uttered wingèd words:
"Telemachos, you have come as a sweet light. I myself thought
I would never see you again when you went by ship to Pylos.
25 But come in here now, dear child, so that in my heart
I may delight to see you here inside, come afresh from elsewhere.
You do not often visit the shepherds and the fields,
But remain in town. Indeed, it has pleased your heart
To look upon the destructive throng of the suitors."
30 Then sound-minded Telemachos answered him:
"So it shall be, father. I have come here on your account,

So that I may see you with my eyes and hear your story
As to whether my mother stays in the halls or already
Some other man has wed her and the bed of Odysseus
Lies with foul spider webs, perhaps, deprived of bedding.   35
Then the swineherd addressed him, the chief of the men:
"Yes, long now indeed does that woman in her enduring spirit
    wait
Within your halls. And the miserable nights
And the days always waste away for her as she sheds tears."
When he had said this, he took the bronze spear from him,   40
Then he himself went in and crossed the stone threshold.
His father Odysseus yielded him a seat as he entered.
But Telemachos, for his part, checked him and spoke out:
"Sit down, stranger. We will find a seat somewhere else
In our hut. Here is a man who will furnish one."   45
So he said. The other went and sat down. Then the swineherd
Spread yellow-green brushwood beneath and fleeces on top.
And there the beloved son of Odysseus took a seat.
The swineherd offered platters of meat slices to them,
Of the roast meat that they had left from eating before.   50
And in baskets he hastily heaped up bread,
And he mixed honey-sweet wine in a bowl of ivy wood.
He himself sat down facing the godly Odysseus.
Then they stretched forth their hands to the food that was laid
    out ready,
But when they had taken their fill of food and drink,   55
Telemachos spoke out to the godly swineherd:
"Father, where did this stranger come from? How did sailors
Bring him to Ithaca? What men did they claim to be?
For I do not think he could have arrived here at all on foot."
Then you addressed him in answer, swineherd Eumaeos: 60
"Well then, my child, I shall tell you all of the truth.
He declares he is of the race of those who live in broad Crete,
And he says he has been to many cities of mortals
In his wandering, for that was the way the god spun his thread.
And now, having escaped from a ship of the Thesprotians,   65
He has come to my hut, and I hand him over to you.
Do as you wish. He declares he is a suppliant to you."
Then the sound-minded Telemachos answered him:
"Eumaeos, this speech you have spoken is distressing.

70 How indeed shall I receive the stranger in my home?
   I myself am young and have not yet trusted my hands
   To defend me against some man when he outrages me first.
   As for my mother, the heart in her breast ponders two ways,
   Either that she remain here with me and attend to the house,
75 Respecting the bed of her husband and the talk of the people,
   Or that she already go at once with whichever of the Achaians
   Is the best man that woos her in the halls and offers the most.
   Yet, indeed, since this stranger has come to your house,
   I shall clothe him in a mantle and a tunic, lovely garments.
80 I shall give him a two-edged sword and sandals for his feet,
   And I shall send him wherever his heart and spirit bid.
   But if you wish to, care for him and keep him in your hut.
   I shall send the garments here myself and all the food
   To eat, so that he will not strain you and your companions.
85 I for my part should not allow him to come there
   Among the suitors, for they have too much reckless
       presumption,
   Lest they mock him, and that be a dread grief to me.
   It is difficult for a single man, even a mighty one,
   To succeed at all against many, since they are far stronger."
90 Then godly Odysseus, who had suffered much, answered him:
   "My friend, since surely it is proper for me to reply,
   My own heart is torn to pieces when I hear
   About the reckless deeds you say the suitors contrive
   In your halls, against the will of a man as good as yourself.
95 Tell me, are you willingly subjected or do the people
   Despise you in the district, yielding to the voice of a god?
   Or do you blame your kinsmen, those on whom a man
   Should rely for fighting, even if a great quarrel arises?
   Would that, with this heart of mine, I were as young as you,
100 Or the child of excellent Odysseus, or that the man himself
   Should come roaming; for there is still a share of hope.
   And may an alien mortal at once cut off my head
   If I did not become a curse to all of those men,
   As I come into the hall of Odysseus, son of Laertes.
105 And if they should beat me, a single man, by their numbers,
   I would rather be killed in my own halls and die
   Than perpetually to look upon these sorry deeds:
   Strangers being maltreated, and men disgracefully
   Dragging the servant women through the lovely halls,

And wine being drawn off, and men eating bread   110
Rashly this way, and limitlessly, acts without end."
Then sound-minded Telemachos answered him:
"Very well, stranger, I shall speak to you truthfully.
The whole district is not hostile or enraged against me,
Nor do I blame any kinsmen, those on whom a man   115
Should rely for fighting, even if a great quarrel arises;
For thus did the son of Cronos make ours a single line.
Arkesios sired Laertes, a single son,
And his father sired Odysseus alone; Odysseus sired me
Alone, and left me in the halls, and got from me no joy.   120
So now there are countless enemies in the house.
All the noblemen who rule over the islands,
Dulichion and Samê and wooded Zacynthos,
And all those who are masters in craggy Ithaca,
Are paying court to my mother and wearing down my home,   125
She neither refuses the hateful wedding nor can she
Make an end of it. But they are wasting my home away
As they devour it. Soon they will tear me to pieces myself.
Well, all these matters lie in the laps of the gods.
Go quickly, father, to constant Penelope.   130
Tell her I am safe and have arrived from Pylos.
I myself shall remain here, but you come back here
When you have told just her. Let no one else of the Achaians
Find out about it, for many devise evils against me."
And you addressed him in answer, swineherd Eumaeos: 135
"I know, I see; you say this to an understanding man.
But come, tell me this, and speak out truthfully,
Should I go or not by the same path to tell Laertes,
That wretched man, who, while he grieved much for Odysseus,
Used to oversee the fields, and with the servants in his house 140
Ate and drank when the heart in his breast bade him to.
But now from the time you were gone in the ship to Pylos,
They say he no longer eats and drinks the way he did,
Nor looks over the fields, but with groaning and wailing
He sits and laments, and the flesh shrinks round his bones."   145
Then sound-minded Telemachos answered him:
"That is the more painful. Still, let us leave him, though we are
    grieved,
For if all things were somehow free for mortals to choose,
We should first choose the day of my father's return.

150 But you, when you have told the news, come back and do not
Wander in the fields after that man. But tell my mother
To send the housekeeper on as soon as possible,
Secretly. And she may announce it to the old man."
He spoke, and roused the swineherd. He took sandals in hand,
155 Bound them under his feet, and went to the city; nor did
The swineherd Eumaeos escape Athene as he went from the
　　　lodge,
But she came up close. She likened her body to a woman's,
Lovely and tall and skilled in excellent tasks.
She stood and appeared to Odysseus at the hut doorway,
160 Nor did Telemachos see her face to face or perceive her.
For in no way do the gods appear clearly to all men.
But Odysseus and the dogs saw her. They did not bark;
They slunk with a whimpering to the other side of the lodge.
She signaled with her eyebrows. Godly Odysseus perceived it
165 And went out of the room along the great farmyard wall
And stood in her presence. Athene addressed him:
"Zeus-born son of Laertes, Odysseus of many devices,
Now is the time, say the word to your son, and do not conceal it
So you may both work death and destruction on the suitors,
170 And come to the renowned city together. Nor shall I
Myself be long from you, as I desire to fight."
Athene spoke and touched him with a golden wand.
At first she placed a cloak and a well-washed tunic
About his shoulders, increased his body and his youth.
175 His skin became dark again, and his cheeks filled out,
And the beard around his chin turned into dark blue.
When she had done this, she went back again, and Odysseus
Went into the hut. His dear son marveled at him.
He cast his eyes the other way, alarmed lest it be a god.
180 And he spoke out to him and uttered wingèd words:
"You appear other to me, stranger, than a moment before.
You have other garments, and your skin is not as it was.
You must be some one of the gods who possess broad heaven.
Well, be gracious, so we may give pleasing sacrifices
185 And well-made golden gifts to you. Be sparing toward us."
Then godly Odysseus, who had suffered much, answered him:
"I am not any god. Why liken me to immortals?
But I am your father for whose sake you are grieving
And suffer many pains, receiving the assaults of men."

When he had said this, he kissed his son and sent a tear to the
    ground   190
Off his cheeks. Before, he had always held them back without
    blenching.
Telemachos—he did not yet believe him to be his father—
Answered him right away with words and addressed him:
"You surely are not my father Odysseus, but some god
Enchants me, so that I may grieve and lament still more;   195
For in no way would a mortal man in his own mind
Devise these things, unless a god came by in person
Who might easily if he wished make one young or old.
Just recently you were an old man and had on sorry clothes.
And now you resemble the gods who possess broad heaven."   200
Odysseus of many wiles addressed him in answer:
"Telemachos, it is not seemly when your father is within
To wonder exceedingly and to be amazed.
No other Odysseus, indeed, shall ever come to you here.
I am the very man; suffering evils, wandering much,   205
I have come in the twentieth year to my fatherland.
And now this is the work of the forager Athene,
Who has made of me what she wishes, for she can do that,
Sometimes in the semblance of a beggar and sometimes
That of a young man who has lovely clothes on his skin.   210
It is easy for the gods who possess broad heaven
To glorify a mortal man or to disfigure him."
When he had said this he sat down. Telemachos
Embraced his noble father and moaned, shedding tears.
In both of them there arose a longing for lamentation.   215
They wailed piercingly and more incessantly than birds,
Sea eagles or falcons with hooked claws whose children
Farmers have snatched off before they were fully fledged.
So they lamented and shed tears from under their eyelids,
And the light of the sun would have gone down on their
    moaning   220
If Telemachos had not at once spoken out to his father:
"In what kind of a ship, dear father, did sailors
Bring you to Ithaca? Who did they claim to be?
For I do not believe you reached here at all on foot."
Then godly Odysseus, who had suffered much, addressed him: 225
"Well then, my child, to you I shall speak out the truth.
The Phaeacians, famous for ships, brought me, who escort

Other men too, whenever anyone reaches their people.
They brought me sleeping in a swift ship on the ocean,
230 Put me down at Ithaca, and gave me glorious gifts,
Bronze and gold in abundance and woven clothing;
These things now lie in caverns, by the will of the gods.
Now I have come here at Athene's instigations,
So we may plan about slaughter for our enemies.
235 Come now, speak out, and number the suitors for me,
So I may know how many men they are, and what sort.
Then as I deliberate in my own blameless heart
I may consider whether we can oppose them ourselves,
Alone without others, or shall seek for others."
240 Then sound-minded Telemachos spoke to him in answer:
"Father, I have always heard of your great renown
For being a skillful fighter with your hands and prudent in
    counsel.
But you speak of something enormous. Awe holds me. It could
    not
Be that two men might fight against so many stout men.
245 Truly, there are not ten of the suitors or twenty only,
But far more. You shall soon know their number here:
Out of Dulichion there are fifty-two
Chosen young men, and six servants to follow them.
Out of Samê there are four and twenty mortal men;
250 Out of Zacynthos there are twenty young men of the Achaians;
Out of Ithaca herself, twelve, all of the best;
And Medon is with them as herald, and the godly singer,
And a pair of servants who are skilled at carving the meat.
If we opposed all of those who are within, I fear
255 In bitterness and dread would you avenge their violence
Now that you have come. But if you can, think of some
    defender;
Take thought for someone well disposed to defend us."
Then godly Odysseus, who had suffered much, addressed him:
"I shall tell you, then, mark it well and listen to me,
260 And consider whether Athene with Father Zeus
Will protect us, or I shall think up some other defender."
Then sound-minded Telemachos answered him:
"These are excellent defenders of whom you speak,
Both seated high upon the clouds, and the two of them
265 Rule over all others, both men and the immortal gods."

Then godly Odysseus, who had suffered much, addressed him:
"Those two, indeed, shall not be for a long time far
From the mighty combat, when the strength of Ares
Is put to the proof in my halls between us and the suitors.
Well now, you go on home at the appearance of dawn   270
And mingle in with the presumptuous suitors,
And the swineherd will bring me later to the town
In the semblance of a beggar, miserable and old.
And if they dishonor me in the house, let the heart
In your own breast endure it that I suffer evilly.   275
Even if they drag me by the feet through the house out the
     doors
Or throw at me with darts, look on and restrain yourself.
No, just order them to cease their foolishness,
Speaking to them with soothing words. And they will surely
Give no heed at all, because for them the fated day stands at
     hand.   280
I shall tell you another thing, and keep it in mind.
When Athene of many plans puts it in my mind,
I shall nod to you with my head, and then you yourself take
     note
How many weapons of war are lying in the halls;
Pick them up and put them in a nook of the lofty chamber,   285
All of them. And appease the suitors deceptively
With soft speeches when they miss them and ask you questions:
'I have put them out of the smoke, since they no longer look
     like those
That Odysseus once left behind when he went to Troy,
But they are befouled, so much has the smoke of the fire got to
     them.   290
And the son of Cronos, too, has put this greater thought in my
     mind:
That, perhaps, drunk with wine, you may set up a quarrel
Among you, wound one another, and disgrace the banquet
And your wooing. For iron of itself draws a man on.'
And for us alone leave two swords and two spears   295
And a pair of oxhide shields to grasp with our hands
So we may rush upon them and capture them. And then
Pallas Athene will charm them, and the counselor Zeus.
I shall tell you something else, and keep it in mind,
If you are indeed truly my own and of our blood: 300

Let no one at this time hear Odysseus is within;
Let Laertes not know it, and not the swineherd,
No one of the servants, not Penelope herself.
Let you and me alone find out the bent of the women,
305 And we shall further try out certain of the menservants,
To see where one honors us and respects us in his heart,
And who does not heed you and dishonors the man you are."
His illustrious son spoke out to him in answer:
"Father, you shall know my disposition, I think,
310 And soon, for no slackness of mind holds me at all.
But I for my part think this will not be an advantage
To the two of us. I ask you to consider it;
A long time in vain would you go and test each person
By visiting the fields. And they in our halls unharmed
315 Devour goods insolently; there is no restraint.
And I ask you to find out for yourself the women
Who dishonor you, and those who are innocent.
As for the men, I myself would not want us to go
To their lodgings to test them; but attend to these matters
     later
320 If you truly know some portent from aegis-bearing Zeus."
And so such things did they say to one another.
Then the well-made ship was brought up to Ithaca
That had borne Telemachos and all his companions from Pylos.
When they had arrived within the very deep harbor
325 They drew the black ship up upon the land themselves
While proud-spirited servants carried their gear off.
At once they brought beautiful gifts to Klytios' house,
And they sent on a herald to the home of Odysseus
With a message to tell the prudent Penelope
330 That Telemachos was in the fields and had ordered the ship
To sail off to the town, so that the goodly queen
Might not fear in her heart and shed a tender tear.
The herald and the godly swineherd met each other
On account of the very same message they were to tell the
     woman,
335 And when they reached the home of the divine queen
The herald spoke out in the midst of the serving maids:
"Your beloved son, my queen, has already come."
And the swineherd, standing near Penelope,
Told her all her beloved son bade him to say.

And when he had told her all he was to deliver,   340
He went on his way to the swine and left the enclosures and the
    hall.
The suitors were grieving and depressed in their hearts;
They went out of the hall along the great wall of the courtyard
And they sat down there out in front of the portals.
Eurymachos, son of Polybos, began speaking to them: 345
"Friends, a great task is arrogantly achieved
By Telemachos, this voyage. We thought he would not achieve
    it.
Come now, let us drag down a black ship, the one that is best,
And gather seamen as rowers, so they may quickly
Give a message to those men to go swiftly home."   350
He had not said all, when Amphinomos saw the ship,
As he turned in his place, inside the very deep harbor;
And men lowering the sails and holding oars in their hands.
He gave a sweet laugh and said to his companions:
"Never mind sending a message now. Here they are inside;   355
Either some god told them this, or else they themselves
Saw the ship coming in that they were not able to catch it."
So he said, and they stood up and went to the strand of the sea.
They dragged the black ship up at once on the dry land
And proud-spirited servants carried the gear off for them.   360
They themselves went off to the assembly together. Nor did
    they
Allow anyone else to sit with them, of young men or old.
Antinoos spoke to them, son of Eupeithes:
"Well now, the gods have delivered this man from harm!
Lookouts were sitting day by day on the windy heights,   365
In quick succession always, and at the setting sun
We never rested a night on land, but on the ocean,
Sailing in the swift ship we awaited godly dawn,
In ambush for Telemachos that we might capture him
And kill him. And meanwhile some god has brought him home. 370
But let us here think of a woeful destruction
For Telemachos, and let him not escape us. I think
These deeds will not be accomplished while he is alive.
He himself is skilled in deliberation and thought,
But the people no longer wholly bear favor toward us.   375
Well, come now, before he convenes the Achaians
Into assembly—for I think he will not let anything go,

But will be angry. He will stand up among all and tell
How we contrived sheer murder for him and did not catch him.
380 And they will not approve when they hear of the evil deeds.
I fear they will do some evil and drive us out
Of our own land, and we shall reach the country of others.
Let us forestall him and take him in fields far from the city
Or on the path. We should then have his living and property
385 To divide duly among us, and then we might give
The house for his mother and for the one who weds her to
    have.
But if this speech displeases you, and you wish
The man to live and have all his paternal goods,
Let us not then gather here and devour his goods
390 In their pleasing abundance, but let each from his own hall
Woo her and seek her with gifts. And she then may wed
Whoever gives the most and comes as the destined man."
So he said, and they all became hushed in silence.
Amphinomos then spoke out to them and addressed them,
395 The illustrious son of King Nisos, son of Aretias,
Who out of Dulichion, grassy and rich in grain,
Was leader of the suitors and pleased Penelope
The most with his speeches, for he practiced good sense.
With favorable intent he spoke out and addressed them:
400 "My friends, I would not myself at all want to kill
Telemachos. Dreadful it is to kill the race
Of kings. But let us first ask the gods for advice
If the decrees of great Zeus do agree with this,
I shall kill him myself and order all others to do so,
405 But if the gods turn aside, I give the order to cease."
So Amphinomos said, and his speech was pleasing to them.
They got up then at once and went to the home of Odysseus,
And when they got there, they took their seats in polished
    armchairs.
But the prudent Penelope had another thought:
410 To appear to the suitors with their presumptuous pride;
For she had heard death was to be in the halls for her son.
The herald Medon, who found out their plans, had told her.
She went on into the hall along with her serving women.
And when the godly woman arrived before the suitors,
415 She stood beside the pillar of the stoutly fashioned roof;
Holding the glistening headbands before her cheeks

She rebuked Antinoos and spoke right out directly:
"Antinoos, for all your pride and evil devices, they say
You are the best of your peers in the land of Ithaca
For advice and speeches. But you are not really so.   420
You madman, why do you devise murder and death
For Telemachos, and do not heed the suppliants
Who have Zeus for a witness? It is not holy to plot ills for one
    another.
Do you not know that your father came here in flight
And in fear of the people? And they were highly enraged   425
Because he had come along with Taphian pirates
And troubled the Thesprotians, who were our close friends.
They wished to destroy him and to tear out his own heart,
And to devour his great and satisfying livelihood.
But Odysseus held them back and restrained them, though they
    wanted that.   430
Now you devour his home without payment, and woo his wife,
And kill off his son, and you anger me very much.
Well, I tell you to stop and to order the others so.
Eurymachos, son of Polybos, answered her:
"Prudent Penelope, daughter of Icarios,   435
Take heart. Do not give heed to these matters in your mind.
The man does not exist, nor shall, nor come to be,
Who would lay hands on your son Telemachos
While I at least am alive and have sight on the earth.
I declare this to you, and it shall surely come to pass.   440
Right away his black blood shall run on my spear,
Since Odysseus, the sacker of cities, many times
Sat me upon his knees and placed a piece of roast meat
In my hands, and also held the red wine up to me.
And so Telemachos is by far the dearest to me   445
Of all men, and I bid him not to tremble for death,
From the suitors at least. But from the gods it is not to be
    escaped."
So he said, cheering her, and himself wrought destruction for
    him.
But she went on into the shining upper chamber
And wept there for Odysseus, her dear husband, until   450
Bright-eyed Athene cast sweet sleep on her eyelids.
At evening the godly swineherd came to Odysseus
And his son. They were preparing dinner attentively,

Sacrificing a year-old swine. And Athene
455 Stood close beside Odysseus, son of Laertes,
Struck him with a wand, and made him an old man again.
She clothed his skin in wretched garments, lest the swineherd
Look straight at him and know him and go announce it
To constant Penelope, and not keep it back in his mind.
460 Telemachos was the first to address a speech to him:
"You have come, godly Eumaeos. What is the news through the
  town?
Are the bold suitors already within and back
From their ambush, or do they still watch for me on my way
  home?"
And you addressed him in answer, swineherd Eumaeos:
465 "I did not bother to ask and inquire about these matters
As I went down through the town. My heart bade me at once,
After I had told the message, to come back here again.
The swift messenger from your companions joined me,
A herald, who first gave the word to your mother.
470 I know something else, for I saw it with my eyes.
Just now over the city where the hill of Hermes is,
I was going along when I saw a swift ship coming on
Into our harbor. There were upon her many men.
It was loaded down with shields and with two-edged spears.
475 And I thought it to be those men, but do not at all know them.
So he said, and Telemachos smiled in his sacred strength.
He looked with his eyes at his father and avoided the swineherd.
And when they had ceased from their toil and made dinner,
They dined, nor did their hearts want for a well-shared meal.
480 But when they had taken their fill of food and drink
They remembered rest, and they took the gift of sleep.

XVII

And when the early-born, rosy-fingered dawn appeared,
Telemachos, the dear son of godly Odysseus,
Bound the beautiful sandals underneath his feet,
And he took the stout spear that fitted in his hand,
Heading for the town, and he spoke out to his swineherd: 5
"Uncle, I am going to the city, so that my mother
May see me; I do not believe that she will cease
From hateful wailing and tearful lamentation
Until she sees me in person. I give you this order:
Lead this wretched stranger to the city, so that there   10
He may beg a dinner. Whoever wishes may give him
A loaf and a cup. It is not possible for me to endure
All sorts of men, with the pains in my heart that I have.
And if the stranger gets very angry, it will be the more painful
For himself. Yes, indeed, I like to speak the truth."   15
Odysseus of many wiles addressed him in answer:
"My friend, I do not wish to be held back myself.
It is better for a beggar to beg dinner in the city
Than in the fields. Whoever wishes will give it to me.
I am not yet of an age to remain at the folds,   20
So as to obey in everything a master who gives orders.
But come, this man that you are bidding will lead me
The moment I get warm from the fire and the sun's heat
  comes.
I have miserably poor clothes on, and I fear the frost
Of morning may overcome me. You say the town is far away."   25
So he spoke, and Telemachos went through the lodge
At a brisk pace; he was sowing the seeds of ill for the suitors.
And when he arrived at the well-situated house,
He stood the spear he carried against a tall pillar.
Then he went in himself and crossed the stone threshold.   30
The nurse Eurycleia was by far the first to see him.
She strewed fleeces upon the cleverly wrought armchairs,

And then she broke out in tears and came straight to him.
The other serving women of hardy-minded Odysseus gathered,
35 And they kissed him affectionately on his head and shoulders.
The prudent Penelope went on out of the chamber,
Resembling Artemis or golden Aphrodite.
Weeping, she threw her arms around her beloved son;
She kissed him on the head and on both lovely eyes.
40 And while she was sobbing she uttered wingèd words:
"You have come as a sweet light, Telemachos. I thought
I would see you no more when you went secretly in a ship
Against my will to Pylos for word of your dear father.
But come, tell me in what way you got sight of him."
45 And sound-minded Telemachos answered her:
"Mother, do not raise lamentation in me, nor arouse
The heart in my breast, since I did escape sheer destruction.
But bathe and put pure garments upon your skin
And go on into the upper chamber with the serving women.
50 Vow to all the gods you will sacrifice full hecatombs
If somehow Zeus may bring about deeds of retribution.
And I shall go on to the assembly, so that I may call
On a stranger who accompanied me hence as I came here.
I sent him on myself with my godlike companions,
55 And I ordered Peiraeos to lead him to the house,
To befriend him kindly and respect him till I should come."
So he said, and for her the speech was without a wing.
She washed herself and put pure garments upon her skin,
Vowed to all the gods she would sacrifice full hecatombs
60 If somehow Zeus might bring about deeds of retribution.
Telemachos then went on through the hall
Holding a spear, and two swift dogs accompanied him.
Moreover, Athene shed a marvelous grace about him.
All the people wondered about him as he came on.
65 The bold suitors gathered together around him,
Speaking fine words but plotting evils in their minds.
And then he avoided the entire group of them.
But where Mentor sat down, and Antiphos and Halitherses,
Who were his father's companions from the beginning,
70 He went and took a seat. They asked him for the details.
Peiraeos, renowned for the spear, came close to them,
Bringing the stranger through the city to the assembly. Not long

Did Telemachos turn aside from the stranger, but stood beside
    him.
First to him did Peiraeos address his speech:
"Telemachos, go urge the women at once on to my house   75
So that I may send the gifts that Menelaos gave you."
Then sound-minded Telemachos answered him:
"Peiraeos, we do not know how the present acts will come out.
If the bold suitors in the halls secretly
Kill me and divide up all the goods of my father,   80
I would rather you gained them yourself than any of those.
But if I myself breed death and destiny for these men,
Then carry them gladly to the house, and I shall be glad."
When he had said this, he led the long-suffering stranger to the
    house.
And when they reached the well-situated hall,   85
They put their mantles down over the seats and armchairs,
Got into well-polished bathtubs, and washed themselves.
When the serving maids had washed and anointed them with
    olive oil,
And thrown woolen mantles around them, and tunics
They got out of the bathtubs and sat on the seats.   90
A handmaid poured water from a pitcher she was carrying,
A lovely golden one, over into a silver basin,
For washing the hands; she set up a polished table alongside.
A respected housekeeper served bread she was carrying,
Laying out many dishes, gracious with the provisions.   95
His mother sat opposite him by the doorpost of the hall,
Leaning back in her seat, turning the fine threads on the distaff.
They stretched forth their hands to the food that was laid out
    ready,
But when they had taken their fill of food and drink,
The prudent Penelope began speaking to them: 100
"Telemachos, when I have gone up into the upper chamber
I shall lie down in my bed, which is made full of groans for me,
Ever sullied with my tears since the time Odysseus
Went to Troy with the sons of Atreus. Nor did you dare,
Before the bold suitors came into this house   105
To tell clearly of your father's return, if you did hear of it."
And sound-minded Telemachos answered her:
"All right, then, Mother, I shall speak the truth to you.
We went to Pylos and to Nestor, shepherd of the people.

110 The man received me and kindly befriended me
   In his lofty home, as a father would his own son
   Come afresh after a time from somewhere else. So the man
   Kindly entertained me with his glorious sons.
   But of hardy-hearted Odysseus, alive or dead,
115 He said he had never heard anything from anyone on earth.
   He sent me on with horses and well-jointed chariots
   To the son of Atreus, Menelaos, famed for the spear.
   There I saw Argive Helen, on whose account
   Trojans and Argives suffered much at the will of the gods.
120 Menelaos, good at the war cry, asked me at once
   What I had come in search of to godly Lacedemon.
   And I declared to him myself the entire truth.
   Then he addressed me and answered me with a speech:
   'Well now, they who are themselves without courage
125 Have wished to lie down in the bed of a stouthearted man!
   As when a deer in the thicket of a mighty lion
   Has put her newborn milk-sucking fawns to sleep,
   And goes questing over the spurs and the grassy gorges
   For grazing, and just then he comes to his own lair
130 And upon the two of them brings a wretched fate;
   So upon these men will Odysseus bring a wretched fate.
   By Father Zeus, Athene, and Apollo, I wish
   He might be as he once was in well-established Lesbos
   When he stood up and wrestled in a fight with Philomelides,
135 Threw him down mightily, and all the Achaians rejoiced;
   As that sort of man might Odysseus contend with the suitors.
   They would all be swift in their doom and bitter in marriage.
   As for what you ask and beseech me about, I myself
   Will say nothing at all off the point, nor will I deceive.
140 But what the unerring old man of the sea told me,
   Not a word of that shall I hide from you or conceal.
   He said he saw him on an island, that he had strong pains
   In the halls of the nymph Calypso, who by compulsion
   Is holding him back. And he cannot reach his fatherland,
145 For he has no ships there with oars, and no companions
   Who might convey him over the broad back of the sea.'
   So said Atreus' son, Menelaos, famed for the spear.
   When I finished this, I went off. The immortals gave me
   A breeze, and they brought me swiftly to my dear fatherland."
150 So he said, and he stirred up the heart in her breast.

And the godlike Theoclymenos spoke among them:
"Respected wife of Odysseus, son of Laertes,
Indeed this man has no clear knowledge, but mark my word;
For I shall prophesy to you truthfully and conceal nothing.
May Zeus now be my witness, first of the gods, and this guest
    table,   155
And the hearth of the blameless Odysseus, to which I have
    come,
That Odysseus is already on his fatherland soil.
He is here, sitting still or moving, and is finding out
These evil deeds, and he breeds evil for all the suitors.
Such was the meaning of the bird I observed as I sat   160
On the well-timbered ship, and declared it to Telemachos."
And then the prudent Penelope spoke to him:
"Would that this speech, stranger, might be fulfilled.
Then you would soon know friendship and many gifts
From me, so that one who met you would call you blessed."   165
And so they said such things to one another.
The suitors out in front of the hall of Odysseus
Were amusing themselves by throwing weights and javelins
On the leveled terrace as before, in their insolence.
And when it was time for dinner, and from everywhere   170
In the fields sheep came that the men drove as they did before,
Then Medon spoke to them, who was most pleasing to them
Of all the heralds, and he attended on them for the meal:
"Young men, now that you have all amused your minds with
    contests,
Come into the house so that we may partake of a meal.   175
It is not a bad thing to take dinner at the right time."
So he said. They stood up, went, and obeyed his word.
And when they had arrived at the well-situated house,
They put mantles down on the seats and on the armchairs;
And they sacrificed great sheep and goats rich with fat,   180
They sacrificed sleek hogs and a heifer of the herd,
Preparing the meal. But Odysseus and the godly swineherd
Were hastening on to go from the field to the city.
The swineherd, chief of the men, began speaking to them:
"Stranger, since you do desire to go to the city   185
Today, as my master commanded, I myself would like
To leave you here as a guardian of the folds,
But I hesitate and fear him, lest afterward

He reproach me for it. Harsh are the rebukes of masters.
190 Come now, let us go. The day is mostly past,
    And soon it will be colder for you, toward the evening."
    Odysseus of many wiles addressed him in answer:
    "I know, I see. You say this to an understanding man.
    Well, let us go. Lead us all the way on yourself,
195 And give me any staff that may have been cut for you
    To support me, since they say the roads are slippery."
    He spoke, and put the sorry wallet around his shoulders,
    Full of rents. And there was a twisted strap on it;
    Eumaeos then gave to him a staff that he liked.
200 The two of them then went on. The dogs and the herdsmen
    Who stayed behind guarded the lodge. He led his master
    To the city in the likeness of a beggar miserable and old,
    Walking with a staff. Sorry clothes were on his skin.
    And when, as they went on along the rugged path,
205 They got near the city, they arrived at a spring,
    Paved and fair-flowing, whence the townswomen drew water,
    Which Ithakos, Neritos, and Polyktor had made.
    About it was a grove of poplars nourished by water
    In a circle on all sides, and cold water flowed down
210 From the rock above. An altar had been built above
    To the nymphs, where all travelers made offerings.
    There Melanthios, son of Dolios, came upon them
    While he was leading goats that were best among all the herds,
    As dinner for the suitors. And two herdsmen followed along.
215 When he saw them he upbraided them and spoke directly,
    A striking, disgraceful speech. He stirred Odysseus' heart.
    "Now a man wholly foul leads a man who is foul;
    So the god always brings a like to his own like.
    Miserable swineherd, where are you leading this wild pig,
220 This tiresome beggar, desecrator of feasts,
    Who stands by many door posts and rubs his shoulders on them,
    Begging for morsels, but not for basins or swords?
    If you give him to me to become a guard of the folds,
    To be a stall sweeper and carry greens for the kids,
225 Then he could drink whey and put on a great thigh.
    But since he has learned foul deeds, he will not wish
    To approach work, but wants to beg through the district
    And to ask food for his insatiable belly.
    I tell you this straight out and it will be fulfilled:

If he ever comes to the home of godly Odysseus,   230
Many stools about his head thrown from the hands of men
Will his ribs wear out as he is tossed through the hall."
So he said, and in his foolishness rushed with a kick
On his flank. But he did not drive the man off the path;
Odysseus stood steadfast. And he deliberated   235
Whether to rush on the other with the staff and take his life
Or to lift him by the middle and dash his head to earth.
But he braced himself and checked his mind. The swineherd
Looked at the other and scolded him; he raised his hands and
    prayed aloud;
"Nymphs of the springs, Zeus's daughters, if ever Odysseus   240
Burned thighs to you, enclosing them in rich fat,
Of lambs or of kids, bring this wish of mine to pass:
May the man himself come, and may some god bring him.
Then he would scatter all these vainglories far and wide
That you bring now in your insolence, forever straying   245
To the town. And evil herdsmen are destroying the flock."
Then Melanthios, herdsman of the goats, spoke to him:
"Well now, what has this dog of pernicious mind said!
Someday I shall take him on a black, well-timbered ship
Far from Ithaca, where he might get me a large fortune.   250
Would that silver-bowed Apollo might shoot Telemachos
Today in the halls, or he be overcome by the suitors,
As Odysseus' day of return has been lost afar."
When he had said this, he left them there as they walked quietly
    on.
Then he went on and swiftly reached the master's house.   255
He went in at once and sat down among the suitors
Opposite Eurymachos, for the man liked him very much.
Those who were serving offered him a portion of the meat
And a respected housekeeper offered bread she was carrying,
To eat. Both Odysseus and the godly swineherd   260
Stood still as they got near. About them came the sound
Of the hollow lyre. For Phemios struck up a song among them.
The other took the swineherd by the hand and addressed him:
"Eumaeos, this is surely the lovely home of Odysseus,
Easy to recognize when seen, even among many.   265
One part is right next to another, and its court is finished off
With wall and copingstones. And there are doors well fenced
In a double gate. No man could look down upon them.

I know that many men are holding banquets
270 In the place, since meat smoke rises from it, and the lyre
Sounds there, which the gods make the companion of a
        banquet."
And you addressed him in answer, swineherd Eumaeos:
"You know it clearly, as you are not otherwise without sense.
So come now, and let us discuss how these acts shall be.
275 Either you first enter the well-situated house
And go among the suitors, and I shall be left behind here,
Or, if you wish, stay back, and I shall go forward myself.
Do not linger, lest someone perceive you outside
And hit you or drive you; I bid you to consider this."
280 Then godly Odysseus, who had suffered much, answered him:
"I know, I see. You say this to an understanding man.
Go forward now, and I shall remain here behind,
For I am not unacquainted with tosses or with blows.
My heart is enduring, since I have suffered many ills
285 On the waves and in war. Let this one be added to them.
There is no way of concealing an eager stomach,
The accursèd thing that gives many evils to men,
On whose account also well-rigged ships set out
Over the barren ocean, carrying evils for enemies."
290 And so such things did they say to one another,
And the dog held his head and his ears up where he lay,
Argos, stout-hearted Odysseus', that he himself
Had once reared and did not enjoy, but he went off beforehand
To holy Ilion. Some time back, young men used to take him out
295 After the wild goats and the rabbits and the deer.
But now he was lying unwanted while his master was gone,
In much dung from mules and oxen, which was heaped
In abundance before the gates, till Odysseus' servants
Should bring it when they had a great plot to fertilize.
300 There the dog Argos lay, full of the vermin of dogs;
And then, when he perceived that Odysseus was nearby,
He fawned over him with his tail and dropped both his ears.
But then he was no longer able to go closer
To his master. The man looked away and wiped off a tear.
305 He hid easily from Eumaeos, and he at once asked a question:
"Great wonder is it, Eumaeos, that this dog lies here in the
        dung;
He is handsome in body, but I do not clearly know

Whether along with this look he used also to be swift to run
Or was simply the sort of table dog that belongs to men
And that masters take care of on account of their graceful look." 310
And you addressed him in answer, swineherd Eumaeos:
"Ah yes, this is the dog of a man who died far away,
And if he were the same in body and in his actions
As when Odysseus left him behind on his way off to Troy,
You would wonder at once when you saw his speed and his
    force.   315
No wild beast that he chased could escape him at all
In the recesses of the deep woods. And tracks he knew well.
Now he is caught in misery, and his master is dead somewhere
Far from his fatherland. The careless women do not tend him.
And the servants, since the masters are holding sway no more, 320
Hence are no longer willing to perform proper tasks.
And broad-seeing Zeus takes away half the excellence
Of a man, from the time the day of slavery comes upon him."
When he had said this he entered the well-situated halls,
And he went straight through the hall to the noble suitors.   325
But the fortune of black death took Argos away
Once he had seen Odysseus in the twentieth year.
God-like Telemachos was by far the first to see
The swineherd coming to the house; and then he quickly
Nodded and called him. The man looked around and took a
    stool   330
That was lying where a server usually sat and carved
Many pieces of meat for the suitors as they dined in the hall.
He brought it to Telemachos' table on the other side,
Put it down, and sat on it himself. And a herald
Brought him a share, set it down, and lifted bread out of a
    basket.   335
Odysseus entered the halls close behind him
In the semblance of a beggar, miserable and old,
Walking with a staff. Sorry garments clothed his skin.
He sat at the ashwood threshold inside of the portals
Leaning on a cypress post that a workman once   340
Had skillfully planed and drawn straight to the line.
Telemachos called the swineherd to him and addressed him;
He took an entire loaf from the beautiful basket
And as much meat as his hands held around it could contain:
"Bring this and give it to the stranger and tell him   345

To go around to all the suitors and beg in turn,
For shame is not a good thing for a needy man."
So he spoke, and the swineherd went when he had heard what
  he said.
He stood close to the man, and uttered wingèd words:
350 "Telemachos gives this to you, stranger, and tells you
To go around to all the suitors and beg in turn,
Since shame, he says, is not good for a needy man."
Odysseus of many wiles addressed him in answer:
"Lord Zeus, grant me that Telemachos be blessed among men,
355 And all that he wants in his mind come about for him."
So he said, and received it with both hands, and set it down
In front of his feet there, upon the disgraceful wallet.
And he ate while the singer was singing in the halls.
When he had had dinner and the godly singer had ceased,
360 The suitors made a din through the halls. And Athene
Stood close beside Odysseus, son of Laertes,
And urged him on to gather loaves from the suitors,
So he might know who were righteous and who lawless;
And yet she did not intend any to escape from misfortune.
365 He went along begging of each man, from left to right,
Stretching his hand every way as though he had long been a
  beggar.
They pitied and they gave, and they marveled at him
And asked one another who he was and whence he came.
And then Melanthios, the goatherd, spoke out among them:
370 "Suitors of the famous queen, listen to what I say
About this stranger here. For I have seen him before.
And surely the swineherd guided him to this place.
But I do not know him clearly, or whence he declares his birth
  to be."
So he said, and Antinoos upbraided the swineherd with a
  speech:
375 "Notorious swineherd, why did you lead this man
To the city? Are there not enough vagrants for us,
Insatiable beggars, defilers of the banquet?
Do you treat it lightly that those who are gathered here
Devour your master's living, that you called this man here too?"
380 And you addressed him in answer, swineherd Eumaeos:
"Antinoos, though you are noble, you have said what is not
  good.

For who invites some other stranger when he comes himself
From elsewhere, unless he is one of the district craftsmen,
A prophet or a healer of ills or a worker of wood
Or a wonderful singer who gives delight as he sings?   385
These are invited among mortals throughout the boundless
     earth.
No one would invite a beggar to eat his substance away!
But always you are harsh beyond the other suitors
To the servants of Odysseus, and especially to me.
I do not care, though, while constant Penelope   390
And god-like Telemachos are alive for me in the halls."
Then sound-minded Telemachos answered him:
"Silence, and please do not answer this man so much with
     words.
Antinoos has the habit of always giving evil provocation
With harsh speeches, and he urges others also to do it."   395
So he said, and he uttered wingèd words to Antinoos:
"Antinoos, you care for me nicely as a father for his son
When you order me to drive the stranger from the halls
With a word of constraint. Let a god not bring this to pass.
Take and give to him; I begrudge it not. In fact, I command it. 400
And do not stand in awe of my mother, or of anyone else
Among the servants who are in the halls of godly Odysseus.
And yet you have no such intention in your breast.
You would rather eat yourself than give to another."
In answer to him, Antinoos addressed him: 405
"High-talking Telemachos, unchecked in your anger, what have
     you said?
If all the suitors should offer him as much as this,
The house would keep him at a distance for three months."
So he said, and out from under the table he brought a footstool
That lay there, on which he held his glossy feet while feasting. 410
All the others gave and filled his wallet with bread and meat.
And soon Odysseus was again ready to go back again
To the threshold and get a taste from the Achaians free.
He stood by Antinoos and addressed a word to him:
"Give, my friend; you do not seem to me to be the worst   415
Of the Achaians, but the best, since you look like a king.
And so you ought to give bread more liberally
Than the others. I shall speak your fame through the boundless
     earth.

For I myself was once blessed, and I inhabited
420 A rich house among men, and gave to a tramp like this
Many times, no matter who came, whatever he needed.
I had numberless servants and many other things
Men have who live well and are called prosperous.
But Zeus, son of Cronos, destroyed me, as he somehow wished;
425 He sent me along with pirates who wandered much,
To go to Egypt, a long journey, so I might die.
I beached my bobbing ships by the Egyptian river,
And then I called upon my trusty companions
To remain there beside the ships and to guard the ships.
430 And I ordered spies to go up on places of lookout,
But they gave in to excess, and, relying on their own strength,
They sacked the beautiful fields of the Egyptians
At once and carried their women and infant children off.
They killed the men. And soon the noise reached the city.
435 They perceived the shouting, and at the appearance of dawn
Came on. The whole plain was filled with foot soldiers and
     horses,
And the flash of bronze. Zeus who hurls the thunderbolt
Threw evil panic among my companions, nor could any
Bear to stay face to face. Ills surrounded us on all sides.
440 Then they slaughtered many of us with the sharp bronze
And led some off alive to work for them under constraint.
But they gave me to a stranger they met bound for Cyprus,
Dmetor, son of Iasos, who ruled over Cyprus by force.
From there have I now come here this way, suffering troubles."
445 Then Antinoos answered him and addressed him:
"What god has brought this trouble, this annoyance at the
     banquet?
Stand as you are in the middle, apart from my table,
Lest you soon arrive at a bitter Egypt and Cyprus,
Because you are some bold and shameless beggar.
450 You stand beside all in turn. And they give to you
Wantonly, since they have no restraint or remorse
At giving of others' goods freely, since each has much."
Odysseus of many wiles withdrew and addressed him:
"Well now, your mind is not a match for your appearance.
455 You would not give salt from your house to your own suppliant,
You who now sit among others' things and cannot bear
To take off a little bread and give it to me; yet much is there."

So he said, and Antinoos was very angry in his heart,
And glaring at him, he uttered wingèd words:
"I think you will no longer withdraw through the hall;   460
In peace, since you are even uttering reproaches."
So he said, and took the footstool and hit his right shoulder
At the very base of his back. He stood there just like a rock,
Steadfast. Nor did the throw of Antinoos make him fall,
But he moved his head in silence, plotting evils deep inside.   465
He went back to the threshold and sat down, and he put
His full wallet beside him and spoke to the suitors:
"Listen to me, suitors of the illustrious queen,
So that I may say what the heart in my breast bids me to.
There is no pain in a man's mind or any grief   470
When he battles over possessions of his own
And is wounded for the sake of his oxen or shining sheep.
But Antinoos hit me on account of my woeful belly,
A cursed thing that gives many evils to men.
But if perchance gods and Furies exist for beggars,   475
May the end of death find Antinoos sooner then marriage."
Then Antinoos, son of Eupeithes, addressed him:
"Sit and eat in peace, stranger, or go somewhere else,
Lest the young men drag you through the halls for what you say,
By the foot or by the hand, and tear you all to pieces."   480
So he said, and they all grew presumptuously angry.
And this is what one of those overbearing young men would
    say:
"Antinoos, you did not do well to hit a hapless wanderer.
You are cursed, if perchance he is some heavenly god.
Yes, the gods in the semblance of alien strangers   485
Do appear in all forms and go about among cities
Looking upon the excess and the good order of men."
So said the suitors, and he did not attend to their speech.
Telemachos was nursing a great grief in his heart
For the struck man, but he cast no tear on the ground from his
    eyelids;   490
But in silence moved his head, plotting evils deep inside.
When the prudent Penelope heard that the man
Was struck in the hall, she spoke out to her servants:
"Would that bow-famed Apollo might so strike the other
    himself."
Then Eurynome, the housekeeper, addressed her in a speech: 495

"Would that there might come a fulfillment for our prayers!
None of these men would get as far as the fair-throned Dawn."
Then the prudent Penelope spoke to her:
"Good mother, they are all foes, since they devise evils.
500 Antinoos most of all is like a black fate.
Some hapless stranger wanders into the house
Begging from the men. Lack of means calls him on.
Then all the others filled him up and gave to him there,
And this one hit him with a footstool at the base of the right
       shoulder."
505 And so did she speak among her serving women,
Seated in her chamber. And godly Odysseus was eating dinner.
She called out to the godly swineherd and addressed him:
"Come, godly Eumaeos, go order the stranger
To come, so that I may embrace him in some way and ask of
       him
510 If he has perchance heard news of stouthearted Odysseus,
Or seen him with his eyes. He looks like a man who has much
       roamed."
And you addressed her in answer, swineherd Eumaeos:
"Well then, my queen, let the Achaians be silent.
The man tells such tales as would enchant your own heart.
515 Three nights I had him, and I held him for three days
In my hut. He first came to me running away from a ship.
Nor did he ever make an end of telling his misfortune.
As when a man looks upon a singer who sings
The words pleasing to mortals that he has learned from the gods,
520 And they endlessly long to hear him whenever he sings:
So that man enchanted me as he sat in the halls.
He says he is a paternal guest-friend of Odysseus
And he dwells in Crete, where the race of Minos is.
And now he has come here this way, suffering pains,
525 Rolling on and on. He claims to have heard news of Odysseus
Near us, in the fertile land of the Thesprotians;
That he is alive and is bringing many treasures to his home."
Then the prudent Penelope spoke to him:
"Come, call him here, so he may speak himself, face to face.
530 And let these men sit sporting either at the doors
Or here through the halls, since their hearts are merry.
Their own possessions lie undisturbed at home,

Bread and sweet wine. These are what their house servants eat,
But they themselves cluster to our house day after day
Slaughtering oxen and sheep and fat goats.   535
They carry on their revel and drink the sparkling wine
Wantonly. Many things are wasted. And there is no man
Of the kind Odysseus was, to ward off harm from the house.
But if Odysseus were to come and reach his fatherland,
With his son he would at once avenge the men's violence."   540
So she said, and Telemachos sneezed loud. About the house
It resounded terribly. And Penelope laughed.
At once to Eumaeos she uttered wingèd words:
"Come to me, and summon the stranger so, face to face.
Did you not see that my son sneezed at all the words?   545
So death will come not unfulfilled for the suitors,
All of them, nor will any ward off death and destiny.
I shall tell you something else; keep it well in mind.
If I acknowledge that he says everything truthfully,
I shall clothe him in a mantle and a tunic, lovely clothes."   550
So she said; the swineherd went when he heard the speech,
Stood close beside him, and uttered wingèd words:
"Father stranger, the prudent Penelope calls to you,
The mother of Telemachos. Her heart bids her to ask
Something about her husband, though she has suffered cares.   555
If she acknowledges that you say everything truthfully,
She will clothe you in a mantle and a tunic, the things that you
    need
The most. And then, begging bread through the district,
You will feed your belly; whoever wishes will give to you."
Then godly Odysseus, who had suffered much, spoke to him: 560
"Eumaeos, straight off I would tell all truthfully
To the prudent Penelope, daughter of Icarios.
For I know well about that man; we have got the same woe.
But I fear the throng of the difficult suitors
Whose insolence and force reach iron heaven.   565
Why, just now, when this man, as I was going to the house
Doing no evil, struck me and presented me with pains,
Telemachos could not at all prevent it, or anyone else.
So now go bid Penelope to remain in the halls,
Though she is eager, till the setting of the sun.   570
Then let her ask me about the day of her husband's return,

Seating me closer to the fire. For the clothes I have
Are woeful. You yourself know it too, since I besought you
first."
So he said. And the swineherd went when he heard the speech.
575 Penelope spoke to him as he went over the threshold:
"Do you not bring him, Eumaeos? What does the wanderer
mean by this?
Does he fear someone excessively, perhaps, or otherwise
Feel ashamed in the house? A tramp who feels shame is a bad
one."
Then you addressed her in answer, swineherd Eumaeos:
580 "He speaks in measure, as anyone else would think
Who would avoid the insolence of presumptuous men.
But he bids you to wait until the setting of the sun;
And this way, queen, it will be far better for yourself
To speak alone to the stranger and to hear his speech."
585 Then the prudent Penelope addressed him:
"The stranger is not senseless; he thinks the way it may be.
For never, in this way, surely, did any among mortal men
So devise reckless deeds in their insolence."
So the woman spoke, and the godly swineherd went off
590 To the conclave of suitors, when he had told her everything.
And at once he uttered wingèd words to Telemachos,
Holding his head close, so the others could not hear:
"My friend, I am going off to guard the swine and the other
things there,
Your living and mine. Let everything here be your affair;
595 Protect yourself first and give heed in your heart
Lest you suffer something. Many Achaians plot evils.
May Zeus destroy them before trouble comes upon us."
And then sound-minded Telemachos answered him:
"So it will be, father. Go when you have had supper.
600 Come at dawn and bring fine victims for sacrifice.
But all these things will be my affair, and the immortals'."
So he said, and the man at once sat on the polished stool,
When he had filled his heart with eating and with drinking.
He went after the swine, and left the enclosures and the hall
605 Full of banqueters. They were enjoying themselves with dancing
And with song, for the evening of the day was already coming.

XVIII

Then up came the beggar of the whole district, who begged
Through the town of Ithaca; he was outstanding for his greedy
  belly,
For incessantly eating and drinking. Nor did he have
Strength or force, but his form was very large to behold.
Arnaios was his name. His queenly mother gave it   5
At the time of his birth. But all the young men called him Iros,[1]
Because he went with a message when anyone asked him.
He came up and tried to drive Odysseus from his own home,
And, upbraiding him, he uttered wingèd words:
"Leave the doorway, old man, lest you soon be dragged off by
  the foot.   10
Don't you understand that they are all winking at me
And call on me to drag you? Still, I am ashamed to.
But get up, lest our quarrel soon come even to fists."
Odysseus of many wiles glowered at him and addressed him:
"My fine friend, I do not do or speak any wrong to you.   15
Nor do I begrudge anyone's giving, even if much is taken.
This threshold can contain us both. There is no need
To begrudge what others have. You seem to me to be
A tramp, like me; and the gods are supposed to bestow wealth.
But do not challenge with your fists too much, lest you anger
  me;   20
Lest, old man though I am, I stain your chest and your lips
With blood. And then there would be still greater peace for me
Tomorrow. And indeed I think you will not return at all
A second time to the house of Odysseus, son of Laertes."
Getting angry at him, the tramp Iros spoke to him: 25
"Well now, how fluently does the wild pig talk,
Like an oven woman; I should devise evils for him,
And beat him with both hands, and knock all his teeth
Out of his jaw to the ground like a crop-devouring sow's.
1. The messenger of the gods.

30 Gird yourself now so all these men may look upon us
   As we fight. How would you contend with a younger man?"
   And so outside in front of the lofty portals,
   On the polished threshold, they grew fierce in full wrath.
   Antinoos noticed them in his sacred might,
35 Laughed out sweetly, and spoke before the suitors:
   "My friends, nothing like this has ever happened before.
   Such a delight has the god brought to this house!
   The stranger and Iros are quarreling with one another
   To battle with their fists. Let us quickly set them together."
40 So he said, and all of them sprang up in laughter
   And clustered about the beggars in their foul clothes.
   Antinoos, son of Eupeithes, spoke out to them:
   "Listen to me, bold suitors, so I may say something.
   These stomachs of goats are lying in the fire that we
45 Have stuffed with fat for dinner and filled up with blood.
   Whoever wins and turns out to be the better man,
   Let him stand up and take whichever one of them he wishes.
   And he may always dine with us, nor shall we allow
   Any other beggar inside to mingle and make requests."
50 So Antinoos spoke, and his speech was pleasing to them.
   Odysseus of many wiles spoke to them with a plan in his mind:
   "My friends, there is no way for an old man worn out with grief
   To fight against a younger. Still, my criminal belly
   Urges me on, that I be overcome with blows.
55 But come, all of you, and swear a mighty oath,
   That no one favoring Iros will recklessly
   Strike me with heavy hand and overpower me for him."
   So he said, and all of them swore as he had asked.
   But when they had sworn and had completed the oath,
60 Telemachos again addressed them in his sacred might:
   "Stranger, if your heart and bold spirit urge you on
   To ward this man off, do not fear any of the other
   Achaians, since he who smites you shall fight with many.
   I am myself the host, and the two kings agree,
65 Antinoos and Eurymachos, both sound-minded men."
   So he said, and they all assented. Then Odysseus
   Girded his rags round his private parts and displayed his thighs,
   Handsome and large; and his broad shoulders appeared,
   And his chest and his powerful arms. Then Athene

Stood near and filled out the limbs of the shepherd of the
    people,   70
And all the suitors were exceedingly amazed.
So one of them would look at his neighbor and say:
"Soon Iros, un-Irosed, shall have an ill he brought on himself,
So great a thigh muscle does the old man show from his rags."
So they said, and the heart in Iros was sorely stirred.   75
And so the servants, when they had girded him, led him by
    force
In his fright. And the flesh trembled all over his limbs.
Antinoos rebuked him and spoke out to him directly:
"You ought not to exist now, ox-braggart, or have been born,
If you tremble before this man and dreadfully fear him,   80
An old man overwhelmed with the grief that has come upon
    him.
But I shall tell you this, and it shall be brought to pass;
If this man overcomes you and turns out the better man,
I shall throw you on a black ship and send you to the mainland,
To King Echetos, destroyer of all mortal men,   85
Who will cut off your nostrils and ears with a sharp bronze
    sword;
He will tear off your private parts and give them to dogs to eat
    raw."
So he said, and still greater trembling seized the other's limbs.
They led him out to the middle; both men held out their hands.
And then godly Odysseus, who had endured much, considered 90
Whether to strike him so his soul would leave him as he fell
Or to strike him softly and stretch him out on the ground;
And as he thought, it seemed to him to be better this way:
To strike softly so the Achaians would not take note of him.
Then they both drew themselves up. On the right shoulder   95
Iros hit him. But the other struck his neck under the ear and
    crushed
The bone inside. At once gory blood came out of his mouth.
He fell bellowing in the dust. He knocked his teeth together,
As he kicked the ground with his feet. Then the noble suitors
Held their hands up and died with laughter. And Odysseus   100
Took him by the foot and dragged him through the door till he
    reached
The courtyard and the doors of the porch. He leaned him up

Against the fence of the courtyard, put his staff in his hands,
And speaking to him, he uttered wingèd words:
105 "Sit there from now on and keep off the swine and the dogs,
And do not be a lord over strangers and beggars,
Woeful as you are, lest you incur a greater evil."
He spoke, and put his sorry wallet around his shoulders,
Full of rents. And there was a twisted strap on it.
Then he went back to the threshold and sat down. But they
110 went inside,
Sweetly laughing, and they welcomed him with speeches.
And this is what one of the overbearing young men would say:
"Stranger, may Zeus and the other immortal gods
Grant you what you wish and is most dear to your heart,
115 Since you have stopped this insatiable man from wandering
In the district. And soon we will bring him to the mainland,
To King Echetos, destroyer of all mortal men."
So he said, and godly Odysseus rejoiced at the omen he heard.
Antinoos put a large stomach before him
120 Full of fat and blood. And Amphinomos
Lifted two loaves out of the basket and gave them to him.
He toasted him with a golden cup and spoke forth:
"Hail, father stranger, henceforth may prosperity
Be yours in the future. But you are held now in many ills."
125 Odysseus of many wiles addressed him in answer:
"Amphinomos, you seem to me to be quite sound minded,
For such was your father, because I heard of his noble renown,
That Nisos of Dulichion was prosperous and good.
They say you are his son; you seem like a discreet man.
130 So I shall speak to you; pay attention and listen to me.
Earth nourishes nothing of slighter account then man
Of all the things that breathe and move on the earth.
For he thinks he will not suffer any evil in the future
As long as the gods provide excellence and his limbs stir.
135 But whenever the blessed gods bring woeful things to pass,
He bears them, too, against his will, in his enduring heart.
The disposition of men who dwell on earth is the same
As the kind of day the father of men and gods may bring.
And I myself was accustomed to be happy among men;
140 But I did much recklessly, yielding to my strength and might,
Relying on my father and on my relatives.
And so let no man ever be lawless by any means.

He should keep the gods' gifts in silence, whatever they give.
So I see the suitors devising such reckless deeds,
Consuming the property and dishonoring the wife   145
Of a man who I think will not be away much longer
From his dear ones and his fatherland. He is very near. May
    some god
Lead you back safely, and may you not encounter that man
At the time he returns to his dear fatherland.
I think when that man enters his hall, the suitors   150
And he shall not be pulled apart without bloodshed."
So he said; he poured libation, and drank honey-sweet wine.
Then he put the cup back in the hands of the chief of the
    people.
The other went through the house, grieving in his own heart,
Nodding his head. For indeed in his spirit he apprehended evil. 155
Yet not even so did he flee fate. Him too had Athene bound
To be overcome in power by the hands and spear of
    Telemachos.
Then he sat down again in the chair from which he had stood
    up.
The bright-eyed goddess Athene put it in the mind
Of Icarios' daughter, the prudent Penelope,   160
To appear to the suitors so she might the most expand
The hearts of the suitors, and might get more honor
From her husband and her son than she had before.
She laughed inanely and spoke quite directly out:
"Eurynome, my spirit longs, as it did not before,   165
To appear to the suitors, though they are detestable;
And I shall say something to my son, that it would be better
Not always to associate with the presumptuous suitors,
Who speak nicely but are thinking of evil for the future."
Then the housekeeper Eurynome addressed a speech to her: 170
"Yes, indeed, child, you have spoken all this properly;
But go, say the word to your son and do not conceal it,
When you have wiped off your skin and anointed your cheeks.
Do not go with your countenance befouled this way
By tears, since it is very wrong to mourn endlessly.   175
Already your son is of the age that you have most
Prayed to the gods to see him at, growing a beard."
And then the prudent Penelope addressed her:
"Eurynome, do not say this, though you care for me,

180 That I should wipe off my skin, and anoint me with oil.
The gods who possess Olympos have destroyed in me
My charm, from the time he went off in the hollow ships.
But give the order for Autonoe and Hippodameia
To come to me, so they may stand by me in the halls.
185 I shall not go alone among the men. I am ashamed."
So she said, and the old woman went out through the hall
To give the word to the women and urge them to come.
But the bright-eyed goddess Athene had another thought.
She shed sweet sleep over the daughter of Icarios.
190 And she sank back in sleep, and all her joints relaxed
There in her armchair, while the divine goddess gave her
Ambrosial gifts, so the Achaians might wonder at her.
First she purified her lovely face with ambrosial beauty
Like that with which the well-crowned Cytherea anoints herself
195 When she goes to the delightful dancing of the Graces;
And then she made her taller and fuller to look upon
And made her to be whiter than sawn ivory.
When she had done that, the divine goddess went off,
And the white-armed servants came out of the hall,
200 Coming up with their voices. Sweet sleep let go of her.
And she wiped her cheeks off with her hands and spoke out:
"In my dread suffering a soft slumber covered me round.
Would that chaste Artemis might bring soft death upon me
At once now, so that I should no longer waste my life away
205 Mourning in my heart and longing for my dear husband,
Who had excellence of all kinds, since he was foremost of the
     Achaians!"
When she had said this, she went down from the glistening
     upper chambers,
Not alone, but two servants followed along with her.
And when the godly woman had come to the suitors,
210 She stood by the pillar of the stoutly fashioned roof,
Holding the glistening headbands before her cheeks.
A devoted servant maid stood near her on either side.
The men's knees were loosened on the spot and their hearts
     were charmed with desire,
And they all voiced the prayer of lying beside her in bed.
215 Then she addressed Telemachos, her beloved son:
"Telemachos, your mind and intent are steadfast no longer.

While you were still a child you managed plans in your mind
    better.
But now that you are big and have reached the measure of
    youth,
And one would say you were the offspring of a prosperous man:
For so an alien mortal would say who saw your beauty and
    stature,   220
Yet your mind and intent are no longer correct,
Since a deed of this sort has been performed in the halls,
In that you have allowed the stranger to be outraged this way.
What now, if the stranger seated in our halls as he is
Should suffer some harm from the miserable maltreatment?   225
Shame and disgrace would come about for you among men."
Then sound-minded Telemachos answered her:
"Mother, I do not hold it against you for being angry.
But I perceive in my heart and know about every matter,
The good and the worse. Until now I was a child.   230
Still, I cannot always have ideas that are sound,
For they dismay me, seated on one side and the other,
Those men who plot evils. And there is no one to help me.
The struggle between the stranger and Iros did not come out
To the suitors' liking—but he was the stronger in might.   235
By Father Zeus, Athene, and Apollo, I wish
The suitors that are now in our house in the same way
Might nod their heads, overcome: both those in the courtyard
And those within the house, and the limbs of each might be
    loosed,
The way that man Iros at the door of the courtyard now   240
Sits nodding with his head like a drunken man,
And cannot stand up straight on his feet or return home,
Wherever that may be, since his precious limbs are loosed."
And so such things did they say to one another.
But Eurymachos addressed a speech to Penelope: 245
"Daughter of Icarios, prudent Penelope,
If all the Achaians through Iasian Argos should see you,
More suitors still would be dining in your halls
From the morning on, since you excel among women
For form and stature, and for a mind well balanced within."   250
Then the prudent Penelope addressed him in answer:
"Eurymachos, the immortals destroyed my excellence

Of form and body at the time the Argives went aboard ship
Toward Ilion, and with them went my husband Odysseus.
255 If that man should come and minister to my life,
My renown would be greater that way, and lovelier,
But now I am grieved. So many ills some god has sent me!
Yes indeed, at the time when he went to leave his fatherland
He took me by the right hand at the wrist and said to me:
260 'My wife, I do not believe the well-greaved Achaians
Will all get back safely uninjured out of Troy,
For they say that the Trojans are men who are fighters,
Both as throwers of javelins and as drawers of arrows,
And mounters of swift horse chariots, such as most quickly
265 Decide the great contention of impartial war.
So I know not if the god will restore me, or I shall be taken
There in Troy. But do look after everything here.
Remember my father and my mother in the halls
As you do now, or even more, when I am gone away.
270 And when you see that my son is growing a beard,
Marry whom you may wish to and leave your own home.'
So the man said. Now all these things are brought to pass.
And there will be a night when hateful marriage shall come
Upon my cursèd self, whose bliss Zeus has taken away.
275 And the dreadful grief reaches my heart and spirit.
This is not the just way established in the past for suitors
Who wish to rival one another and pay court
To a good woman and the daughter of prosperous man.
Such men as those are bring oxen and goodly sheep,
280 A banquet for the lady's friends, and give glorious gifts,
But they do not consume another's livelihood scot free."
So she said; godly Odysseus, who had endured much, rejoiced
That she extracted their gifts from them and charmed their
    hearts
With soothing speeches, but her mind devised other things.
285 Then Antinoos, the son of Eupeithes, addressed her:
"Daughter of Icarios, prudent Penelope,
Let whoever of the Achaians wishes bring gifts here,
And you receive them. For it is not good to refuse a gift.
And we shall not go to our fields or anywhere else
290 Until you have married the noblest of the Achaians."
So Antinoos said, and his speech was pleasing to them.
Each one sent for a herald to bring his gifts.

For Antinoos one brought a great, beautiful tunic,
Embroidered. And twelve brooches were on it in all,
Made of gold, fitted with well-fastening clasps.   295
One brought for Eurymachos a necklace cunningly wrought
Of gold, strung with amber beads, and it was like the sun.
For Eurydamos two servants brought in earrings
With three droplets, clustering. Much grace shone from them.
And from the lord Peisander, son of Polyktor,   300
A servant brought a necklace, a beautiful ornament.
Each of the Achaians brought some other lovely gift.
Then the godly woman went up to the upper chambers,
Where servants followed her bearing the beautiful gifts.
The men turned then to dancing and delightful song   305
And took their pleasure, and waited for evening to come.
As they took their pleasure black evening came upon them.
Right away they stood three braziers up in the halls
To give light: they put seasoned pieces of wood around,
Dried a long time, very parched, newly split with the ax.   310
And they mixed torches between. The maids of stouthearted
    Odysseus
Kept their light up high, taking turns. But he himself,
Zeus-born Odysseus of many wiles, spoke out to them:
"You maids of Odysseus, the master who is gone so long,
Do come to the halls where the respected queen is;   315
Twist up her distaff wool for her and do her pleasure,
Seated in the hall, or else card the wool with your hands,
And I myself shall furnish light to all these people.
Even if they wish to await the fair-throned dawn,
They will not overcome me; I can hold out very well."   320
So he said, and they laughed and looked at one another.
But fair-cheeked Melantho upbraided him shamefully;
Dolios fathered her, and Penelope cared for her,
And reared her as her own child, and gave her toys to her liking;
Yet even with that, she did not keep Penelope's grief in mind;   325
But she had lain with Eurymachos, and loved him.
And with reproachful speeches she rebuked Odysseus:
"Wretched stranger, you are a man knocked out of his mind,
As you do not wish to go and sleep in the bronzesmith's house,
Or, say in the public court; but you speak very much here   330
Boldly among many men, nor are you at all frightened
In your heart. Wine possesses your mind, or your mind is always

The way it is now, so that you utter vanity.
Are you beside yourself for beating the tramp Iros?
Take heed lest a better man than Iros soon stand up against
335   you
Who would beat you around the head with his stout hands
And send you from the house, defiling you with much blood.'
Odysseus of many wiles glowered at her and spoke:
"Soon I shall tell Telemachos what you say, bitch,
340 When he comes here, so he may cut you up limb from limb."
When he had said this he terrified the women with his words.
They went through the hall, and the limbs of each one went
    slack
In alarm. For they thought that he had spoken the truth.
And he himself stood by the flaming braziers keeping the light
    up
345 And looked at all the men. The heart in his breast planned
Other matters, and those were not to be unachieved.
Athene by no means allowed the bold suitors
To keep from grievous outrage, so that still more pain
Might enter the heart of Odysseus, son of Laertes.
350 Eurymachos, son of Polybos, began speaking to them,
Abusing Odysseus, and he caused laughter in his companions
"Listen to me, suitors of the illustrious queen,
So I may tell you what the heart in my breast bids me to.
Not without the gods has this man reached the house of
    Odysseus;
355 Indeed, the light of the torches seems to me to be his own,
From his head, since there are no hairs on it in the least."
He spoke, and addressed Odysseus, sacker of cities:
"Stranger, would you like to labor, if I should take you on,
At the field's very verge—the pay will be enough for you—
360 Gathering stones for the walls and planting tall trees?
There I myself shall furnish unfailing bread,
Clothe you in garments, and give you sandals for your feet.
But since you have learned foul deeds, you do not wish
To approach work, but want to beg through the district
365 So that you may have food for your insatiable belly."
Then Odysseus of many wiles addressed him in answer:
"Eurymachos, I wish a contest of work might come between us
In the spring season, when the long days come around,
In the grass, and I held a well-bent sickle myself

And you held the same kind, so we might test us at the work,   370
Fasting right up until dusk, and the grass should still be there;
And if there were oxen to drive, the best there are,
Great tawny ones, the pair of them filled up on grass,
The same age, equal at plowing, their strength not slight,
And the field were four lengths and the clod should yield to the
    plow;   375
Then you should see if I cut ahead an unbroken furrow.
And if the son of Cronos should raise up a battle somewhere
On this day, and I should have a shield and two spears
And a helmet all of bronze and fitted to the temple;
Then you should see me mingling in the forefront of combat,   380
Nor would you address me in reproach of my belly.
But you are quite insolent and your mind is unbending.
Perhaps you think yourself a great and mighty man
Because you associate with small men of no worth.
But if Odysseus should come and reach his fatherland,   385
Right away the portals, although they are very broad,
Would be narrow for you as you fled through the entrance
    outdoors."
So he said, and Eurymachos got still angrier in his heart.
Glowering at him, he uttered wingèd words:
"Wretch, I soon shall bring evil to pass for you, since you   390
Speak boldly among many men. Nor are you at all frightened
In your heart. Wine posesses your mind, or your mind is always
The way it is now, so that you utter vanity.
Are you beside yourself for beating the tramp Iros?"
So he said, and he took hold of a footstool. Odysseus   395
Sat down at the knees of Dulichian Amphinomos
In fear of Eurymachos. But that one struck the wine server
On his right hand; the pitcher clattered as it fell on the ground.
The man himself groaned and fell on his back in the dust.
The suitors made a din through the shadowy halls.   400
And this is what one of them, looking at his neighbor, would
    say:
"I wish that the stranger had strayed elsewhere and perished
Before coming. So he would not have set such a noise among us.
And now we are contending over beggars, and no delight
Shall be in the noble banquet, but worse matters win out."   405
And Telemachos spoke to them in his sacred might:
"You fools, you are enraged and no longer hide in your hearts

Your eating and drinking. One of the gods stirs you up.
But since you have dined well, go on home and lie down,
410 Whenever the spirit bids. I shall not pursue anyone."
So he said, and they all bit their lips with their teeth
And wondered at Telemachos, that he spoke boldly.
Then Amphinomos spoke to them and addressed them,
The illustrious son of lord Nisos, the son of Aretias:
415 "My friends, surely no one should become enraged
At a just saying, and rebuke someone with hostile words.
Do not maltreat the stranger at all, or any one
Of the servants who are in the halls of godly Odysseus.
Come now, let a wine server pour the first drops in the cups,
420 So we may pour libation and go on home to sleep.
And let the stranger go into the halls of Odysseus,
In the care of Telemachos; for he has reached his dear home."
So he said, and spoke a speech pleasing to all of them.
The hero Moulios, the herald from Dulichion, mixed
425 A bowl up for them. He was a servant of Amphinomos.
He gave it in order to all. They poured libation
To the blessed gods and drank the honey-sweet wine;
But when they had poured libation and drunk all they wished
They went off, each one to his own home to sleep.

So godly Odysseus was left behind in the hall
Devising slaughter for the suitors, with Athene's aid.
At once he uttered wingèd words to Telemachos:
"Telemachos, we must put the weapons of war inside,
All of them, and beguile the suitors deceptively   5
With soft speeches, when they miss them and ask you questions:
'I put them out of the smoke since they no longer look like those
That Odysseus once left behind when he went to Troy.
But they are befouled, so much has the smoke of the fire got
    to them.
And some god has put this other, greater thought in my mind: 10
That besides, drunk with wine, you might set up a quarrel
Among you, wound one another, and disgrace the banquet,
And your wooing too. For iron of itself draws a man on.'"
So he said. And Telemachos obeyed his dear father.
He called the nurse Eurycleia and spoke to her: 15
"Good mother, come hold the women back in the halls,
So that we may put away the weapons of my father up into the
    chamber,
The fine ones that smoke tarnishes uncared for in the house
Since my father went off, and I was still a foolish child.
Now I wish to put them away where the fire's smoke will not get
    to them."   20
Then his dear nurse Eurycleia spoke to him:
"My child, would that some time you might get hold of
    prudence
To take care of your house and watch over all your goods.
But come, who will go get a light and carry it for you?
You do not let the maids, who might have given light, go
    ahead."   25
Then sound-minded Telemachos answered her:
"This stranger. I shall not let any man go idle

Who has touched my rations, though he has come from far
   away."
So he said, and for her the speech was without a wing.
30 She shut the doors of the well-situated halls.
Odysseus and his illustrious son both leaped up
And carried the helmet plumes and the bossed shields in,
And the pointed spears. Pallas Athene in front of them
Held a golden lantern and made a beautiful light.
35 Then Telemachos at once spoke to his father:
"Father, this is a great wonder I see before my eyes.
Indeed, the walls of the halls and the lovely pedestals,
The fir-wood beams and the pillars holding them high,
Appear bright to my eyes as if from a glittering fire.
Some god must be inside, one of those who possess broad
40   heaven."
Then Odysseus of many wiles addressed him in answer:
"Silence. Keep this in your mind and ask no question.
This is the rule of the gods who possess Olympos.
You go lie down, and I shall stay behind here,
45 So I may stir up still more your mother and the serving maids.
And she, as she laments, will ask me for details."
So he said, and Telemachos went out through the hall
Under the shining torches to lie down, to the chamber
Where he went to bed before whenever sweet sleep came upon
   him.
50 He lay down there then also and awaited the godly dawn.
But godly Odysseus was left behind in the hall
Devising slaughter for the suitors with Athene's aid.
And the prudent Penelope went out of her chamber
In the semblance of Artemis or golden Aphrodite.
55 They put a chair by the fire for her where she used to sit,
A chair whorled with ivory and silver that Ikmalios
The craftsman had once fashioned; to it he had attached
A footstool under the feet; and over it a large fleece was
   thrown.
Then the prudent Penelope sat down on it.
60 White-armed serving women came out of the hall
And were taking away a great amount of bread, and the tables,
And the cups from which the insolent men had drunk.
They threw the fire from the braziers to the ground and heaped
Much fresh wood upon them for light and for warming.

Melantho upbraided Odysseus again a second time;   65
"Stranger, will you still bother us here even now through the
    night,
Prowling through the house; and will you be ogling the women?
Well, go on outdoors, you wretch, and enjoy your meal,
Or soon you will be struck with a firebrand and go outdoors."
Odysseus of many wiles glowered at her and spoke: 70
"You terror, why do you hold at me so in rancorous spirit?
Is it because I am dirty and wear foul garments on my skin
And beg through the district? Necessity drives me on.
This is the way that beggars and wandering men are.
I myself was once blessed, and I inhabited   75
A rich house among men, and gave to such a wanderer
Many times, no matter who came, whatever he needed.
I had numberless servants and many other things
Men have who live well and are called prosperous,
But Zeus, son of Cronos, destroyed me, as he somehow wished. 80
So take heed, woman, lest soon you, too, lose all the grace
In which for the present you excel among the serving maids,
Lest perhaps your mistress get angry and bear hard on you,
Or lest Odysseus come. For there is still a share of hope.
And if he has died, as you think, and is no more to return,   85
Yet already, thanks to Apollo, he has a son like himself,
Telemachos. And no women in the halls who acts recklessly
Escapes his notice, because he is no longer so young."
So he said, and the prudent Penelope heard him.
She rebuked her servant and spoke out to her directly: 90
"Bold woman, fearless bitch, you indeed do not escape my
    notice
When you do this enormous deed, that you shall wipe off on
    your head.
And you know this full well, as you heard me say it myself,
That I intended to ask the stranger in my halls
About my husband, since my griefs come thick and fast."   95
She spoke, and said a speech to the housekeeper Eurynome:
"Eurynome, bring a chair and a fleece upon it here
So that the stranger may sit down and speak with me,
And listen; I should like to ply him with questions."
So she said, and the woman very quickly brought a well-planed
    chair   100
And set it up, and upon it she threw a fleece.

Then godly Odysseus, who had endured much, sat down there.
And the prudent Penelope began speaking between them:
"Stranger, I myself shall ask you this question first:
105 What men are you from? Where are your city and parents?"
Odysseus of many wiles addressed her in answer:
"My good woman, no one among mortals on the boundless
     earth
Would find fault with you. Your renown reaches broad heaven,
As though of some blameless king who in a god-fearing way
110 Holds sway over numerous and valiant men,
Who upholds good laws, and his black earth produces
Wheat and barley, and his trees are laden with fruit.
His sheep bear young without fail, and the sea provides fish
From his good leadership, and the people excel under him.
115 And so ask me anything else now in your house,
But do not inquire of my race and my fatherland,
So that you may not fill my heart up further with pains
While I remember. I am a man of much grief. There is no need
For me to sit wailing and moaning in another's home,
120 Since it is always worse to grieve endlessly,
Lest one of the maids resent it, or you yourself,
And say my tears flow because my mind is heavy with wine."
And then the prudent Penelope answered him:
"Stranger, truly the immortals destroyed my excellence
125 Of form and body at the time the Argives went aboard ship
Toward Ilion, and with them went my husband Odysseus.
If that man should come and minister to my life,
My renown would be greater that way, and lovelier.
But now I am grieved, so many ills has some god sent me!
130 All the noblemen who rule over the islands
Of Dulichion and Samê and wooded Zacynthos,
And who dwell round about sunny Ithaca itself,
Woo me against my will and are consuming my house.
And so I have no regard for strangers or suppliants,
135 Nor for heralds at all, who are craftsmen of the district;
But, longing for Odysseus, I pine away in my heart.
They are eager for marriage, and I weave deceits.
First some god inspired my mind with the thought of a robe;
I should set up a great loom in the halls and weave on it
140 A large and delicate fabric. I told them at once:
'Young men, my suitors, since godly Odysseus is dead,

Wait, though you are eager for this marriage of mine, till I finish
This robe, so that the yarn may not waste in vain,
This burial sheet of hero Laertes for the time
When the ruinous fate of long-sorrowful death seizes him,   145
Lest one of the Achaian women in the district blame me
If he who had won so much lie without covering.'
So I said, and the bold spirit was persuaded in them.
Every day I kept weaving there on the great loom,
And the nights I undid it when I had the torches set up.   150
So for three years I fooled the Achaians and persuaded them.
But when the fourth year came and the seasons came on
As the months waned, and many days came to an end,
Then indeed through my maid servants, uncaring bitches,
They came and caught me, and all shouted at me together.   155
And so I finished it, though unwilling and under duress.
And now I can neither escape marriage nor find
Any further plan. My parents urge me on very much
To marry, and my son chafes at those who devour his living,
And he notices it; for he is already a man quite able   160
To care for the sort of house to which Zeus gives renown.
But tell me of your descent, wherever you are from,
For you are not from the oak of ancient tale or from rock."
Odysseus of many wiles addressed her in answer:
"Respected wife of Odysseus, son of Laertes,   165
Will you never leave off inquiring of my descent?
Well, I shall speak out to you, and you will give me to more
    woes
Than those I am held in. For this is the rule, when a man
Has been away from his fatherland as long as I now have,
Wandering to many cities of mortals, suffering pains.   170
Yet even so I shall tell you what you ask and inquire about:
There is a certain land, Crete, in the midst of the wine-faced
    ocean,
Lovely and fertile, circled by the sea. Many men
Are in it, innumerable, and ninety cities are there;
One tongue is mingled with others. There are Achaians,   175
Great-hearted true Cretans and Cydonians,
Dorians, of three settlements, and godly Pelasgians.
And among those is Cnossos, a great city, where Minos,
The intimate of great Zeus, ruled nine years as king.
The father of my father, great-hearted Deucalion.   180

Deucalion begat me and the lord Idomeneus.
And that man went off up to Ilion in the curved ships
With the sons of Atreus. Aithon is my well-known name.
I was the younger by birth; he was older and more valiant.
185 And there I myself saw Odysseus and gave him guest gifts.
For in fact, the force of the wind had brought him over toward
    Crete
When he was eager for Troy, driving him off course past Malea.
He anchored at Amnisos, where the cave of Eileithyia is,
A difficult harbor, and he barely escaped the storms.
190 He went up to the city at once and asked for Idomeneus
And said he was his guest friend, a dear and respected one.
But the tenth or eleventh dawn had already come for the man
Since he had been gone in the curved ships to Ilion.
I led him to my house and entertained him well,
195 Befriending him kindly, as there was much in my home.
To him and to the others, his companions who followed him
I gave barley gathered from the region and sparkling wine
And oxen for sacrifice so their hearts might be satisfied.
There the godly Achaians remained for twelve days.
200 A great North Wind held them back, and did not allow them
To ride at anchor near land; some harsh god raised it up.
The thirteenth day the wind fell, and they put to sea."
He spoke many falsehoods and made them seem like the truth.
Tears flowed from her as she listened and her flesh melted.
205 Just as snow melts down upon the peaks of the mountains
Which the East Wind melts when the West Wind pours it
    down,
And when the snow melts the flowing rivers are full;
So her lovely cheeks melted as she poured down her tears,
Weeping for her husband who was sitting by. Odysseus
210 Felt pity in his heart for his wife as she lamented,
But his eyes stood fast, as though they were horn or iron
Untrembling in his eyelids. And by guile he hid his tears.
But when she had her fill of tearful lamentation,
She once more answered him and addressed him, saying:
215 "And now, stranger, I think I shall test you out,
If truly in that place with his godlike companions
You entertained my husband in your halls, as you say.
Tell me what sort of clothes he had on over his skin,

What sort of man he was, and what companions went with
    him."
Odysseus of many wiles addressed her in answer: 220
"My good woman, it is hard to say, for a man who has been so
    long
Parted, since already it is the twentieth year
From the time he went thence and left my fatherland.
But I shall tell you the way my heart pictures it for me:
Godly Odysseus had on a purple mantle of wool,   225
A double one. And the brooch upon it was made of gold,
With twin sockets. And on its face it was skillfully wrought:
In his front paws a dog was holding a dappled fawn
And gazed at it while it writhed. All men marveled to see
How the one, being of gold, gazed at the fawn he throttled,   230
And the other strove to get away as he writhed with his feet.
I noticed the tunic over his flesh glistening
The way the husk does on an onion that is dried,
So soft it was, and it was shining like the sun.
Many women indeed looked with wonder upon him.   235
I shall tell you something else, and keep it well in mind:
I do not know if Odysseus had these clothes on his skin from
    home,
Or if some companion gave them as he went on the swift ship,
Or perhaps some guest friend, since Odysseus was dear
To many men. For few of the Achaians were equal to him.   240
And I myself gave him a bronze sword and a lovely double-
    folded
Cloak of purple and a tunic with a fringe on it,
And I sent him off with honor on his well-timbered ship,
And a herald a little older than he was himself
Followed him. I will tell you the sort of man he was, too: 245
He was bent in the shoulders, black-skinned, with a wooly crown;
Eurybates was his name. Odysseus honored him foremost
Among his companions, because he had a mind that matched
    his own."
So he said, and roused in her still more desire for weeping
When she recognized as sure ones the signs Odysseus gave her.   250
And when she had her fill of tearful lamentation,
She replied to him with a speech and addressed him:
"And now, stranger, though you were pitied by me before,

You shall now be beloved and respected in my halls.
255 I myself gave him those garments that you speak about
From my chamber, after folding them; and I put on the shining
　　brooch
To be an ornament for him. But I shall not welcome him again
On his return home to his dear fatherland.
So did Odysseus go off by an evil fate on a hollow ship
260 On his way to see evil Ilion, the unspeakable."
Odysseus of many wiles addressed her in answer:
"Respected wife of Odysseus, son of Laertes,
No longer mar your lovely skin, nor waste your heart
Lamenting for your husband. I do not blame you at all.
265 For indeed one would mourn a wedded husband she had lost,
To whom she had coupled in love and borne children, even
Another sort than Odysseus, who they say is like the gods.
But cease from lamentation and hearken to my speech.
I shall tell you unerringly and shall not conceal
270 That I have already heard about the return of Odysseus;
He is nearby in the rich land of the Thesprotians,
Alive. And he is bringing many excellent treasures,
Begging them through the land. But his trusty companions
And his hollow ship he lost on the wine-faced ocean.
275 Going from the island Thrinacria. At him did Zeus
And the Sun get angry, for the companions killed his cattle.
All of them perished in the much-surging sea.
But a wave threw him on the ship's keel upon the mainland,
The country of the Phaeacians, who are close kin to the gods.
280 They honored him heartily as they would a god,
And gave him many things, and wished themselves to send him
Homeward unharmed. And long ago would Odysseus have
　　been here,
But this course seemed to him in his heart to be better:
To get together goods while going to many lands,
285 Because Odysseus knows beyond all mortal men
About great gains, and no other person might contend with
　　him.
So Pheidon the king of the Thesprotians told me.
He swore to me personally, pouring a libation in his house,
That a ship had been drawn down and companions were ready
290 Who would conduct him to his beloved fatherland.
But he sent me off first. For a ship happened to come

Of Thesprotians headed for Dulichion, rich in wheat,
And he showed me all the possessions Odysseus had gathered.
They would support each man in turn to the tenth generation,
So many were the treasures that lay in the lord's halls.   295
He said that man had gone to Dodona in order to hear
The plan of Zeus from the lofty-leaved oak of the god
As to how he might return to his beloved fatherland,
Openly or in secret, as already he had been long away.
And so he is safe and very near, and he will come   300
Soon, nor will he be absent much longer, far
From his friends and fatherland. Indeed, I shall give you an oath:
Zeus now be my first witness, the highest and best of the gods,
And the hearth of blameless Odysseus to which I have come:
That all these things shall come to pass as I say.   305
Within the light of this very month will Odysseus be coming
   here
While one moon is waning and another is on the rise."
Then the prudent Penelope answered him:
"Would that this saying, stranger, might be brought to pass,
And then you would soon know friendship and many gifts   310
From me, so that a man who met you might call you blessed.
And yet it seems to me in my heart it will be this way:
Odysseus will not come home again, nor shall you be granted
An escort, since there are no masters in the house of the sort
That Odysseus was among men, if he ever existed,   315
To send respectable strangers off and receive them.
Well now, servants, wash him off and lay him down a bed
Of bedclothes and of mantles and of glistening blankets
So that he may reach, well-warmed, Dawn of the golden throne.
And very early in the dawn wash him and anoint him,   320
So he may think of a meal seated in the hall within
Beside Telemachos. And it will be very painful
For whoever of these grievous men annoys him. He shall not
Gain anything here any more, though he be dreadfully angry.
How shall you learn about me, stranger, that I at all excel   325
Among other women for purpose and a thoughtful plan,
If, squalid and clothed in evil garments, you dine
In the halls? Men come to their growth just a tiny while.
On whoever is himself harsh and versed in what is harsh
Do all mortal men invoke the curse of future pains   330
While he is alive, and all jeer at him when he dies.

Whoever is himself blameless and versed in what is blameless,
For him do strangers carry renown far and wide
Among all men, and many speak of him as noble."
335 Then Odysseus of many wiles addressed her in answer:
"Respected wife of Odysseus, son of Laertes,
Mantles and glistening blankets have in fact been hateful to
　　me
From the time when I first left behind the snowy mountains
Of Crete, going upon the ship with its long oars.
340 I shall lie down, as indeed I spent slumberless nights before.
Yes, for many nights in an ill-favored bed
I have rested and waited for the fair-throned Dawn.
No water for washing my feet is at all pleasing
To my heart. Nor shall any woman touch our feet
345 Among those who are active for you in your house,
Unless there is some agèd woman with a sense of devotion,
Someone who has suffered in mind as much as I have myself:
I shall not hold it against her if she touches my feet."
And then the prudent Penelope spoke to him:
350 "Dear stranger, never yet has a man so sound in mind
Of strangers from far away come more welcome to my house,
Because you so thoughtfully speak of all that is sound.
I have an old woman whose mind is packed with thoughts,
Who nourished that hapless man well and brought him up,
355 Taking him in her own hands when his mother first bore him.
She shall wash your feet, though indeed her strength is slight.
Come and stand up now, prudent Eurycleia;
Wash a man the same age as your master. Perhaps Odysseus
By this time is just like him in his hands and feet,
360 For quickly in misfortune do mortals become old."
So she said, and the old woman covered her face with her hands,
Shed hot tears, and uttered a speech of lamentation:
"Alas, for you, my child, I am helpless. Zeus hates you
Beyond other men, though you have a god-fearing heart.
365 No mortal ever yet burned so many fat thighs or sacrificed
Such choice hecatombs to Zeus, who hurls the thunderbolt,
As you bestowed on him, praying that you might come
To a sleek old age and rear your illustrious son.
For you alone is the day of return now all taken away.
370 And so perhaps the women jeered at him also
Among far-off strangers when he reached someone's home,

As these bitches, all of them here, are jeering at you.
And now, to avoid their reproach and their many insults,
You do not allow them to wash you. But me did Icarios'
   daughter,
The prudent Penelope, ask, and not against my will.   375
So I will wash your feet on Penelope's own account,
And on your own, since the heart is aroused within me
By sorrow. And now understand the speech that I speak:
Many long-suffering strangers have reached this place:
I think I have never yet seen one who resembles him   380
As you resemble Odysseus, in voice, body, and feet."
Odysseus of many wiles addressed her in answer:
"Old woman, that is what all men say who have seen us both
With their eyes, that we are very similar to one another,
As, indeed, you yourself have discerned and said."   385
So he spoke, and the old woman took a glittering basin
That she used for washing feet; she poured in much water,
The cold; then she transferred in the hot. Odysseus
Was sitting by the hearth, and suddenly turned toward the
   darkness.
For at once he was apprehensive in heart lest when she touched
   him   390
She notice his scar and the facts become apparent.
She went near and was washing her master, and right away knew
The scar which once a boar dealt him with its shining tusk
When he had come to Parnassos to see Autolycos and his sons,
His mother's noble father who excelled among men   395
In trickery and oath making. The god Hermes himself
Endowed him, for he burned the thighs of lambs and kids
Pleasing to the god, who zealously attended the man.
Autolycos had gone to the rich land of Ithaca
And found a son newly born to his own daughter.   400
Eurycleia placed him upon the man's own knees
As he finished dinner, and spoke out to him directly:
"Autolycos, now find yourself a name you may give
To the dear son of your child; he has been much prayed for."
Then Autolycos answered her and addressed her: 405
"My son-in-law and daughter, give him the name I say.
I myself come here as one who has been enraged at many,
At men and at women, throughout the much-nourishing earth,
And let him be named Man of Wrath: Odysseus. For my part,

410 When he reaches his prime, and comes to the great house
    Of his mother, to Parnassos where I have my possessions,
    I shall give him some from them and send him back in joy."
    Odysseus went for them, so the man might give him glorious
        gifts.
    Autolycos and the sons of Autolycos greeted him
415 With handclasps and welcomed him with soothing speeches.
    The mother of his mother, Amphithea, embraced Odysseus
    And kissed him on the head and on both lovely eyes.
    Autolycos called to his illustrious sons
    To get dinner ready. They heeded as he urged them on.
420 And at once they drove in a male ox five years old.
    They flayed it and worked round it and dismembered it all
    And cut it up skillfully and pierced it on spits,
    Roasted it carefully, and distributed the portions.
    So then for the whole day till the setting of the sun
425 They dined, nor did their hearts want for a well-shared meal.
    And when the sun went down and the darkness came on,
    They lay down to sleep and took the gift of slumber.
    And when the early-born, rosy-fingered dawn appeared,
    They went on the hunt, both the dogs and themselves,
430 The sons of Autolycos. With them godly Odysseus
    Went along. They approached the sheer mountain covered with
        woods
    Of Parnassos, and soon they reached the windy ravines.
    At that moment the Sun was freshly striking the fields
    Up from the deep stream of gently flowing Oceanos,
435 And the beaters reached the glen. In front of them
    Dogs moved on, tracking the footprints, and behind them
    Came the sons of Autolycos. With them godly Odysseus
    Moved close to the dogs, brandishing a long-shadowed spear.
    And there in a thick-copse was lying a great boar.
440 The blowing winds' watery force did not blow through to it,
    Nor did the Sun strike it with the beams of his rays,
    Nor did the rain get all the way through, so thick
    It was, and a plentiful deposit of leaves was there.
    The beating of the feet of men and dogs came round to him
445 As they came rushing on. Facing them out of the thicket
    He bristled his back well, glanced fire with his eyes,
    And stood very close to them. Odysseus first of all
    Rushed on, holding the long spear up in his stout hand,

Eager to hit him. The boar got the start and struck him
Above the knee, and gashed his flesh deep with a tusk,   450
Charging at him slantwise, but did not get to the man's bone.
Odysseus wounded him, hitting him on the right shoulder.
And the point of his shining spear went straight on through
    him.
He fell in the dust, squealing, and his spirit flew off.
The beloved sons of Autolycos attended to the boar   455
And bound up the wound of excellent, godlike Odysseus
Skillfully. And with an incantation they held back
The black blood. At once they reached their dear father's home.
Autolycos and the sons of Autolycos healed him
Well, and they provided him with glorious gifts,   460
And sent him in joy speedily to his dear fatherland,
To Ithaca. His father and queenly mother welcomed him
On his return, and they inquired about the details
Of how he had suffered the scar. He told them about it fully.
How the boar had struck him with his shining tusk while he was
    hunting   465
When he had gone to Parnassos with the sons of Autolycos.
The old woman took the scar in the palms of her hands and
    knew it
As she touched it; she let the foot drop that she held,
And his shin fell into the basin and the bronze clattered.
It tipped back to one side and the water spilled out onto the
    ground.   470
Both delight and pain gripped her mind, and her two eyes
Filled with tears, and her resonant voice was held back.
She touched Odysseus' chin and spoke to him:
"Indeed you are Odysseus, dear child; not even I
Knew you at first, till I had touched my master all over."   475
She spoke, and then glanced at Penelope with her eyes,
Wishing to tell her that her dear husband was within.
But the other could not sight her face to face or perceive her,
For Athene had turned her mind. Odysseus groped for her
With his hands and took her by the throat with his right hand,   480
And with the other he drew her closer to himself and spoke:
"Good mother, why do you wish to destroy me? You brought
    me up
At your breast yourself. Now, having suffered many pains,
I have come in the twentieth year to my fatherland.

485 Since you have recognized me, and a god put it in your heart,
Be quiet, lest someone else in the halls find out.
For I shall speak out as follows, and it shall be fulfilled;
If a god does subdue the noble suitors underneath me,
I shall not hold off from you for being my nurse
490 When I kill the other serving women in the halls."
And then the prudent Eurycleia addressed him:
"My child, what sort of a speech has got past the bar of your
teeth?
You know how much my strength is steadfast and unyielding.
I shall hold out like iron or some rigid stone.
495 I shall tell you another thing, and keep it well in mind.
If a god does subdue the noble suitors underneath you,
Then I shall tell you about the women in the halls,
Those that dishonor you and those that are innocent."
Odysseus of many wiles addressed her in answer:
500 "Good mother, why tell me of them? There is no need.
I myself shall observe and know each one quite well.
But keep your story in silence and turn it over to the gods."
So he said, and the old woman went on through the halls
To bring water for the feet, since the first had all been spilled.
505 And when she had washed him and anointed him richly with oil,
Then Odysseus drew the chair up closer to the fire
To warm himself. And he hid the scar in his rags.
Then the prudent Penelope began speaking between them:
"Stranger, I myself shall ask just this little thing;
510 For indeed it shall soon be the hour for pleasant slumber.
Sleep is sweet, whomever it seizes, though he has cares.
However, to me some god has given unmeasured grief.
For I enjoy my days in lamentation, mourning
And looking after my tasks and those of the servants in the
house.
515 But whenever night comes and slumber seizes them all
I lie in my bed, and thronging about my throbbing heart,
The sharp anxieties plague me as I lament.
As when the daughter of Pandareus, the nightingale of the
green,[1]
Sings beautifully when spring has freshly risen,
520 Seated amid the thick foliage of the trees,

1. Aedon ("nightingale, singer") killed her son Itylos by mistake and was
turned into a bird.

And, often modulating, pours out her loud-sounding song,
Lamenting her dear son Itylos, child of lord Zethos,
Whom one day she killed with a sword unwittingly;
So my heart is aroused, divided this way and that,
Whether I should wait with my son and steadfastly guard   525
All my property, the maids and the high-roofed house,
Respecting the bed of my husband and the talk of the people,
Or by this time should follow the best of the Achaians
Who woos me in the halls and offers endless bridal gifts.
My son while he was yet childish and weak of mind   530
Would not let me marry and leave my husband's home;
But now that he is big and has reached the measure of youth,
He implores me to go home again out of the hall,
Chafing at the property that the Achaians consume.
But come, listen to this dream and interpret it for me: 535
Twenty geese are eating the wheat in my house,
Out of the water, and I am warmed to look on them.
Then a great crooked-beaked eagle came off a mountain,
Broke all their necks and killed them. They were heaped
Together through the halls, and soared to the divine air.   540
But I wept and lamented in the very dream,
And the fair-haired Achaian women gathered about me,
As I piteously grieved that the eagle killed my geese;
But he came back and perched on a projecting rafter,
And he checked me and spoke out with a mortal voice: 545
'Take courage, daughter of widely renowned Icarios,
Not a dream it is, but a good vision, that will come to pass:
The geese are the suitors, and I who previously
Was the eagle have come back now as your own husband,
Who shall inflict on all the suitors a sorry destiny.'   550
So he said, and then honey-sweet sleep let me go.
And looking over the geese in the halls, I perceived
That they were pecking up wheat at the trough where they
    did before."
Then Odysseus of many wiles addressed her in answer:
"My good woman, there is no way to interpret this dream   555
By twisting it off another way, since Odysseus himself
Has shown how he will achieve it. Destruction is plain for the
    suitors,
All of them; and not one shall ward off destiny and death."
And then the prudent Penelope spoke to him:

"Stranger, hard to handle and confused in their stories do
560 dreams
Come, and not all in them is brought to pass for men.
For double are the portals of flickering dreams.
One set is made of horn, the other of ivory.
And as for those that come through the sawn ivory,
565 They deceive, carrying words that will not be fulfilled;
But those that pass on outside through the polished horn
Do fulfill the truth whenever any mortal sees them.
But I do not think my awesome dream has come
From these gates. That would truly be welcome to me and to
      my son.
570 I shall tell you something else, and keep it well in mind:
This dawn of evil name shall come that will make me leave
The home of Odysseus, for now I will set up a contest
Of axes, which the man used to stand up in a row
In his halls, as trestles, all twelve of them.
575 He would stand at a great distance and shoot an arrow through.
And now I will set up this contest for the suitors:
The one who most nimbly strings the bow in his hands
And shoots an arrow through all twelve of the axes,
Him will I follow, leaving this very lovely
580 Home of my marriage, full of the goods of life,
Which I think I shall ever remember even in dreams."
Odysseus of many wiles addressed her in answer:
"Respected wife of Odysseus, son of Laertes,
Do not delay this contest any longer in the house.
585 Odysseus of many wiles shall come to you in this place
Long before these men who handle this well-made bow
Have stretched the bowstring and shot an arrow through the
      iron."
And then the prudent Penelope spoke out to him:
"Stranger, if you should like to sit by me in the halls
590 And delight me, sleep would never be shed on my eyelids.
But it is not possible for men to be without sleep
Forever. The immortals have set down a limit
For everything among mortals on the grain-giving earth.
Well, I shall go up myself into the upper chamber
595 And lie down in my bed, which is made full of groans for me,
Ever sullied with my tears since the time Odysseus
Went off to see evil Ilion, the unspeakable.

There I shall lie down. You lie down in this house,
Spreading a bed on the ground; or let them put bedding down
   for you."
When she had said this, she went up to the glistening upper
   chambers,   600
Not alone, but with her went the others, her serving women.
She entered the upper chamber with her serving women
And then wept for Odysseus, her dear husband, until
Bright-eyed Athene cast sweet sleep upon her eyelids.

XX

But godly Odysseus went to bed in the portico.
Under him he spread an undressed hide, and above
Many fleeces of the sheep the Achaians had been sacrificing.
Eurynome threw a mantle on him when he lay down.
5 Then Odysseus lay awake devising evils in his heart
For the suitors. And the women who up to then
Used to lie with the suitors went out of the hall,
Entertaining one another with laughter and with mirth.
As for him, the heart was aroused in his own breast.
10 He deliberated much in his mind and in his heart,
Whether to rush among them and bring death on each one
Or else allow them to lie with the bold suitors
A last and final time. The heart within him growled;
As when a bitch standing over her feeble puppies,
15 Not recognizing a man, growls and is eager to fight,
So his heart growled within him, indignant at their evil deeds.
But he struck his breast and rebuked his heart in a speech:
"Stand it, my heart. You stood something still more shameful
On the day the Cyclops with irresistible force devoured
20 My mighty companions. And you endured, until a plan
Led you out of the cave when you thought you were to die."
So he said, and upbraided the heart in his own breast,
And so his heart kept enduring steadfastly
In submission. But he himself turned this way and that,
25 As when a man shifts an intestine full of fat and blood
On a great blazing fire quickly this way and that
And longs for it to be roasted very rapidly;
So this way and that did he toss about, pondering
How he might lay his hands upon the shameless suitors,
30 Being one man against many. Athene came close to him,
Descending from the sky; she likened her body to a
woman's.
She stood above his head and addressed a speech to him:

"Why are you awake, ill-fated beyond all mortal men?
This is your house, and this is your wife in the house,
And your child, the kind anyone would long to have for a son."   35
Odysseus of many wiles addressed her in answer:
"Yes, in all this, goddess, you have spoken properly.
But this is what the heart in my breast worries somewhat about:
How I might lay my hands upon the shameless suitors,
Being a single man, but they are always within, in a body,   40
And I also think over this greater point in my mind:
If I were to slay them with your help and that of Zeus,
Where would I get away? I ask you to think of that."
Then the bright-eyed goddess Athene addressed him:
"Stubborn man, some will trust an inferior companion   45
Who is a mortal and does not know such wisdom as mine.
But I myself am a god, who constantly protects you
In all your trials. I shall speak to you openly.
If fifty troops of articulate men in ambush
Were to stand around us, striving to kill us in war,   50
Yet should you drive off their cattle and goodly sheep.
But let sleep take you. It is also a trouble to keep watch
And lie awake all night. You shall soon rise up from your ills."
So she said. And she shed sleep over his eyelids;
Then the divine goddess herself went back to Olympos.   55
While sleep, the looser of the limbs, seized him, loosing
The troubles of his heart, his wife, who had a sense of
    devotion,
Woke up and wept while sitting up in her soft bed.
And when she was sated in her own heart with weeping,
The divine woman prayed to Artemis first of all: 60
"Artemis, queenly goddess, daughter of Zeus, would that now
You might strike my chest with an arrow and take my life away
At this very time, or that a storm would now snatch me up
And depart carrying me forth upon the murky ways,
And throw me in the streams of backward-flowing Oceanos;   65
As when storms snatched up the daughters of Pandareus,
Whose parents the gods destroyed, and they were left
    themselves
Orphaned in the halls. Divine Aphrodite tended them
With cheese and with sweet honey and with pleasant wine.
Hera endowed them beyond all other women   70
With form and wisdom. Chaste Artemis gave them stature,

And Athene taught them how to do illustrious tasks.
When divine Aphrodite proceeded to tall Olympos,
To Zeus who hurls the thunderbolt, to ask for an outcome
75 Of lusty marriage for the maidens, as he knows all things well—
What is fated and what not fated for mortal men—
At that time did whirlwinds snatch the maidens away
And give them to the hateful Erinyes to take care of.
So may those who hold Olympos's hall annihilate me,
80 Or may fair-braided Artemis strike me, so that
With Odysseus in my mind's eye, I may go beneath the hateful
　　earth,
Lest perchance I gladden the thought of a lesser man.
But it is an unendurable evil when anyone
Weeps by day, when his heart is abundantly grieved,
85 And sleep holds his nights: it brings forgetting of all
Things good and evil when it closes about his eyelids,
But even the dreams that some god sent me were evil.
For this night again there slept beside me one like the man
　　himself,
As he was when he went off with the host. And my heart
90 Rejoiced, since I thought it not a dream, but a waking fact."
So she said. And at once the golden-throned Dawn came.
Godly Odysseus heard her voice as she was weeping,
And then he thought it over; she seemed to him in his heart
Already to know him and be standing at his head.
95 He gathered up the mantle and the fleeces in which he slept
And put them on a chair in the hall; he carried the hide out,
Set it outside, and raised his hands in prayer to Zeus:
"Father Zeus, if you gods have brought me willingly,
Over dry ground and wet sea, to my land, when you had hurt
　　me much;
100 Let someone inside wake up and tell me an omen,
And outside let another portent appear from Zeus."
So he said in his prayer, and the counselor Zeus heard him,
And he thundered at once from glittering Olympos
High up out of the clouds. Godly Odysseus rejoiced,
105 And a woman grinding sent an omen out of the house nearby
Where the mills were set for the shepherd of the people,
And at them twelve women in all usually plied the work,
Producing barley grain and wheat flour, marrow of men.

The others were sleeping, since they had ground up the
  wheat.
But one had not yet ceased, the weakest; she was still working. 110
She stopped the mill and said a word, a sign to her master:
"Father Zeus, you who rule over the gods and men,
Greatly have you thundered out of the starry heaven,
Nor is there a cloud anywhere. You show this as a portent to
  someone.
Fulfill now, even for my poor self, what I say: 115
May the suitors this day for the last and final time
Partake of a delightful banquet in the halls of Odysseus,
Those who have undone my knees in heart-hurting toil
To make barley flour. May they dine now for the last time."
So she said, and godly Odysseus rejoiced at the omen and
  thunder   120
Of Zeus. For he expected him to take vengeance on the guilty.
The other serving women in the lovely house of Odysseus
Woke up and kindled an unwearying fire on the hearth.
Telemachos, a man like a god, rose up from his bed
And put on his clothes. He put his sharp sword round his
  shoulder   125
And bound the lovely sandals beneath his shining feet.
Then he took his stout spear pointed with sharp bronze,
Went to stand on the threshold, and spoke to Eurycleia:
"Good mother dear, how have you honored the stranger in the
  house?
With bed and food? Or does he lie uncared for entirely?   130
For that is the way my mother is, though she be discreet;
Indeed, among articulate men she honors the worse one
Impulsively, and the better man she sends off with no honor."
And then the prudent Eurycleia addressed him:
"Child, please do not now blame one who should not be
  blamed.   135
He sat and drank wine, in fact, as long as he wished to.
He said he was not hungry for food, for she asked him.
But when he would think about going to bed and sleep,
She ordered the servants to spread the bedding down.
Then, like a man wholly woeful and lacking his fate,   140
He did not wish to lie down to sleep on a bed and in blankets,
But on an undressed oxhide and the fleeces of sheep

He lay down in the portico. We put a mantle on him ourselves."
So she said, and Telemachos went out through the hall
145 Holding his spear. And two swift dogs followed with him.
He went on to the assembly to join the well-greaved Achaians.
Then to the serving maids the godly woman called,
Eurycleia, daughter of Ops, the son of Peisenor:
"Come here. Some of you get busy and sweep the house,
150 Sprinkle it, and throw down purple coverlets
On the well-fashioned chairs; others wipe off with sponges
All of the tables, and clean the mixing bowls out,
And the well-wrought two-handled cups. Others of you go
To the spring for water, and come bringing it quickly.
155 For the suitors will not be long absent from the hall:
They will come very early, since it is a feast day for one and all.
So she said. They listened closely to her and obeyed her.
Twenty of them went on to the dark-watered spring,
And the rest busied themselves skillfully through the house.
160 Then the lordly menservants came in. And these
Split pieces of wood up skillfully and well. The women
Came back from the spring. The swineherd came after them,
Leading on three porkers who were the best of all.
And he let them out to feed in the lovely enclosures.
165 Then he himself spoke to Odysseus with soothing words:
"Stranger, do the Achaians look on you in any way better?
Or do they dishonor you in the halls as they did before?"
Odysseus of many wiles addressed him in answer:
"Eumaeos, may the gods avenge the injury
170 That those insolent men have recklessly devised
In another's home, and they have no share of shame."
And so they said such things to one another;
But Melanthios the goatherd came up close to them,
Leading goats that were outstanding in all the flocks
175 As a meal for the suitors. Two herdsmen followed with him,
And they tied the goats up inside the resounding portico;
And then he himself spoke out to Odysseus with taunts:
"Stranger, will you now still give trouble in the house,
Begging of the men, and you will not go on outdoors?
180 I think the two of us will not be separated wholly
Till we have tasted fists, since indeed you do not beg
Decently. And there are other banquets of the Achaians, too."
So he said, and Odysseus of many wiles said nothing,

But moved his head in silence, deliberating evils.
Philoitios, a chief of men, came up as a third among them,   185
Driving a sterile heifer for the suitors, and fat goats.
Ferrymen had brought them over, who also conduct
Other men, whoever may come up to them.
And he tied the beasts up well under the resounding portico.
He himself stood close by and questioned the swineherd: 190
"Who is this stranger, swineherd, who is newly arrived
At our house? Out of what men does he declare he is?
Where indeed are his race and his fatherland soil?
He is ill-fated, yet he looks in form like a lordly king.
But the gods do afflict much-wandering men   195
Whenever they weave a fate of sorrow, even for kings."
So he said, stood close, and pledged him with his right hand,
And speaking out to him he uttered wingèd words:
"Hail, father stranger; may bliss come to pass for you
Hereafter. But, now at least, you are held in many ills.   200
Father Zeus, none of the gods is more destructive than you.
You do not pity men when once you yourself give them birth,
Getting them involved in misfortune and wretched woes.
I sweated when I thought, and my eyes were filled with tears
To remember Odysseus, since I believe he too   205
Wanders among men wearing such tatters as these,
If he is yet alive and sees the light of the sun.
But if he is already dead and in the halls of Hades,
Alas then for blameless Odysseus who put me as a small boy
In charge of oxen in the land of the Cephallenians.   210
Now they have grown numberless, nor did any race
Of broad-browed cattle give better increase for any man.
Others order me to drive them in for themselves to eat,
Nor do they care in any way for the son in the halls,
Or tremble at the surveillance of the gods. They strive even now 215
To divide the goods of the master who is gone so long.
But this thing the heart inside my own breast turns over
Many times: it is very bad while the son is alive
To go off to the land of others with the oxen and all
Among alien men. But it is more dreadful to remain here   220
And undergo pains while abiding by the oxen of others.
Indeed, I would have fled long ago and come to another
Proud king, since matters are no longer to be borne.
But still I think of that hapless man, if from somewhere

225 He may come and make the suitors scatter through the halls."
Then Odysseus of many wiles addressed him in answer:
"Herdsman, you do not seem like a bad or senseless man,
And I know for myself that prudence attains your mind.
So I shall speak out to you and swear a great oath on it:
May Zeus now be my witness first of the gods, and this guest
230   table,
And the hearth of blameless Odysseus, to which I have come;
While you are in this place Odysseus shall come home
And you shall see with your own eyes, if you desire,
The suitors being slaughtered who are lording it here."
235 Then the man who was a herdsman of the oxen spoke to him:
"Stranger, would that the son of Cronos might bring this to pass!
You should learn what my strength is and how my hands go
    with it."
And so Eumaeos prayed the same way to all the gods
That many-minded Odysseus should return to his own home.
240 Such matters did they speak of to one another.
Meanwhile the suitors were contriving death and destiny
For Telemachos; still a bird came to him on the left,
A lofty-flying eagle and he held a trembling dove.
Amphinomos spoke out to them and addressed them:
245 "My friends, this plan shall not concur with our wish,
The murder of Telemachos. Let us take thought for a banquet."
So Amphinomos said, and his speech was pleasing to them.
They went into the house of godlike Odysseus,
And they put mantles down on the seats and on the armchairs.
250 Then they sacrificed great sheep and goats rich with fat,
They sacrificed sleek hogs and a heifer of the herd.
Then they roasted the entrails and distributed them
And mixed wine up in bowls. And the swineherd passed the
    cups.
Philoitios, a chief of men, passed out bread to them
255 In lovely baskets, and Melanthios poured the wine.
Then they stretched forth their hands to the food that was
    laid out ready.
Telemachos, managing for advantage, sat Odysseus down
Inside the well-built hall next to the stone threshold,
Setting down an insignificant stool and small table.
260 Beside him he put portions of entrails and poured wine
In a golden cup, and addressed a speech to him:

"Sit in this place now and drink your wine among the men.
I myself shall personally hold off the jibes and the fists
Of all the suitors, since this house is not public
But belongs to Odysseus, and he gained it for me.   265
As for you, suitors, keep your hearts in check from taunting
And from using your fists, so no strife or quarrel may arise."
So he said, and they all bit their lips with their teeth
And wondered at Telemachos that he spoke boldly.
Then Antinoos, the son of Eupeithes, addressed them: 270
"Achaians, let us accept the speech of Telemachos,
Though it is a harsh one. He speaks with great threat to us.
For Zeus, son of Cronos, did not allow it, or by now
We would have stopped him in the halls, clear speaker though
    he be."
So Antinoos said. But the man gave no heed to his speech.   275
Meanwhile, heralds were leading a sacred hecatomb to the gods
Through the town. And the long-haired Achaians gathered
Under the shadowy grove of far-darting Apollo.
When they had roasted the top parts of meat and drawn it off,
They divided up the portions and shared in the glorious feast. 280
Those who were serving placed beside Odysseus a portion
Equal to what they got themselves, as Telemachos,
The beloved son of godly Odysseus, had ordered.
And Athene by no means allowed the bold suitors
To refrain from grievous outrage, so that still more pain   285
Might enter the heart of Odysseus, son of Laertes.
There was a man among the suitors who had a lawless mind.
Ktesippos was his name, and in Samê he made his home.
Relying on his own prodigious property,
He wooed the wife of Odysseus who was gone so long.   290
He then spoke out before the insolent suitors:
"Listen to me, bold suitors, so I may say something.
This stranger has long had, as is seemly, a share
Which is equal. It is not good or just to slight
The guests of Telemachos, whoever comes to this house.   295
Come then, I too shall give him a gift, so that he also
May give a prize to the water pourer or someone else
Of the servants who are in the home of godly Odysseus."
When he said this he threw an ox's foot from his stout hand,
Picking it up from the basket where it lay. And Odysseus   300
Dodged it by quickly ducking his head, and smiled in his heart

A very scornful smile. It struck the well-built wall.
Telemachos rebuked Ktesippos in a speech:
"Ktesippos, this was much better for you in your heart
That you did not hit the stranger. He dodged the missile
305   himself.
    For I would have struck you through the middle with my sharp
      spear,
    And your father would be arranging a tomb for you, not a
      wedding,
    Right here. So let no one show any unseemly deeds
    In my house. For I am now aware and know the facts,
310 The good ones, and the worse. I was a foolish child before,
    And still we endure these things as we look on them,
    While sheep are being slaughtered, wine is being drunk, and
      bread
    Being eaten. It is hard for one man to check many men.
    Come then, do me no more evil in your hostility.
315 If you are already eager to kill me with the bronze,
    I should prefer that; it would be better by far to die
    Than perpetually to look upon these sorry deeds,
    Strangers being maltreated and men disgracefully
    Dragging the servant women through the lovely halls."
320 So he said, and all of them grew hushed in silence.
    Finally Agelaos, son of Damastor, spoke out:
    "My friends, surely no one should become enraged
    At a just saying and rebuke someone with hostile words.
    Do not maltreat the stranger at all, or any one
325 Of the servants who are in the halls of godly Odysseus.
    I myself would say to Telemachos and his mother
    A mild speech that should please the hearts of both of them.
    So long as the spirits in your breasts were expecting
    That many-minded Odysseus would return to his own home,
330 There was no resentment that you waited and kept the suitors
    In check within the house, since that was preferable
    If Odysseus had returned and did get back to his house.
    But now it is clear already he is to return no more.
    Come then, sit beside your mother and tell her this:
335 To marry him who is the best man and provides the most,
    So you may possess all your paternal goods in joy,
    Eating and drinking, and she may tend to the house of another."
    Then sound-minded Telemachos answered him:

"Agelaos, by Zeus and the pains of my father, who may
Have perished or have wandered far from Ithaca,   340
I shall not delay my mother's wedding at all. I bid her
To marry whom she wishes, and I shall add on endless gifts.
But I am ashamed to drive her out of the hall against her will
By a word of constraint. May a god not bring this to pass."
So Telemachos said. But Pallas Athene aroused   345
Quenchless laughter in the suitors and set their wits astray.
They were already laughing with the jaws of other men,
And they were eating meat spattered with blood. Their eyes
Filled up with tears and their hearts sensed an anguish coming.
Godlike Theoclymenos also spoke out among them: 350
"Wretched men! What evil is this you suffer? Your heads
And faces are shrouded in night, and your knees beneath;
Wailing blazes up, and your cheeks are covered with tears,
The walls and the lovely pedestals are sprinkled with blood.
The porch is full of phantoms; the courtyard is also full   355
Of those eager for Erebos under the dusk. The sun
Has perished out of heaven, and an evil mist has rushed in."
So he said, and all of them laughed sweetly at him.
Eurymachos, son of Polybos, began speaking to them:
"This stranger newly come from elsewhere is out of his mind.   360
So send him at once, young men, out of the house outdoors
To go to the place of assembly, since it seems like night to him
    here."
Then godlike Theoclymenos addressed him:
"Eurymachos, I do not ask you to furnish guides for me.
I have my eyes and my ears and both of my feet,   365
And the thought in my breast is not at all shabbily formed.
With their help I shall go on outdoors, since I perceive
An evil coming on you, that no one of you suitors
Who outrage men in the home of godlike Odysseus
And devise reckless deeds shall escape from or avoid."   370
When he said this he went out of the well-situated house
And came to Peiraeos, who kindly welcomed him.
Then all the suitors, looking at one another,
Provoked Telemachos, laughing about his guests.
And this is what one of those overbearing young men would say: 375
"Telemachos, no one is worse off with guests than you;
Insofar as you have for one of them this filthy tramp
Who requires bread and wine and is not at all skilled

At tasks or in strength, but is just a burden on the land.
380 Moreover, this other man has stood up to prophesy.
But if you listen a little to me it would be far better.
Let us throw the guests into a ship with many oarlocks
And send them to Sicily, where you would get a worthwhile
price."
So the suitors said. But he did not heed their speeches.
385 No, he glanced at his father in silence, ever on watch
For the time when he might lay hands on the shameless
suitors.
The daughter of Icarios, prudent Penelope,
Put down a beautiful stool opposite
In the halls where the men were and listened to the words of
each.
For the men themselves while they laughed and prepared a
390 dinner,
Sweet and satisfying since they had sacrificed many animals.
No other more joyless supper might ever come to be
Than the one the goddess and the mighty man were soon
To set out. For the others were first to contrive sorry deeds.

Now the bright-eyed goddess Athene put it into the mind
Of Icarios' daughter, the prudent Penelope,
To set the bow before the suitors and the gray iron
In Odysseus' halls as a contest and a start for slaughter.
She stepped up on the high stairway of her quarters   5
And in her stout hand took hold of the well-curved key,
A lovely one of bronze. And an ivory handle was on it.
And she went on with her serving women into a chamber,
The last room, where the treasures of her lord were lying,
Bronze and gold and iron that was highly wrought.   10
There a springy bow was lying, and also a quiver
For arrows, and in it were many arrows that bring grief;
These gifts a friend had given him who met him in Lacedemon,
Iphitos, son of Eurytos, who was like the immortals.
The two of them came upon each other in Messene,   15
In the house of skillful Ortilochos. Odysseus
Had gone there after a debt that the whole people owed him.
Messenian men had taken up three hundred sheep
And their shepherds out of Ithaca in many-oared ships.
For their sake Odysseus had gone a long way on his errand   20
While a boy. His father and the other elders had sent him forth.
And Iphitos came after horses, twelve females of his
That he had lost, along with unweaned, work-enduring mules.
Then these, indeed, brought upon him murder and destiny
When he went in the presence of the stout-hearted son of Zeus, 25
The mortal Heracles, who was experienced in huge deeds
And slaughtered the man as a guest in his own house,
A cruel wretch, as he did not respect the gods' wrath or the
    table
That he had set before him. And then he killed the man himself.
He himself kept the mares with the powerful hooves in his halls. 30
Seeking these, the man met Odysseus and gave him the bow,

Which great Eurytos had carried before, and then
Had left when he died to his son in the lofty house.
Odysseus gave him a sharp sword and a mighty spear,
35   The start of a close-binding friendship; but they did not know
One another at the table, since before that Zeus's son slew
Iphitos, son of Eurytos, a man like the immortals,
Who gave him the bow. And never would godly Odysseus
Take it when he went off on the black ships to war.
40   But he left it lying there in the halls as a reminder
Of his dear friend. And he did carry it in his own land.
And when the divine woman had arrived at her chamber
And had gone over the oak threshold that a craftsman once
Skillfully planed for her and straightened with a line—
45   He fitted doorposts up and set shining doors on them—
Right away she quickly took the thong from the hook,
Inserted the key, and shot back the bolts of the door,
Aiming them straight; and they groaned like a bull
Feeding in a meadow, so loud did the lovely door sound
50   As it was struck by the key and was quickly opened wide.
She stepped up on the lofty planking. And there chests
Were standing, inside of which fragrant clothing was stored.
From there she stretched herself up and reached the bow
    from its peg,
Along with the bow case that surrounded it handsomely.
55   She sat down right there, putting it on her own knees,
And wept aloud as she took down her husband's bow.
And when she had her fill of tearful lamentation,
She went on into the hall among the noble suitors,
Holding in her hand the springy bow and the quiver
60   For arrows. In it were many arrows that bring grief.
Her servants brought her a case in which iron lay
In plenty, and so did bronze, the prizes of her lord.
And when the godly woman had come to the suitors,
She stood beside the pillar of the stoutly fashioned roof,
65   Holding the glistening headbands before her cheeks.
A devoted servant maid stood near her on either side.
At once she spoke out to the suitors and addressed a speech to
    them:
"Listen to me now, bold suitors, you who have always
Beset this house, perpetually eating and drinking
70   While my husband has been gone away for a long time.

You could make up no other story as an excuse
Than that you wanted to marry me and make me your wife.
Well, come now, suitors, since this appears as your prize.
I will set up the great bow of godly Odysseus.
The one who most nimbly strings the bow in his hands   75
And shoots an arrow through all twelve of the axes,
Him will I follow, departing from this very lovely
Home of my marriage that is full of the goods of life,
Which I think I shall ever remember, even in dreams."
So she said, and she called to Eumaeos, the godly swineherd,   80
To set up for the suitors the bow and the gray iron.
Eumaeos took them, weeping, and he set them out.
The herdsman for his part wailed when he saw his master's bow.
Then Antinoos rebuked them and spoke out to them directly:
"Foolish yokels, who consider only the things of the day.   85
You wretches, why are you dripping tears? Why arouse
The heart in the breast of a woman whose heart lies in pain
In any case, since she has lost her dear husband?
But sit down and eat in silence, or else go on
And wail outdoors, leaving the bow behind right here,   90
An inviolable contest for the suitors. So I think
This polished bow is not to be strung easily,
And there is no man present among all of you
Of the kind Odysseus was. I saw him my own self,
And I do remember him though I was still a foolish child."   95
So he said, but even so the heart in his breast hoped
To string the bowstring and shoot an arrow through the iron.
Yet he was destined to be the first to taste an arrow
From the hands of blameless Odysseus, whom he was flouting
    just then
As he sat in the halls, and he was rousing all his companions.   100
Telemachos spoke out to them in his sacred might:
"Well, Zeus, son of Cronos, has made me lacking in sense.
My dear mother says, even though she is prudent,
That she will follow another and leave this house behind.
Yet I am laughing and am pleased in my senseless heart.   105
Come now, you suitors, since this appears as the prize,
A woman whose like now exists not in the Achaian land,
Not in sacred Pylos or in Argos or Mycenae,
Or in Ithaca herself, or upon the black mainland.
You know it yourselves. Why need I praise my mother?   110

Come, do not put it off with excuses or turn away
From stringing the bow any more, so we may see.
And I my very own self might make a try at the bow.
If I were to string it and shoot an arrow through the iron,
115 My queenly mother would not leave me in any grief
If she went off with another, since I should be left behind
As already one able to take up my father's fine weapons."
He spoke, and put the purple tunic off his shoulders,
Sprang upright, and off his shoulders took the sharp sword.
120 First he stood up the axes, digging one long trench through
For all of them, and he straightened it with a line,
And stamped earth down about them. Wonder seized all who
saw
How neatly he stood them, but he had never viewed them
before.
He went and stood on the threshold and tested the bow.
125 Three times he made it quiver, striving to draw it,
And three times he slackened his strength, hoping in his heart
To string the bowstring and shoot an arrow through the iron.
And he would have drawn it the fourth time, bending it with
his strength.
But Odysseus nodded and checked him, impelled as he was.
130 Then Telemachos spoke out to them in his sacred might:
"Well, how weak and cowardly I shall be even in the future,
Or else I am too young and cannot yet rely on my hands
For warding some man off if he gets angry first.
Come now, you who are superior to me in strength,
135 Try the bow out and let us conclude the contest."
So he said, and put the bow away from him on the ground,
Leaning it against the tight-fitted, well-made doors.
And then he leaned a swift dart against its fine tip.
Then he sat back down on the chair from which he had stood.
140 Antinoos, the son of Eupeithes, spoke out to them:
"Rise, all my companions, in order, from left to right,
Beginning at the place from which the wine is poured."
So Antinoos said, and his speech was pleasing to them.
Leodes, son of Oinops, was the first to stand up.
145 He was their soothsayer, and he always sat
Furthest in by the lovely mixing bowl. To him alone
Was recklessness hateful; he resented all the suitors.
He was the first then to take the bow and the swift dart.

He went and stood on the threshold and tried out the bow.
He did not string it. Before that, drawing it up,   150
He tired his soft, unworn hands. And he spoke to the suitors:
"My friends, I cannot string it. Let another take it.
Many excellent men shall this bow have bereaved
Of life and spirit, since it is better by far
To die than to live and miss what perpetually   155
We are gathered for here, expectant day after day,
And even now someone hopes in his mind and desires
To marry Penelope, the wife of Odysseus.
But when he has seen the bow and tested it out,
Let him then woo some other of the well-gowned Achaian
   women   160
And seek her in marriage with gifts. She then may wed
Whoever gives the most and comes as the destined man."
When he had said this he put the bow away from him,
Leaning it against the tight-fitted, well-made doors.
And then he leaned the swift dart against its fine tip.   165
Then he sat back down on the chair from which he had stood.
But Antinoos rebuked him and spoke out to him directly:
"Leodes, what sort of speech has got past the bar of your teeth?
A wretched and grievous one. I am angered as I hear it,
If this bow indeed shall deprive excellent men   170
Of spirit and life, when you cannot string it yourself.
Your queenly mother did not bear you as the sort of man
Who would be capable of drawing a bow and arrows;
But other noble suitors shall quickly string it."
So he said, and he called to Melanthios, the goatherd.   175
"Come, Melanthios, and kindle a fire in the halls.
Put a large stool down alongside and a fleece upon it,
And bring in a great round piece of the fat from inside,
So we young men, when we have warmed it and rubbed it with
   grease,
May try the bow out and may conclude the contest."   180
So he said. Melanthios at once kindled a quenchless fire,
Brought in a stool, put it down, and set a fleece upon it.
Then he carried in a great round piece of the fat from inside.
This the young men tried, when they had warmed it. But they
   were not
Able to string it: they were far too lacking in strength.   185
Antinoos and godlike Eurymachos, chief of the suitors,

Still held back. They were by far the best in excellence.
Accompanying each other, the oxherd and the swineherd
Of godly Odysseus had both gone out of the house.
190 Divine Odysseus came after them from the house himself.
And when they were outside of the doors and the courtyard
He raised his voice and addressed them with soothing speeches:
"Oxherd, and you, swineherd, shall I tell you something
Or keep it to myself? My heart bids me to speak.
195 How would you fend for Odysseus if he came from somewhere
Very suddenly this way and some god had brought him in?
Would you fend for the suitors or fend for Odysseus?
Speak the way your heart and your spirit command you to."
Then the man who was in charge of the oxen addressed him:
200 "Father Zeus, would that you might fulfill this wish,
That the man himself might come, and some god might bring
     him.
You would learn what my strength is and how my hands go with
     it."
And so Eumaeos prayed the same way to all the gods
For many-minded Odysseus to return to his own home.
205 And when he had recognized their unerring intent,
He answered them right away and addressed them with a
     speech:
"Here I am, home, myself, having suffered many pains;
I have come in the twentieth year to my fatherland.
I realize that you alone of the servants I come to
210 Are longing for me. I have heard none of the others
Praying for me to reach home again on my return,
And I shall speak the truth to you both as it shall be.
If a god indeed subdues the noble suitors beneath me,
I shall give you both wives and provide you with property
215 And houses built close to my own. Then you shall be
Companions and kinsmen of Telemachos and myself.
Come now, I shall show you another manifest sign
So you may know me well and trust me in your hearts:
A scar a boar once inflicted on me with his shining tusk
220 When I went to Parnassos with the sons of Autolycos."
When he had said this he drew his rags away from the great scar.
Both of them, when they had seen and well noted the details,
Wept and threw their arms around the skillful Odysseus,
And they kept kissing him, embracing his head and shoulders.

Odysseus kept kissing their heads and hands the same way.   225
The light of the sun would have gone down on them as they
    moaned
If Odysseus himself had not checked them and spoken out:
"Stop wailing and lamenting, lest someone come out
Of the hall, see us, and then tell it within too;
But go inside, each in turn and not all together,   230
I first, and you afterward. And let this be made the sign.
When all the others, the whole number of noble suitors,
Will not allow the bow and quiver to be given to me,
Then you, godly Eumaeos, carry the bow through the house,
Place it in my hands, and then tell the women   235
To lock up the closely fitted portals of the hall,
And if anyone inside hears in our enclosures
A groaning and beating of men, let her not go forth
Out the door at all, but be there in silence at the task.
And you, godly Philoitios, I order to bolt the gates   240
Of the courtyard with a bolt, and quickly lash on the cord."
When he had said this he entered the well-situated halls.
Then he went and sat down on the stool from which he had
    stood,
And the two servants of godly Odysseus also went in.
Eurymachos was already turning the bow in his hands,   245
Warming it here and there in the fire's flame. But he could not
String it that way; his mighty heart swelled heavily.
Angered, he uttered a speech and spoke out directly:
"Well now, there is grief in me for myself and for all.
Not for the marriage, though distressed, do I moan so greatly.   250
There are many other Achaian women, some in this very
Sea-circled Ithaca; and some in other cities.
But if we are to such a degree lacking in the force
Of godlike Odysseus that we cannot string his bow,
It is a disgrace even for men in the future to hear of."   255
Then Antinoos, son of Eupeithes, spoke to him:
"Eurymachos, it will not be so. And you know it yourself.
For now through the district is a feast day of that god,
A holy one. And who would bend the bows? Put them down
Quietly. But as for the axes, suppose we let them   260
All stand. For I think no one will come into the hall
Of Odysseus, son of Laertes, and carry them off.
Come now, let the wine-pourer begin the rite with the cups,

So we may pour libation and lay down the curved bows.
265 And at dawn summon Melanthios, the goatherd,
To bring the goats that are far outstanding in all the herds,
So that, setting out thighs to Apollo, famed for the bow,
We may try the bow out and conclude the contest."
So Antinoos said, and his speech was pleasing to them.
270 Heralds poured out water for them over their hands.
Young men were filling bowls up to the brim with drink.
And served round to all, putting the first drops in the cups.
When they had poured libation and drunk what their hearts
    wished,
Odysseus of many wiles spoke to them with a trick in mind:
275 "Listen to me, suitors of the illustrious queen,
So I may tell you what the heart in my breast bids me to.
Eurymachos especially and godly Antinoos
Do I beseech, since he spoke properly when he said:
We should let the bow go now, and leave the matter to the gods,
280 And at dawn the god will give the strength to the one he wishes.
Come then, give me the polished bow, so that among you
I may test out my strength and hands, whether the force
Is in me still that once was in my supple limbs,
Or whether wandering and lack of care have ruined me already."
285 So he said, and they all grew insolently angry,
Fearing that he might put the string on the polished bow.
Antinoos rebuked him and spoke out to him directly:
"Wretched stranger, you have no sense, none in the least.
Are you not content to dine among us exalted men,
290 Secure, not to be deprived of food at all, and to hear
Our speeches and our discourse? Nor does anyone else,
Whether stranger or beggar listen to our speeches.
Honey-sweet wine besets you, that harms other men, too,
Whoever takes it down in gulps and drinks to excess.
295 Wine blinded the Centaur too, illustrious Eurytion,
In the hall of great-spirited Perithöus,
When he came to the Lapiths. After his mind was blinded with
    wine
He went mad and did evils in the house of Perithöus.
Distress seized the heroes. They leaped and dragged him
    outdoors
300 Through the forecourt and sheared his ears and nostrils off
With the pitiless bronze. Then he grew reckless in his mind

And went on, bearing madness in his impetuous heart.
From that came the quarrel between Centaurs and men.
But first for himself he found evil, being heavy with wine,
And so I declare great trouble for you if you should string   305
This bow. You would not encounter any gentle use
In our district. We should send you speedily
To King Echetos, the destroyer of all mortal men,
In a black ship. And you would not be saved there. But drink
Quietly, and do not wrangle with men younger than you."   310
And then the prudent Penelope answered him:
"Antinoos, it is not good or just to slight
The guests of Telemachos, whoever comes to this house.
Do you think, if this stranger does string the great bow
Of Odysseus, relying on his hands and his mighty force,   315
That he will lead me to his home and make me his wife?
He himself has never yet thought this in his breast.
Let no one of you dine here grieving in his heart
On that account, since it is not seemly at all."
Eurymachos, son of Polybos, answered her: 320
"Daughter of Icarios, prudent Penelope,
We do not think this man will lead you home. It is not seemly,
But we are ashamed at the rumor among men and women,
Lest sometime some other foul person of the Achaeans may say:
'Yes, far inferior men are wooing the wife   325
Of an excellent man and cannot string his polished bow.
But someone else, a beggar, who came on his wanderings,
Easily strung the bow and shot through the iron.'
So they would say, and this would be a reproach to us."
Then the prudent Penelope spoke to him: 330
"Eurymachos, there is no way that good reports may exist
In the district for those who dishonor and devour
A noble man's home. And why make a reproach of this?
The stranger here is very large and of a well-knit frame.
He declares he is by descent a good father's son.   335
Come now, give him the polished bow, so we may see.
For this do I proclaim, and it shall be brought to pass.
If he does string it and Apollo gives him the praise,
I shall clothe him in a mantle and a tunic, lovely clothes.
I shall give him a sharp javelin, a defense against dogs and men, 340
And a two-edged sword. I shall give him sandals for his feet
And send him wherever his heart and spirit bid."

Then sound-minded Telemachos addressed her in answer:
"My mother, as for the bow, none of the Achaians has more
    power
345 Then I have to give or refuse it to whomever I wish.
Not any of those who rule in craggy Ithaca
Or who rule over the islands towards horse-pasturing Elis.
None of them will compel me against my will even from giving
This bow once for all to the stranger to take off, if I wish.
350 But go into the house and attend to your own tasks,
The loom and the distaff, and give orders to your servants
To set at the work. The bow shall concern all the men
But me especially. For the power in the house is mine."
She was amazed at him, and back into the house she went.
355 The sound-minded speech of her son she took to heart.
She went into the upper chamber with her serving women,
And then wept for Odysseus, her dear husband, until
Bright-eyed Athene cast sweet sleep upon her eyelids.
Then the divine swineherd took the curved bow, and was
    carrying it,
360 And all the suitors made an outcry in the halls.
This is what one of those overbearing young men would say:
"Where are you carrying the curved bow, miserable swineherd,
You vagabond? Soon the swift dogs you reared yourself
Shall eat you amid the swine, apart from men, alone,
365 If Apollo is gracious to us, and the other immortal gods."
So they said; but he carried it and put it right where he was,
Afraid because many made an outcry in the halls.
But Telemachos from the other side shouted a threat:
"Uncle, bring the bow out. You will soon not do well to heed
    all,
370 Lest, though younger than you, I drive you to the fields
And throw stones at you. I am mightier than you in strength.
Would I were that much mightier in strength and with my hands
Than all of the suitors who are inside the halls.
Then I should soon send one of them grimly on his way
375 Out of our house, since they are devising evils."
So he said, and all of the suitors sweetly laughed
At him, and they relaxed their oppressive anger
Toward Telemachos. The swineherd carried the bow through
    the house,
Stood beside skillful Odysseus, and put it in his hands.

Then he called forth the nurse Eurycleia and addressed her: 380
"Prudent Eurycleia, Telemachos orders you
To lock up the closely fitted portals of the hall.
And if anyone inside hears in our enclosures
A groaning and a beating of men, let her not go forth
Out the door at all, but be there in silence at the task."   385
So he said, and for her the speech was without a wing.
She locked up the doors of the well-situated halls.
Philoitios hastened in silence out of the house,
Outdoors, and locked up the gates of the well-fenced court.
Under the portico lay the papyrus-fiber cable   390
Of a bobbing ship. With it he tied the gates, entered,
And then went and sat down on the stool from which he had
        stood
And looked at Odysseus. He was already handling the bow,
Turning it in all directions, testing it this way and that,
For fear worms had eaten the horns while the master was away. 395
And this is what one of them, looking at his neighbor would
        say:
"This is some fancier and an expert with bows,
And perhaps such as these are lying in his home too,
Or else he wants to make one, he handles it so
This way and that in his hands, the beggar skilled in evils."   400
And another of the overbearing young men would say:
"Would that he might encounter profit only to the degree
That he shall ever be able to string this bow himself."
So the suitors said. But Odysseus of many wiles,
At once when he raised the great bow and viewed it on all
        sides—   405
As when a man skilled at the lyre and at singing
Easily stretches a string over a new peg,
Tying at both ends the flexible gut of the sheep—
So without effort did Odysseus string the great bow.
He took it in his right hand and tested the cord.   410
It sang sweetly beneath like a swallow in its sound.
Great distress came upon the suitors, and the skin of all
Turned color. Zeus thundered greatly, showing signs.
Then godly Odysseus, who had endured much, rejoiced
That the son of crooked-counseling Cronos sent him a portent. 415
He took a swift arrow that lay by him on the table,
Bare. The others were lying within the hollow quiver,

The ones the Achaians were soon to experience.
He put it to the bridge, drew the string and the notches,
420 And shot the arrow right from there, sitting on the stool,
Aiming it straight, and he did not miss one handle tip
Of all of the axes. The arrow heavy with bronze
Went straight on out the end. He spoke to Telemachos:
"Telemachos, the stranger seated in the halls
425 Does not discredit you. I did not miss my aim,
Nor did I toil long to string the bow. My strength is steadfast still
And is not such as the suitors scorn, despising me.
And now it is time for the Achaians to have a meal prepared
In the light, and then to make sport in other ways
430 With singing and the lyre; they are the ornaments of a feast."
So he said, and signaled with his eyebrows. Telemachos,
The dear son of godlike Odysseus, girded on his sharp sword,
Put his own hand round his spear, and stood close to him
Beside his armchair, equipped with the glittering bronze.

Then Odysseus of many wiles bared himself from his rags
And sprang upon the great threshold, holding the bow
And the quiver full of arrows. He poured the swift shafts out
There before his feet. And he spoke out among the suitors:
"This inviolable contest has been brought to an end.   5
And now I shall know another mark that no man has ever hit,
If I happen to hit it, and Apollo grant me glory."
So he said, and aimed a bitter arrow at Antinoos.
The man was about to lift up the lovely libation cup,
A gold double-eared one, and he held it up in his hands   10
So that he might drink wine. There was no thought of slaughter
In his heart. Who would think a single man among so many
As the banqueters were, though he was very powerful,
Would bring upon him an evil death and black fate?
Odysseus took aim and shot him with an arrow in the throat;   15
The point of it went straight on through his tender neck.
He leaned to one side and the cup fell from his hand
As he was hit; at once a thick spurt of human blood
Came through his nostrils. He quickly pushed the table from
    him,
Striking it with his foot. He spilled the food on the ground,   20
And the bread and roast meat were defiled. The suitors made
A din through the halls when they saw the man fall.
They rose up from their chairs, panicking through the house,
Peering on all sides along the well-constructed walls.
And nowhere was there a shield or stout spear to be grasped.   25
They upbraided Odysseus with words full of rage:
"Stranger, to your ill do you shoot at men. You shall no longer
Enter other contests; now your sheer destruction is certain.
Now you have slain the mortal who was the greatest by far
Of the young men in Ithaca. So vultures shall eat you here."   30
Each man guessed so, since they thought he had killed the man
Without wanting to. And the fools did not perceive

That already the bonds of destruction were fastened on them all.
Odysseus of many wiles glared at them and spoke:

35　"Dogs, you thought I would no longer come home in return
From the land of the Trojans; and so you wore my house away
And slept alongside my serving women by force
And underhandedly courted my wife while I was myself alive,
And you did not fear the gods who possess broad heaven,

40　Or that there would be any vengeance of men in time to come.
Now the bonds of destruction are fastened on you all."
So he said, and sallow fear got a grip on all of them.
Each one peered for where he might flee sheer destruction.
Eurymachos alone spoke to him in answer:

45　"If indeed you are Ithacan Odysseus, who have come,
You have rightfully told all this that the Achaians have done:
Many wicked things in the halls, and many in the fields.
And here he lies already who was guilty of them all,
Antinoos. He it was who instigated these deeds,

50　Not so much wanting or desiring the wedding at all,
But plotting other acts which the son of Cronos did not bring
　　about
For him: that over the well-tilled land of Ithaca
He might himself be king, and might kill your son in ambush.
Now he is slain, as was his due. Spare your people

55　And we shall give satisfaction in the land hereafter
For all that has been drunk up and eaten in the halls,
Each one bringing separately a recompense worth twenty oxen,
And we shall give bronze and gold in return till your own heart
Is softened. Till then no one would blame you for getting
　　angry."

60　Odysseus of many wiles glared at him and spoke:
"Eurymachos, not if you gave me all the paternal goods
That you possess, and any others you added from somewhere,
Not even then should I yet stay my hands from slaughter
Until the suitors had paid for all their insolence.

65　And now it lies with you either to fight face to face
Or to flee, whoever would avoid death and destiny.
But I think that no one shall escape sheer destruction."
So he said; and their knees and their own hearts went slack
On the spot. And Eurymachos addressed them yet again:

70　"My friends, this man will not check his invincible hands,
But once he has taken the polished bow and quiver

He will shoot from the smooth threshold until he has killed
All of us. But let us remember the ardor of battle;
Draw your swords out and hold the tables up in the way
Of the swift-fated arrows. And let us all go at him   75
In a body, hoping we may force him from the threshold and the
  doorway.
And may come to the town, and an alarm quickly be raised.
And soon then this man would have shot for the last time."
When he had spoken so, he drew out his keen sword
Of bronze, sharpened on both sides; and sprang on the man   80
With a terrible cry. At the same time godly Odysseus
Shot off an arrow, and he hit his chest by the nipple;
He drove the swift shaft into his liver. And from his hand
He let the sword drop to the ground. He fell down sprawling
Doubled up on the table. He spilled the food on the ground,   85
And the two-handled cups. He beat the earth with his forehead,
Agonized in his heart. He kicked the armchair with both feet.
And made it shake. A mist was shed over his eyes.
Amphinomos charged upon the mighty Odysseus
Rushing up against him, and he drew his sharp sword   90
That the man might somehow yield the door to him.
    Telemachos
Was too fast for him, and hit him from behind with a bronze
  spear
In the middle of the shoulders, and drove it through his chest.
He made a noise falling and struck the ground flat with his
  forehead.
Telemachos sprang away, leaving his long-shadowy spear   95
There in Amphinomos. For he greatly feared that, as he drew
  out
The long-shadowy spear, some Achaian might thrust him
  through
By rushing on with a sword, or hit him as he stooped forward.
He ran on and very quickly reached his dear father.
He stood close beside him and uttered wingèd words: 100
"Father, I shall now bring you a shield and two spears,
And a helmet all of bronze, fitted to the temples.
I shall put it on me when I come, and I shall give other
  arms
To the swineherd and the oxherd. It is better to be armed."
Odysseus of many wiles addressed him in answer: 105

"Bring them on the run, while the arrows may defend me,
Lest they force me out the doors, single man that I am."
So he said, and Telemachos obeyed his dear father.
He went on into the chamber where lay the glorious arms.
110 And from that place he took away four shields, eight spears,
And four bronze-fitted helmets with shaggy horsehair plumes;
He came carrying them and very soon reached his dear father.
He himself put the bronze on over his flesh first of all.
The two servants put their fine armor on the same way.
115 They flanked the skillful and subtle-minded Odysseus.
He himself, so long as there were arrows to defend him,
Kept aiming at the suitors in his house one by one
And always hit his mark. They fell one after another.
But when the arrows had all left the master as he shot,
120 He leaned the bow to stand it up against the doorpost
Of the well-built hall, against the resplendent walls.
He himself put the four-layered shield round his shoulders
And placed on his mighty head the well-fashioned helmet
With a horsehair crest; terribly the plume nodded on top of it.
125 And he took two valiant spears fitted out with bronze.
There was a certain side door in the well-built wall
Along the highest point of the well-based hall's threshold.
It was a way to the passage, and well-fitted doors held it.
Odysseus ordered the godly swineherd to stand close to it
130 And watch over it. It was the one single way of approach.
Then Agelaos spoke to them, declaring his speech to all:
"My friends, will not someone go up through the side door
And tell the people, so an alarm may quickly be raised,
And then this man would soon have shot now for the last time."
135 Then Melanthios, herdsman of the goats, spoke to him:
"There is no way, Zeus-bred Agelaos. The court's fine doors
Are dreadfully close, and the mouth of the passage is hard,
And a single man who was valiant could hold back all.
But come, I shall bring you arms to gird yourselves with
140 From the chamber. Within, I think, and nowhere else
Have Odysseus and his glorious son put their armor up."
When he had said this, Melanthios, the goatherd, went up
To Odysseus' chambers through the slits of the hall.
There he took out twelve shields and as many spears
And as many bronze-fitted helmets with shaggy horsehair
145   plumes.

He came out and brought them quickly and gave them to the
  suitors
Then Odysseus' knees and his heart went slack
When he saw them putting on the armor and brandishing
The long spears in their hands. It seemed to him a great task.
Right away he uttered wingèd words to Telemachos: 150
"Telemachos, some one of the women in the halls
Stirs up an evil battle against us, or Melanthios does."
Sound-minded Telemachos addressed him in answer:
"Father, I myself made this mistake, and no one else
Is guilty. I left the closely fitted door of the chamber   155
Hanging open. One of them spied it better than I.
But go, godly Eumaeos, and close the door
And observe whether one of the women is doing this,
Or Melanthios, son of Dolios, the one I think."
And so they said such things to one another.   160
Then Melanthios, the goatherd, went again to the chamber
To bring the fine armor. The godly swineherd perceived him
And at once he addressed Odysseus, who was near:
"Zeus-born son of Laertes, Odysseus of many devices,
That destructive man who we ourselves think is the one   165
Is going to the chamber. And tell me unerringly
Whether I should kill him if I am more powerful,
Or bring him here to you to pay for the many
Insolences this man has plotted in your house."
Odysseus of many wiles addressed him in answer: 170
"Indeed, Telemachos and I shall hold the noble suitors
Inside of the halls, though they may struggle very much.
But both of you twist his feet behind him and his hands
  above,
Throw him into the chamber, and bind planks behind him,
And then fasten a plaited rope to the man himself.   175
Drag him up the lofty pillar and bring him near the beams
So he may long be alive and suffer oppressive pains."
So he said. They hearkened closely to him and obeyed him.
They went on into the chamber unseen by the man inside;
He in fact was searching a corner of the chamber for the arms. 180
The two remained standing on either side of the posts.
When Melanthios, the goatherd, was going over the threshold
Carrying a fine-horned helmet in one of his hands
And in the other a broad, old shield spattered with mold

185 Of the hero Laertes, which he used to bear as a young man—
But at this time it was laid by, and the seams of its thongs were
    loose—
The two rushed upon him, seized him, and dragged him inside
By the hair; they threw him, grieved at heart, on the ground.
They bound his hands and his feet with a spirit-hurting bond,
190 Turning it around very thoroughly and well, as the son
Of Laertes had ordered, godly Odysseus, who had endured
    much.
They fastened a plaited rope to the man himself,
Dragged him up the lofty pillar, and brought him near the
    beams.
Then you spoke and taunted him, swineherd Eumaeos:
195 "Now, indeed, Melanthios, you will keep watch the whole night,
Lying down in a gentle bed, as is fitting for you.
Nor shall the early-born, golden-throned one as she comes
From the streams of Oceanos escape your view at the time
You drive goats for the suitors to prepare a feast in the house."
200 And so he was left there, stretched in the ruinous bond.
The two put on armor, closed the shining door,
And went to the skillful crafty-minded Odysseus.
There did they stand, breathing force, the four of them
On the threshold, but there were many noblemen within the
    house.
205 Athene, daughter of Zeus, came to close quarters with them,
Likening herself to Mentor in form and in voice.
Odysseus rejoiced to see her, and spoke to her:
"Mentor, fend off harm; remember the dear companion
Who used to do you good. You are the same age as I."
210 So he said, thinking it was Athene, rouser of the people.
The suitors on the other side made a din in the halls.
Agelaos, son of Damastor, reproached her first:
"Mentor, let Odysseus not win you over with speeches
To fight against the suitors and to defend himself,
215 For I think our own purpose shall be carried out this way;
When we have killed these men, the father and the son,
Then you yourself shall be slain with them for what you plan
To do in the halls. You will pay it here with your own head,
And when we have deprived you of your power with the sword,
220 All the possessions you have, both indoors and out
We shall mix with those of Odysseus, and we shall not

Allow your sons to live in the halls or your daughters
Or your devoted wife to move round in the city of Ithaca."
So he said, and Athene grew very angry in her heart,
And she upbraided Odysseus with angry words: 225
"No longer, Odysseus, have you a steadfast mind or strength
As when, over white-armed Helen, who had a noble father,
You fought the Trojans, always relentlessly, for nine years
And in the dreadful combat slaughtered many men,
And Priam's broad-streeted city was taken by your plan.   230
How is it that now, when you have reached your home and
    possessions,
You wail about being valiant against the suitors?
Come now, old friend, stand by me and see the deed,
So you may see what sort Mentor, son of Alkimos, is
To repay well-doing in the midst of hostile men."   235
So she said, and did not yet wholly give him victory
With decisive strength, but still tested the power and strength
Both of Odysseus and of his glorious son.
Then she herself rushed up and sat upon the roof
Of the smoky hall facing them, in the form of a swallow.   240
Agelaos, the son of Damastor, urged on the suitors,
And so did Eurynomos, Amphimedon, Demoptolemos,
Peisander, the son of Polyktor, and skillful Polybos,
Who were by far the best of the suitors for excellence
Of those who were still living and fighting for their lives.   245
The bow and frequent arrows had already overcome the others.
Agelaos spoke to them, declaring his speech to all:
"My friends, this man shall soon hold back his invincible
    hands.
Mentor has gone from him, uttering empty boasts,
And they are left alone out in front of the gates.   250
Do not all of you let your long spears fly together.
Come now, you six hurl your javelins first, so that Zeus
May perchance grant that Odysseus be hit and we gain glory.
For the rest there will be no trouble when this man has
    fallen."
So he said, and they all threw their javelins as he bade,   255
Eagerly. But Athene made them all of no effect.
One of them hit against the pillar of the well-based hall,
Another one hit against the closely fitted door
And another's bronze-heavy ash spear fell on the wall.

260 And then, when they had avoided the spears of the suitors,
Godly Odysseus, who had endured much, began speaking to
   them:
"My friends, let me say myself that we, too, right now
Should shoot into the throng of suitors who are striving to kill
   us
And strip our armor, adding this to their former evils."
265 So he said, and all of them hurled their sharp spears,
Aiming them straight. Odysseus slew Demoptolemos;
Telemachos, Eurypades; and the swineherd, Elatos;
The man who was in charge of the oxen slew Peisander.
All these together bit the broad floor with their teeth,
270 And the suitors drew away into the corner of the hall.
But the others rushed on them and drew spears out of the dead.
Then the suitors hurled their sharp spears right away,
Eagerly. But Athene made their number of no effect.
One of them hit against a pillar of the well-based hall,
275 Another one hit against the closely fitted door,
And another's bronze-heavy ash spear fell on the wall.
Yet Amphimedon hit Telemachos' hand at the wrist
With a glancing blow, and the bronze wounded his outer skin.
Ktesippos grazed Eumaeos with a long spear on the shoulder
280 Above his shield. It leaped off and fell to the ground.
Then those round the skillful and subtle-minded Odysseus
Hurled their sharp spears into the throng of the suitors.
Then Odysseus, sacker of cities, hit Eurydamas.
Telemachos hit Amphimedon, and the swineherd hit
   Polybos;
285 And then the man in charge of the oxen hit Ktesippos
Upon the chest, and he spoke right out with a boast:
"Son of Polytherses, you lover of jeers, never again
Yield wholly to folly and talk big; but turn the tale over
To the gods, since they are more powerful by far.
290 This is a guest gift in return for the foot you once gave
To godlike Odysseus as he went begging in the house."
So said the driver of the crumple-horned cattle. Odysseus
Wounded the son of Damastor at close hand with a long spear.
Telemachos wounded Leocritos, son of Euenor,
In the middle of the flank with a spear; he drove the bronze
295   through him.

The man fell on his face and struck the ground flat with his
    forehead.
Then Athene held up the aegis deadly to mortals,
On high from the roof. The minds of the men were dismayed.
They fled through the hall like cattle in a drove
That a darting gadfly, when it is stirred up, stampedes   300
In the season of spring, when the days are getting long.
And then, as falcons with bent claws and hooked beaks
Come down from the mountains and dash upon the birds—
These are driven over the plain cowering from the clouds,
But the others pounce on them and kill them; and no help   305
Comes, and no escape, and men rejoice at the chase—
So they rushed on through the house upon the suitors
And struck them one after another. Their wretched groaning
Rose as their heads were struck. The whole ground ran with
    blood.
Leiodes rushed on and seized Odysseus by the knees,   310
And imploring him, he uttered wingèd words:
"I pray to you, Odysseus, respect me and pity me.
Never yet, I say, have I spoken or done anything reckless
To any woman in the halls. But I kept stopping
The other suitors when anyone did such things.   315
But they did not heed me and keep their hands from evil,
And so in their recklessness they have come to a wretched fate.
Yet I who as a soothsayer among them did nothing evil
Shall be laid low, since there is no future grace for good deeds."
Odysseus of many wiles glared at him and spoke: 320
"If you indeed declare you are a soothsayer among them,
You are likely to have prayed many times in the halls
That the end of a sweet return be kept far from me;
That my beloved wife follow you and bear you children.
And so you may not escape death that brings bitter pain."   325
When he had said this, he seized in his stout hand a sword lying
    there
That Agelaos had let fall to the ground when he was killed.
With it he drove through the middle of the man's neck.
His head as he spoke was mingled with the dust.
And the son of Terpes, the singer, still tried to avoid black
    death,   330
Phemios, who sang for the suitors under constraint.

He stood holding the clear-toned lyre in his hands
Close to the side door, and he was thinking two ways in his
　mind,
Whether to abandon the hall and take a seat
335 At the well-made altar of the great Zeus of the Court,
Where Laertes and Odysseus had burned many thighs of oxen,
Or to rush up and implore Odysseus at his knees.
And so, as he thought, it seemed to him to be better
To take hold of the knees of Odysseus, son of Laertes.
340 He put his hollow lyre down upon the ground
Between the mixing bowl and the silver-studded chair
And rushed up himself and took Odysseus by the knees,
And imploring him, he uttered wingèd words:
"I pray to you, Odysseus; respect me and pity me.
345 There will be grief for yourself hereafter if you slay
A singer like me who sings for gods and for men.
I am self-taught, and a god has planted all kinds
Of lays in my mind. I am fit to sing before you
As before a god. And so do not be eager to cut my throat.
350 And Telemachos, your beloved son, may tell you this:
That not at all by my wish or need did I frequent
The suitors in your house to sing for them at their feasts.
But, being far more, and stronger, they brought me by
　constraint."
So he said, and Telemachos in his sacred might heard him.
355 At once he addressed his father, who was close beside him:
"Hold off, do not wound this guiltless man with the sword.
Let us also spare the herald Medon, who always
Looked after me in our house when I was a child,
Unless indeed Philoitios or the swineherd has slain him
360 Or he came on you as you were stirred up in the house."
So he said, and Medon, who was sound of mind, heard him.
He lay crouching underneath an armchair and had covered
　himself
With the new-flayed skin of an ox, to avoid black fate.
He rose at once from beneath the chair, took the oxhide off,
365 Then rushed up and grasped Telemachos by the knees,
And imploring him, he uttered wingèd words:
"My friend, here I am, myself. Hold! Tell your father;
Lest in his greater strength he kill me with the sharp sword,
From his anger at the suitors who have devoured his goods

In the halls, and the fools did not honor you at all."   370
Odysseus of many wiles smiled at him and spoke:
"Take courage, as indeed this man has rescued you and saved
    you,
So that you may know in your heart and even tell someone else
How doing good deeds is much better than doing bad.
But come out of the hall and sit down outdoors in the court   375
Away from slaughter, you and the singer full of stories,
Till in the house I have myself taken care of what I must."
So he said, and the two of them went out of the hall.
They both sat down before the altar of great Zeus
And peered round on all sides, ever expecting slaughter.   380
Odysseus peered round his house lest some one of the men
Might still be concealed alive, avoiding black fate.
But he saw they had all fallen, in great numbers,
In blood and dust, like fish that the fishermen
Have drawn up on the curved beach out of the hoary sea   385
In a net that has many meshes; and all of them
Are heaped up on the sands longing for the waves of the sea;
But the sun in his shining is taking away their life;
So then the suitors were heaped up on one another.
Then Odysseus of many wiles addressed Telemachos: 390
"Telemachos, go and call the nurse Eurycleia for me,
So that I may tell her what it is my desire to tell."
So he said, and Telemachos obeyed his beloved father.
He shook the door and spoke to the nurse Eurycleia:
"Rise and come here, old woman, you who were born long ago,   395
And who watch over our serving women in the house.
Come, my father calls you, so he may tell you something."
So he said, and for her the speech was without a wing.
But she opened up the doors of the well-situated halls
And came on out. Telemachos went on ahead to lead.   400
Then she found Odysseus among the bodies of the slain,
Bespattered over with blood and with gore like a lion
Who goes along when he has eaten from an ox of the field,
And all his breast and also his cheeks on either side
Are bloody, and his face is terrible to look upon;   405
So was Odysseus bespattered, on his feet and his hands above.
Now when she saw the corpses and the unspeakable blood,
She made ready to exult, since she beheld a huge deed.
But Odysseus checked her and held her, eager as she was,

410 And speaking out to her, he uttered wingèd words:
"Old woman, rejoice in your heart; hold back and do not exult.
It is not holy to boast over men who have been slain.
The gods' fate has worsted these men, and their cruel deeds,
For they honored no one of the men upon the earth,
415 Either evil or noble, whoever encountered them.
And so in their recklessness they met a sorry fate.
Come now, and tell me about the women in the house,
Which ones dishonor me and which ones are innocent."
Then his beloved nurse Eurycleia spoke to him:
420 "All right, then, my child, I shall tell you the whole truth:
There are fifty women of yours inside the halls,
Serving women whom we have taught how to do their tasks,
How to card wool and how to endure servitude;
Of these, twelve in all have gone the way of shamelessness
425 And do not honor me or Penelope herself.
Telemachos grew up recently, and his mother has not
Allowed him to give orders to the serving women.
Well, now, let me go up to the glistening upper chamber
And tell your wife, in whom some god has induced sleep."
430 Odysseus of many wiles addressed her in answer:
"Do not wake her up yet. Go in and tell the women
To come, the ones who devised sorry deeds in the past."
So he said, and the old woman went on through the hall
To announce this to the women and to hasten their coming.
435 But he himself called Telemachos and the oxherd
And the swineherd to him and uttered wingèd words:
"Begin now to carry the corpses, and command the women;
And then have the tables and the beautiful armchairs
Cleaned off with water and with the porous sponges.
440 And when you have set in order the entire house,
Bring the serving women on out of the well-based hall
Between the round-room and the excellent fence of the
     courtyard,
And strike them with the long-edged swords until you have
     taken
The lives of all away, and they have forgotten the love
They had under the suitors, when they lay with them
445 secretly."
So he said, and the women all came in a body together,
Lamenting dreadfully and shedding a swelling tear.

Then they first carried away the bodies of those who were dead
And they set them down under the portico of the well-fenced
   court,
Propping them on one another. Odysseus gave the orders,   450
Urging them on himself. They bore them out by constraint.
And then the tables and the beautiful armchairs
They cleaned off, with water and the porous sponges.
Then Telemachos, the oxherd, and the swineherd
Scraped down the floor of the stoutly built house with shovels. 455
Those servants kept carrying the scrapings and put them
   outdoors.
And when they had set in order the entire hall
They led the serving women out of the well-based hall
Between the round-room and the excellent fence of the court.
They cooped them in a narrow place, from which was no way to
   escape.   460
And sound-minded Telemachos began speaking to them:
"I would not take away with a clean death the lives
Of these women who have heaped reproaches on my head
And upon my mother, and have slept with the suitors."
So he said, and a cable from a dark blue-prowed ship   465
He threw round a pillar of the great round-room and tied
   it on,
Tightening it high up, so none could reach the ground with her
   feet.
As when either thrushes with their long wings or doves
Rush into a net that has been set in a thicket,
As they come in to roost, and a dreadful bed takes them in;   470
So they held their heads in a row, and about the necks
Of all there were nooses, that they might die most piteously.
They struggled a little with their feet, but not very long.
They brought Melanthios through the forecourt and the yard,
Cut off his nose and ears with the pitiless bronze,   475
And tore off his private parts for the dogs to eat raw,
And chopped off his hands and feet in their furious spirit.
Then, when they had washed off their hands and their feet,
They went into the house of Odysseus, and the work was done.
And he addressed Eurycleia, his beloved nurse: 480
"Bring brimstone, old woman, the cure of ills; bring me fire
So that I may purge the hall. You yourself go tell
Penelope to come here with her attendant women

And urge all the serving women in the house to come."
485 Then the dear nurse Eurycleia spoke to him:
"Yes, my child, you have said these things properly.
Come now, I shall bring you a tunic, a mantle and clothes
So your broad shoulders may not be covered with rags this way
As you stand in the halls. It would be a cause of blame."
490 Odysseus of many wiles addressed her in answer:
"First of all now let a fire be made for me in the halls."
So he said, and his dear nurse Eurycleia did not disobey.
Then she brought in fire and brimstone, and Odysseus
Thoroughly purged house and courtyard and hall.
495 The old woman went off through the fine halls of Odysseus
To announce this to the women and hasten their coming.
They came out of the hall bearing torches in their hands.
They gathered round Odysseus and greeted him in welcome;
They kissed him and embraced his shoulders and his head
500 And his hands. And a sweet longing took hold of him
For moaning and wailing; in his mind he recognized them all.

XXIII

The old woman went chuckling on into the upper chamber
To tell her dear mistress that her husband was inside.
Her knees moved quickly and her feet stumbled along.
She stood above her head and addressed a speech to her:
"Wake up, Penelope, dear child, so you may see   5
With your own eyes what you desire all your days.
Odysseus has come and reached home, though arriving late.
He has killed the bold suitors who disturbed his house
And devoured his property and oppressed his son."
And the prudent Penelope spoke to her: 10
"Dear mother, the gods have made you mad, who have the
      power
To make a man senseless, even one who is quite sensible;
And also they put the slack-minded on the way of prudence.
They have injured you, you were balanced in mind before.
Why do you mock me who have a heart full of grief,   15
To tell me these wild things and wake me out of the sweet
Sleep, which has bound me and shrouded my own eyelids?
Never have I had such a sleep from the time Odysseus
Went off to see evil Ilion, the unspeakable.
But come now, depart and go back into the hall.   20
For if anyone else of the women who belong to me
Had come to tell me this and waked me from sleep,
I myself should soon have sent her off hatefully
To go back again to the hall. In this, old age shall help you."
The beloved nurse Eurycleia then spoke to her: 25
"I am not mocking you, dear child, but it is true;
Odysseus has come and reached his home, as I say;
He is that stranger whom they all dishonored in the halls.
Telemachos has known for a long time he was within
But concealed out of prudence the purpose of his father   30
Till he might take revenge on the insolent men for their
      presumption."

So she said. The woman rejoiced, leaped out of her bed,
Embraced the old woman, and shed a tear from her eyelids.
Speaking out to her, she uttered wingèd words:
35 "Come now, dear mother, and tell me unerringly,
If he has truly arrived at his home, as you say,
How did he set his hands upon the shameless suitors,
A lone man, when they always stayed in a body inside?"
Then the beloved nurse Eurycleia spoke to her:
40 "I did not see or learn it, but I heard only the noise
Of men being killed. In a corner of the well-built chambers
We sat terrified, and the well-fitted doors held us
Until the time when your son Telemachos called me
From the hall. His father sent him out to call me.
45 Then I found Odysseus standing among the bodies
Of the slain. They surrounded him on the hard-stamped ground
Lying one upon the other. Your heart would have warmed to see
    him
Bespattered over with blood and with gore like a lion.
And now all of them are at the gates of the courtyard
50 In a heap, and he is purging the beautiful house,
Having kindled a great fire. He sent me to call you.
But come with me so you may both enter into gladness
In your own hearts, since you have suffered many ills.
And now this long desire is already fulfilled;
55 He has himself come alive to his hearth and found in the halls
Both you and his son. Though the suitors acted to him
Evilly, he has punished them all in his own house."
And then the prudent Penelope spoke to her:
"Dear mother, do not chuckle yet and make a great boast,
60 For you know how welcome in the halls he would appear to all,
And especially to me and the son that we both had.
But this story is not really so, the way that you tell it.
Some one of the immortals has killed the bold suitors,
Offended at their heart-hurting insolence and evil deeds,
65 For they honored no one of the men upon the earth,
Either evil or noble, whoever encountered them.
So they suffered evil through their recklessness. And Odysseus,
Far from Achaia lost his return, and is lost himself."
Then the beloved nurse Eurycleia answered her:
70 "My child, what sort of word has got past the bar of your teeth,
To say that your husband who is within at the hearth

Would never come home? Your heart is ever untrusting.
Well, then, I shall tell you another manifest token:
The scar a boar once dealt on him with a shining tusk
I noticed as I washed it. And I wanted to tell it   75
To you yourself. But he seized my mouth with his hands
And did not let me speak, in his resourcefulness of mind.
Come along, then, and I shall myself stake my own person.
If I deceive you, kill me with a most piteous death."
And then the prudent Penelope answered her: 80
"Dear mother, the counsels of the ever-living gods
Are hard for you to comprehend, though you are very shrewd.
In any case let us go to my son, so I may see
The suitors dead and also the man who has killed them."
When she had said this she went down from the upper chamber.
  Her heart   85
Pondered much whether to question her dear husband at a
  distance
Or to stand beside him and clasp and kiss his hands and head.
When she had gone on in and crossed the threshold of stone,
She sat across from Odysseus, in the gleam of the fire
By the other wall. And he sat against a tall pillar   90
Looking down, waiting to see if his goodly wife
Would say something to him when she saw him with her eyes.
But she sat a long time in silence, and stupor came over her
  heart.
With her gaze sometimes she looked him full in the face,
And sometimes did not know him for the vile clothes he had on
  his skin.   95
Telemachos rebuked her and spoke out to her directly:
"My mother, cruel mother, you have a heart that is harsh!
Why do you turn from my father so and do not sit
Beside him and ply him with speeches and question him?
No other woman, indeed, with a resisting heart   100
Would so stand off from the husband who had suffered many
  ills
And come back for her in the twentieth year to his fatherland.
Always the heart in you is harder than a stone."
And then the prudent Penelope spoke to him:
"My child, the heart within my breast is amazed,   105
And I am not at all able to speak a word or to ask
Or to look him in the face directly. If really

He is Odysseus and he has arrived home, we two
Shall know one another, and more fully. There are signs
110 For us that the two of us know, hidden from others."
So she said, and godly Odysseus, who had endured much, smiled.
At once he uttered wingèd words to Telemachos:
"Telemachos, permit your mother to test me out
Within the halls. She shall quickly discern even better.
115 Now, because I am dirty and have bad clothes on my skin,
She does not respect me and does not yet say I am he.
But let us consider how it shall come out for the best.
For whosoever kills a single man in the district,
Though there be not many advocates for man thereafter,
120 He flees, abandoning his kinsmen and fatherland.
And we have killed the mainstay of the city, the very best
Of the youth in Ithaca. I bid you to consider this."
Then sound-minded Telemachos answered him:
"Look to these matters yourself, dear father. They say
125 Your counsel is the best among men, nor could any
Other man among mortal men contend with you.
We shall follow along with you eagerly; I do not think
We should lack any courage so far as we do have power."
Odysseus of many wiles addressed him in answer:
130 "Well then, I shall tell you what seems to me to be best,
First of all wash yourselves and put tunics on,
And order the serving women in the halls to take their clothes.
Then let the godly singer, holding his clear-toned lyre,
Be the leader for us in a reveling dance,
135 So a listener outside would think this was a wedding,
One who walked on the road, or one of those who dwell
     round about;
So that a wide report about the slaughter of the suitors
Shall not first get through the town, before we have gone outside
To our own well-wooded land. And then afterward
140 We may think of any advantage the Olympian may bestow."
So he said, and they listened closely and did not disobey.
And first they washed themselves off and put on tunics,
And the women adorned themselves, and the godly singer took
The hollow lyre and aroused the desire among them
145 For sweet melody and also for excellent dancing.
The great house about them resounded at the feet
Of men frolicking and of women with lovely gowns.

And this is what a man who heard them outside the house
   would say:
"Someone indeed must have married the much-wooed queen.
The cruel woman, she did not hold out for her wedded husband 150
And tend the great house steadfastly till he arrived."
So a man would say: they did not know what had been done.
But the housekeeper Eurynome washed great-hearted Odysseus
Inside his own house and anointed him with olive oil.
She put a lovely mantle and a tunic over him.   155
Then Athene poured much beauty upon his head,
Made him bigger to look at and stouter, and made his hair
Flow in curls upon his head like the hyacinth flower.
As when some man overlays gold upon silver,
A skilled man whom Hephaistos and Pallas Athene have taught 160
Art of all kinds, and he turns out graceful handiwork;
So she poured grace upon his head and his shoulders.
He stepped from the bathtub in form like the immortal gods,
And he sat back down on the chair from which he had risen,
Across from his wife, and he addressed a speech to her: 165
"Strange woman, those who have their home on Olympos put in
   you
A heart implacable beyond that of womankind.
No other woman, indeed, with a resisting heart
Would so stand off from the husband who had suffered
   many ills
And come back for her in the twentieth year to his fatherland.   170
Come now, old mother, spread me a bed, so that I
May lie down alone, for the heart in this woman's breast is iron."
And then the prudent Penelope answered him:
"Strange man, I do not at all exalt myself or slight you,
Nor am I too much amazed. I know well the sort of man you
   were   175
When you went off from Ithaca on the long-oared ship.
Come now, Eurycleia, spread for him the thick bed
Outside the well-based bedroom which the man made himself.
Put the thick bed out for him there and throw bedding on,
Blankets and mantles and the glistening coverlets."   180
So she said, testing her husband. But Odysseus
Grew angry and spoke to his wife, who had a sense of devotion:
"My wife, this is a heart-hurting speech you have made.
Who has put my bed elsewhere? That would be hard

185 Even for one very skilled, unless a god came in person,
And easily, if he wished, might put it in another place.
No mortal man alive, not even one in his vigor,
Could dislodge it easily, since a great token was made
In the well-wrought bed. I worked on it, and nobody else.
190 The long-leaved bush of a wild olive grew inside the yard
Flourishing in bloom. It was thick as a pillar is.
So I built the bedroom round it till I finished it
With close-fitted stones and roofed it well up above.
And I put portals on it, jointed and closely fitted.
195 Then I cut off the crown of the long-leaved wild olive;
Chopping the stump from the root up, I hewed it with the
    bronze ax
Well and skillfully, and straightened it with a line.
When I had fashioned the bedpost, I bored it all with an auger.
Starting with that, I hewed out a bed till I finished it,
200 Adorning it with gold and silver and ivory.
And I stretched over it an oxhide thong shining with purple.
So I declare this token to you. I do not know at all
Whether the bed is still steadfast, wife, or already
Some man has put it elsewhere, cutting the olive base beneath."
205 So he said, and her knees and her own heart went slack
As she recognized the steadfast tokens Odysseus had shown to
    her.
Then she wept, ran straight over, and threw her arms
About the neck of Odysseus, kissed his head and spoke:
"Do not scowl at me, Odysseus, since in everything else
210 You have been the wisest of men. The gods have given us woe
Who begrudged it to us that, staying with one another,
We should enjoy our vigor and reach the threshold of age.
But be not angry at me now for this, and do not resent
That I did not embrace you this way when I saw you first,
215 For always the spirit in my precious heart went cold
Lest someone among mortals come and deceive me
With speeches. Many men think up evil devices.
Nor would Argive Helen, who was a child of Zeus,
Have lain in love and in bed with an alien man
220 If she had known that the warlike sons of the Achaians
Were to bring her back home to her dear fatherland.
Yes, a god stirred her up to do a sorry deed.

She did not lay up in her heart beforehand that woeful
Madness, out of which, from the first, sorrow reached us too.
But now, since already you have declared very plain tokens   225
About our bed, which no other mortal has seen,
But you and I alone, and one single handmaiden,
Aktoris, whom my father gave me when I came here,
She who tended for us the doors of the stout bedchamber;
Now you have convinced my heart, harsh indeed though it be."   230
So she said. In him rose a still greater desire for wailing.
He wept, holding his pleasing wife, who had a sense of devotion.
As when land appears welcome to men who are swimming,
Whose well-made ship Poseidon has dashed in the ocean
As it was driven on by wind and a solid wave,   235
And few have escaped from the hoary sea onto the mainland
By swimming, and much brine has caked upon their skin,
And they walk up on land glad, having fled misfortune,
So welcome was her husband to her as she looked upon him.
In no way could she quite let her white arms go from his neck,   240
And rosy-fingered Dawn would have appeared while they
     wept
If the bright-eyed goddess Athene had not had another thought.
She held the night long on its course, and then kept
The golden-throned Dawn upon Oceanos, and did not allow her
To yoke her swift-footed horses that bear light to men,   245
Lampos and Phaethon, who are the colts that bring the dawn.
Then Odysseus of many wiles spoke to his wife:
"My wife, we have not yet come to the end of all
Our trials, but a measureless labor yet remains,
A long and a hard one that I must wholly carry out.   250
So did the soul of Tiresias prophesy to me
On the day when I went down into the house of Hades
Seeking a return for my companions and myself.
But come, let us go to bed, my wife, so that now
We may lie down and take pleasure beneath sweet sleep."   255
And then the prudent Penelope addressed him:
"The bed shall be for you indeed whenever you wish
In your heart, since the gods have made you to arrive
At your well-established home and your fatherland.
But since you have thought of it and a god has put it in your
     heart,   260

Come tell me of the trial, since hereafter I think,
I too shall hear of it; and it is no worse for me to learn of it at
    once."
Then Odysseus of many wiles addressed her in answer:
"Strange woman, why do you strongly urge me and bid me to
    speak?
265 Well, I will tell it myself and shall not conceal it.
But your heart shall not rejoice, nor do I myself
Rejoice, since he ordered me to visit many towns
Of mortals, holding in my hands a well-fitted oar,
Till the time I come unto those who do not know
270 The sea and do not eat a food that has been mixed with salt,
And where they do not know about ships with purple cheeks
Or about well-fitted oars that are the wings for ships.
He told me a very clear token; I shall not conceal it:
When another wayfarer has confronted me
275 And said I had a winnowing fan on my gleaming shoulder,
He bade me to fix my oar then into the earth
And offer fine sacrifices to lord Poseidon,
A ram, a bull, and a boar, the mounter of sows,
Then to go back home and sacrifice sacred hecatombs
280 To the immortal gods who possess broad heaven,
To all of them in order. Far from the sea will death come
Ever so gently, to my person, and slay me
Worn out with sleek old age. And the people about me
Will be happy. He told me all this would come to pass."
285 And then the prudent Penelope spoke to him:
"If the gods do bring a better old age to pass,
Then there is hope for you there will be an escape from evils."
And so they said such things to one another.
Meanwhile Eurynome and the nurse prepared the bed
290 With soft bedclothing, underneath shining torches.
And when they had made haste and strewn the thick bed,
The old woman went back into the house to lie down
And Eurynome, servant of the chamber, conducted them
With a torch in her hand as they went on to bed.
295 She led to the bedroom and went away again. They then
Arrived happily at the site of their old bed.
But Telemachos, the oxherd, and the swineherd
Stopped the men's feet from dancing and stopped the women
    too,

And went to bed themselves through the shadowy halls.
The two, when they had taken their pleasure of delightful love, 300
Enjoyed themselves with stories, talking to one another:
She, the godly woman, told how much she endured in the
    halls
To look upon the destructive throng of the suitors
Who on her account had slaughtered oxen and goodly sheep
In numbers, and much wine had been drawn off from the jars.   305
And Zeus-born Odysseus told of the many cares he had brought
Upon men, and the many he had suffered himself in his woe.
He told them all, and she enjoyed hearing, nor did sleep
Fall upon her eyelids before he had told it all.
He began how first he had conquered the Cicones and then   310
Had gone to the fertile land of the Lotus-eating men,
And all the Cyclops did, and how he made him pay the
    penalty
For the valiant companions he ate and did not pity.
And how he got to Aeolos who at first kindly received him
And sent him on. But it was not yet his lot to reach   315
His dear fatherland; but a storm snatched him up again
And bore him heavily groaning on the fish-laden ocean.
And he told how he reached Lestrygonian Telepylos,
Whose men destroyed his ships and all his well-greaved
    companions.
Odysseus alone got away from them with his black ship.   320
And he told about Circe's wiles and resourcefulness,
And how he went down to the dank dwelling of Hades
So he might consult the soul of Theban Tiresias
In a ship with many oarlocks and saw all his companions
And the mother who bore him and reared him when he was
    small,   325
And how he listened to the voice of the chanting Sirens,
And how he reached the Wandering Rocks and dread Charybdis
And Scylla, which men have never yet escaped unharmed.
And how his companions slew the oxen of the Sun,
And how high-thundering Zeus struck the swift ship   330
With a smoldering thunderbolt, and his noble companions died
All together, but he himself escaped the evil fates.
And how he reached the island Ogygia and the nymph Calypso.
She held him back, longing for him to be her husband
In the hollow caves, and she nourished him and said   335

She would make him immortal and ageless all his days,
But she never persuaded the heart within his breast.
And he told how, having suffered much, he came to the
   Phaeacians
Who honored him heartily the way they would a god
340 And conducted him in a ship to his dear fatherland,
Giving him bronze and gold and clothing in abundance.
This was the last tale he told, when sweet, limb-loosing sleep
Came upon him, releasing the cares of his heart.
Then the bright-eyed goddess Athene had another thought.
345 When she had supposed in her heart that Odysseus
Had taken pleasure with his wife of the bed and of sleep,
At once from Oceanos she roused the early born one
Of the golden throne to bring light to men. Odysseus
Rose from his soft bed and laid a charge on his wife:
350 "My wife, we are already glutted, the two of us,
With many trials. Here you wept for my troublesome return,
But, while I was wanting to go, Zeus and the other gods
Held me back in pains from my own fatherland.
Now since we have arrived at the bed of much desire,
355 Give heed to the goods which are mine in the halls.
As for the sheep of mine the presumptuous suitors pillaged,
Many others I shall myself plunder back; still others the
   Achaians
Shall give me until they have filled up all the folds.
And then I shall go on myself to the well-wooded land
360 To see my noble father, who is heavily grieved for me.
And, my wife, I charge you this, prudent as you are:
At once at the rising of the sun the report will travel
About the suitors whom I slaughtered in the halls.
Go into the upper chamber with your serving women
365 And sit, and do not look at anyone or ask any question."
He spoke, and put the lovely armor about his shoulders.
He roused Telemachos, the oxherd, and the swineherd
And ordered them all to take the war gear in their hands.
They did not disobey, but armed themselves in bronze.
370 They opened the doors and went out. Odysseus led.
Light was on the earth already, and Athene hid them
In night and led them rapidly out of the city.

And Hermes of Cyllene summoned forth the souls
Of the suitors, and he held in his hand the lovely gold wand
With which he enchants the eyes of those men he wishes,
And others he wakens even when they are asleep.
He stirred them with it and drove them. They followed
   squeaking,   5
As when bats in the corner of a prodigious cave
Squeak as they fly when one of them falls away
From the cluster on the rock where they cling to one another;
So they squeaked as they went together. And Hermes,
The deliverer, led them on along the dank ways.   10
They went past the streams of Oceanos, past the White Rock;
Past the gates of the Sun also, and the district of dreams
Did they go. And at once they reached the asphodel meadow
Where the souls dwell, phantoms of those who are worn out.
They came upon the soul of Achilles, son of Peleus,   15
The soul of Patroclos and of excellent Antilochos,
And of Ajax, who was the finest in body and form
Of all the Danaans, after the excellent son of Peleus.
So they thronged around that man, and right close to them
The soul of Agamemnon came on, the son of Atreus,   20
Grieving. And the others drew in together, all those
Who had died with him and met their fate in Agisthos' house.
The soul of the son of Peleus spoke out to him first:
"Son of Atreus, we thought you were dear beyond other heroes
To Zeus who hurls the thunderbolt, for all your days,   25
Because you were lord over many valiant men
In the land of the Trojans where we Achaians suffered pains.
And yet the destructive fate that no one who is born
Can avoid was destined to come early upon you as well.
Would that when you were enjoying the honor of which you
   were master   30
In the land of the Trojans, you had met death and destiny!

Then all the Achaians would have made you a funeral mound
And you would have won great glory for your son hereafter.
As it is, you were fated to be caught in a grievous death."
35 Then the soul of the son of Atreus spoke to him:
"Blessed are you, son of Peleus, godlike Achilles,
You who died in Troy far from Argos. Around you, others,
The best sons of the Achaians and of the Trojans were killed
Contending over you. You in a whirling cloud of dust
40 Lay great and greatly fallen, having forgotten horsemanship.
And we contended the whole day. Nor would we at all
Have stopped the battle if Zeus had not stopped it with a storm.
But when we had brought you up on the ships out of battle,
We set you down upon a bier and cleaned off your lovely skin
45 With warm water and oil, and the Danaans shed
Many hot tears over you and sheared off their hair.
Your mother came from the sea with the deathless girls of the sea
When she heard the report. A prodigious cry arose
Over the ocean, and a trembling seized all the Achaians,
And they would have sprung up and gone to the hollow ships
50 If a man had not restrained them who knew many ancient matters,
Nestor, whose advice had also before seemed best.
With good intent he spoke out to them and addressed them:
"Hold back, Argives; do not flee, young Achaians. His mother
55 This is, here from the sea with the deathless girls of the sea;
She has come to be beside her son who has died."
So he said, and the great-hearted Achaians were held back from flight.
About you stood the daughters of the old man of the sea,
Wailing piteously; they clothed you in ambrosial garments.
60 All the nine Muses, changing off with lovely voice,
Sang a dirge. There you would have seen none of the Argives
Who did not weep, so stirring was the clear Muses' song.
Seventeen days for you, and also the nights alike,
Did we lament, both immortal gods and mortal men.
65 On the eighteenth we gave you to the fire and about you
Killed many fat sheep and cattle with crumpled horns.
You were burned in the clothes of the gods and with much oil

And with sweet honey. Many of the Achaian warriors
Marched around the fire in armor while you were being burned,
Foot soldiers and horsemen, and a great din arose.   70
But when the flame of Hephaistos had made an end of you,
At the dawn, Achilles, we gathered your white bones
In unmixed wine and in oil. And your mother gave
A golden two-handled jar. She said it was a gift
Of Dionysos, the work of highly renowned Hephaistos.   75
So in it, glorious Achilles, your white bones lie,
Mingled with those of dead Patroklos, Menoitios' son;
Apart are those of Antilochos, whom you honored
Above all your other companions after the dead Patroklos.
And then we, the sacred army of Argive spearmen, heaped   80
A great and excellent funeral mound up over them
On a strand jutting forward on the broad Hellespont,
So that it might be seen far over the ocean by men,
Both those who are born now and those who shall be hereafter.
And your mother asked the gods for beautiful prizes   85
And set them up for a contest amid the best of the Achaians.
Already you have been present at the burial of many men,
Of warriors; when, because a king has passed away,
The young men gird themselves and prepare for the prizes.
But you would have marveled in your heart most to see those,   90
The beautiful prizes that the goddess set up for you,
Thetis [1] of the silver foot. You were very dear to the gods.
So you did not lose your name even when you died, Achilles.
There shall be noble renown for you always among all men.
But what pleasure did I have, when I had wound up the war?   95
For Zeus planned woeful destruction for me on my return
At the hands of Aigisthos and my accursèd wife."
And so they said such things to one another.
The Runner, the slayer of Argos, came up close to them,
Leading the souls of the suitors subdued by Odysseus.   100
The two, marveling, went straight up when they saw them.
The soul of Agamemnon, son of Atreus, recognized
The dear son of Melaneos, renowned Amphimedon,
For he was a guest friend of his who dwelt in Ithaca.
The soul of the son of Atreus spoke out to him first: 105
"Amphimedon, what did you suffer to go under the gloomy
    earth,

1. A sea nymph and mother of Achilles.

All you chosen men of the same age? Not otherwise
Would someone pick out and gather the best men in a city.
Was it that Poseidon overcame you in your ships
110 By raising up oppressive winds and giant waves,
Or did hostile men ravage you upon the mainland
As you were cutting off their cattle and fine flocks of sheep,
Or as they were fighting on behalf of their city and women?
Tell me what I ask—I declare I am your guest friend.
115 Do you not remember when I came there to your house,
Urging Odysseus on to come along to Ilion
With godlike Menelaos upon the well-timbered ships?
An entire month we spent crossing the whole broad ocean
Since we could scarcely persuade Odysseus, the sacker of cities."
120 And then the soul of Amphimedon addressed him:
"Glorious son of Atreus, Zeus-nourished Agamemnon,
Lord of men, I do remember all the things you say,
And I shall tell you everything truthfully and well,
The evil end of our death, the way it came about.
125 We wooed the wife of Odysseus, who was gone so long;
She neither refused the hateful wedding nor carried it out,
Contriving for us death and black destiny;
And she devised in her mind this other deceit:
She set a great loom in the halls, and on it she wove
130 A large and delicate fabric. She told us at once:
'Young men, my suitors, since godlike Odysseus is dead,
Wait, though you are eager for this marriage of mine, till I finish
This robe, so that the yarn will not waste in vain,
The burial sheet of hero Laertes for the time
135 When the ruinous fate of long-sorrowful death seizes him,
Lest one of the Achaian women in the district blame me
If he who had won so much lay without covering.'
So she said, and the bold heart was persuaded within us.
Then every day she kept weaving there on the great loom,
140 And in the nights she undid it when she had the torches set up.
So three years she fooled the Achaians and persuaded them.
But when the fourth year came and the seasons came on
Of the waning months and many days came to an end,
Right then one of the women who perceived it clearly told it.
145 And we happened upon her undoing the shining fabric.
Then she finished it, though unwilling and under duress.

And when, having woven the great fabric and washed it,
She showed forth the robe that resembled the sun or the moon,
Just then some evil god led Odysseus from someplace
To the verge of the field where the swineherd had his home.   150
There, too, the beloved son of Odysseus had come
When he went from sandy Pylos in his black ship.
The two of them, contriving an evil death for the suitors,
Had arrived at the city of great renown. Odysseus
Was last, and Telemachos led the way ahead of them.   155
The swineherd brought the man, who wore vile clothes on his
    skin
And resembled a wretched beggar who was an old man
Walking with a staff. He had sorry clothes on his skin.
None of us could recognize that it was he
When he appeared suddenly, not even those who were older,   160
But we rebuked him with missiles and evil speeches.
Still, he held out all the while with enduring heart
When he was being beaten and rebuked in his own halls.
But when the purpose of aegis-bearing Zeus aroused him
He took up the beautiful weapons with Telemachos   165
And placed them in the chamber and locked the fastenings,
And resourcefully he gave the order to his wife
To set before the suitors the bow and the gray iron,
A contest and start of slaughter for us in our dread fate.
No one of us was able to stretch out the string   170
Of the mighty bow, for we were too weak by far.
But when the great bow came into Odysseus' hands,
Then all of us made a common outcry with speeches,
Not to give him the bow, however much he might say.
Telemachos alone urged him on and gave him the order.   175
Then godly Odysseus, who had endured much, took it in his
    hand,
Easily strung the bow and shot through the iron.
He went and stood on the threshold, poured the swift arrows out,
Peering round terribly, and hit King Antinoos.
And then on the others he let the groan-carrying darts fly,   180
Taking aim straight across. And they fell thick and fast.
It was known then that one of the gods was their helper for
    them.
For at once they went on through the house in their rage

And killed them one after another. A sad groaning
Rose as their heads were struck. The whole ground ran with
185   blood.
Agamemnon, this is the way we perished, we whose bodies
Are still lying uncared for now in the halls of Odysseus.
For the dear ones in the home of each man do not know it yet,
Those who, when they have washed the black gore from the
        wounds,
190   May lay us out weeping. For that is the prize of the dead."
Then the soul of the son of Atreus spoke out to him:
"Blessed son of Laertes, Odysseus of many wiles,
Truly you have won a wife of great excellence.
How good was the mind of blameless Penelope,
195   Daughter of Icarios, who remembered Odysseus well,
Her wedded husband! And so the fame of her excellence
Shall never die. The immortals shall make for men on the earth
A delightful song about constant Penelope.
Not so did the daughter of Tyndareus [2] devise her evil deeds,
Who killed her wedded husband; and a hateful song shall there
200   be
Among men, and she will bestow a harsh reputation
On womankind, even on one who is good in what she does."
And so they said such things to one another,
Standing in the halls of Hades under the depths of the earth.
205   The others, when they had gone out of the city, quickly reached
The fine, well-worked field of Laertes that Laertes had once
Acquired for himself when he had toiled very hard.
There his home was. And all around it a shed ran
In which the bondservants who did the tasks at his
        pleasure,
210   Took their meals and sat down and went to sleep.
In it there was an old Sicilian woman, who carefully
Attended to the old man in the field far from the city.
There Odysseus addressed a speech to his servants and his son:
"Come on inside of the well-built house now, and at once
215   Make a sacrifice of the best of the swine for dinner
And I shall test my own father out for myself,
Whether he recognizes me and perceives me with his eyes,
Or does not know me since I have been away for a long time."

2. Clytemnestra.

When he had said this, he gave the arms of war to the servants.
They went then swiftly into the house. But Odysseus   220
Went close to the fruitful vineyard to try him out.
As he entered the large orchard he did not find Dolios
Or any of the servants or their sons. They were gone off
Gathering wall-stones that would serve as a fence
For the vineyard. And the old man led the way for them.   225
He found his father alone in the well-laid vineyard,
Digging around a plant. He had a dirty tunic on,
A sorry patched one. And greaves of oxhide were bound
In patches on his calves to keep him from getting scratched.
He had gloves on his hands on account of brambles. On his head 230
He was wearing a goatskin cap, cherishing his grief.
When godly Odysseus, who had endured much, perceived the
    man
Worn down by age and with a great grief in his mind,
He stood under a stately pear tree and shed a tear,
And then he turned over in his mind and in his heart   235
Whether to kiss and embrace his father and tell the details
Of how he had come and arrived at his fatherland
Or should first ask him for details and test him out.
To him as he thought about it this seemed to be better:
To test him out at first with words of bantering.   240
With this in mind, Odysseus went directly to him.
The man was holding his head down and digging around the
    plant.
Standing beside him, his illustrious son spoke out:
"Old man, no lack of skill is yours as you tend
The orchard, but good care is yours. Nothing at all,   245
No plant, no fig tree, no vine, no wild olive tree,
No pear tree, no leek bed in the garden is without your care.
I shall tell you something else, and do not feel rage in your
    heart;
Your person is not well cared for, but along with woeful old age
You have a foul squalor and are wearing sorry clothes.   250
Not for idleness, surely, does your master not take care of you;
And nothing about your appearance conforms to the slave
In form or in stature. You look like a man who is king.
You look like such a man, who, when he has washed and eaten,
Should sleep softly. For this is the just way of old men.   255

Come, tell me this, and speak out truthfully:
Of whom among men are you slave? Whose orchard do you
   tend?
Tell me this really, so I may know it well,
If this place we reach is truly Ithaca, as this man
260 Has told me who met me just now when I was coming here.
He is not very clever, for he did not venture to tell
The details or to listen to my speech when I inquired
About my guest friend, whether he still lives and exists
Or is already dead and in the halls of Hades.
265 I shall speak out to you; understand and hear me well.
I once entertained a man in my dear fatherland
When he came to our place, and no other mortal yet
Among alien strangers came dearer to my house.
He declared his descent was from Ithaca, and he said
270 His father was Laertes, son of Arkesios.
I led him into my house and entertained him well,
Befriending him kindly, as there was much in my home,
And I provided him with the gifts of a guest, fitting ones;
First I gave him seven talents of well-wrought gold,
275 And I gave him a mixing bowl all of silver decked with flowers,
Twelve mantles of single fold, and as many coverlets,
And as many lovely robes, and as many tunics besides,
And in addition four shapely women who were versed
In excellent tasks, the ones he wished to pick out himself."
280 Then his father answered him, shedding a tear:
"Stranger, you have indeed come to the land you ask about;
But insolent and reckless are the men who possess her.
In vain you bestowed these gifts, if you gave countless ones.
But if you had found him alive in the land of Ithaca
He would have requited you well with gifts before sending you
285 back,
With good hospitality, which is right toward the man who
   begins it.
But come now, tell me this, and speak out truthfully:
How many years ago is it you entertained that man,
Your hapless guest, my son, if he ever existed,
That ill-fated man? Perhaps far from his friends and his
290 fatherland
The fish in the ocean have devoured him, or on the mainland
He has become the prey of wild beasts and birds. His mother

And father, we who had him, did not lay him out and mourn,
Nor did his richly dowered wife, the constant Penelope,
Wail for her husband on his bier and close his eyes,   295
As it is seemly to do. For that is the prize of the dead.
And tell me this really, so I may know it well:
What men are you from? Where are your city and parents?
Where indeed does the swift ship stand that brought you here
And your godlike companions? Or did you come as a passenger   300
On the ship of others who put you ashore and went away?"
Odysseus of many wiles addressed him in answer:
"All right, I shall tell you everything truthfully:
I am from Alybas, where I live in my famous halls.
I am the son of Lord Apheidas, the son of Polypemon.   305
My own name is Eperitos. But some god drove me astray
To come here from Sicania against my will.
My ship is moored yonder by the fields apart from the city,
But with regard to Odysseus, this is the fifth year
From the time he went away and left my fatherland,   310
That ill-fated man. Still, as he went, he had birds of good omen
On the right, in which I rejoiced as I sent him off.
And he rejoiced as he went. The hearts in us hoped yet
To exchange hospitality and give glorious gifts."
So he said, and a black cloud of grief covered the other.   315
He picked up the ashen dust in both of his hands
And heavily moaning poured it over his gray head.
The other's heart was aroused, and a piercing throb had already
Struck through his nostrils when he saw his dear father.
He leaped up, kissed, and embraced him, and spoke to him: 320
"Here I am, father, the very man you ask about;
I have come in the twentieth year to my fatherland.
But hold off from weeping and tearful lamentation.
I shall tell you right out; nevertheless, we must hurry.
I have slain the suitors within our own halls,   325
Punishing their heart-hurting injury and evil deeds."
And then Laertes answered and spoke out to him:
"If you are my son Odysseus who have arrived here,
Tell me now some very plain sign, so I may be convinced."
Odysseus of many wiles spoke to him in answer: 330
"First of all, take notice with your eyes of this scar
That a boar inflicted on me with shining tusk on Parnassos
When I had gone there. You and my queenly mother sent me

To my mother's dear father Autolycos, so I might get
335 Gifts that when he came here he promised me with a nod.
Come now, and in the well-laid vineyard I shall also tell you
The trees that you gave me once, and I asked you for each,
Myself as a child, following you through the yard. We went on
Through these very ones, and you named them and told me of
  each.
340 You gave me thirteen pear trees and ten apple trees
And forty fig trees. You named the vine rows the same way
To give me fifty of them. And throughout the grape season
Each was fruitful in turn. And there all sorts of clusters are
  on them
Whenever the seasons of Zeus weigh them down from above."
345 So he said. The man's knees and his own heart went slack
When he recognized the sure tokens Odysseus had shown him.
He threw his arms round his dear son and went faint for breath
As godly Odysseus, who had endured much, grasped him.
But when he caught his breath and the spirit was brought to
  his mind,
350 He answered him right away and addressed him with a speech:
"Father Zeus, you gods are still on tall Olympos, if truly
The suitors have paid for their reckless insolence.
But now I dreadfully fear in my mind that the Ithacans
Will soon all come against us here and send messengers
355 Everywhere to the cities of the Cephallenians."
Odysseus of many wiles answered him and spoke:
"Take courage, and do not give heed to this in your mind.
But let us go to the house that lies close to the orchard.
For there did I send Telemachos forth, and the oxherd
360 And the swineherd, to prepare a meal as soon as they could."
As they said this the two went on to the lovely house.
There, when they had reached the well-situated home,
They found Telemachos, the oxherd, and the swineherd
Carving abundant meat and mixing the sparkling wine.
365 Meanwhile the Sicilian servant woman in his house
Washed Laertes and anointed him with olive oil,
And she put a lovely mantle round him. Then Athene stood
  near
And filled out the limbs of the shepherd of the people.
She made him taller than before and stouter to look upon.

He stepped out of the bathtub. His dear son was amazed at
    him;   370
As he saw him, the man looked like the immortal gods.
Then addressing him, he uttered wingèd words:
"My father, surely one of the ever-living gods
Has made you better to look on in form and stature."
Then sound-minded Laertes said to him in reply: 375
"Father Zeus and Athene and Apollo, would that I were just
    the way
As I was when I took Nerikos, the well-built citadel,
A headland on the shore, when I ruled the Cephallenians;
That way I might have been yesterday in our own halls,
Bearing armor on my shoulders, to stand by and ward off   380
The suitors. So in the halls I would have loosed the knees
Of many of them. In your mind you would have rejoiced."
And so such things did they say to one another.
But when the others had ceased from work and prepared dinner
They sat down one after another in seats and in armchairs,   385
Then they laid their hands on the meal. The old man Dolios
Came near, and with him were the sons of the old man,
Wearied from their tasks, since their mother had gone and
    called them,
The old Sicilian woman who fed them and carefully
Tended to that old man, since old age had taken hold of him.   390
And then, when they had seen Odysseus and noticed him
In their hearts, they stood in the halls amazed. And Odysseus
Addressed them with soothing speeches and spoke to them:
"Old man, sit down to eat; fully forget your wonder,
For we have waited a long time in the halls in desire   395
Of laying our hands on the bread, always expecting you."
So he said, and Dolios came straight to him, stretching forth
Both his hands. He took Odysseus' hand and kissed his wrist.
And speaking out to him, he uttered wingèd words:
"My friend, since you have returned to us who longed for that   400
But never thought to see it—the very gods themselves brought
    you—
Good health and great welcome! May the gods grant you
    wealth!
And tell me this truly, so I may know it well:
Does the prudent Penelope already clearly know

₄₀₅ You have returned here, or shall we send her a messenger?"
Odysseus of many wiles addressed him in answer:
"Old man, she knows already. Why need you bother about
     this?"
So he said, and the other sat down again on the polished stool.
And the sons of Dolios around glorious Odysseus
Greeted him with speeches the same way and clasped his
₄₁₀   hands.
They sat down one after another beside their father Dolios.
And so they busied themselves with a meal in the halls.
Now the messenger Rumor went everywhere fast through the
     town
Declaring the suitors' hateful death and destiny.
₄₁₅ When all had heard it, they strayed in from every side
With murmur and groaning in front of Odysseus' halls.
They carried their corpses, each from his house and buried
     them.
They sent those from other cities, each one to his home,
Putting them upon swift ships for the fishermen to bring them.
Then they went in a body to the places of assembly, grieving in
₄₂₀   heart.
And when they were gathered and had come together,
Eupeithes stood up among them and spoke to them,
As unforgettable grief lay on his mind for his son
Antinoos, the first one whom godly Odysseus had slain.
₄₂₅ Shedding tears for him, he spoke out and made a speech:
"Friends, this man has planned a huge deed against the
     Achaians.
Some men he led away in ships, many noblemen,
And he lost the hollow ships, and he lost the men.
Others he killed when he came, the best Cephallenians by far.
₄₃₀ Come now, before this man may get quickly to Pylos
Or to godly Elis where the Epeians rule;
Let us go. Or else hereafter we shall always be disgraced.
These deeds are a shame to learn about, even for future men;
Unless we avenge us on the murderers of our kinsmen and sons.
₄₃₅ To my mind at least it would not then be sweet to live,
But I would die as soon as I could and be among the dead.
Come then, lest those men get a start on us crossing the sea."
So he said, shedding a tear. Pity seized all the Achaians.
Medon and the divine singer came up close to them

Out of the halls of Odysseus, since sleep had let them go.   440
They stood in their midst. Amazement seized every man.
Then Medon, who was sound in knowledge, spoke out to them:
"Listen to me now, Ithacans. Odysseus has not
Planned these deeds against the will of the deathless gods.
I myself saw an immortal god who stood close beside   445
Odysseus and resembled Mentor in every way.
Now the deathless god appeared in front of Odysseus
Encouraging him, and now he aroused the suitors
And rushed on through the hall. They fell down one upon the
    other."
So he said, and sallow fear got hold of all of them.   450
Then the old hero Halitherses spoke to them,
The son of Mastor; he alone saw both before and after.
With good intent he spoke out and addressed them:
"Hear me now, Ithacans, in what I am to say:
My friends, these deeds have come about through your
    wickedness.   455
You did not obey me or Mentor, shepherd of the people,
To make your sons cease from their stupidities.
They did a huge deed in their evil recklessness,
Wasting away the goods and dishonoring the wife
Of an excellent man. They thought he would come no more.   460
And now, so be it. Obey me in what I say,
And let us not go, so no one may find self-inflicted pain."
So he said, but they rushed on with a great war cry,
More than half of them, while the others stayed in a body
    there,
For his speech did not please their minds, but they were
    persuaded   465
By Eupeithes.[3] And then at once they ran on for their armor.
When they had put the glittering bronze round their skin
They gathered in a body before the town with a broad
    dancing-place.
Eupeithes was the leader for their foolishness.
He thought he would avenge his son's murder, but he was not   470
Destined to get back; there he was to meet his fate.
Then Athene spoke out to Zeus, the son of Cronos:
"Our father, son of Cronos, highest of all rulers,
Tell me when I ask, what plan of yours is concealed here?

3. The name means "Good Persuader."

475 Will you fashion further an evil war and dread battle,
Or will you establish friendship between both sides?"
And cloud-gathering Zeus addressed her in answer:
"My child, why do you ask me and question me about this?"
Why did you not think out this idea by yourself,
That Odysseus might indeed take vengeance on them when
480   he came?
Do as you wish, but I will tell you what seems fitting.
Since godly Odysseus has done vengeance on the suitors,
Let them solemnize an oath, that he may always reign.
And let us bring about oblivion for the murder
485 Of their sons and kinsmen. Let them love one another
As before, and let there be abundant wealth and peace."
When he said this, he aroused Athene, who was eager before.
She went down in a rush from the summits of Olympos.
And when the men had taken their fill of mind-honeying food,
Godly Odysseus, who had suffered much, began speaking to
490   them:
"Let someone go out and see lest they are coming close."
So he said, and the son of Dolios went out as he bid.
He went and stood on the threshold and saw them all close.
Right away he addressed wingèd words to Odysseus:
495 "Here they are nearby. Let us quickly arm ourselves!"
So he said. They rose up and got their armor on,
Four including Odysseus, and the six sons of Dolios,
And among them Laertes and Dolios put armor on,
Gray though they were, warriors by necessity.
500 And when they had put the glittering bronze round their skin,
They opened the doors and went out; Odysseus led.
Athene, daughter of Zeus, came up close to them,
Likening herself to Mentor in form and in voice.
Godly Odysseus, who had endured much, rejoiced to see her;
505 At once he spoke out to his dear son Telemachos:
"Telemachos, you will soon learn, now you have come yourself
To where men are fighting and the best ones are judged,
Not to disgrace the family of your fathers, who before
Were distinguished for strength and prowess on the whole
     earth."
510 Then sound-minded Telemachos said to him in answer:
"In my present spirit, dear father, you will see, if you wish,

That, as you say, I shall not at all disgrace your family."
So he said, and Laertes rejoiced and spoke a word:
"What a day is this for me, dear gods! I greatly rejoice
That my son and my grandson contend over excellence."   515
Bright-eyed Athene stood beside him and addressed him:
"Son of Arkesios, dearest by far of all my companions,
When you have prayed to the bright-eyed maid and to Father
    Zeus,
Brandish your long-shadowy spear at once and hurl it forth."
So she said, and Pallas Athene breathed great strength into him. 520
Then he prayed to the daughter of the mighty Zeus
And brandished his long-shadowy spear at once and shot it
    forth.
He hit Eupeithes through the bronze cheek piece of his helmet.
This did not keep the spear back; the bronze went right
    through.
He made a crash as he fell, and his armor clattered upon him.   525
Odysseus and his glorious son fell upon the fighters in the front
And struck at them with their swords and their two-edged
    spears.
Now they would have destroyed all and made them without
    return,
If Athene, the daughter of aegis-bearing Zeus, had not
Shouted with her voice and restrained the whole host: 530
"Ithacans, hold off from war, which is disastrous,
So you may separate without bloodshed as soon as you can."
So did Athene say. And sallow fear got hold of them.
As they were afraid, all their arms flew out of their hands
And fell on the ground, as the goddess uttered her voice.   535
They turned back toward the city, longing for life.
Godly Odysseus, who had endured much, shouted dreadfully.
He bunched himself up and swooped down like a high-flying
    eagle.
Then the son of Cronos shot a smoldering thunderbolt.
It fell before the bright-eyed daughter of the mighty father.   540
Then bright-eyed Athene spoke out to Odysseus:
"Zeus-born son of Laertes, Odysseus of many wiles,
Hold off and cease from the strife of impartial war,
Lest Zeus, the broad-seeing son of Cronos, in some way get
    angry."

545 So Athene said. He obeyed, and rejoiced in his heart.
Then Pallas Athene, daughter of aegis-bearing Zeus,
Established oaths for the future between both sides,
Likening herself to Mentor in form and in voice.

Glossary

Achaians   a collective appellation of the Greeks besieging Troy

Achilles   the captain of the Myrmidons and the greatest hero of the Greeks at Troy

Aeolos   lord of the winds

Agamemnon   the leader of the Greeks at Troy; killed by Clytemnestra on his return home

Agelaos   son of Damastor and a suitor of Penelope

Aiaia   the legendary island home of Circe

Aietes   the king of Colchis; father of Medea and brother of Circe

Aigisthos   the cousin of Agamemnon and lover of Clytemnestra; after Agamemnon's murder, he became king of Mycenae

Ajax   (1) son of Telamon; second to Achilles in prowess among the Greeks at Troy
      (2) son of Oileus

Alcinoos   grandson of Poseidon; king of the Phaeacians at Scherie

Alcmene   the wife of Amphitryon and mother of Heracles

Amphimedon   a suitor of Penelope killed by Telemachos

Amphinomos   a suitor of Penelope killed by Telemachos

Anticleia   the daughter of Autolycos, wife of Laertes, and mother of Odysseus

Antilochos   a son of Nestor killed at Troy

Antinoos   son of Eupeithes; the ringleader and most insolent of Penelope's suitors

Antiphates   king of the Lestrygonians

Antiphos   one of Odysseus' crew eaten by the Cyclops

Aphrodite   daughter of Zeus; the goddess of love

Apollo   son of Zeus and brother of Artemis; the god of sun and light

Ares   son of Zeus; the god of war

Arete   the queen of the Phaeacians; wife of Alcinoos and mother of Nausicaa

Argos   the general name for Agamemnon's kingdom

Artemis   daughter of Zeus and sister of Apollo

Athene   the goddess of the arts and special patron of Odysseus

Atlas   the father of Calypso and the supporter of the pillars of heaven

Autolycos   the grandfather of Odysseus

Cadmos   founder of Thebes

Calypso   a goddess living on Ogygia; daughter of Atlas; Odysseus stays with her for seven years

Charybdis   a legendary whirlpool opposite Scylla

Cicones Thracian allies of the Trojans raided by Odysseus
Circe an enchantress living in Aiaia; daughter of the sun
Clytemnestra wife and murderer of Agamemnon
Creon a king of Thebes
Cronos one of the older gods; the father of Zeus, Poseidon, Hera, Hades
Cyclopes a lawless race of giants met by Odysseus

Danaans like "Achaians," a general designation for the Greeks at Troy
Delos an Aegean island sacred as the birthplace of Apollo and Artemis
Demodocos the blind bard of the Phaeacians
Diocles the son of Ortilochos, living at Pherai
Diomede the ruler of Argos; a major Greek hero at Troy
Dodona site of an ancient oracle of Zeus

Elpenor one of Odysseus' crew; he falls off Circe's roof
Erebos outer darkness for the dead
Erinyes goddesses who fulfill curses and avenge crimes
Eumaeos the faithful swineherd of Odysseus
Eupeithes the father of Antinoos; killed by Laertes
Euryalos a Phaeacian youth who taunts Odysseus
Eurycleia the nurse of Odysseus and housekeeper in his palace
Eurylochos the chief companion of Odysseus
Eurymachos a suitor of Penelope's killed by Odysseus
Eurynome a servant of Penelope's
Eurynomos an Ithacan suitor of Penelope's

Hades the god of the underworld
Halitherses an Ithacan; son of Nestor and friend of Odysseus
Helen wife of Menelaos; carried off by Paris to Troy
Hephaistos son of Zeus and husband of Aphrodite; god of fire and the forge
Hera queen of the gods; wife and sister of Zeus
Hermes son of Zeus; messenger of the gods and guide of the dead
Hyperion cognomen of the sun god

Ktesippos from Samê; one of the suitors of Penelope

Icarios the father of Penelope
Idomeneus the grandson of Minos and king in Crete
Ilion another name for Troy
Iros nickname of Arnaios, the beggar at Ithaca

Laertes the father of Odysseus and former king at Ithaca
Laodames a Phaeacian; son of Alcinoos
Lestrygonians a tribe of savage giants whose king was Lamos
Leto the mother of Apollo and Artemis

Megapenthes an illegitimate son of Menelaos
Melanthios son of Dolios; the faithless goatherd of Odysseus
Menelaos brother of Agamemnon and husband of Helen; co-commander of the Greeks at Troy

Mentes king of the Taphians, in whose guise Athene visits Telemachos
Mentor an Ithacan friend of Odysseus, in whose guise Athene guides
  Telemachos to Pylos
Minos legendary king of Crete and a ruler in the underworld
Mycenae the chief city of Homeric Greece and residence of Agamemnon
Myrmidons the followers of Achilles at Troy

Nausicaa Phaeacian princess, the daughter of Alcinoos and Arete
Nausithoos the colonizer of Scherie; son of Poseidon and father of
  Alcinoos
Neleus the founder of Pylos; son of Poseidon and father of Nestor
Nestor the aged king of Pylos and chief adviser for the Greeks at Troy
Nisos father of Amphinomos

Ogygia the legendary island home of Calypso
Oedipos a king of Thebes; son of Laios and Epicaste (in Homer)
Orestes son of Agamemnon; kills Clytemnestra and Aigisthos in aveng-
  ing his father's murder
Orion mighty hunter slain by Artemis; he appears as a constellation
Ortilochos a nobleman living at Pherai

Pallas an epithet of Athene
Patroclos the alter ego of Achilles at Troy; his death inspires Achilles
  to return to battle
Peiraios son of Klytios and companion of Telemachos
Peisander a suitor of Penelope's
Peisistratos Nestor's youngest son; Telemachos' companion on his
  journey to Sparta
Perimedes one of Odysseus' crew
Persephone the daughter of Zeus and Demeter; queen of the under-
  world
Pheidon king of the Thesprotians
Phemios son of Terpis ("Pleasure") and bard at Odysseus' palace
Philoitios the faithful herdsman of Odysseus
Phorcys a lesser sea divinity, the grandfather of the Cyclops
Polybos an Ithacan, the father of Eurymachos; also the name of a
  Phaeacian
Polyphemos a Cyclops, son of Poseidon
Poseidon son of Cronos and brother of Zeus; god of the sea, especially
  hostile toward Odysseus
Priam the aged king of Troy killed by the Greeks

Scylla a monster inhabiting a sea cave opposite Charybdis
Sirens two enchantresses luring sailors to destruction by their songs
Styx "Hateful" river of the underworld

Tiresias the blind seer of Thebes summoned by Odysseus on his visit
  to Hades
Theoclymenos a seer at Ithaca, friend of Telemachos
Theseus the great legendary hero and king of Athens

Thetis   a sea nymph and mother of Achilles
Tyndareus   from Sparta; father of Clytemnestra

Zeus   son of Cronos; king of the gods and specifically the god of the sky and of weather

The Greek World WITH PLACES MENTIONED IN The Odyssey

A map of probable locations for legendary places mentioned in The Odyssey

Backgrounds

J. A. DAVISON†

The Homeric Question

It is convenient (and, I hope, legitimate) to consider Homeric scholarship since 1910 under six headings, derived from Mülder's principles.

I. The artistic unity of the poems has been proclaimed by almost every literary critic of importance since Aristotle, and is supported not only by the opinion of ordinary readers (a fact emphasized from different points of view by books such as E. Drerup's *Das Homerproblem in der Gegenwart* and J. A. Scott's *The Unity of Homer* of 1921, J. T. Sheppard's *The Pattern of the Iliad* of 1922, and A. Rüegg's *Kunst und Menschlichkeit Homers* of 1948), but also by recent researches into the composition of the poems, whether they deal with one or other poem as a whole, or with problems of detail. As a result of these and other studies, a belief in the unitary plan of the Homeric poems can now be firmly based upon the evidence for design which both poems provide.

II. We have next to grapple with the problem of the inconsistencies in language, equipment, religion, and social customs, as well as those in the narrative. To do this, it is essential to begin by studying the case for the prosecution, as it is presented by the revisionists, among whom Wilamowitz must take pride of place (*Die Ilias und Homer* of 1916 and *Die Heimkehr des Odysseus* of 1927 are classics of Homeric scholarship), and the interpolationists, especially G. M. Bolling (*The External Evidence for Interpolation in Homer* [1925], *The Athetized Lines of the Iliad* [1944], *Ilias Atheniensium* [1950—an attempt to reconstruct the Pisistratean text] and Miss H. L. Lorimer (*Homer and the Monuments* [1950]). Many of the counts in the indictment are unreal, but even after all the unrealities are removed, no amount of self-deception on the part of believers in the unity of the poems can alter the fact that a serious case remains for them to answer; and the question is whether it is possible to show that these inconsistencies are compatible with

† From *A Companion to Homer*, ed. J. B. Wace and Frank H. Stubbings (New York: Macmillian & Co., 1963), pp. 254–259. Reprinted by permission of Macmillan & Co. and St. Martin's Press, Inc.

the purpose for which the poem was planned. In the sixth and fifth centuries, at least, the Homeric poems were recited at periodical festivals by professional singers or rhapsodes competing for prizes (Hdt. v. 67, Plat. *Ion*); and at Athens these competitions were so regulated that the poems had to be recited in sequence ([Plato] *Hipparch.* 228 в). Earlier poetical competitions (not necessarily for heroic poetry) are mentioned, both at festivals (Delos—*Hymn to Apollo* 149–50) and at the funerals of great men (Chalcis—Hes. W. & D. 654–9). It is thus at least possible that the Homeric poems were originally composed for the purpose for which they were used in historic times—to be the text for rhapsodes in a public competition. Only so, it seems, would it be possible to gather a continuing audience for the minimum time which would be necessary for the performance of a complete poem (with relays of reciters the *Iliad* would require three full days, the *Odyssey* not much under three days). In that case some, at least, of the inconsistencies, especially those in the narrative, can be explained as the sort of things which do occur in works intended for popular entertainment (ἀγωνίσματα ἐς τὸ παραχρῆμα ἀκούειν, in Thucydides's terminology)—either the audience would not notice them or would not care if they did, or they were what the audience expected in tales of mediaeval chivalry. That the poet should have admitted such lapses may lower him in critical eyes; but no poet can be popular for long who writes over his audience's head, and in any case we must allow for the dual nature of works of art. The element of perfection in the Homeric poems (Jean Wahl's 'monde achevé') is there for the person who reads them at about the speed at which they were intended to be performed (hence the importance of Ronsard's sonnet, referred to in note 25); the imperfections (the 'monde inachevé') become visible only when the poem is read slowly and dissected under the academic magnifying-glass. Other inconsistencies, especially those in language or equipment, are due to the nature of the epic language, which is the product of a long professional tradition and deals largely in formulae and similes; the formulae especially tend to preserve many linguistic and cultural fossils, much in the same way as modern English preserves many forgotten quotations and dead metaphors.

III. That the *Iliad* and *Odyssey* are the products of a long literary evolution is accepted to-day by every serious scholar, and since in them the evolution of the Greek epic poem may be said to have 'attained its nature', they may be regarded logically as the end of that evolution. The remote date at which the evolution must have begun is attested by the fossil forms in the epic language (Arcado-Cypriot and Aeolic words and forms; words which seem to be used in different, even contradictory, senses; irrelevant formulae; and so on), by the metre, by the persistence of Mycenaeanisms in armament, domestic equipment, social customs, and even (though less obviously) in religion, by the allusions to a surprisingly wide range of myths, many going back into the Mycenaean period (or even earlier), and by what we can learn from the poems themselves (and especially from the *Odyssey*) about professional bards, their training and their relations with their public, in what we may call 'pre-Homeric' times. The 'Homeric' language then was not used, and the myths were not told, for the first time in the *Iliad* and *Odyssey*; and this has important consequences for any attempt to prove the early existence of our *Iliad* or *Odyssey* from incidental occurrences in early poems, and especially in elegy, of short phrases which also occur in the *Iliad* or *Odyssey*, or to prove the early existence of any particular epic poem from representations of its known subject-matter in early art. A short phrase, even a whole line, may be simply an epic formula; a scene which seems to illustrate heroic life on a vase or brooch or shield-strap or comb, even if it can be identified with absolute certainty, need not necessarily illustrate any poem known to us —Phoenix in the *Iliad* (I 524–5) is our witness that the heroes who lived before Agamemnon had their *vates sacri*, whose works may well have been known to late Geometric artists.

IV. This leads us to the question of the sources of the *Iliad* and *Odyssey*; here again all the works of the evolutionists are relevant, and among them we may note especially C. Robert's attempt to establish objective criteria by which the different strata in a poem can be distinguished. Internal evidence gives us some idea of the material on which 'Homer' worked; the *Odyssey* speaks several times of οἶμαι ('paths'), which are either collections of stories or longish continuous poems from which some part can be extracted, to be sung in hall after dinner, and the components of such an οἶμη are once called κλέα ἀνδρῶν ('tales of men'—θ 73–4), a phrase which looks back to two passages in the *Iliad* (I 524–5 τῶν πρόσθεν . . . κλέα ἀνδρῶν | ἡρώων and 189, where Achilles sings them to the φόρμιγξ). It was presumably in these οἶμαι, knowledge of which was a monopoly of professional bards (θ 480–1), that the stories were preserved which formed the basis for the *Iliad* and *Odyssey*; and both poems make it clear that their stories were already known in essentials to the audience. Thus attempts to analyse the sources of the Homeric epics operate mainly with pre-Homeric epic poems, and with them we return to something very like Grote's view of the *Iliad*; and Focke has argued cogently that the *Odyssey* too is an expansion (by a poet of talent, though not perhaps of genius) of an original *Odyssey* which was by a great poet. We must suppose that the cyclic poems were formed in the same way, out of pre-Homeric οἶμαι; it is thus natural that many *motifs* are common to the Homeric poems and to one or other of the cyclic epics.

V. No one, that I know of, now believes that the *Iliad* or the *Odyssey* was created by joining together 'loose songs' into 'a sequel of songs and rhapsodies' in such a way that the original components could be simply uncoupled from one another and resume an independent existence. All the researches into the relative chronology of the various elements in the poems show that 'older' and 'younger' elements (whether archaeological, linguistic or social) interlock (perhaps the best example is the occurrence of the unquestionably ancient boar's tusk helmet in K, a book in which the language is characteristically modern and even 'post-Odyssean'). We may therefore deny that the *Iliad* and *Odyssey* were created directly out of lays in the Lachmannian sense; but we cannot deny that there are blocks which seem to be closely inter-connected, and may have originally formed parts of separate οἶμαι (or even κλέα ἀνδρῶν), as for example T-E, H-Θ, K, and ι-μ.

VI. Mülder's conclusion, that the *Iliad* (and, by legitimate extension, the *Odyssey*) can have been created only by a poet, and not by a *Bearbeiter*, by evolution, or by accident, depends for its cogency on one's own estimate of the poetic value of the plan and its accomplishment. The question is no longer whether the poems are composite, but whether the composition is good and the pieces of which it is composed are well chosen, well shaped, and well arranged—mosaic can be a great art, and even the humble patchwork quilt may be beautiful. In judging this aspect of the poems, it is well to stress the way in which the story is told; the arrangement is not what mediaeval critics called the *ordo naturalis* ('Begin at the beginning, go on to the end, and then stop'), but the much more complex *ordo artificialis*. Formally, the *Iliad* (the real title of which must have been *The Wrath of Achilles*) deals with only a few days, relatively speaking, in the tenth year of the siege of Troy. Using this short episode as his framework, the author has built up around it by means of reminiscences and prophecies almost the whole story of the Trojan war from the marriage of Peleus and Thetis down to the establishment of the Aeneadae at their town in the Troad as Priam's successors; thanks to these reminiscences and prophecies, together with the tales and anecdotes about past events elsewhere in the heroic world (Elis, Aetolia, Thessaly, Lycia, etc.), the main narrative is displayed against a background of past history, and also put to some extent in perspective by occasional reminders to the audience of what has happened since those days. The *Odyssey* follows a similar, though somewhat simpler, plan; it is noteworthy that it almost never overlaps the *Iliad*, although it fills several gaps left by the *Iliad* between the death of Hector and the sack of Troy. In both these poems a sense of narrative strategy is shown which is paralleled in Greek literature only by Herodotus, and in Latin is approached only by the *Aeneid*; nothing like it is found again in literature until the Renaissance, and then only in one or two poems, of which *Paradise Lost* perhaps comes nearest to the Homeric standard. It does not seem that any of the modern heroic poems which are invoked by the believers in the comparative method shows anything like the narrative strategy of the *Odyssey*, not to mention the *Iliad*; the more elaborate modern poems may qualify for the title οἴμη, but they are not fully-developed epic poems. It is on the narrative strategy and the character-drawing (both unsurpassed in later times) of the Homeric poems that the claim of their author (or authors) to a place among the great poets finally rests. We cannot say that the same person composed both poems, but there can hardly be a doubt that each was given its present form by a single person with all the resources of a professional bard at his finger-tips, or that the author of the *Odyssey* was intimately acquainted with the *Iliad*.

Two points still await consideration: the date of the poems, and the question of writing. The belief in the artistic unity of our *Iliad* and *Odyssey* can rest only upon the assumption that the textual tradition of the two poems is at least as reliable as that of Pindar; and this can be true only if (*a*) the poems were preserved in writing from the moment of composition by some self-perpetuating corporation (such as the Homeridae), (*b*) the copy brought to Athens in the sixth century was obtained from that corporation (if so, it would explain the authority which it obviously enjoyed), (*c*) the Panathenaic text was scrupulously preserved from excisions or interpolations (the conditions of its use would presumably guarantee that), and (*d*) the text which was victorious over all competitors in the second century B.C. was an accurate copy of the Panathenaic text. Not one of these things can be proved; but none is impossible, or even improbable, and if they are true, it follows that the text of the poems, as reconstructed by the normal processes of textual criticism from the Byzantine MSS. and checked with the papyri of the period after 150 B.C., must be taken to be as accurate a representation as is now attainable of the original text as it was first written. From this text there cannot be any rejection of passages as interpolations or revisions; what is in it must be accepted as it stands, and either explained or admitted to be inexplicable with our present knowledge. In that case the *terminus post quem* for the composition of the *Iliad* will be the latest datable archaeological object mentioned in it. The archaeologists have still to determine the identity and date of this object, but it will be surprising if the suggested *terminus post quem* is found to lie after, or many years before, 700 B.C. The *terminus ante quem* for the *Odyssey* seems to be, at latest, the founding of Naucratis (Rhys Carpenter, *op. cit.* 100), *i.e. circa* 620. Between these two extremes, to account for the universal belief in pre-Alexandrian times that both poems were by the same man, a single working life-time should cover their creation. In any case, if we put the creation of the *Iliad* and *Odyssey* at the end of the eighth or in the first half of the seventh century, all difficulties about the use of writing in their composition disappear, and there is no gap to be accounted for between the Homeric poems and the earliest surviving lyric and elegiac poetry of the late eighth and seventh centuries. The earlier literature has perished, either because it was not committed to writing or (perhaps more probably) because it was out-classed and to some extent swallowed up by the new poetry of the early seventh century.

The theory thus advanced seems to me to come nearer to satisfying the requirements of the evidence now available than any other; but, like all theories, it is only provisional, and may be destroyed by the discovery of new evidence or by the reflections of other minds upon the existing evidence. The 'revolutions of learning' are not (*pace* Dr. Johnson) merely circular, keeping the human mind 'in motion without progress'. In the Homeric scholarship of the last three centuries we may watch the progressive application to the old problems of new types of evidence and new methods of interpretation. To this progress all the scholars whom I have named, and many whom I have not named, have made their several contributions; and even apparently retrograde movements have sometimes proved to be the starting-point for new advances. 'Other men have laboured and ye are entered into their labours.'

G. S. KIRK†

Heroic Age and Heroic Poetry

The narrative oral poet sings of the deeds of heroes, usually heroes of the past, and sometimes too of gods, giants or folk-tale figures. This heroic poetry is nearly always sung in lines with a uniform metrical pattern, a rapid and flowing rhythm like that of the Homeric hexameter or the looser decasyllable of Serbo-Croat verse. Metrical regularity is essential for learning and composing long oral poems; though in some traditions, especially those affected by Latin, quite complex factors like rhyme, alliteration or division into stanzas may be added. Even with the help of an easy and regular rhythmical framework, a restricted and standardized poetical vocabulary, and the great powers of memory of the non-literate, the oral heroic poet must almost invariably be a professional or semi-professional, one who begins his training as a boy and thereafter has constant practice.

Songs sung from memory need not only be narrative ones, though there is often little or no surviving evidence of other cat-

---

† From G. S. Kirk, *The Songs of Homer* (Cambridge: Cambridge University Press, 1962), pp. 56–61, 63–69, and 280–281. Reprinted by permission of the publisher.

egories. Work-songs, dance-songs and dirges must always have had a place in the kind of culture that gave rise to the oral narrative poet, and in some societies gnomic and didactic oral poetry flourished too. Yet songs of these other genres were in most ways less important than the heroic songs: they were shorter, often less formally arranged, and less closely associated with the nobility. Two common features of nearly all kinds of oral poem, however, are that they were composed and remembered without the aid of writing and that they were sung or chanted, usually to a musical accompaniment. Poems are songs, and the Homeric word for a poet is ἀοιδός (aoidos) or singer, one who accompanies himself on the lyre-like instrument known in Homer as the *kitharis* or *phorminx*.

It is strange that great heroic narrative poems of comparable structure and ideology should have grown up in different periods and parts of Europe: the Homeric poems in early Iron Age Greece, the Teutonic poems, including *Beowulf* and the *Nibelungenlied*, in the 4th to the 8th centuries A.D., the Celtic narratives in Ireland and Wales (in which, however, prose saga was mixed with poetry), especially down to the 13th or 14th century, the great Norse poems and sagas which flourished from the 9th to the 13th century, and the Russian and South Slavic heroic epics which have developed from the 14th century to the present day—not to speak of Finnish heroic songs, or the *Chanson de Roland*, or the Byzantine epic of Digenes Akritas, or the much earlier and rather different Near Eastern tradition exemplified in the stories of Gilgamesh and Keret or in the Babylonian creation hymn. In some of these, especially the Scandinavian and Near Eastern poems, the element of magic, demonology or folk-tale is much stronger than in Homer. In others, like the *Chanson de Roland*, writing has played some part. Yet the heroic quality and the oral quality remain predominant. The reason for the similarity of these products is that they arose from basically similar cultures; each of them derives from a Heroic Age or its immediate successor. The main components of such an age, which tends to occur in the development of many different nations, seem to be a *penchant* for warfare and adventure, a powerful nobility, and a simple but temporarily adequate material culture devoid of much aesthetic refinement. In such conditions the heroic virtues of honour and martial courage dominate all others, ultimately with depressive effects on the stability and prosperity of the society. It is usually during the consequent period of decline that the poetical elaboration of glorious deeds, deeds that now lie in the past, reaches its climax; though narrative songs are a favourite recreation of the tired warrior throughout the whole heroic period.

The Homeric epic, developed in its monumental form by about 700 B.C., is an outcome of the in most ways typical Heroic Age of the late Mycenaean period, an age which had ended, historically speaking, as far back as 1100. That a tradition of oral heroic song maintained itself for so long, and grew to so late and stupendous a culmination, is surprising enough. But fortunately the final collapse of the Mycenaean system, drastic as it was, had not produced a total dispersal of population; many survivors were able to cultivate and transmit the memory of the heroic past. Another event which fortified the Greek heroic tradition throughout a post-heroic age was the submergence of writing for a period of several centuries; and this in its turn had been helped by the laborious and imprecise nature of the Mycenaean script. During the period of total illiteracy of the 11th and 10th century oral poetry would be as much a necessity of life as it ever had been before—perhaps more so. Other heroic ages in other lands tended to be followed much more rapidly by the spread of writing, and their oral traditions may have been relatively less pure; though in parts of Europe an oral tradition has continued for even longer than four hundred years, because until recently writing never touched more than a small minority of the population. Even in Mycenaean Greece only a small minority seems to have been literate; from the 7th century onwards, on the other hand, the impact of writing on the Greeks was rapid and pervasive.

In spite of these and other differences between one nation and another the concept of the Heroic Age as a recurrent phenomenon in the development of cultures, especially in Europe, is valid and useful; its isolation is largely the work of H. M. and N. K. Chadwick. It allows us to understand the picture of the *aoidos* or professional singer as given in the Odyssey, and to envisage the way in which Homer himself—the first 'monumental' poet, that is—may have grown out of such a figure. It allows us, too, to credit the successors of singers like Demodocus with songs longer and more complex than those mentioned in the Odyssey, songs of the scale of *Beowulf* or the earlier Icelandic sagas. Yet the concept of the court poet of the Heroic Age must be diversified by the study of the popular or market-place poet. This is the kind that survives most tenaciously when a Heroic Age is ended and when the noblemen's houses are divided or abandoned. The court minstrel is the typical poet in the Heroic Age, but we must be careful not to regard the composers of the Iliad and Odyssey as necessarily resembling that kind of singer in every respect. These poems were brought to perfection long after the Achaean Heroic Age had ended. Their audience must have included comparatively rich patrons and noblemen, but also, probably, the general populace in various kinds of gathering. . . . Heroic poetry appeals to the people as well as to heroes and their descendants; and the oral poets that can be studied best, those of modern Yugoslavia, have for long been popular poets who sing in coffee-houses, not court poets. Yet their subjects are mainly heroic and aristocratic.

The Languages of Formulas in Homer

The case for describing Homer as an oral poet would be incomplete if it depended solely on the importance of the minstrel in other heroic or post-heroic societies, together perhaps with the description of Phemius and Demodocus in the Odyssey and the absence of writing from Greece during much of the interval between the downfall of Mycenae and the probable date of the Iliad. Some or all of these factors, however, interpreted with varying degrees of accuracy, had led many critics, even before Milman Parry, to conclude that Homer composed in a very different manner from Apollonius of Rhodes, Virgil or Milton. Furthermore the language of the poems had for long been closely scrutinized, and by the early 1920's Witte, Meister, Meillet and others had made a strong case for its classification as a formalized and traditional development, in which alternative dialect forms, for example, were chosen mainly to suit the requirements of metre. Of Parry himself, whose importance was generally overlooked until some time after his premature death in 1935, much has now been written. His contributions to Homeric scholarship are twofold: he saw the relevance of the modern oral poetry of Yugoslavia and succeeded in recording a great deal of it; and he demonstrated beyond doubt that Homer was an oral poet, depending on a gradually evolved traditional store of fixed phrases which covered most common ideas and situations—a store that was neither unnecessarily luxurious nor restrictively parsimonious.

These essential qualities of the oral poet's treasury of verbal formulas were termed by Parry *economy* and *scope*. Düntzer and a few others had already recognized that the many recurrent phrases in Homer, most obviously the name-epithet formulas like 'divine Odysseus' and 'gleaming-helmeted Hector', were used in a way that was not just haphazard or unimaginative, but on the contrary was somehow essential to the poet. Parry first showed that such fixed phrases in Homer composed a system so tight and logical that it could only be the outcome of many generations of refinement. This process of refinement consisted in the rejection of the otiose—the merely decorative alternative —and the consolidation and expansion of whatever was functional and organic. Now the Homeric hexameter verse tends to be more or less self-contained in meaning; its ending usually coincides with a major or minor pause, the end of a sentence or clause or at least the point at which a predicate is divided from its subject. This means that there is plenty of opportunity for the repetition of whole lines, the verse being treated as a formula; and in fact about one-third of the verses in the Iliad and Odyssey recur at least once. It is more important, however, that the verse itself is divided into smaller sections by word-breaks which are part of its structure; and into these sections are fitted recurrent phrases or sense-units. The most important internal divisions, which must coincide with a gap between words, are the compulsory main caesura in the third foot, either male or female (i.e. after the first syllable of that foot, the 'strong' position, or after its first trochee, $-\cup$, the commoner 'weak' position); the extremely common 'bucolic' diaeresis before the fifth foot; and the word-break after the first measure of the fourth foot in many lines which contain a female, or trochaic, main caesura. The intervals between the beginning of the verse and the male caesura, or between the male, female, fourth-foot or bucolic caesuras and the end of the verse, are the main places in which standard phrases or fixed formulas are employed. Since the verse-end is marked by the fixed rhythm $-\cup\cup-\cup$ (as opposed to all other parts of the line, where the spondee can be substituted for the basic dactyl at will) the poet must first be sure of filling the latter part of the line. Thus the majority of fixed phrases are designed to fill out portions of the verse-end. At the beginning of the verse the commonest formula-lengths are the whole portion down to the main caesura, or less often the first one-and-a-half feet. . . .

There is, in fact, amazingly little unnecessary reduplication of formulas in Homer. To take the large number of name-epithet phrases in the nominative case: the table on pp. 50f. of Parry's classic study, *L'Épithète traditionnelle chez Homère* (Paris, 1928), shows that for eleven prominent gods and heroes there are no less than 824 uses of 55 different formulas in the Iliad and Odyssey as a whole. These formulas, some of which are of course very frequent (πολύμητις Ὀδυσσεύς comes 81 times) are those which fill out the four commonest metrical segments of the verse. . . . Out of the 824 uses only 15, involving only three different formulas, are reduplicative in the sense of being exact metrical equivalents of other commoner ones. . . . Thus in the extensive name-epithet nominative system there is an astounding *economy* of phrases, not more than 5 per cent of reduplication. At the same time the coverage or *scope* is almost equally striking. The four main parts of the verse to be filled, in the case of these eleven prominent characters, make a possibility of 44 name-epithet groups. Two of these positions cannot in any case be filled by particular names because of their metrical value, but out of the 42 remaining we find formulas for no less than 37, making roughly 88 per cent perfect coverage.

This degree of scope and economy cannot be accidental; nor can it be the creation of a single poet. No one singer could construct a system so rich in metrical alternatives and at the same time so closely shorn of unfunctional variation. Even a pen and paper composer would be hard pressed to achieve such a system, and to do so he would have to behave not like a poet but like a cryptographer—or a classical scholar; and his effort would be quite pointless, since the only reasonable purpose of such a construction is to enable the oral, non-literate poet both to assimilate and to increase a great stock of traditional heroic song. The system is so extensive because for generation after generation individual singers had added a fresh phrase here and another there, as the necessity of their particular contexts demanded; it is so economical, spare and thrifty because needless alternatives —a mere encumbrance to the singer—were systematically if gradually discarded. Human skills being fallible, and the crea-

tive urge not always responding to systems, a new and unfunc-
tional alternative would naturally be added from time to time,
so that the economy at any one period would never be quite
complete.

Closer examination of the details of the formular system
shows how it helps the poet to remember traditional verses; for
if a line is divided into three familiar phrase-units, say, rather
than ten or a dozen word-units, it is obviously easier to remem-
ber and reproduce. It also helps him to compose his own fresh
lines with the minimum of effort. Epithets are standardized not
only for people but also for many familiar objects, and once
again they vary according to the portion of verse that it is
desired to fill. If the idea 'of a ship' has to be expressed in the
latter part of a verse, the ship will be described as 'equal',
'curved around' or 'dark-prowed' simply according as the final 2,
$2\frac{1}{2}$ or $3\frac{1}{4}$ feet have to be filled—in other words, according as
the phrase has to succeed the bucolic, hephthemimeral or
trochaic caesura. The formulas are νηὸς ἐίσης, νεὸς ἀμφιελίσσης and
νεὸς κυανοπρῴροιο: note that the form of the word 'ship' itself
is varied solely for metrical convenience. If the case is changed,
and a dative, for example, is needed after the bucolic caesura—
because the other concepts to be expressed use the whole of
the verse up to that point—then the epithet may have to be
changed too, and νηὸς ἐίσης becomes νηὶ μελαίνῃ. That is not be-
cause ships in the dative are any blacker and less equal than
those in the genitive, nor is it because a ship in a particular
context is envisaged as black rather than equal: it is black simply
and solely because after the word νηί, and to fill the measure
$\cup - \underline{\cup}$, we require an epithet of that value beginning with a con-
sonant—since νηί ends in a vowel. ἐίση will not do and μελαίνῃ
will. Prepositions, too, can be incorporated in these noun-epithet
groups, and may require fresh epithets with new metrical values:
thus 'on a ship', if it is to fill the last $2\frac{1}{2}$ feet, for instance, entails
replacing the standard epithet of the simple noun-epithet group
in that place, namely 'curved around', by the shorter word 'hol-
low'—κοίλης ἐπὶ νηός in place of νεὸς ἀμφιελίσσης.

Other common types of formula express the verb, or the verb
and its object, and so on, and are designed to fill either the first
or the second part of the verse and often to be mated with an
appropriate subject-formula in the other part. Thus αὐτὰρ ὁ
μερμήριξε, or τὸν δ' αὖτε προσέειπε, or αὐτὰρ ἐπεί τό γ' ἄκουσέ, for in-

stance, may be followed by an 3¼-foot noun-epithet group beginning with a consonant. Such formulas are themselves often built up from shorter fixed components—thus there are many different phrases beginning with αὐτάρ: αὐτὰρ ὁ with different verbs, αὐτάρ ἐπεί or ἐπειδή, αὐτὰρ ἔβη and so on. . . .

The singers of the Ionian oral tradition sometimes adapted a phrase to a new position or a new use without much conscious thought, by ear and by instinct. The formula in its standard use and form had a familiar metrical value, and it seems to have been assumed, sometimes wrongly, that this value persisted even after the standard form had been slightly altered; or perhaps it would be truer to say that there was no conscious assumption of any kind, that this problem is one that often does not occur to the oral singer. Thus μερόπων ἀνθρώπων, for example, is a well-known formula, evidently developed for use in a genitive case, which occurs at the verse-end seven times in the Iliad and twice in the Odyssey. Once in the Iliad it is successfully adapted to the dative, μερόπεσσι βροτοῖσιν, but at XVIII. 288 we see that at some stage some not very careful singer required a *nominative* phrase meaning 'men' for the same part of the line, and so transposed the familiar formula into μέροπες ἄνθρωποι, thus producing a technical fault of metre. In performance the singer would presumably disguise this fault by artificially prolonging the -ες, and the audience would probably not notice the difference. Similarly many Homeric instances of hiatus—that is, of irregularly leaving a final vowel unaffected before a succeeding initial vowel—are the result of the minor adaptation of fixed phrases; though Parry exaggerated when he made this the primary cause of metrical anomalies, since many cases of hiatus are caused by the loss of digamma or other initial semi-vowels, or by the assumption of such a loss, or by a feeling that hiatus sometimes did not matter at the major divisions of the verse. An analogous result of the careless placing of formulas is inappropriateness not of metre but of sense. Thus the basic idea 'with the hand' is often expressed by the formula χειρὶ παχείῃ, in which the epithet 'thick' helps to fill up the part of the verse following the bucolic caesura. When this epithet is applied not to the powerful fist of a warrior, which must have been its usual and so 'proper' function, but to the ladylike hand of the refined (sometimes over-refined) Penelope, the result, if it is noticed at all, is ludicrous. The same is the case with 'blameless Aegisthus'

(1.29) and perhaps with the revolting Irus's 'lady mother' (18.5)—I am not sure that in the last case any contradiction would be felt. These are obvious and familiar cases, but there are others in which the redeployment of a formula reveals itself in more subtle ways; thus one of a pair of repeated passages may reveal itself as adapted from the other—or from the type of which the other is a fair representative—because of the forced adjustment of a component formula.

What is the minimum length of a formula? The maximum may be several complete lines, composing a passage which is repeated whenever a typical scene, like the preparation of a meal or sacrifice or the launching or beaching of a ship, is to be described. The minimum may be two words like ὣς φάτο or Τρώεσσι δέ, if we insist on the formula as a phrase-unit. But even single words have definite formular tendencies, since they gravitate strongly to certain positions in the verse according to their metrical value; and there are fewer exact metrical alternatives of single words having a similar meaning than one would find in written poetry—though more than in the case of most formular phrases. The fixity of position of individual words within the line is indeed remarkable, though it quite escapes the notice of most readers or hearers. The longer the word the less remarkable this fixity becomes; there are only two positions which a word like φιλοπτολέμοισι, for example, can occupy without disturbing the natural articulations of the hexameter line. Yet even disyllables like ἦτορ or δῶμα show a strong preference for one or perhaps two positions in the verse, whereas there are theoretically several in which they could occur . . . ; and παιδός, παιδί regularly avoid the line-end (only once in 61 uses), while παῖδα and the plural forms do not. Sometimes this preference is due to the fact that the word in question occurs predominantly in a particular formula, itself restricted in position. Where this is not the case the tendency toward fixity arises in part out of the pure mechanics of the hexameter verse, a subject which we do not yet fully understand; but at least a perusal of Eugene O'Neill Jr.'s article on metrical world-types in the Greek hexameter shows that the tendency had reached a considerable degree of formalization or stylization in the Homeric poems. Thus metrical word-values, rather than particular single words, are formular in Homer, and this apparent restriction, like that imposed by fixed phrases, was of a kind to help rapid composition rather than to hinder it. The singer begins to crystallize a thought of which the pivotal concept is 'house': he assigns δῶμα, for instance, to its preferred position, and can then confidently fit verbal and other nominal formulas round it. His verse is made with the minimum of conscious effort.

The Oral Tradition and the Advent of Writing

I hope to have outlined the broad principles of formular composition and to have shown by a small number of examples that Homer manifests the scope and economy of a developed oral tradition. To illustrate all the complexities and potentialities of this type of composition would need a complete book; not even Parry produced such a comprehensive explanation, nor is one necessary. What is necessary is to grasp the principle. One consequence of Parry's demonstration is that every single line of the great poems must be assessed in terms of a traditional and formalized language and a traditional subject-matter. Fulsome lip-service has been paid to Parry's conclusions, and some scholars have even been tempted to make the one-sided claim that the only way in which Homeric scholarship can progress is by closer examination of the formular system. In spite of this, relatively little has been achieved since Parry died.

Even less attention has been given to post-Homeric hexameter poetry from this viewpoint. Hesiod's *Theogony* and the fairly copious fragments of his Catalogue poetry are composed in a distinctly Homeric style, somewhat debased but traditional in essence. There are many new phrases, some of them repeated several times and tending to become fully formular; these are confined primarily to fresh subject-matter. Where the subject is traditional—as for example in many of the Catalogue fragments —the traditional language is used, though often with drastic adaptations. The subject of *Works and Days*, on the other hand, is so different from those of the regular heroic narrative that hundreds of new words and phrases are needed. Native Boeotian poets may have developed a tradition which included didactic and gnomic poetry, so that even the non-Homeric language of *Works and Days* may still be oral and formular in character. Unfortunately there is no contemporary material for comparison, nor have the economy and scope of the new phrases been evaluated in detail; but Hesiod could well have used the aid of writing, in some way or other, in the genuine parts of this later poem. The earlier 'Homeric' Hymns, particularly those to Demeter, Apollo, and Aphrodite, are probably entirely oral. They depart from Homeric vocabulary often enough, and have many new phrases; but these, especially the decorative and lyrical ones, are in the style of certain relatively late elements in Homer, like the Beguilement of Zeus in Iliad xiv and xv, which there is no reason to associate with writing and which indeed preserve a scope and economy which preclude it. As for the few surviving fragments of the poems of the Homeric Cycle, they are for the most part easily distinguishable in style from Homer. The later Cyclic poems, like the *Telegony* of Eugammon, almost certainly belong to written literature. The earlier, like the *Aithiopis* and the *Iliou Persis* of Arctinus, may have been composed not long after 700 in the decadent oral manner of certain later expansions of Homer. . . .

Nevertheless by the probable time of composition of the *Theogony,* the *Aithiopis,* and the *Hymn to Demeter,* none of which is likely to be very much later than 650, writing was reaching the point at which it could be used for literary purposes. Archilochus, who was certainly a literate composer, refers to an eclipse of the sun which must be that of 648. Moreover *graffito* inscriptions on certain unambitious pots show that writing was used in different parts of the Greek world, and sometimes for casual and inessential purposes, as early as the last decades of the 8th century. The Dipylon prize jug with a hexameter couplet to the effect that the best of the dancers (? shall receive this prize) is datable from its shape and decoration seen that these special occasions are not particularly likely to have provided the conditions to elicit an exceptionally large-scale poem, and I think it quite possible that the humbler and more frequent occasions would have been no worse, and perhaps better, in this respect. *Weddings* in Yugoslavia, Hungary, Greece and many other traditionally peasant communities sometimes still last for as long as a week, and are most commonly arranged for the slack times of a farmer's year. Eating, drinking, telling stories, singing and listening to songs are the main occupations. In Muslim Yugoslavia the month of Ramadan, with its nights devoted to eating and drinking, is the chief occasion for a singer to deploy his repertoire to the full, and best provides a continuous audience. No such comparable festival existed in ancient Greece, but weddings and perhaps funerals—humble no less than aristocratic—and small horse-fairs and the like would in some cases have lasted long enough for the development and singing even of a song as vast as the Iliad. It could have been in such circumstances as these that Homer first strung together elements of his Trojan repertoire—much of it acquired from older singers—so as to form a coherent poem with one or two strong central themes.

The truth remains that none of these possible occasions—feast or festival, fair or wedding or funeral or informal gathering in market-place or tavern—seems to possess any special quality that could easily and naturally have actually *elicited* a large-scale epic. The concept of the oral poem as functional is a useful one—but it is not going to help us much with the monumental poem, simply because by the normal canons of heroic song this kind of poem is an aberration. Rather I believe we should accept that the chief factor in the making of the new literary form was not function or occasion, but—and this is horribly obvious once one comes to say it, though it has been avoided like the plague by most Homeric critics in the last sixty years—the special ability, aims, imagination and reputation of a particular singer; the singer in fact who compounded the first large-scale Iliad and who was known as Homer. An outstandingly accomplished singer may be seen to acquire a tremendous reputation in any oral society, first in his own district and then further afield; often he may acquire a prestige equalling that claimed by Demodocus in the Odyssey. I am driven towards the provisional conclusion that it was this prestige that enabled Homer to outstrip normal performances, normal audiences and normal occasions—that enabled him to *impose* his own will and his own vast conception on his environment, so as eventually to produce an Iliad. Admittedly if circumstances were such that no one would listen to a poem of this length, or more or less take in its whole span, the Iliad would hardly have survived in the tradition—unless it could be recorded in writing without delay, which ... I regard as an improbable and unnecessary hypothesis. But there is no reason to suspect that circumstances *were* such—weddings and fairs, to look no further, could have provided audiences consistent enough to encourage the great singer, if only his own powers and reputation were high enough to hold them. The crucial factor was the creative imagination, the singer of outstanding brilliance and an exceptionally large Trojan repertoire who suddenly saw that many of its songs could be interlocked to make a complete and universal Trojan song. This was not like the evolution of tragedy, for example, each stage of which may have seemed a logical development from the last; it was more like the evolution of the monumental Geometric amphora or crater. The evidence of archaeology does not suggest that pots become systematically larger and larger until eventually one was made that was seven feet tall, but rather that there was a leap from the largeish pot to the perfectly colossal one, a leap which must have been made for the first time by a particular potter who suddenly had a flash of ambition and the inspiration of sheer size, and at the same time realized that he possessed the necessary materials and technique. This kind of leap, incidentally, is far easier to understand in one man than in a group or a corporation—though others will inevitably follow the example of magnitude once it has been given.

M. I. FINLEY†

Wealth and Labor in the *Odyssey*

A deep horizontal cleavage marked the world of the Homeric poems. Above the line were the *aristoi*, literally the "best people," the hereditary nobles who held most of the wealth and all the power, in peace as in war. Below were all the others, for whom there was no collective technical term, the multitude. The gap between the two was rarely crossed, except by the inevitable accidents of wars and raids. The economy was such that the creation of new fortunes, and thereby of new nobles, was out of the question. Marriage was strictly class-bound, so that the other door to social advancement was also securely locked.

Below the main line there were various other divisions, but, unlike the primary distinction between aristocrat and com-

† From M. I. Finley, *The World of Odysseus* (New York: The Viking Press, 1954), pp. 49–73. Reprinted by permission of the author, Chatto & Windus, Ltd., and The Viking Press, Inc. Copyright 1954 by M. I. Finley.

moner, they seem blurred and they are often indefinable. Not even so simple a contrast as that between slave and free man stands out in sharp clarity. The word *drester*, for example, which means "one who works or serves," is used in the *Odyssey* for the free and the unfree alike. The work they did and the treatment they received, at the hands of their masters as in the psychology of the poet, are often indistinguishable.

Slaves existed in number; they were property, disposable at will. More precisely, there were slave women, for wars and raids were the main source of supply, and there was little ground, economic or moral, for sparing the lives of the defeated men. The heroes as a rule killed the males and carried off the females, regardless of rank. Before offering up his prayer for his son, Hector, who knew his own doom, said to his wife: "But I care not so much for the grief of the Trojans hereafter . . . as for yours, when one of the bronze-clad Achaeans will carry you off in tears; and you will be in Argos, working the loom at another woman's bidding, and you will draw water from Messeis or Hypereia, most unwillingly, and great constraint will be laid upon you."

Hector did not need Apollo's aid in foretelling the future. Never in Greek history was it otherwise; the persons and the property of the vanquished belonged to the victor, to be disposed of as he chose. But Hector showed gentle restraint, for his prophecy was not complete. The place of slave women was in the household, washing, sewing, cleaning, grinding meal, valeting. If they were young, however, their place was also in the master's bed. Of the old nurse Eurycleia, the poet reports that "Laertes bought her with (some of) his possessions when she was still in the prime of youth . . . but he never had intercourse with her in bed, and he avoided the anger of his wife." It was the rarity of Laertes' behavior, and the promise of his wife's wrath, that warranted the special comment. Neither custom nor morality demanded such abstinence.

It is idle to seek for numbers here. Odysseus is reported to have had fifty female slaves, but that is surely a convenient round figure, used for the household of King Alcinous of the Phaeacians too. A few men were also in bondage, such as the swineherd Eumaeus, an aristocrat by birth, who had been kidnaped when a child by Phoenician traders and sold into slavery. Like the women, the male slaves worked in the home, and in the fields and vineyards, never abroad as servants or orderlies.

Of the Ithacans who were not slaves, the free population who were the bulk of the community, some were surely independent householders, free herders and peasants with their own holdings (although the poet tells us nothing about them). Others were specialists, carpenters and metal workers, soothsayers, bards, and physicians. Because they supplied certain essential needs in a way that neither the lords nor the nonspecialists among their followers could match, these men, a handful in numbers, floated in mid-air in the social hierarchy. Seers and physicians might even be nobles, but the others, though they were close to the aristocratic class and even shared its life in many respects, were decidedly not of the aristocracy, as the treatment and behavior of the bard Phemius attest.

Eumaeus, we remember, called these specialists *demioergoi*, literally "those who work for the people" (and once Penelope attached the same classificatory label to the heralds). From the word, used in the Homeric poems only in these two passages, it has been suggested that the *demioergoi* operated in a way well known among primitive and archaic groups, the Kabyle of Algiers, for instance: "Another specialist is the blacksmith, who is also an outsider. The villagers lend him a house, and each family pays him a fixed portion of his yearly salary in grain and other produce." Unfortunately the evidence for the world of Odysseus is far from clear or decisive. Once when Nestor, at home, wished to make sacrifice, he ordered his servants, " 'Bid the goldsmith Laerces come here, that he may gild the horns of the cow'. . . . And the smith came, with the smith's tools in his hands, the instruments of his craft, anvil and hammer and well-made fire-tongs, with which he worked the gold. . . . And the old horseman Nestor gave gold, and the smith then skillfully gilded the horns." Neither the status of the goldsmith nor even his domicile is indicated here, unlike the passage in the *Iliad* about the great "unwrought mass of iron" which Achilles offered from his booty for a weight-throwing contest. The iron was to be both the test and the prize for the winner. He will have it, said Achilles, "to use for five full years, for neither the shepherd nor the plowman will have to go into town for lack of iron, but this will furnish it."

Although nothing is ever said about remuneration, it does not necessarily follow that each family in the community gave the smith, or the other *demioergoi,* a fixed annual maintenance quota. They could have been paid as they worked, provided only that they were available to the public, to the whole *demos.* That availability would explain the word well enough.

Eumaeus indicated still another special quality of the *demioergoi* when he asked "who ever summons a stranger from abroad . . . unless he be one of the *demioergoi*" (again with a parallel among the Kabyle). Were they, then, traveling tinkers and minstrels, going from community to community on a more or less fixed schedule? Actually the logic of Eumaeus's question is that all invited strangers are craftsmen, not that all craftsmen are strangers. Probably some were and some were not, and, of those who were, none need have worked on a circuit at all. The heralds were certainly permanent, regular, full-scale members of the community. The bards may have wandered a bit (in the poet's own day they traveled all the time). Regarding the others, we are simply not informed.

Indispensable as the *demioergoi* were, their contribution to the quantity of work performed on an estate was a very small one. For the basic work of pasturage and tillage in the fields, of stewardship and service in the house, there was no need of specialists: every man in Ithaca could herd and plow and carve, and those commoners who had their own holdings worked them themselves. Others made up the permanent staffs of Odysseus and the nobles, free men like the unnamed "carvers of the meat," who were an integral part of the household. Still others, the least fortunate, were *thetes,* unattached, propertyless laborers who worked for hire and begged what they could not steal.

"Stranger," said the leading suitor Eurymachus to the beggar (Odysseus in disguise), "would you be willing to work as a *thes,* if I should take you in my service, on a farm at the border—you can be sure of pay—laying walls and planting tall trees? There I would furnish you ample grain and put clothes on your back and give you shoes for your feet." Ample grain and clothes and shoes made up the store of a commoner's goods. But Eurymachus was mocking, "creating laughter among his companions," at the direct inspiration of Athena, who "would by no means permit the arrogant suitors to refrain from heart-rending scorn, so that the pain might sink still more deeply into the heart of Odysseus son of Laertes."

A little of the joke lay in the words, "you can be sure of pay."

No *thes* could be sure. Poseidon once angrily demanded of Apollo why he of all the gods should be so completely on the side of the Trojans. Have you forgotten, Poseidon asked, how, on order from Zeus, "we worked as *thetes* for one year, for an agreed-upon pay," for Laomedon, king of Troy, building the wall around the city and herding cattle? And how, at the end of the year, Laomedon "deprived us of our pay and sent us off with threats?" The real joke, however, the utter scornfulness of Eurymachus's proposal, lay in the offer itself, not in the hint that the pay would be withheld in the end. To see the whole point, we turn to Achilles in Hades rather than to Poseidon on Olympus. "Do not speak to me lightly of death, glorious Odysseus," said the shade of Achilles. "I would rather be bound down, working as a *thes* for another, by the side of a landless man, whose livelihood was not great, than be ruler over all the dead who have perished."

A *thes*, not a slave, was the lowest creature on earth that Achilles could think of. The terrible thing about a *thes* was his lack of attachment, his not belonging. The authoritarian household, the *oikos*, was the center around which life was organized, from which flowed not only the satisfaction of material needs, including security, but ethical norms and values, duties, obligations, and responsibilities, social relationships, and relations with the gods. The *oikos* was not merely the family, it was all the people of the household and its goods; hence "economics" (from the Latinized form, *oecus*), the art of managing an *oikos*, meant running a farm, not managing to keep peace in the family.

Just what it meant, in terms of customary or legal obligation and in a man's own familial life, to be a permanent but free member of the *oikos* of another is by no means clear. Negatively it meant considerable loss of freedom of choice and of mobility. Yet these men were neither slaves nor serfs nor bondsmen. They were retainers (*therapontes*), exchanging their service for a proper place in the basic social unit, the household—a vicarious membership, no doubt, but one that gave them both material security and the psychological values and satisfactions that went with belonging. Altogether the chief aristocrats managed, by a combination of slaves, chiefly female, and a whole hierarchy of retainers, supplemented by *thetes*, to build up very imposing and very useful household forces, equipped to do whatever was required of a man of status and power in their world. The hierarchy of retainers, it should be added, reached very high indeed. As a child Patroclus was forced to flee his home. Peleus received him in his palace and "named him retainer" of young Achilles. The analogy that comes to mind at once is that of the noble page in some early modern court, just as "lord Eteoneus, the ready retainer of Menelaus" who met guests at the door and poured the wine for them, might well have been the counterpart of a Lord Chamberlain.

A *thes* in Ithaca might even have been an Ithacan, not an outsider. But he was no part of an *oikos*, and in this respect even the slave was better off. The slave, human but nevertheless a part of the property element of the *oikos*, was altogether a nice symbol of the situation. Only twice does Homer use the word that later became standard in Greek for a slave, *doulos*, which seems etymologically tied to the idea of labor. Otherwise his word is *dmos*, with its obvious link with *doma* or *domos*, a house; and after Homer and Hesiod *dmos* never appears in literature apart from a few instances of deliberate archaizing, as in Sophocles and Euripides. The treatment of the slaves was essentially milder and more humane than the pattern familiar from plantation slavery. Eumaeus, a favorite slave, had even been able to purchase a slave for himself. To be sure, a dozen of the slave girls were hanged in the midst of the carnage of Odysseus' successful return, but it was the method of their execution alone that distinguished them from the lordly suitors, who died by the bow and the spear.

There was little mating of slave with slave because there were so few males among them. Nearly all the children born to the slave women were the progeny of the master or of other free males in the household. Commonly, in many different social systems, as among the Greeks later on, such offspring were slaves like their mothers: "the belly holds the child," say the Tuareg nomads of the Sahara in explanation. Not so in the world of Odysseus, where it was the father's status that was determinative. Thus, in the fanciful tale with which Odysseus sought to conceal his identity from Eumaeus immediately upon his return to Ithaca, his father was a wealthy Cretan, his mother a "bought concubine." When the father died the legitimate sons divided the property, giving him only a dwelling and a few goods. Later, by his valor, he obtained to wife the daughter of "a man of many estates." The slave woman's son might sometimes be a second-class member of the family, but even then he was part of that narrower circle within the *oikos* as a whole, free and without even the stigma of bastardy in our sense, let alone the mark of slavery.

Fundamentally the difference between the ordinary landowner and the noble lay in the magnitude of their respective *oikoi*, and therefore in the numbers of retainers they could support, which, translated into practical terms, meant in their power. Superficially the difference was one of birth. At some past point, remote or near in time, either conquest or wealth created the original separation. Then it froze, continued along hereditary lines, was given divine sanction through genealogies that assigned every noble family a god for an ancestor, and was called a blood-distinction.

The nature of the economy served to seal and preserve the class line. Wherever the wealth of the household is so decisive, unless there is a measure of mobility in wealth, unless the opportunity exists to create new fortunes, the structure becomes caste-like in its rigidity. This was the case in Ithaca. The base of the *oikos* was its land, and there was no way, under normal, peaceful conditions, to acquire new land in the settled regions. Hypothetically one might push to the frontier and take up vacant land, but few men actually did anything so absurd and foolhardy, except under the most violent compulsions. It was not out of mere sentiment for the fatherland that banishment was deemed the bitterest of fates. The exile was stripped of all ties that meant life itself; it made no difference in this regard whether one had been compelled to flee or had gone from home in the search for land by free choice.

The primary use of the land was in pasturage. To begin the story of his adventure among the Cyclopes, which he told at the court of Alcinous, Odysseus underscored the primitive savagery of the one-eyed giants. First of all, they had not learned the art of agriculture: "they neither plant anything nor till." Nevertheless, Odysseus' own world was one of pasturage, not of tillage (unlike the Greek world at the time of Homer himself and of Hesiod, when agriculture had moved to the fore). Greek soil is poor, rocky and waterless, so that no more than twenty per cent of the total surface of the peninsula can be cultivated. In places it once provided excellent pasturage for horses and cattle; virtually all of it is still, in our day, good for the smaller animals, sheep and pigs and goats. The households of the poems carried on a necessary minimum of plowing and planting, especially on orchard and vine-land, but it was their animals on which they depended for clothing, draft, transport, and much of their food.

With their flocks and their labor force, with plentiful stone for building and clay for pots, the great households could almost realize their ideal of absolute self-sufficiency. The *oikos* was above all a unit of consumption. Its activities, insofar as they were concerned with the satisfaction of material wants, were guided by one principle, to meet the consuming needs of the lord and his people; if possible by the products of his estates, supplemented by booty. But there was one thing which prevented full self-sufficiency, a need which could neither be eliminated nor satisfied by substitutes, and that was the need for metal. Scattered deposits existed in Greece, but the main sources of supply were outside, in western Asia and central Europe.

Metal meant tools and weapons, but it also meant something else, perhaps as important. When Telemachus had concluded his visit at the palace of Menelaus in Sparta, in search of news about his father, his host offered him, as a parting gift, "three horses and a chariot-board of polished metal and . . . a fine goblet." The young man demurred. "And whatever gift you would give me, let it be treasure. I will not take horses to Ithaca. . . . In Ithaca there are neither wide courses nor any meadowland." The Greek word customarily rendered by "treasure" is *keimelion*, literally something that can be laid away. In the poems treasure was of bronze, iron, or gold, less often of silver or fine cloth, and usually it was shaped into goblets, tripods, or caldrons. Such objects had some utilitarian worth and they could provide aesthetic satisfaction too, but neither function was of real moment compared to their value as symbolic wealth or prestige wealth. The twin uses of treasure were in possessing it and in giving it away, paradoxical as that may appear. Until the appropriate occasion for a gift presented itself, most treasure was kept hidden under lock and key. It was not "used" in the narrow sense of that word.

When Agamemnon was finally persuaded that appeasement of Achilles was absolutely essential to prevent the destruction of the Achaean forces, he went about it by offering amends through gifts. His offer included some to be presented at once, others on conditions of victory. And what a catalogue it was: seven cities, a daughter to wife with a great dowry "such as no one ever yet gave with his daughter," the girl Briseis, over whom the quarrel had broken out, seven captive women from Lesbos skilled in crafts, twelve prize-winning racehorses, and his choice of twenty Trojan women when the war was won. These, apart from the horses, were the utilitarian gifts. But Agamemnon began with none of them; first came "seven tripods that have never been on the fire and ten talents of gold and twenty glittering caldrons," and further on, from the anticipated Trojan spoils, as much gold and bronze as his ship would hold.[1] That was treasure, and its high importance is marked by the care with which it is enumerated here and again later in the poem. Menelaus's gift to Telemachus, all treasure, reappears four more times in the *Odyssey*, in three different books.

Whatever its purpose or its source, metal created for the individual *oikos* a special problem in the distribution of goods. For the most part distribution was internal and hence no problem at all. Since there has never been a world of Robinson Crusoes, the simplest human groups perforce have a mechanism, and it is the same one that served, with some extension, even the most elaborate princely *oikos*. All the productive work, the seeding and harvesting and milling and weaving, even the hunting and raiding, though performed by individuals, was carried on in behalf of the household as a whole. The final products, ready for consumption, were gathered and stored centrally, and from the center they were redistributed—in the authoritarian household, by its head at a time and in a measure he deemed appropriate.

It made no difference in essence whether the family members within the household were no more than a husband, wife, and child, or whether the *oikos* was that of King Priam of Troy, with his fifty sons and their wives, twelve daughters and their husbands, and his uncounted grandchildren; or the more reason-

---

1. *Iliad* 9.121–56. In Plato's will, preserved by Diogenes Laertius, *Lives* 3.41–43, the itemized bequest included "three minas of silver, a silver bowl weighing 165 drachmas, a small cup weighing 45 drachmas, a gold ring and gold earring weighing 4½ drachmas together." This is treasure, now narrowed to gold and silver, and, like Agamemnon's it is made up indifferently of metal and metal objects.

able example of Nestor at Pylos, with six sons and some sons-in-law. The sons possessed arms and treasure of their own, from gifts and booty, as the wives and daughters had their fine garments and jewels. But unless the males left the paternal household and established their own *oikoi*, their personal property was an essentially insignificant factor. Normally, the poems seem to say, although the evidence is not altogether clear and consistent, the sons remained with their father in his lifetime.

Architecturally the heart of the system was the storeroom. Preparing for his journey to Pylos, Telemachus "went down to his father's spacious, high-ceilinged storeroom, where gold and copper lay piled up, and clothing in chests, and fragrant oil in plenty; and there stood jars of wine, old and sweet, filled with the unmixed divine drink, close together in a row along the wall." And of course it contained arms and grain in quantity. More than three hundred years after Homer the Athenian Xenophon, a gentleman farmer and no tribal chieftain or king, still placed proper care of the storeroom high on the list of wifely virtues.

It was when distribution had to cross *oikos* lines that the creation of new and special devices became necessary. Wars and raids for booty, indistinguishable in the eyes of Odysseus' world, were organized affairs, often involving a combination of families, occasionally even of communities. Invariably there was a captain, one of whose functions was to act as the head and distribute the booty, all of which was first brought to a central storage point. Division was by lot, much like the division of an inheritance when there were several heirs. For example, not all of Odysseus' homecoming adventures were tragic. Two or three times he and his men had the pleasant opportunity to raid. "From Ilion," he began the account of his wanderings, "the wind bore me near to the Cicones, to Ismarus. There I sacked the city and killed the men; taking the women and many goods, we divided them, so that no one might go cheated of his equal share through me."

Forcible seizure, followed by distribution in this fashion, was one way to acquire metal or other goods from an outside source. Some scholars think that the kernel of historical truth in the tale of the Trojan War is precisely such a mass raid for iron supplies. Whether they are right or not, there were surely many smaller Trojan wars to such a purpose, against Greeks as well as against barbarians. But the violent solution was neither always feasible nor even always desirable; if the aggrieved party were strong enough it invited retaliation, and there were times and conditions when even the fiercest of the heroes preferred peace. An exchange mechanism was then the only alternative, and the basic one was gift-exchange. This was no Greek invention. On the contrary, it is the basic organizing mechanism among many primitive peoples, as in the Trobriand Islands, where "most if not all economic acts are found to belong to some chain of reciprocal gifts and counter-gifts."

The word "gift" is not to be misconstrued. It may be stated as a flat rule of both primitive and archaic society that no one ever gave anything, whether goods or services or honors, without proper recompense, real or wishful, immediate or years away, to himself or to his kin. The act of giving was, therefore, in an essential sense always the first half of a reciprocal action, the other half of which was a counter-gift.,

Not even the parting gift was an exception, although in this one instance there was an element of risk. The last of the recognition scenes in the *Odyssey*, between the hero and his aged father, began in the customary fashion, with Odysseus claiming to be someone else, a stranger from another land in search of information about "Odysseus." Your son, he said to Laertes, visited me about five years ago and received the proper gifts. "Of well-wrought gold I gave him seven talents, and I gave him a bowl with flower designs, all of silver, and twelve single cloaks and as many carpets and as many fine mantles, and as many tunics besides, and in addition four pretty women skilled in excellent work." Laertes wept, for he had long been satisfied that his son had perished, and he could think of no better way to reveal that fact to the stranger than by commenting on the gift situation. "The countless gifts which you gave, you bestowed in vain. For if you had found that man still alive in the land of Ithaca, he would have sent you on your way well provided with gifts in return."

Then there is the interesting scene in the opening book of the *Odyssey*, in which the goddess Athena appeared to Telemachus in the shape of Mentes, a Taphian chieftain. When she was ready to part, the young man followed the expected custom: "Go to your ship happy in your heart, bearing a gift, valuable and very beautiful, which will be your treasure from me, such as

dear guest-friends give to guest-friends." This created a very deli-
cate situation for the goddess. One did not refuse a proffered
gift, yet she could not accept it under the false pretense of her
human disguise. (Gods as gods not only accepted gifts from
mortals, they expected and demanded them.) Being the clever-
est of the gods, Athena unhesitatingly found the perfect solu-
tion. "Do not detain me any longer as I am eager to be on my
way. The gift, which the heart of a friend prompts you to give
me, give it to me on my return journey that I may carry it
home; choose a very beautiful one, that will bring you a worthy
one in exchange."

Telemachus had said nothing about a counter-gift. Yet he
and "Mentes" understood each other perfectly: the counter-gift
was as expected as the original gift at parting. That was what
gift-giving was in this society. The return need not be forthcom-
ing at once, and it might take several forms. But come it nor-
mally would. "In a society ruled by respect for the past, a tradi-
tional gift is very near indeed to an obligation." No single detail
in the life of the heroes receives so much attention in the *Iliad*
and the *Odyssey* as gift-giving, and always there is frank refer-
ence to adequacy, appropriateness, recompense. "But then Zeus
son of Cronus took from Glaucus his wits, in that he exchanged
golden armor with Diomedes son of Tydeus for one of bronze,
the worth of a hundred oxen for the worth of nine oxen." The
poet's editorial comment, so rare for him, reflects the magnitude
of Glaucus's mistake in judgment.

There was scarcely a limit to the situations in which gift-giv-
ing was operative. More precisely, the word "gift" was a cover-
all for a great variety of actions and transactions which later
became differentiated and acquired their own appellations.
There were payments for services rendered, desired, or antici-
pated; what we would call fees, rewards, prizes, and sometimes
bribes. The formulaic material was rich in such references, as in
the lines with which Telemachus and twice Penelope responded
to a stranger's favorable interpretation of a sign from the gods:
"Stranger, would that these words be fulfilled! Speedily should
you become aware of friendship and many gifts from me, so
that whoever met you would congratulate you."

Then there were taxes and other dues to lords and kings,
amends with a penal overtone (Agamemnon's gift to Achilles),
and even ordinary loans—and again the Homeric word is always

"gift." Defending himself for having lent Telemachus a ship with which to sail to Pylos and Sparta seeking information about Odysseus, a young Ithacan noble made this explanation: "What can one do when such a man, troubled in heart, begs? It would be difficult to refuse the gift." In still another category payment for service was combined with the ceremonialism necessary to an important event. There is much talk in the *Odyssey* about the "gifts of wooing," and the successful suitor, who reminds one of nothing so much as the highest bidder at an auction, in turn received his counter-gift in the dowry, without which there could be no marriage. The whole of what we call foreign relations and diplomacy, in their peaceful manifestations, was conducted by gift-exchange. And even in war occasions presented themselves, as between Diomedes and Glaucus, for example, or Ajax and Hector, when heroes from the two contending sides stopped, right on the field of combat and before the approving eyes of their fellow heroes, and exchanged armor.

Odyssean trade differed from the various forms of gift-exchange in that the exchange of goods was the end itself. In trade things changed hands because each needed what the other had, and not, or only incidentally, to compensate for a service, seal an alliance, or support a friendship. A need for some specific object was the ground for the transaction; if it could be satisfied by other means, trade was altogether unnecessary. Hence, in modern parlance, imports alone motivated trade, never exports. There was never a need to export as such, only the necessity of having the proper goods for the countergift when an import was unavoidable.

Laertes bought Eurycleia "with (some of) his possessions . . . , and he gave the worth of twenty oxen." Cattle were the measuring stick of worth; in that respect, and only in that sense, cattle were money. Neither cattle, however, nor anything else served for the various other, later uses of money. Above all, there was no circulating medium like a coin, the sole function of which was to make purchase and sale possible by being passed from hand to hand. Almost any useful object served, and it is noteworthy that the measure of value, cattle, did not itself function as a medium of exchange. Laertes bought Eurycleia for unspecified objects worth twenty oxen; he would never have traded the oxen for a slave.

A conventional measuring stick is no more than an artificial language, a symbol like the X, Y, Z of algebra. By itself it cannot decide how much iron is the equivalent of one cow, or how much wine. In Adam Smith's world that determination was made through the supply-and-demand market, a mechanism utterly unknown in Troy or Ithaca. Behind the market lies the profit motive, and if there was one thing that was taboo in Homeric exchanges it was gain in the exchange. Whether in trade or in any other mutual relationship, the abiding principle was equality and mutual benefit. Gain at the expense of another belonged to a different realm, to warfare and raiding, where it was achieved by acts (or threats) of prowess, not by manipulation and bargaining. Gain from trade was "greedy gain."

The implication that exchange rates were customary and conventional seems unavoidable. That is to say, there was no constituted authority with the power to decree a set of equations—so much of X for so much of Y. Rather the actual practice of exchange over a long period of time had fixed the ratios, and they were commonly known and respected. Even in the distribution of booty, where a central authority, the head of the *oikos* or a king or commander-in-chief, took charge, he was obviously bound by what was generally deemed to be equitable. The circumstance that no one could punish him for flouting custom, as in the conflict between Agamemnon and Achilles, is irrelevant to the issue. For the very fact that just such a situation gave the theme for the *Iliad* illustrates how dangerous the violation could be. In this world custom was as binding upon the individual as the most rigid statutory law of later days. And the participant in an exchange, it may be added, had the advantage over the passive participant in the distribution of booty. He could always refuse to go through with the transaction if the rules were manifestly being upset, or if he merely thought they were.

None of this is to say that no one ever deliberately profited from an exchange. But the exceptional instance is far less noteworthy than the essential point that, in a strict sense, the ethics of the world of Odysseus prohibited the practice of trade as a vocation. The test of what was and what was not acceptable did not lie in the act of trading, but in the status of the trader and in his approach to the transaction. So crucial was the need for metal that even a king could honorably voyage in its search.

When Athena appeared to Telemachus as Mentes, the Taphian chieftain, her story was that she was carrying iron to Temesa in quest of copper.[2] That gave no difficulties, and her visit ended with the colloquy regarding costly gifts between guest-friends.

A stranger with a ship was not always so welcome or so free from suspicion. He might have been Odysseus before Ismarus, or Achilles: "Twelve cities of men have I destroyed from ship-board and eleven on foot, I say, in the fertile region of Troy; from all these I took out much good treasure." No wonder that some Greeks eventually objected to Homer as the teacher of the Hellenes. Glorification of piracy, disapproval of theft (seizure of goods by stealth), and encouragement of robbery (seizure of goods and persons by physical prowess)—truly this seemed a world of mixed-up moral standards. "Theft of property is mean," protested Plato, "seizure by force shameless; none of the sons of Zeus delighted in fraud or violence, nor practiced either. Therefore, let no one be falsely persuaded by poets or by some myth-tellers in these matters."

Yet there was a pattern and a consistency in the moral code; and it made sense from the premises. The distinctions rested on a specific social structure, with strongly entrenched notions regarding the proper ways for a man to behave, with respect to property, toward other men. Upon his arrival among the Phaea-cians, but before he had identified himself and told of his wan-derings, Odysseus was entertained by King Alcinous. Following the feast, the younger nobles competed in athletics. After a time the king's son Laodamas approached Odysseus and invited him to participate.

"Come, stranger and father, you enter the games, if per-chance you are skilled in any; you seem to know games. For there is no greater fame for a man, so long as he is alive, than that which is made by foot and hand."

Odysseus asked to be excused, pleading the heavy burden of his sorrows. Another young aristocrat then interposed. "No indeed, stranger, I do not think you are like a man of games, such as there are many among men; but like one who travels with a many-benched ship, a master of sailors who traffic, one

2. Neither Taphos nor Temesa is otherwise known as a place name, and the many attempts, all failures, to identify them with one or another mining region illustrate once again the futility of such "historicizing" of the Homeric poems.

who remembers the cargo and is in charge of merchandise and greedy gains."

The insult was unbearable under all circumstances, and to Homer's audience it must have carried an added barb when directed against Odysseus. There was something equivocal about Odysseus as a hero precisely because of his most famed quality, his craftiness. There was even a soft spot in his inheritance: his maternal grandfather, the goodly Autolycus, "surpassed all men in thievishness and the oath, for that was a gift to him from the god Hermes." Later the doubts of many Greeks turned to open contempt and condemnation. "I know full well," says Philoctetes in the Sophoclean play, "that he would attempt with his tongue every evil word and villainy." What saved the Homeric Odysseus was the fact that his guile was employed in the pursuit of heroic goals; hence Hermes, the god of tricks and stealth, may have given him the magic with which to ward off Circe the witch, but it was Athena who was his protector and his inspiration in his heroic exploits. To the insult in Phaeacia he first replied with an indignant speech, but Odysseus, of all men, could not establish his status with words. Having finished his reply, he leaped up, seized a weight greater than any the young men had cast, and, without removing his garment, threw it far beyond their best mark.

Possibly there were men, a very few from among those who were not men of games, living in the interstices of society, who traveled in many-benched ships and trafficked. Yet there is no single word in either the Iliad or the Odyssey that is in fact a synonym for "merchant." By and large, the provisioning of the Greek world with whatever it obtained from the outside by peaceful means was in the hands of non-Greeks, the Phoenicians in particular. They were really a trading people, who sailed from one end of the known world to the other, carrying slaves, metal, jewelry, and fine cloth. If they were motivated by gain— "famed for ships, greedy men"—that was irrelevant to the Greeks, the passive participants in the operation.

The need for metal, or any similar need, was an oikos affair, not an individual matter. Its acquisition, whether by trade or by raid, was therefore a household enterprise, managed by the head. Or it could be larger in scale, involving many households acting cooperatively. Internally, the situation was altogether different. Trade within the household was impossible by definition: the *oikos* was a single, indivisible unit. Because a large sector of the population was enmeshed in the great households, it was too withdrawn from any possibility of trade, external or internal. The *thetes*, finally, were absolutely excluded; having nothing, they had nothing to exchange.

That leaves the non-aristocratic, small-scale herders and peasants. In their households shortages were chronic, if not absolute as a consequence of a crop failure or a disaster to their flocks, then partial because of an imbalance in the yield. Their troubles are not the subject of heroic poetry, and neither the *Iliad* nor the *Odyssey* is informative in this regard. The inference is permissible, however, that some of their difficulties were alleviated by barter, primarily with one another, and without the instrumentality of a market or fair, absolutely unknown in this world. They exchanged necessities, staples, undoubtedly on the same principles of equivalence, ratios fixed by custom, and no gain.

Herders and peasants, including the *thetes*, always had another resource to draw upon. They could work. As with trade, so with labor, the society's moral judgment was directed not to the act itself but to the person and the circumstance. Back in Ithaca, but still disguised as a beggar, Odysseus, in reply to Eurymachus's mocking offer of employment, challenged the suitor to a plowing contest—just as, in his proper guise, he boasted of his superior bowmanship or his weight throwing. But Odysseus was not required to plow in order to live. In fact, it is obvious that, though he knew how to till and herd and build a raft, he rarely did any work on his estate except in sport. That was the great dividing line, between those who were compelled to labor and those who were not. Among the former, the men with the inspired skills, the bards and the metalworkers and the others, were an elite. Above all, the test was this, that "the condition of the free man is that he not live under the constraint of another." Hence there was a sharp line between those who, though they worked, remained their own masters, the independent herders and peasants, and on the other side the *thetes* and the slaves who labored for others, whose livelihood was not in their own hands. The slaves, at least, were usually the victims of chance. The *thes* was in that sense the worst of all: he voluntarily contracted away his control over his own labor, in other words, his true freedom.

Much of the psychology of labor, with its ambivalence

between admiration of skill and craft and its rejection of the laborer as essentially and irretrievably an inferior being, found its symbol on Olympus. Having humanized the gods, the bard was consistent enough to include labor among the heavenly pursuits. But that entailed a certain difficulty. Zeus the insatiable philanderer, Apollo the archer who was also a minstrel, Ares the god of battle—these were all embodiments of noble attributes and activities, easily recreated in man's image. But how could the artisan who built their palaces and made their weaapons and their plate and their ornaments be placed on equal footing with them, without casting a shadow over the hierarchy of values and status on which society rested? Only a god could make swords for gods, yet somehow he must be a being apart from the other gods.

The solution was neatly turned, very neatly indeed. The divine craftsman was Hephaestus, son of Hera. His skill was truly fabulous, and the poet never tired of it, lingering over his forge and his productions as he never sang of the smith in Ithaca. That was the positive side of the ambivalence. The other was this: of all the gods, Hephaestus alone was "a huge limping monster" with "a sturdy neck and hairy chest." Hephaestus was born lame, and he carried the mark of his shame on his whole personality. The other gods would have been less than human, in consequence, were Hephaestus not to be their perennial source of humor. Once, when Zeus and Hera were having a fearful quarrel, the limping god attempted the role of peacemaker, filling the cups with nectar for all the assemblage. "And unquenchable laughter was stirred up among the blessed gods as they watched Hephaestus bustling about the palace." And the social fabric of the world of Odysseus was saved.

In fact, the mirror-image on Olympus was still more subtle. In art and craftsmanship, Athena was frequently linked with Hephaestus, as in the simile in which a comparison is drawn with a goldsmith, "a skillful man whom Hephaestus and Pallas Athena taught all kinds of craft (*techne*)." But there was absolutely nothing deformed or the least bit comical about Athena, deservedly her father's favorite among the gods. It was unnecessary to apologize for Athena's skill with her hands, for the pattern with respect to work differed somewhat for women. Denied the right to a heroic way of life, to feats of prowess, competitive games, and leadership in organized activity of any kind, women worked, regardless of class. With her maids, Nausicaa, daughter of the Phaeacian king, did the household laundry. Queen Penelope found in her weaving the trick with which to hold off the suitors. Her stratagem, however, of undoing at night what she had woven in the day, repeated without detection for three full years until one of her maids revealed the secret, suggests that her labor was not exactly indispensable. The women of the aristocracy, like their men, possessed all the necessary work skills, and they used them more often. Nevertheless, their real role was managerial. The house was their domain, the cooking and the washing, the cleaning and the clothes-making. The dividing line for them was rather in the degree to which they performed the chores themselves—between those who supervised, working only to pass the time, and those whom circumstances compelled to cook and sew in earnest.

MARTIN P. NILSSON†

[Homeric Anthropomorphism and Rationalism]

. . . The words of Andromache after Hektor's death are significant of the total disappearance of the old understanding of the meaning of funeral gifts:

O yea, no profit to thee—they shall not swathe thee on the pyre;
But to be for thine honour in Troy-town's sons' and daughters' eyes.

The continued cult of the dead man, the offerings upon the tomb, are not mentioned and seem no longer to exist. With the cessation of these the power of the dead over the living is broken.

In connexion with this change is associated a revision and a weakening of the ideas about that part of man which lives on after death, and about its existence. That which survives man is *psyche*, the soul, the shade: it is nothing more. It is true that the most important descriptions of the souls are contained in

† From Martin P. Nilsson, *A History of Greek Religion* (London: Oxford University Press, 1949), translated by F. J. Fielden, pp. 137–140, 159–163, and 170–172. Reprinted by permission of the publisher.

the two Nekyiae, which are later additions to the *Odyssey*. With a faint squeak as of bats—here the old idea of the bird-like appearance of the soul is seen—the souls of the murdered suitors follow Hermes, their guide, into the underworld. Odysseus three times seeks in vain to embrace his mother's shade; she yields before his grasp. The 'impotent heads' of the souls have neither flesh nor bone; they flit away like dreams. Like a phantom the still unburied Patroklos shows himself to Achilles, in all things, even in size, resembling the dead man; the vision draws from Achilles the significant cry:

O strange! then even in Hades' homes—and I knew not this—
They have spirit and shape ($\psi\nu\chi\grave{\eta}$ $\kappa\alpha\grave{\iota}$ $\epsilon\check{\iota}\delta\omega\lambda o\nu$), albeit in these
   no life there is.

As in the Nekyia, the shade of Patroklos vanishes 'like smoke with a rustling sound.' In the Nekyia the prevailing idea, although it is not consistently carried out, is that the souls have no consciousness and can acquire this only by drinking the blood of the sacrificial animal, an idea which originates in the blood-offerings poured out upon the grave. The souls are shades possessing neither strength nor consciousness, and such figures there is no need to propitiate and worship. A continued existence of this kind is of no value to man.

Rather would I be a hireling to drudge in the fields all day
With a landless master, who sparely would feed me and niggardly
   pay,
Than over the hosts of the dead which have perished a sceptre to
   sway,

Achilles replies to Odysseus. The life after death becomes so pale and empty that it is not far from non-existent. The man who makes Death and Sleep twin-brothers and calls death 'a brazen sleep' does not really believe in any future life.

The kingdom of the dead is modelled upon these ideas. There the detested Hades rules, the most odious of all gods to men, and his consort, the dreaded Persephone. His kingdom is dark and noisome. Its terror chiefly lies in the fact that the way back is closed to any who have once passed within its portals. Hades is the strong custodian of the gates; his dog is mentioned in connexion with the Herakles myth. Pylos, where Herakles strove with Hades, is originally nothing else than the gate of the realm of the dead. The idea of a common kingdom of the dead is naturally much older than Homer and recurs among most other peoples. It arises of itself as soon as man, in order to depict the life hereafter, makes use of the ever-present analogy with human life. It generally exists without difficulty side by side with the idea that the dead man lives and is active in his grave, but in Homer it has completely prevailed and may be said to be a kind of anthropomorphism. The life after death has been brought closer to the life on earth but has also lost its power and intensity. Instead of a copy it has become a pale shadow.

The kingdom of the dead lies beneath the earth, for there the dead are buried. During the battle of the gods Hades springs up in terror from his throne, for he is afraid that the roof over his head will fall in. Where are its gates? In later times grottoes and deep lakes were thought to be entrances to Hades. The idea is certainly old, but for a seafaring people, who naïvely imagined the earth to be a flat disk surrounded by the Ocean, the world had an extreme edge, and over this men passed into the realms below. On this idea is based the famous description of Hades in the journey of Odysseus to the underworld, but it exists also in the *Iliad*. Patroklos exhorts Achilles to bury his body as soon as possible, for the shades will not permit him to pass the river which bounds the kingdom of the dead. This is a transposition to the Homeric world of ideas belonging to the old belief that a man who has not been buried can find no peace; if his body does not rest in the ground he must wander about unceasingly like a lost spirit. Accordingly Odysseus on his visit to the lower regions meets the shipwrecked Elpenor before any other shades; for he has not yet been buried.

The bond between the two worlds of the living and of the dead has been weakened but by no means severed, and the doctrine that this bond was broken by the burning of the corpse overstates the case. The poet certainly makes the shade of Patroklos declare that after his burial he will never come back, but this is merely an expression adapted to the particular occasion and must not be erected into a general theory. Homeric ideas are not without mutual contradictions. Passages have already been adduced to show that burial was regarded as necessary, since without it the dead man would not be admitted into the kingdom of the dead; but not withstanding this it is declared in numerous instances that the slain go down to the dwellings of Hades, and Achilles himself says of the shade of the unburied Patroklos that it dwells there. Cremation by no means originated in a desire to be liberated from the troublesome claims of the dead; it is an old funeral custom alongside of which the notion of the continued life and activity of the dead in the grave can still exist and does exist in later times. In the expression 'appease in the fire' ($\pi\upsilon\rho\grave{o}\varsigma\ \mu\epsilon\iota\lambda\iota\sigma\sigma\acute{\epsilon}\mu\epsilon\nu$) lies neither more nor less than the old idea of burial as the undisputed right of the dead, the same feeling that forbids the Homeric warrior to refuse burial even to a dead foe....

... The man of the people sees from below what the nobility views from above. The nobility in its turn views from below the class of highest rank, that of the gods. And it is precisely of their relationship to man that the above two words are used. The thirst for fame and an unlimited self-esteem urge the man of the nobility forwards, and when misfortune overtakes him it is described as the envy of the gods; the gods regard his success as beyond what human powers should achieve. The explanation is constantly present: it is used when a bowstring breaks in the fight, so that the foe escapes the shot; Calypso thinks that the gods grudge a goddess life with a mortal man. The expression finally becomes stereotyped; Penelope says that the jealousy of the gods had prevented her and Odysseus from living together. Thus anthropomorphism found in the settled order of society the ultimate barrier between gods and men. The Greeks never lost sight of the idea and the problem involved in it. Insolence towards the gods must be regarded by any genuine religious feeling as the most deadly ethical and religious sin. That it was not so regarded by the Greeks was due to their anthropomorphism, which made the gods resemble men and then measured them by the same moral standards as mankind.

Actually, no living person has ever seen a god, and Homer makes the gods associate personally only with favoured fabulous peoples such as the Ethiopians and the Phaeacians. But he is not consistent; on rare occasions a god does reveal himself to certain heroes in an untransformed shape. Rationalism overcame the difficulty that the gods were so frequently supposed to intervene in human affairs and were yet nowhere to be seen by supposing that they assumed human shape. This device is characteristic of Homer's divine apparatus, and popular belief assisted it. There was thought to be something mysterious about the stranger, and it was upon occasion believed that a god was concealed under his form.

Religious experience had still less to say about the activities of the gods than about their epiphany. Many had doubtless experienced the intervention and influence of a god, but simple religious feeling does not ask how or by what agency this comes about. It sees something which it must ascribe to divine power, it knows its prayer to be answered; with this it is satisfied and inquires no further. Rationalism succumbed to the temptation of representing the influence and intervention of the gods in a visible form credible to ordinary reason. Anthropomorphism by investing the gods with human shape had shown the way. What best accorded with reality was to make a god intervene in the disguise of a human being.

This became the normal fashion in which the gods are made to intervene, but there are certain distinctions. Zeus directs the battle from afar by means of his will and the messages he sends. He intervenes personally but once, when he hurls the lightning before the horses of Diomedes. Apollo strikes Patroklos with his powerful hand, and the armour falls from the hero's body. He goes before Hektor with the aegis and smoothes out with his feet the ditch around the Greek ships as easily as a child at play fills up a hole in the sand. But he never condescends to the office of a squire or to pure deception as Athena does. The intervention of the other gods displays still less of the divine power, is still more strongly humanized. Athena in the *Odyssey* becomes a familiar spirit, except that she is not invoked and compelled to appear but comes freely and spontaneously.

Another rationalistic explanation of the presence of the gods and of certain of their actions is the cloud or darkness which is always at hand when a god wishes to appear among men or to help and save one of his favourites. The gods sit upon the wall of Troy and descend to the fight hidden in a cloud. They withdraw heroes from the contest by wrapping them in a mist; Athena covers Odysseus in the same way when he walks into the town of the Phaeacians, and also when he returns to Ithaca. Apollo protects Hektor's body with a mist. When a cloud lies spread over Olympus and when Zeus on Ida sits enthroned upon a cloud we have a reminiscence of visible Nature. At a later stage the cloud becomes a means of making invisible, resembling the helmet of Hades, the magic hat of our popular belief, and it is probably a rationalistic adaptation of this old popular idea. It is significant of the desire to visualize things that the cloud finally becomes a garment which the gods cast over their shoulders. The outstanding instance is that of Ares turning aside from the fight and sitting in a cloud against which he has leaned his spear. The converse notion of a cloud or darkness covering a person's eyes and preventing him from seeing seldom occurs.

At every point of human life Homer recognizes the influence of a divine power. The gods are the donors of physical and mental advantages, skill, and wealth. The prophetic eye of Calchas, Skamandrios' skill in hunting, Phereklos' art of ship-building, the house-wife's art of weaving, the sceptre of the Pelopides, the armour of Achilles, Pandaros' bow—all are the gifts of the gods. They are lords of the fates of men. They grant the fall of Troy, a safe home-coming, bride and children. The issue of the contest between Hektor and Achilles, the kingship in Troy, Penelope's hand, all these lie in the lap of the gods. They exalt and they cast down, they send prosperity and misfortune. Above all they are lords of life and death. The idea of an all-powerful conscious government of the universe has arisen, a government not according to a uniform plan but in accordance with a single will. It has been much disputed what is the relationship of the individual god's own will to this general idea. The question cannot be decided in the dogmatic fashion usually adopted in the discussion. We must appeal to religious experience, remembering that this finds no insuperable difficulty in allowing contradictory ideas to persist alongside of one another, and does so all the more easily the older and simpler they are.

Hitherto we have been principally concerned with the poet's own presentation, in particular with his divine apparatus. We have every reason to suppose that this form is adopted by the poet for the purpose of describing the relationships of the gods among themselves and to men, a description which is part of his poetic scheme, but that it does not accord with the Homeric man's real beliefs and expectations in regard to his gods. A means of distinguishing between the poetic presentation and the religious experience and belief has been furnished us in the observation that the gods are treated quite differently in the poet's own presentation and in the speeches which he puts into the mouths of men. The divine apparatus belongs to the former, the speech of men does not make use of it. Where the poet can tell exactly which god it was that intervened, the human character, in reference to the same events, will speak quite vaguely about a *daimon* or some god or the highest god of all, Zeus. There is no mention of Athena in Odysseus' own story of his adventures; in the poet's account she is the ever-present protectress. Exceptions occur, but they belong, characteristically enough, to the special spheres of activity of certain gods, originating in ancient cult and belief: a sudden death is ascribed to the arrows of Apollo and Artemis, the turmoil of the sea to Poseidon, the gift of artistic skill to Athena, the scourge of famine to Demeter's wrath. The king is under the protection of Zeus, but the personal protecting goddess belongs to the myth and therefore to the divine apparatus. With certain definite and easily determined exceptions, therefore, the people of Homer do not make individual gods responsible for all the experiences which they attribute to divine intervention. And these form a large element in their life. . . .

Here, however, we find once again the idea of the universal 'power', even though in a disguised form, developed by the increasing tendency to reflection upon the destinies of human life. For the different events in life have not each a separate *moira* as they have a separate *daimon*. Just as the word is one, so also are events manifestations of one *moira*. The word is nowhere found in the plural except in one late passage, in which personification has already taken place.

This circle of ideas moreover was exposed to the influence of mythological conceptions, which in part contributed to anthropomorphize *moira* and in part to develop fatalism. Just as the *moira* of death is assigned upon the day of birth, so the idea arises that the whole course of life is predetermined at birth. We see it in the well-known image of the destinies that the gods or the powers spin and wind for men, as the spun thread is wound upon the distaff, destinies, that is to say, which the gods allow to come upon them. This predetermination arises from the folk-tale motif of the gifts which the gods bring men on their birthdays or wedding-days, gifts which are to serve them in life. The myths of Meleager and Herakles are examples of this motif. The developing idea of the portion, *moira*, laid hold upon it, and thus arose the notion that fate, the course of life, is determined at birth.

Moira and the *daimones* upon one side, and the gods upon the other represent two stages in religious evolution. The one is earlier and less definite, but has developed in a later and peculiar manner; the other is younger and is characterized by individual and highly specialized anthropomorphic figures. The latter are therefore incapable of appearing as the causes of all the emotions, all the events in which man feels the working of a higher power. The Homeric gods were obliged on account of their special character to leave one sphere of activity to 'power' and 'the powers'. As they themselves were to a great extent Nature-gods, this sphere became first and foremost the life of man in so far as it is not determined by Nature. The limits are neither fixed nor clearly drawn. The word *daimon* also includes 'god', and 'god' can also be used indefinitely or collectively to denote 'power'. As soon as 'power' has gained substantival denomination, for instance, as *moira*, the tendency to personification makes itself felt, and anthropomorphism follows in the train of personification. One god, Zeus, is of so universal and all-embracing a nature that his influence can be traced everywhere. He rules destinies as Moira does, because he, like her, is an expression for the all-embracing 'power'.

The two systems, that of the gods and of 'power', stand upon different foundations: the powers remain behind upon the old foundation which the gods have abandoned. The dispute as to the relationship between the gods and Fate is from the point of view of the history of religion a dispute about words. Simple faith has no difficulty in acquiescing in such contradictions. But the two systems may come into conflict with each other. Homer has left *naïveté* behind and is a rationalist. Logic has, therefore, imposed a problem upon religion. Sometimes, with the simplicity of an earlier time, the gods and *moira* are unconcernedly placed side by side: sometimes *moira* is conceived as determined by the gods and Zeus. Zeus feels himself able to correct *moira*, and refrains from doing so not from lack of power but upon the exhortation of Hera. One system is here subordinated to the other. *Moira* is not taken seriously; we have merely one of the customary conflicts between two gods. But as soon as the underlying sense of order, and therefore of something determined by Fate, was taken seriously, the conflict was brought to a head. The problem was momentous, for the very existence of religion was ultimately involved in it. Religion in the proper sense was not strong in Homer, and this fact is in great measure due to the powerful rivalry of the other system.

It sometimes happened that 'power' received a name adapted to its particular expression. Ate (Blind Folly) is one, but there are several: Strife (Eris), Fear (Deimos, Phobos), Uproar (Kydoimos), in fact perhaps even Ares (the Destroyer) himself, all belong to the same company. These powers are written with capital letters and are called gods, but they are without personality and individuality because they are each nothing but a power of a certain kind. They are personifications. Personification is not an abstraction belonging to a late and far advanced period, as is often said; it is the bastard descendant of 'power' and the god. In its train followed allegory, and of this too there are elaborate examples in Homer. In regard to religious problems, he left a rich and fatal inheritance to later ages, both positively and negatively.

The Odyssey
in Antiquity

Samples of Reactions to Homer in Antiquity

For a millennium and a half, Homer occupied a central position in Greek culture, as a sacred text and then as a schoolbook. His very centrality, from the poet Pindar in the sixth century on, meant that comment on him would be imbedded in a much larger context, or used as a point of reference, as Aristotle uses him when writing about Greek tragedy in the excerpts quoted below.

The "Homer" of Aristotle, of course, existed as the most eminent of a group of ancient epic poets whose texts are lost to us, though descriptions of them are given in the anthology-handbook (*Chrestomathy*) of Proclus, who probably wrote in the second century A.D. His account of the *Telegony*, a sort of sequel to the *Odyssey*, given below, was meant to provide information about an important part of the tradition studied in the rhetorical schools of the Roman Empire. Nero's tutor, the philosopher Seneca, in the first century A.D. used *The Odyssey* as a basis for moralizing. Longinus, a critic who wrote perhaps a shade earlier, was using Homer and other writers to make distinctions for a similar audience.

Something of the ancient notion that Homer was a sacred text may have led the neo-Platonic philosopher Porphyry (232–305) to base what others have taken as a whole mystic system on one passage of the *Odyssey*. His *On the Cave of the Nymphs*, key extracts of which appear below, allegorizes Homer powerfully enough to have impressed Renaissance and Romantic hermeticists, right down to Blake.

All this time, and later, the text of Homer was receiving commentary in the schools. Large portions of the vast annotation, the *scholia*, have come down to us, and we also have the thousands of pages of such notes gathered by Eustathius, a late twelfth-century Greek Orthodox bishop, who compiled from various sources his own compendious commentary on the poem. Brief extracts of both are given below.

PINDAR

Nemean VII†

If one has luck in his deeds, he comes on a honeyed cause
In the Muses' flowings. Mighty feats
Hold much darkness when they are lacking hymns.
But for fair deeds we know a mirror with one way,
If for Memory of the shining diadem
A reward of efforts is found in the glorious songs of verse.
Wise men know a wind when it is coming
Two days off, nor are injured for gain.
Rich and poor past the bound of death
Go together. I think the tale
Of Odysseus has got greater than the suffering,
Through sweet-voiced Homer,
Since for lies there stands in him with suasive means
The lofty, yes. Skill cheats, leading
Along with myths. A blind heart
Does the main throng of men possess. If it had been
His to see the truth, powerful Ajax
Would not have driven the clear sword
Through his chest in anger.

Lines 14–27

PROCLUS

The Telegony‡

After the *Returns* comes the *Odyssey* of Homer, and then the *Telegony* in two books by Eugammon of Cyrene, which contain the following matters. The suitors of Penelope are buried by their kinsmen, and Odysseus, after sacrificing to the Nymphs, sails to Elis to inspect his herds. He is entertained there by Polyxenus and receives a mixing bowl as a gift; the story of Trophonius and Agamedes and Augeas then follows. He next sails back to Ithaca and performs the sacrifices ordered by Teiresias, and then goes to Thesprotis where he marries Callidice, queen of the Thesprotians. A war then breaks out between the Thes-

† Translated by Albert Cook.

‡ From Proclus, *Chrestomathy*, in *Hesiod*, translated by H. G. Evelyn-White (Cambridge, Mass.: Harvard University Press, Loeb Classical Library edition, 1964).

protians, led by Odysseus, and the Brygi. Ares routs the army of Odysseus and Athena engages with Ares, until Apollo separates them. After the death of Callidice Polypoetes, the son of Odysseus, succeeds to the kingdom, while Odysseus himself returns to Ithaca. In the meantime Telegonus, while travelling in search of his father, lands on Ithaca and ravages the island: Odysseus comes out to defend his country, but is killed by his son unwittingly. Telegonus, on learning his mistake, transports his father's body with Penelope and Telemachus to his mother's island, where Circe makes them immortal, and Telegonus marries Penelope, and Telemachus Circe.

PORPHYRY

De Antro Nympharum in Opuscula Selecta†

Because he has not made mention of the matters transmitted in accordance with fact (*historia*)—the geographers writing about the island have clearly mentioned no such cave on the island as Kronios says—and because he would be poetically unconvincing if he had expected to be believed when he had imagined a place of such circumstances that some men in Ithaca had fashioned passages for both men and gods, . . . so it is quite clear not only to the wise, but also to ordinary people, that in these details the poet speaks through allegory and through enigma.

Sections II–III, pp. 55–56

The naiad nymphs are souls going toward their birth. . . . And what is holy to them on earth would be a pleasant and shadowy cavern according to the image of the universe, in which as in the holy of holies the souls linger. . . . "Sea-purple veils". —Well, on the bones and about the bones is flesh; the former in living animals are stone or like stone, whence these bones are made of no other material, but are spoken of as being of stone. The "sea-purple veils" would be the flesh interwoven with blood. . . . [As for the bees and their honey] the theologians use honey for many and varied symbols because of its composition from many powers, and since it has the power to heal and preserve.

Sections XII–XV, p. 65

† Edited by Nauck (Leipzig, 1886).

. . . And so the cave has not one gate but two . . . one that is proper for gods and those who are good, the other for mortals and those who are inferior.

Section XXXI, p. 77

And the olive tree is not "at the head of the harbor"—by any chance, but it sustains itself the middle of the cave, planted, in addition to the cave-image of the universe as a symbol of the thought of god. For it is a plant of Athena, and Athena is thought.

Section XXXII, p. 78

ARISTOTLE

From *Poetics*†

The *Iliad* is at once simple and "pathetic" and the *Odyssey* complex (for "recognition" scenes run through it), and at the same time "ethical."

1459^b14

Other poets appear themselves upon the scene throughout, and imitate but little and rarely. Homer, after a few prefatory words, at once brings in a man, or woman, or other personage; none of them wanting in characteristic qualities, but each with a character of his own.

1460^a8

. . . But Homer, as in all else he is of surpassing merit, here too—whether from art or natural genius—seems to have happily discerned the truth. In composing the *Odyssey* he did not include all the adventures of Odysseus—such as his wound on Parnassus, or his feigned madness at the mustering of the host—incidents between which there was no necessary or probable connection; but he made the *Odyssey,* and likewise the *Iliad,* to center around an action that in our sense of the word is one.

1451^a22

† From S. H. Butcher, *Aristotle's Theory of Poetry and Fine Art* (London: Macmillan & Co., Ltd., 1911). Translated by S. H. Butcher.

. . . But once the irrational has been introduced and an air of likelihood imparted to it, we must accept it in spite of the absurdity. Take even the irrational incidents in the *Odyssey*, where Odysseus is left upon the shore of Ithaca. How intolerable even these might have been would be apparent if an inferior poet were to treat the subject. As it is, the absurdity is veiled by the poetic charm with which the poet invests it.

1460ª35

SENECA

From *Epistles*†

You ask where Ulysses will have wandered instead of acting so as to keep us from always wandering? There is no time to listen for whether he was tossed between Italy and Sicily or outside the world known to us—nor could he have wandered so long in a space so narrow. The storms of the soul toss us daily, and inquity drives us into all the ills of Ulysses. The beauty is not lacking to assail our eyes, nor is an enemy lacking. Here wild monsters delighting in human gore; there the subtle blandishments of gold, shipwreck, and every kind of evil. Teach me how to love my fatherland, my wife, my father; how, even shipwrecked, I may steer towards honor. Why do you ask if Penelope was immodest or caused scandal to her age? If she suspected before she knew for sure that the man she saw was Ulysses? Teach me what modesty is, and the amount of good there is in it, and whether it be located in the body or the soul.

LXXXVIII. 7–8

LONGINUS

On the Sublime

Yet throughout the *Odyssey*, which for many reasons we must not exclude from our consideration, Homer shows that, as genius ebbs, it is the love of myth that characterizes old age. There are indeed many indications that he composed this after

† Seneca, *Epistles*, translated by Albert Cook.

the *Iliad* beside the fact that throughout the *Odyssey* he intro-
duces as episodes remnants of the adventures at Ilium; yes, and
does he not in this poem render to his heroes their meed of lam-
entation as if it were a debt long due? In fact the *Odyssey* may
be called an epilogue to the *Iliad*:

> There then Ajax lies, great warrior; there lies Achilles;
> There, too, Patroclus lies, the peer of the gods in counsel;
> There, too, mine own dear son.

It was, I imagine, for the same reason that, writing the *Iliad* in
the heyday of his genius he made the whole piece lively with
dramatic action, whereas in the *Odyssey* narrative predominates,
the characteristic of old age. So in the *Odyssey* one may liken
Homer to the setting sun; the grandeur remains without the
intensity. For no longer does he preserve the sustained tension
of the great *Iliad* lays, the consistent sublimity which never
sinks into flatness, the flood of moving incidents in quick suc-
cession, the versatile rapidity and actuality, brimful of images
drawn from real life. It is rather as though the Ocean had
shrunk into its lair and lay becalmed within its own confines.
Henceforth we see the ebbing tide of Homer's greaatness, as he
wanders in the incredible regions of romance. In saying this I
have not forgotten the storms in the *Odyssey* and such incidents
as that of the Cyclops—I am describing old age, but the old age
of a Homer—yet the fact is that in every one of these passages
the mythic dominates the actual. . . .

There is another justification for our considering the *Odyssey*
as well as the *Iliad*. I wanted you to realize how with the
decline of their emotional power great writers and poets give
way to character-study. For instance, his character-sketches of
the daily life in Odysseus's household are in the style of some
comedy of character.

10. Well, then, let us see further whether we could find any-
thing else that can make style sublime. Since with all things
there are associated certain elements, essentially inherent in
their substance, it follows that we shall find one factor of sub-
limity in a consistently happy choice of these constituent ele-
ments, and in the power of combining them together as it were
into an organic whole. One writer for instance attracts the
reader by the selection of ideas, another by the soldering of
these selected. Sappho, for instance, never fails to take the emo-
tions incident to the passion of love from the symptoms which

accompany it in real life. And wherein does she show her excellence? In the skill with which she selects and combines the most striking and intense of those symptoms.

DEMETRIUS

On Style

Homer uses such means sometimes in order also to make a scene more intense and telling. When he is jesting he is all the more fearful, and he seems to have been the first to devise fearful pleasantries, as in the passage describing that most unpleasant personage the Cyclops: "Noman will I eat last, but the rest before him"—that "guest-gift" of the Cyclops. No other detail reveals so clearly the grimness of the monster—not his supper made from two of the comrades of Odysseus, nor his crag-door, nor his club—as this show of urbanity.

SCHOLIA†

Graeca in Homeri Odysseam

They say in the myth that Poseidon went to the Ethiopians at a certain season and was honored by them. But in the allegory, Poseidon is a term for water. Since water, that is, the ocean, circles the whole earth, and because the Nile at a certain season waters the land of the Ethiopians and makes the trees grow, on this account they say Poseidon, or water, is honored by them as the cause of many good things for them.

I, 15, on *Odyssey* I.22

[*Drugs of such devices*]—or those discovered by the intelligence ["devices"] and proposed by the [drugs] theoretical skill —both the theory of medicine and that which leads through general discourse and method to a knowledge of the parts. And the parts of this are the semiotic, the etiological, and the practical. And of the one, that which proceeds through its effects.

† *Scholia, Graeca in Homeri Odysseam*, edited by W. Dindorf (London: Oxford University Press, 1895). Translated by Albert Cook.

And the parts of this, in turn, are the dietetic, the chirurgical, and the pharmaceutic.

I, 194, on *Odyssey* IV.227

If the gods do not drink anything but nectar, how did Calypso "mix" it with water? Simply before pouring in by the old custom. For they poured into a horn [*keras*] and drank. So "mixing" [*kerase*], as Aristotle and Porphyry say, meant not adding water as another ingredient, but simply pouring in.

I, 251, on *Odyssey* V.93

[*And if he has come down as one of the immortals*] If a god comes in human form, the gods plan something strange. For the gods have never yet appeared to us in altered form, but manifestly. And he says they appear to us manifestly not only in sacrifice, but in person.

I, 342, on *Odyssey* VII.199

[*And the Lotus-Eaters did not plot destruction*] Being just men, they do not gain over by force, but by persuasion. And the "oud" ... medont'" ["they did not intend"] shows it was not by their will that the destruction came about.

II, 414, on *Odyssey* IX.92

The Cyclops in Homer was not one-eyed by nature, but he had lost his other eye through some misfortune. For he had two eyebrows. For he says in [line 389] "eyebrows and eyelids."

II, 434, on *Odyssey* IX.383

The Gods call it "moly." He does not say what men call it. Indeed, he introduced it as unknown to men.

II, 467, on *Odyssey* X.305

Why did Circe fear the sword of Odysseus, since she was a goddess? We say that daimons who live a long time, but are nevertheless subject to death, the poet habitually calls "gods." Or else Circe fears the sword from her nature as certain daimons also fear certain other materials. So too did Dionysius say in his "Treatise on Stones," "By nature is crystal and holy jasper repugnant to Bogeys and other phantoms."

II, 469, on *Odyssey* X.323

And how did trees stand in water? We say by imagination, for the punishment of Tantalus.

I, 523, on *Odyssey* XI.588

Allegorically [holy cave of the nymphs] designates the cave as the universe, the nymphs as the souls, the bees the same too, and men as bodies. And the two doors of the bodies are the exit, or birth, and the entrance for souls, in which nothing of the bodies comes in, but only souls. For they are immortal.

I, 562, on *Odyssey* XIII.103

EUSTATHIUS

Commentarii ad Homeri Odysseam

"As a steward of the winds Aeolus is spoken of not only allegorically, but according to the truth of history. A man is shown to be wise and honored for predicting the blowing of the wind.

On *Odyssey* X.21–23, p. 364

"It is fitting that Circe has four servants as the myth has fashioned it, and they are clearly nymphs the ones that, as poetry tells, are born from springs and groves and rivers and such, showing them to be certain powers of nature; and more, the ones who serve luxuries for Circe, through the birth of animals and seasonal fruits, and elemental causes of other things ... And some of the old interpreters say—discordantly and confusedly, though they were on the right track—that Circe is the year and her four servants the four seasons.

On *Odyssey* X.248, p. 384

"Eratosthenes said jokingly, in referece to the mythical and incredible nature of Odysseus' wandering, that the locations of his travels would be established by anyone who found the cobbler who sewed the bag the winds were kept in."[1]

[Eratosthenes is the great Alexandrian geographer.]

On *Odyssey* X.19, p. 365

1. Translated by Bernard Knox.

Criticism

JEAN RACINE

[Homer Begins Modestly]†

Horace praises the beginning of this poem in his *Art of Poetry* and says that Homer is very far from the practice of those poets who make big promises at the start of a work and fall afterwards to the ground. Homer, instead, begins modestly and then shows big things.

Homer leaves Ulysses on Calypso's island during the first four books and does not have him appear till the fifth.

JOHANN WOLFGANG VON GOETHE

From *Letters*‡

I sought to subsume the law of [narrative] retardation under a higher law, and it appeared to belong under this: one could know—yea must know—the outcome of a good poem. The pure and simple "How" should really make for the interest....

The *Odyssey* delays, so to speak, in its smallest parts, and thereby it is affirmed and assured perhaps fifty-fold that the matter will have a happy outcome. So many foreshadowings and predictions that anticipate the end give a counterbalance, I think, to the perpetual delay.

No. 303 (22 April 1797), Vol. I, p. 350

Besides, one would have to struggle against the *Odyssey*, which has already taken away [from a tale of voyage] the most interesting motifs. The arousal of a woman's feeling through the arrival of a stranger,—the loveliest motif—is not to be undertaken any more, given Nausikaa....

For us inhabitants of the mainland it is only the mores in the poem that charm us really. Our imagination rises to the descriptions in it only in an imperfect and sorry way. In what a lustre,

† Jean Racine, *Oeuvres* (Paris: Pléiade, 1966), II, 725. Translated by Albert Cook.

‡ H. S. Chamberlain, ed., *Briefwechsel zwischen Schiller und Goethe* (Jena, 1905). Translated by Albert Cook.

though, did this poem appear to me when I read its Cantos in
Naples and Sicily! It is as when one puts varnish on a painting
whose colors have sunk in; the work appears at once clear and
in harmony. I confess it no longer seems a poem but Nature
itself, something the more necessary with those ancients when
their works were read in the presence of nature. How many of
our poems would stand up if read in the market place or under
the open sky!

No. 424 (16 February 1798), Vol. II, pp. 48–49

EZRA POUND

[The Homeric World]†

The Homeric world, very human. The *Odyssey* high water
mark for the adventury story, as for example Odysseus on the spar
after shipwreck. Sam Smiles never got any further in preaching
self-reliance. A world of irresponsible gods, a very high society
without recognizable morals, the individual responsible to him-
self.

G. E. DIMOCK, JR.

The Name of Odysseus‡

"There is no way to stand firm on both feet and escape trouble."
Odyssey 5.413–4

In a way, the whole problem of the *Odyssey* is for Odysseus to
establish his identity. "After all, who knows who his father is?"
says Telemachus in the first book. "My son, if he really ever
existed," says Laertes in the last. To establish his identity Odys-
seus must live up to his name.

---

† Ezra Pound, *Guide to Kulchur* (New York, New Directions Publishing
Corporation, n.d.), p. 38. Copyright © 1970 by Ezra Pound. All rights
reserved. Reprinted by permission of New Directions Publishing Corpora-
tion.

‡ From *The Hudson Review*, IX, No. 1 (Spring, 1956), pp. 52–70.
Reprinted by permission of the publisher. Copyright © 1956 by *The
Hudson Review*, Inc.

This is not a new idea. A nameless ancient commentator has puzzled editors by glossing *Hēbēsas* in line 410 of the nineteenth book with *odyssamenos*. *Hēbēsas* means "when he has grown up," a meaning with which *odyssamenos* has nothing to do; but as we shall see, the scholiast means that for Odysseus to grow up, to achieve his full stature, will be for him to "odysseus"—to live up to the meaning of his name, whatever that may be.

"To odysseus" (*odyssasthai* in Greek) is usually said to mean "be wroth against," "hate," and to be connected with Latin *odisse*. Historically speaking, this may be true. For the *Odyssey's* poetical purposes, however, the verb denotes a more general sort of hostility, which Homer is at pains to define. In the fifth book the nymph Ino explains it as "planting evils," without specifying what sort of hostility is in the mind of the planter. It is true that Poseidon, who happens to be the planter in this case, is angry; but Zeus, who also odysseuses Odysseus, is not. In the nineteenth book Odysseus' grandfather Autolycus indicates that it is not a question of anger; asked to name the baby, he replies,

> "I have odysseused many in my time, up and down the wide world, men and women both; therefore let his name be Odysseus."

Now, all we know from the *Odyssey* about Autolycus' career is that he was the foremost liar and thief of his day. Most naturally, by "odysseusing many" he means that he has been the bane of many people's existence. The secret of his palpable success would seem to be that he has never given a sucker an even break, and he wants his grandson to be like him. In the career of Autolycus, and in the attitude which it implies, we are much closer to the *polytropon* "crafty" of the *Odyssey's* first line, than to the *mēnin* "wrath" of the *Iliad's*. So let us think no more of "wrath," which implies provocation and mental perturbation, but rather of a hand and mind against every man, by nature, or as a matter of policy. Autolycus' own name does not suggest "Lone Wolf" for nothing. These considerations, and others, lead me to think that in the *Odyssey odyssasthai* means essentially "to cause pain (*odynē*), and to be willing to do so." We need not draw the line between subjective and objective here, any more than we need do so in the case of the word "suffer." Where did Odysseus "suffer" the "woes" of the *Odyssey's* fourth line: "on the high seas," or "in his heart"? Just as "suffer" brings to mind both the external and internal aspects of being a victim, so "odysseus" implies subjectively and objectively what it is to persecute. For what it is worth, the seven-odd instances of the verb outside the *Odyssey* show nothing inconsistent with this meaning.

Autolycus, then, we discover in the nineteenth book, intended Odysseus to be a causer of pain. He has been one all along, of course. Perhaps the most prominent fact about him is that more than any other man he was responsible for taking Troy; and what it means to sack a city, we know from the simile at the end of book eight. Odysseus

> wept as a woman weeps when she throws her arms around the body of her beloved husband, fallen in battle before his city and his comrades, fighting to save his town and his children from disaster. She has found him gasping in the throes of death; she clings to him and lifts her voice in lamentation. But the enemy come up and belabor her back and shoulders with spears, as they lead her off into slavery and a life of miserable toil, with her cheeks wasted by her pitiful grief.[1]

Less than a hundred lines later, at the beginning of his tale, Odysseus will say,

> The same wind as wafted me from Ilium brought me to Ismarus, the city of the Cicones; I sacked the place and killed the men; their wives, together with much booty, we took out of the city and divided up.

As has been well observed, the Sack of Ismarus is the Sack of Troy in its predatory essentials, with the glamor stripped off. This attitude Odysseus will maintain to the end. "The cattle which the suitors have consumed," he says in the twenty-third book, "I will for the most part make up by raiding on my own; the Achaeans will give others." Perhaps worse than this, Odysseus' going to Troy caused Telemachus grievous mental suffering, wasted Penelope's nights in tears, and reduced Laertes, his father, to misery and squalor; his absence killed his mother, Antikleia.

So conceived, Odysseus is not an attractive character. In fact the poem implies a good deal of criticism of the Autolycan attitude. As Mr. H. N. Porter once pointed out to me, one of the first things we hear about the hero is his predilection for poisoned arrows. Athene, disguised as Mentes, tells Telemachus,

---

1. This quotation is from E. V. Rieu's excellent translation. So, in whole or in part, are many of the passages which follow.

He was on his way from Ephyre, where he had stayed with Ilus
Mermerides—he went there in his fast ship to get a mortal
poison to smear his bronze-tipped arrows with. Ilus wouldn't give
it to him in fear of the eternal gods. But my father [Zeus?] gave
him some. He was terribly fond of him.

Much better, one would think, for Autolycus to have adopted
Eurycleia's suggestion of Polyaretus as a name for the baby:
"He's our 'Answer to Prayer' (*polyaretos*)," she remarked as she
put the child on his grandfather's lap. But Autolycus preferred
a name that most would regard as ill-omened.

For in spite of the fact that Odysseus is so obviously a causer
of pain, the name which Autolycus wished on him strikes one as
ironical. Up to the nineteenth book, Odysseus has been referred
to as odysseused rather than odysseusing: "Why do you odys-
seus him so, Zeus?" Athene asks, before the poem is well under
way; Ino and Odysseus both say that Poseidon is odysseusing
him; finally, as we read the Autolycus passage, we are aware that
Odysseus has just told Penelope that Zeus and the Sun-god
odysseused her husband. In the *Odyssey's* proem itself, the hero
seems essentially the sufferer: he is the *polytropos* man, the
Tutolycan rogue who treats the world as his enemy, but who
sacks Troy only to be driven far astray thereafter, and take a
beating. In the process, we are told, he is to win his *psyche*,
which means loosely his life, and more properly the image of
life after the liver is gone—in other words something very like
identity—but the whole business seems unpleasant, to say the
least.

To understand the satisfaction involed in injuring and
suffering and the connection between them, we must return to
the nineteenth book and the scholiast's note. The giving of the
name is coupled with the adventure in which Odysseus first
lives up to it. *Hēbēsas* is in fact *odyssamenos*. "When he has
grown up," the hero, as though undergoing an initiation, wins
Autolycus' favor and recognition by going on a boar hunt; as
causer of pain he kills the boar; as sufferer he is slashed by it,
thus acquiring the scar important in identifying him later. The
pain given and received results in joy:

> Autolycus and the sons of Autolycus
> Efficiently healed him and loaded him with presents;
> Rejoicing they dispatched him rejoicing to his beloved
> Ithaca. His father and his good mother
> Rejoiced at his return, and asked for each particular
> Of how he got his scar.

The suffering results from the doing, and is inseparable from it in the recognition and satisfaction produced by this exploit. Not simply "how he killed the boar" but "how he got his scar," is for Odysseus' parents the measure of their son.

To be Odysseus, then, is to adopt the attitude of the hunter of dangerous game: to deliberately expose one's self, but thereafter to take every advantage that the exposed position admits; the immediate purpose is injury, but the ultimate purpose is recognition and the sense of a great exploit. Odysseus killed a boar to win his name; he went to Troy to enlarge it; in order to keep it, he will presently kill 108 suitors in as cold blood as he can manage.

In the adventure with the Cyclops, Odysseus inflicts pain in order to identify himself, and in so doing challenges the hostility of the universe. Polyphemus' pain is obvious. Even Euripides could not have dwelt more explicitly than Homer on the boring of the red-hot stake into the great eyeball, the sizzling of the eye's fluid, and the crackling of its roots. By virtue of this deed of horror, Odysseus, until now *Outis* "nobody" as far as Polyphemus is concerned, puts himself in a position where he can tell the monster who he is, can cry his name aloud to the Cyclops' face. This cry of defiance is thought to be foolish of the wily Odysseus, no less by his crew than by the critics, but it is in reality, like the boar hunt, a case of deliberate self-exposure for the purpose of being somebody rather than nobody.

To blind the son of Poseidon, and then to defy him, is both to challenge nature to do her worst, and to demonstrate her ultimate impotence to crush human identity. It is challenging nature in the sense that the sailor does, every time he goes to sea. The hero's colonizing eye as he approaches the Cyclopes' island, the remark that they have no ships or shipwrights, the shipbuilding technique employed in blinding Polyphemus and the mention of axe, adze and auger, the tools which enabled Odysseus to leave Kalypso and set sail on his raft, all this sounds very much as though Odysseus' crime against Poseidon were the crime of all those who go down to the sea in ships. But Poseidon will not get his revenge. In the *Odyssey* navigation is a practical possibility; the elements are conquered. So to blind Polyphemus is to convict savage nature of impotence and blindness. She is indiscriminate in her blows. Her most hostile efforts, like the rocks thrown by Polyphemus, are as likely to wash the

hero to safety as they are to drive him into danger. Thus the
power of the elements does not render Odysseus' identity mean-
ingless. Rather he makes sense, and the elements do not. This, I
think, is the significance of the general assumption in the *Odys-
sey* that Poseidon will give Odysseus his bellyful of trouble
before he reaches his home, but will not kill him.

Polyphemus and Poseidon, however, are more than the hostil-
ity of inanimate nature. There is no "inanimate nature" in
Homer anyway. They prefigure all the overt savagery which the
universe presents, human and divine. This savagery is as able to
breach the conventions, hospitality and the rest, among the civi-
lized suitors in Ithaca, or the hypercivilized Phaeacians (remem-
ber Euryalus), as it is among the cannibal Laestrygons, or
among the Cyclopes. If Poseidon and Polyphemus are the hos-
tile aspects of this world, it is not foolish for Odysseus to cry his
name in defiance of them, and so be subject to Polyphemus'
rock-slinging and his curse; or rather, the foolishness or good
sense of the action is not the point. To pass from the darkness
of the cave into the light, to pass from being "nobody" to
having a name, is to be born. But to be born is to cast one's
name in the teeth of a hostile universe; it is to incur the enmity
of Poseidon. In such a world, what better name could be found
than Odysseus, "Trouble"? ("Trouble" is perhaps as good a
translation of Odysseus' name as any. When a character in a
western movie says, "Just call me Trouble, stranger," we take
him to be a hostile type who makes trouble for other people,
and so presumably for himself also.)

That braving Polyphemus is being born is not my metaphor;
it is Homer's. In the nineteenth book Odysseus hints to Penel-
ope that her husband has undergone a birth somewhere over-
seas:

> He put in at Amnisis, where the cave of Eileithuia is, in a
> difficult harbor; he barely escaped the gales.

Eileithuia is goddess of childbirth. But in the nineteenth book
this is merely a way of reminding us of the Polyphemus adven-
ture and possibly of Kalypso as well. In the ninth book, as Pol-
yphemus is in the act of rolling the stone from the mouth of the
cave, we are told of his anguish for the second time. We already
know how his eye hurts, but this time we hear that he is "tra-
vailing in pain"; *ōdinōn odynēsi* are the words used. Whether or
not we hear in them the name of Odysseus, we should not fail

to reflect that *ōdinō* means essentially "to be in labor of child-birth." We are born for trouble, the adventure of the Cyclops implies, yet to stay in the womb is to remain nobody. There is security of a sort in being nobody, but as the Cyclops promises, Nobody will be devoured in the end, though last of all.

For there are more insidious threats to identity in the *Odyssey* than those which Polyphemus represents, the dangers and sufferings consequent upon taking on the world as one's enemy. Trouble is difficult and dangerous, but it can lead to identity. Security, on the other hand, is inevitable oblivion. The narrative proper of the *Odyssey* begins as follows:

> By now all the others, as many as had escaped sheer destruction, were at home. Odysseus, alone of all, wanting his home and his wife, a queenly nymph held prisoner, Kalypso, divine goddess, in her hollow cave, begging him to be her husband.

This is the state of affairs which the fifth book will develop. He wants home and a wife. He has a cave and a goddess. Why do all the gods but one pity him for this? Odysseus has realized the tired soldier's or sailor's dream, an immortality of comfort and physical satisfaction, with no troubles. But Odysseus would rather die, as Athene says. Everybody sees this paradox and understands the flaw in this paradise: such an existence has no meaning. But it adds something, I think, to see life on Ogygia in terms of identity and nonentity. Kalypso is oblivion. Her name suggests cover and concealment, or engulfing; she lives "in the midst of the sea"—the middle of nowhere, as Hermes almost remarks—and the whole struggle of the fifth book, indeed of the entire poem, is not to be engulfed by that sea. When the third great wave of book five breaks over Odysseus' head, Homer's words are: *ton de mega kyma kalypsen*—"and the great wave engulfed him." If this wave had drowned him, it would have been a "vile death," surely, as Odysseus remarks at the beginning of the storm. Much better, he says, to have died where "the spears flew thickest" at Troy; then he would have had "recognition," *kleos*. People would know about him and his death. Odysseus does not wish he were back with Kalypso. Though she offered immortality, not death—an immortality of security and satisfaction in a charming cave—it is still an immortality of oblivion, of no *kleos*, of nonentity. Leaving Kalypso is very like leaving the perfect security and satisfaction of the womb; but, as the Cyclops reminds us, the womb is after all a deadly place. In the womb one has no identity, no existence worthy of a name. Nonentity and identity are in fact the poles between which the actors in the poem move. It is a choice between Scylla and Charybdis—to face deliberately certain trouble from the jaws of the six-headed goddess, or to be engulfed entirely by the maelstrom. One must odysseus and be odysseused, or else be kalypsoed.

Odysseus did not always live up to his name. There was one occasion when oblivion seemed almost preferable to trouble. His name seemed to have lost its magic. Hence his failure with the Laestrygonians, and the necessity of winning back his identity in the Circe episode.

While we remember Polyphemus ("Much-fame") in connection with Odysseus, we are very apt to forget Antiphates ("Against-renown"), the Laestrygonian king. In the Laestrygonian affair Odysseus himself avoids the encounter, and loses his whole fleet. In this, his least creditable adventure, he never makes his identity felt. The Laestrygonians don't know who he is, or care. Yet Odysseus survives. With poetic rather than nautical logic, he escapes by virtue of having left his ship in an exposed position, while the rest of the fleet trusts itself to the security of the fiord and is lost.

Odysseus in the land of the Laestrygonians is not the Odysseus whom we saw with Cyclops, though in both cases he has to do with cannibal giants. Avoiding the encounter here is perhaps as sensible as avoiding the Planctae, but there are other reasons why Odysseus is not up to it. In the interim, as we have said, his name has lost its magic. "Trouble," intended to mean success, has seemed to be failure. Aeolus has listened with interest to the tale of prowess at Troy and has sent Odysseus on his way, insuring that he will have, for once, a remarkably painless trip. But in sight of the goal, trouble strikes. Aeolus, seeing in this a sign that heaven is inveterately hostile to Odysseus, banishes him from his sight. Such trouble means to Aeolus not identity, but oblivion. Odysseus himself has nearly reached a similar conclusion. Since leaving Troy he has sacked Ismarus in characteristically ruthless fashion and rejected the passive peace of Lotosland. By handling the situation in a manner worthy of Autolycus, he has been able to cry his name in defiance of Polyphemus. He has come within sight of his home. He has done all this only to find his achievement undone at the first relaxation of his mistrustful watchfulness. Small wonder that success on these terms should seem impossible. As the winds sped Odysseus out of sight of Ithaca, "I debated," he says, "whether to leap from my ship and end it all in the sea" (embracing thus the "vile death" of the Kalypso episode), "or whether to bear my misery and remain among the living." He adopts a sort of compromise: "I endured and I remained; *kalypsamenos* I lay in my ship," he puts it, meaning that he had wrapped his head in his cloak. This is the Odysseus who fails to confront Antiphates.

After the discouragement of the Aeolus episode, it is natural that life's difficulties should appear as insuperable as the Laestrygonians; but Odysseus will find the courage to go on. After the Laestrygonian experience his depression is shared by his men. Two days they all lie in weariness and woe on Circe's beach. But against this sea of troubles Odysseus takes arms, a spear and a sword. As he once killed a boar, he now kills a stag. This puts heart in Odysseus' men: "diskalyposed" (ek de kalypsamenoi) they revive. Odysseus now makes a remarkable speech:

> Friends, we don't know where the darkness is, or where the dawn; where the sun that shines for mortals rises, or where it sets. Still let us quickly consider whether any resource can still be found. I for one don't think so.

The point, as Odysseus goes on to suggest, is whether they must indeed make themselves known and ask the inhabitants of the island for their route, perilous though it has proved to confront Polyphemus and Antiphates. In other words, shall they turn their backs on the comparative security of their present oblivion? Characteristically, this wider implication is stressed by a pun—a blatant pun which has been used before, in the Cyclops passage. "Whether any resource can still be found," sounds in Greek almost precisely like "Whether any of us is going to go on being nobody." "I for one don't think so," is Odysseus' comment. They have been "nobody" for some time, in fact ever since Aeolus refused to recognize their claims as human beings. This cannot go on, as the pun implies. The time has come when Odysseus must stand and be recognized.

Without taking account of the pun, critics have interpreted this passage as Odysseus at the end of his human resources, about to apply for divine aid. The moly plant, soon to be granted, becomes for them almost a symbol of grace. This is fair enough in its way. Identity in the Odysseus is in some sense a gift of the gods. But "from the gods who sit in grandeur, grace comes somehow violent."[2] Odysseus doesn't pray for grace; he exacts it, first by killing the stag and then by threatening Circe and forcing her to swear to do him no harm. Hermes, Autolycus' patron, puts him up to the threatening, but it is quite in accord with Odysseus' name and nature anyhow. We remember the oaths exacted from Helen and Kalypso. In the present instance Odysseus remains nobody, a denatured wolf or lion like Circe's other victims, until sword to throat, he makes her recognize him and speak his name. Prior to this, despite the introductory formula "he took my hand and spoke my name," Hermes had not named the hero; he only named his passive aspect, *O dystēne* "poor wretch." But with the gift of moly, "black at the root, but with a flower like milk," Hermes seems to restore the magic of the name of Odysseus. However black its first effects, it will ultimately flower with balm and solace. Though she "struck [him] with her rod and named" him, Circe gives Odysseus no name at all until the hero seems "like one eager to kill her"; once having recognized him as "Odysseus *polytropos*" however, she uses his name every chance she gets, four times with full titles: "Zeus-sprung son of Laertes, expedient Odysseus." By choosing to live up to his name with Circe, Odysseus restored its magic; he had to in order to get anywhere, and so to be anybody, at all.

For Odysseus to choose to pursue the path of his painful identity as he did on Circe's beach, is to win power over, and recognition from, that ambiguous daughter of Sun, the life-giver, and Ocean, the all-engulfing. It is also to accept pain as the only real basis of meaning in this life or the next. This is the secret of Teiresias.

To achieve the goal of recognition and identity, and to learn the secrets of the abyss, are equally to row upon the sea of trouble. This is the meaning of the apparently witless question, "What ship brought you to Ithaca, for I do not think you came on foot," and of Antikleia's first words to her son in the underworld:

My child, how did you come beneath the misty dark, alive as you are? It is hard for the living to get a sight of all this. For in between are great rivers and dreadful streams, first Ocean, which

2. Aeschylus, *Agamemnon* 182–3 (Lattimore's translation).

there is no way to cross on foot, if one does not have a well-built ship.

But with Aeolus the question arose, is such sea-faring endurable? To ask this question is "to enquire of Teiresias" (*Teiresiēs* in Homer); for Teiresias' name is the weariness of rowing. *"TEIReto d' andrōn thymos hyp' EIRESIĒS alegeinēs,"* Odysseus says of his crew after Aeolus denied them: "*Worn* was my men's spirit by the woeful *rowing*." To enquire of Teiresias is to ask the meaning of trouble.

This is why Odysseus is not so much interested in what the prophet has to say of the troubled future—"You seek homecoming sweet as honey, noble Odysseus; heaven will make it hard for you"—as he is in recognition, in the meaning of his own painful and pain-producing existence:

> Doubtless the gods had all that in store for me. But tell me: I see here the shade of my dead mother; she sits in silence near the blood, and has not the strength to look her son in the face or speak to him. Tell me, lord, how might she recognize the man I am?

His mother's recognition contains a blow. It was Odysseus' sweet nature, she says, that killed her. Thus it appears that even in his gentlest aspect, Odysseus gives pain. He is, after all, soft as well as hard. The predatory brooch, dog throttling fawn, pinned on him by Penelope as he left for Troy, is coupled with a second mark of identification, equally important: the shirt which gleamed on his body

> like the skin of a dried onion—so gentle it was to the touch, and at the same time bright, like the sun; many were the women who admired it.

Yet Odysseus' soft side can be as painful, or as fatal, as his hardness. The love, not the hate he inspired, killed the dog Argus and wasted Penelope's nights in tears. Antikleia recognized at least part of her son's nature by dying for the love of him.

Agamemnon, dead by no sweet nature, but rather by the treacherous hand of his wife, also recognizes Odysseus; despite Penelope's virtue, he had better not, Agamemnon thinks in contrast to Antikleia, tell his wife everything. Neither of these recognitions, neither the first, evoking the hero's sweetness, nor the second, calling upon his guile, can bring Odysseus much comfort as to the value of life as Trouble. Achilles on the other hand makes it clear that it is something to be alive at all, and furthermore his concern for his son's prowess reminds us that Telemachus too, promises to become a credit to his father. Still, neither simple existence, nor existence continued through a worthy son, is of the essence. Ajax' silence, though eloquently expressive of the power of Odysseus as injurer, is discouraging; but the climax of recognition is reached when Heracles, whose "seeming" is hell's own picture of hostile ferocity, but whose reality "dwells in bliss among the immortals," equates Odysseus to himself:

> One look was enough to tell Heracles who I was, and he greeted me in mournful tones. "Zeus-sprung son of Laertes, expedient Odysseus—unhappy man! So you too are working out some such miserable doom as I was slave to when the sun shone over my head. Son of Zeus though I was, unending troubles came my way. . . . a master far beneath my rank . . . sent me down here to bring away the Hound of Hell. And under the guiding hands of Hermes and bright-eyed Athene, I did succeed in capturing him and I dragged him out of Hades' realm."

Not just Heracles, but all these people (except Ajax) explicitly recognize Odysseus; still excepting Ajax, all but Antikleia, who appropriately calls him "my child," use Odysseus' full titles. Each sees him differently, and to a greater or less degree, truly. To all of them he means, in one way or another, pain. To Antikleia he is the pain of a lost child; Agamemnon connects him with the pain and betrayal that marriage may bring; Achilles is reminded of the ultimate pain of being dead, Ajax of wounded honor. Heracles sees in him the "unending troubles" of life under the sun. For the secret of life which Odysseus has come to the realms of the dead to discover is the necessity of pain, and its value. The generations of woman ("and each proclaimed her bringing-forth") may be for good or ill, involving Zeus or Poseidon indifferently. Man's fate may seem to be Tantalus' endless craving, never satisfied; or Sisyphus' endless striving, never successful; life's basis may even by Tityus' vultures, a great gnawing in a great belly, as Odysseus several times suggests (7.216–21; 15.343–4; 17.286–9; 18.53–4). Yet Minos continues to pass his judgments, and Orion to pursue his quarry. Heracles has his heavenly, as well as his hellish aspect—and so does Odysseus, "Trouble." Ajax feels only Odysseus' hellish side, but Heracles implies that a life of pain, given and received, snatches something from Death himself. This is the secret of Teiresias, the answer to the weariness of rowing. To know himself as Trouble, and to be so known by others, is the only way for Odysseus to possess his identity.

There is no human identity in other terms than pain. To escape Kalypso, Odysseus needs a ship (4.559–60, 5.16–7), and so must accept the weariness of rowing. To see life in any other way is to live in a dream-world, as the Cyclopes do, and the Phaeacians. To avoid trouble, the Phaeacians withdrew, we are told, from their ancestral conflict with the Cyclopes. The conflict is indeed ancestral, for the Cyclopes are as savage as the Phaeacians are civilized; but both are out of touch with reality. Polyphemus thinks he can act with impunity, "for we are much mightier than the gods," but he succumbs to Trouble in the shape of a clever "weakling" and a skin of wine. The Phaeacians on the contrary trust in their piety. Nausicaa thinks that no one could possibly come "bringing enmity, for we are dear to the gods." This she says of Odysseus, Enmity himself. To her, he is either an object of pity or a dream come true:

> Doubtless she has picked up some castaway from his ship [she thinks of someone as remarking of her], a foreign man, since there is nobody like that nearby [or "those nearby are nobodies"], or else in answer to her hopes a god, long prayed for (polyaretos), has come down from heaven to keep her all her days.

Eurycleia's "Polyaretus" fits Odysseus in the sense that his return to Ithaca in his hostile might is something to pray for, but he is not what Nausicaa would pray that he be. Nausicaa is victimized by her too trusting love for him, and his visit is ultimately disastrous for her people. The *Odyssey* has its dream-worlds, and, "near to the gods," Scheria is one of them. Its queen, "whose name is Prayed-for" (*Arētē d'onom' estin epōnymon*), suggests her antonym, Odysseus, who, the poem later tells us, might have been Polyaretus, but was not. "So let his name be Trouble" (*to d' Odysseus onom' estin epōnymon*), Autolycus will say in the nineteenth book.

Odysseus no more can exist in the dream-world of Alcinous and Arete, where woman rules man and rowing is no trouble, than he can with Kalypso. In a world without trouble love must be as little serious as the affair of Ares and Aphrodite. With Nausicaa there is no scope for the relationship which Odysseus describes to her:

> There is nothing nobler or more admirable than when two people
> who see eye to eye keep house as man and wife, *confounding*
> *their enemies* and delighting their friends, as they themselves
> know better than anyone.

How can love be really felt, without pain? Therefore, after arriv-
ing exhausted, naked, and unknown on Scheria, Odysseus must
somehow so impress the inhabitants that they will send him on
his way, neither killing him as enemy nor overmuch befriending
him and settling him down with Nausicaa. This he accom-
plishes primarily by means of his well-advertised Tale of Woe.
It is received with mingled horror and fascination. Avid for its
miseries the Phaeacians certainly are. This supports our impres-
sion that their dream-world, lacking pain, is human life
manqué. On the other hand, after the simile of the woman led
into captivity, it is easy to assume Phaeacian feelings of horror
at Odysseus' brutal account of the Sack of Ismarus. The recog-
nition accorded the tale is equivocal: "Phaeacians," Arete asks
during the intermission, "what do you think of this man, his
size and strength and wit?" A dubious answer is implied in Alci-
nous' polite comment:

> O Odysseus, when we look at you we don't find you a bit like a
> liar and thief, [or "your *Outis* looks to us like a liar and thief"]
> such as the black earth produces in such far-flung numbers—
> thieves piling lie on lie, and where they get them all from nobody
> knows; your words are charming, there is good sense in them, and
> you tell your story as skillfully as a bard, the grim sufferings of
> yourself and all the Argives.

After all Odysseus has shown himself to be a pirate, and it is
worth noting that Alcinous' remarks occur half-way through the
story of the underworld, before the value of pain is established.
But for the Phaeacians this is never established. Their rowing is
without drudgery, for all their sea-faring. At the end of the tale
Alcinous will tell the guest he once thought of as a son-in-law
that he is sure he will never come back. One doesn't quite know
whether the Phaeacians are bestowing on Odysseus more wealth
that he won at Troy in recognition of his exploits, or as an invi-
tation to leave the country; for it was Odysseus' stated willing-
ness to stay a year that brought forth Alcinous' remarks about
liars and thieves. In Odysseus the Phaeacians enjoy Trouble
vicariously, but ultimately dismiss him. We may be pretty sure

that, for their "painless escorting of strangers," Poseidon's threat to "surround (*amphikalypsai*) their city with mountains" will come off. Just as he turned their ship to stone, he will bar them from the sea, and therefore from any chance of future identity. The price of no trouble is oblivion.

Teiresias implies three modes of pain: first, pain administered, like the slaying of the boar and stag, or the blinding of Polyphemus. Odysseus, Teiresias predicts, will kill the suitors. Second, there is the pain of the resisted impulse. Odysseus must restrain his predatory impulses when he comes upon the cattle of the Sun. Third, to plant the oar, the symbol of the weariness of rowing, among those "who do not know the sea, nor eat their food mixed with salt, nor know of red-prowed ships, nor balanced oars, which are a vessel's wings" is to introduce the idea of trouble to those who, like the Phaeacians, are not sufficiently aware of it. In establishing his identity, Odysseus must use these three modes of pain.

It is sufficiently clear how administering pain by killing the suitors and threatening their kinsmen with annihilation serves to establish Odysseus in Ithaca. The second mode is subtler. It would seem a denial of Odysseus' name for him to boggle at a little cattle-rustling. That he does so leads some to suppose that his adventures are intended to purge him of the brutalizing effects of the Trojan campaign and bring him home readjusted to civilian life. But the temptation of the cattle of the Sun is more like the temptation of the Lotos than like the Sack of Ismarus. It is a temptation not to crime but to oblivion. To fall for it is the typical weakness of the "innocent" crew, as the proem suggests. Faced with the Planctae, the Reefs of Hard Knocks, they drop their oars. Knowing the mortal danger in eating the Sun's cattle, they do not know it thoroughly enough to forego the immediate satisfaction of eating when they are hungry. Forgetful of homecoming and identity itself, they eat. Of all that band only Odysseus can resist such impulses and hang on interminably, as he does clinging to the fig tree above Charybdis, refusing to drop and be comfortably engulfed.

Odysseus is a master of the delayed response, of the long way round, of the resisted impulse. That is the reason he is able to keep his identity intact. It is courting oblivion to rush blindly into love, as Nausicaa did, and as Penelope, even when reunited with her husband, did not. In Circe's bed, Odysseus would have become just another denatured wolf or lion, if he had not first with a show of hostility made sure of his integrity. As in love, so with eating. Man is a predatory animal; to eat he must kill; but he must know what he is doing. He must not, like the crew and the suitors, take life as a table spread before him, insufficiently aware of the presence of enemies.

He must not even take life as a song, though the episode of the Sirens suggests that this is the most irresistible of impulses. The Phaeacians are certainly not proof against it. Alcinous may think that the meaning of life's pain is that

> the gods were responsible for that, weaving catastrophe into the pattern of events to make a song for future generations,

but pain must be experienced, not just enjoyed as after-dinner entertainment. Therefore the Phaeacians are victimized by Odysseus' Tale of Woe. Odysseus on the other hand is proof against the Sirens and their singing of "all things that happen on this fruitful earth," just as he is against the Lotos and against Circe. He is steadfast in enduring Teiresias' second mode of pain, the pain of the resisted impulse.

"The steadfast," says a priest in *Murder in the Cathedral*, "can manipulate the greed and lust of others, the feeble is devoured by his own." This leads us from the second mode of pain to the third—introducing the idea of trouble to those insufficiently aware of it. Odysseus in his steadfastness knows the pain of the thirst for life, the danger it leads to, and the trouble involved in successfully gratifying it. He knows it so well ("he saw the cities of many men, and knew their mind"), that he can use this knowledge in manipulating others, for the purpose of getting himself recognized as Trouble. One picture of this is Odysseus in the underworld, sword in hand, controlling the access of the ghosts to the blood. Manipulating the Phaeacians chiefly through their itching ears, he introduces himself to them as Trouble, and wins survival and homecoming. In the second half of the poem, using his lying tales, his wife, and the good things of his house as bait, he maneuvers the upholders and the defilers of his household alike into a position where, bow in hand and arrow on string, like Heracles in the underworld, he can make himself really felt.

For Odysseus to establish his identity at home, manipulation is necessary, manipulation even of those who favor him. It is difficult to get people to accept pain. Even the suitors do not dispute that he was a good king; unfortunately this is not enough to maintain his position in Ithaca. He must get both his pleasant and his hostile aspect recognized at the same time. When they finally are, near the end of the last book, this is signalized by the curious salutation of Dolius, the last to join forces with him: *oule te kai mala chaire,* he says, "hail and rejoice!" But *oule* is an exceedingly rare word, and its auditory suggestions of *oulos* "baneful," and *oulē,* the famous scar, will be felt—something like "Bane and Weal!" For the scar which the boar gave him is in particular the mark of Odysseus as Trouble. Antikleia ("Opposed-to-fame"), in her recognition of her son in the underworld, did not seem to understand the scar's full meaning, but it is easy for Eurycleia ("Far-fame") to accept it. After touching the scar as she washed his feet,

> joy and pain seized upon Eurycleia at the same time; her eyes filled with tears, and the voice caught in her throat. Touching his chin she said to Odysseus: "Surely you are Odysseus, dear child —and I didn't know my master until I had felt all of him!"

Eurycleia knows both aspects. It is she who has to be restrained from howling in triumph over the dead suitors. Telemachus is not much of a problem either. "I am no god;" Odysseus says, "Why do you think I am an immortal? No, I am your father, for whom you groan and suffer so much pain, accepting the insults of your fellows." Telemachus' difficulty is to determine whether Trouble is a miserable wretch in filthy rags or a very god for splendor. We have met this ambiguity before in the double nature of Heracles.

Penelope's recognition is harder to win. She knows Odysseus' soft garment, and her own hands pinned on him the badge of the dog and fawn; but the predatory side of him she cannot accept. Troy is to her not a great and necessary exploit, but something he merely "went to see," and for this she cannot forgive him. To her Troy is not a source of renown, but "Evil Ilium, not to be named." If Odysseus' manipulation, or his knowledge of the mind of man ever fails, it is with her. In their false-recognition scene, his riddle-name is *Aithōn,* the "blaze" which melts her (19.204-9) but which she cannot face (19.478). In spite of all the help her disguised husband can give her, she reacts to her dream of the eagle, Odysseus, killing her geese, the suitors, not by preparing for his "return," but by deciding, at last, to give him up for good. After the suitors are dead, and Odysseus has had his bath, she still holds out. Even the appeal to her desire as a woman, effective though it was with Kalypso, Nausicaa, and Circe, doesn't work; Odysseus, it appears, will have to sleep alone. In exasperation he asks who moved his bed. In spite of all he has done to make permanent their marriage and the symbol of it, he still cannot tell, he admits, "whether it still stands or whether by now someone has moved it elsewhere, and cut through the trunk of the olive." By this bed and by this exasperation she knows him; flinging her arms around his neck, "Odysseus, don't scold me," she cries, giving him his true name at last. Later, she will accept trouble in more detail. The "immeasurable toil" still to come, none other than the planting of Teiresias' oar, she elects to hear of immediately, though in the first book, after ten years, she could not bear to hear the bard singing of the return from Troy. In the end she takes delight in hearing "all the woes Zeus-sprung Odysseus inflicted on others, and all he himself toiled and suffered." She has accepted the meaning of the name of Odysseus.

Teiresias implied that to win identity one must administer pain, resist all impulses to ignore it, and plant the idea of it in the minds of others. Hence the curious behaviour of the hero in making himself known to Laertes. Checking his own tears and resisting the impulse to "kiss his father and embrace him, and tell him all, how he had come and was back at home," Odysseus instead teases the suffering old man with the pain of the loss of his son. This is the pain which killed Antikleia, but it now serves to make clear to Laertes and Odysseus what they mean to each other.

Laertes knows Odysseus by his scar, but also by some fruit trees, given to Odysseus as a boy, which the old man is still tending for him. There is something obviously fruitful in the pain of this relationship between father and son, and the sense of the boar-hunt exploit is there too, especially when later the old man delights to see "son and grandson vying in prowess" in the fight with the suitors' kinsmen. The fruitfulness of trouble has been hinted all along, particularly by the image of the olive.

There is the double olive thicket which shelters the hero, naked and alone on Scheria; the green olive stake which puts out Polyphemus' eye; and notably the great olive trunk which makes one corner of Odysseus' bed. The recurrent phrase, *kaka phyteuein* "to plant evils," points to the same fruitfulness. Therefore we can be sure that the life of pain contemplated in the *Odyssey* is fruitful, not sadistic. The ultimate object is recognition and the sense of one's own existence, not the pain itself. The pain necessary to win recognition may be as slight as the show of anger to Penelope, or as great as the blinding of Polyphemus, but in some degree pain will be necessary. Nothing less than the death of 108 suitors (to say nothing of the faithless maids), and the readiness to kill the suitors' kinsmen, will get Odysseus recognized in Ithaca. Once recognition is achieved, however, pain is pointless. At the very end of the poem, Odysseus "swooping like an eagle" on the fleeing ranks of the suitors' adherents, "might have killed them all." Then, "Zeus-sprung son of Laertes, expedient Odysseus, stop!" Athene cries, ". . . lest Zeus be angry at you." The daughter of Zeus herself, as Circe and others have done before her, now hails Odysseus with the rolling epithets of his full titles. Killing beyond the point of this recognition would anger Zeus, would violate the nature of things. But has Zeus not been angry all along at the hero "who received so many buffets, once he had sacked the sacred citadel of Troy?" No. The universe is full of hostility, it includes Poseidon, but it is not ultimately hostile. Zeus has been showing Odysseus not anger, but a terrible fondness, to echo Athene's words quoted early in this paper.

It is thus that the *Odyssey* solves the problem of evil, which it raised at line 62 of the first book. "Excessive suffering," says Zeus, or words to that effect, "is due to folly." " So it is," replies Athene; "but what about Odysseus? Why do you odysseus him so, Zeus?" It is a good question; Zeus admits that Odysseus is the wisest of mankind; yet he permits Poseidon to persecute him. It is a good question, and it contains its own answer. In exposing Odysseus to Poseidon, in allowing him to do and suffer, Zeus is odysseusing Odysseus, giving him his identity. In accepting the implications of his name, Trouble, Odysseus establishes his identity in harmony with the nature of things. In the ultimate sense he is "Zeus-sprung," one whose existence is rooted in life itself.

GABRIEL GERMAIN

Polyphemus and African Initiation Rites†

We are now ready to advance the following conclusions:

1. The theme of the Cyclops constitutes a special case in the vast group of tales about ogres. This theme is well defined by its characteristic traits: the single eye of the monster, the puncturing of that eye, flight under the cover of a ram. The outline and the atmosphere remain identical.

2. In treating the theme the way it does, the *Odyssey* distinguishes itself fundamentally from parallel tales (even from the ones closest to it, those of the Caucasus and Berber Morocco) by the contamination which it effects with another theme from folklore: that of deception by means of a name. Moreover, it enriches the folklore with all its borrowing from an already developed dramatic and poetic imagination; but, by interesting contrast, it nevertheless remains very close to the particular logic which governs popular narratives. It receives—it does not *invent*—the historical base. The master of the *Odyssey*, whose much more modern intellectual qualities are affirmed by the general construction and detail of the poem, would not have known how to imitate folklore on this point, even if he had thought of it. If some tales of Hackman's collection are suspected of literary influence, the relative ease with which this is disclosed makes the authenticity of the other tales still more convincing; for them it does not pose a serious question. Besides, if literature often finds its source in the popular tradition, has not the popular tradition sometimes been known to grant its riches to a purely literary theme?

3. It is fitting, then, that one seek in this tradition the explanation of the Odyssean narrative, looking as much at its general spirit as at certain details whose original foundation that narrative has obscured.

Under these conditions, the interpretation of stories about ogres from primitive sources is to be taken into serious consideration. P. Saintyves has connected the stories of the "Petit

---

† From Gabriel Germain, *Genèse de l'Odyssée* (Paris: Presses Universitaires de France, 1954), pp. 76–81. Translated by Clement Goodson. Reprinted by permission of the publisher.

Poutet" (Tom Thumb) series with initiation ceremonies for young men, and the result seems interesting enough for us to try the same method here, *mutandis mutandi.*

The scene, we have said, is almost always in a deserted place. It seems unusual for the heroes to meet a whole population of ogres. The *Odyssey* furnishes Polyphemus with companions, but it leaves us ignorant—we insist on this point—of whether they have the same tastes as him. He remains nothing less than the monster who lives alone ($o\hat{\iota}os$), far away from and in front of the others ($\dot{a}\pi\acute{o}\pi\rho o\theta\epsilon\nu$), always apart ($\dot{a}\pi\acute{a}\nu\epsilon\nu\theta\epsilon\nu$). His kith live within calling distance, but Ulysses is able both to arrive and to escape without passing under their eyes.

It is true that solitude is propitious to the crime without being an inevitable condition for it. It would therefore be possible to seek no more distant explanation for it if what followed did not call for it. Now isolation is obligatory in those tribal initiations in which the secret of the initiation must be absolute. That is why "houses of initiation" are, most frequently, huts built apart from the villages, in the forests. But caves are used as well when they can be found. The facts are too well known to need insistence.

One of the essential characteristics of initiation is its representation of a first death of the novice, which permits him to be reborn again as a transformed being. This is not the place to enumerate all the ways known which simulate that death; only one is of interest here, because it shows in what direction we must look for the origin of the type of the ogre. This is the practice of certain tribes of New Guinea who lend the cabin of initiation a vaguely human form, with a mouth through which the adolescent is passed. He is then considered devoured. But the monster relents through the gift of a boar and consents to reject his prey, who retains the traces of a bite: circumcision. In these and similar rites we may see the explanation for which we are looking.

It is necessary to pick up here, with particular attention, a small but, for the interpretation of our Berber tales, very important fact: in the Magoussaoua of the Sahara, already cited, in the course of initiation, "at the culminating point of ecstasy," the young men are wounded sexually by a leopard—that is, by an initiatory instructor with a leopard mask—from whom it is thought that they suffer a bite. The same mask is used by certain of Adamaoua (Negroes of the western Cameroons), by the man who practises circumcision. Now, we recall that it is a leopard which plays the role of ogre in Text B of these tales. The ritual attachment of this detail appears, from this point on, quite probable.

Let us now go into the house of initiation, ready to consume whatever presents itself, for a moment or for several years. We always find there one, or several, terrifying personages. With the Australians, it is a mythical being called Thuremlin, or Daramulun, or Thrumalun, or Tavanyaika, or Katajalina, or Tumana, or Eruba, or Witurna, or Tundun. The *tubuan* of the Solomon Islands; the magician of the lower Congo; and the celestial, masked visitor of the Fuegians assume, in their dress, frightening aspects as well. The mask is conspicuous among many "primitives," in all ceremonies which have to do with both scaring the uninitiated and "severing the initiating official from his usual surroundings" until he is identified more or less with the being which he represents; as such, his design always answers to "an anti-realistic effort." Failing the mask, the initiator is at least covered with feathers and daubed with color.

It is not so astonishing, then, that ogres easily grow to the height of a house or are distinguished by a deformed face. The ones we are concerned with here conform to the common rule. The form of Polyphemus is like a mountain rather than a man. The Berber monsters, badly disengaged from animality, find their real prototype at the southern edge of the Sahara or with the Sudanese. There, where the "leopard" does not bite the circumcised initiate, he at least steps in to test his courage. "A leopard mask frightens the young initiate in the passage of a subterranean cavern."

We begin to understand the deformity which appears to our voyagers: the single eye. But it is possible to be even more precise. For the primitive mentality, which is extremely conformist, any individual who is not "like everyone else" is disquieting and malevolent. This is carried so far that certain African peoples kill or abandon children whose teeth do not come in in the usual order. Even today, in the popular or infantile environments of Europe, deformities sometimes activate a kind of unconscious hostility, the legacy of ancestral fears. It is easy to see why the masks of the initiators seek grimacing expressions: they really terrify those for whom they are meant; it is only to more evolved spirits that they appear grotesque.

It is quite certain that even today, in North Africa, the

person with one eye is considered charged with a baneful power. The same is true among certain black peoples.

In Irish legends, numerous malevolent personages, possessors of supernatural powers, have only one foot, one hand, one eye. Others, who are not at all misformed by nature, have paid for the acquisition of their magic powers by a mutilation of this kind. Similarly, in Germanic traditions, Odhinn had to lose an eye in order to understand the runes.

The invention of the one-eyed ogre is, on the basis of these diverse sources then, quite easy to explain. We have indicated examples of it outside our group of narratives. We also find at least one case of an ogre with three eyes.

T. W. ADORNO

Odysseus, or Mythos and Enlightenment†

Just as the story of the Sirens affirms the interlocking relation between mythos and rational labor, so does the *Odyssey* bear complete witness to the dialectic of enlightenment. The epic appears, in its oldest layer at least, to be tied up with mythos: its adventures derive from folkloristic transmission. But while the Homeric spirit takes possession of myths—organizes them, so to say—it comes also to contradict them. The familiar equation of epic and mythos, which has in any case been discarded by recent classical philology, has been shown by philosophical criticism to be deceiving. The two concepts diverge. They mark two phases of an historical process which can be recognized at the seams of Homeric narrative itself. Homeric diction creates a universality of language if it does not already presuppose this; it dissolves the hieratic social order through the esoteric shape of its presentation, even where it glorifies that same order; to sing of the wrath of Achilles and the wanderings of Odysseus is already a nostalgic stylization of that which no longer can be sung, and the hero of the adventure proves to be the very prototype of bourgeois individuality, whose conception derives from

† From Max Horkheimer and Theodor W. Adorno, *Dialektik der Aufklärung: Philosophische Fragmente* (Amsterdam: Querido Verlag N. V. 1947). Excursus I, "Odysseus oder Mythos und Aufklärung," pp. 58–83. Translated by Clement Goodson. Reprinted by permission of the publisher.

that central self-assertion whose preconceptual model the wandering hero furnishes. In the epic—this opposite of the novel in its philosophy of history—we still find novelistic strains, and the venerable cosmos of the Homeric world, filled as it is with significations, is revealed as the achievement of orderly reason, which destroys mythos by means of rational order, in which this same reason mirrors mythos....

In Homer, epic and mythos, form and content do not so much separate as come to settlement. This aesthetic dualism testifies to a tendency regarding a philosophy of history. "The apollonian Homer is just the transmitter of that universal human artistic process to which we owe the concept of Individuation."[1]

The myths themselves have been suppressed in the layers of content in Homer; but the report of them, the unity which has been forced onto diffuse tales, is nonetheless the description of the path of flight of the subject in the face of mythical powers. This is true in a deeper sense in the *Iliad*. The wrath of a Mycenean son of a goddess against the rational leader-king and organizer, the undisciplined inactivity of that hero, and finally an understanding of this victorious victim of death by way of the Greek national need—no longer just a tribal one—achieved through mythical loyalty to dead companions: these are strands which hold fast this twisting mixture of prehistory and history. This is as much more valid for the *Odyssey* in its contiguity to the form of the novel of adventure. In the exposure of a single surviving ego to a manifold fate, it stamps enlightenment onto mythos. The course of wandering from Troy to Ithaca is the course of the infinitely weak subject's engagement of the power of nature: the path of the self, coming for the first time into self-consciousness, through the world of myth. The preconceptual world is secularized in the space through which the hero travels; old demons people its distant edge and the islands of the civilized Mediterranean Sea, driven back to rock and cave from which, once—in the horror of prehistory—they came into being. The adventures provide each place with its name; and from them a rational view of space is derived. The shivering shipwreck victim anticipates the work of the compass. The very physical weakness of this man to whom no part of the sea is

1. Friedrich Nietzsche, *Works*, vol. 9, p. 289.

unknown aims at disarming these mythical forces. But the simple failure of truth in the myths (the fact that sea and earth are not actually inhabited by demons—a fantasy and diffusion accountable to the received folk-religion) comes to be seen by the matured hero as "error" in the face of his resolute goal of self-preservation, of his return to home and possessions. The adventures which Odysseus endures are all of them dangerous enticements which draw the self away from the track of its logic. He gives himself up time and again to new experience, tests it as an uninitiated but eager learner, even sometimes as a foolish curiosity-seeker, in the same way that a mime-actor probes insatiably around in his role. "But where there is danger, there grows/ Too the force that saves":[2] knowledge, in which his identity is constituted and which enables him to live through his wanderings, has its substance in the experience of the manifold, the distracting, the dissolving; and the knowledge-able, enduring hero is the same one who, at his boldest, gives himself up to the threat of death and by this becomes durable and strong in life. This is the secret object of contest between epic and mythos: the self does not make adventure out of obstinate opposition, rather it comes to create its own obstinacy by means of this opposition, a stark unity in a world of multiplicity which negates that unity. Odysseus, like the heroes of all real novels after him, gives himself away in order that he may come to win himself; the distancing from nature which he effects is realized in the abandonment to nature which in every episode he eschews; and, ironically, the relentless force which he commands triumphs—he comes home relentless hero, as judge and avenger of the heritage of the forces he escaped. The identity of self in Homer is so much a function of the realm of the uni-dentified, of dissociated, inarticulate myths, that it is compelled to borrow itself from these. The internal, organizational form of individuality—time—is still so weak that the unity of adventure, externally—its succession of spatial changes of stage—remains the geographical centers of local deities toward which the storm diverts him. Whenever, historically, the self has again experienced such a weakening, or the artistic representation presumes such weakness in the reader, the story of life again slides off in a succession of adventures. Laboriously and revocably, historical

2. Friedrich Hölderlin, "Patmos," in Collected Works, Leipzig, p. 230.

time is discharged in a portrait of journey through space, from the irrevocable scheme of all mythic time.

Cunning is the agent of the self: it enables the hero to withstand adventure, throw himself away, maintain himself. The sailor Odysseus cheats the natural deities as a civilized traveler cheats the savage, offering him colored glass beads in exchange for ivory. It is only occasionally that Odysseus appears in the role of trader. At these times gifts of guest-friendship are given and taken. The Homeric gift of guest-friendship stands somewhere between barter and sacrifice. As a sacrifice it exists to satisfy blood lost, whether that of a foreigner or that of a resident besieged by pirates, and to obtain a vow of peace. At the same time, though, the principle of equivalency is enunciated in the gift of guest-friendship: the host obtains, actually or symbolically, the equivalent value of his gesture while the guest gets provision for his journey, enabling him in some important way to reach home. If the host obtains no negotiable ware for his troubles, he can still figure that he or one of his relations has at some time been similarly received: as a sacrifice to the gods of the elements, the gift of guest-friendship is also a rudimentary kind of insurance in the face of their power. The extensive and dangerous sea travel of early Greece offers an empirical condition for this expedient. Poseidon, Odysseus's elemental enemy, himself thinks in concepts of equivalence, even as he continues to wreak hardship: Odysseus obtains at the stations of his wanderings more in gifts than his portion of the booty at Troy would have been, had he been able to convey it to Ithaca without Poseidon's interference. . . .

The moment of deception in the victim is the prototype of Odyssean cunning just as many of Odysseus's tricks are introduced as a kind of offering to the nature deities. These deities are outwitted by the solar deities as well as by the hero. The Olympic friends of Odysseus use the visit of Poseidon to the Ethiopians, backwoodsmen who worship and offer huge sacrificial victims to him, to lead their ward out of danger. Deception is involved even in the sacrifice which Poseidon gratefully accepts: the enclosure of the amorphous god of the sea at a fixed locality, his holy precinct, contains his power as well, and he is forced to forego his huge meal of Ethiopian oxen in order to vent his rage on Odysseus. All sacrifices by men, systemati-

cally carried out, deceive the god for whom they are intended:
they subordinate him to the primacy of human purpose, dissolve
his power, and his deception is perfectly achieved by the unbe-
lieving priest who carries it out in the believing community.
The quality of cunning arises from the cult. Odysseus himself
functions as both victim and priest. By the calculation of his
own activity he effects the negation of power toward which that
activity contrives. So it is that he wins his declining life by bar-
gaining. But deception, trick, and rationality by no means stand
in simple opposition to the archaic principle of sacrifice.
Through Odysseus, the moment of deception in the victim, per-
haps the most profound base of the character of appearance in
mythos, is raised to self-consciousness. The realization that sym-
bolic communication with the deity by means of sacrifice is not
real must be a primal experience. The sacrificial substitute, glori-
fied by recent irrationalists, cannot be separated from the deifi-
cation of the sacrificed, from the deception worked by the
priest: rationalization of death through the apotheosis of the
chosen. Something of this sort of deception, which elevates the
weak human being to the role of bearer of the divine substance,
has been noticeable ever since in the ego, which owes the sacri-
fice of the present to the fact of the future. Its substance is
appearance, like the immortality of victims of battle. Not with-
out cause was Odysseus mistaken by many as a deity. . . .

It is formulaic for the cunning of Odysseus that the detached,
instrumental spirit—yielding to Nature in resignation—gives
Nature some of her own and deceives her in the process. The
mythical monsters into whose realm of power he falls present
fossilized agreements and demands from prehistory. The older
folk-religion presented itself thus to the developed patriarchal
time in its scattered relics: beneath the Olympian heaven they
became figures of abstract Fate and obscure Necessity. That it
would have been impossible to choose some other route than
the one between Scylla and Charybdis, one may rationalistically
come to understand as the mythic transformation of the superi-
ority of the ocean current to the small ships of antiquity. But in
the mythically objectified translation, the natural condition of
might and powerlessness has already assumed the character of
the just condition. Scylla and Charybdis have a right to what-
ever comes between their teeth, just as Circe has a right to
change the shape of the unprotected and Polyphemus the right
to the bodies of his guests. Every one of the mythical figures is

obliged always to do the same thing. Each exists in repetition: their failure would be their end. All bear strands of that which is grounded by Olympian decree in the punishment myths of the underworld—Tantalos, Sisyphus, the Danaids. They are figures of compulsion: the horrors which they commit are the curse that weighs upon them. Mythic inevitability is defined by the equivalence between that curse, the misdeed that atones for it, and the guilt which grows out of it, which guilt reproduces the curse. All justice in hitherto existing history bears the trace of this schema. In mythos, every moment of this circular track satisfies the previous one and helps to install the guilt-connection as law. This is what Odysseus comes up against. The self represents rational universality against the inevitability of fate. But because the self discovers the universal and the inevitable to be interlocked, his understanding assumes a necessarily confined form—that of the exception. He must extract himself from the enclosing and threatening conditions of justice which are to some extent prescribed for every mythical figure. He satisfies the imperative of justice in such a way that it loses its power over him—he confines this power. It is impossible to hear the Sirens and not fall to them: he does not try to defy them. Defiance and infatuation are one, and he who defies them loses with that the mythos to which he stands in relation. The quality of cunning is a kind of rational defiance. Odysseus does not try to travel any other route than the one past the island of the Sirens. He also does not try to presume on the superiority of his knowledge and freely listen to the temptresses, imagining his freedom to suffice as protection. He makes himself insignificant, the ship assumes its predestined, fatal course, and he realizes that he, as listener, is still subject to them, though consciously distanced from nature. He keeps the covenant of his bondage to himself and he still struggles at the mast, trying to throw himself into the arms of the seductresses. But he has found a hold in the covenant through which he escapes the fulfillment of the decree. The prehistoric covenant does not specify whether the victim, passing through Scylla and Charybdis and listening to the song, must be bound or unbound. Bondage first belongs to a stage in cultural development at which prisoners are not immediately killed. Odysseus recognizes the archaic superiority of the song and, being technologically enlightened, he has himself bound. He is aroused by the song of desire and frustrates it as he does death. The bound listener wants to go to the Sirens as much as anyone else. Only he has struck upon an arrangement by which he, though subject to them, is not in fact subjugated. He cannot with all the force of his desire (which reflects the force of the demi-goddesses themselves) go to them, because his rowing companions are deaf not only to the demi-goddesses but also to the desperate cry of their commander. The Sirens have what is theirs, but it already has been neutralized in bourgeois prehistory and become a longing for that which has passed. The epic is silent about what happens to the seductive singers after the ship has disappeared. But in tragedy it must have been their last hour, as it was for the Sphinx when Oedipus solved the riddle, fulfilling her command and overturning her in the process. Since the fortunate (or unfortunate) encounter of Odysseus with the Sirens, all songs have been upset, and the whole of Western music suffers from the absurdity of song in civilization —with which absurdity, however, the moving power of all art music dispenses.

With the breaking of agreement by the verbal observation of it, the historical position of speech is altered: it starts to become designation. The mythic fate (*Fatum*) was one with the spoken word. The circle of performance, to which the maxims of the unalterably executed about fate belong, still does not recognize the difference between word and fact. The word is destined to have immediate power over the object; expression and intention run together. The quality of cunning consists in taking advantage of the distinction. One fastens on the word in order to change the object. In this way the consciousness of intention emerges: Odysseus, in his need, becomes aware of dualism as he discovers that the same word may mean various things. Because the hero, as well as no-man, is referenced by the name *outis*, he is able to break the name taboo. . . . Self-preservational cunning lives on that ruling process of refinement between word and object. The two contradictory acts of Odysseus in his encounter with Polyphemus, his obedience to the name and his dissociation from it, are in fact the same. He knows himself even as he renounces himself as "no man," he saves his life even as he makes it disappear. . . .

One of the first adventures of the actual return to Ithaca reaches very far indeed back in time, even farther back than the barbaric age of grimaced demons and magical gods. It deals with the tale of the Lotus-eaters. He who partakes of their food is subjugated just like anyone who hears the Sirens or is touched by the staff of Circe. But nothing unpleasant awaits the man who thus succumbs: "But from the Lotus-eaters no evil befell the men / Of our crew" (IX.92). Forgetfulness and the dissolution of his will threaten him. The curse damns him to nothing more than the primitive state without work and struggle in the "fruitful field" (XXIII.311). "He who tasted of the lotus plant, sweeter than honey / Thought no more of pronouncement nor of the future; / But tried out the industry of the Lotus-eaters / Remaining to pick lotus and renounce his home" (IX.94). Such an idyl, which is reminiscent of the happiness of a narcotic drug —with the help of which, in hardened social orders, underprivileged classes are made capable of bearing the unbearable— cannot be permitted, for reasons of self-preservation, by their social order. . . .

The next shape to which Odysseus is driven in his wanderings —to be driven out of one's course and to be crafty are equivalents for Homer—is that of the Cyclops Polyphemus, who bears his single eye, large as a wheel, as a mark of this same preconceptual world: the one eye recalls the nose and the mouth, more primitive than the symmetry of the eyes and ears, which —in the unity of two convergent perceptions—first provides identification, depth, and objectivity. He nevertheless represents a later development than the Lotus-eaters, the actual barbaric age of hunters and shepherds. The definition of barbarism coincides, for Homer, with the stipulation that no systematic agriculture be practiced and therefore still no systematic, gradually arranged organization of work and society be achieved. He calls the Cyclopes the "unlawed arrogant" (IX.106) because (and herein lies something like a secret admission of guilt by civilization itself) they "depend on the deathless gods / Nor plant with their hands nor cultivate plants, / But these grow unsown and unploughed / Wheat, barley and vine, which bears / The wine of fine grape-clusters and the rain of Zeus makes them grow" (IX.107–11). This plenitude needs no law, and the civilized accusation of anarchy sounds almost like a denunciation of plenitude itself. "For them there are no council meetings and no laws / But they inhabit the crowns of high-lying mountains / In hollow caves, each proclaiming the law / For his own children and wives, nor do they care about the others" (IX.112–15). This is already a patriarchal, tribal society based on the

repression of the physically weak, but not yet organized on the
principle of private property and its hierarchy, and it is the dis-
connectedness of those who dwell in the cave that accounts for
the lack of objective law and with it the Homeric reproach of
reciprocal indifference, of their wild condition. In this the prag-
matic fidelity of the narrator contradicts at a later place his own
civilized judgment: at the desperate cry of the blinded Cyclops
his tribe comes out to help him in spite of that "indifference,"
and only Odysseus's name-trick keeps these foolish creatures
away, standing beside their own kind. Stupidity and lawlessness
appear as the same attribute: if Homer calls the Cyclops that
"monster knowing the state of lawlessness" (IX.428), this
means not just that his thought does not respect the laws of civ-
ilization, but also that his thought itself is lawless, unsystematic,
and rhapsodic; just as he is unable to deal with a lesson in bour-
geois thought—the way in which his uninvited guests are able
to escape the cave by fastening themselves to the sheep's under-
sides instead of riding upon them—so the sophistical double
sense of Odysseus's false name does not occur to him. . . .

CEDRIC H. WHITMAN

The *Odyssey* and Change†

The *Odyssey* is the work of a master, though perhaps of a
master whose zenith, as Longinus suggests, has gone by.

Whether or not it was the same master who wrote the *Iliad* is a
question which must probably remain unanswered, except in
the personal convictions of individuals. Suffice it to say here
that, for all the real and even extreme contrast between the two
poems, there has yet to be produced a single cogent argument
to the effect that they must belong to different hands, or differ-
ent eras. Arguments drawn from minor points of subject matter,
such as Phoenicians, the knowledge of riding astride of horses,
familiarity with Egypt, and all such, provide intolerable exam-
ples of argument from silence, at best, and at worst betray con-

† From Cedric H. Whitman, *Homer and The Homeric Tradition* (Cam-
bridge: Harvard University Press, 1958), pp. 286–289. Reprinted by per-
mission of the publisher. Copyright 1958, by the President and Fellows of
Harvard College.

victions about Homer more positivistic than well-informed. Attempts on linguistic grounds to prove the *Odyssey* later fail utterly; the epic language, save for what differences must exist because of the differences in the setting and the story, is the same for both poems, and in the *Odyssey* no neologisms exist of such a convincing sort that we must put the poem very much later than the *Iliad*. Also, on the grounds of oral theory, the *Odyssey* cannot be pushed very far into the period when literacy and a changing society were popularizing the various forms of lyric poetry, and relegating oral composition to the obscure corners of the Greek world. If the *Odyssey* belonged in any real sense to the seventh century, it must have been composed in some such obscure corner by a poet with old-fashioned tastes, bent on following in the wake of the *Iliad*, and essentially unmoved by the world around him. If such a poet existed—and many may have—it is hard to see how his work ever became known as Homer's. In the seventh century, the least of poets signed his work, and even the poems of the *Cycle* have names other than Homer's (and sometimes several) attached to them. To say the least, it is an uneconomical hypothesis to put the *Odyssey* so late. Both great epics belong to the most mature period of oral composition; both reflect the synthetic and formalized vision of the heroic Bronze Age in essentially the same way; both have ecumenical breadth, and tend to draw into their schemes large sections of the myth of Troy not immediately involved in the plot; both are complex, monumental, and retrospective; and both show much in common with the Athenian artistic approach, at once vivid, lucid, and subtle.

Such basic similarities point to similar poetic concerns and a similar period of composition. But if one looks at certain differences of compositional approach, one may be able to guess the relation between the two poems a little more accurately. That the *Odyssey* is later than the *Iliad* most will agree, albeit the agreement is often based on the groundless assumption that the *Odyssey* is more "civilized," because more concerned with civilization as such, and the *Iliad* more primitive. The reverse could be asserted with equal truth, and, in any event, the *Iliad* penetrates further into the frontier mysteries of human psychology. But the relative outlooks upon character and experience cannot be decisive in such a matter. More significant is the relative structure of the two poems. The *Iliad*, as already shown, follows a strict Geometric design comparable to nothing except the sepulchral vases of the Dipylon. Very little of the sort occurs in the *Odyssey*, and where it does occur, asymmetrical elements are more frequent, the responsions less careful and less significant. The antithetical polarities of the hysteron-proteron technique enhance meaning in the *Iliad*; insofar as they exist in the *Odyssey*, they are somewhat perfunctory, and the sense of form which one derives from the poem comes far less from repeated or inverted themes and episodes than from the substance of the narrative itself, its progress through time, and its achievement of a long-awaited end. The *Iliad* is tightly designed in every instant; the *Odyssey* sings itself, proceeding with a natural, leisurely pace, entirely suited to the prevailing mood of a large landscape with figures. For this reason, perhaps, the *Odyssey* has far fewer similes than the *Iliad*: the latter concentrates on one *mise en scène*, one major action, one monolithic idea of the heroic; visions of the rest of the world therefore knot themselves into hard images which cluster luminously around the rush of action. The *Odyssey* has a wider lens; it peers less deeply, but takes time to describe. Its object, like that of its hero, is often simply to see:

> Standing there, divine long-suffering Odysseus gazed.

And there is very little which Odysseus will not take time to look at. The same objective scrutiny falls on Cyclops, Circe, the suitors, Eumaeus' steading, the gardens of Alcinous, the faithless maidservants, and weeping Penelope—"eyes like horn or iron." The *Odyssey* keeps building scenic episodes, typical and often static, and in these lie its chief symbols, not, as in the *Iliad*, in continuous and ever-shifting motifs.

This is not to say, however, that no evidences of Geometric design are to be found in the *Odyssey*. Certain parts, especially the *Adventures* and the Phaeacian episode, show conscious scenic antithesis and framing patterns. The *Adventures* are particularly elegant, grouped as they are around the supreme adventure, the Journey to the Dead. This central episode, with its retrospect upon the whole heroic tradition in the ghosts of Ajax, Achilles, Agamemnon, and Heracles, and its mysterious prospect of peace at last and "death from the sea" in the prophecy of Teiresias, is carefully framed, first by the two Elpenor episodes, and then by the two scenes with Circe. For the rest, the

poet summarizes two out of every three adventures rather
briefly, and dramatizes one at greater length, so that the pattern
of Odysseus' narrative is as follows:

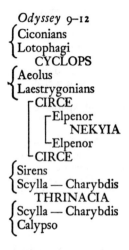

Odyssey 9–12
{ Ciconians
{ Lotophagi
    CYCLOPS
{ Aeolus
{ Laestrygonians
    CIRCE
       Elpenor
         NEKYIA
       Elpenor
    CIRCE
{ Sirens
{ Scylla — Charybdis
    THRINACIA
{ Scylla — Charybdis
{ Calypso

Calypso, of course, is dramatized in her own right in Book 5,
but not in the narrative of the hero. Book 8 offers, perhaps, a
more interesting Geometric structure. Here Odysseus is deliber-
ately contrasted with his Phaeacian hosts, who grow more and
more impressed and mystified by him until finally nothing will
satisfy save the full narrative of his adventures. The whole book
turns on the two principles of music and gymnastic, keynotes of
civilization to the Greek mind, and both highly developed by
the peace-loving and somewhat soft Phaeacians. Odysseus
proves the supremacy in bodily arts of the lonely and experi-
enced hero over those who dwell in the ivory tower on the edge
of the world. As for music, he is not a singer, but he emerges as
the living substance of the heroic lays of Demodocus, which are
mere amusement to the Phaeacians. Of Demodocus' three
songs, the middle one of Ares and Aphrodite, with its ring of
Olympian laughter, is a lighthearted romance appropriate to the
people who love warm baths and bed; the first and the last are
Trojan songs appropriate to Odysseus, deeply involved with his
identity, and prompting those tears which in turn lead to the
full revelation of his experience. Few episodes in Homer are
more skillfully handled than the Eighth *Odyssey*; form and pur-
pose are truly one:

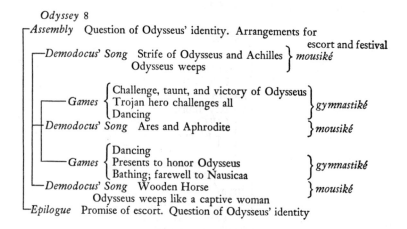

Odyssey 8
Assembly   Question of Odysseus' identity. Arrangements for
                                                    escort and festival
    Demodocus' Song   Strife of Odysseus and Achilles } *mousiké*
                        Odysseus weeps

        Games { Challenge, taunt, and victory of Odysseus }
                 Trojan hero challenges all   } *gymnastiké*
                 Dancing
        Demodocus' Song   Ares and Aphrodite   } *mousiké*

        Games { Dancing
                 Presents to honor Odysseus   } *gymnastiké*
                 Bathing; farewell to Nausicaa
        Demodocus' Song   Wooden Horse   } *mousiké*
                 Odysseus weeps like a captive woman
Epilogue   Promise of escort. Question of Odysseus' identity

ANNE AMORY

The Reunion of Odysseus and Penelope†

At this point, the poet cannot pause for a detailed explanation of Penelope's state of mind and reasons for deciding to set the contest now. He simply states that Athene inspired her to go and get the bow (21.1–2). For those who misunderstand the role of the gods in Homer, Penelope's decision here inevitably seems abrupt and unmotivated, and Athene's intervention appears an arbitrary resort to a *dea ex machina*. But Homer habitually objectifies internal mental processes in the figures of gods, and always with due regard for the psychological reality of his characters. Here Athene's intervention is a kind of short-hand for a psychological process at a moment when the narrative is too crowded to permit fuller presentation, but it also symbolizes the fact that Penelope, acting only on intuition, without a full knowledge of the situation, does just the right thing at the right time.

There are several other indications in what follows that Penelope is acting without full conscious knowledge either of the sit-

† From Charles H. Taylor, Jr., *Essays on the Odyssey* (Bloomington, Ind: University of Indiana Press, 1963), pp. 113–117. Reprinted by permission of Charles H. Taylor, Jr.

uation or of her own emotions. When she takes down Odysseus' bow she weeps for a while, but no explanation of her tears is given, as it is on the other occasions when she weeps. It is not hard to furnish reasons. She weeps, in part, simply because the bow reminds her of Odysseus, just as Eumaeus and Philoetius weep when they see it (21.82–83). Sheer nervous tension, too, accounts for her tears, since she is committing herself to a course of action which is irrevocable, and about whose outcome she feels the utmost anxiety. Nonetheless, the absence of any stated reason suggests that Penelope herself does not entirely know why she weeps, because she does not really know how she feels.

Next, when she makes her announcement to the suitors, she does not give the reason which the suitors might expect—that she has at last given up hope of Odysseus' return. Instead she speaks rather as if she were calling the suitors' bluff. First she says they have feasted in Odysseus' house while he was absent and could not put forward any pretext except that they wished to marry her. Then without any transition, she simply goes on —"Come now, since the contest is ready" (21.73).

She watches silently while the suitors one after another try, and fail, to string the bow. Leodes, the first to try, speaks a word of ill omen for the suitors: "This bow will strip many good men of their life and soul" (21.153–154). Antinous replies angrily that he is talking nonsense, but Odysseus, Telemachus, and Penelope, who have understood the import of Theoclymenus' vision, would take Leodes' speech as a confirmatory *klēdōn*.

Eventually Odysseus, who has in the meantime disclosed himself to Eumaeus and Philoetius, comes forward and asks to try the bow so that he can see if any of his old strength remains. The suitors are afraid he may succeed (having seen him at work on Irus) and Antinous violently denies his request. But Penelope intervenes and tells Antinous not to insult Telemachus' guests. "Do you suppose," she goes on, "that the stranger will expect to marry me if he succeeds in stringing Odysseus' great bow? I am sure such a thought hasn't entered his mind" (21.312–317). Eurymachus replies that, of course, they do not expect the beggar to marry Penelope. But they are concerned about what the common people will say—that they have been unable to measure up to the man whose wife they are courting, while some poor beggar was easily able to string the bow (21.321–329).

Penelope retorts that they need not be so careful of their reputations, which have suffered already because of their disgraceful behavior. Even if the stranger should succeed, it would be no reflection on them, for he is big and well-built and claims to come of a noble family. She promises that if the stranger strings the bow she will give him clothes and arms and send him wherever he wishes to go.

Penelope's speeches are most delicately done and show to the best advantage on the assumption that her recognition of Odysseus is still mostly unconscious. If she has definitely recognized him, as Harsh thinks, her words seem a little bland; we expect a sharper edge of double meaning. If she has no suspicions of his real identity, as many scholars assume, they are too apropos. Even the pressing claims of Greek hospitality do not demand her lavish promises. And why should she champion the beggar's request at all, or why should the idea that he might marry her need disclaiming? He has only asked to string the bow, not to enter the contest. As it is, she hovers charmingly between saying almost too much and not quite enough.

What she says is the literal truth, as far as the action which will result from the contest is concerned. The beggar will not marry her, for he has done that already. She will furnish him with new clothes and arms, but they will be his own. She will send him where he wants to go, but he will not want to go anywhere, except to her—at least for the moment. At the same time, her words are almost startlingly removed from the truth of what she will feel when she knows the result of the contest. This is a very curious state of affairs, appropriate only to the particular way in which the story is told in our *Odyssey*.

There is one other consideration that is often overlooked in assessing Penelope's reasons for setting the contest of the bow at this moment. The contest itself is a means of divination. One modern critic complains that Penelope might "just as well have invoked the chances of the lot."[1] Indeed she might, and with good reason, according to ancient belief. For subjecting an important choice to an apparently chance process, including that of drawing lots, was a regular means of ascertaining the will of the gods and insuring the right choice. Hence Penelope, since her feelings are too complex and contradictory to guide her

1. W. J. Woodhouse, *The Composition of Homer's Odyssey* (London: Oxford University Press, 1930), pp. 82–83.

clearly, is doing the only safe thing in resorting to the contest. For if the omens are right, if the stranger had good reason for his advice, then she is doing exactly what Odysseus wants her to do. If, on the other hand, the omens are wrong and her trust in the stranger a result of self-deception, so that one of the suitors may win the contest, then she will at least be marrying a man who is the least inferior to Odysseus. If, that is, any one of the suitors succeeds; there is after all a good chance that none will, so that if Odysseus is neither present nor coming, the contest will prove merely another delaying device, as her web was in the original version of the story (see notes 46 and 55).

In the revenge theme, the stringing of the bow is itself an omen of success for Odysseus, for it assures him that his old prowess is still intact. This decisive moment is preceded by a *klēdōn*, marked by similes, and followed by an omen. The suitors make scornful remarks when Odysseus first picks up the bow; one wishes that the bow may be as likely to give him profit or delight (*onesios*) as he is likely to succeed in stringing it (21.402–403). But Odysseus fits the string to the bow as easily as a bard strings his lyre, and the first arrow sings like a swallow. The suitors, at last realizing that their doom is at hand, turn pale, while Zeus thunders giving signs (*sēmata*), and Odysseus rejoices at the omen (*teras*).

When the battle begins, the long sequence of omens in the *Odyssey* is almost complete. There is only one more real omen, at the very end of the poem. Zeus hurls a thunderbolt to convince Odysseus that he must not continue the fight with the Ithacans (24.539–540). Zeus is the special protector of kings in Homer, and it is possible to interpret this omen as a symbol which marks the final supremacy of the true king returned. On the other hand, the action of the end of the *Odyssey* is only sketched in rapidly, because the major significant themes have been completed. Zeus' thunderbolt accomplishes something that the poet wants in the action—which is the simplest function of omens in the narrative of Homer—and the symbolic overtones are only lightly sounded.

Meanwhile there remains Athene's appearance during the slaying of the suitors. The incident is a perfect illustration and summary of the principles which govern the action of the gods in the Homeric poems. At a critical point in the battle Athene appears in the guise of Mentor, an old friend of Odysseus.

Odysseus greets her joyfully, just as if he thought it was Mentor himself, but he knows, or suspects, that it is really Athene (22.210). The suitors also address Athene as if she were Mentor, but without any suspicion of her real identity. She then turns to Odysseus and accuses him of being less brave now than he was at Troy fighting for Helen's sake, although he should be braver when fighting for his own possessions (22.226–235). The goddess does not bring immediate victory; she flies up to the roof, leaving Odysseus on his own. At this the suitors rally and attack. But Athene makes their spears miscarry, while helping Odysseus' party to hit their targets. Only at the very end does she raise her aegis and spread panic among the remaining suitors.

In this scene, Athene's speech represents Odysseus' own momentary fear of failure when his arrows are gone (21.147–149) and the way in which he regains his courage by reminding himself that he survived Troy and is now fighting for something more important to him personally. Athene's appearance as Mentor represents the suitors' feeling that they will not be able to defeat Odysseus; her disappearance indicates their surge of confidence as they remind themselves of their far superior numbers and realize the weakness of Odysseus' position. Their confidence is overconfidence, however, and they miss their aim. The raising of the aegis is a sign of the decisive moment in any battle where one side breaks completely. The whole scene is a fine blending of the miraculous and the natural, and a good example of the economy of narrative and impressiveness of dramatic effect which epic gained by using the gods as it did.

ALBERT COOK

The Man of Many Turns†

The epic poem is all-embracing; it is comprehensive, rather than encyclopedic, in character. It is their focus, more even than their lack of verse form, which deprives *Finnegans Wake* or *La Comédie Humaine* of an epic aura, and which almost gives one to *War and Peace*. The distinction, while elusive, is nicely illustrated by the contrast between the encyclopedic *Tesoro* of

† From Albert Cook, *The Classic Line* (Bloomington, Ind.: Indiana University Press, 1966), pp. 120–137. Reprinted by permission of the publisher.

Dante's master Brunetto Latini and the comprehensiveness of the *Divina Commedia* itself.

The code that is to press the mortality of the hero, the verse style that is to sound the depths of his objectified feeling, though they must derive from tradition, cannot simply be received from it, even if the tradition be that of the man's earlier work.

An epic poem must find its embodiment in a wholly adequate fable. The test of adequacy is not to be found in some generality such as War, the subject of many long poems, or Wandering, the subject of many others. An epic adequacy, moreover, cannot be said to be guaranteed by the resonance of an archetypal plot. Poems with stories, short and long, in all conventions, draw as heavily on the archetypal situation as they do on the rhythmic emphasis of a meter—that is to say all but universally —and perhaps for related reasons. It may be said, in brief, that epic adequacy resides in some myth that can unify all the incidents of a given poem into a view of experience large enough to pose completeness for the life of the protagonist. The poet's great task of invention is finding the myth for his particular poem, a problem that Homer had to solve by centering on Achilles no less than Milton did by centering on Adam. Such adequacy may not be gained by merely choosing a subject which superficially resembles some other adequate myth. Each epic, to possess its own universality, must fully articulate the view it envisions on ground it wins for itself. It is the poet of *Beowulf* who makes his myth superior to that of the *Waltharius*. Looking at epic poems after the fact, we can remark on the aptness of the invention: if such aptness were completely bound up with generic laws, we would have more epic poems than we do. Getting the right myth and a "classic line" together at full pitch is one of the rarest of literary acts.

So Homer—if we may conceive of the same man moving on with the same traditional equipment from *Iliad* to *Odyssey*— did not repeat himself by selecting some similar myth. He did not go on to the Seven Against Thebes or some other war, as Apollonius superficially chose Jason because Odysseus had been done, as Statius and so many others opted for their own or another national myth of war, aping the *Iliad*. Nor did he handle his verse in quite the same way.

Homer managed the complexity of the *Iliad* by coordinating an entire society at war. This achievement was unique, and since it was, it could not serve him for a poem which presents a like complexity in the sequential experience of a single hero.

Achilles stands at the center of the *Iliad*, but his world measures him. Odysseus, however, measures his world as he moves through it. And it does not alter him; he remains the same from first to last, not only in the actual time span of the poem, but also, essentially, over the twenty years of his wanderings.

In his dominance of the action he resembles Beowulf, Roland, and the Cid. But their experience is also single, while Odysseus goes through varieties of experiences that intimately mirror his complexity while testing his mind and emotions. In its characteristically light and subtle way, the *Odyssey* exhibits a hero whose experience is internalized; whose psyche is plumbed. So the heroes of the best epic poems after Homer—Aeneas, Dante, Adam—resemble Odysseus more closely than they do Achilles. And Pound has taken Odysseus in *The Cantos* for the persona most fit to mirror his varieties of experience.

The actual fable (*logos*) of the *Odyssey* is short, as Aristotle points out. And yet the poem is complexly interwoven (*peplegmenon*). This is because we have recognition (*anagnorisis*) throughout, he says, and this simple term serves as well as any other to describe Homer's mediation between his single hero and the hero's manifold experience.

The poem insists on this singleness, and this complexity, in its very first line:

Ἄνδρα μοι ἔννεπε Μοῦσα, πολύτροπον, ὃς μάλα πολλὰ

Tell me, Muse, about the man of many turns, who many . . .

Man, the first word. Complexity is named twice, in *polutropon*, "of many turns," and also in *polla*, "many."

Odysseus' situation deepens in time, and the situation of the poem deepens as it progresses; yet Odysseus' adequacy remains everywhere the same in all its aspects (*polutropos*). Only by a kind of alteration of the substance of the poem can we accept Cedric Whitman's reading of a developing self for Odysseus. His wholeness appears from the beginning in the memory of friends and comrades about him, in the persistence of his return, in his adroitness at meeting the enigmas of societies so variable that beside them the forms of Proteus which Menelaus must master seem simple indeed.

Through all the "change" of the poem—the term is Whitman's—Odysseus, by intelligence and striving (as the opening tells us) copes consistently with minds and peoples:

> Tell me, Muse, about the man of many turns, who many
> Ways wandered when he had sacked Troy's holy citadel;
> He saw the cities of many men and he knew their thought.

The variations of scene in the Odyssey involve a progression from the young to the mature (Telemachus to Odysseus), from the old to the new (Ithaca to a Phaeacian present), from the single to the complex (Nestor to Menelaus; Calypso to and through Circe), from the hostile to the hospitable (Ciconians to Phaeacians), from the natural to the fantastic (Ciconians to Hades, to the Oxen of the Sun groaning on the roasting spits), from the known Troy far from home to the remote Phaeacia whence Odysseus may soon sail for Ithaca.

Underlying these progressions is the psyche of the hero, broad because we have narrow ones (Nestor, Telemachus) for comparison. And since everyone's experience is appropriate for his character, the experience becomes a figure of the extent and complexity and subtlety of his inner life.

Applying this principle of congruence between a man's self and his destiny to the smaller characters, to the other peoples, we may apply it *a fortiori* to Odysseus. In this principle lies the canon of unity for the whole poem. Character in the *Iliad* is a given affirmation of a man's stable situation. In the *Odyssey* the situation is in flux, which means not that character changes, but that the flux of situation itself is seen to rest obscurely on the predisposition of the person or persons involved, character as fate.

The heroes return from war on voyages that are revelatory to us of their very selves. The simple Nestor had a straight return, the proud Agamemnon a disastrous one. The subtle and elegant Menelaus, a slighter of the gods, finds a return which tests his subtlety. Prompted by a nymph, he must first grapple with Proteus' sleepy noon disguises on lonely Pharos; then sacrifice in Egypt to the gods. Far more various are the wanderings of Odysseus, and consequently far more famous is Odysseus himself. He is outstanding in all virtues (IV, 815: *pantoies aretesi*[1] *kekasmenon*). And the fullness of his humanity is mirrored in his wanderings.

---

1. The plural here forbids our reading *aretesi* in anything like a Platonic sense.

Telemachus, too, voyages to learn to become like his father, to overcome his excessive respect (*aidos*, III, 24). He already has too much of what Achilles had too little. As the disguised goddess of wisdom says to him:

> Few are the sons who are equal to their fathers;
> Most are worse, but few are better than their fathers.
> If you would not be a coward hereafter, and senseless,
> If the counsel of Odysseus has not forsaken you wholly,
> Your hope in that case is to bring these deeds to pass.
>
> (II, 276–280)

Telemachus passes over into his manhood; it is through him, as he moves into the present of the poem, that the narrative begins, evoking both memory and futurity in the longing for Odysseus, and also the dim sense that the father who has been gone so long may have come to his mortal end.

Telemachus, risking a voyage to learn the facts about his father, learns that no simple facts are forthcoming, because facts undergo the alteration of memory; the glorious Trojan war that Nestor tells about, in which he and Odysseus were equal counsellors, does not seem the exploit that subtle Helen and Menelaus remember, focusing as it does on the deceptions of the wooden horse.

How a man sees things depends on who he is; Intelligence is the presiding goddess. These gods are not objective, standing for the unknown-and-visible, as in the *Iliad*. They are clear in the *Odyssey*, and yet they too vary according to the observer, who is then himself objectively presented in the foreground of the poem. To Menelaus they are beings who must be propitiated. Nestor sees them as stubborn (III, 147), Helen as capable of great favor (IV, 220–222), the Phaeacians as always benign. At the same time this particular people takes the gods with sophisticated familiarity and humor, laughing at Demodocus' tale about Ares and Aphrodite; adultery occasions mirth for them—the very evil that Penelope has been avoiding for twenty years.

Character is fate: who a man is also determines how far he goes, how widely he is tested, what sort of a home he has made his own. In this sense men get exactly what they deserve, a moral transparently presented at the very outset in Zeus' speech to Athene and the other gods:

> Well now, how mortal men do accuse the gods!

They say evils come from us, yet they themselves
By their own recklessness get pains beyond their lot.

The Phaeacians are near to the gods (V, 35); they dwell far away from other mortals, having been close to the challenging Cyclops. Their location and their way of life are taken altogether for a total character that compasses Odysseus at this stage, but does not absorb him.

Each man is closed in the world of his own perceptions, and so is each people. Each place visited is an episode for the variable Odysseus, as in a lesser way for his searching son. Nestor lives a simple life, his boys doing his work for him. It is a comfortable life, too; there are smooth stones before his palace. Beyond his imagination, overland from his territory, lies the elegant court of Menelaus, come upon characteristically in the midst of a wedding celebration. In that court there is a dominance of ceremoniousness all but total. But neither of Telemachus' hosts exhibits any trait so surprising as the near-supernaturalism of the Phaeacians, who also marry their cousins; or the out-and-out incest of the forever dining children of Aeolus.

Pain[2] befalls man, but the gods have taken pain away from the Phaeacians. With pain, the gods have taken away the sort of wholeness exemplified, as always, by Odysseus, who lands naked and hungry on *their* shore just before finally going home. Nestor can face pain in nostalgia, but Menelaus can stand little pain. His "heart breaks," he tells us, when he learns from Proteus that he must sail the relatively little distance from Pharos to Egypt. And he has small patience for combat, as his words imply:

> quick is the glut of cold lamentation
>
> (IV, 103)

Helen passes to her guests a drink with a nepenthe in it, to make the drinker so forget all his pain that:

> He would not shed a tear down his cheeks the whole day long,
> Not if his mother and his father were both to die,
> Not if right in front of him his brother or his dear son
> Were slaughtered with bronze, and he saw it with his own eyes.
>
> (IV, 224–7)

Through the formality of Helen and Menelaus there is felt a

2. George Dimock finds pain the pervasive theme of the *Odyssey*, deriving Odysseus' name from the verb for suffering.

certain coldness. And to Odysseus the Phaeacians display a child-
ish eagerness, for all their own elegance. Menelaus has the
servants bathe Telemachus, a task Nestor assigned to his own
daughter. Anxious about their cleanliness, Menelaus orders the
bath as soon as they arrive; Nestor has had it done as a send-off.
Such coldness, in this poem of heartfelt pain and joy, may evi-
dence cruelty. Menelaus mentions casually that if Odysseus
should care to settle nearby, he would gladly sack and depopu-
late a city for his old friend.

Each character, of place and society, becomes objectified in
the comparing eye of the visitor; Telemachus, like his father,
can compass the varieties by encountering them. Home is the
norm, and Ithaca—unlike Aegea or Ogygia or Phaeacia or Pylos
or Argos—has no special features other than the chaos into
which it has fallen.

Odysseus discovers himself on his way home. The wideness of
the way, the wideness of the character destined for so much
turning, becomes apparent by comparison with the briefer ways
of others, and by the more circumscribed societies, each of
which objectifies a whole moral attitude and destiny: a charac-
ter (*ethos*) of the sort Aristotle asserted this poem to be woven
from (*peplegmenon*).

Ithaca lacks the heightened felicity of Lacedaemon and
Phaeacia, their ordered painlessness and easy delight. Subject to
pain and chaos, it is the more rooted in the human variety
known and sought by its absent overlord, and it stands waiting
in memory, changing in reality, for his rearrival. When he does
arrive, his reinstitution must be so deliberate as to take nearly
half the poem. While Odysseus wanders, Ithaca stands in
unseen relation to him, though from the beginning it is por-
trayed in its changed reality. Perpetually the poem holds his
biased and unswaying nostalgia in a comparison, often unex-
pressed, between home and the place of sojourn. Explicitly he
declares that Calypso surpasses Penelope in appearance and
form, but such ideal excellence pales before the real rootedness
of his mortality. Telemachus, in refusing Menelaus' gift of
horses, admits that Ithaca affords poor pasturage; but he persists
in his superlative praise of the island:

> In Ithaca there are no broad courses or any meadow;
> It has pasture for goats and is pleasanter than a horse pasture.

> But none of the islands that lie by the sea has good meadows
> Or a place for driving horses, and Ithaca surpasses them all.
>
> (IV, 605–8)

So he feels; and so does his father, enough to strain his ingenuity to return there.

This epic hero substitutes supple intelligence for the courage and prowess of the Cid, Beowulf, and Achilles. He follows not a code but the course of his own longing, an inner canon the poem sets out as equally to be trusted. Consistently, then, he does not gather all he knows in order to face the unknown. He acts on hunches (Lestrygonians) or social canniness (Phaeacia) or a surfaced feeling (Calypso) or luck (Circe) or improvised plan (Cyclops). In a sense there is nothing he can rely on as known, because he always copes with a wholly new situation in utter ignorance:

> For I have arrived here as a long suffering stranger
> From afar, from a distant land; so I know no one
> Of the men who conduct this city and its fields.
>
> (VII, 22–25)

He faces not the unknown but the new, not death but transience. Transience, itself a consequence of mortality and a kind of figure for it, replaces death in the imaginative vision of this epic. Longing for permanence drives the resourceful Odysseus round the changing seas and years.

Home itself changes, in the relentless metamorphosis of a third of a life-time. Permanence and change, satisfaction and longing, joy and pain, foresight and happenstance—these never get fixed in hard opposition because Odysseus moves too fast and copes too variously. His fable allows him to embody all these complexities without setting one stiffly against another; without overembroiling himself in any, and also without slighting the real difficulty or allure of a single one.

It is not death he must face. From the present time of the poem on, that risk is slight. In this epic, a life rounds itself out by return to an original mature circumstance that the very course of life has altered.

Change brings pain, and yet the joy of changelessness among the lotus eaters or the Phaeacians lacks the fullness of changeful life. Death may be taken as a fearful circumstance and at the same time as bland fact. The death of his mother Anticleia is spoken of matter-of-factly (XIII, 59) in a salutation wishing joy.

In the seeming universality of transience, arrival seems forever debarred, and Odysseus comes back a second time to Aeolus, who will not help him; to Circe, who greets him with a warning. Back again he comes, also, to Scylla and Charybdis. Death lies as a test in the future. Though the hero's own death is vague and remote, he must risk it and pass its country in order to return. Odysseus can get back only by visiting the dead, all the way past the eternally shrouded Cimmerians. Even then it takes the escort of the Phaeacians, who are near to gods, to get him back. The Phaeacian vessel, moving like a star, unerringly and effortlessly swift, bears Odysseus in a sleep "most like to death" (XIII, 879-92) to the home he has not been able to sight for twenty years.

Odysseus has changed so much himself, and Ithaca has become so remote to him, that he does not know where he is when he wakes up there. Of the disguised Athene he asks a question at once obvious and profound: are the inhabitants hospitable or wild?

All is old, and all is new. If Odysseus did not recognize old elements in any new situation, he could not exercise his many wiles. If he did not have to confront the new, there would be less need for any wiles at all.

The need dwindles at the end, but it has not disappeared. At the end of his life he must undertake another journey across the sea and set up a sacrifice to Poseidon among men who do not know the sea (XI, 12 ff).

Odysseus stands midway between the easier returners, achievers of a simpler permanence, Menelaus and Nestor, and those who have died on the return, the victims to change, Agamemnon and Ajax, not to mention all his own followers.

Permanence brings joy, transience, pain. The living sustain a subtle balance between permanence and transience, and so between joy and pain. The sea is sparkling but treacherous; to the solitary Odysseus Ogygia is joyful for its unearthly beauty but painful for its not being home. Pain coalesces with joy, or else a life is shown to lack the epic wholeness: if pain becomes total, one is to die; if joy fully dominates, one enters the lifeless permanence of the Lotus Eaters and the Phaeacians, whom Odysseus' long tale of suffering fills not with tears like his own but with a feeling of charm, the poem twice says (*kelethmos*: XI, 334; XIII, 2).

To return brings joy but causes pain. It is of the joy of return that Agamemnon speaks (IV, 522)—he who least of all would have cause to remember that joy. Yet the pain of becoming reinstated in a changed home offsets, precedes, and intensifies, the joy of restitution.

In his coping, Odysseus works his way through contrarieties; pain and suffering he names at once when he is asked what his wanderings have brought. Joy can be as much a trial as pain; heartbroken with longing on Calypso's isle, he refuses her blissful immortality but enjoys her in the cave. He lives a year with Circe. The Lotus Eaters, and Phaeacians, and the Sirens all promise—the first could even fulfill—a painless existence wherein the pain might be obviated and even the longing be gone. But the fullness of life demands the wholeness of longing; and Odysseus, delighted and also pained, pushes on to his return. All sufferings of wandering are told, after the tears of a delightful song, to the banqueting, hedonistic court of an Alcinoos who has already promised escort home. The habit of Ithaca counters the novelty of the strange delights, and yet habit too is the enemy of the remembered home: Odysseus stays seven years on Calypso's island.

Within its scheme of variety, this broad poem can vary the key of an alternation between joy and pain without changing its tone. Each episode has a different flavor of joy or pain. As Odysseus sails away from Cyclops, he gets exulting delight in exchange for teeth-gnashing despair. Aeolus occasions first impulsive gladness and then a resigned, fearful despondency. An ocean of moods for the longing hero is held in the single vision of the poem.

2

The poem sustains a sense of the hero's fine equanimity in transience and permanence, in sorrow and joy, by having placed him in a flexible situation where he transcends every person and every people he meets. The equanimity of the hero also enters the verse, for example in its descriptions of the visible world through which Odysseus moves.

A fine veil of poetry, simple and delectating, limns the changing landscapes, none so fully described as Ithaca, and all consequently more immediately redolent of an almost lyric singleness, a seemingly mythic signification. But the significance merely impresses in passing, and does not construct allegories. What are the Cimmerians at the bounds of the deep-flowing ocean, shrouded in darkness and cloud, who never see the beams of the sun or the starry heavens? They are far (Ithaca is nearness) and shrouded (the mists part often in the clarity of the Adriatic sun; Ithaca sees sun and starry heavens). They stand before the underworld, sharing some of its obscurity.

As Stella points out, the fruits and trees of this landscape are described more realistically than the fabulous vegetation found not only in the jewelled forests of Gilgamesh, but in such Greek legends as the Golden Apples of Hesperides. Yet as Max Treu says, we cannot distinguish between fairytale and real in the landscape descriptions of the *Odyssey*. Its epithets are at once evocative and descriptive, far looser than those in the *Iliad*:

> The sun arose, leaving the *lovely* lake,
> Into the *much-bronze* heaven, where for immortals it shone,
> And for mortal men upon the *life-giving* earth.
>
> (III, 1–3)

All the grandeur of the *Iliad*, as Longinus says, but less intensity. *Polychalchon*,[3] much-bronze, sets off no contrasts between "lovely" and "life-giving." The attributions are not faceted situationally, as they are in the *Iliad*. They merely rise to their seemingly haphazard descriptiveness, and their rightness seems to reside somewhat in a mythic resonance. The real and the fairy-tale are mingled in the memory of the recounting Odysseus and the perceptions of the poem's hearer. Against the joy of a given place stands the hero's own pain; against the beauty of life the hard risk of death, and the difficult, losing battle against time. At the end of all the easy hospitalities of Phaeacia, of the checked Circe, of Calypso, lies the difficult restitution in Ithaca. The transience of an arriver's longing, of the guest's contingency, clings to the poetry, for Odysseus' longing son as for himself:

> And they came to hollow Lacedaemon full of ravines.
>
> (IV, 1)

This is a new sight to Telemachus, a temporary one; his enjoyment of the visual loveliness, the presence of this poetic line in the narrative, is tinged with his fearful search for light

3. Even if this word carries a memory of an Aegean primitive concept of a bronze heaven, as Stella asserts, we must decide what the epithet denotes in the poem.

about his father. Helen's nepenthe does not last for him, though it may for the Lacedaemonian court.

> They when they saw it
> Wondered at the house of the king nourished by Zeus;
> Like the beam of the sun it was or like the moon.
>
> (IV, 43–5)

But the sun goes down, the moon rises, and by day or night there is toil. Lacedaemon for the son, like Phaeacia or Ogygia for the father, is a delightful interlude, something unreal in the reality of life. A man who has a full life on his hands can see the loveliness, along with some of the unreality. His eyes enjoy the glitter, but his heart is in his mouth; the words catch the glitter, the rhythm moves wave on nostalgic wave in the feeling of the poem.

The hexameter—lightly!—bears the burden of sadness, reiterating in its "disappointed" last foot the sorrow of the total fable. Poetry makes people weep in the *Odyssey*, even finally in the Phaeacian court. Odysseus himself weeps to hear of Troy, though he weeps behind his veil.

"The accents of the Homeric hexameter are the soft rustle of a leaf in the midday sun, the rhythm of *matter*"—Spengler's fine ear has picked up the characteristic rhythm of the *Odyssey*. Not, I feel, of the *Iliad*. In both poems, of course, quantity determines the main rhythm, and not accent. Where Vergil patterns the subordinate accents, Homer lets them fall where they may. This randomness in the *Iliad* produces a surging afflatus, rather the way the free meter of the ballad does. In the *Odyssey*, I do not hear these free syllables as surging. The unaccounted accents play, as it were, over the surface of the statement, as the words themselves seem to do. In the *Iliad* the unaccounted accents do a more strenuous work, and yet are closer to prose in their lack of emphasis; in the *Odyssey* they twitch the veil of the poetry, rhythmically carrying a sense of the variety of life.

The poetry reveals its lightness in the very particularity of its designations; it touches lightly on literalness, and quite haphazardly (*pace* Auerbach). All is known, but the known is a mystery. Home remains the same, but time changes it. Take the line about the constellation Bear, "which they also call by the name Wagon":

οἴη δ' ἄμμορός ἐστι λοετρῶν Ὠκεανοῖο.

And it alone has no share in the washings of Ocean.

(v, 275)

The statement conveys a literal piece of astronomical fact, but with a light resonance that lies in each word. *"Oie,"* alone, echoes the aloneness of Odysseus. "Has no share," or "unfated" (*ammoros*): in the very negation lies a whole sense of fate, at once specific and general. The "washings" (*loetroi*) are carrying Odysseus too; he is caught in the wash of the ocean stream above which gleams the Bear. In its suggesting of analogy, though, the line is not metaphoric. It merely speaks of the natural world, the stars and the sea, in words that usually apply to man, and so it hints at a participation in a total situation which is not patterned but merely moves ahead in its predictable but incalculable alterations. This hint is absent from the line when it occurs in the *Iliad* merely to describe a point of Achilles' shield.

And the tone of the poem, the fine veil of what, for lack of a more delicate term, we may call irony—that tone veils all the actions and the landscapes. The hexameter carries that tone, forbidding, as it were, even the most dire incident from carrying a tragic cast. The elegiac becomes a delectated likeness. At the height of the grisly Cyclops episode, a joke: Odysseus is "no man." Homer may have got this joke from a folk-tale or not; it has the same effect in the poem, the consonant presentation of an exultant joy within a crushing sadness.

Through its tone of equanimity, the verse conveys pain and joy without setting one paradoxically off against the other, as the *Iliad* somewhat schematically sets the actuality of pain against the memory of joy. The veil of mystery covers everything in the *Odyssey*; yet everything also shows through the tonal veil. Deception comes up again and again, the host of disguises and feints and subtle unmentioned calculations and adjustments which every character makes, and preeminently the resourceful Odysseus. Even gods deceive; right at the start in Book I they quickly hold their committee meeting about Odysseus, while his enemy Poseidon, the opposition, is conveniently far away among the Ethiopians.

For all the deceptions, clarity. For all the caprice, justice. For all the wanderings, return. Here the world is utterly clear and whole, and utterly mysterious. Its clarity is its mystery, the poetry is declaring. The same blue Aegean washes real and miraculous shores, and the real and the miraculous differ only in incidental, equally perceptible details, which the poetry proffers:

> On the hearth a big fire was burning, and the smell from afar
> Of cedar and easy-split pulp was exhaled to the island
> As it blazed. She within, singing in a lovely voice,
> Going to and fro at the loom, wove with a golden distaff.
> Wood was growing around the cave in abundance,
> Alder and black poplar and well-scented cypress,
> Where the birds with their long wings went to sleep,
> Horned owls and hawks and, with their long tongues,
> Salt water crows, who are busy with the things of the sea.
>
> (v, 59–67)

A superlative place, but with a quality finely perceptible as of itself; distinct from the superlative of Lacedaemon or Phaeacia or Aeaea. The cave, the trees, the birds, and later the springs and meadows, characterize the physical world of Calypso, which is at the same time her world of spirit, just as the deepness of Ithaca resides for the poetry, as for the naming Telemachus, in the very physical homeliness and roughness of the place.

Often we are given designations for the sea, wine-faced or grey, Protean as the numberless lands are different. Yet each is clear and whole unto itself, each capable of receiving at times the enumerative detail Auerbach claims is typical of the *Odyssey* generally.

Homer, however, is not so enumerative in his verse as Auerbach claims. The poet does tend to linger over detail of the narrative, as Auerbach follows Schiller in asserting; but not utterly for the sake of the detail. If we cannot read some other significance into the detail—the ritual use of Calypso's trees, for example—we cannot obliterate significance either. Certainly to assert that Homer tells "everything" would be to make him inarticulate. He must select, though more abundantly than the inspired author of *Genesis*.

Nor can it be said, with Auerbach, that the *Odyssey* has no "background," no hidden depths of motive. It is all foreground, to be sure, but a light irony holds all the detail. That light irony constitutes the background, the delicate and profound sense of success in transience, of unfinality in any terror, which renders the epic sense of life to the *Odyssey*, lightening the poetry and unifying the fable; so that the poem stands as something at once close to what we expect from a novel in its incident, and yet utterly different from a novel in its final bearing.

3

In all the alterings of circumstance, in all the pains, the hero's self remains wholly adequate in its adaptability (*polutropos*)— and without being defined. To take Odysseus' wanderings as deepening him, the way Cedric Whitman does, involves reading the significance of the places he visits as allegory or symbol. They do have the ring of archetype, and they do figure a total spiritual condition, each of them, mysteriously. Yet to read their significance as symbol or allegory is to pierce the veil of mystery. The depth is all on the surface, a sunlit mystery. No totality glides like a Moby Dick in the darkness beneath these waters. To interpret the surface of this poem metaphorically is to translate the surface as gaining significance from some depth; but the significances are all there on the surface, embodied simply in landscape and lightness of gesture.

Achilles develops and realizes his manhood. Odysseus moves ahead with his into time, changing only as he ages, while events at once tax and fortify him. He simply exists. No coordinated social world can deepen him; there is only the series of unpredictable surfaces, each complete and partial in itself, which he shows himself capable by meeting, and whole by transcending. Intelligence attends him from first to last, and the manifestation of Athene at his landing on Ithaca attests no special consideration, no final success, but only a momentary embodiment, as the world of his striving has actualized itself under his feet without his being aware of it.

When Odysseus speaks to himself, as he does after having set out from Ogygia (V, 299ff), the soliloquy explores no motive but merely develops and estimates the incidence of misfortune. Once again, it is all on the surface: the depth inheres in the irony with which it is presented, an irony so slight as to seem transparent, vanishing at a breath.

The irony may at numerous moments emerge into event. Odysseus slights Calypso in his account to Arete, falsifies his contact with Nausicaa, and delicately implies a refusal of Alcinous' marriage offer by mentioning in the course of his narrative how he has often refused such offers elsewhere. Menelaus, who had to wander years because he had slighted the gods, gives Telemachus a libation bowl! So, the poem hints, he has learned his lesson. Athene sacrifices to her enemy Poseidon. But the events need not be ironic; they may be deadly serious, and irony is still conveyed in the uniform tone of the verse.

Without the *poetry*, the flexible Odyssean hexameter, the

humor would be episodic, and so would the nostalgia. The variety of incident would then merely add up to a superficial romance of the picaresque with some fine detail and occasional lyric moments, rather like the *Lusiads*. But in the *Odyssey* nostalgia comments on humor. Humor and nostalgia blend but do not fuse in the epic unity of this poem, lighter than the *Iliad*, but no less profound.

Suffering, even the dark terror of Cyclops or Odysseus' wholesale slaughter of the suitors, is kept serenely in vision, as it is not in even so equanimous a comedy as the *Tempest*. Only loosely can the *Odyssey* be called a comedy, or even a comic epic. It is an epic whose lightness compasses comic events, and also tragic; that allows of both tragic and comic events without inventing a whole philosophic relation for them (or a Dantesque justification) beyond the unitary tonal feeling of myth and verse.

JOHN H. FINLEY, JR.

The Heroic Mind†

In the seventeenth book of the *Odyssey* when Odysseus, still in the guise of a beggar, at last first approaches his house and the dog Argus, left behind twenty years before and now old and neglected, sees his master, lowers his ears, wags his tail, but lacks strength to move, does Odysseus commiserate with him or pat him? On the contrary, after secretly wiping away a tear, he says to his companion the swineherd, "What a handsome dog there on the dung-heap! But was he fast in the chase or simply a table-dog?" And the swineherd gives the expected answer, "That is the dog that Odysseus left behind when he went to Troy, and none was faster or braver to track down beasts in the depths of the thick woods." Odysseus enters the house, and the dog dies, the first to have recognized him at home. He had for a dog the virtue that Hector's helmet had for a helmet. Each, like all the other people and objects in the poems, keeps its inherent nature, and a chief marvel of the poems might be said to be the ineffable act of concentration whereby men and women, great

† From John H. Finley, Jr., *Four Stages of Greek Thought* (Stanford: Stanford University Press, 1966), pp. 4–9 and 18–21. Reprinted by permission of the publisher. © 1966 by the Board of Trustees of the Leland Stanford Junior University.

people, small people, towns, fields, animals, seas, rivers, earth, sky, and the lucent gods themselves, remain each distinct while jointly comprising the brilliant world.

How conceive the working of such a mind? Theoretical answers, though hardly complete, go a certain distance, and chief among them, it scarcely needs be said, is the work of the Californian Milman Parry, who died at thirty-three in 1935 after revolutionizing Homeric studies. Apparently as early as when he first read Homer in college, he thought him so unlike other poets that he must have composed in some unusual way. This different way, Parry came to think, was the so-called oral method of composition which he spent his short life elaborating, partly by theory, partly by learning Serbian and coming to know at first hand the oral poetry of Jugoslavia. Briefly put, this theory of oral composition postulates two main conditions: first, a body of legend about bygone heroes whose feats gathered about a few famous enterprises; second, and more crucial, a body of language passed from generation to generation but freshly used and slightly changed by each age and singer that enabled singers to compose complete verses as they went along. The familiar Homeric line introducing a speech may illustrate in small the complex process: "Him answering addressed swift-footed Achilles." The line falls into halves: Achilles at the end, how he spoke at the start. Now Parry noted that any other character, if provided with a suitable epithet, might metrically replace Achilles at the end of the line, a character with a long name like Agamemnon being joined with a short epithet, a character with a short name like Zeus with a long epithet. Similarly at the start of the line "answering" was not the only stance in which a character might speak; he might do so "standing up," "with a scowl," "with good intent," "fainting," or in a number of other ways that—and this is the important point—are metrically equivalent to "answering." Taken together, the options at the end and at the start of the line give the singer a set of choices by which he may introduce any character speaking in some fitting way. One may not call such a line memorized in the usual sense of the word; rather, it is composed from memorized elements, proves metrical because these elements were so intended, suits all the characters and many kinds of situations because its terms had been perfected for that purpose—in short, lets the singer simultaneously advance his story and compose a verse.

Needless to say, this simple example does small justice to the subtle tradition that supplied a singer with fit and metrical words in the quick moment when he needed them, supplied him too with procedures and motifs for describing battles and banquets and messages and a thousand such recurrent events, supplied him even with the tone and cast of a gallery of characters. The extraordinary fact that one must keep recalling is that through the centuries when the art was elaborated no one ever read a poem or had in fact learned anything by reading; in everyone's mind, singer and listener alike, lay the words of the poetic tradition that he had known since childhood and that alone lifted above the small present its arc of completer relevance and meaning. If everyone in a part of his being thought in this greater language and even Achilles in the *Iliad* is pictured as solacing himself by singing, some people by special gifts lived themselves more fully into it, each necessarily in his own way, since, though the language was traditional, it was not fixed in books but had to be recreated by each man, inevitably with the changes that time and temperament dictated. How the Homeric poems came to be written down when the very nature of the art implies the lack of writing is another kind of question, fixed in circumstance and doubtless lost beyond recall. Homer lived in Ionia—so much ancient tradition and his language make clear—in the late eighth century, it is thought, when writing was first emerging beside the oral art. Was he recognized as so great that professional singers, perhaps of his own family, wanted his songs as heirloom of their guild, and did some clever young man—a grandson, one would like to think— see how writing could serve the purpose? If one can only guess in such matters, the oral character of the poems is beyond guess, and it is this that brings us back to the crystalline Homeric world of Hector's helmet and the dog Argus. The helmet shines and the dog was swift, partly because Homer's epithets, that functional element of his oral style, declared them such. Similarly all the other characters and objects of the poems keep identities that the very nature of oral verse-making compelled them to keep. Had Homer conceived the thought of substituting new words and epithets for the received, he would in that act have become a literary poet, and the clear world of his recurrent shapes would have vanished.

Yet that world stayed fixed and clear not only by reason of the oral style, but because Homer and presumably his audience as well thought and wanted it such. The legendary figures of Troy and Mycenae, Ithaca and Pylos, lived on untouched by the thought that they were only thoughts. Hence we return to more elusive questions: what is implied by this unfaltering confidence in outer reality, and why has it so deep a grip on us? It may be said of literary styles that the more elaborate their structures, the more these reflect a man's conscious and ordering thought, and, by the same token, the less they reflect external objects. Thought proceeds by scheme and sequence; it manipulates, puts things where it wants them, makes different designs from any that the eyes see, and, what is more, knows that it is doing so. Conscious art selects from nature and by selecting adds. In the process the forms of nature inevitably take second place; their edges are blunted to fit the ruling design, and the complex final effect, being composed of many parts, diminishes the being of any one part. Yet the price of this triumph is violation of our senses. We evidently see at any moment a sequence of sharp particulars—light at a window, a tree trunk, the gray of a rock—single, peremptory impressions, moving in endless specificity across our vision. A part of our life belongs to them; we know the world and feel at home in it not least through these sure reminders. Happiness, one sometimes thinks, is clarity of vision, moments when things stand clear in sharpest outline, undimmed by familiarity as if revealed for the first time. Such moments bring back, so to speak, the memory of Eden sparkling on the first day of creation, the tree of life soaring in the middle, and if Eden be related to our childhood, they bring back childhood too. In this spirit Gladstone entitled his book on Homer *Juventus Mundi,* the world's youth—evidently not because the *Iliad* is comforting but because it is clear. Literary history abounds in reactions against elaborate and mental styles —for example, in recent times that of Hemingway against, say, Henry James. I remember from an otherwise forgotten story of Hemingway a sentence about a bare light bulb glaring in a diner; the sentence was complete; one saw just that. No more than Hector's shining helmet did the light bulb announce a happy ending, yet it was to this extent happy and confident: it signified impressions that one could trust. However intoxicating the attractions of intellect and however essential to the structures by which we live, something in us wants also the clear signals of the senses by which alone the world is made fresh and definite.

Now, needless to say, words and thoughts, being products of our minds, cannot capture reality, which remains beyond us, an object of faith, not of knowledge. Presumably no leaf or blade of grass or person or object exactly resembles another, but being unable to comprehend a world of unutterable and endless differences, we, as Aristotle said, put things into classes, and keep our sanity by speaking of oak tree or maple tree, man or woman, Frenchman or Englishman—just as if one of these quite resembled another. . . . Agamemnon concludes, "Thus not even in death did you lose celebrity; forever among all men will your great fame endure, Achilles. But where for me is this regard, after I wound the skein of war? At my return Zeus devised grim ruin for me at the hands of Aegisthus and my baleful wife." After this interchange they notice the ghosts of the suitors; and when Agamemnon asks them who they are and is told, he breaks into passionate praise of Odysseus: felicitous man, he got in Penelope a prudent and faithful wife, report of whose merit will never die but will be fashioned by immortals into song for earthly men. Here at the end of the poem Penelope shares the honor that Odysseus has had throughout it, and husband and wife emerge together as the fit and joint theme of poetry.

Now two of the most gifted recent writers on Homer, Schadewaldt and Whitman, emphasize in ways that may be omitted here the degree to which both the *Iliad* and the *Odyssey* are composed with a sense of the whole Trojan tradition; they illuminate it, sum it up, complete it. If so, this nearly final scene of the *Odyssey* gives something like the ultimate judgment. Of the three greatest figures, one, Agamemnon, though a king on earth and the most powerful of known men, is effectively eliminated; he died miserably, and if his death did not fit his life, it bears on and relates to it. The two remaining figures, Achilles and Odysseus—or in the latter case, the paired figures of Odysseus and Penelope—contain the sum and meaning. Of Odysseus, more in a moment by way of conclusion; of Achilles, he is in the keeping of the Muses. So Pindar later thought in a noble poem on the mingled ruin and grandeur of the Persian war; Achilles remained to him the example of those who had died, and then as formerly the Muses alone give comment. His fame approached him, so to speak, not from the front with foreseen and calculable invitation, but unexpectedly, out of disillusion, anger, and self-reproach. Yet he remains described by the first brightness of expectation that took him to the unknown of Troy, and by his affinity with the measureless sea that shines beyond the fixed and bounded present. The *Iliad*, like all tragedies but seemingly more clearly than any other, is at one and the same time paradoxically very dark and very bright: dark in the actual unfulfillment of what might have been expected and seemed possible, bright in the ardor of that expectation and its persistence over change. Hector's shining helmet and all the other clear and beautiful objects that comprise the visible flash of the world fit and solicit the ardor of this response.

Finally, to turn to Odysseus, the sea that partly describes Achilles obviously describes him too—it is his teacher and he its aptest pupil—but in a somewhat different way. Hector in the *Iliad* is a figure of the land, and the water that identifies him is the benign flow of streams and springs; in his last flight from Achilles, he runs beside the hot and cold springs where the wives and daughters of the Trojans had washed their shining clothes "in peacetime before the sons of the Achaeans came." Land and springs comprise an idyl of peace. Achilles in the *Iliad* is associated also with fire—the fire both of glory and of ruin—and his destruction of Hector and by implication of Troy suggests the lightning stroke that destroys the benign but impermanent house. The house is human; the lightning half-divine. These elements recur with changed suggestion in the *Odyssey*. One never quite knows whether Odysseus likes or dislikes his travels; we first see him on a headland of Calypso's island willing to die if he may only see the smoke upleaping from his rooftop at home; wrecked later at sea, he wishes that he might have died at Troy. Yet his insatiable curiosity keeps him in the Cyclops's cave when his companions want to leave, and he has to be reminded that he has stayed a year with Circe. He is marked by the sea, which makes him the great man that he is, yet in his humanity he renounces it for home. Two episodes describe his choice and its result. The first is when Calypso, justly claiming to be more beautiful than Penelope, offers him agelessness and immortality if he will stay with her; though aware of her divine beauty, he refuses. A famous description had recounted the island's ravishing freshness; in renouncing it, he gives up the eternity of nature—as it were, of untracked beaches and blue water forever flowing in and out of caves—in favor of his mortal identity at home. The second episode is the prophecy of the seer Teiresias in the underworld. Odysseus will indeed reach home, says the seer, but then must take an oar on his shoulder and seek a land where men are ignorant of salt and where a passerby, spying the oar, will call it a winnowing fan; he must then build an altar and sacrifice to Poseidon; returning home, he will rule in peace over a happy people and reach a shining old age, and a gentle death will come to him from the sea. Odysseus is like a runner who cannot stop at once on finishing a race; he must exorcise and placate some restlessness of the sea that survives in him; even when he does so and has pacified Poseidon, something of the sea will return in his death. This wonderful prophecy declares him the reconciler of two worlds; he does achieve home and is profoundly grateful to have done so, yet he would know its virtues less fully than he does—would miss its wonder—if travel had not taught him. He ends, if one may put it so, by crossing to the other side of the measureless sea of Achilles' youth, and the land that he finds is different from Hector's land, because return is different from never having gone away, and attainment different from keeping. In like spirit, the former destructive fire now becomes purifying. A sulphurous thunderbolt destroys Odysseus's companions when they have sinfully eaten the cattle of the sun, and he purifies his house with sulphur after killing the suitors. The fire of the *Odyssey* is that of the hearth and of life itself. On finishing his last battle with the sea and reaching much-spent the land of the Phaeacians, he finds shelter in a fall of olive leaves beneath thick intertwined boughs, as a man on a remote farm shelters a brand beneath the black ash, saving the seed of fire.

CHARLES SEGAL

Transition and Ritual in Odysseus' Return†

Passage, transition, change: the most familiar phenomenon of human life, and also the most difficult to comprehend. It is no

† N.B. This paper is a revised and expanded form of an essay which appeared in *Masterpieces of Western Literature: Contemporary Essays in Interpretation*, eds. Alex Page and Leon Barron (Dubuque, Iowa: W. C. Brown Co., 1966). I am grateful to the editors and publisher for permission to reuse some of this material here. Translations, unless otherwise noted, are by the author. From *La Parola Del Passato*, September–October, 1967, pp. 321–342. Reprinted by permission of the publisher.

wonder that this theme, in one form or another, is one of the central concerns of Greek philosophy, from Heraclitus and Parmenides to Plato and Aristotle. In placing at the center of the *Odyssey* the hero's passage from the marvels of Phaeacia to Ithacan reality and probability, Homer sets out in high relief, for the first time in Western literature, man's sense of the inexhaustible mystery of the changes of state or being, outward and inward, that constitute his life.[1]

The universal fact of change in human life is symbolized in the *Odyssey*, as throughout Western literature, by the journey itself.[2] Yet Homer's hero, unlike Dante's or Tennyson's Ulysses, does not simply travel in search of new experiences. His journey is a *return*. Thus we are anchored in the world of his human past, Ithaca and the Greek mainland, in the first four books before we are allowed to follow Odysseus over distant seas. We are first shown the past which is to be regained and the weakened order which is to be restored.

In most societies changes of state are marked by rituals which help define the change, visibly confront its reality, and orient the individual in the new world he has entered. Such rituals, or *rites de passage*, seem to follow a more or less constant pattern and to show three major phases. They comprise, according to Van Gennep, *rites of separation, rites of transition, and rites of incorporation*.[3] This division is useful for analyzing Odysseus' return. The journey between Troy and Ogygia constitute a gradual *separation* from his Trojan warrior past (compare the widespread concern for the de-sanctification of the returning warrior most familiar, perhaps, from the Roman practices of lustration). The sojourn with the Phaeacians is a primarily *transitional* situation, succeeding the total suspension from 'reality' on Ogygia and preceding the re-entrance into Ithaca. The Ithacan adventures, then, are mostly concerned with his *reincorporation* into the society he left behind, and fittingly culminate in a re-

---

1. For the significance of the Phaeacian episode and the hero's reclaiming of his humanity, see C. P. Segal, *The Phaeacians and the Symbolism of Odysseus' Return*, "Arion", 1, no. 4, 1962, 17–64.
2. For the symbolic implications of the journey in the 'epic of quest', see Gertrude R. Levy, *The Sword from the Rock* (London, 1953), chap. 5 and *passim*.
3. Arnold van Gennep, *The Rites of Passage* (1908; Engl. Transl., Chicago, 1960), 21 and *passim*; also the introduction by Solon T. Kimball, vii ff.

enactment of marriage. The analogies should not be pressed, and there is a certain overlapping, naturally. Yet both the schema of the ritual and the structure of the poem share a common perception of a universal experience in human life.

The significance of the broad movement of the Return is reflected in various specific situations of transition throughout the poem; and these transitional situations are reinforced in turn by certain recurrent themes or motifs, well-known in almost every mythic journey, as for instance the crossing of water, the changing of clothes, the sharing of food. Such themes in their various repetitions throughout the work gain a deepening symbolic significance, an effect which is totally consistent with the nature of oral epic which proceeds in terms of repeated themes or groups of themes, contracted, expanded, elaborated, as the poet requires.[4] The verbal repetition of the particular formula or formulas involved in such motifs often underlines the thematic repetition.[5] Indeed, the Homeric oral formulaic style itself almost 'ritualizes' such actions, presents them as rituals,

4. For the recurrent theme in oral epic see Albert B. Lord, *The Singer of Tales* (Harvard Studies in Comparative Literature, vol. 24; Cambridge, Mass., 1960), 148: 'Each theme small or large—one might say, each formula—has around it an aura of meaning which has been put there by all the contexts in which it has occurred in the past. It is the meaning that has been given it by the tradition in its creativeness. To any given poet at any given time, this meaning involves all the occasions on which he has used the theme, especially those contexts in which he uses it most frequently; it involves also all the occasions on which he has heard it used by others, particularly by those singers whom he first heard in his youth, or by great singers later by whom he was impressed. To the audience the meaning of the theme involves its own experience of it as well. The communication of this supra-meaning is possible because of the community of experience of poet and audience'. See in general chap. 4. 'The Theme' and especially pp. 89–91 and 109 for ritual elements in recurrent epic themes. For the symbolic possibilities on the level of the formula rather than the theme see Cedric H. Whitman, *Homer and the Heroic Tradition* (Cambridge, Mass., 1958), chaps. 1 and 6.

5. The formula in Homer may be defined as a recurrent unit of fixed metrical value; and for the orally composing poet this unit, rather than the individual word, serves as the building block of his hexameter line. These formulas may consist of a noun plus fixed epithet, like 'rosy-fingered dawn', or a recurring predicate, like 'so speaking he went off'. I use the term 'formulaic', however, somewhat more broadly here, to apply also to the repeated passages of one or more lines that describe certain standard actions, like bathing, eating, the embarkation of ships. On the formula in general see Lord (above, note 4) chap. 3.

frozen and stylized into a set pattern. These formulas, then, provide a familiar and constant background for the newness which Odysseus is ever encountering in the exotic world of his adventures.

Yet there is a latent tension between the formulaic language of the *Odyssey* on the one hand and the richness of the hero's experiences and the fabulousness of the poem's far-flung geography on the other, a tension which marks a step beyond the *Iliad*. In the *Iliad* style and matter are more fully one. They fuse more harmoniously in the poem to produce its atmosphere of grandly austere concentration, its unrelenting insistence on the tragedies focused and held before our eyes. In the *Odyssey* action and structure are less fully unified and more multifarious than in the *Iliad*, and the formulaic language too is perhaps somewhat more loosely used.[6]

On the other hand, the *Odyssey* makes use of those primitive strata of myth and ritual that have so intrigued scholars like J. A. K. Thomson, Gertrude Levy, and, more recently, Gabriel Germain. Perhaps the very forces that were causing the loosening of the severer structure and style of the *Iliad* also stimulated interest in the primitive reaches of mythic lore behind elements like Ogygia, Circe, the Cyclops, the Phaeacians. The *Odyssey's* greater openness of style, by comparison to the *Iliad*—for which Cedric Whitman has suggested analogies with the Proto-Attic style in pottery—leaves it receptive to the strange, shadowy figures of the pre-heroic past.

The ritual elements of the *Odyssey*, then, should be considered in close connection with these roots in folk-tale and in the common Mediterranean (and Bronze Age) storehouse of fable and legend. The blending of these common Aegean elements with the formal, demanding qualities of the Greek epic hexameter makes the *Odyssey* a poem which, like its hero, straddles two worlds, whereas the *Iliad* plants itself gigantically and immovably in one.

Deeply underlying these themes of transition is a basic mythical pattern fundamental to the epic of quest or search, namely the cyclic alternation of life and death; the rediscovery of 'life'

6. For this relative looseness of language and structure in the *Odyssey* see D. Page, *The Homeric Odyssey* (Oxford, 1955), *passim*; Whitman (above, note 4), 287 ff.; G. S. Kirk, *The Songs of Homer* (Cambridge, 1962), 167, 206, 355 ff., especially 361–62.

after a period of sterility, darkness, imprisonment; the ultimate victory of life over death, of order over disorder. This kind of epic, of which *Gilgamesh* is the prototype, embodies the experience (to quote G. R. Levy) 'of loss and segregation, the temptations of love and fear, the vision of death and the return of the hero to the starting point, changed by the knowledge and acceptance of defeat'.[7] The *Odyssey*, though undoubtedly based on such a mythic pattern, transcends it by turning its significance away from the originally ritually enacted death and rebirth of cosmic divinities to the realities and possibilities of human action and human nature. Yet beneath the man-centered action the underlying mythic structure still makes itself felt and gives the poem what Northrop Frye calls the 'encyclopaedic range' of high epic, an inclusiveness which embraces symbolically the totality of human experience.[8]

I define ritual in this context as a regularly performed action carried out in a stylized manner to indicate a significant contact with supernatural powers which themselves embody the basic mysteries of our existence. It is possible that some of these transitional situations in the poem dimly echo *actual* transitional rituals of a remote past. Here, however, I am not concerned with survivals of actual rituals, but rather with the literary function of situations of transition in the poem as a work of art. Even in this limited sense, the ritual elements open into the realm of the sacred and the numinous and thus add a significant dimension to the poem's meaning. For a society such as Homer's the 'sacred and the profane' as Mircea Eliade has shown, are still closely united, and the division between man's physical and spiritual life is much less clear than in the modern Western world.

It should, then, be possible to follow the unfolding of the Return through an examination of some of the recurrent motifs that involve or accompany transition. Those which I shall consider are *sleep*, the *bath*, *purification*, and the *threshold*. All, as will appear, are somehow associated with the mystery of passage between worlds, and all belong to the realm of experience where known and unknown cross. Only the middle two, however, Purification and the Bath, can properly be said to be of a ritual nature. The other two, Sleep and the Threshold, can perhaps

7. Levy (above, note 2), 21–22.
8. N. Frye, *Anatomy of Criticism* (Princeton, 1957), 218 ff.

best be described simply as themes of significant transition. In them all, however, is reflected the fullness of the Return, the hero's gradual reclaiming of all that is his own—country, wife, son, father: in short, the wholeness of his humanity.

Sleep. Sleep is perhaps the most obvious means of transition between the real and unreal worlds. Odysseus' Return from the Phaeacians is an awakening out of a sleep 'likest to death' (13.80). Like any passage of change of state, sleep is ambiguous. It can be like death or it can restore to new life. On his wanderings in the fantasy world Odysseus is wary of sleep. As he sails from Calypso's island, Ogygia (5.271), he is the man of alert wakefulness who has learned not to trust sleep. When he has yielded to it, it has brought disaster, as on the voyage from Aeolus' island (10.31 ff.) or on Thrinacia (12.338). It is only when he arrives on Scheria, the Phaeacians' homeland, that sleep becomes positive and restorative. At first he resists it, as he did earlier in the wanderings, fearing wild animals (5.470–73); but the olive thicket saves him, and Athena 'poured sleep upon his eyes, that she might ease him soon of his toilsome weariness' (5.491–93). The next night he sleeps in Alcinous' palace in perfect security, 'on the well-bored bed, under the resounding portico' (7.345). Thus as he emerges from the fantasy world, or at least from its more dangerous aspects, he can yield to sleep in safety. So when the efforts of the Return have been made, he can sleep on the Phaeacians' ship, though they pay dearly for the effortlessness and safety of his passage (see 13.134 ff.).

Sleep seems to frame Odysseus' entire return. On Scheria, the bridge between the fantasy world and reality, he sleeps on arrival and departs in sleep. Later, in the repetition of his Phaeacian adventures to Penelope, the theme of sleep frames his tale. His account to her is introduced thus: 'And she took pleasure in hearing, nor did any sleep fall upon her lids until he had related everything' (23.308–309). His tale ends: 'This was the last tale he spoke of when sweet sleep that looses the limbs came upon him, loosing the cares of his heart' (23.342–43).

Further, Hermes who will bring the message which sets in motion Odysseus' return arrives on Ogygia carrying 'the wand with which he charms the eyes of whomever he wishes and awakens them, in turn, when sleeping' (5.47–48). He then reappears as escorter of the dead with the same wand (and almost the same two lines) immediately after the reunion of Odysseus and Penelope at the beginning of Book 24. Hermes and the dead suitors mark the threatening complement to the life Odysseus has regained. As the god of both sleep and awakening, Hermes unites in himself the poles of failure and success, dream and reality (compare his function of guiding Priam through the limbo between the two camps in *Iliad* 24). Thus on the one hand Hermes is connected with sleep, dormancy, death—that which Odysseus experiences in his 'concealment' on Calypso's island. On the other hand he is connected with the hero's rewakening to conquest over beautiful enchantresses (it is he shows Odysseus how to overcome Circe) or with conquest (of a different kind) over treacherous enemies. It is thus fittingly Hermes and his wand that appear at the beginning and end of the journey. Through them the magical potency of sleep marks the initial stages and the final fulfilment of the hero's Return.

These passages and the recurrence of Hermes and his wand at the two ends of the journey home make the entire Return appear under a great metaphor of sleeping and awakening. Part of Odysseus sleeps and rests until Athena begins to promote the awakening into the real world. On the divine level, she is the real motive force behind the return; she initiates it, unlike Hermes, who is only an agent, a mechanism fulfilling that which has already been set into motion by the will of the gods. It is interesting that Athena too is often the dispenser of sleep in the *Odyssey*, and there is perhaps a deeper connection between her other functions in the poem and her ministrations of sleep. It is perhaps *because* she is the divine force most clearly behind the Return that she controls the mechanism of sleeping and waking, knowing when withdrawal and stillness are necessary and when, the process of recovery and integration complete, the mind may again awaken to the light of reality.

Sleep has a special importance for Penelope. She, indeed, is more frequently associated with sleep than anyone else in the *Odyssey*. Her sleep often follows grief and weeping. It is a constant reminder of the emptiness of her bed, and hence perhaps a retiring back into herself until Odysseus comes. Athena, as the ministrant of sleep for her, may be associated with her deep womanly trust in the return of her husband and her wholeness as the wife of Odysseus. Hence her sleep, as a communion with that trust through the goddess who is contriving her husband's return, is often restorative and soothing (see 4.839–40, 18.187 ff).

Yet sleep is also a sign of her passivity and the static condition of her world without Odysseus. It is in her sleep that she is acted upon by Athena, as in the two passages just cited. Sleep, however, is not a means of change and passage for her in the same way that it is for Odysseus (as in Books 6 and 13). Crucial events occur while she sleeps, such as Telemachus' departure for the mainland at the end of Book 4, and especially the slaying of the suitors. In the latter case, in fact, she says she has never slept so soundly since Odysseus left for Troy (23.18–19). Her sleep during the struggle with the suitors has some analogies with Odysseus' landing on Ithaca: she awakens (or rather is, to her displeasure, awakened, 23.15–17) to find reality changed, to be told of the fulfilment of the hoped for Return; and, like Odysseus in Book 13, she cannot recognize the truth until later. For her, however, sleep is rather a sign of the suspended condition of her life and removal from the action going on about her than the renewal of strength for positive action of her own. Her nature is to wait and hope, and sleep keeps her fresh for the time when the Return is accomplished.

Yet her sleep, as a communion with her past, restores the beauty that Odysseus knew before the war. In the deep sleep which precedes her tempting of the suitors in Book 18, Athena carefully enhances her beauty (18.187 ff.). And with the return of her beauty of past years comes also the resurgence of her longing for her husband. Thus it is here that her recollection of Odysseus' departure is keenest, and she relates at length his parting words of twenty years before (257–70). It is interesting not only that Penelope should choose to report at such length —which she never does elsewhere—an intimate moment with her long-absent husband, but also that she should do so at the very time when she is trying to coax presents from her wooers. It is more interesting still that Odysseus, present in disguise, should be pleased (18.281–83). It is as if her sleep and Athena's ministrations have reawakened in her a more vivid sense of the past, through which Odysseus recognizes in truth the wife he left behind. He knows, as the suitors do not, that 'her mind is eager for other things' (18.283).

In this unexpected flashback of Penelope's into the past, there seems to be also an ironical foreshadowing of the near future wherein the past will in fact be restored. The desire of the suitors is described with the phrase, 'but thereupon their knees were loosed'. (τῶν δ' αὐτοῦ λύτο γούνατα, 18.212). The

phrase refers not only to erotic desire, but also to death or to
the sinking despair at the fear of death. In fact this very expres-
sion describes the suitors' reaction when Odysseus prepares to
turn the deadly bow upon them (22.69).[9] There are other
ironic foreshadowings here in Book 18, as when the suitors 'die
with laughter' (18.100). In this connection it has often been
suggested that from this point on there is operating within
Penelope an intuitive or subconscious recognition of her dis-
guised husband which prepares her for the 'real' recognition in
Book 23.[1] If so, it is again sleep which creates the setting for
this pre-recognition, serving as the essential mediator between
past and future, illuminating past happiness with the stark light
of present longing.

Penelope's sleep in Book 18, like Odysseus' in Book 13, is
compared with death: 'Would that chaste Artemis would send
so soft a death', 18.201–2. Sleep, death, change form a related
cluster of motifs in the Return, but differ in their significance
for Odysseus and Penelope. Her sleep after Telemachus' asser-
tion of his authority over the Bow (21.354–58) and during the
slaughter does, in fact, mark a crucial passage, but one of which
she remains oblivious until later. Because, as a woman, Penel-
ope has not Odysseus' active control over her environment, the

9. Note also the similar 'and their knees were loosed', in a sinister sense
elsewhere in Book 18, e.g. 238, 242, 341. This mixture of the sinister and
the erotic in the 'loosing of the knees' is taken up later in the book in
Odysseus' banter with the maids who have become paramours of the suit-
ors. He assures them that he will be able to supply light for all, even if
they wish to stay up till dawn: οὔ τι με νικήσουσι, 'They will not conquer
me', or as R. Fitzgerald translates (*The Odyssey*, New York, 1963), 'They
cannot tire me out' (18.319), at which the maids laugh and glance at one
another (18.320). This possible *double entendre* in 'loosing the knees' is
reflected in the twofold use of the closely related adjective, *lysimelēs*, 'loos-
ing the limbs'. On the one hand, it is an epithet of sleep in *Odyssey* 20.57
(note too that it is an epithet of death, *thanatos*, in Euripides, *Suppliants*,
47). On the other hand, it is often an epithet of *Eros*, love, in early Greek
poetry: Hesiod, *Theogony* 121 and 911; Sappho, frag. 137 Diehl (= 130
Lobel-Page); *Carmina Popularia* 44.3 Diehl (= 873.3 Page); and cf. also
Alcman 3.61 Page.
1. For the most recent discussion of Penelope's 'recognition' of Odysseus in
Book 18 see Anne Amory, *The Reunion of Odysseus and Penelope*, in
Essays on the Odyssey, ed. Charles H. Taylor Jr., (Bloomington, 1963),
100 ff. Also Philip W. Harsh, *Penelope and Odysseus in Odyssey XIX*,
"AJPh" 71, 1950, 1–21, esp. 10 ff. For a different interpretation see now
G. F. Else, *Homer and the Homeric Problem* (Lectures in Memory of
Louise Taft Semple, Cincinnati, 1965), 47–50.

transitions for her are veiled in sleep; and, unlike Odysseus, she does not even know that a transition is being made. Yet for her, as for Odysseus in Book 13, sleep marks a communion, through a kind of death, with a dormant wholeness of self and precedes its vital awakening into life.

The Bath. The bath is a long established sign of welcome (see *Genesis* 18.4) and mark of accepting a stranger into a new environment. It indicates for him a point of crucial entrance, and washing by water probably retains a certain ritual significance as the ceremony marking this tradition. It is also obviously connected with birth and hence rebirth (see *infra* p. 340). Like other transitional situations, the bath has an essential ambiguity. It is physically pleasant (cf. the Phaeacians' pleasure in 'warm baths', 8.249), yet involves a potentially dangerous exposure. This latter aspect of the bath is familiar from the post-Homeric version of the return of Odysseus' less fortunate companion, Agamemnon. Through the bath also changes can occur, changes both in appearance (as frequently in the *Odyssey*) and in mood.

Here too the Homeric formula helps underline the ritual element involved, for, as one would expect, similar formulas are used in nearly all the bathing scenes. There is, of course, a great deal of variety even here, but practically the same pair of lines occurs near the beginning of each instance of bathing ('X washed Y and anointed him with oil and put a beautiful cloak around him': cf. 3.466–67, 4.49–50, 4.252, 6.227–28, 8.454–55, 10.364–65, 17.88–89, 23.154–55, 24.366–67).

Like sleep, the bath, through its outward function as a sign of welcome, can emphasize the danger of the passage to a new situation.[2] Such is the bath Helen gave Odysseus at Troy when he entered the city in disguise (4.242 ff.). A bath may also be only partially accepted. Thus Circe has Odysseus bathed as a sign of her acceptance of him and his successful passage through the danger of her enchantments (10.348 ff.). Her bath has all the sensuous accompaniments that a bath by Circe should have (see esp. 359–60, 362–63), including the four

2. For a possible image of bathing in a situation of dangerous passage see 12.237, where the seething of Charybdis is compared to water boiling in a caldron (*lebes*). Contrast the Phaeacians' friendly gift of a tripod and caldron in 13.13, implements associated with bathing. For the soothing and gentle connotations of bathing see also Pindar, *Nemean* 4.4–5.

maidservants born 'from springs and groves and from sacred rivers' (10.350–51). But still all this 'pleased not' Odysseus' heart (373), and his grief for his companions disturbs the usual smooth flow of formulaic motifs. Here the purely physical restorative powers of the bath do not operate on the man who seeks a restoration of another kind. When the companions are changed back, however, all are bathed (10.449–51) and happily spend an entire year with her.

Two instances of bathing are of especial interest, that on Scheria in Book 6 (216 ff.) and Odysseus' bath by his nurse in Book 19 (343 ff.). In the first passage Odysseus, for the only time in the poem, is bathed in 'the flowing streams of a river' (6.216), the 'beautifully flowing river' which saved him from the sea and the rocks (5.441 ff.). The sweet waters succeed the 'salt water';[3] and Odysseus' washing off of the 'salt sea water' (6.219, 225–26) marks his return to safety, the end of his duel with the sea and Poseidon. Yet he refuses to let Nausicaa's maids bathe him, out of reluctance to be seen nude by 'fair-tressed maidens' (220–22), especially after the ravages of the sea ('he appeared frightful to them, all befouled by the sea', 6.137). His refusal is perfectly in keeping with the situation: he shows a tactful delicacy of feeling in not offending the young girls on whom his salvation depends. Yet such an attitude toward nudity is unusual in the epic.[4] Odysseus' refusal, then, may be more than embarrassment. It may indicate also his hesitation to be drawn into his new environment more than is necessary, bathing being the sign of welcome and acceptance. When he was luxuriously bathed by Circe, after all, he spent a whole year. Now, ready for his Return to Ithaca, he wishes to keep his distance from new involvements. Hence he bathes alone and thus keeps outside of the gaiety, youthful beauty, and carefree energy of the Phaeacian girls. He is bathed later by Arete's servants only when he is assured of his return (8.449

3. Note the use of the phrase 'salt water' three times in close succession of Charybdis: 12.236, 240, 431. Compare also the single occurrence of the phrase 'sweet water' of the safe harbor on Thrinacia (12.306). Thrinacia is, in fact, a place of shelter as long as the Sun's cattle are not harmed.

4. For the usual absence of such self-consciousness about nudity and bathing see W. B. Stanford, *The Odyssey of Homer* (ed. 2, London, 1958–61), on 3.464. G. Germain, *Genèse de l'Odyssée* (Paris, 1954), 310 ff. would explain the irregularity of this modesty by the influence of the Near East and the oriental sacral significance of nudity.

ff.). The refusal is thus perhaps another instance of his removal from the Phaeacians, and an indication of his increasing readiness to separate himself from the fantasy world. His nakedness in bathing (6.222) would also be a symbolical revelation of his identity which he correspondingly holds back from the Phaeacians until he can reveal himself in his own terms, terms which now look back to the real world he is ready to reenter (9.19 ff.): 'I am Odysseus, son of Laertes, ... and I dwell in far-seen Ithaca'.

The bathing by Eurycleia in Book 19 (343 ff.) is, like the first Phaeacian washing, a ritual which is not fully or perfectly performed. Again Odysseus holds back, permitting himself to be washed only by an old servant, 'who has endured in her heart such things as even I have endured' (347). His refusal to let himself be washed by the younger servants, as in the Nausicaa episode, marks his insistence on re-entering his world only under the sign of the suffering and ageing that have become integral parts of him. Thus he seeks out the servant with whom he has the greatest bond of suffering (see 360, 374, 376–78).

Here too is fused the double significance of the bath as ritual entrance and means of revealing identity. Eurycleia's dropping of the basin with a loud clang when she feels the scar (467–70) indicates the interruption of the proper ritual and underlines the ambiguity of Odysseus' position, that what should be a welcoming and safe gesture, the bathing of the master in his own house, is, in fact, fraught with danger. The re-entrance is a perilous one, and accordingly so indicated. Correspondingly, the revelation of his identity would be dangerous, as Odysseus firmly points out to his nurse (479–90). The scene, as noted above, recalls a corresponding situation of danger from which Odysseus escaped triumphantly, his bathing by Helen in Troy (4.252 ff.). The similarity is bitterly paradoxical, for on Ithaca he is now as much in the house of his enemies as he was at Troy. The clang of the basin may, furthermore, indicate not only the interruption or unpropitious execution of the due ceremony, but perhaps also serves as an evil omen for the suitors (like the clanging of the pitcher in 18.397), for the ritual of the bath marks Odysseus' official 'entrance' into the life of the palace.

Odysseus' final bath in Book 23 (152 ff.) seals the fulfillment of his Return and immediately precedes his recognition by Penelope. Here at last he is bathed openly in his own house without mishap, and no longer, as in Book 19, as a stranger.

Athena, directress of his return to himself, enhances his beauty in lines repeated from the similar scene at his arrival in Scheria (23.157–62=6.230–35). Thus the beginnings of his Return are brought full circle with its completion. Both crucial entrances are marked by a welcoming ceremony and divine aid. There is, however, a major difference: washed up from the sea on Scheria, among strangers, he bathes himself, alone, in a river; here, on Ithaca, he is washed by his housekeeper Eurynome, not merely under the shelter of a regular human dwelling, but in his own house. The difference is significant of the differences between the two realms: isolation, wandering, exposure to the elemental forces in the world *versus* society, stability, safety amid the reestablished order of human civilization. Yet Athena presides over both scenes as the constant element. She reveals in the grizzled warrior the young husband who left twenty years before. The decisive recognition by the bed can thus follow immediately thereafter (23.171 ff.).

Finally, in Book 24, the bathing of Laertes (365–71) marks the extension of the process of rebirth and rejuvenation brought about by Odysseus. This passage is useful for illustrating how the formulaic style reinforces the ritual repetition. The formulas used of Laertes here repeat those used in the bathing and miraculous enhancing of Odysseus' stature in the preceding book:

μείζονα δ' ἠὲ πάρος καὶ πάσσονα θῆκεν ἰδέσθαι

(She made him larger and stouter to look upon than before, 24.369).

. . . μείζονά τ' ἐσιδέειν καὶ πάσσονα . . .

. . . larger and stouter to look upon . . . , 23.157).

The same formula, naturally, also introduces both bathing episodes:

τόθρα δὲ Λαέρτην μεγαλήτορα ᾧ ἐνὶ οἴκῳ
ἀμθίπολος Σικελὴ λοῦσεν καὶ χρῖσεν ἐλαίῳ

(Then a Sikel maidservant washed and anointed with oil great-hearted Laertes in his own house, 24.365–66).

αὐτὰρ 'Οδυσσῆα μεγαλήτορα ᾧ ἐνὶ οἴκῳ
Εὐρυνόμη ταμίη λοῦσεν καὶ χρῖσεν ἐλαίῳ

(Then Eurynome the housekeeper washed and anointed with oil great-hearted Odysseus in his own house, 23 153–54).

The close formulaic and thematic (*i.e.* ritual) linking of these two baths is, of course, expressive of the meaning of Odysseus' Return. For both men this bath marks a return to 'their own house', that is, to their rightful position of authority both within and without: they both recover a lost vitality as father and king. The archetypal pattern of the restoration of the dead or maimed king is operative, in a sense, for Laertes as well as for Odysseus. Odysseus, to be sure, is now king (see, e.g. 24.501: αρχε δ' 'Οδυσσεύς, 'Odysseus led them'); yet Laertes performs a kingly action, as of old, in being the first to strike down his enemy (24.520 ff.).[5]

Thus Odysseus' reentrance into the fullness of his past life, with its human ties, recreates also those lives which wait on his; and they too are washed of their previous sufferings and prepared to resume a fullness of existence which had been lost.

Purification. The bathing episodes can be seen also as a ritual cleansing. But it is fire that replaces water as the purifying element in the crucial transition after the killing of the suitors and their accomplices (22.481 ff.). Odysseus refuses Eurycleia's offer to exchange his rags for more decent garb, and insists on first purging the house with fire and sulphur: 'Let there first of all (*prōtiston*) be fire in my halls' (491). It is perhaps felt that only the violence of fire, by a kind of homoeopathy, is sufficient to purge away the destructive aspects of the Return which culminate in the suitors' death. Indeed the thoroughness of this purgation—the only one of its kind in the *Odyssey*—is perhaps one of the poet's means of indicating that he recognizes and wishes to mitigate the brutality involved in the suitors' slaughter, the maids' execution, and the mutilation of Melanthius.

For Odysseus too, fire is the final exorcism of the violence of the past years. Leaving behind now the war and the destructive monsters of the journey home, he must nevertheless reenter his house as he left it, a warrior, under the sign of violence—the blood-splattered lion and the purifying fire.

The picture of Odysseus as a blood-splattered lion at the end of the slaughter is the image which Euricleia reports to Penelope at the beginning of the following book: 'You would have been warmed in spirit', she tells her just-awakened queen (23.47 ff.), 'to have seen him splattered with blood and gore, like a

5. Note that earlier too (24.353–55) Laertes is the first to assess the danger of reprisal from the suitors' families.

lion'. The lion image re-evokes the Iliadic world which the hero has been so long in leaving. At the same time it is natural for the elderly servant to see in Odysseus the terrible warrior who has made good his return. She sees the outward, grim, one might say 'official' aspect of Odysseus. The warrior too, though speaking kindly words, was Penelope's last picture of her husband, as it recurred to her mind in Book 18. But in the final recognition between them, she will look deeper into the past for another image: 'For we have signs', she says, 'hidden, which we alone know, apart from others'.

The fire at the end of Book 22, ordered by the returned master from the faithful servant, helps make the palace his own again and rids it of the intrusive influences of the past. Only gradually, however, will Odysseus undergo the 'stepping-down' process to become again the familiar husband and 'gentle father'. He is curt and imperious in rejecting the clothes Eurycleia offers (22.485 ff.) and perhaps implicitly rejects also the bath that would naturally accompany such a change of raiment. The other participants in the slaughter wash immediately after the deed and the execution of the delinquent maids: 'Then washing off their hands and feet they went to Odysseus in the house, and the deed was accomplished' (22.478–79). And it is at this point that Odysseus calls for sulphur and fire. There is no bath for him until Book 23, line 154, immediately before the recognition by the bed. For him the destructive, purifying force of fire precedes restorative waters at this point of crucial transition. It is only *after* this purgation that he is ready to reassume the positive elements in his life, to shed his rags (23.155), claim the living bed (23.181 ff.), and appear again as Penelope's husband.

This purification of the past parallels and completes another loss by fire and sulphur in the past, the blasting of his ship by Zeus' lightning off Thrinacia at the end of Book 12: 'The ship was filled with sulphur and the companions fell from the ship' (12.417; cf. also Odysseus' tale to Eumaeus, 14.305–315). Ship and companions, the unstable remnants of his Trojan past, are purged away before the total isolation of Ogygia. This purgation is necessary and implicit in the preceding adventures, wherein Odysseus moves further and further from the heroic world into experiences of an increasingly private nature (Circe, the Sirens, the visions in Hades, Calypso). Thus it leaves Odysseus totally alone, cut off from his remaining human ties, 'suspended' (12.432 ff.) over the abyss, surrounded by death. It also marks the transition to his greatest point of isolation, the seven years with the goddess Calypso, who would complete his separation from the mortal world and make him, like herself, immortal.

The sulphur and fire in his halls, then, mark the end of his isolation and the return to his full human position. Here it is at his command that the sulphur is brought: he is again in a world which he can understand and control, and in it he has reestablished his rightful authority. With the return of the legitimate king order is restored and disorder purged away. In Book 12 the purgation is followed by loss and death; in Book 22 by recovery and life. Both have been necessary, and the second naturally succeeds the first; but both also constitute a purgation of the forces which prevent the full Return.

Odysseus' successful purgation through blood and fire contrasts with a bloody purgation of a different outcome, the death of Agamemnon. The blood of the murdered king 'seethes upon the ground' (11.420, δάπεδον δ' ἅπαν αἵματι θῦεν). The verb θῦεν (probably related to the Latin *fumus*)[6] suggests smoke or fire and, in its context here, perhaps purgation also. It points, in any event, to another level of contrast between Agamemnon's and Odysseus' return: there is an opposition not only of death to life, failure to success, but also of pollution to purification. The parallel with Odysseus' return is pointed up by the repetition of this half-line in the slaughter of the suitors (22.309); and the half-line occurs but once more in Homer when the suitors describe their death to Agamemnon in Hades (24.185=22.309). There is a significant inversion of the theme in this repetition, for it was first Agamemnon who described to Odysseus the 'seething' of his own (and his companions') blood (11.420); it is now Odysseus' vengeful shedding of blood that is described to him (24.185).

The situations too are similar in other ways, for both slaughters occur at a banquet, amid tables and feasting. At the same time the death of Agamemnon is felt as a sinister ritual. He is, as it were, 'sacrificed' like an ox ('as one would kill an ox at the trough', 11.411=4.535, and cf. Aegisthus' sacrifices, 3.273–75). The parallels complete a carefully developed antithesis between

6. On θῦεν here see Stanford (above, note 13), *ad loc.* and E. Boisacq, *Dictionnaire étymologique de la langue grecque* (Paris, 1916), 356, 360.

the two returns. Agamemnon fails at his point of crucial transition as Odysseus succeeds at his. Both returns at their completion contain ritual elements involving fire and sacrifice. In Agamemnon's return this significant entrance and the ritual motifs accompanying it have their full measure of potential destructiveness. For him, these purgative and ritual associations bring only defilement and pollution. For Odysseus, the 'seething' blood and sulphurous fire are succeeded by water and the restorative, cleansing bath.

Threshold. The crossing of the threshold, since it marks the passage between known and unknown, is, like bathing or the receiving of guests, a significant, danger-fraught act. To primitive (and non-primitive) peoples even today the threshold is an important transitional point, safeguarded by magical representations or good-luck charms. It is, of course, but one example of the many dangerous entrances or guarded gates to be encountered in every epic journey into the unknown, from *Gilgamesh* on. The threshold in the *Odyssey* serves as the human, comprehensible counterpart to such mysterious entrances as the double-portalled 'misty cave' on Ithaca in Book 13, the crucial juncture between worlds.

At the beginning of the human action in the poem, when Athena begins to set in motion Odysseus' Return and Telemachus' journey, she appears to the latter 'on the threshold of the court' (1.104) as he is thinking of his father's return and the expulsion of the suitors. His inviting her within the house is the initial sign of his new spirit of manly independence that will now take him to the courts of the heroes on the mainland.

In Odysseus' journey the threshold is more involved with dangerous and supernatural elements. The Cyclops' great stone bars his threshold (9.242) and makes the passage out one of the greatest tests of Odysseus' wit and courage. In his entrance into and passage out of the Phaeacian kingdom the crossing of thresholds receives special attention. Alcinous' threshold, like Aeolus' palace, is of bronze, and Odysseus approaches it with anxious thoughts (7.82–83), to be succeeded by wonder (see 7.134), until he crosses it to find the Phaeacians engaged in pious libations (7.135 ff.).

For the Phaeacians as well as for Odysseus this entrance is a tense situation, for the treatment of a stranger is always a delicate and dangerous matter. Coming from the unknown and

potentially hostile outside, he must somehow be incorporated
into the familiar, made a part of what is friendly and 'normal'.
For Odysseus there is also his accumulated experience of other
ways, not all friendly, in which a stranger may be treated. Thus
at this point of crucial transition, the silence (7.154) empha-
sizes the tension and the 'in-between' state of Odysseus. The
tension is resolved and the full entrance effected by a succession
of ritual acts. Echenaos breaks the silence with the suggestion of
a libation to Zeus 'who attends suppliants worthy of respect'
(165). Then King Alcinous takes Odysseus by the hand (a sig-
nificant establishment of physical contact: cf. 3.36 ff.) and seats
him upon a 'bright chair' in the place of his own son, Laodamas
(167-70). Odysseus is then washed (172-74); a table is set
(174); and a common meal shared (175-77). The due libation
to Zeus 'who attends suppliants worthy of respect' (181=165)
is then carried out (179 ff.). Here not only the ritual acts them-
selves, but the familiar formulas in which they are described
strike a reassuring note and mark the successful completion of
an important stage in the Return.

When Odysseus is about to leave Phaeacia and make the
final crossing of waters back to the mortal world, the threshold
underlines once more the significance of the passage. His last
conversation among the Phaeacians is with Arete, their queen:
'Fare you well, O Queen, all the time until old age and death
come which come upon men. But I depart. Do you in this
house take joy in children and people and Alcinous the king! So
saying, *over the threshold he crossed*, noble Odysseus' (13.59–
63). He then boards the swift ship and embarks for Ithaca, his
mind fully turned, in this conversation, toward the human
world he is about to re-enter.

When Odysseus, returned to Ithaca, approaches his palace,
he sits disguised as a beggar, actually *upon* 'the ash-wood thresh-
old within the doors' (17.337–40). He thus occupies now in
squalor the very point of entrance to what he has so long
sought. Later, in 20.258, Telemachus seats Odysseus further
inside, 'by the stone threshold', but still just barely within his
house. In the contest of the Bow, then, it is perhaps significant
that Telemachus tries it at the threshold (21.124), whereas
Odysseus shoots from his seat to the door (21.420–23). He thus
not only demonstrates his masterful ease with the bow but also
establishes his rightful position *inside* the palace. Finally, at the

beginning of the slaughter Odysseus 'lept upon the great threshold' (22.2), and later 'the four stand upon the threshold, but within the house are many men and noble' (22.203–4). Here the proper place of inner and outer is again reversed, and the rightful possessor must for the last time make good his claim and establish his identity through a dangerous passage. Here also the transition to a new condition is underlined by a throwing aside of clothing: Odysseus throws off his rags (22.1) to reveal himself to the suitors and leaps upon the threshold.

Afterwards, when Penelope is informed, she wonders 'whether she should address her dear husband from a distance or stand beside him and kiss his head and take his hands'. She then 'crosses over the stone threshold' and sits 'opposite Odysseus' (23.86–89). These lines also recall Odysseus' significant entrance among the Phaeacians in the seventh Book, where he hesitates before crossing the threshold (7.82–83=23.85–86). Also the description here of Penelope sitting 'in the light of the fire' (23.89) recalls Arete sitting by the fire in that scene in the seventh Book (cf. 7.153–4; also 6.305).[7] There Odysseus supplicated Arete directly upon his crossing the threshold into Alcinous' hall, and then sat himself 'on the hearth by the fire' (7.153–54). Thus a striking combination of transitional themes connects the two episodes: in both the hero confronts a queen, and in both hesitation at the threshold is combined with sitting by the fire. Here, then, is another linking of the beginnings of the Return with its completion. Yet now it is Penelope rather than Odysseus who initiates the crucial passage back to reclaim what has been lost. After the man has won his way back by his strength and endurance and by the constant exercise of his will and reason, then the final movement of acceptance, the spontaneous rekindling of the intimate tie between them, is left to the woman. Here too it is the woman who will test the man who has been the tester on so many other occasions.

7. The theme of sitting by the fire is developed also in the first meeting of Odysseus and Penelope. First in 17.572 Odysseus sends word to Penelope through Eumaeus that it would be better to meet him in the evening, 'seating me nearer the fire'. Then in 19.55 when Penelope comes down from her chamber she is given a seat 'by the fire'; and finally Odysseus, just before she addresses him and immediately after his bath by Eurycleia, draws his stool 'closer to the fire' (19.506). The theme of meeting by the fire thus prepares for and is duly completed by the final meeting 'by the fire' in Book 23.

The Return of Odysseus has been described above in terms of a reawakening. It appears also as a rebirth. The theme of bathing, as suggested earlier, has obvious connections with birth and rebirth. Occurring at points of significant entrance, it naturally accompanies the exchange of age and debility for youth and freshness. In one of the most important of crucial entrances the connection is made quite explicit. The nurse who bathes Odysseus in Book 19 is an obvious maternal figure, and she is made to remember vividly here the actual birth of Odysseus and his naming by his grandfather (19.399 ff. and cf. especially 400, 'new-born child', and 482–83, 'Why do you wish to destroy me, my nurse? For you yourself nursed me at your breast').[8]

Birth and death, then, the ultimate and most mysterious passages of human life, underlie the overall rhythm of the Return and oscillate ambiguously in it in a kind of contrapuntal movement. In order to obtain passage back to mortal life, Odysseus must visit the land of the dead. The knowledge of his own death gained from this visit is present to him even at the moment of joyful reclaiming of his human life and his spouse: 'O wife, we have not yet come to the limit of our trials, but afterwards there will be still measureless toil, much and difficult', he begins, and goes on to tell her, reluctantly, of Teiresias' prophecy of his death (23.248). Earlier, Odysseus regarded his Phaeacian landing as a rebirth and thanked Nausicaa for 'giving him life' (8.468). It is of course fitting that the fresh princess should be the restorer of life to the exhausted warrior; yet his sleep on the ship which brings him back to the mortal world and fulfils the Phaeacians' promise is 'most like to death' (13.80). In the same contrapuntal fashion, the dead suitors are paraded off by Hermes 'leader of souls' (*psychagogos*) as the grim counterpart to Odysseus' successful return to full 'life'.

Odysseus' 'rebirth', however, is a source of life also for those who waited: son, wife, father. It is also a rebirth for Odysseus' line, marked in the joyful utterance of Laertes, himself rejuvenated after his bath (24.365 ff.), when he sees 'son and grandson striving concerning excellence' (24.515). Odysseus' return to his human position is here fulfilled in terms beyond himself; and he

8. The connection between Eurycleia's bathing of Odysseus and the theme of birth is stressed by Charles Baudouin, *Le triomphe du héros* (Paris, 1957), 45 ff., who would go so far as to regard the scar as a 'signe de naissance'.

stands in the middle-as the link between generations, between past and future. This rebirth is transferred also into moral and social terms at the very end of the *Odyssey*: the interference of the gods ends the cycle of strife and assures 'wealth and peace in abundance', as Zeus had promised Athena (24.486). The poem thus ends with the order of Zeus with which it began; and the promised restoration of the land comes with the Return of the rightful king and 'gentle father', as foreshadowed in Odysseus' first words with Penelope on his return, when he addresses her, disguised as a beggar, in the darkened halls:

> My lady, never a man in the wide world
> should have a fault to find with you. Your name
> has gone out under heaven, like the sweet
> honor of some god-fearing king, who rules
> in equity over the strong: his black lands bear
> both wheat and barley, fruit trees laden bright,
> new lambs at lambing time—and the deep sea
> gives great hauls of fish by his good strategy,
> so that his folk fare well. (19.107–114, Fitzgerald's translation).

Though Penelope and Odysseus have not yet explicitly recognized one another, they meet here both as the individual characters they are and as the archetypal King and Queen, the partners in a Sacred Marriage, whose union symbolises the ever-renewed fertility of the earth and the fruitful harmony between society and cosmos. This second level of their meeting is an important part of the 'encyclopaedic range' of the epic mentioned earlier.

The ritual elements which have been stressed throughout this essay not only add to the poem the larger dimension of meaning suggested in the preceding paragraph. They also point to an artistic function behind a basic component of the poem's style: the 'ritualizing' quality of the repeated formulas. Through the repetition of the verbal formulas, the recurrent acts of sleep, bathing, entrance, departure, etc. come to stand out in their full ritual character, with the overtones of meaning carried by that ritual character for a society such as Homer's. One may regard this cooperation of matter and style as a happy 'by-product' of Homeric language. Yet there may be an inner congruence between the material and the style, a congruence that grows out of the culture itself and its means of apprehending and ordering the world. The outwardly inflexible demands of the oral style, in other words, seem to suit the ritual modes of thought which doubtless helped to create the style in the first place. These are modes of thought in which recurrent cycles of loss and regeneration, alienation and rediscovery, death and rebirth are celebrated as the fundamental facts of existence and form an organic link between human life and the natural world. Such cyclical patterns are *both* metaphor and reality; and the ritual patterns discussed here help unite the two, for ritual itself partakes of both play and seriousness, both imaginary projection and realistic confrontation.

The very fabric of Homer's language, then, presents the expected, re-enacted situations which comprise the Return through the equally predictable, crystallized, 'ritualized' expressions which make up the formulas. These recurrent formulaic expressions themselves intimate the steady sameness, the shared narrowness, the richness in limitation which form the substance of that for which the hero has journeyed back to Ithaca.

Here, then, the contrast between the circumscribed, formulaic language of the *Odyssey* and the richly varied, brightly colored adventures it describes gives the poem its special unity. This unity is, in a sense, also the meaning of the poem: its movement between exploration and return, between the exotic and the familiar, between the open possibilities of the free traveler who consorts with goddesses and the accepted constraints and rewards of the land-dweller who is bound to a mortal woman.

PAOLO VIVANTE

Time and Life in Homer†

This indefinite sense of human time cannot come gratuitously, like an idle dream. As everything in Homer, it must be occasioned by material conditions, it must be prompted by a vital need. What is required is a distance between the characters. There must be a man that is cherished or feared, alive but absent, whose destiny is not known. Friends or enemies visual-

† From Paolo Vivante, *The Homeric Imagination: Homer's Poetic Perception of Reality* (Bloomington, Ind.: Indiana University Press, 1970). Reprinted by permission of the publisher. Copyright © 1970 by Indiana University Press.

ize him far away. Only then can thoughts focus anxiously upon a given object, and yet be free to wander unencumbered by its immediate presence. In such a way the life of an absent character can be mentally realized. His distant experiences are questioned, imagined, tentatively followed in their possible course, and not represented as objective data. The momentary occasion of a day or of a night must be left out of account. Time is here an indeterminate lapse of life, subjectively felt and yet posited in the world at large.

The *Odyssey* fosters this sensibility. We are made aware of it right at the beginning. For Odysseus emerges, as it were, out of nowhere. As he is first presented, his feet do not rest on any ground, he does not stand out in a particular stance, as Achilles and Agamemnon do at the beginning of the *Iliad*. He is unmistakably himself, but only by being strongly entrenched in our imagination. His prominence is due to a certain aura rather than to a single action. Where is he? When will he come? His image is in everyone's mind, remembered, expected, fixed in no given time or place, helplessly out of range.

The first book of the *Odyssey* gathers very quickly various threads of time around absent Odysseus. Telemachus sees him in his mind's eye, imagining the storms that might have killed him. Phemius sings the return of the Achaens, recalling the destinies of the expedition which carried him away. Penelope hears and bids the minstrel stop, protesting her life-long grief for his absence. The suitors pursue their quest, scarcely concealing how they fear his return. All these characters survey the life of Odysseus in their persistent thoughts; and Odysseus is, in turn, a theme which keeps in unison their moods and their actions. A lapse of indefinite years is thus covered in brief outline.

Such a rendering of time would have been impossible, if Odysseus had been pictured in Ithaca, furthering his cause. His encompassing presence could leave no room for vague expectation or regret. But, as it is, his distance opens up the prospect of things to come and memory fills his vacant place with images from the past. It is as if the poet had no other means to suggest such an extension in time. For it was not his genius to depict changing situations in the manner of a novelist or a historian; and now the radiance of a distant image afforded him an effective medium: here was a man whose spell could reverberate into a whole age.

The distance of Odysseus is essential to the sense of time in the *Odyssey*. Existence thereby recedes more and more from what is immediately visual. It becomes a course of life to be endured or struggled for—a destiny summing up all the days in its own terms. It is so throughout the poem. See how, under the approaching shadow of Odysseus, the quality of each character grows into what it is. Telemachus becomes resolute. The suitors are obstinate. Penelope is faithful. It could not be otherwise: they are weathered by fear or hope, and their feelings have matured into a habit of mind. Everyday business here becomes perfunctory. In Penelope's case, for instance: the daily tasks—which elsewhere in Homer are so self-sufficient—become for her an excuse, a device to keep alive, like the weaving of the famous web which seems to allegorize her long resistance.

Odysseus, on the other hand, thinks of Ithaca. This thought is a driving force, turning his scattered exploits into phases of a long effort. His endurance has a counterpart in that of Penelope: at a different pole of the earth there is a longing which is parallel to his own, affecting his own; and deeply related feelings converge from different angles, gathering all accidental happenings into one great protracted strain.

It is remarkable how this encompassing effect of time ultimately rests, once again, on the spell of the Homeric image—just as in the quick exchanges of the *Iliad*, but much more extensively. For that same spell works now on a larger range, over the distance that separates the characters; and it is the same character that exerts it throughout the poem. Odysseus is πολύτλας, "much suffering" by definition; and his very name evokes his destiny. But it is as if the burden of his epithet overflowed into his words, into his very features. For his sufferings are his great theme whenever he gives a condensed account of himself (cf. *Od.* 5. 222; 7. 24, 147, 152, etc.). Similarly, they are ever borne in mind whenever he is seen, remembered, imagined by others (cf. *Od.* 14. 42; 1. 161, 195, 235, etc.). As these instances accumulate, they haunt the mind of the reader. It is as if, each time, we saw Odysseus against a deepening background. Insofar as his suffering is expressed in a mere epithet, it is crystallized into his image; and we have no more than a heroic attribute. But, as the poem develops, this suffering is seen in a different light. We become aware of a capacity to suffer, to endure, to strive year after year. The heroic image is trans-
dreams and visions which kept her waiting for so long, shreds of

formed into a complex character. Another Odysseus arises before us. Grief and hope have sobered him. His experiences advance in time; and all the dangers or wonders of isolated moments take their allotted place in the large vital movement of his life.

It is, of course, Odysseus himself who gives the full account of his experiences, speaking directly to the Phaeacians. But he arrives from far away. The distance which separated him heretofore from his listeners still isolates him. He is there in their midst; but removed into a world of his own by the legend that has gathered around him, by a past which is all one with the spell of his presence. Here at last a direct contact takes place— not suddenly, fleetingly, as in the scenes of the *Iliad*, but after a long suspense, the intervening distances at last cut short. As the long-suggested image strikes the beholder, the history of a whole lifetime is prefigured even before it is told.

The way in which Odysseus gradually reveals himself to the Phaeacians in the eighth book of the *Odyssey* is visual rather than verbal. He is not simply a stranger saying who he is and recounting his past. His identity seems to transpire, hinted by the wonder of his first appearance, by the wisdom of his words, by the power of his weatherworn limbs. Then the minstrel sings about Troy, and he weeps. His tears offer a glimpse of the actual truth, so that when he finally says his name, it hardly comes as a surprise. It is as if the image of Odysseus hovered in the consciousness of the audience right from the beginning. But what was just divined or known by hearsay is now made flesh and bones, and the timeless suggestion of a distant glory is transposed into the record of a man, legend is turned to self-confession, fame to subjective acknowledgement. The whole Trojan cycle becomes just a phase in a man's life. In that Phaeacian land where gods often consort with men Odysseus insists upon his human character: not only is he a mortal, but the most wretched of mortals. Only with this premise could his story be told in terms of human experience. But, at the same time, he has to rise to the full measure of his own prefigured image, in response to the expectation of those who are there before him questioning and wondering. His past must be elicited from his present spell, and not only from his tales. This is why he does not proceed to give an orderly account of his adventures from first to last. He begins, rather, with the last one —with the journey which brought him there from Calypso's island, as a wanderer, a suppliant. It is his presence there and then which matters most—a wonder for all to witness and account for. And later, when he actually recounts his return from Troy, it is as if his story were a means of self-realization. His past actions are each a parcel of the life which is gathered within him; and time is like the shadow of his image, indefinitely prolonged. He is not only surveying things gone by, he is giving a proof of himself. His relation with the audience is here essential. The listeners progressively contemplate, admire, learn, know; and their knowledge is in turn a new feeling for what they apprehended at first sight. What amazes them is not so much the narrative itself as the narrator who grows upon them as he speaks. His personality, surmised at first, is now recomposed more clearly in its human terms; and we have no chronological sequence of mythical ventures, but the progressive revelation of a man's life—a living process rather than a cycle artificially contrived.

The way in which Odysseus makes himself known in Ithaca is worked out in the same spirit. Again we have the penetrating spell of his image; again the questioning gaze of those who see him, and the distances finally cut short, an interval of absence which must be filled, words which recompose the lapse of time.

Only the circumstances are different than they were in the land of the Phaeacians. Odysseus is now transformed into an old beggar by Athena; and, when the occasion calls for it, again into a young man. These transformations, of course, are required by the plot. But we may also see them in a different light. His appearance as an old man can be justified in an ideal sense. It is an alteration, a disguise worked by the years of absence, a screen which gives way at an even pace with the process of recognition which exhumes the past.

Odysseus seems to emerge more and more clearly out of his rags. He becomes a power in Ithaca even before it is known who he actually is. For his relation with the island becomes more meaningful from hour to hour. He is moving into the circuit of old affections. His bodily presence gradually absorbs them all; and he advances dramatically to take his rightful place, filling the gap of separation and estrangement, retrieving an identity which seemed out of reach. Finally he is made one with the image which had haunted for so long the mind of his people.

His progress in Ithaca is at once a recovery of the past. As he

advances, his background is enlarged. For, almost unintention-
ally, he attracts or challenges whomsoever he happens to meet;
and long-standing attitudes are immediately brought into play.
Thus Eumaeus is stirred to instant sympathy and impassioned
recollection, while Odysseus, standing before him in his rags,
participates in the drama of Ithaca with increasing intensity, as
if he were drawing new blood from his ancient roots. Now a
mysterious familiarity draws them closer to one another. He
appears enhanced by an unexpected prestige, so keenly does he
realize the true state of the island, so strongly does he judge and
forecast the course of events. Who might this stranger be?
Even before this is known, he is made to bear the mark of his
true character, just as the makeshift story which he composes
about himself comes as a preface to the true one, almost an alle-
gory of his life, an intimation of his identity.

His broadening role also means an enrichment of his person-
ality. Here again the element of time is important. For now a
more intimate side of his life is opening up, a side of him which
had remained concealed so far. Its values come upon him as a
distinct awareness of facts and of people in their long careers.
Penelope, Telemachus, Laertes, Anticleia now take their perti-
nent part in his introspection, and a whole portion of his past
becomes intrinsic to his being. At a certain point, it is as if the
burden of this past could no longer be contained within him, as
if recognition were inevitably imminent through some force of
its own.

It is extraordinary how his increasing awareness is matched by
an increasing transparency of his image to the eyes of others.
More and more does the beggar appear like Odysseus, as he
meets the taunts of the suitors and of the handmaids, as he
endears himself to Penelope; more and more, accordingly, does
his life unfold. The climax comes, of course, when Euryclea,
washing him, recognizes the famous scar. But a premonition
haunts her beforehand. At that moment her feelings for Odys-
seus are singularly stirred; and, as in a vision, she says to him:
"Woe is me, o son, for your sake; how helpless I am. Zeus has
especially spurned you in spite of your goodness" (*Od.* 19. 363
ff.). Then, turning to the beggar: "Even so, I think, the attend-
ants of far-off strangers have scoffed at him, as now these
shameless ones were scoffing at you" (Ibid. 370 ff.). Finally a
sympathetic insight flashes upon her: "My heart is all astir with

your woes. But listen . . . of all the many wretched wanderers that have come in the past to this house, none have I seen so resembling Odysseus as you" (Ibid. 377 ff.).

The feeling of recognition becomes contagious. The sight of the beggar unmistakenly evokes the destiny of Odysseus. A little later Philoitios echoes the words of Eurycleia: "O father Zeus, none of the gods brings more woe than you. You do not take pity upon men though yourself you bring them to birth, and you plunge them in misery and grief" (*Od.* 20. 201 ff.). Then turning to the beggar: "I perspire as I see you, tears rise up in my eyes, remembering Odysseus; for he too, I think, is clothed in such rags a wanderer among men" (Ibid. 204 ff.).

Recognition is the key word here. It implies a recovery of wasted times, values made good again, features retraced to their ancient integrity. To see, to know, to rediscover are now all one. The eyes of the characters are endowed with a particular insight which seems to penetrate beyond the surface. Odysseus, on his part, stands transfigured by the impact of attentive looks. The past blends with the present, shimmering through his outlines. The work of memory is wonderfully quickened. Unwittingly he bears in himself his story.

After a long time people are altered, and yet essentially the same. Their lives might be suggested by their features. It is so with Odysseus: his long suffering is witnessed by the wrinkles that disfigure him, while the power of his limbs still betrays his native prowess. All this is quite natural; but the plot seems so designed as to isolate and stress these effects of time. More and more do we realize that Odysseus' transformations at the hand of Athena acquire in this context a meaning which goes beyond that of a mere stratagem. If he appears now young now old as befits the occasion, is not this a way of rendering visually the suggestions of memory and of present awareness? Penelope, at the end (*Od.* 23. 93 ff.), sits wondering. It is of no help that Odysseus should be made to assume again the splendor of his youth (Ibid. 156 ff.). Her silence conceals the effort to realize the unity of these varied appearances, to make the real coincide with its idealization. She must reconcile her long-matured restraint with her present longing. What are these transformations to her eyes? Who is Odysseus? The husband she remembers, the begger she has just been talking to, the bright metamorphosis now displayed before her? All these are like illusions which time has played upon her baffled consciousness—the dreams and visions which kept her waiting for so long, shreds of her brooding experience which must now be made into one coherent whole. Here is a heart-searching task which Homer does not, cannot retrace in its subjective, passionate phases, but, again, through the glimmer of shifting appearances.

Penelope cannot resist for long. She must reply to Odysseus' entreaty. When she does so, it as if his transformation into a young man awaked in her the feelings of her earlier life. "I am not proud, I am not disdainful, I am now coming back to myself; I remember how you looked when you sailed away in the long-oared ship," she says (*Od.* 23. 174 ff.). We are reminded of the scene in which Helen is carried back to a past experience by a far different transformation.

Returning or welcoming back after twenty years is an engrossing experience, especially when those who meet again are an Odysseus and a Penelope. In long regret they have idealized one another; and now they stand out for what they are, weathered by the years. Here is a dissonance between the mental image and the real one. Pent-up feelings suddenly concur to fill up the gap, to restore the harmony. Now more than ever can a long lapse of time be mentally realized. The initial shock clears the way. It was characteristic of Homer to concentrate upon such a moment, to work it up with all the wonder it naturally implies. A miraculous coincidence seemed to occur—destiny joining in with a spontaneous movement of human sympathy. Euripides must have had something like it in mind in his *Helen* when he wrote "to recognize a friend is a god" (*Hel.* 560). Homer could not be so abstract. He brought into play Athena's spell, the transformation of Odysseus.

A long-awaited moment, when it comes, puts everything else in the shade. Our feelings magnify it, gathering into it all that in the past was missed or vaguely anticipated. But Homer could not render it as pure inner experience. He conceived it visually, dramatically. Hence Odysseus' changing image, hence the devious ways of his return to Penelope. There is no passionate celebration, no tender recollection. We have, instead, overtures, approaches, meetings that become more and more pressing, shifting appearances that become more and more significant. All this is carried out as by a divine spell; but the element of wonder is made convincing and forcible insofar as it stresses the human tensions implied in each scene. Thus Odysseus' transfiguration, as we have seen, reflects Penelope's feeling of duration and change, of expectation and fulfillment. It is as if time had discharged upon a visual form the burden of persistent longings.

As in the *Iliad*, the images are suddenly brought before one another and reveal themselves. But here the meeting comes after a long climax; and the crowning moment must be made relevant to a previous story, broad vicissitudes of life compressed into the imagery and action of single scenes. The extent to which this could be done is no small proof of artistic power—of how the bulky epic material could be made to suggest, if not to express directly, the delicate complexities of human time.

Memories are stirred up almost unwittingly when people meet again at length. Time gathers spontaneously from many sides: what strikes a common chord comes to the fore, no matter when or where it happened. This is human time, this is life. And yet a survey of one's life is something different. It requires that an individual be followed in the course of his existence. What matters is not so much the significance of single occasions as a sense of continuity, of development, of growth. The idea of time must thus be gleaned from the signs of a vital spark that perseveres in its activity. We shall have to look for it in the notion of existence itself, and not in the self-revelation of characters that meet in dramatic moments.

In fifth century Greek, just as in English, the word "life" means both the fact of being alive and its duration. We easily abstract the sense of time from that of a vital organic principle and, by doing so, we make the word "life" synonymous with experience, history, biography (as when we say "a happy life" or "the life of Shakespeare"). It is not so in Homer. The temporal meaning is only implied. There are no such abstractions as time and life. These are ideal values, submerged as yet in the material which is their source. We find, instead, a stress on those organs or things which make life possible—what nourishes, what breathes, heart, spirit. Herein lies a vital function. By its very nature it yields a sense of time—a common capacity to be, to live, to resist, to endure.

The language of Homer will give us a cue. There are many words which might be translated as "life"; but not one which normally carries with it a sense of duration. What prevails is everywhere the idea of a vital force or sustenance whose extension in time may be indirectly conveyed by the context, as if the animate vigor were all there waiting to be drawn out. What we mean by "life span," "lifetime" is not something taken for granted; it is a value which is inferred from observing the ways of nature.

EDWIN DOLIN

Odysseus in Phaeacia†

The poet of the Odyssey was bold, and nowhere in the poem more so than in the Phaeacian episode,[1] where his artistic ambition required that he take on the many problems involved in placing his epic hero, the proud conqueror of Troy, in the con-

† From *Grazer Beitraege* 1 (1973). Reprinted by permission of Editions Rodopi and Edwin Dolin.

1. For discussion of the Phaeacian episode, see C. R. Beye, *The Iliad, the Odyssey and the Epic Tradition* (New York, 1966), pp. 194–199; S. Besslich, *Schweigen-Verschweigen-Uebergehen* (Heidelberg, 1966), pp. 42–47, 143–147; F. Bliss, "The Structural Unity of Odyssey 8," *Bucknell Review* XVI.3 (1968), pp. 57–73; W. Burkert, "Das Lied von Ares und Aphrodite," *Rheinisches Museum* CIII (1960), pp. 130–144; H. W. Clarke, *The Art of the Odyssey* (Englewood Cliffs, N.J., 1967), pp. 45–56; A. S. Cook, *The Classic Line* (Bloomington, Ind., 1966), pp. 120–137; G. E. Dimock, Jr., "The Name of Odysseus," in *Essays on the Odyssey*, ed. C. H. Taylor, Jr. (Bloomington, Ind., 1963), also in *Homer: Twentieth Century Views*, ed. by G. Steiner and R. Fagles; F. Eichhorn, *Homers Odyssee* (Goettingen, 1965), pp. 16–21, 54–56, 60–63; U. Hoelscher "Das Schweigen der Arete," *Hermes* LXXXVIII (1960), pp. 257–265; W. Mattes, *Odysseus bei den Phaeaken* (Wuerzburg, 1958); K. Reinhardt, *Tradition und Geist* (Goettingen, 1960), pp. 112–124; G. P. Rose, "The Unfriendly Phaeacians," *Transactions and Proceedings of the American Philological Association* 100 (1969), pp. 387–406; W. Schadewaldt, "Kleiderdinge," *Hermes* LXXXVII (1959), pp. 13–26; C. P. Segal, "The Phaeacians and the Symbolism of Odysseus' Return," *Arion* I, No. 4 (Winter 1962), pp. 17–64; W. B. Stanford, *The Ulysses Theme* (Oxford, 1954); C. H. Taylor, Jr., "The Obstacles to Odysseus' Return," in *Essays on the Odyssey*, ed. C. H. Taylor, Jr. (Bloomington, Ind., 1963); C. H. Whitman, *Homer and the Heroic Tradition* (Cambridge, Mass., 1958), pp. 285–309. On the picaresque, see C. Guillén, *Literature as System* (Princeton, N.J., 1971), pp. 71–106. On the Odysseus-Polyphemus episode, see E. M. Bradley, "The Hybris of Odysseus," *Soundings* LI (1968), pp. 33–44; C. S. Brown, "Odysseus and Polyphemus," *Comparative Literature* XVIII (1966), pp. 193–202; A. J. Podlecki, "Guest-gifts and Nobodies," *Phoenix* XV (1961), pp. 125–133.

dition of what we today would call a picaro. For this seems to be the correct name for the role seemingly awaiting Odysseus at his arrival, almost dead, on the beach of Scheria. He is a wanderer, alone in a foreign land, with no resources except his brain and tongue, and with a compelling reason to conceal his real identity. A condition as precarious and exposed as this would seem to demand that the hero play the picaro part to the full by devising for the occasion a new, safe and useful identity. The great surprise of the Phaeacian episode of the *Odyssey*, as well as the motive that binds it together from beginning to end, is that Odysseus does not, finally, choose to play the picaro part. Past master of deception and false personae, he nevertheless renounces these weapons and tells the truth about his name and, even more unpicaresque, about the reason why that name is so perilous for himself and for others.

But the decision for truth, a dangerous truth, is not made immediately. Between his arrival at the palace of Alcinous and the banquet the following evening there intervenes a time during which he carefully avoids any form of self-identification, either true or false. Why? What prevents this quick-witted extemporizer from taking the appropriate decision, whichever it is, almost immediately? Among the various possible answers to this question, the most generally adequate would seem to be that Odysseus is, during this time, *uncertain* about which course to take, the safe lie or the dangerous truth.

The facts which make a choice between these alternatives necessary were disclosed to Odysseus when he met a young girl, who is Athena in disguise, while walking from the beach to the city of the Phaeacians on the evening of his first day. The girl's information is of fundamental importance to Odysseus, whom we know as Poseidon's hated enemy (5.282 f., 6.324–331). First the girl mentions that the Phaeacians' skill with ships had come as a gift from Poseidon (7.34). Then she explains that the Phaeacian royal family is directly descended from this god (7.56–66). Earlier Odysseus had already heard from Nausicaa that the Phaeacian agora is centered on Poseidon's shrine (6.266).

Even a less prudent man than Odysseus would be compelled to pause at this news and wonder how ready Alcinous and the Phaeacians would be to help him if they knew the ominous nature of his connection with the god who dominates their nation and life. Under these circumstances it is only to be expected that Odysseus should give Alcinous, Arete and the Phaeacian nobles even less information about himself than he had previously given Nausicaa on the beach. There his account of himself included mention of having stopped once at Delos while leading a large army, and of having just now come from Ogygia. But in the palace before the royal family and court he has not a word to say about any aspect of his past except the immediate trip from Ogygia. In fact, he lets pass two opportunities to make a self-identification, one indirect, the other direct.[2] Then, on the following day, during an assembly in the agora, he again rejects an opportunity to give his name. Later this same day, challenged and insulted during the athletic contests, he slips to the extent of revealing that he has been a prominent warrior at Troy, but his self-control reasserts itself before a specific name or identifying detail is disclosed.

One artistic purpose of the outburst at the athletic contests is to emphasize for us the strain that prolonged reticence is causing the hero. A decision one way or another must be made soon, because the ship which will carry Odysseus to safety cannot sail without a destination, and the name of the destination would, if not inevitably, at least normally, be accompanied by the name of the traveller. After having been the recipient of so much courtesy, merely to say "take me to such-and-such a port," with nothing more, would imply an attitude perilously close to coldness and ingratitude, or even contempt. The strain of reticence is made all the more burdensome by the obvious readiness of Alcinous to accept the stranger on any terms he gives. Almost any story would do, apparently, and Odysseus is the man to produce just the right one for the circumstances. Thus there is a stranger with a compelling reason to deceive and a host who is beyond any expectation susceptible to deception. What is restraining Odysseus? Only, it would seem, this same phenome-

2. Alcinous' reference to the possibility that Odysseus is a god (7.199) as an indirect invitation to Odysseus to identify himself is supported by *Iliad* 6.128. Odysseus' reference to Poseidon at 7.271 does not constitute a change from his policy of delay, or an anticipation of his self-revelation in Book 9. In saying to Alcinous and Arete that "Poseidon the earth shaker raised up a great trouble against me" he assumed they would understand him as merely using common language to refer to trouble at sea, not as suggesting any special reason for Poseidon to be angry with him as an individual.

nal trustfulness, generosity and nobility of the Phaeacian king. With any one else there would have been no grounds for hesitation. The most impressive and utilitarian lies would have been forthcoming with no delay. But with Alcinous—! If any man could be trusted to keep his promise, no matter what the consequences, it was he. Odysseus is faced with the surprising prospect that to tell the truth is for once a real and valid option.

By the evening of his second day in Scheria, Odysseus has apparently reached a decision on which option to take. He suggests to the court bard that he sing the episode of the Trojan horse,[3] because he foresees the effect that this theme will have on himself, tears, just as he foresees the effect his tears will have on Alcinous, another appeal to the stranger for his name and that of his city.[4] This time, since Odysseus has himself arranged for the question to be asked, we know that he is going to respond affirmatively to his host's appeal. But we do not know the content of his answer, only that there will be one. He could choose to lie, along the lines of his later story to Eumaeus, with a statement that he is so-and-so from Crete and would like passage to Ithaca in order to collect a debt. Brought that far by the Phaeacians, he would manage the rest of the way to Crete by himself.

3. In Book 8 Demodokos sings first of the Trojan War as something in the future, a foretold success (8.73–82) and the phrase used to describe the song is *klea andron*, the same phrase, invoking the glamor of saga, that was used to describe Achilles' song at *Iliad* 9.189. Finally, Demodokos, at Odysseus' suggestion, sings of the last victorious event of the Trojan War, Odysseus' mixture of deceit and violence, the wooden horse filled with soldiers. But Odysseus' reaction to this victory is a flood of tears like those of a woman being dragged away from her husband dying in front of his captured city. In other words, the thought of his victory brings to Odysseus, ten years and much suffering later, not a sense of satisfaction and self-congratulation, but a feeling of desolate, hopeless grief. The conqueror now knows what it is to be conquered. This is a fundamental perspective of the *Odyssey*, a view of the self-glorifying, warrior world of saga from a critical angle. It seems unlikely to be an accident that the epithet *ptoliporthios*, "sacker of cities," is chosen by Odysseus to proclaim himself to the Cyclops and is then repeated by the Cyclops when he curses Odysseus. The concept expressed by this epithet is the subject of Demodokos' song of the Trojan horse, which is followed immediately by the simile of the captured woman forced away from her dying husband. The man who ten years before was proud of having sacked cities now cries like a woman whose city has been sacked.

4. See Eichhorn, *op. cit.*, p. 9.

A feasible solution, but any tendency towards adopting it is destroyed for Odysseus by the language which Alcinous uses to him at this decisive moment:

> A guest and suppliant is held equal to a *brother*
> By a man who has even a little grasp with his wits.
> So, in your cunning notions, do not yourself conceal
> What I ask you about. . . . (8.546–549, italics mine)[5]

The message is clear, Alcinous is as committed to the stranger as he would be to his blood brother. Furthermore, Alcinous makes a pointed contrast between himself and his guest. The stranger has "cunning notions" (*noemasi kerdaleoisin*). In fact, *kerdaleos* implies the stranger is not only secretive, but self-seeking, in sharp contrast to Alcinous himself. But there is more than reproach in this speech. Alcinous also produces new information, which dramatically involves not merely his own well-being but that of the whole Phaeacian people in the decision about to be made by the foreigner whom no one knows:

> . . . once I heard my father Nausithous
> Say this: he asserted that Poseidon bore ('would bear'
>   alternate reading) a grudge
> Against us, because our convoys are safe for all men.
> He said a well-made ship of the Phaeacian men
> Coming back some time from an escort on the murky sea
> Would be dashed and a great mountain would hide our city
>   round.
> So the old man said. And the god will either fulfill it
> Or it will be unfulfilled, as his spirit desires.
> Come, tell me this and speak out truthfully,
> Where have you wandered. . . . (8.564–673)

The introduction of this ominous prophecy is Alcinous' proof that he is willing to incur a serious risk to himself and his own in return for an expression of trust from his "brother." Why should his "brother" refuse to incur a risk comparable to his host's, if he is truly the man he has been taken for? The lines constitute an appeal for a relationship on a high ethical level, that of two courageous men who are willing to face danger for the sake of their friendship, two brothers or two *hetairoi*, "com-

5. The idea of the comrade-brother recurs at the end of this speech, 584–586. The translation is from Albert Cook, *The Odyssey* (New York, 1967). Other verse quotations are from the same translation.

rades," on the epic scale of Achilles and Patroclus.

Confronted by an appeal as direct, total and challenging as this, the stranger at last gives a commensurate response:

> I am Odysseus, son of Laertes, who for my wiles (*doloisin*)
> Am of note among all men, and my fame reaches heaven.
>
> (9.19 f.)

What is implied by Odysseus' use of the word *doloisin*, "deceit," is that Alcinous was perceptive in attributing to his guest "cunning notions" (*noemasi kerdaleoisin*). He *is* a cunning man, ever seeking his own advantage, openly or secretly. He *could* have deceived Alcinous before, if he had wished, and might deceive him yet. All this is admitted by Odysseus' word *doloisin* in response to Alcinous' words *noemasi kerdaleoisin*. But the prospect of future deception is countered and rebutted by the content of the story Odysseus tells in reply to Alcinous' appeal. If Alcinous will risk an act of anger from Poseidon for friendship's sake, Odysseus in turn will risk a test of that friendship by disclosing why Alcinous' apprehensions about Poseidon are even better founded than he could have imagined. Alcinous had assured Odysseus of his truthworthiness. What Odysseus tells him now will put that assurance to a severe test. The confessional narrative of Odysseus' crime against Poseidon is Odysseus' gift to Alcinous, and is given on the terms Alcinous proposed, the confrontation of danger. The stranger begging for the Phaeacians' help is the enemy of the Phaeacians' stern god, on whose good will they depend absolutely.

This is the opposite of what a picaro could be expected to say. It is unnecessary, excessive frankness. Even if Odysseus had wished to make some gesture of friendship, he could have stopped with his name and some innocuous adventures. The name would have been risk enough, for how was Odysseus to know whether or not there was some prophecy known to Alcinous specifically naming Odysseus, as had been the case with Circe and Polyphemus? But Odysseus does not choose to make merely a partial gesture. He tells everything, not only the fact of Poseidon's hatred, but why Poseidon hates him. To tell this is to go beyond anecdote and externals. It is to confess a personal guilt which lays bare the whole ambiguous nature of the heroic life, the very life that is now providing the tone for Alcinous' and Odysseus' mutual understanding.

Contrary to the warnings of his crew, so Odysseus declares to Alcinous and the Phaeacians in the course of his narrative of the most crucial and pivotal episode of the whole *Odyssey*, he went into the cave of the Cyclops. Trapped but not outwitted, Odysseus gives a false name and then succeeds in blinding Polyphemus and escaping to sea. But once there, contrary again to the warnings of his crew, he proudly shouts out his true name to the enraged monster, curses him and at that moment hears the Cyclops' curse on him in return. From that point Odysseus is "hated by the blessed gods" (10.74) and wanders onwards leading his comrades from disaster to ruin.[6]

Thus Odysseus' story is a boldly candid response to Alcinous' challenge, since it places the enmity of Poseidon and the risks it occasions in central focus. But it is also a self-accusation, the confession of a fatal destructive act of egotism. That heroic, gloating, taunting self-advertisement of so many years before—

> Cyclops, if some one among mortal men should inquire
> Of you about the unseemly blindness in your eye,
> Say that Odysseus, sacker of cities, blinded it,
> The son of Laertes, whose home is in Ithaca. (9.502–505)

—that proclamation had originally been an act of pride and hate. But now, repeated in the context of his helplessness in Scheria, it is an act of humility. The contrast between the arrogant conqueror represented in the narrative and the lonely wanderer who speaks the narrative is total. The man who made that boast ten years ago had let his success in the violence of the Trojan War confuse his sense of reality. The consequences are still being unfolded at the very moment he recreates the distant event to his audience. Odysseus is, in effect, explaining to the innocent what it means to be a bloody-handed, cunning man of war. It means being precisely what *he* is, right there in front of them, defeated by the very values of courage and vengeance-seeking that had made him victorious in the first place. Through Alcinous the Phaeacians had asked to be taught this lesson and had offered in exchange what they had to give, the risk of final severance from the world of men. As Odysseus speaks and the weight of his long punishment at the hands of Poseidon grows ever more clear, they cannot help but be aware

6. For the curse of Polyphemus and Odysseus' sense of responsibility for its consequences, see Reinhardt, *op. cit.*, pp. 47–112.

of the reality of their own risk and of the mysterious mesh of all
these destinies. Once the Phaeacians had lived close to the
Cyclopes, and had been injured by them. But Alcinous' father,
Nausithoos, had settled them far from both Cyclopes and
humans (6.2–8). Yet now this wanderer is here bearing the
mark of the Cyclopes in his misery and asking the Phaeacians to
incur danger so that he can be safe. It is as though his presence
were a reminder that their kinship with the Cyclopes through
their ruler could not be evaded. Both Polyphemus and Alcinous
are descendants of Poseidon. No matter how drastic the dis-
tance in space and custom that the Phaeacians have put
between themselves and the Cyclopes—scorn of the gods vs.
piety, murder of guests vs. hospitality, unorganized social struc-
ture vs. highly organized social structure, no technology vs.
developed technology—they have not escaped their old enemies.

   Odysseus has now restored the contact that Nausithoos had
broken. Odysseus has been harmed by the Cyclopes, as had the
Phaeacians. He has escaped, and so had they. But there is this
difference between them. The curse is over for Odysseus. He has
come full circle, from one kind of self-proclamation involving
cursing and being cursed, to another kind of self-proclamation
involving prayers for blessing on others and for an end of the
curse on himself. The remainder of Poseidon's anger will fall on
the Phaeacians instead of on him: a returning Phaeacian ship
will be stricken and the threat of enclosure by a mountain will
hang menacingly over the city (13.125–187).

   Such is the price Alcinous will have to pay for having received
Odysseus as a brother. That he is conscious of the complexity of
the situation enclosing him while Odysseus tells his story is
made clear by what he says during the pause in the narrative in
Book 11:

> Odysseus, as we look on you, we would not think you
> To be a deceiver and cheat the way many men are
> Whom the black earth nourishes, and are widely dispersed,
> Fashioning falsehoods. . . . (11.363–366)

These words, at first view surprisingly blunt, are an acknowl-
edgement of Alcinous' understanding that Odysseus *could* have
deceived him and had reason to do so, but evidently has not.
Taken with Alcinous' renewed assurance of help and additional
gifts, the lines constitute a reaffirmation of the basis of the rela-

tionship between the two men, mutual trust. They understand each other. Odysseus wants desperately to go home and would do it honestly, without lies, if possible. Alcinous longs to participate in the heroic world from which his Phaeacian destiny has separated him, and to so participate he is willing to risk final severance from the human world, and perhaps worse, for who knows exactly what Poseidon will do?

Alcinous' dangerous longing is comprehensible in view of his lineage and family history. Did not his father give heroic names to him and to his dead brother, Courageous and Man-Breaker (Alcinous, Rhexenor)? His father's name, Swift-with-Ships (Nausithoos), was different, not comparable to the warrior names of the *Iliad*. True to this name, Swift-with-Ships had fled far from war with the violent Cyclopes, but he had furnished his two sons with the same kind of name as their grandfather, the king of the violent, powerful giants, Eurymedon, Wide-ruling, an epic, heroic name. Alcinous' dead brother, Rhexenor, is gone now, no breaker of men. But Odysseus, who has broken many, is there and knows so well the cost of such a life. He is a man such as his brother, Rhexenor, might have been, if he had lived; this is what Alcinous sees in Odysseus, a brother restored.[7]

The subtle relationship of appeal and hesitant response between Alcinous and Odysseus is the principle of composition in the Phaeacian episode. But it might have been otherwise. There are other ways, other atmospheres and other moods in which the poet could have brought his hero home. For example, the tone could have been wholly heroic. The Phaeacians would, in such a version, have no connection with Poseidon; Odysseus would meet the king's only *son*, not his only daughter; would identify himself immediately, instead of delaying, and then show his mettle in a military campaign important to his host, who would, in gratitude, have sent him home in a ship, not magical, but effective in the ordinary epic fashion.

Or the tone of the episode could have been entirely picaresque. The Phaeacians would be dependent on Poseidon, suspi-

7. If Odysseus, as the restored Rhexenor, married Nausicaa, as Alcinous had suggested (7.313), each brother would have married the other's daughter, so the family, in this ideal eventuality, would have had something of the symmetrical exclusiveness of the family of Aeolus, king of the winds, another entity immune in the vastness of the sea.

cious of the stranger and hostile to him. Odysseus would in self-defense seduce the princess, deceive the royal parents and win his passage home by cleverness.[8]

It should not be decided too quickly that the existing Phaeacis is obviously and inevitably what the poet had to do, whereas alternative versions are impossible. What a poet is going to do is never obvious until he does it. What we can see from posing the hypothetical heroic and picaresque versions is that neither permits the existing Alcinous-Odysseus relationship with its mutual commitment to danger, nor do they permit the drama of the meeting of a man who has challenged the Cyclopes and is the enemy of Poseidon with another man who has been protected from the Cyclopes, is a friend of Poseidon, and yet finds himself committed to the other. The Phaeacian episode acquires its peculiar atmosphere from the mingling, although in unequal measure, of two tones, the heroic and the picaresque, like a musical composition in which two rhythms are used at once, or rather like one in which an alternative to the dominant rhythm is constantly suggested.

It would seem evident that the poet who composed the Phaeacis as it stands in the present *Odyssey* (Books 6–8, 13) also refashioned the traditional material used in Odysseus' adventure-narrative (Books 9–12) so as to integrate the two sections. What the adventure-narrative of Books 9–12 was like before its refashioning by the *Odyssey* poet is open to many suggestions. However, a few details may seem more probable than others. For example, the hero of earlier versions probably coolly maintained his clever pseudonym, Noman, with the Cyclops, instead of proudly identifying himself, and so escaped the disaster of the curse of Polyphemus, who in that version ridiculously and uselessly implored the god to punish "nobody." As a consequence the troubles which befell the hero's comrades in those earlier versions were not his fault at all, but their own, as indeed the proem of the *Odyssey* asserts.

In those earlier versions the comrades were destroyed by their own foolishness. Odysseus never lost his cool self-possession, was never overcome by pride and vain self-glorification. What the poet gained from reshaping the older versions is a hero not simply defeated, but also profoundly guilty; and, among other things, an

8. For suggestions in the present text of what the heroic alternative might have been like, cf. 14.316–319, 13.223; for the picaresque alternative, cf. 13.254–255, 13.291–299.

episode, the Phaeacis, in which that defeated, guilty hero is permitted to be true, instead of false, both to his dark past and to the human beings who enable him, finally, to escape from it.

CHARLES DORIA

[Aphrodite and Ares]†

"The Story of Aphrodite and Ares" (*Odyssey* 9.266–366) is interesting because it is a burlesque of the *Odyssey* as seen through the eyes of love. All the key themes of the *Odyssey* are there: the handsome suitor, the clever husband, the neglected wife, Homecoming, Travel, and the Timely Warning/Prophecy. But does love triumph? No, money and the claims of respectable morality do. In the *Odyssey* the domestic love of Odysseus and Penelope rises above the eroticism of Calypso and Circe, the innocence of Nausicaa, and the adventuristic heroism of Antinous and the Suitors. Yet the curious thing is that while we see the *Odyssey* as an epic, we consider the Story of Aphrodite and Ares a love story. This, I suppose, is because of what the characters say they are doing: Ares and Aphrodite talk only of bed and pleasure, Odysseus and Penelope of family, prosperity, tranquillity and the re-establishment of what one assumes is really the established order.

CLEMENT GOODSON

Homer and *Ouranos*‡

The name trick of Odysseus, his deception of the Cyclops Polyphemus by the word *outis* (no-man), has been described as a paradigm for the human discovery of the fundamental deceit of all language. Truncating the word from its usual referent, Odysseus alters the ground of the Cyclops's relation to language, his unthinking equation of words and things:

Odysseus discovers in words what developing bourgeois society

† Charles Doria, from "Studies in Translation," Doctoral Thesis in Comparative Literature, State University of Buffalo, 1970.

‡ Published here for the first time by permission of the author.

calls formalism . . . out of the formalism of mythical names and
rules which, like nature, would rule indifferently over men and
history, nominalism, the prototype of bourgeois thought,
emerges.[1]

Polyphemus's name is a product of this formalism: his fellow
Cyclopes address him thus (the word means "much-speaking")
in response to his agonized cries. And though he attempts to
communicate the substance of Odysseus's trick to his own kind,
his words fail him; he cannot signify the linguistic act itself,
cannot articulate the workings of a trick whose logic escapes
him even as he suffers its dire consequences.

The name trick signals Odysseus's seminal reformulation of
the world he traverses; his experience forges in him a sense of
the permeability of that world, its access of penetration by the
powerful instrumentality of human consciousness. The larger
homeric consciousness partakes of this revelation: to render the
tale thus is to have internalized its logos, to have realized a cul-
tural sophistication that permits this sort of joke to have the
force of myth. The homeric act finds its center in the fitting of
the roots and rhythms of a received tongue to a genuinely
visionary grasp of human experience strung together from the
mythemes, the story-units of myth, which the poet receives by the
same cultural process that gives him language. What the cun-
ning Odysseus works on the powers that inhibit his return,
Homer may be thought to work on the raw mythical materials of
his song.

The homeric world, the space his characters traverse, is the
product of an habitually fabricating consciousness. Homer's cre-
ation of world is heuristic—ever shifting, probing, and remaking.
He creates the field of human experience as Odysseus tests the
limits of human experience, and his own search is a preliminary
exploration of its axes. It is a mistake to attribute to him a
finished model of natural space, much less the geographical: for
him the formulation of space can have only a tentative solution.
Received critical opinion holds that Homer conceives the ele-
ments of the natural world as a coherent and stable physical
system. Succinctly, this system is reconstituted as follows:

> The surface of the earth would, as the dome above and the circle
> of the horizon suggest, naturally be conceived as circular, the
> Roman *Orbis terrarum*, and was apparently so conceived by the

1. Max Horkheimer and Theodor W. Adorno, *Dialektik der Aufklärung*
(Amsterdam, 1947), p. 77.

early Greeks—as a disk or cylinder. Above this was the dome of ouranos, conceived apparently as a hard shell, arching down to the surface of the earth at the rim, round which okeanos flows so that the stars are washed by the water of the latter.[2]

If this rigidly conceptual vision of space existed at all, it existed outside of the homeric epics. While there is sound evidence that, for instance, the shape of a war shield and its outer rim are conceived by Homer as structurally related to the earth and the river *okeanos* which surrounds it, [3] there is no evidence that this is a fixed conception, a spatial absolute to which he conforms and systematically refers. There is, further, no evidence that he thought of *ouranos*, "sky," as a "solid hemisphere like a bowl."[4] His use of the word suggests something very different.[5] He uses it in connection with two distinct referents—a solid, shining ceiling above the earth; and the space inhabited and charged by the gods, especially Zeus. These significations cannot be rigorously separated in context; residue of each may be presumed to remain in every act of signification. There is, further, a set of contexts relating to the heavenly bodies which breaks importantly with the conceptual implications of both of these referents. It reveals in this the nominal ground of the homeric imagination and the unsettled nature which it envisions.

He uses the word *ouranos* first to mean the solid ceiling of the sky. Atlas is said by Athena (*Od*. I, 53-4) to hold the great pillars that keep *ouranos* and *gaia* (generally, the ground of the earth) "apart." The relation of *ouranos* to *gaia* is thus an architectural one; it is that of a ceiling raised from a floor by columns, as in a megaron, and implies in this their separation. This architectural metaphor is anticipated a few lines earlier in the description of the gathering of the gods "in the palace-chambers of Zeus at Olympos." (*Od*. I, 27). The logic of this metaphor

2. Richard B. Onians, *The Origins of European Thought* (Cambridge, 1954), p. 249. Onians speculates interestingly about the relation of the elements of the world to the structure of an egg and it seems clear that Epicurus, for instance, rather systematically developed this conception, with the Orphic cosmogoners following him in this. But it would be a mistake to suggest that Homer shares this view. It seems, rather, a later development.
3. Homer, *Iliad* XVIII, 606-7: "On it he placed the great might of Okeanos River / Along the outer rim of the wisely made shield." See also G. S. Kirk and J. E. Raven, *The Presocratic Philosophers* (Cambridge, 1966), pp. 11-19. Translations from Homer are based on Cook and Lattimore.
4. Kirk and Raven, p. 10.
5. Cf. M. L. West, Hesiod. *Theogony* (Oxford, 1966), p. 127. West notes in passing that the space of *ouranos* has been misconstrued.

probably does not lie in imaginative description of natural features of a mountain. Zeus in his aspect of mediator among the gods and agent of justice for gods and men alike is understood as inhabiting internal, architectural space. We may think here of Minos, a son of Zeus, seated in "the wide-gated house of Hades," "dealing out justice to the dead." (*Od.* XI, 569–71).

The force of these metaphors is, clearly, to anthropomorphize and thus lend logic and credence to the difficult-to-conceive processes of divine principle: how it is, specifically, that the ceiling of the sky does not fall down, and how a man's fate is constituted. Zeus talks in this scene first of the fate of Aigisthos, and Athena follows him, calling Odysseus's misfortunes to the attention of the gathering. The evocation of the divine palace here suggests that the familiarity and cultural significance of Mycenaean royal architecture made it a sound base for the description of other systems. In the first instance, the balance of natural elements is involved; in the second, in a different way, divine balance in the disposition of fate. Palace architecture embodies a complex sense of social order, and the Mycenaean palaces in issue here were certainly emblems of the power of their royal inhabitants.[6]

Although this is the only instance in which Homer chooses to make the connection so explicitly, the architectural conception is implicit in his attribution of metallic solidity to *ouranos*. He calls it *chalkēon* (brazen) and *poluchalkon* (great-brazen);[7] he also calls it *sidēreon* (made of iron).[8] The variance here suggests that it is, in the first instance, its solidity that makes it like metal. This variety of metallic epithet corresponds to his variety of use in sea epithets: the gray sea and wine-dark sea, especially. Variety of naturalistic condition may be the impulse here—a brazen *ouranos* for the brightness of sunshine and *ouranos* made of iron for an overcast sky—though this is impossible to determine from context.

Another instance of the implied solidity of *ouranos* occurs in the description of a burning sacrifice to Apollo in the first book of the *Iliad*:

And they sacrificed to Apollo, performing hecatombs

6. Jean-Pierre Vernant, *Les origines de la pensée grecque* (Paris, 1969), p. 30.
7. *Iliad* XVII, 425; and *Iliad* V, 504 and *Odyssey* III, 2.
8. *Odyssey* XV, 329 and XVII, 565.

Of bulls and goats along the barren sea's beach.
The smell of the burning, curling round the smoke, reached oura-
    nos. (*Il.* I, 315–317)

The verb here indicates *ouranos* as a concrete destination.[9] A
similar usage occurs at a feast in the *Iliad*. Hector commands
the preparations:

... and pile up much cut wood,
So that all night and until early-born dawn
We may burn many fires, and the brightness reach to ouranos. (*Il.*
    VIII, 507–9).

On other occasions the "reach to ouranos" expression is used
more colloquially.[1] The disguised Odysseus, replying to Penel-
ope's initial questions about his home and parents, replies,
"... your renown reaches broad ouranos" (*Od.* XIX, 108)—in-
volving its sense as the divine location but making it, in this same
attribution, concrete as well. Circe, relating to Odysseus the
way of his return, describes the crag of Scylla which "reaches
to broad ouranos" (*Od.* XII, 73). This is similarly colloquial
though far more concrete; it defines Scylla as supernatural in
spatial proportion and involves the sense in which *ouranos* is
associated with the divine mountain Olympos—a sense dis-
cussed below. By invoking the space of divinity it strikes Scylla
out of nature and the realm of ordinary experience.[2]
    A further use of *ouranos* in this concrete sense occurs three
times in the *Iliad*.[3] This is illustrated by a homeric simile
describing the marching Achaeans:

As destructive fire lights up a huge forest
On the peak of a mountain, and the flare appears far away,
So from the godly bronze of the marching men
The gleam, shining all through the aither, reached to ouranos.
    (*Il.* II, 455–8)

9. It is noteworthy in this connection that Aristotle gives *horon einai tōn
anō*, "the boundary of those things above," as the etymology of *ouranos*.
This is uniformly rejected by philologists. See *De Mundo* in *Aristotelis
Opera* (Berlin, 1960), v. I, p. 400 A7. Also Hjalmar Frisk, *Griechisches
Etymologisches Wörterbuch*, Lieferung 15 (Heidelberg, 1965), pp. 446–7.
1. See *Odyssey* XV, 329 and XVII, 565 for similar uses.
2. There is an especially interesting use of *ouranos* as a spatial quantifier
in the *Iliad*: "... as far below Hades as *ouranos* stands from earth" (*Il.*
VIII, 16).
3. The undiscussed use occurs at *Iliad* XVII, 425.

Again, *ouranos* is understood as an actual, physical boundary, like the roof of a house to an observer inside. Elsewhere Athena is seen to leap from this boundary, suggesting how very literally its solidity is imagined:

Speaking this he roused Athena who was already eager,
And she in the shape of a broad-winged, thin-crying hawk
Leaped down from ouranos through the aither.   (*Il*. XIX, 349–51)

This use also invokes the association of *ouranos* with divine space, though its usual abstraction—as if that space were not continuous with the space inhabited by mortal men—is here breached by the unusually concrete image.

Finally, there are two identical passages in the *Iliad* describing Athena's descent to battle from the "threshold" of Zeus:

Hera then swiftly felt for the horses with a whip;
And moving by themselves the gates of ouranos, guarded by the
     Hours, bellowed—
Those Hours to whom vast ouranos and Olympos is entrusted,
Both to open up thick darkness and also to close it. (*Il*. V, 748–51;
     and VIII, 392–5)[4]

Commentators have tried to make this conform to a naturalistic conception of the sky by explaining these gates as a thick cloud which the Hours open and shut like a trap door.[5] But they clearly refer to this same solid ceiling. As in Athena's descent as a hawk, the space of *ouranos* is divine as well as architectural in conception. Here it is imagined as having gates, an attribution thoroughly incongruous to a ceiling. The poet would seem here to continue invoking the architectural model while abandoning representational consistency within the confines of the model: gates are architectural elements, even if they are not found in ceilings. Homer's imagination does not ask a greater consistency. It does uniformly ask the reduction of divine space to human terms and to one set of terms; within these, however, it is generally free to operate. This is an indication of the real latitude of the poet's spatial imagination. Space remains equivocal for him and in process of definition.

The use of the word *ouranos* to signify the space of the gods

4. The somewhat irregular instance of the singular verb used with "ouranos and Olympos" may be related to an understanding of the two nouns as a single spatial unit. This accords with a possible earlier sense of *olympos* as "mountain," generically.

5. See thus H. G. Liddell and R. Scott, *A Greek-English Lexicon*, 9th edition, rev. H. S. Jones (Oxford, 1966), p. 1273.

is illustrated in the same gathering scene in the first book of
the *Odyssey*. Replying to Athena's charge that he is angry at
Odysseus, Zeus states,

How could I ever forget godlike Odysseus
Who excels in thought among mortals, and for the sacrifices
He has given the immortal gods who possess broad ouranos. (*Od.* I,
   65–7)

In the *Iliad*, Poseidon describes the division of the natural
elements among himself and his brothers:

Everything was divided three ways, each of us receiving his due,
And when the lots were shaken I drew the gray sea to live in always;
Hades drew the misty darkness below,
And Zeus drew broad ouranos, in the aither and the clouds.
But earth and high Olympos are common to the three of us. (*Il.*
   XV, 189–93)

In the first of these passages the sense of *ouranos* as a solid ceil-
ing is submerged; the eminent attribute of the sky is divine pres-
ence, rather like the English word "heaven." The word is used
emblematically rather than descriptively, in an almost trans-
spatial sense. The second passage includes naturalistic description
and certainly involves the concept of a solid ceiling, suffused by
clouds and the fiery upper air. It clarifies the relation between
the two referents of *ouranos*.

   There are several passages in Homer which attest a connec-
tion between the word *ouranos* and the word *olympos*. Nilsson[6]
points out that *olympos*—evidently a pre-Greek word that may
have meant "mountain," generically, before it came to signify a
specific one—is actually one with *ouranos* in its sense of the
rather abstract space of the gods which exists outside the vault
of the sky and of which Zeus is lord in dominion. So in the
Iliad Thetis, a sea-nymph,

. . . arose from the waves of the sea
Early in the morning and went up to vast ouranos and olympos. (*Il.*
   I, 496–7)

And Zeus, tricked by Hera,

. . . swore a strong oath
Lest ever again to olympos and starry ouranos
Mischief, who misleads everyone, return. (*Il.* XIX, 127–9)

6. Martin Nilsson, *Geschichte der Griechischen Religion* (München,
1941), v. I, p. 354.

The space of *ouranos* remains abstract in these passages; the adjective *megan* (vast) is, in the one, too vague to be helpful visually. And in neither does the connection with the divine mountain modify the word spatially (in the exclusively physical sense) except perhaps to reiterate its size; rather, as a loose spatial synonym, it blocks out the cosmographically specific signification. The word remains, in its uses here, a formulaic attribution of divinity with little or no reference to the structure of the physical universe.

There is, finally, an interesting deviation from the normative senses of *ouranos*. A single example should illustrate the force of this usage. Homer on two occasions refers to an *ouranos* "crowned"—once (*Od.* V, 303) with clouds, by Zeus, and once (*Il.* XVIII, 485) with heavenly bodies.[7] This is a peculiarly flat metaphor for a description of the relation of such elemental forces; it is strictly one-dimensional, stating only the fact of the relation. If we were to extend its implications *ouranos* would become, perhaps, a head. But the metaphor defies, in fact, elaboration. It is eminently unconceptual. The deviance from the terms of the usual sense of *ouranos* (especially its architectural sense) suggests recourse to a nominal *ouranos*, however it is conceptually integrated to the spatial field of the natural world. These passages revert to this preconceptual base in their lack of final definition: they are phenomenologically residual and do not submit to the analytical process that characterizes Homer's refabrication of the natural world. Homer may understand *ouranos* as a ceiling or an abstract attribute of divinity (or both at once), but he is in any case reliant on its nominal existence. *Ouranos* is—as the word is, so is its referent.

This is a characteristic nominalism that Homer cannot escape without evading the responsibility of the very mythos that is the unformed matter of his creation. If his conception of cosmic space demands a reduction of its physical axes to a single terminal field, these contexts of *ouranos*—the only ones in which he truly deviates from the interlocking terminal field that has been described—would seem to bypass that condition by

7. Several other passages describe the heavenly bodies' relation to *ouranos* in a similar way. Among these is the simple *ouranos asteroeis*, starry sky (*Il.* VI, 108; V, 769, and elsewhere). Hesperus, the evening star, is said to "stand" in *ouranos* (*Il.* XXII, 318); and the sun is said to perish completely from *ouranos* (*Od:* XX, 356–57), evidently a reference to an eclipse. These uses are all acceptable phenomenologically but fail to relate conceptually to *ouranos* conceived as a solid ceiling.

ignoring the spatiality of the objects they treat. If the clouds and heavenly bodies cannot be structurally related to an *ouranos* conceived as architectural, they are returned to their ground state as words. They revert in this to the nominalism of myth and to the implicit unity that homeric epic imposes on material that resists integration to its constructs.

The referents of *ouranos* remain diverse after Homer and extend the spatial configuration to which he assimilates it. Hesiod elevates *ouranos* to an inhabited deity as the son of Erebos and Gaia,[8] and Orphic cosmogoners pick up this strain.[9] The abstract space of divinity is elevated in this conception to proto-divinity. Aeschylus and Plato both use the phrase "those from ouranos"[1] to signify the gods, continuing Homer's sense of its divine habitation. Empedocles, inheriting the architectural metaphor, describes *ouranos* as "solid";[2] and it was described by Zeno as the "outer limit of the aither."[3] There are late instances of its use to describe a vaulted roof, the palate of the mouth, and a tent.[4]

8. Hesiod, *Theogony*, 127 ff.
9. See Kirk and Raven, pp. 38–43.
1. Aeschylus, *Prometheus*, 897: Plato, *Republic*, 508a.
2. The word he uses is *steremnion*. Empedokles, in H. Diels, *Die Fragmente der Vorsokratiker* (Berlin, 1903), v. I, p. 209.
3. Zeno the Stoic, I.33.
4. Liddell and Scott, p. 1273.

Selected Bibliography

Related works available in English, in addition to those excerpted above.

Arnold, Matthew. "On Translating Homer," London, 1861; and "On Translating Homer; Last Words," London, 1862. Often reprinted. The best normative description of Homer's style.

Carpenter, Rhys. *Folk Tale, Fiction, and Saga in the Homeric Epics.* Berkeley, Calif., 1958. An engaging discussion of the interweaving of anthropological and archeological factors relating to Homer.

Graves, Robert. *The Greek Myths.* London, 1955. Based on authoritative German sources, this is the most engaging handbook on myth available in English.

Havelock, Eric. *Preface to Plato.* Cambridge, Mass., 1963. An inquiry into the intellectual implications of the use of Homer in classical Athens, notably by Plato.

Lorimer, H. L. *Homer and the Monuments.* London, 1950. An exhaustive survey of archeological evidence bearing on Homer.

Onians, R. B. *The Origins of European Thought.* London, 1951. A study of the philosophical implications underlying the exact meanings of certain words in Homer.

Parry, Milman, *The Making of Homeric Verse: Collected Papers of Milman Parry,* edited by Adam Parry. Oxford, 1971. The classic statements of the great discoverer of oral composition practices in early poetry. Hitherto available only in journals, such as *Harvard Studies in Classical Philology,* XLI, pp. 73–147, and *ibid.,* XLIII, pp. 1–50.

Snell, Bruno. *The Discovery of Mind,* translated by Thomas Rosenmeyer, New York, 1960 [1953]. A study of Homer's method of perception, on the evidence of his vocabulary, and the development of that method in later Greek thought.

Wace, A. J. B., and F. H. Stubbings. *A Companion to Homer.* London, 1962. A compendious collection of essays by specialists on nearly all phases of Homer.

Supplementary Bibliography

Works are not listed which have been excerpted in this collection.

EDITIONS

Stanford, W. B. *The Odyssey.* 2 vols. London, 1962, 4.

LINGUISTIC AIDS

Chantraine, P. *Grammaire homérique.* 2 vols. Paris, 1948, 1953.
Cunliffe, R. J. *Lexicon of Homeric Dialect.* London, 1924.
———. *Lexicon of Homeric Proper Names,* London, 1931.
Dunbar, H. *Concordance to Odyssey and Hymns of Homer.* London, 1880.

BACKGROUND

Adkins, A. W. H. *Merit and Responsibility: A Study in Greek Values.* Oxford, 1960.
Allen, T. W. *Homer: the Origins and the Transmission.* Oxford, 1924.

Bérard, Victor. *Les Phéniciens et l'Odyssée*. Paris, 1927.
Chadwick, H. M. *The Heroic Age*. Cambridge, 1912.
Harrison, J. E. *Myths of the Odyssey*. London, 1882.
Mireaux, E. *Daily Life in the Time of Homer*, translated by Iris Sells. London, 1959.
Nilsson, M. P. *Homer and Mycenae*. London, 1933.
Thomson, J. A. K. *Studies in the Odyssey*. Oxford, 1914.
Webster, T. B. L. *From Mycenae to Homer*. London, 1958.

CRITICISM

Basset, S. E. *The Poetry of Homer*. Berkeley, Calif., 1938.
Myres, John L. *Homer and His Critics*, edited by Dorothea Gray. London, 1958.
Parry, M. *Collected Papers*. London and New York, 1971.
Scott, J. A. *The Unity of Homer*. Berkeley, Calif., 1921.
Stanford, W. B. *Ambiguity in Greek Literature*. Oxford, 1939.
———. *Greek Metaphor*. Oxford, 1936.
———. *The Ulysses Theme*. Oxford, 1954.
Taylor, C. H., ed. *Essays on the Odyssey*. Bloomington, Ind., 1963.
Woodhouse, W. J. *The Composition of Homer's Odyssey*. Oxford, 1930.